MW01114804

THE CAMBRIDGE HANDBOOK OF THE LAW OF THE SHARING ECONOMY

This handbook grapples conceptually and practically with what the sharing economy – which includes entities ranging from large for-profit firms like Airbnb, Uber, Lyft, TaskRabbit, and Upwork to smaller, nonprofit collaborative initiatives – means for law, and how law, in turn, is shaping critical aspects of the sharing economy. Featuring a diverse set of contributors from multiple academic disciplines and countries, the book compiles the most important, up-to-date research on the regulation of the sharing economy. The first part surveys the nature of the sharing economy, explores the central challenge of balancing innovation and regulatory concerns, and examines the institutions confronting these regulatory challenges. The second part turns to a series of specific regulatory domains, including labor and employment law, consumer protection, tax, and civil rights. This groundbreaking work should be read by anyone interested in the dynamic relationship between law and the sharing economy.

NESTOR M. DAVIDSON joined the Fordham University School of Law in 2011 and was named the Albert A. Walsh Professor of Real Estate, Land Use, and Property Law in 2017. Professor Davidson is an expert in property, urban law, and affordable housing law and policy, and serves as the faculty director of the law school's Urban Law Center. Professor Davidson practiced with the firm of Latham and Watkins, focusing on commercial real estate and affordable housing, and served as Deputy General Counsel at the US Department of Housing and Urban Development.

MICHÈLE FINCK is Senior Research Fellow at the Max Planck Institute for Innovation and Competition and lecturer in EU Law at Keble College, University of Oxford. She previously worked at the London School of Economics and holds a doctorate in law from the University of Oxford. Dr. Finck researches the interaction between regulation and technology, and has particular expertise on the sharing economy, distributed ledger technology, and the legal treatment of (big) data. She is the author of "Blockchain Regulation and Governance in Europe" (Cambridge University Press, 2018).

JOHN J. INFRANCA is Associate Professor of Law at Suffolk University Law School. Infranca previously worked as a legal fellow at the Furman Center for Real Estate and Urban Policy. Professor Infranca's scholarship focuses on land use regulation and affordable housing policy, property theory, and law and religion. His publications include "The Sharing Economy as an Urban Phenomenon" (with Nestor Davidson) and "Spaces for Sharing: Micro Units amid the Shift from Ownership to Access."

The Cambridge Handbook of the Law of the Sharing Economy

Edited by

NESTOR M. DAVIDSON

Fordham Law School

MICHÈLE FINCK

University of Oxford

JOHN J. INFRANCA

Suffolk University Law School

CAMBRIDGE
UNIVERSITY PRESS

CAMBRIDGE
UNIVERSITY PRESS

University Printing House, Cambridge CB2 8BS, United Kingdom

One Liberty Plaza, 20th Floor, New York, NY 10006, USA

477 Williamstown Road, Port Melbourne, VIC 3207, Australia

314–321, 3rd Floor, Plot 3, Splendor Forum, Jasola District Centre, New Delhi – 110025, India

79 Anson Road, #06-04/06, Singapore 079906

Cambridge University Press is part of the University of Cambridge.

It furthers the University's mission by disseminating knowledge in the pursuit of education, learning, and research at the highest international levels of excellence.

www.cambridge.org
Information on this title: www.cambridge.org/9781108416955
DOI: 10.1017/9781108255882

First published 2018

Printed in the United States of America by Sheridan Books, Inc.

A catalogue record for this publication is available from the British Library.

ISBN 978-1-108-41695-5 Hardback

To Clare, ever and always inspiring – ND
To Moritz and my parents, for their boundless support – MF
To Erin and Leo, with whom I am fortunate to share my life – JI

Contents

Figures

Tables

Contributors

Aurélien Acquier is Full Professor in Management, Organization, and Society at ESCP Europe. His research explores how new organizational forms (such as global value chains, sharing economy, etc.) impact responsibility and governance issues. He has recently edited a special issue in *Technological Forecasting and Social Change*: "Promises and Paradoxes of the Sharing Economy: An Organizing Framework" (2017).

Antonio Aloisi is a Max Weber Postdoctoral Fellow at the European University Institute, Florence. He has a PhD in Legal Studies (Business and Social Law) from Bocconi University, Milan. His dissertation is titled "Facing the Challenges of Platform-Mediated Labour: The Employment Relationship in Times of Non-Standard Work and Digital Transformation." In 2016, he was a visiting researcher at the Saint Louis University School of Law. His current research activity focuses on the individual and collective dimensions of non-standard forms of employment, including platform labor and work in the gig economy.

Erez Aloni is an assistant professor at the Peter A. Allard School of Law at the University of British Columbia. His research focuses on legal regulation of adult relationships. His work examines the way that diverse laws affect a family's well-being and assesses how those laws create effects – socioeconomic and otherwise – on society at large. He has also written on pluralistic theory and the way it can inform regulatory dilemmas concerning family law and other areas, such as the emerging market of the platform economy.

Mohammad Amir Anwar is a researcher at the Oxford Internet Institute, University of Oxford and Research Associate at the School of Tourism and Hospitality, University of Johannesburg. He is a human geographer by training with interests in the fields of economic and development geography, poverty, labor, and social movements in Africa and India. His current work focuses on the information economy and digital gig work in Africa. He has a forthcoming book chapter with Mark Graham on digital labor in *Digital Geographies* (2018).

Jordan M. Barry is Professor of Law at the University of San Diego School of Law. He teaches and writes in the areas of tax law and policy, corporate law and finance, and law and economics. He has also taught at the University of Michigan Law School and the UC Berkeley School of Law. He has published numerous articles, including, most recently, "Regulatory Entrepreneurship" (2017). Prior to joining the faculty at USD, Professor Barry practiced law in the New York office of

Fried, Frank, Harris, Shriver & Jacobson and clerked for the Honorable Jay Bybee of the United States Court of Appeals for the Ninth Circuit. Professor Barry is a graduate of Cornell University and Stanford Law School, where he served as Managing Editor of the *Stanford Law Review*.

Ray Brescia is the Hon. Harold R. Tyler Chair in Law and Technology and Professor of Law at Albany Law School. He is formerly the associate director of the Urban Justice Center, a Skadden Fellow with the Legal Aid Society of New York, a Staff Attorney with the New Haven Legal Assistance Association, and law clerk to the late Constance Baker Motley, United States District Judge for the Southern District of New York. He is a coeditor, with John Travis Marshall, of *How Cities Will Save the World: Urban Innovation in the Face of Population Flows, Climate Change, and Economic Inequality* (2016).

Bryant Cannon is Deputy Attorney General with the California Department of Justice in the San Francisco office. He represents state agencies in a wide range of federal and state environmental, natural resources, land use, and other litigation matters, including enforcement and defense actions. Among other areas of research, he has written on the regulatory environment affecting the sharing economy: "A Framework for Designing Co-Regulation Models Well-Adapted to Technology-Facilitated Sharing Economies" (2015).

Valentina Carbone is Full Professor of Supply Chain Management and Sustainable Business Models at ESCP Europe. Her current research covers the sustainable dimension of SCM, corporate social and environmental responsibility, sharing and circular economy business models.

Miriam A. Cherry is Professor of Law and Codirector of the William C. Wefel Center for Employment Law at Saint Louis University Law School. Professor Cherry is a graduate of Harvard Law School and Dartmouth College, an author of 30 articles, and a member of the American Law Institute. She is an international expert on work, technology, and corporate social responsibility. Professor Cherry's coedited book, *Invisible Labor: Hidden Work in the Contemporary World*, was published in 2016.

Hanna Chung has been Deputy Attorney General with the California Department of Justice where her work focused on criminal appeals. She has previously written on the regulatory environment affecting the sharing economy: "A Framework for Designing Co-Regulation Models Well-Adapted to Technology-Facilitated Sharing Economies" (2015).

Peter Coles is Head Economist at Airbnb, where he has worked since November 2015. Previously he was Head Economist and Director of Global Strategy at eBay, and before that a professor at Harvard Business School. His expertise is in the fields of marketplace design, data, strategy, and public policy. Much of his research relates to reducing frictions in marketplaces, and he helped design a "signaling mechanism" used by the American Economic Association to match students with jobs: "Preference Signaling in Matching Markets" (2013).

Nicola Countouris is Professor in Labour Law and European Law at the Faculty of Laws of University College London. His main areas of research and work are employment law and EU law, with a particular interest in the regulation of personal work relations in a comparative and supranational perspective. He has acted as an independent expert for the ILO and the ETUC on topics surrounding the regulation of the employment relationship and the "gig economy," and his works include *The Legal Construction of Personal Work Relations* (2011), coauthored with Professor Mark Freedland.

Nestor M. Davidson joined the Fordham University School of Law in 2011 and was named the Albert A. Walsh Professor of Real Estate, Land Use, and Property Law in 2017. Professor Davidson is an expert in property and urban law, and affordable housing law and policy, and serves as the faculty director of the law school's Urban Law Center. Professor Davidson practiced with the firm of Latham and Watkins, focusing on commercial real estate and affordable housing, and served as Deputy General Counsel at the US Department of Housing and Urban Development.

Niamh Dunne is Associate Professor in the Law Department of the London School of Economics and Political Science, where she teaches and researches in the area of competition law. She is the author of *Competition Law and Economic Regulation* (2015).

Michael Egesdal is a data scientist at Airbnb, where he has worked since February 2016. He received his PhD in economics from Harvard University in 2016, with a focus on industrial organization. His prior work includes research on the estimation of game-theoretic structural models.

Ingrid Gould Ellen is the Paulette Goddard Professor of Urban Policy and Planning at NYU Wagner and a faculty director of the NYU Furman Center. She is author of *Sharing America's Neighborhoods: The Prospects for Stable, Racial Integration* (2000), and many peer-reviewed articles about housing and neighborhoods.

Michèle Finck is Senior Research Fellow at the Max Planck Institute for Innovation and Competition and a Lecturer in EU law at Keble College, University of Oxford. Her research focuses on the interaction between technological change and regulation with a special focus on (big) data, blockchains, and the sharing economy.

Charlotte Garden is an associate professor and Co-Associate Dean for Research & Faculty Development at Seattle University School of Law, where she teaches constitutional law and labor law. Her scholarship focuses on collective labor rights, especially the intersection of labor law and the First Amendment. Her most recent article, "Disrupting Work Law: Arbitration in the Gig Economy," appears in *University of Chicago Legal Forum*. She also writes for popular outlets such as *The Atlantic* and SCOTUSBlog, and drafts amicus briefs in labor law cases.

Andrea Geissinger is a PhD student in business administration at Örebro University School of Business and the Ratio Institute in Stockholm, Sweden. She holds an MSc from Stockholm Business School and a BA from LMU in Munich, Germany. She has a strong interest in societal change processes facilitated by technological drivers of change in markets and organization. More specifically, her main research focuses on the specific challenges and opportunities that arise out of the sharing economy for individuals and organizations alike, such as digital trust, sustainability, and innovations in business models.

Mark Graham is Professor at the Oxford Internet Institute, Senior Research Fellow at Green Templeton College, and Faculty Fellow at the Alan Turing Institute. His research focuses on economic development, labor, power, participation, and representation. You can read more about his work at www.markgraham.space.

Janice C. Griffith is Professor of Law at Suffolk University Law School, in Boston, Massachusetts, and served as the University's Vice President for Academic Affairs from 2008 to 2011. Before coming to Suffolk University, Professor Griffith taught at Georgia State University College of Law and served as its Dean from 1996 to 2004. Previously she taught at Quinnipiac University School of Law and the University of Bridgeport School of Law. Nationally recognized as a scholar in state and local government law, she has published articles on federalism, housing, transportation, public finance, land use, home rule, open space protection, comparative urban law, and regional governance. She is one of the authors of a leading case book titled *State and Local Government in a Federal System*. Before entering academia, Professor Griffith served in New York City's government as a Division Chief in the Office of Corporation Counsel and as General Counsel and Assistant Administrator of the Housing and Development Administration. She was an associate with the Wall Street law firm of Hawkins, Delafield and Wood before holding these governmental posts. Professor Griffith received a JD from the University of Chicago Law School and an AB degree from Colby College.

Leah Chan Grinvald is Associate Dean of Academic Affairs and Professor of Law at Suffolk University Law School, in Boston, Massachusetts. She teaches and researches in the area of intellectual property law, focusing on enforcement of IP laws, both domestic and international. Prior to Suffolk University, Professor Grinvald was Assistant Professor of Law at Saint Louis University School of Law. Before entering academia, Professor Grinvald was Global Corporate Counsel at Taylor Made Golf Company, Inc., based in Carlsbad, California and previously practiced at two international law firms. Professor Grinvald is a graduate of NYU School of Law and The George Washington University.

John J. Infranca is Associate Professor of Law at Suffolk University Law School. Professor Infranca's scholarship focuses on land use regulation, affordable housing policy, property theory, and law and religion. Infranca previously worked as a legal fellow at the Furman Center for Real Estate and Urban Policy, where he focused on land use regulation and affordable housing policy. He also served as a law clerk to Judge Julio M. Fuentes of the United States Court of Appeals for the Third Circuit and Judge Berle M. Schiller of the United States District Court for the District of Pennsylvania. His publications include "The Sharing Economy as an Urban Phenomenon" (with Nestor Davidson) and "Spaces for Sharing: Micro Units amid the Shift from Ownership to Access.".

Jamila Jefferson-Jones is Associate Professor of Law at the University of Missouri, Kansas City. She teaches courses in Property, Real Estate Transactions, and Housing Law. Professor Jefferson-Jones has written a number of law review articles and book chapters on the sharing economy generally and is an emerging expert on the housing segment of the sharing economy. She also served as the founding Vice Chair of the American Bar Association Section of State and Local Government Law Sharing Economy Committee. Professor Jefferson-Jones is a graduate of Harvard Law School. Prior to entering academia, she practiced law at firms in the District of Columbia and in her hometown of New Orleans.

Sonia Katyal is the Chancellor's Professor of Law and the Codirector of the Berkeley Center for Law & Technology. She joined the Berkeley Law faculty in 2015 from Fordham Law School, where she had served as the Joseph M. McLaughlin Professor of Law and the Associate Dean for Research. Professor Katyal's research focuses on the intersection of technology, intellectual property, and civil rights. Before entering academia, Professor Katyal was an associate specializing in intellectual property litigation in the San Francisco office of Covington & Burling.

Rosalie Koolhoven (University of Groningen, the Netherlands) studied International and European Law in Nijmegen (the Netherlands), Coimbra (Portugal), and Osnabrück (Germany) where she obtained her PhD in "unjustified enrichment law." She did internships a.o. at the European Court of Justice in Luxembourg. At Groningen, Professor Koolhoven's research and teaching has focused on property, access to resources, and the sharing economy. She joined the Department of Law & IT – now Transboundary Legal Studies – of the University of Groningen in 2016 to develop and teach a new interdisciplinary course on the circular and sharing economy. Her interest lies in the growth and potential of these "new economies," as they are enabled by ICT, putting traditional principles of property and contract law to the test.

Christopher Koopman is Senior Director of Strategy and Research at the Center for Growth and Opportunity at Utah State University. He is also Senior Affiliated Scholar at the Mercatus Center at George Mason University. Koopman earned his JD from Ave Maria University and his LLM in law and economics at George Mason University.

Nancy Leong is Professor of Law at the University of Denver Sturm College of Law, where she teaches courses relating to constitutional law and civil rights. She is the author of over 30 law review articles. Her recent scholarship has appeared or will appear in the *California Law Review, Georgetown Law Journal, Harvard Law Review, Northwestern University Law Review, Stanford Law Review, Virginia Law Review,* and *Yale Law Journal,* among many others. Professor Leong is the recipient of numerous awards and honors. She received the University of Denver's school-wide Distinguished Scholar Award for the 2017–2018 academic year, and her research was selected for presentation at the 2016 Yale/Stanford/Harvard Junior Faculty Forum.

Xiaodi Li is a doctoral fellow at the NYU Furman Center and a PhD candidate at NYU Wagner. She is interested in housing policy in the digital age, with a focus on short-term rental regulation. Xiaodi holds a BS from Tsinghua University School of Economics and Management (China) and an MA in Public Policy from Cornell University.

Sarah E. Light is Assistant Professor of Legal Studies and Business Ethics at the Wharton School of Business at the University of Pennsylvania, where she teaches Environmental Management, Law, and Policy. Light's research examines issues at the intersection of environmental law and business and technological innovation. Her articles have addressed the regulatory implications of the rise of transportation platforms like Uber and Lyft, as well as the development of autonomous vehicles; and the US military's role in stimulating private technological innovation to reduce fossil fuel use in what Light has called the Military-Environmental Complex. She also writes about the role of non-traditional institutions as sources of environmental governance, including the Department of Defense and the private sector through private environmental governance. Her articles have appeared in and are forthcoming in *The Stanford Law Review,* the *Duke Law Journal,* the *UCLA Law Review,* the *Vanderbilt Law Review,* the *Emory Law Journal* and the *Stanford Environmental Law Journal,* among others.

Orly Lobel is Don Weckstein Professor of Law at the University of San Diego and received her doctoral and law degrees from Harvard University. She is the award-winning author of several books and numerous articles. She is a prolific speaker, commentator and scholar who travels the world with an impact on policy and industry. Her best-selling book *You Don't Own Me: How Mattel v. MGA Entertainment Exposed Barbie's Dark Side* (2017) has been nationally and internationally acclaimed and received rave reviews from the *Wall Street Journal*, the *Financial Times*, the *New Yorker*, NPR, *Modern Law*, *Times Higher Education*, the *Washington Blade*, and more. Her book *Talent Wants to Be Free: Why We Should Learn to Love Leaks, Raids and Free Riding* (2013) is the winner of several prestigious awards, including Gold Medal Axiom Best Business Books 2014, Gold Medal Independent Publisher's Award 2014, the 2015 Gold Medal of Next Generation Indie Books, and Winner of the International Book Award. Lobel writes in the area of employment law, intellectual property law, regulatory policy, and behavioral law and economics.

Derek McKee is Professor of Law and Codirector of Programs in Common Law and Transnational Law at the Université de Sherbrooke. He first studied law at McGill University before obtaining his doctorate in law from the University of Toronto. He also served as law clerk to Chief Justice Beverley McLachlin of the Supreme Court of Canada in 2006–2007. His teaching and research focus on administrative law, tort law, and transnational law, including the relationship between domestic and international law in Canada. He is the editor, with Finn Makela and Teresa Scassa, of a volume entitled *Law and the "Sharing Economy": Regulating Market-Based Online Platforms* (forthcoming).

Stephen R. Miller is Professor of Law and Associate Dean for faculty development at the University of Idaho College of Law. He is a coauthor of *West's Land Use and Sustainable Development Law*. He holds a JD from the University of California, Hastings College of Law, a master's in city and regional planning from University of California, Berkeley, and an undergraduate degree from Brown University.

Matthew D. Mitchell is Senior Research Fellow and Director of the Project for the Study of American Capitalism at the Mercatus Center at George Mason University. He is also an adjunct professor of economics at Mason. In his writing and research, he specializes in public choice economics and the economics of government favoritism toward particular businesses, industries, and occupations. Mitchell has testified before the US Congress and has advised several state and local government policymakers on both fiscal and regulatory policy. His research has been featured in numerous national media outlets, including *The New York Times*, the *Wall Street Journal*, the *Washington Post*, *US News and World Report*, National Public Radio, and C-SPAN. He is the coauthor, with Peter J. Boettke, of *Applied Mainline Economics: Bridging the Gap Between Theory and Policy*. Mitchell received his PhD and MA in economics from George Mason University and his BA in political science and BS in economics from Arizona State University.

Mareike Möhlmann works as Assistant Professor in the Information Systems and Management Group at Warwick Business School. Previously, she worked as a postdoctoral researcher at the Stern School of Business at NYU. She obtained her doctoral degree at the University of Hamburg and holds an MSc from the London School of Economics. Her research focuses on how digital technologies change businesses, society, and human interaction. In particular, she is curious about collaborative consumption or sharing economy services, P2P platforms, digital trust, and algorithmic management.

Bronwen Morgan is Professor of Law at UNSW Sydney, Australia and recently completed an Australian Research Council Future Fellowship on the intersection of social movements and social enterprise. She is the coeditor of *Law for a New Economy: Enterprise, Sharing, Regulation* (2018).

Shu-Yi Oei is Professor of Law at Boston College Law School. Oei's recent work has focused on innovations in the arena of human capital investments and the taxation and regulation of new industries such as the gig economy. Her research interests also include social insurance and economic security, and domestic and international tax enforcement and administration. Her recent works on the sharing economy include "Can Sharing be Taxed?" (2016) (with Diane Ring).

Katerina Pantazatou is Associate Professor in Tax Law at the University of Luxembourg. Katerina has been a visiting researcher at Harvard Law School and at the Institute for Austrian and International Tax Law (WU) as an Ernst Mach scholar. Her research focuses on the taxation of the digital economy and the interaction between corporate governance and taxation.

Luca Ratti is Associate Professor in European and Comparative Labor Law at the University of Luxembourg and an Internal Fellow of the Robert Schuman Institute of European Affairs, Luxembourg. After a period as visiting post-doc in the United Kingdom, he served as Senior Researcher and Adjunct Professor in Labor Law and Social Security at the University of Bologna since 2012, where he also obtained his Doctorate in 2007. His works include "Online Platforms and Crowdwork in Europe: A Two-step Approach to Expanding Agency Work Provisions?" (2017).

Daniel E. Rauch is a 2016 graduate of Yale Law School. His previous works include "Like Uber, but for Local Government Law: The Future of Local Regulation of the Sharing Economy" (2015) (with David N. Schleicher) and "School Choice Architecture" (2015).

Diane M. Ring is Professor of Law and the Dr. Thomas F. Carney Distinguished Scholar at Boston College Law School. She researches and writes primarily in the fields of the sharing economy, international taxation, corporation taxation, and ethics. Her works on the sharing economy include "The Tax Lives of Uber Drivers: Evidence from Internet Discussion Forums" (2017) (with Shu-Yi Oei).

Brishen Rogers is Associate Professor of Law at Temple University. His research focuses on labor/employment law, and on the relationship between law and the political economy. He is currently writing a monograph with MIT Press on how the current wave of technological innovation is altering the political economy of work and work regulation. His previous works on such issues include "The Social Costs of Uber" (2015) and "Basic Income in a Just Society" (2017).

Naomi Schoenbaum is an associate professor of Law at George Washington University Law School whose research centers on employment law, family law, anti-discrimination law, and gender. Her work has addressed the legal regulation of critical but often overlooked relationships in the market, such as those between coworkers and those between workers and customers, as well as the design of anti-discrimination law. Her current research is focused on discrimination and intimacy in the sharing economy, unsexing the law of pregnancy, and the law's increasing turn to ignorance to achieve anti-discrimination goals. Her work has appeared in numerous law journals, including "The Law of Intimate Work" in the *Washington Law Review*, as well as popular publications such as *Slate* and *The Atlantic*.

Guido Smorto is Full Professor of Law at the University of Palermo (Italy) and Faculty Affiliate at the Internet Interdisciplinary Institute (IN3) – Barcelona (Spain). His most recent articles focus on the platform economy, with a special emphasis on European law. On these topics, beside scholarly works and non-academic articles, he has published a report on behalf of the EU Commission and a research paper for the EU Parliament, and contributed as an expert to the 2017 EP Resolution on the collaborative economy.

Arun Sundararajan is Professor of Business and the Robert L. and Dale Atkins Rosen Faculty Fellow at New York University's Stern School of Business, and an affiliated faculty member at NYU's Center for Data Science and Center for Urban Science and Progress. His award-winning book, *The Sharing Economy* (2016), has been translated into Mandarin Chinese, Japanese, Korean, Vietnamese, and Portuguese. He has authored over 50 peer-reviewed scientific papers, written over 35 op-eds, and has given hundreds of talks globally. His scholarship has been recognized by numerous Best Paper awards, two Google Faculty awards, an Axiom Best Business Books Award and a Thinkers50 Radar Thinker Award. He is a member of the World Economic Forum Global Future Council on Technology, Values, and Policy. He has provided expert testimony about the digital economy to the United States Congress, the European Parliament, the Federal Trade Commission, the White House and a range of regulators globally. He is an advisor to organizations that include the Female Founders Fund, Walmart Corporation, the Internet Society of China, OuiShare, and the National League of Cities.

Elizabeth Tippett is Associate Professor at the University of Oregon School of Law, as well as the Faculty Codirector of the Conflict and Dispute Resolution Master's Program. She researches business ethics, employment practices, and decision-making. Her research has been cited by state and federal courts, including two opinions by the United States Court of Appeals. She is a coauthor of the West Academic textbook, *Employment Discrimination & Employment Law: the Field as Practiced.* In 2017, she testified before a committee of the United States House of Representatives regarding attorney ethics.

Rebecca Tushnet is the inaugural Frank Stanton Professor of First Amendment Law at Harvard Law School. After clerking for Chief Judge Edward R. Becker of the Third Circuit and Associate Justice David H. Souter on the Supreme Court, she practiced intellectual property law at Debevoise & Plimpton before beginning teaching. Her publications include "Registering Disagreement: Registration in Modern American Trademark Law" (2017), "Worth a Thousand Words: The Images of Copyright Law" (2012), and "Copy This Essay: How Fair Use Doctrine Arms Free Speech and How Copying Serves It" (2004). With Eric Goldman, she publishes a casebook on advertising and marketing law, and has a forthcoming book on images in intellectual property law. Her work currently focuses on copyright, trademark, and false advertising law and their relationship to the First Amendment. Her blog, at tushnet.blogspot.com, is part of the ABA's Blawg Hall of Fame. Professor Tushnet helped found the Organization for Transformative Works, a nonprofit dedicated to supporting and promoting fanworks, and currently volunteers on its legal committee. She received Public Knowledge's IP3 Award for Intellectual Property in 2015.

Manoj Viswanathan teaches both doctrinal and experiential tax courses at UC Hastings College of the Law. His research focuses on tax policy, economic development, and the regulation of tax-exempt organizations. He received his LLM and JD from New York University School of Law, and undergraduate and graduate degrees from the Massachusetts Institute of Technology.

Katrina M. Wyman is the Sarah Herring Sorin Professor of Law at New York University School of Law. Her publications include "Taxi Regulation in the Age of Uber" (2017) and "Problematic Private Property: The Case of New York Taxicab Medallions."

Kellen Zale is an assistant professor at the University of Houston Law Center, where she writes and teaches in the areas of property, real estate, land use, and local government law. She received her AB from Princeton University and her JD from Duke University. Prior to joining the University of Houston, she was a Westerfield Fellow at Loyola University New Orleans College of Law, and an associate attorney in the Los Angeles office of Gibson, Dunn & Crutcher. Her scholarship has appeared, or is forthcoming, in the *Stanford Law Review, University of Colorado Law Review, Arizona State Law Journal,* and *Ecology Law Quarterly,* among others.

Acknowledgments

We thank the Suffolk Law School Faculty Initiatives Fund for supporting a workshop for contributing authors. We also thank Anthony Balzano and Louis Cholden-Brown for their tireless assistance and Heather Addison, Laura Blake, Liz Davey, Sara Marchington, and Deborah Renshaw for their careful editing. And we express our deep appreciation to Matt Gallaway for his inspiration and guidance in this project.

Introduction

That you are reading the *Cambridge Handbook of the Law of the Sharing Economy* is a testament to the rise of a global phenomenon that just a decade ago had barely begun to emerge, let alone to transform economies and regulation. It was only 2007 when Joe Gebbia and Brian Chesky created a website they called airbedandbreakfast.com in honor of the air mattresses they were planning to rent out on the floor of their living room. Today Airbnb claims more than 3,000,000 listings worldwide in more than 65,000 cities in over 191 countries. Uber did not launch until 2010 – as a black car hailing service (its ubiquitous UberX service launched two years later) – and has likewise spread worldwide, expanding significantly beyond its original business model of shared driving.

The rise of online platforms facilitating the sharing and pooling of everything from rooms to cars to food to money to clothes to people's skills and time is not only changing markets for goods and services. These platforms, and the individuals who use them, are also interacting in often unforeseen ways with existing regulation and posing challenges for regulators. This Handbook was born of an ambition to grapple conceptually and practically with what the rise of the sharing economy means for law and how law, in turn, is shaping critical aspects of the sharing economy.

That inquiry is important in its own right, as the challenges wrought by platforms are upending significant areas of regulation in legal system after legal system. But the interaction between the sharing economy and law is also critical and timely as a case study in the many and varied legal responses to innovation and disruption. This dynamic is hardly new and one can point to any number of other examples of similarly significant shifts, but as with so much of our society, the pace of change is cycling ever more rapidly and old institutions – as the scholars collected in this volume can attest – are adapting in surprising and vital ways.

A WORD ON NOMENCLATURE

Before we turn to details of the substance of the Handbook, we wanted to pause on the question of nomenclature – an issue that pervades the discourse. This Handbook uses the term "sharing economy" in reference to a diverse range of activities, subsets of which are variably referred to as the "peer-to-peer," "platform," "on demand," "gig," and "collaborative" economy. The phrase "sharing economy" has faced significant criticism. As numerous commentators have observed, highly visible and often controversial firms like Uber, Lyft, and Airbnb, which are often referred to as part of the sharing economy, do not, in fact, facilitate the gratuitous sharing of goods and services. Rather they facilitate commercial transactions between two parties: sellers or providers of goods and services and buyers or users. For this reason many prefer the term peer-to-peer, which suggests that, in most cases, the parties on either side of these exchanges are not professionals and that, in many cases, their activity is simply a side gig that makes use of the spare capacity of a resource they already own. But this description proves inaccurate for a significant number of providers, as some individuals work full time as a driver for Uber or Lyft or rent out multiple apartments on Airbnb. Others prefer the term platform economy, which focuses on the digital platforms and apps through which transactions are brokered. In many instances these platforms enable users to obtain goods and services "on demand." But this term can also be under-inclusive, as it may fail to include those components of the broader sharing economy that do in fact reflect a traditional understanding of "sharing," such as neighborhood tool libraries, which also may not rely upon a digital plat-form to facilitate exchanges.

Cognizant of these limitations, this Handbook uses the term "sharing economy" because it is the most ubiquitous term for referring to a myriad of new mechanisms for facilitating the exchange of goods and services, often provided by individual, small-scale actors. The Handbook embraces a very broad conception of the "sharing economy," including large for-profit firms like Airbnb, Uber, Lyft, Taskrabbit, and Upwork, as well as smaller, nonprofit collaborative initiatives, including lending libraries, maker spaces, and fab labs, through which individuals can obtain temporary access to a particular resource. Throughout the Handbook individual authors will, at times, spe-cify their own, perhaps narrower definition and scope of the economic activity they are discussing.

AN OVERVIEW OF THE HANDBOOK

This Handbook is divided into two broad parts. The first offers an overview of the nature of the sharing economy, explores the central challenge of balancing innovation and regulatory concerns, and then examines the institutions confronting these regulatory challenges. In the second part, the book turns to a series of specific regulatory domains. Since the project began, the global regulatory environment has continued to evolve, and new regulatory concerns have emerged, but a core set of legal questions continues to dominate. With details that vary across different legal systems, the critical regulatory questions that the sharing economy raises involve protections for workers and platform providers and conversely, consumer welfare for those using sharing platforms for goods and services; tax compliance; and, of course, civil rights. With both parts, this Handbook seeks to be timely in a fast-moving regulatory environment and offer depth across a range of regulatory domains.

One of the sharing economy's most noteworthy features is that it has spread across the globe irrespective of geographical borders. To account for that reach, the Handbook adopts a com-parative perspective. Our authors document the impact the sharing economy has had across jurisdictions, particularly in the United States and in the European Union, but also beyond. This rich range of perspectives reveals that while the impact and consequences of the sharing economy are often deeply linked to place, many of the benefits and challenges encountered are similar irrespective of place.

Just as digital platforms themselves operate across borders, the sharing economy's disruptive effects cannot be pinned down to a specific jurisdiction. With this in mind, the Handbook unites authors from a wide range of backgrounds to document the regulatory responses that have been adopted as a consequence of the sharing economy's emergence. The hope is to create a cross-jurisdictional debate on these aspects, and enable regulators to learn from experiences elsewhere. The comparative perspective is one of the Handbook's distinguishing features and we encourage readers to not limit themselves to the chapters specifically related to their own jurisdiction as experiences elsewhere might provide just as much insight as those at home.

With these goals in mind, what follows provides an overview of how the Handbook progresses.

SECTION 1

The Handbook's first section examines the nature of the sharing economy and its growing importance. Aurélien Acquier argues that peer-to-peer digital platforms like Uber and Airbnb – the most visible and controversial parts of the sharing economy – are not a radically new phenomenon. While they depart from the traditional model of the hierarchical and integrated firm, Acquier invokes organizational theory and business history to contend that these platforms represent "a digital reincarnation of the 'putting-out system.'" Akin to that pre-industrial form of business organization, peer-to-peer platforms outsource work to individuals who own their own means of production. Yet even as they depart from a managerial understanding of the firm, these platforms accord with a financial vision that casts the firm as a nexus of contractual relationships.

Such relationships depend, to a significant degree, on trust. Mareike Möhlmann and Andrea Geissinger provide a sociological account of the historical evolution and transformation of trust. They examine how platforms build trust between strangers in a cumulative fashion, relying on a variety of digital cues, such as peer reviews, which foster both interpersonal and institutional trust. These platform-mediated trust cues, which might, they propose, one day be accumulated into a form of digital social capital, have important regulatory implications.

While, on the one hand, the sharing economy might be understood in terms of small-scale, peer-to-peer transactions reliant on digital trust, the significant volume of such small transactions can produce negative cumulative effects. Kellen Zale argues that scale is a defining feature of the sharing economy and one that must be better understood in order to craft more effective regulatory responses. Traditional justifications for the regulatory leniency afforded to small-scale activities are less convincing when applied to the large number of such activities facilitated by third-party platforms functioning as network orchestrators.

Section 1 concludes with a more granular examination of peer-to-peer platforms in relation to a typology of business models. Relying on field research into 30 sharing initiatives in Europe, Aurélien Acquier and Valentina Carbone situate a range of sharing economy initiatives in relation to their mechanisms of value creation, scaling potential, and social innovation impacts. They conclude that the sharing economy's potential for promoting social innovation depends, in significant part, on the decisions and efforts of governments, academic institutions, and social actors.

SECTION 2

The sharing economy has engendered a range of innovations, transforming transportation, lodging, lending, and other sectors. Section 2 examines how to balance the desire to encourage beneficial innovations with the demand for appropriate and effective regulation. Orly Lobel begins the section by examining how platforms serve to lower transactions costs and improve deal-making. She argues that regulators must consider how platform innovations might make certain traditional regulations redundant.

Matthew D. Mitchell and Christopher Koopman examine the emergence of the sharing economy in the transportation sector and how public and private models of regulation have been deployed to create order in a context of disruptive innovation. On the basis of this analysis they establish a typology of four distinct types of regulation that have been adopted to date.

In spite of their young age, sharing economy platforms have accumulated significant market power. Niamh Dunne considers the implications of that state of affairs from the European perspective, drawing attention to the limits of competition law in addressing negative social and economic consequences.

In light of the lack of solid data, speculation often surrounds the sharing economy's impact on a given sector or space. Peter Coles, Michael Egesdal, Ingrid Gould Ellen, Xiaodi Li, and Arun Sundararajan offer new empirical evidence regarding actual Airbnb usage patterns across New York City. Combining a rich mix of data from various sources, including from the platform itself, they illustrate how Airbnb's effect on the city's housing market has changed over time.

Katrina Wyman looks at sharing in the mobility sector and the emergence of the category of transportation network companies (TNCs) in the United States as a novel form of regulation. Comparing TNC regulation to traditional taxi regulation, she highlights that TNCs are able to address long-standing concerns while also reinforcing established problems of industry capture.

SECTION 3

Section 3 examines various regulatory strategies that have been adopted as a response to the sharing economy's emergence. The contributions examine different aspects of the regulatory challenges triggered by the emergence of the sharing economy but agree that regulatory responses must fit the sharing economy's specific characteristics.

The sharing economy encompasses a wide range of phenomena. Its actors are equally diverse and include peers or nonprofessional providers, who offer a surplus of time, skills, or goods, as well as highly professionalized actors who harness the platform economy model. Erez Aloni illustrates how such pluralism burdens any regulatory response and argues that the state should establish a series of valuable alternative regulatory regimes that can protect individuals from related risks.

Raymond Brescia illustrates that the very features that make the sharing economy attractive as a business model, including decentralization, the reliance on trust as an engine for economic exchange, and new technological possibilities, also make it difficult to regulate. Relying on new governance approaches, he suggests that regulation must be matched to the sharing economy's uniqueness in order to balance innovation and consumer protection.

Licenses are often at the center of controversies surrounding the sharing economy. Derek McKee illustrates, drawing on the Canadian example, that despite claims to the contrary platform-based business models have not rendered established licensing regimes obsolete. Industry self-regulation is shown to be unable to do away with known licensing problems as it raises the same concerns of inefficiency and political arbitrariness so that alternative regulatory models should be considered.

Bryant Cannon and Hanna Chung posit that regulation ought to echo the sharing economy's inherent attributes. With this in mind they put forward a proposal for a co-regulatory model able to account for specific market behaviors.

Stephen R. Miller draws attention to the data collected by platforms and underlines the potential of data for urban governance from a historical perspective. Taking the example of sharing economy platforms as collectors of data, he explores the legal and political implications of urban data-based decision-making.

SECTION 4

The sharing economy has spread irrespective of geographical boundaries and affects regulators at various scales of public authority. Considering the large variety of potential regulators, this section attempts to determine which levels of public authority are best placed to address the sharing economy.

The sharing economy is a predominantly urban phenomenon. Nestor Davidson and John Infranca explore the implications of the place of the sharing economy, highlighting that sharing platforms are often able to address urban challenges and leverage features of urban life. Exploring the role of local governments as early sharing economy regulators, they argue that even as other levels are now also stepping in, a degree of local autonomy ought to be preserved.

While the local level was the first to be immediately affected by the rise of sharing platforms, other actors have gradually become involved in their regulation. Sarah Light examines the federalism implications of the sharing economy in the United States, highlighting the regulatory role of the federal government.

Janice Griffith, on the other hand, explores the role of state governments in the United States. Considering that the sharing economy can affect statewide and local interests, her contribution presents guidelines for the delineation of the governance level best suited to regulate sharing economy activities.

The sharing economy is thus a phenomenon that affects numerous levels of public authority. Daniel Rauch explores why, considering its multilevel nature, local governments have become such important actors in the regulation of the sharing economy, and raises the question of whether they can and should play such a prominent role.

Questions regarding the most adequate scale of regulation have also emerged in the European Union. Michèle Finck explores whether there is a place for the EU to regulate aspects of the sharing economy. Answering this question affirmatively, she then attempts to determine which regulatory model is best suited for digital data-driven platforms.

Bronwen Morgan examines the question of the most adequate scale of regulation from the Australian perspective. She draws attention to the fact that definitions of the sharing economy are disputed and adopts the framework of "platform cooperativism" to present a distinctive vision of multi-scalar relationships between the local, national, and international dimensions of platform regulation.

SECTION 5

Section 5 of the Handbook shifts focus from understanding the sharing economy and its regulatory landscape at a macroscopic level to the first of a series of explorations of specific regulatory domains, namely the critical arena of labor and employment. To begin, Elizabeth Tippett offers a cogent overview of the legal standards that govern whether the law classifies workers as independent contractors or employees. She then homes in on ways that existing doctrine can facilitate employer noncompliance with and avoidance of employee protections and ways the legal system might address those challenges.

Brishen Rogers next turns to ways that the sharing economy is particularly impacting low-wage workers. Rogers usefully disaggregates two aspects of organization in low-wage labor markets: statutory entitlements for those firms' workers and the firms' technological and regulatory sophistication as well as market impact. From this typology, Rogers suggests some avenues of reform of the disadvantages of informality and low quality of work in the sharing economy.

Miriam Cherry and Antonio Aloisi offer a different set of reform proposals, centered around the idea of a hybrid classification between employee and independent contractor. Bringing a keen comparative perspective, Cherry and Aloisi explore the use of a third category to cover non-standard workers in Canada, Italy, Spain, Germany, and South Korea, concluding that there are significant limitations to this model and instead advocating for a default rule in the sharing economy that workers should be classified as employees or something resembling that classification.

Finally, turning to other parts of the globe, Mark Graham and Mohammad Amir Anwar focus on the role of digital labor, and its developmental impacts, in low- and middle-income countries in Africa and Asia. They examine how, through models of cooperative work, labor practices in the sharing economy might be made fairer for workers throughout the world.

SECTION 6

How sharing economy firms classify workers – whether as independent contractors or employees – has significant tax consequences. Section 6 explores the range of tax issues raised by the sharing economy, from the perspective of individual sharing economy workers, the platforms themselves, and taxing authorities. Shu-Yi Oei and Diane Ring examine the myriad of tax issues – including classification, documentation, and compliance challenges – sharing economy workers in the United States must confront. They highlight the complexities of existing requirements for workers and outline a range of proposed reforms. As they note, how the tax system responds to work in the sharing economy will affect the sector's growth and development.

Manoj Viswanathan shifts the focus to examine tax compliance issues and potential changes to better balance the interests of sharing economy workers and federal, state, and local taxing authorities. In addition to income tax compliance, the sharing economy raises a range of issues for the assessment and collection of wage, sales, occupancy, and property taxes. Viswanathan suggests that, to be successful, tax compliance efforts must enlist sharing economy companies, who have access to the information and resources necessary to improve reporting and compliance.

A lack of uniformity and the absence of regulation at the EU level makes it inherently difficult to discuss taxation of the sharing economy in the European Union. Katerina Pantazatou provides an overview of taxation in the EU generally and the taxation of the sharing economy in particular. She then presents some of the specific initiatives different EU Member States have taken with regard to taxation of the sharing economy and identifies the tensions these can create in relation to EU law in other areas. Pantazatou argues that the EU should take comprehensive action in relation to the sharing economy, at a minimum establishing general guidelines for Member States.

Finally, Jordan Barry concludes the tax law section by turning back to the question of how to balance regulation and innovation. He uses the sharing economy as a focal point for analyzing the relationship between the federal income tax system in the United States and innovation. Barry questions whether tax law acts as an effective tool for encouraging technological or trans-actional innovation. Instead, he suggests, the innovations that mark the sharing economy, by exacerbating gray areas in the tax code, might spur regulators to clarify these areas, advancing the tax system itself.

The sharing economy, of course, involves not only producers but equally importantly consumers matched through platforms. This next section explores a variety of issues involving consumer protection and privacy. Rebecca Tushnet examines a set of related challenges arising from the collapse of distinctions between speech and commerce, between public and private, and between work and voluntary "sharing," which once marked regulatory domains. This has placed stress on false advertising protections, online conflicts of interest in testimonials, and in creative uses of agency law to hold platforms liable. In the online world of the sharing economy, Tushnet argues, consumer welfare law can adapt through other means of linking responsibility for an entity's acts to another entity.

Turning to another important legal regime implicated in the sharing economy, Sonia Katyal and Leah Chan Grinvald argue that trademark is determinative for the success or failure of platform companies. This centrality plays out across a spectrum of trademark interactivity, and Katyal and Grinvald offer an insightful typology of how trademark interacts with platform entrepreneurship. The chapter then explains the ways that design and architectural form challenge – but create opportunities for – the modernization of trademark law.

Rosalie Koolhoven shifts focus to European private law, canvassing contract law across European Member States as a complement to European law on the question of the liability of platforms for harms caused by providers. Koolhoven unpacks the different ways Member States address sharing economy matching services, arguing that the core contracts that define the relationship between platforms and providers obligate platforms to pursue third-party interests, which is to say consumer interests. As Koolhoven argues, consumer protection law varies across the EU, but has surprising strength grounded in private law.

Finally, Guido Smorto challenges claims for lighter regulation in light of arguments for new paradigms of choice. Instead, Smorto argues, platforms use boilerplate, technological architecture, and algorithms to assert power over providers and consumers. In light of a detailed analysis of the terms and conditions of these techniques, Smorto concludes that law must protect what he describes as weaker parties in the sharing economy.

The sharing economy has sadly proven that the pathologies of the physical world all too often carry over to the platform, raising significant concerns for anti-discrimination law. Charlotte Garden and Nancy Leong begin the Handbook's exploration of these dynamics by excavating the landscape of responsibility for platform companies. Such firms, Garden and Leong argue, are suffering from an "identity crisis," both embracing and distancing themselves from the commercial relationships they foster. Law has accordingly struggled with whether platforms genuinely neutrally enable dyadic relationships between others or instead actively participate in a triadic relationship. Surfacing this key tension can help shape legal responses across discrimination law and public accommodations, but more broadly for the general responsibility of platforms.

Naomi Schoenbaum next turns to the ways in which the sharing economy augurs a shift in the place of intimacy and its relationship to equality. Sharing-economy transactions, Schoenbaum notes, tend to involve personal space, with platforms highlighting personal relationships to foster trust. This economic intimacy, however, has raised concerns with race and sex discrimination, and major platforms have moved to depersonalize transactions. As Schoenbaum concludes, there are costs to this rebalancing between equality and intimacy.

Jamila Jefferson-Jones takes an empirical turn, given evidence of pervasive discrimination in the sharing economy, particularly with short-term rentals. Jefferson-Jones provides an exegesis of the ways anti-discrimination laws in the United States apply to new models of short-term rentals, with particular focus on the question whether individual hosts or platform firms should be liable for discrimination. As Jefferson-Jones argues, in the context of race and disability, there are serious impediments to applying traditional anti-discrimination paradigms to the sharing economy, and she offers reform proposals.

The Handbook's exploration of the challenges of discrimination concludes with an analysis by Nicola Countouris and Luca Ratti of EU anti-discrimination responses. Countouris and Ratti argue that there is important potential in EU equality law to combat discrimination, given the law's broad scope and dual nature as both an economic and a fundamental social right. However, Countouris and Ratti caution that this potential may not be realized, given some structural doctrinal deficiencies in EU equality law as interpreted and applied by the Court of Justice of the EU (CJEU).

CONCLUSION

The sharing economy's rapid growth has disrupted existing business models and displaced incumbent industries. It has created challenges for all levels of governments as they struggle to enforce existing regulations or create new regulations amid a climate of innovation and uncertainty. And for individuals it has, in some cases, rendered work more precarious, tax compliance more challenging, and discrimination even more pernicious.

The rapid growth and change that mark the sharing economy also make it difficult for scholars who seek to understand and evaluate it. As such, the contributions in this Handbook try to take a step back at a moment in time when the sharing economy, while not entirely new, is still in its adolescence, and to offer perspective on where this new economy came from, how it is developing, and how it is being shaped by, but also transforming, existing areas of law. We hope that, by establishing a deep, multi-disciplinary, and comparative understanding of the law of the sharing economy as it stands today, in 2018, the Handbook will frame for discussion going forward the issues, questions, and challenges that regulators, individual citizens, and scholars must continue to grapple with in the decades ahead.

PART I

Understanding the Sharing Economy and Its Regulatory Landscape

What Is the Sharing Economy and Why Is It Important?

Uberization Meets Organizational Theory

Platform Capitalism and the Rebirth of the Putting-Out System

Aurélien Acquier

INTRODUCTION

At first sight, peer-to-peer digital platforms undoubtedly appear as a radically new phenomenon. Most of them were created less than a decade ago: Airbnb was founded in 2008, Uber in 2009, Lyft in 2012. While these corporations are still in their infancy when compared to most large-scale capitalist enterprises that have dominated capitalism since the second industrial revolution, they have, in a surprisingly short period of time, brought about major economic and social transformations. Much has been written about the competitive transformations and disruptive pressures created by platforms like Airbnb or Uber on century-old companies and professions;[1] about the ongoing rise of self-employed versus salaried work and the emergence of a "gig economy"[2] with its associated regulatory challenges;[3] new forms of collaborative consumption and exchange based on "stranger sharing";[4] and about the dynamics of peer and open-source production.[5]

There is little doubt that platforms largely depart from the traditional bureaucratic and hierarchically integrated firm that has long dominated capitalism and organizational theory.[6] As digital organizations, platforms convey the countercultural and libertarian values that marked the origins of the internet,[7] and tend to promote decentralization and horizontal forms of peer-to-peer collaboration. Internet and digital organizations are often analyzed as a field of alternative, collaborative, and democratic forms of organization,[8] de-hierarchized systems based on "Holacracy,"[9] open-source

---

[1] *See* C. M. Christensen, M. E. Raynor, and R. McDonald, *What Is Disruptive Innovation?* December Harv. Bus. Rev. 44–53 (2015); A. Sundararajan, *The Sharing Economy* (2016).

[2] G. Friedman, *Workers Without Employers: Shadow Corporations and the Rise of the Gig Economy*, 2 Rev. Keynes. Econ. 171–88 (2014).

[3] III R. L. Redfearn, *Sharing Economy Misclassification: Employees and Independent Contractors in Transportation Network Companies* (2016).

[4] Y. Benkler, *"Sharing Nicely": On Shareable Goods and the Emergence of Sharing as a Modality of Economic Production*, 114 Yale Law Sch. Leg. Scholarsh. Repos. 273–358 (2004).

[5] M. Bauwens, *The Political Economy of Peer Production*, CTheory 12–1. (2015).

[6] W. R. Scott and G. F. Davis, *Organizations and Organizing: Rational, Natural, and Open System Perspectives* (1st ed., 2014).

[7] F. Turner, *From Counterculture to Cyberculture: Stewart Brand, the Whole Earth Network, and the Rise of Digital Utopianism* 1 (paperback ed., 2008).

[8] F. Laloux, *Reinventing Organizations* (2015).

[9] B. J. Robertson, *Holacracy: The New Management System for a Rapidly Changing World* (1st ed., 2015). Holacracy is one of many concepts that promote a new approach to management and leadership in opposition to the traditional hierarchical bureaucracy. According to its founder, Brian J. Robertson, holacracy is a management model based on self-engagement, individual initiative, and distributed leadership.

production,[10] or spaces for noncommercial collaboration allowing the emergence of shared goods.[11] In general, peer-to-peer platforms are imbued with a strong post-bureaucratic flavor.[12]

For academics trained in organization theory, these new organizational forms pose a challenge. Are organization theories still relevant to make sense of this new breed? In the end, why wouldn't digital platforms disrupt organization theory itself, just like Uber and Airbnb disrupted the taxi and hotel sectors? In this chapter I use organizational theory and business history to question the newness of peer-to-peer platforms and develop an organizational analysis of digital platforms such as Uber and Airbnb and more generally of platform capitalism.[13] By "platform capitalism," I refer to a set of organizations carrying out productive and for-profit activities through digital platforms that arrange transactions between providers and customers. Two definitional remarks: as defined in this chapter, "platform capitalism" only constitutes one part (arguably the most visible and controversial) of what is commonly referred to as the sharing economy. Therefore, this chapter does not cover the entire and broader field of the sharing economy, which also builds on logics derived from the access-based economy and community-based economy,[14] and involves a variety of value-creation models.[15] Second, this chapter does not look at platforms for sharing information between peers (social networks like Facebook, Twitter, etc.); instead, I will focus on peer-to-peer transactional platforms whose primary function is to intermediate between peer-based supply and demand for commercial transactions.[16]

My central argument in this chapter is that the emergence of platform capitalism should be understood as a digital reincarnation of the "putting-out system,"[17] a pre-industrial organizational form that preceded the emergence of manufacturing and the managerial corporation. In this system, merchants outsourced work to individuals who produced goods at home and owned their own means of production. The current return of this mode of production creates major challenges, for organizational theory, the governance of platforms, and individuals.

This chapter is structured in three parts. First, I discuss how platform capitalism is challenging two fundamental tenets of organizational theory. In the second section, I explore platform capitalism from a historical perspective. I first examine – and then challenge – the idea that algorithmic management marks a rebirth of Taylorism.[18] Moving beyond this perspective, I develop

---

[10] E. S. Raymond, *The Cathedral & the Bazaar: Musings on Linux and Open Source by an Accidental Revolutionary* (1st ed., 1999).

[11] Y. Benkler, *The Wealth of Networks: How Social Production Transforms Markets and Freedom* (2006); D. Jemielniak, *Common Knowledge? An Ethnography of Wikipedia* (2014).

[12] A. Acquier, T. Daudigeos, and J. Pinkse, *Promises and Paradoxes of the Sharing Economy: An Organizing Framework*, 125 Technol. Forecast. Soc. Change 1–10 (2017).

[13] P. C. Evans and A. Gawer, *The Rise of the Platform Enterprise: A Global Survey* (2016); N. Srnicek and L. De Sutter, *Platform Capitalism, Theory Redux* (2017); Sundararajan, *supra* note 1.

[14] Acquier et al., *supra* note 12.

[15] *See* Acquier and Carbone, this volume.

[16] Evans and Gawer, *supra* note 13.

[17] D. A. Hounshell, *From the American System to Mass Production, 1800–1932: The Development of Manufacturing Technology in the United States. Studies in Industry and Society* (1984).

[18] The term Taylorism is used in reference to the managerial doctrine founded by Frederick Winslow Taylor, also known as "scientific management." Taylorism emerged as one of the first systematic managerial doctrines of work design, at the end of the nineteenth and beginning of the twentieth century; *see* F. W. Taylor, *Shop Management* (1903); F. W. Taylor, *The Principles of Scientific Management* (1911). Taylor developed a systematic method for re-engineering work using scientific principles, relying on the use of science and rationality (instead of empiricism and workers' autonomy) and on a stark differentiation between work engineers (in charge of designing and controlling

two propositions that I believe are central to conceptualizing the organizational models of peer-to-peer platforms. First, I argue that the emergence of transactional platforms can be viewed as the organizational outcome of the ongoing financialization of firms and individuals, which began in the 1970s and 80s. Second, I argue that this logic replaces the managerial organization by pre-capitalist forms of labor organization, in a type of putting-out system powered by digital technologies. In the third section, I explore the challenges of this analysis in terms of the governance of platforms.

I WELCOME TO THE NEW – AND STRANGE – WORLD OF PLATFORM CAPITALISM

Peer-to-peer platforms challenge fundamental tenets of both the economic and sociological view of the firm, arguably the two major traditions of organizational theory. For organizational analysis rooted in the economic tradition, *platforms erode the boundaries between markets and firms.* Since Ronald Coase's foundational article on "the nature of the firm" and Oliver Williamson's subsequent Transaction Cost Theory,[19] it has generally been acknowledged that firm and market are two fundamentally different mechanisms for coordinating transactions. In this perspective, business coordination is based on a centralized hierarchy, standardization and planning, which reduces uncertainty. It constitutes an alternative to market coordination, which by nature is more heterogeneous, uncertain, free, and regulated by price. This fundamental distinction – often used in organization theory textbook introductions – obviously does not apply to platforms like Uber, Airbnb, Taskrabbit, and others, which organize transactions between providers and customers who are independent of the platform. Neither full markets, nor full hierarchies, they constitute hybrid governance structures that are best described as "market organizations."[20] Such hybrids render obsolete the idea of a fundamental difference between organizational and market functioning.

Platforms are also shaking up some fundamental tenets of the sociological tradition of organizational analysis, as *relations of social and economic domination are no longer based on the cleavage between capital and labor.* Since 1865 when Marx theorized relations of domination in the capitalist regime, it has been accepted that conflicts concerning value production and value capture revolve around the distinction between capital holders on one side and labor providers (who exchange work for a salary) on the other.[21] This fundamental distinction between capital and labor, which has infused a long tradition of research in the sociology of labor, is also being shaken by the emergence of platforms. Indeed, platform workers, whether Uber drivers or Airbnb hosts, possess (or at least provide) the capital needed to perform their activity. In the strange world of platform capitalism, workers are capitalists without power, exploited by the virtual managers (algorithms) of companies without employees!

---

work) and workers (in charge of execution). Taylorism has been associated with mechanization, mass production, standardization of processes, automation, extreme specialization of work, and negative consequences for workers such as alienation and de-skilling of the workforce; *see* G. Friedmann, *The Anatomy of Work: Labor, Leisure, and the Implications of Automation* (1961).

[19] R. Coase, *The Nature of the Firm.* November Econ. NSG (1937); O. E. Williamson, *The Economic Institutions of Capitalism* (1985).

[20] R. Makadok and R. Coff, *Both Market and Hierarchy: An Incentive-System Theory of Hybrid Governance Forms*, 34 Acad. Manage. Rev. 297–319 (2009).

[21] K. Marx, *Salaires, prix et plus value* (2010).

II FROM FIRMS TO PLATFORMS: FINANCIALIZATION AND THE REBIRTH OF THE PUTTING-OUT SYSTEM

History is an indispensable tool for contextualizing and analyzing how these organizational innovations function and understanding their implications. In this section, I discuss the emergence of platforms in light of business history and the transformation of the firm.

A *A Reincarnation of Taylorism?*

Sociologists of work have recently taken an interest in the impact of algorithms on work. Rather than study the work of programmers who design algorithms (digital white collars), they explore the hidden and dark side of "digital labor," the emergence of a new type of work that is often low-skilled and globalized.[22] This research explores how a new class of specialized workers, often referred to as "digital pieceworkers,"[23] sells its labor on micro-task platforms similar to Amazon's Mechanical Turk platform.[24] Through such platforms, companies offer micro-tasks to individuals dotted around the world who perform them in exchange for micro-wages. Earning anywhere from a few cents to a few dollars per task, individuals assist the algorithms by completing or configuring them: they input data for a few seconds, verify files, transcribe, translate, correct, code, take photos, put items in order, click on a page, etc.

Echoing academic work on algorithmic management,[25] a recent *Financial Times* article invokes this historical perspective.[26] Detailing the working conditions of delivery drivers and couriers for UberEats and Deliveroo in London (in the food delivery sector), the article draws an analogy between these new forms of labor organization and Taylorism. It underlines how algorithms measure and monitor the activity of couriers in real time and make managerial decisions, such as automatically excluding a member from the platform for any deviation from expected standards. These tools are used for measuring productivity, timing activities, and remote monitoring, which largely echo the scientific management of Frederick Taylor.[27] The article cites Jeremias Prassl, professor of law at Oxford University: "Algorithms are providing a degree of control and oversight that even the most hardened Taylorists could never have dreamt of."

For these new proletarians of the early twenty-first century, the limitations, fears, and criticisms leveled at the Taylorist organization of labor one hundred years ago seem to be largely transposable to these contemporary forms of work. Digital work is characterized by a clear separation between the conception and execution of work, which ultimately places the individual in the service of the algorithmic machine, in a digital version of *Modern Times*. Work on such micro-task platforms is reduced to an extremely fragmented and alienating task, the individual to an

---

[22] C. Fuchs, *Digital Labour and Karl Marx* (2014); T. Scholz (ed.), *Digital Labor: The Internet as Playground and Factory* (2013).

[23] D. Cardon and A. A. Casilli, *Qu'est-ce que le digital labor ?* (2015).

[24] Beyond its mode of operating, the reference to the "Mechanical Turk" is particularly revealing of the platform's underlying vision: to make work literally "invisible"; *see* P.-Y. Gomez, *Le travail invisible: enquête sur une disparition* (2013). The original Mechanical Turk was an elaborate fake automaton, designed at the end of the eighteenth century to trick people into believing that it was an automaton equipped with artificial intelligence that could play chess against humans. Outwardly, the Mechanical Turk looked like a machine, but in reality it was controlled by a human chess player hidden inside. Amazon's Mechanical Turk metaphor reveals the concept behind the platform: using invisible human labor to create the illusion of an automaton and assist the algorithms.

[25] M. K. Lee, D. Kusbit, E. Metsky, and L. Dabbish, *Working with Machines: The Impact of Algorithmic and Data-Driven Management on Human Workers.* 1603–12 (2015).

[26] S. O'Connor, *When your Boss is an Algorithm*, Financ. Times, Sept. 8, 2016 at 10.

[27] *Supra* note 18.

operator, with the same effects in terms of deskilling, dehumanization, and loss of meaning in work as in Taylorist forms of organization.[28] The Taylorist engineering dream of a completely mechanized and rationalized organization appears to be alive and well if we consider Uber's plans for autonomous vehicles, which reflect its desire to get rid of its drivers, in a universe where the service would be entirely robotized, mechanized and free of human work. In this corner of the digital universe, human work is seen as a necessary evil, a relic that serves to supply an algorithmic chain that appears to have replaced the physical production line of the factory.

Many traces of Taylorism seem to be present in digital work: a mechanistic vision of the organization, a scientific dream of organizational control through technology, the stopwatch timing of operators and a sharp separation between design and execution where the worker is just an extension of the machine. However, the Taylorist analogy has several limitations and should be nuanced on three important points. First, the level of workers' autonomy differs vastly from one platform to the other, resulting in varying degrees of prescription, to use Taylorist language. While the degree of prescription appears to be high on platforms like Mechanical Turk or Uber – where the organization sets prices and operating processes that must be followed by operators – other platforms such as Etsy, Airbnb, or Upwork (a global freelancing platform) allow service suppliers significantly more autonomy and are less obtrusive in the types of interaction between transaction partners. Similarly, crowdfunding platforms claim to act as mere brokers: they impose very few conditions on their users, either on the nature of projects to be financed, their operation or the responsibility of the project initiators.

Second, while Taylorism is characterized by a transformation of work, achieved by breaking down tasks and recomposing processes, things are more complex for platforms. In the case of Uber, the activity is only reconceived marginally: the driving activity is not radically transformed (it is still performed by a driver who has freedom of choice in terms of routes, trips/riders, driving, working hours, etc.). Rather than imposing a standardized process or redesigning the work by fragmenting it, the platform intensifies control by introducing performance evaluations by the customer, the driver, and the platform.

Finally, digital labor is quite unlike the social organization of Taylorism. As several business historians have pointed out, Taylorism is closely associated with the emergence of large firms, salaried employment, and labor unions.[29] Through the systematic study and engineering of work, Taylorism radically redefined the nature of work and its processes. Such a transformation entailed the creation and recognition of hierarchical power in the workshop, and a relationship of subordination between the worker and the organization. Along with the emergence of Taylorism, the responsibility for work was transferred from the individual to the organization, and salaried employment was generalized as a way of regulating work in the firm. Through this mechanism, the firm took on responsibility for workers' skills, the means of production, and working conditions and it established long-term employment relations – quite the contrary of platform capitalism, which emphasizes the independence and autonomy of workers.

In the end, while some platforms echo the technical aspects of Taylor's dream, they seem to be completely at odds with the social organization (the managerial firm and work subordination) that underpinned Taylorism.

---

[28] Friedmann, *supra* note 18.

[29] *See* A. Hatchuel, Coordination and Control, in *The IEBM Handbook of Organizational Behaviour* 330–38 (A. Sorge and M. Warner eds., 1997); D. Nelson, *Frederick W. Taylor and the Rise of Scientific Management* (1980); D. Savino, *Louis D. Brandeis and His Role Promoting Scientific Management as a Progressive Movement*, 15 J. Manag. Hist. 38–49 (2009); C. D. Wrege and R. G. Greenwood, *Frederick W. Taylor, The Father of Scientific Management: Myth and Reality* (1991).

B From the Managerial Firm to the Financial Platform

The organizational logic of platform capitalism must also be understood as the product of a process of financialization that progressively replaced the logics of managerial capitalism, a process that has been described in detail by Gerald Davis.[30] The organizational model of the traditional – and integrated – managerial firm was generalized during the second industrial revolution and the twentieth century. As Alfred Chandler has shown, with the emergence of large firms, the central driver of the economy and innovation shifted from the "invisible hand of the market" to the "visible hand of managers."[31] Through their power, the managers rationalized firms and organized their operations. The firm concentrated power and gathered together unique competences, whether in terms of product creation (unprecedented in technical complexity and scale), the organization of labor and production (as attested by Taylor's efforts in the organization of work), marketing or market power.

In the 1930s, Berle and Means underlined the issues of control and governance raised by this managerial revolution, especially in relation to shareholders.[32] In the managerial firm, management became more and more concentrated, while shareholding became more and more diffused. Managers took over the running of the firm. Their accountability toward distant and fragmented shareholders was limited. In the 1960s and 1970s, many observers worried about the considerable influence that managers exerted on society. Galbraith criticized the way firms neutralized the laws of supply and demand with their economic power, intervened in democratic choices through political influence and shaped consumers' intimate desires through marketing.[33] In the era of managerial capitalism, big business, now an institution, prioritized its own development and preservation, adopting a dominant role over markets and society.

However, the story did not end there, and the 1970s paved the way for the market's comeback. The transformation was both academic and ideological, occurring against a backdrop of the rise of neoliberalism and the democratization of capital markets, boosted by academic research in finance. In 1965, Henry Manne published an article advocating the deregulation of financial markets in order to better discipline managers.[34] Corporate governance had to be overhauled: putting shareholders back at the center, increasing financial transparency, and discouraging any managerial underperformance with the constant threat of being taken over by a competitor or investor. In 1976, Jensen and Meckling laid the foundations of agency theory, a theory of the firm that runs counter to the notion of the firm as an institution (the managerial firm) and instead depicted it as a simple "nexus for contracting relationships" whose nature is not fundamentally different from the market.[35] According to this theory,

> contractual relations are the essence of the firm... most organizations are simply legal fictions which serve as a nexus for a set of contracting relationships among individuals... Viewed this way, it makes little or no sense to try to distinguish those things that are "inside" the firm (or any other organization) from those things that are "outside" of it. There is in a very real sense only a multitude of complex relationships (i.e., contracts) between the legal fiction (the firm) and the owners of labor, material and capital inputs and the consumers of output... We seldom fall into

---

[30] G. F. Davis, *Managed by the Markets: How Finance Reshaped America* (2009).

[31] A. Chandler, *The Visible Hand: The Managerial Revolution in American Business* (1977).

[32] A. A. J. Berle and G. C. Means, *The Modern Corporation and Private Property* (1933).

[33] J. K. Galbraith, *The New Industrial State*, The James Madison Library in American Politics. (1967).

[34] H. G. Manne, *Mergers and the Market for Corporate Control*, 73 J. Polit. Econ. 110–20 (1965).

[35] M. C. Jensen and W. H. Meckling, *Theory of the Firm: Managerial Behavior, Agency Costs and Ownership Structure*, 3 J. Financ. Econ. 305–60 (1976).

the trap of characterizing the wheat or stock market as an individual, but we often make this error by thinking about organizations as if they were persons with motivations and intentions.[36]

In agency theory, the firm should not be viewed as an entity with clear boundaries and responsibilities. For the proponents of agency theory, the view of the firm as a legal "person" (or a "body," as suggested by the term in-corporation) is strongly misleading: considering the firm as an entity is a mere "legal fiction," which simply allows the organization to conclude contracts under the law. Consequently, firms should not be viewed as institutions or persons, but as mere platforms for contracting among parties. This financial vision of the firm as a nexus of contracts radically departs from the managerial perspective which depicted the firm as a central social entity or institution. In this new perspective, workers are no longer "inside" the firm, and they have no more rights than any other stakeholder.

These new doctrines of markets and companies gave rise to a series of legal transformations in the 1980s in the United States – mainly urged by Ronald Reagan – which would pave the way for financial capitalism.[37] Following these transformations, companies brought market mechanisms into their internal functioning on a massive scale, as attested by waves of outsourcing, the dismantling of conglomerates, efforts to refocus on their core business, the hiring of temporary workers, and the emergence of global value chains, through which a myriad of independent firms contribute to the production of a single product. In the world of financial capitalism, the firm is no longer a player on its own; it has become a tool for shareholder value maximization. The aim is no longer to grow and to protect the firm from market competition, but to maximize its flexibility and profitability.

From this point of view, platform capitalism appears to be a logical outgrowth of financial capitalism. Drawing on the power of digital technologies, companies like Uber and Airbnb seem to be the very incarnation of the "nexus of contracts" type of firm. These market-organizations are essentially constituted of a light, flexible central structure that takes the logic of outsourcing to its extreme for all productive activities, except marketing and digital development. The role of the platform is basically to conclude contracts, implement algorithms, handle intermediation and control, and conduct massive investments in marketing and algorithmic development. But platforms have very few assets and are not responsible for production as they claim to act as a mere intermediary. These organizations tend to shift issues of insurance, quality of service, working hours, conditions, and taxation to individuals.[38] This is perfectly consistent with Jensen and Meckling's theory of the firm: as the firm does not exist as an entity, it is misleading to think that the firm has social responsibility.

The transformation is considerable: while the managerial firm organized and transformed work, the platform concludes contracts, outsources work, and controls it remotely. The locus of work is no longer inside the firm. The firm was an institution; now it is just a market.

C *A New Form of Putting-Out System, Powered by Silicon Valley*

Digital platforms do not possess any productive assets. It is up to the "workers" to obtain and provide the capital necessary to perform the work, and to bear any associated risks. Individuals must obtain and use their own capital (a car for ride-share drivers, a property for Airbnb) before they can work. This situation is reminiscent of the putting-out system (or "domestic system"). In

---

[36] *Id.* at 310–11.
[37] Davis, *supra* note 30.
[38] *See* Smorto, this volume.

this mode of production, which appeared in Europe in the sixteenth century before the manu-facturer, farmers would make use of slack periods to perform domestic (often textile) work for merchants with whom they had a commercial relationship.[39] The farmers worked from home, generally using their own tools. In the putting-out system, the merchant also provided the raw materials (the cloth) needed for the activity. This pre-capitalist framework is reflected in many characteristics of current work arrangements via platforms: the disappearance of a workspace managed by the employer, the independence of workers whose relationship with the business intermediary is not hierarchical but commercial, the difficulty of creating a form of collective representation or union, the difficulty of drawing a clear boundary between the domestic and professional spheres, the phenomenon of holding multiple jobs and secondary income activities (which recalls "slashers" – people who combine multiple careers) rather than pursue a single full-time activity, and finally individual self-organization (individuals determine their own level of engagement with the platform).

In this context, the distinction between capital and work does not constitute a criterion by which to understand relations of power and exploitation. As productive capital is outsourced and often widely distributed, it is their relative market power that determines the balance of power between platforms and workers. The power of Airbnb and Uber is that of the merchant, business intermediary, or broker who aggregates demand.

Why are such pre-capitalist organizational arrangements making such a comeback today? From an economic point of view, information technology has considerably improved control (using rating tools and online reputation scores) and reduced the risk of carrying out transactions between peers who did not previously know each other. Technology reduces transaction costs, making the market more attractive than organizational integration for an entire range of activ-ities.[40] From a more ideological point of view, these forms of pre-capitalist organization are very consistent with the ideal of a financialized vision of the firm based on massive outsourcing and market coordination. Platforms thus enjoy greater legitimacy with investors who see the market as the most legitimate mechanism of coordination (as opposed to government regulation, pro-fessional autonomy, or organizational integration).

III THE NEO PUTTING-OUT SYSTEM: CONSEQUENCES AND IMPACTS

A *Consequences at the Individual Level: Platforms, Managerialization, and Self-Financialization*

For individuals, the return of the putting-out system is bringing about major transformations. The "financialization of daily lives"[41] is an ongoing process that increases asset inequalities among individuals and redefines individual identities according to a financial logic.[42]

---

[39] Hounshell, *supra* note 17.

[40] *See* Williamson, *supra* note 19, and also Lobel, this volume, for such an analysis. Platform opponents argue that part of this cost advantage is artificially facilitated by the fact that a large part of the platform economy activity occurs in a non-regulated zone, belonging to the informal economy and often outside the law (accusations of undeclared or concealed work, undeclared rentals, non-payment of occupancy tax, lack of social protection for workers, etc.), which allows these activities to avoid taxation on labor and capital (*see* Tom Slee, *What's Yours Is Mine: Against the Sharing Economy* (2015)). Some would also argue that such "cost advantage" also results from the significant amounts of ven-ture capital that allows these firms to cushion losses.

[41] R. Martin, *Financialization of Daily Life, Labor in Crisis* (2002).

[42] G. F. Davis and S. Kim, *Financialization of the Economy*, 41 Annu. Rev. Sociol. 203–21 (2015).

Platform organizations do not own productive assets. Instead of building a competitive advantage from complex and unique assets, platforms massively outsource them and compete with ordinary resources.[43]

At the same time, issues related to the value and uniqueness of assets are being transferred to individuals. For platform workers, owning valuable and strategic assets is necessary to make a profit in the peer-to-peer economy. In this "Resource-Based View of the individual,"[44] the ability to generate profits from platform capitalism is directly proportionate to the value of the personal assets – material or immaterial – that individuals bring to the platform. Platforms therefore constitute a mechanism through which individual patrimonial inequalities may be reproduced and exacerbated. Airbnb provides a striking illustration of this mechanism: the analysis of data produced by the InsideAirbnb.com website shows that in Paris, like most other world cities that are so attractive to tourists, short-term rentals are two to five times more profitable than traditional rentals.[45] This effect is mediated by the location of the property: in Paris, profitability and occupancy rates are inversely proportional to distance from the most touristy neighborhoods.[46]

Potential profits to be made from platform capitalism appear to be proportional to the value and rarity of the assets individuals possess: while an individual can generate very significant profits from renting an unusual property in a sought-after tourist neighborhood in Paris, profits are much lower for ordinary properties in less touristy neighborhoods or in the nearby suburbs. The profit potential is structurally lower for individuals whose capital endowment is less specific and less valuable. This is the case for Uber drivers, whose asset is just a car. In such markets, barriers to entry are much lower and the service provided is rather standard, which results in stiff competition among substitutable drivers, and in an unfavorable power relationship between drivers and the platform. And at the base of the pyramid, bike couriers are even more substitutable, with even lower profit perspectives.

Beyond the fact that these processes exacerbate inequalities among individuals – those with the most valuable assets are more likely to profit from these new models – they contain the seeds of a transformation of individuals, who increasingly integrate financial and managerial logics in their own way of functioning.[47] To extract value from platform capitalism, individuals must constantly monetize and maximize the value of their own assets. This means, for example, that individuals may, when buying a new property, integrate the potential profit that could be obtained by regularly listing their property on Airbnb or another rental platform. Their capital is both tangible and intangible: individuals must preserve their online visibility and reputation, manage trust, adopt transparent behavior, integrate an ethic of evaluation

---

[43] F. Fréry, X. Lecocq, and V. Warnier, *Competing with Ordinary Resources*, MIT Sloan Manage. Rev. (Spring 2015).

[44] I use the term in reference to the "Resource-Based View of the firm"; *see* Birger Wernerfelt, *A Resource-Based View of the Firm*, 5(2) Strategic Mgmt. J. 171–80 (1984); Jay Barney, *Firm Resources and Sustained Competitive Advantage*, 17(1) J. Mgmt. 99–121 (1991). In this theory of corporate strategy, the sustained strategic advantage of a firm results from its ability to hold resources that are valuable, rare, non-imitable, and non-substitutable.

[45] *See* Gay Justine, *A Paris, la location Airbnb rapporte 2,6 fois plus que la location classique*, JDN (Journal Du Net), Mar. 30, 2016, www.journaldunet.com/economie/immobilier/1175834-location-airbnb-versus-location-classique/.

[46] Coles et al. in this volume study Airbnb data in New York to compare the profitability of short- versus long-term rental in various districts. Their data reveal that the profitability ratio of short- versus long-term rental is higher in outlying, middle-income neighborhoods. This is in the specific context of New York, where strict city regulations were introduced in recent years to regulate Airbnb and limit the development of short-term rentals.

[47] P. Fleming, *The Human Capital Hoax: Work, Debt and Insecurity in the Era of Uberization* 38 Organ. Stud. 691–709 (2017); C. J. Martin, *The Sharing Economy: A Pathway to Sustainability or a Nightmarish Form of Neoliberal Capitalism?* 121 Ecol. Econ. 149–59 (2016); D. Murillo, H. Buckland, and E. Val, *When the Sharing Economy Becomes Neoliberalism on Steroids: Unravelling the Controversies*, 125 Technol. Forecast. Soc. Change 66–76 (2017).

by peers and cultivate their social and professional network to ensure future opportunities. In this perspective, any asset (tangible or intangible) may be seen as an idle resource whose value can and should be maximized. The new "*homo collaborans*" calculates, makes choices, and integrates a financialized ethic in which he/she constantly manages his/her own value. Recalling Foucault, information technologies and platforms may be analyzed as technologies of self-government that redefine the way individuals perceive, define, and project themselves.[48] In this new domestic system, rather than a simple contractor, the worker is being transformed into an entrepreneur who has to cope with risks, be adaptable, and manage his/her image, reputation, and networks.

B *Governing the Neo Putting-Out System: Can Platforms be Made Socially and Legally Responsible?*

By marking a rebirth of the putting-out system, peer-to-peer platforms constitute a radical organizational innovation that profoundly differs from the managerial firm. This creates many regulatory voids, as most of the existing regulatory framework was developed in the context of the managerial corporation, with clear boundaries, salaried employment relationships, and assets owned and controlled by the corporation. By contrast, platforms are set in a much blurrier landscape, where workers act as independent contractors, with unclear boundaries between market and hierarchy, between the professional and domestic spheres, where work situations vary greatly in terms of autonomy or economic dependency, and where behavior is controlled and governed by algorithms rather than formal rules, authority, or hierarchy.[49] In such a context, determining what/who is inside or outside the organization is difficult, as is deciding where platforms' responsibilities start and end in relation to those of the individuals using them.[50] As Garden and Leong argue in this volume, platforms are confronted with an identity crisis of their own making. This identity crisis concerns their ambiguous nature, standing in between positions of simple matchmakers and true service providers.

To add to this regulatory complexity, peer-to-peer platforms have scaled up local transactions at a tremendous pace in a surprisingly short period of time, generating massive externalities both in size and scope.[51] In Paris, for example, Airbnb has been accused of taking tens of thousands of apartments out of the individual rental market in just over five years. According to some press articles, in 20,000 of these cases, the owners were acting illegally in 2016 as they did not declare the associated rental income.[52] These activities are criticized for contributing to the rise of real estate and rental prices, illegal rentals, and the exacerbation of inequalities in assets. In 2015, the entire neighborhood of Barceloneta (in Barcelona) rose up against the multiplication of nuisances caused by these new practices.[53]

One fascinating aspect of platforms concerns the way their social and legal responsibilities are being framed in reaction to such controversies and externalities. There is no clear answer to the

---

[48] M. Foucault, *Discipline and Punish: the Birth of the Prison* (1979).

[49] L. Lessig, *Code and Other Laws of Cyberspace* (1999).

[50] *See* Cherry and Aloisi, this volume.

[51] *See* Zale, this volume.

[52] Marine Lassery, *Airbnb: 20.000 logements seraient dans l'illégalité à Paris*, Les Echos, May 30, 2016, www .lesechos.fr/30/06/2016/lesechos.fr/0211082718653_airbnb---20-000-logements-seraient-dans-l-illegalite-a-paris .htm#WdpPeXGx8iKAkHci.99.

[53] *See* Stephen Burgen, *Barcelona Cracks Down on Airbnb Rentals with Illegal Apartment Squads*, The Guardian, June 2, 2017, www.theguardian.com/technology/2017/jun/02/airbnb-faces-crackdown-on-illegal-apartment-rentals-in-barcelona.

question of who should be held accountable for the controversies generated by platforms: the state – for failing to adequately regulate or supervise platform exchanges, the platforms themselves, or the individuals using them? Such situations echo what Rittel and Webber and Reinecke and Ansari call "wicked problems," i.e. complex issues involving multiple actors, rationalities, and shared and blurred responsibilities.[54] In such complex situations, the role and responsibility of individuals and platforms are hard to define ex-ante, and must be settled as controversies arise. A key question is to analyze how *responsibilities are being attributed to actors and organizations*. One avenue of research is to study the processes by which platforms are held accountable and responsible (or resist such efforts), calling on cross-disciplinary perspectives between sociology, law, and management.

Different approaches are currently being explored by regulators to govern the platform economy. One approach consists in taking action against the platforms themselves and holding them accountable for wider social and legal responsibilities. The intent is to treat these "market-organizations" like more traditional – and easier to regulate – managerial organizations. Examples of this approach include the recent case of Uber being stripped of its London license because of a lack of social responsibility and failure to address user safety concerns.[55] Other related initiatives seek to reclassify commercial relationships as salaried employment contracts. In France, Urssaf (an organization that collects social security contributions) has followed such a path, as have thousands of Uber drivers in the United States, through a class action suit brought in 2014.[56] In both cases, the goal is to convert the commercial contract between workers and platforms into an employment contract, provided it can be proven that there is a relationship of subordination between workers and the platform. However, such efforts have not had significant success either in France or the United States so far.[57]

Reclassification is a potential threat for all platforms that exert a strong level of prescription and control over work processes, or use strict evaluation and performance mechanisms. At the same time, because of their organizational novelty, digital platforms create new work situations that challenge old criteria used by regulators to establish an employment relationship. A Belgian startup called *Click and Walk* provides an illustration of this difficulty.[58] This company, which employs about ten people, could unintentionally be transformed into a large multinational enterprise with 300,000 employees, if an overly restrictive definition of subordination were adopted. Indeed, the micro-task platform has been under investigation since June 2016 by the central office that combats illegal work in France in relation to the undeclared work of some 300,000 European "*clicwalkers*" (160,000 of whom are in France). These individuals carry out micro tasks (paid between 1 and 6 euros) that involve walking around in stores, taking photos of products, and transmitting them to the platform to verify the availability and positioning of

[54] H. W. J. Rittel and M. M. Webber, *Dilemmas in a General Theory of Planning*, 4 Policy Sci. 155–69 (1973); J. Reinecke and S. Ansari, *Taming Wicked Problems: The Role of Framing in the Construction of Corporate Social Responsibility: Taming Wicked Problems*, 53 J. Manag. Stud. 299–329 (2016).

[55] Sarah Butler and Gwyn Topham, *Uber Stripped of London Licence Due to Lack of Corporate Responsibility*, The Guardian, Sept. 22, 2017, www.theguardian.com/technology/2017/sep/22/uber-licence-transport-for-london-tfl.

[56] Christophe Alix, *Devant la justice, l'Urssaf perd face à Uber*, Liberation, Mar. 17, 2017, www.liberation.fr/futurs/2017/03/17/devant-la-justice-l-urssaf-perd-face-a-uber_1556255.

[57] In the United States, a specific difficulty is due to the massive use of class action waivers that prevent platform workers from engaging class action suits against platforms to obtain employment reclassification (*see* Tippett, this volume).

[58] Arnaud Touati and Camilia Billon, *Le travail dissimulé, nouveau mal de l'économie collaborative*, Maddyness, July 28, 2016, www.maddyness.com/entrepreneurs/2016/07/28/travail-dissimule-clic-and-walk/.

products on the shelves. The grounds for investigation are that the company evaluates worker performance and bases the payment of funds on the quality of the work provided (mainly the quality of photos). This case illustrates the need to rethink the concept of subordination in the context of the neo putting-out system created by platforms that are neither pure market (which would involve independent contractors), nor pure hierarchy (which would involve employees). Efforts are currently being undertaken to better respond to this new context: some explore the possibility of creating a new employment category;[59] others underline the need to revise and adapt existing proxies for employment classification to the reality of digital platforms.[60] These initiatives also recognize the need to better assess the variety of work situations that exist on peer-to-peer platforms. Emerging models suggest that two variables may be relevant to differentiate four types of work situation on platforms: the degree of economic dependency of workers vis-à-vis a given platform, i.e. the existence of other economic alternatives for them to make a living, and their degree of autonomy at work, i.e. their ability to set their prices and self-organize their working processes.[61]

A second approach is to tackle regulatory issues by targeting individual users of the platforms. Instead of targeting platforms, several regulatory initiatives focus on users and have come up with new forms of taxation, laws, protection, and support for digital workers.[62] In the case of France, the parliament voted at the end of 2016 in favor of a series of measures to tax the sharing economy.[63] Legislators decided to tax every activity that is not strictly speaking "sharing," but which generates a profit for the provider. Furthermore, this taxation complies with annual thresholds for transactions, beyond which the private individual may be considered a professional. Once an individual exceeds these limits (€8,000 per year for the rental of objects, €23,000 for property rentals) they must enroll in the independent workers' social security regime (RSI). This aims to take into consideration individual roles and levels of activity that separate the domestic sphere from a professional activity. Beyond these fiscal issues, many public or private initiatives aim to give more thought to forms of social protection and risk sharing for freelance workers.

A third approach is to challenge the dominance of exploitative platforms by encouraging the emergence of competing platforms based on alternative models of governance that are more favorable to the workers and customers who use them. Numerous debates have arisen around platform cooperativism, promoting the idea that platforms can be made to serve the interests of digital workers through cooperative governance.[64] Other initiatives, like La Ruche qui Dit Oui! (The Food Assembly), defend a logic of social innovation and advocate the emergence of hybrid organizations that simultaneously pursue economic and societal goals.[65] These initiatives seek to develop platforms with a "limited profit" objective, allowing an acceptable distribution of income among stakeholders and the pursuit of the initiative's societal goal, while financing the economic development of the platform. With the recent ban of Uber from the city of London,

---

[59] *See* Cherry and Aloisi, this volume, for a review of initiatives worldwide.

[60] *See* Smorto; Tippett, this volume.

[61] K. M. Kuhn and A. Maleki, *Micro-entrepreneurs, Dependent Contractors, and Instaserfs: Understanding Online Labor Platform Workforces*, 31 Acad. Manag. Perspect. 183–200 (2017).

[62] *See* Pantazatou, this volume, for an overview in the European Union.

[63] Ulrika Lomas, *French Lawmakers Approve Tax Hike on Sharing Economy*, Tax-News, Nov. 1, 2016, www.tax-news .com/news/French_Lawmakers_Approve_Tax_Hike_On_Sharing_Economy____72629.html.

[64] T. Scholz and N. Schneider, *Ours to Hack and to Own: The Rise of Platform Cooperativism, a New Vision for the Future of Work and a Fairer Internet* (2016).

[65] *See* Acquier and Carbone, this volume.

voices have emerged to explore nonprofit, cooperative, or community-based ride-sharing platform alternatives, following the philosophy of RideAustin, which was launched after Uber and
Lyft left the city of Austin in 2016.[66]

CONCLUSION

As a significant organizational innovation and social phenomenon experiencing fast growth,
platform capitalism is generating a large amount of debate about its social impacts and responsibilities. In this chapter, I have examined the emergence of platforms through the lens of business
history and organization theory to develop the following ideas and propositions:

- Peer-to-peer digital platforms constitute a new organizational archetype in the landscape of
  organizations. For productive activities, these "market-organizations" differ radically from
  the managerial firm that has prevailed since the second industrial revolution and which
  was the cornerstone of the existing regulatory framework of business.
- Viewing platforms as a return of the Taylorist work organization misses part of the complexity of this transformation, because Taylorism was based on hierarchical coordination, the
  transformation of work and the managerial/integrated firm. Instead, platform organizations
  have more to do with processes of financialization (which affect both organizations and
  individuals) and a theory of the firm that views the firm as a network of contracts rather
  than an institution.
- From an organizational point of view, the rise of platforms marks the rebirth of the putting-
  out system, where digital tools are used as controlling devices. In this neo putting-out
  system, work is controlled through algorithms rather than managerial hierarchy, and
  power relationships are based on market power instead of hierarchical power. In this new
  economy, work situations are very diverse in terms of worker autonomy and economic
  dependence.
- Given this new context, we need to rethink and update established concepts, such as the
  way we define subordination to determine employment relationships. As the concept of
  subordination was historically framed around notions of managerial control and internal-
  ization/control of assets by the firm, it no longer fully reflects the new realities, and should
  thus be re-conceptualized and adapted accordingly.

As a closing remark, organizational theory has traditionally approached organizations in two
ways: on the one hand, "organization" can refer to an activity or a process of organi*zing*,
shaping behaviors and structure; on the other hand, "the organization" can be viewed as an
object, a subject, or an entity. This latter substantive view of the organization is often used
when we refer to the organization as a firm, a corporation, or an institution with social or
legal responsibilities. Platforms and the rebirth of the putting-out system create significant
tensions between these two views of the organization. As entities, these market-organizations
are small "liquid organizations," with fluid and evanescent structures.[67] At the same time,
they generate pervasive effects on society. Platforms do a large amount of organizing through

---

[66] Sam Levin, *"There is Life After Uber": What Happens When Cities Ban the Service?* The Guardian, Sept. 23, 2017,
www.theguardian.com/technology/2017/sep/23/uber-london-ban-austin.

[67] Z. Bauman, *Liquid Modernity* (2012); J. Kociatkiewicz and M. Kostera (eds.), *Liquid Organization: Zygmunt Bauman
and Organization Theory. Routledge Studies in Management, Organizations and Society* (2014).

algorithms: prescribing work, setting up a social order, shaping relations and interactions between producers and clients, transforming individual identities, etc.[68] Clearly, the scope of these organizing processes goes far beyond the current legal boundaries of platforms. This mismatch between "organizing as a process" and "organization as an entity" is probably one of the root causes of the social controversies and current regulatory conundrums surrounding platform capitalism and the sharing economy. Understanding how such liquid organizations, which produce such pervasive effects on society, may be governed and regulated constitutes an exciting and urgent field for research, which calls for interdisciplinary collaborations between history, sociology, organizational theory, and law.

---

[68] Viewed this way, platforms not only blur the distinction between organization and market, but also that between organization and society. From a theoretical point of view, this explains the increasing difficulty of distinguishing between the sociology of organizations, sociology of technical objects, and general sociology.

2

Trust in the Sharing Economy

Platform-Mediated Peer Trust

Mareike Möhlmann and Andrea Geissinger

INTRODUCTION

The sharing economy is a new phenomenon that has transformed business practices in numerous industries, resulting in the creation of the most valuable privately owned US tech start-ups of all time: the accommodation-sharing platform Airbnb ($30 billion), and the personal transportation network Uber ($68 billion).[1] Owing to its disruptive impact, the appropriateness of the term "sharing economy" is still debated, with a plethora of similar terms invoked by researchers: collaborative consumption, crowd-based capitalism, the platform economy, and access-based consumption.[2] Producing a clear definition of the concept's boundaries thus presents a challenge. In this chapter, we take the sharing economy to mean digitally enabled, peer-to-peer exchange platforms for goods and services that connect spare capacity with demand or offer access-over-ownership by enabling renting, lending, reselling, or swapping.[3]

The extensive spread of digital technologies and the internet has created numerous options for interaction and communication with others online. Exposure to an immense volume of information and a variety of products and services is resulting in heightened complexity,[4] with Luhmann describing this complexity as "the unexpected surprise, the inaccessible."[5] The growing digitization of the modern world creates an increasingly anonymous and impersonal society that many perceive to be unpredictable and uncertain.[6]

Sharing goods and services via the internet is based on the fundamental mechanism of de facto strangers starting to interact with each other in the digital sphere. Therefore, as in any

---

[1] See B. Stone, *The $99 Billion Idea: How Uber and Airbnb Fought City Hall, Won Over the People, Outlasted Rivals and Figured Out the Sharing Economy*. Bloomberg Businessweek, Jan. 26, 2017, www.bloomberg.com.

[2] R. Botsman and R. Rogers, *What's Mine is Yours: The Rise of Collaborative Consumption* (2010); F. Bardhi and G. M. Eckhardt, *Access-Based Consumption: The Case of Car Sharing*, 39(4) J. Consumer Res. 881–98. (2012); M. Möhlmann, *Collaborative Consumption: Determinants of Satisfaction and the Likelihood of Using a Sharing Economy Option Again*, 14(3) J. Consumer Behav. 193–207 (2015); A. Sundararajan, *The Sharing Economy: The End of Employment and the Rise of Crowd-Based Capitalism* (2016).

[3] M. Avital, J. M. Carroll, A. Hjalmarsson, N. Levina, A. Malhotra, and A. Sundararajan, *The Sharing Economy: Friend or Foe?* Paper presented at the 36th International Conference on Information Systems, Fort Worth, TX (2015); Bardhi and Eckhardt, *supra* note 2; R. Belk, *You Are What You Can Access: Sharing and Collaborative Consumption Online*, 67(8) J. Bus. Res. 1595–2000 (2014); Botsman and Rogers, *supra* note 2; Möhlmann, *supra* note 2.

[4] N. Luhmann, *Risk: A Sociological Theory* (1994); P. Sztompka, *Trust: A Sociological Theory* (2000).

[5] N. Luhmann, Familiarity, Confidence, Trust: Problems and Alternatives, in *Trust: Making and Breaking Cooperative Relations* 94–107, 96 (D. Gambetta ed., 2000).

[6] K. Cook, M. Levi, and R. Hardin, *Whom Can We Trust? How Groups, Networks and Institutions Make Trust Possible* (2009); A. Giddens, *The Consequences of Modernity* (1990); Luhmann, *supra* note 4; Sztompka, *supra* note 4.

(online or offline) business setting, the presence of trust is a major precondition for successful transactions in the sharing economy. Trust allows humans to form communities, cooperate with each other and even, at times, find solutions beyond plain self-interest. Trust affects how we form relationships with our family and friends, and why and how we develop business relationships or decide to buy products in the marketplace.[7] Indeed, trust can help to alleviate the uncertainty that is often felt in a complex environment, and as such, "one should expect trust to be increasingly in demand as a means of enduring the complexity of the future which technology will generate."[8]

The concept of trust is thus of key relevance to the sharing economy, which is charting new territory characterized by high uncertainty and dynamic change processes.[9] Joe Gebbia, co-founder of Airbnb, suggests that "the sharing economy is commerce with the promise of human connection. People share a part of themselves, and that changes everything."[10] In placing people and human interactions at its core, the sharing economy seeks to mitigate our inherent stranger-danger bias by designing and facilitating trust-building capacities between strangers whose interactions are enabled through digital platforms.

Drawing on the literature on digital platforms,[11] the main argument of this chapter is that trust in peer-to-peer contexts is reliant upon sharing economy platforms' capacity to foster platform-mediated peer trust, by effectively enabling trust to be built between strangers through the use of trust-enhancing digital cues.[12] We adopt a sociological point of departure to understand trust in the context of the sharing economy. This stands in contrast to the economic literature, which often considers trust as an "implicit form of contracting" when describing certain transaction situations (such as in the setting of the sharing economy). In this regard, economists usually draw on theory addressing transaction costs when discussing trust. However, from a sociological perspective, and in related (information systems) management literature, trust is understood as a more comprehensive concept, also capturing underlying framework conditions such as personal character traits that might be highly influenced by socialization processes and the institutional settings in which individuals act.[13] Nevertheless, due to the fundamental role of trust, there are no clear disciplinary boundaries to the concept *per se*. Economists and sociologists both incorporate and build upon each other's perspectives on trust within their respective discussions.

We start by discussing the historical expansion of trust in societies. We explain how trust evolved and transformed from family- and institutional-based trust to platform-mediated peer trust in the context of the sharing economy. We also discuss how the sharing economy refers to trust in multiple entities, and what the interplay of such multiple trust entities might look like. We then conceptualize how trust cues allow us to move toward platform-mediated peer trust.

---

[7] Cook et al., *supra* note 6; Sztompka, *supra* note 4; L. G. Zucker, *Production of trust: Institutional sources of economic structure, 1840–1920*, 8 Res. Org. Behav. 53–111. (1986).

[8] N. Luhmann, *Trust and Power* 16 (1979).

[9] F. Mazzella, A. Sundararajan, V. D'Espous, and M. Möhlmann, *How Digital Trust Powers the Sharing Economy*, 30 IESE Insight 24–31 (2016); Möhlmann, *supra* note 2; M. Möhlmann, *Digital Trust and Peer-to-Peer Collaborative Consumption Platforms: A Mediation Analysis*. Research paper, Leonard N. Stern School of Business, New York University, New York (2016). DOI: 10.2139/ssrn.2813367; Sundararajan, *supra* note 2.

[10] J. Gebbia, *Joe Gebbia: How Airbnb Designs for Trust [videofile]* (2016), www.ted.com.

[11] *See* A. Hagiu and D. Spulber, *First-Party Content and Coordination in Two-Sided Markets*, 59(4) Mgmt. Sci. 933–49 (2013); G. Parker and M. Van Alstyne, *Two-Sided Network Effects: A Theory of Information Product Design*, 51(10) Mgmt. Sci., 1494–504 (2005).

[12] Möhlmann, *supra* note 9.

[13] Zucker, *supra* note 7.

Lastly, we present the outlook for digital trust capabilities with a brief discussion of regulatory challenges.

I A HISTORICAL PERSPECTIVE: FROM INSTITUTIONALIZED TRUST TO PLATFORM-MEDIATED PEER TRUST IN THE SHARING ECONOMY

We argue that trust and trustworthiness in the sharing economy stem from interpersonal relationships that expand outwards in a "radius of trust," including trust mediated by digital platforms.[14] We take our point of departure from Mayer et al.'s definition of trustworthiness as a "willingness to be vulnerable to the actions of another party, based on the expectation that the other will perform a particular action important to the trustor, irrespective of the ability to monitor or control that other party."[15] Mayer et al. take this interpersonal perspective as a starting point for further contemplation of organizational trust.

In the historical evolution of trust systems over the last few centuries, trustworthiness and trust were initially bestowed only on members of one's family and close family friends, who formed an intimate, homogeneous community with shared norms and sets of behaviors that facilitated honesty and cooperation.[16] According to sociologists, in such contexts, trust is intertwined with the concept of social capital. Coleman argues that social capital can be defined by its function: it inheres in the structure of relations between and among actors. It is not lodged either in the actors themselves or in the physical implements of production, but is usually built among members of closed networks, such as communities with frequent interactions and close family, religious, and community affiliations.[17]

With the development of economic trade, having a reputation for being a trustworthy partner increased one's potential to maximize economic self-interest and promote future financial success.[18] Being perceived as trustworthy was an important attribute as trade extended beyond one's immediate community circle.[19] Increased trade exchanges led to the formation of governmental and political institutions that shifted trust from a reputational base to the establishment of exchange regulations and rules, such as through the emergence of legally binding contracts between different parties that are enforceable based on jurisdiction.[20] As trust was now placed in established institutions instead of personally known individuals, this allowed the development of business contacts even between strangers with no previous interactions or direct social ties.

These processes of formalization and centralization were further intensified by the emergence of information technologies and breakthroughs in transportation, enabling businesses to serve customers without the necessity for local proximity.[21] This gave rise to corporations with large-scale global operations and a worldwide customer base. In order to take advantage of economies of scale and scope, corporate brands were established, which substituted for the trust

---

[14] F. Fukuyama, *Trust: The Social Virtues and the Creation of Prosperity* (1995).

[15] R. C. Mayer, J. H. Davis, and D. F. Schoorman, *An Integrative Model of Organizational Trust*, 20(3) Acad. Mgmt. Rev. 709–34, 712(1995).

[16] K. Cook, *Trust in Society* (2001); R. D. Putnam Bowling Alone: America's Declining Social Capital *in Culture and Politics* 223–34. (L. Crothers and C. Lockhart eds., 2000).

[17] J. S. Coleman, *Social Capital in the Creation of Human Capital*, 94 Am. J. Soc. S95–S120 (1988).

[18] Mazzella et al., *supra* note 9.

[19] Sztompka, supra note 4.

[20] K. S. Cook, R. Hardin, and M. Levi, *Cooperation Without Trust?* (2005); Mazzella et al., *supra* note 9; Zucker, *supra* note 7.

[21] Mazzella et al., *supra* note 9.

formerly placed in formal contracts and regulations by assuring customers of the brands' value propositions, regardless of geolocation.[22]

As digital technologies have continued to develop, our social world has undergone tremendous shifts in how we communicate with each other, how we conduct business, and how we consume products and services. The emergence of digital platforms based on network algorithms that connect millions of people around the globe has paved the way for digital ventures tapping into the potential of networks and digital crowds. Social networks now have the capacity to mediate trust relationships,[23] since trust is more likely to arise in a network of likeminded people sharing a joint identity.[24] Such mutual trust leads to expectations of reciprocity, even in the absence of robust organizational structures such as governmental and political institutions.[25] As with trust in very close social contexts, such as among family members and friends, the key to trust among members of digitally enabled networks is social capital.

The emergence of digital trust cues, such as peer reviews, offers opportunities to access social capital accumulated by other members of online communities. This new digital infrastructure, with its simplicity, immediacy, and speed, undermines state regulations and governmental interventions, which are often complex, costly, and lengthy, enabling trust to be built among individuals embedded in these digital networks.[26] This is arguably an essential building block for a peer-based sharing economy. Building on the success of network companies such as Facebook and eBay, digital connections between strangers are easily established, which in turn facilitate sharing activities in the marketplace.[27] Yet, if large-scale online interactions and transactions are to be truly fruitful, our profoundly rooted stranger-danger bias must be overcome. Leveraging the full potential of digital technologies and the embryonic peer-based economy requires a carefully calibrated trust system.[28]

II PLATFORM-MEDIATED PEER TRUST IN THE SHARING ECONOMY: TRUST IN MULTIPLE ENTITIES

Trust has traditionally been portrayed as a dyadic relationship between a trustor and a trustee; yet, in many transactions associated with the sharing economy, at least three parties are involved: the (digital) platform provider and a pair of peers acting on that platform. Thus, the conventional dyadic relationship between trustor and trustee is extended to a triad.[29]

Platforms act as intermediaries, matching peers and taking over certain tasks to ensure smooth transactions.[30] In the context of the sharing economy, the digital platform commonly represents

---

[22] *Id.*; Sundararajan, *supra* note 2.

[23] Cook et al., *supra* note 6; Cook et al., *supra* note 20; M. Foddy and T. Yamagishi, Group-Based Trust, in *Whom Can We Trust? How Groups, Networks and Institutions Make Trust Possible* 17–41 (K. Cook, M. Levi, and R. Hardin eds., 2009).

[24] R. Kramer, M. B. Brewer, and B. A. Hanna, Collective Trust and Collective Action in Organizations: The Decision To Trust as a Social Decision, in *Trust in Organizations: Frontiers of Theory and Research* 357–89 (R. M. Kramer and T. R. Tyler eds., 1996).

[25] Foddy and Yamagishi, *supra* note 23.

[26] Mazzella et al., *supra* note 9; Möhlmann, *supra* note 9; Sundararajan, *supra* note 2.

[27] Mazzella et al., *supra* note 9; Möhlmann, *supra* note 9; Sundararajan, *supra* note 2.

[28] Mazzella et al., *supra* note 9.

[29] F. Hawlitschek, T. Teubner, M. Adam, N. Borchers, M. Möhlmann, and C. Weinhardt, *Trust in the Sharing Economy: An Experimental Framework*, in Proceedings of the 37th International Conference on Information Systems 1–14 (2016); Möhlmann, *supra* note 9; T. A. Weber, *Intermediation in a Sharing Economy: Insurance, Moral Hazard, and Rent Extraction*, 31(3) J. Mgmt. Info. Sys. 35–71 (2014).

[30] *See* Hagiu and Spulber, *supra* note 11; Parker and Van Alstyne, *supra* note 11.

a company or an organization, with some of those platforms profiting from a strong brand image. Peers who conduct sharing activities on this platform may be either contractors or private individuals (e.g. Airbnb guest and host, Uber driver and customer).[31] This set-up of actors enables us to identify different trust relationships, both peer to peer, and between peers and the digital platform. This entanglement of trust entities results in blurred boundaries between service users, the service provider, and peers offering goods or services, leading to "firm–market hybrids" characterized by high levels of perceived complexity in peers sharing on these platforms.[32]

Based on the triadic nature of platform-mediated peer trust, we differentiate between interpersonal and institutional trust.[33] Interpersonal trust lies at the core of trust in the sharing economy since it refers to relationships between peers acting on these platforms. The sharing platform provider enables interpersonal trust, while at the same time being dependent on being perceived as a trustworthy institution itself.

As a starting point for the interpersonal dimension, we draw on Mayer et al.'s definition of trustworthiness, introduced earlier.[34] This differentiates between three dimensions of trustworthiness: ability, benevolence, and integrity. Ability refers to a trustee's relevant skills, competencies, and enabling characteristics, such as driving skills for a driver listed on the city-to-city ride-hailing service, BlaBlaCar. Benevolence is a perception that the trustee has good intentions, such as an Airbnb host motivated to offer guests the best experience rather than solely making a profit. Integrity refers to the principles of the trustee that the trustor thinks are acceptable. This might refer to the fact that the trustee's actions are in line with promises made, for instance concerning the condition of an item that is rented out. These three dimensions have been discussed or empirically measured by many scholars,[35] some of whom have addressed trust in the context of online marketplaces and e-commerce and the sharing economy.[36] As the sharing economy is based on human interactions, the interpersonal trust element is arguably more significant than in other online transactions, such as e-commerce. Sharing economy activities tend to be characterized by greater social interaction among peers than in the more impersonal transactions conducted on platforms such as eBay and Amazon.[37] Social interactions on Amazon are usually limited to communication with the delivery driver at the final stage of the transaction process, whereas sharing economy settings usually involve closer personal interactions, as when driving in a car together or spending the night in a host's apartment and having dinner together.

In addition to interpersonal trust levels, in the context of the sharing economy, the institutional aspect of trust is equally important. Over the years, scholars have developed various theories of the concept. Zucker takes a neo-institutionalist sociological approach.[38] She identifies institutional aspects, such as underlying structures and assurances that are evident in societal

---

[31] Möhlmann, *supra* note 9.
[32] Sundararajan, supra note 2; Möhlmann, *supra* note 9.
[33] Möhlmann, *supra* note 9.
[34] *See supra* note 15.
[35] O. Schilke and K. Cook, *Sources of Alliance Partner Trustworthiness: Integrating Calculative and Relational Approaches*, 36(2) Strategic Mgmt. J. 276–97 (2015).
[36] On online marketplaces and e-commerce *see* D. H. McKnight and N. L. Chervany, *What Trust Means in E-Commerce Customer Relationships: An Interdisciplinary Conceptual Typology*, 6(2) Int'l. J. Electronic Com. 35–59 (2001); P. A. Pavlou and D. Gefen, *Building Effective Online Marketplaces with Institution-Based Trust*, 15(1) Info. Sys. Res. 37–59 (2004). On the sharing economy *see* F. Hawlitschek, T. Teubner, and C. Weinhardt, *Trust in the Sharing Economy*, 70(1) Die Unternehmung: Swiss J. Bus. Res. & Practice 26–44 (2016); Möhlmann, *supra* note 9.
[37] Möhlmann, *supra* note 9.
[38] *Supra* note 7.

contexts, to be a crucial trust-building mechanism. Generally speaking, the functioning of our society depends largely on structural cues established both formally in terms of rules and regulations and informally in terms of cultural norms and values.[39] Shapiro refers to institutional trust as a belief in the security of a situation, for instance based on guarantees or security nets.[40] Thus, institutional trust may refer to a variety of mechanisms, processes, and structural assurances that are in place – this might be particular frameworks, or rules and regulations. In a broad sense, it may refer to legislation and policies enforced by governmental and legal institutions; it may also refer to institutional security provided by digital or sharing economy platforms embedded in these legal systems. Institutional trust mechanisms may be implemented to facilitate transactions on digital platforms, such as by providing specific certifications or facilitating safe escrow services.[41] These are discussed in more detail later.

Having discussed the different notions and characteristics of trust entities, we need also to address the relationships and interconnections between the multiple parties involved in sharing economy transactions. Several authors address the interplays between diverse trust entities. Stewart uses the label "trust transfer," theorizing that trust may be transferred from one source to another in a hierarchical order.[42] Möhlmann also suggests that trust in the sharing economy may be a hierarchical construct.[43] She argues that trust in a platform provider or brand as an organization leads to trust in the peers with whom one is sharing, allowing spillover effects between different trust entities. In particular, such trust hierarchies may be evident at early stages of trust relationships, when users have little familiarity with a sharing economy service. We expect the process of trust transfer to apply as well to low levels of trust. Thus, trust can also be lost by the same mechanism. For instance, public scandals, such as those that have recently affected Uber,[44] might affect the brand of a sharing economy platform, and, in turn, lower consumers' trust in the platform more generally.

Fukuyama refers to a "radius of trust," a term later adapted by Sztompka to become "circles of trust."[45] The authors argue that trust spans personal relationships, functional systems, and abstract social objects, and that these circles are all interconnected. However, behind the entire trust circle lies a "primordial form of trust – in people and their actions."[46] At the core of the trust circle are our closest family and friends; next, we place our trust in people fulfilling familiar social roles (such as doctors, professors, and judges) and social groups (football clubs or student clubs), followed by institutions and organizations. Trust in technological systems, as well as trust in the overarching social system or the current social order, lie on the outer perimeters of the trust circle.[47]

Applying this logic to the sharing phenomenon, we observe that sharing economy platforms bridge the different trust circles. Interpersonal trust in peers is located at the very core of the trust circle. Digitally matched peers tend to have real-life contacts following their initial interactions on a sharing economy platform – for example, when using sharing economy services such as

---

[39] *Id.*

[40] S. P. Shapiro, *The Social Control of Impersonal Trust*, 93(3) Am. J. Soc. 623–58 (1987).

[41] *See, e.g.*, McKnight and Chervany, *supra* note 36; Pavlou and Gefen, *supra* note 36; Zucker, *supra* note 7.

[42] K. J. Stewart, *Trust Transfer on the World Wide Web*, 14(1) Org. Sci. 5–17 (2003).

[43] Möhlmann, *supra* note 9.

[44] M. Möhlmann and L. Zalmanson, *Hands on the Wheel: Navigating Algorithmic Management and Uber Drivers' Autonomy*, in Proceedings of the International Conference on Information Systems (ICIS 2017), Dec. 10–13, Seoul, South Korea(2017).

[45] Fukuyama, *supra* note 14; Sztompka, *supra* note 4.

[46] Sztompka, *supra* note 4, at 46.

[47] Sztompka, *supra* note 4.

Airbnb or Uber. However, sharing economy platforms must also establish institutional trust, at the outskirts of the trust circle, as platforms engage in more traditional organization–customer relationships with participating peers.

III DIGITAL TRUST CUES: TOWARD PLATFORM-MEDIATED PEER TRUST IN THE SHARING ECONOMY

Recent research has investigated the success of sharing economy platforms in building trust. For example, Mazzella et al. surveyed European users of the city-to-city ride-sharing service, BlaBlaCar, a platform that brokers empty car seats to passengers who want to travel long distances.[48] The authors asked participants about their various levels of trust in a diverse range of people (family, friends, colleagues, and neighbors) as well as in BlaBlaCar members with full digital profile details. Trust levels in the latter were ranked third (88 percent) after family (94 percent) and friends (92 percent); thus, users trusted BlaBlaCar members with full digital profiles almost as much as their family and friends. Much lower trust levels were attributed to colleagues (58 percent), neighbors (42 percent), and social media contacts (16 percent). How can we explain this confidence and trust in total strangers in the sharing economy? Various digital trust cues facilitate trustworthiness and trust between people who have never met in real life. We argue that such cues enable both relational and calculative trust to be built.[49]

Relational trust-building mechanisms refer to the attitudinal and social underpinnings of trustworthiness, based on joint values and individual or group identities. This rationale takes a sociological and psychological perspective on trust, and places social relationships at the center of trust considerations. Thereby, it refers not only to trust relationships with family and friends, but also with colleagues, business partners, and even strangers.[50]

Calculative trust-building mechanisms refer to hierarchical controls and measures to prevent undesired actions. Calculative trust is based on rational calculations and economic considerations of whether or not to trust. As such, calculative trust offers one example of how an economic principle might impact the social interaction of individuals. Enforcement of calculative aspects in the sharing economy may be pursued by the parties already discussed in the context of institutional trust. First, regulations and policies may be enforced by governmental and legal institutions, for instance to ensure that potential fraud can be prosecuted. Despite ongoing digital disruption, a worldview that produces trust through institutionalized trust production mechanisms, such as legal contracts and legislative rule,[51] is still considered to be fundamental and must be acknowledged when designing for trust online. Hence, it is paramount that legislators, regulators, businesses, and the public alike accept their respective significance for establishing institutionalized trust in new business models that emerge from continuous digital innovations. Legally binding rules for service-providing peers in accordance with labor market laws or tax regulations need to be put in place. As such, institutionalized trust can set the scene for enabling higher levels of digital trust based on the notion of peer-sharing. Second, as a result of the evolution of new digital trust cues, digital or sharing economy platforms embedded in such legal systems may enforce further calculative aspects. Such platforms act as monitoring and potentially sanctioning agents that hold peers accountable and responsible, with the capacity

---

[48] Mazzella et al., *supra* note 9.
[49] Kramer et al., *supra* note 24; Schilke and Cook, *supra* note 35.
[50] Kramer et al., *supra* note 24; Schilke and Cook, *supra* note 35; Mayer et al., *supra* note 15.
[51] Zucker, *supra* note 7.

to enforce certain sanctions independently. This may include banning peers who engage in deviant behavior on the platform.[52]

We argue that, in the context of the sharing economy, digital trust cues enable trust between multiple parties involved in the trust-building process. They have the capacity to build both interpersonal and institutional trust, by triggering relational as well as calculative aspects. Ongoing research has started to unveil key digital trust-building cues.[53] Sharing economy platforms constantly introduce new and innovative trust cues that support the trust-building process. Consequently, it can be argued that such trust cues are cumulative in nature: The more cues a sharing platform provides, the more likely it is that trust is produced. These cues are leveraged to establish trust in digital platforms in general, and in the sharing economy in particular:

1) *Peer reputation:* In large and internationally distributed sharing economy networks, personal, first-hand experience of a particular peer is likely to be nonexistent. In this case, digital reputation based on peer ratings serves as a fundamental pillar for assessing whether trust is well placed, and as a legitimizing credential.[54] Peer ratings offer opportunities to access digital social capital accumulated by other members of an online sharing platform. More recently, sharing economy platforms have implemented two-way ratings, or so-called simultaneous reviews, to deal with reciprocal peer review behavior, which has been shown to result in inflated and non-credible review scores. Simultaneous review scores only become public after each party has reviewed the other.[55]

2) *Digitalized social capital:* Connecting a peer's profile with other social media networks on a sharing economy platform opens up the potential to accumulate digital social capital, and to carry it from one digital network or platform to another. Digital platforms now allow users to display the number of social media contacts they have in common with other users, including mutual Facebook friends or LinkedIn contacts. Accumulating social capital from different contexts increases the volume of feedback cues, and thus has the capacity to build trust.[56]

3) *Provision of information:* When building trust online, displaying one's full name, age, and descriptions of particular skills, competencies, and general interests are as fundamental as uploading one's picture.[57] This information is crucial in providing a first impression of a peer with whom one is interacting online. Relevant information or descriptions of the goods or services offered through the sharing economy platform, such as the interior design of an apartment offered via Airbnb or the model of car used for a joint car-ride on BlaBlaCar, also have the capacity to build trust.

4) *Escrow services:* The platform provider often facilitates financial transactions between peers acting on sharing economy platforms. Some platforms have extended security systems, meaning that money may be withheld if the service is not provided as promised or expected.[58]

5) *Insurance coverage:* Communicating the details of the insurance that is covering the transactions on a particular sharing economy platform can build trust.[59] The fact that peers

---

[52] Sztompka, *supra* note 4.
[53] *See* Mazzella et al., *supra* note 9; Möhlmann, *supra* note 9.
[54] Mazzella et al., *supra* note 9; McKnight and Chervany, *supra* note 36.
[55] G. Bolton, B. Greiner, and A. Ockenfels, *Engineering Trust: Reciprocity in the Production of Reputation Information*, 59(2) Mgmt. Sci. 265–85 (2012); Möhlmann, *supra* note 9.
[56] Mazzella et al., *supra* note 9; Möhlmann, *supra* note 9.
[57] Hawlitschek et al., supra note 29; Mazzella et al., *supra* note 9.
[58] Mazzella et al., *supra* note 9; Pavlou and Gefen, *supra* note 36; Möhlmann, *supra* note 9.
[59] Mazzella et al., *supra* note 9; Möhlmann, *supra* note 9; Sundararajan, *supra* note 2.

rather than professionals might provide the actual sharing economy service might lead to risky incidents in which no trained staff are available to handle potentially dangerous situations. In addition, there might be considerable costs involved in negative incidents – ranging from destroyed Airbnb apartments to car accidents when taking an Uber.[60]

6) *Certification and external validation*: Some platform providers in the sharing economy foster secure and safe transaction processes using a form of digitally displayed certification or validation, for instance for telephone numbers, external social network profiles, or apartment pictures. Platforms may either establish internal certification systems or involve trusted third parties in the validation process. Such third parties include government institutions (government IDs), trusted consumer and trade associations, and companies specializing in certification.[61]

In addition to these digitally displayed trust cues, the personal characteristics of the trustor are a crucial building block for trust. Such personal characteristics are a result of socialization, sometimes even a result of childhood experiences or deeply inherited interaction patterns.[62] One particular characteristic is trust propensity, which refers to the general tendency of trustors to trust in a particular person or thing.[63] Trust propensity levels might differ across cultural contexts. Many authors theorize trust propensity as a major factor in trust relationships. Following this logic, Mayer et al. identify it as a key factor in their integrative model of trust.[64]

Another trust-building factor is the trustor's familiarity with aspects of the sharing economy. Luhmann argues that a familiar environment is a prerequisite for trust: "Trust has to be achieved within a familiar world, and changes may occur in the familiar features of the world which will have an impact on the possibility of developing trust in human relations.[65] Familiarity may apply to different aspects of the sharing economy. An individual may be familiar with interacting with strangers in general, with other services associated with the sharing economy, or with a particular sharing economy service. For example, one individual may be more inclined to trust the provider of a sharing economy platform for accommodation (such as Airbnb) following an initial positive experience of using a different online sharing platform (such as BlaBlaCar). Another individual may be more willing to trust the Airbnb platform following a previous positive experience with this particular platform. A history of interactions between an individual and a platform provider hence increases familiarity, which in turn increases the likelihood of establishing trust.[66]

IV OUTLOOK: ARE WE ENTERING A NEW ERA OF SHARED TRUST?

It remains to be seen whether trust in the sharing economy is well placed with regard to its many promises to foster smarter, more environmentally conscious consumption, as well as to enable a more just society characterized by meaningful human connections. Criticism is increasingly being raised about the potentially negative impacts of the sharing economy, in particular concerning tax legislation, labor market rights, and other legal implications.[67]

---

[60] Möhlmann, *supra* note 9.

[61] Mazzella et al., *supra* note 9; Pavlou and Gefen, *supra* note 36; Sundararajan, *supra* note 2.

[62] Zucker, *supra* note 7.

[63] Möhlmann, *supra* note 9.

[64] Mayer et al., *supra* note 15.

[65] Luhmann, *supra* note 8; *supra* note 5, at 94.

[66] Möhlmann, *supra* note 2.

[67] S. R. Miller, *First Principles for Regulating the Sharing Economy*, 53 Harv. J. on Legis. 147–202 (2016); S. Oei, and D. Ring, *Can Sharing Be Taxed?* 93(4) Wash. U.L. Rev. 989–1069 (2016); R. L. Redfearn, *Sharing Economy*

The notion of platform-mediated peer trust has important implications for regulation. Its multiple-entity characteristic may lead to a distribution of responsibilities to all parties involved, including sharing economy platform providers as well as pairs of peers on the supply and demand sides, such as Airbnb guests and hosts or Uber drivers and customers. We have discussed the potential for platforms to act as monitoring bodies, and potentially even to impose sanctions on actors exhibiting deviant behavior.[68] Since platforms facilitate transactions between peers, they can trace all interactions taking place through their digital channels, enabling them to engage in monitoring. However, in order for such shared responsibility to be acceptable in global networks, negotiation of the general norms, rules, and moral codes of a globalized society is required, as well as measures to prevent platform providers from making potentially inappropriate decisions. For instance, owing to the simple fact that platform providers are operating worldwide on the internet without distinct geolocations, background expectations and globally acceptable cultural trust cues need to be redefined.[69] As of now, global sharing firms are in the lead with regard to transforming societal norms, rules, and moral codes. With their ability to facilitate trust between strangers, sharing economy actors have initiated a societal shift that might alter the functioning of society on a larger scale. It is therefore crucial that representatives of civic society deliberate about whether or not pioneering actors in the sharing economy should play a dominant role in negotiating how such a globalized society should be organized. It can also be argued that the next wave in sharing should be actuated by public discourse on how to utilize the possibilities demonstrated by global sharing firms.

How should governments, regulators, and legislators respond to such challenges? One option is to establish institutionalized trust, in the form of globally binding regulations and legislation. Another option is to emphasize the major structural conditions for building trust in any society: inherent transparency and public and societal debate.[70] Governments, regulators, and legislators must rise to the challenge of restructuring our society for the digital age. Such bodies must renegotiate the digital social order while not overprotecting the status quo with excessive litigation, but instead making space for innovation and structural change. A prime example of a successful initiative is demonstrated by the city of Amsterdam. The "Amsterdam Sharing City" project is a hub of various sharing pilot projects including businesses, NGOs, and local governments with the common goal of remodeling Amsterdam as a "city that has sharing on its mind."[71] We argue that, regardless of the wider impact of the sharing model on society, as a result of the availability of new trust-building mechanisms, "stranger sharing" is a phenomenon that enlarges our circle of human interaction.[72] As this chapter contends, establishing trust between de facto strangers is essential for any sharing economy platform. The recent success of such platforms is a good indicator that digital trust cues fulfill this purpose. Arguably, without designing for digital trust, the sharing economy might never have emerged.[73]

Interesting possibilities for further enhancement of trust in digital settings remain to be explored. While the facilitation of peer reputation on platforms is relatively common practice these days, in the future digital trust might be accumulated into a form of trust capital that

---

Misclassification: Employees and Independent Contractors in Transportation Network Companies, 31(2) Berkeley Tech. L.J. 1023–56 (2016).

[68] Sztompka, *supra* note 4.

[69] Zucker, supra note 7; Sztompka, *supra* note 4.

[70] Sztompka, *supra* note 4.

[71] *See* Amsterdam Sharing City, www.sharenl.nl/amsterdam-sharing-city.

[72] J. Schor, *Debating the Sharing Economy*, Great Transition Initiative (2014), greattransition.org/publication/debating-the-sharing-economy.

[73] Botsman and Rogers, *supra* note 2.

could be utilized and exported, not just on a single platform, but on a plethora of platforms and applications, similar to the notion of digital social capital that allows users to display Facebook friends or LinkedIn contacts exported from other digital networks. The possibilities as well as the dangers of mapping peer ratings and reviews onto one's digital persona across platforms are manifold. On the one hand, the accumulation of digital trust capital that is easily accessible everywhere might foster an even deeper capacity for digital trust. On the other hand, such an amount of sensitive information about individuals is also prone to risks regarding cyber security, data exploitation, and surveillance issues. As different levels of trust propensity are accounted for in various cultural settings, further explorations should be undertaken in order to shed light on where and how digital trust cues need to be modified and adapted in order to foster digital trust adequately.

Furthermore, rapid advancement in blockchain technology offers new potential to facilitate direct peer interaction in the sharing economy,[74] particularly since distributed ledger technologies, "smart contracts," and other applications leverage the need for mediating platform providers. This would entail a move toward decentralized, autonomous organizations.[75] Without the need for a mediating platform provider, peer trust has the potential to be even more crucial – a "new currency" for our future peer economy.[76]

Joe Gebbia may romanticize the phenomenon in saying that "the connection beyond the transaction is what the sharing economy is aiming for"; however, building trust between strangers may be the true achievement of the sharing economy model.[77] More discussion is needed regarding the potential for digital trust to transform our stranger-danger bias into perceiving strangers as friends whom we have not yet met.

---

[74] Sundararajan, *supra* note 2.
[75] S. Javenpaa and R. Teigland, Trust in Digital Environments: From the Sharing Economy to Decentralized Autonomous Organizations, in Proceedings of the 50th Hawaii International Conference on Systems Science, 5812–16 (2017).
[76] Botsman and Rogers, *supra* note 2.
[77] Gebbia, *supra* note 10.

3

Scale and the Sharing Economy

*Kellen Zale**

INTRODUCTION

This chapter explores the role of scale in the sharing economy.[1] On one hand, companies such as Uber, Lyft, and Airbnb have amassed multi-billion dollar valuations by facilitating millions – even billions – of home-sharing and ride-hailing transactions. On the other hand, each individual, peer-to-peer transaction – between host and guest on Airbnb, or driver and passenger on Lyft and Uber – is a small-scale, *de minimis* contributor to the overall extent of home-sharing and ride-hailing activity occurring on these platforms.

This dichotomy of scale – large amounts of small-scale activity – is key to the tremendous growth of the sharing economy. However, when "everything is small,"[2] the regulatory challenge is immense. As scholars have recognized in a range of legal contexts, from environmental law to administrative law to tax law, "[i]t is very expensive and difficult to regulate … where the scale of the business organizations is relatively small and the number of business actors is large."[3]

I suggest in this chapter that scale is a defining feature of the sharing economy and that effective governance of the sharing economy requires a more complete understanding of the role of scale. As small-scale activities that once fit criteria for regulatory leniency occur in increasingly large numbers, the regulatory calculus changes. Traditional models used to distinguish between those activities that should be regulated and those that should be treated with regulatory leniency, like the commercial–personal dichotomy, are inadequate when confronting an economy based on multi-billion dollar companies facilitating individuals using personal assets for commercial purposes. Large numbers of small-scale activities, facilitated by third-party platforms using a network orchestrator model, are falling outside the reach of existing regulation, from employment

---

* This chapter is derived from a longer law review article that appeared in the *San Diego Law Review*. *See* Kellen Zale, *When Everything is Small: The Regulatory Challenge of Scale in the Sharing Economy*, 53 San Diego L. Rev. 949 (2016).

[1] There is no single, agreed upon definition of what counts as the sharing economy; the term "sharing economy" is itself a subject of contention. *Id.* In this chapter, the sharing economy refers to peer-to-peer transactions for access to goods and services facilitated by third-party platforms, with a focus on the prominent sectors of home-sharing and ride-hailing.

[2] *See* Uri Friedman, *Airbnb CEO: Cities Are Becoming Villages*, Atlantic (June 29, 2014), www.theatlantic.com/international/archive/2014/06/airbnb-ceo-cities-are-becoming-villages/373676/ (quoting Brian Chesky, CEO of Airbnb: "At the most macro level, I think we're going to go back to the village … everything will be small.").

[3] David Barnhizer, *Waking from Sustainability's "Impossible Dream": The Decisionmaking Realities of Business and Government*, 18 Geo. Int'l Envtl. L. Rev. 595, 672–73 n.172 (2006).

laws to fair housing laws, because those regulations are ill-suited to the sharing economy's particular configuration of scale. Recognizing the role of scale in the sharing economy is a crucial step to adapting our governance tools to address negative cumulative impacts[4] and regulatory fractures[5] resulting from large numbers of small-scale home-sharing and ride-hailing activities.

This chapter proceeds in three parts. Section I provides an overview of the role of scale in the sharing economy, analyzing how companies such as Airbnb and Uber have leveraged the network orchestrator business model to facilitate massive numbers of small-scale transactions.

Section II situates the issue of scale in the broader regulatory context by unpacking the governance responses to small-scale activities. I discuss why small-scale activities are often subject to regulatory leniency, and how the governance response tends to shift as small-scale activities increase in number.

Section III develops the case for a regulatory response to scale in the sharing economy on three grounds. First, negative cumulative impacts may result from large numbers of small-scale home-sharing and ride-hailing activities, such as decreased long-term rental availability or increases in vehicle congestion and emissions. Second, existing regulations are ill-suited to the three-sided, network orchestrator model of the sharing economy, and the failure to address this misfit is producing regulatory fractures that threaten to undermine civil rights laws and other important public policies. Finally, the traditional justifications for regulatory leniency for small-scale activities do not apply with full force to the networked peer-to-peer activities occurring in the sharing economy.

I SCALE IN THE SHARING ECONOMY

The growth of – and controversies surrounding – the sharing economy have been the subject of extensive media coverage, as well as a growing body of legal literature. The goal of this section is not to repeat those accounts, but rather to provide a snapshot of the sharing economy that highlights the role of scale.[6]

While the scale of peer-to-peer activity occurring in the sharing economy is unprecedented, the underlying activities are not new. Versions of home-sharing and ride-hailing have been in existence long before the emergence of Uber and Airbnb.[7] Arrangements such as offering a room in one's home to boarders or travelers,[8] or using gypsy cabs, or carpooling, all predate the sharing economy.[9] However, transaction costs previously limited such activities to an

---

4 Cumulative impacts occur when activities, which individually may have only *de minimis* impacts, result in aggregate negative impacts when repeated by numerous individual actors. Zale, *supra* note * at 971.

5 The term "regulatory fractures" is drawn from Saskia Sassen's scholarship on the informal economy and refers to a situation in which "[activities] diverge from the model for which extant regulations were designed… [and] take on a recognizable shape of their own, it becomes meaningless to speak of regulatory violations." Saskia Sassen, *The Informal Economy: Between New Developments and Old Regulations*, 103 Yale L.J. 2289, 2291 (1994).

6 The discussion here is broadly applicable to the range of activities occurring in the sharing economy, but examples are primarily drawn from two prominent sectors of the sharing economy: home-sharing and ride-hailing.

7 *See* Kellen Zale, *Sharing Property*, 87 U. Colo. L. Rev. 501 (2016).

8 Boarding or homestay arrangements in the pre-sharing economy could be on short-term (nightly) or longer-term (weekly or monthly) basis. *See id.* at 517, 572 (discussing short-term accommodation provided to travelers and lodgers); *see also* Emily M. Speier, *Embracing Airbnb: How Cities Can Champion Private Property Rights Without Compromising the Health and Welfare of the Community*, 44 Pepp. L. Rev. 387, 392–93 (2017) (discussing the history of rooming houses in the United States and noting that workers staying in such accommodation typically stayed for short periods of time).

9 *See* Saskia Sassen, *The Global City: New York, London, Tokyo* (2nd edn. 2001) (discussing informal transportation in the underground economy).

ad-hoc or informal basis, or to within close-knit communities. Not only could it be difficult to find someone to enter into a short-term rental or ride arrangement for specific dates or locations, but there were also a range of risks, from concerns about safety to questions about how to ensure payment. Thus, until recently, the short-term accommodation and point-to-point transportation sectors were characterized by a few relatively larger entities – such as hotels and taxi companies – which could take advantage of economies of scale to lower transaction costs.

The scale of activities changed, however, when companies like Airbnb and Uber entered the scene. Previously expensive, inconvenient, or risky exchanges have become almost instantaneous, thanks to technology such as GPS location services, smartphones, and app software. Trust verification mechanisms, such as background checks, two-way user reviews, and external payment processing have reduced the transaction costs and lowered (though not entirely eliminated) risks involved in peer-to-peer transactions.

As a result, massive numbers of people are now engaging in one-time, small-scale transactions.[10] Uber has provided more than two billion rides worldwide[11] and has a greater market share than taxis in a growing number of cities.[12] Airbnb has more short-term accommodation listings than the world's largest hotel chains.[13] Almost three-quarters of all US residents have participated in some aspect of the sharing economy.[14] Airbnb and Uber have two of the three highest valuations of venture-backed private corporations globally.[15]

Yet, at the same time, each individual homesharing or ride-hailing transaction represents only a small fraction of the overall amount of activity being facilitated by companies like Airbnb and Uber. This combination of massive numbers of small-scale individual transactions being facilitated by a central entity is an example of what is known in the economic literature as the network orchestrator model. A network orchestrator is a company that facilitates a network of users whose activities in turn create value for the company. This business model leverages a phenomenon known as network effects, which occur when the value of a good or service increases as the number of people using it increases.[16]

---

[10] Some users of sharing economy services are more than one-time participants. However, even high-volume Airbnb hosts or frequent Uber riders would be considered small-scale actors, since their activities still contribute only a small amount to the overall number of transactions occurring on the platforms. Small-scale in this sense thus refers to the relative amount of activity contributed by a participant (such as an Uber driver or passenger, or Airbnb host or guest) to the overall amount of activity occurring on the platform, not the relative amount of activity contributed by any one participant compared to another participant on that platform. The latter distinction between "high-volume" participants and low-volume participants does become relevant when considering how to design regulatory responses. *See infra* Section III.

[11] Brian Solomon, *Uber Just Completed its Two Billionth Ride*, Fortune (Jul. 18, 2016), www.forbes.com/sites/briansolomon/2016/07/18/uber-just-completed-its-two-billionth-ride/ - 43f99a3f5224.

[12] Andrew Bender, *Uber's Astounding Rise: Overtaking Taxis in Key Markets*, Forbes: Travel (Apr. 10, 2015, 11:42 AM), www.forbes.com/sites/andrewbender/2015/04/10/ubers-astounding-rise-overtaking-taxis-in-key-markets/#5285824322ef.

[13] Vicki Stern et al., *Hotels: Is Airbnb a Game-Changer?*, Barclays, at 1, 4, 13 (Jan. 16, 2015) (reporting that Airbnb had a 20 percent share of "hotel" rooms in New York City and predicting it to double in market share in the next twelve months).

[14] Aaron Smith, *Shared, Collaborative, and On Demand: The New Digital Economy*, Pew Research Center, May 19, 2016, www.pewinternet.org/2016/05/19/the-new-digital-economy/

[15] *See* Scott Austin et al., *The Billion Dollar Startup Club*, Wall St. J. (Feb. 18, 2015), http://graphics.wsj.com/billion-dollar-club/ (listing Uber's valuation as $68.0 billion and Airbnb's as $25.5 billion as of September 2016).

[16] Carl Shapiro and Hal R. Varian, *Information Rules: A Strategic Guide to the Network Economy* 174–75, 183–84 (1999) ("The value of a network goes up as the square of the number of users.").

Network effects create positive externalities because each individual user's decision to participate in the network benefits not only that user, but also other participants, the public, and the network orchestrator. For example, participants in a ride-sharing network like Uber or Lyft benefit because the more people join the network, the more likely passengers will be able to find drivers who are available, and the more likely drivers will be able to find passengers in need of rides. The public can also benefit because the network may make it more feasible to achieve socially desirable activity that was previously difficult to coordinate. For example, shared-ride services like UberPool and LyftLine have the potential to make a form of carpooling a far more viable option than it has previously been, with the potential for less congestion and lower emissions, outcomes that would benefit not only network participants but also members of the public at large.

Finally, network effects benefit network orchestrators. The more individuals that join a network, the more valuable the network becomes. For example, since Uber and Lyft collect a commission from each ride, the more users there are on the network, the more rides are likely to occur, and the more commissions the company will collect. And because network effects are self-perpetuating, the more small-scale transactions, the better. As Reid Hoffman, founder of LinkedIn, put it: "First-scaler advantage beats first-mover advantage."[17]

Network orchestrators like Uber and Airbnb have not only facilitated large numbers of ride-hailing and home-sharing transactions; they have also created massive data networks. While pre-sharing economy ride-hailing and home-sharing activities – gypsy cabs, renting rooms to boarders – were largely ad hoc, one-time, unmonitored (and often unmonitorable) transactions, companies like Uber and Airbnb have data about every transaction that occurs on their network. Difficult questions, beyond the scope of this chapter, are raised about the value of this data and how it should be used, but the existence of the data presents both a challenge and opportunity for governance of the sharing economy.

The particular configuration of scale in the network orchestrator model of sharing economy companies differs from traditional business models in other significant ways. Unlike their non-sharing economy competitors, such as taxi companies or hotels, network orchestrators like Airbnb and Uber do not own (and therefore do not incur the costs associated with) the underlying assets that are the subject of their business model. Instead, the companies leverage the assets of network participants – i.e. the Airbnb host's home, the Uber driver's car – thereby reducing the companies' risks and expenses.

Furthermore, unlike the traditional two-sided business model – between industry and consumers – the sharing economy's model is a three-sided one involving platforms, users (i.e. ride-hailing passengers or home-sharing guests), and providers (i.e. ride-hailing drivers or home-sharing hosts). Many in the last category – providers – would be treated as consumers under the two-sided model, but their role under the three-sided model is murkier. These individuals supply goods and services, but they are not necessarily professionals. Instead, they typically use personal assets – such as their own vehicles and private residences – for commercial purposes part of the time, while retaining those assets for personal use at other times.

---

[17] Reid Hoffman, *Expertise in Scaling Up Is the Visible Secret of Silicon Valley*, Fin. Times (Sept. 12, 2015), www.ft.com/content/39001312-4836-11e5-af2f-4d6e0e5eda22.

II REGULATION AND SCALE

As the previous section discussed, the sharing economy utilizes the network orchestrator model to harness the power of large numbers of small-scale transactions. Yet despite the massive numbers associated with the sharing economy, companies in the sharing economy have often focused on the smallness of peer-to-peer transactions. Lyft's tagline is "Your friend with a car."[18] Uber says it is "Everyone's private driver."[19] Airbnb claims its "greatest achievements aren't monumental … They're the small, meaningful connections that happen between us every day."[20] Even the terms "peer-to-peer" and "sharing economy" convey smallness, by "keep[ing] the focus on the people who provide the services – and off the platforms."[21]

By focusing on smallness, rather than their multi-billion-dollar valuations and the massive numbers of transactions being facilitated, corporations such as Airbnb and Uber have tapped into a powerful framing device. In a wide range of legal contexts, regulatory systems treat small-scale activities with reduced stringency, either completely exempting them from regulation or subjecting them to lowered levels of regulatory oversight.

The justifications for regulatory leniency for small-scale activities fall into five categories: (1) the *de minimis* character of the activities; (2) privacy and autonomy concerns; (3) enforcement costs; (4) fairness concerns; and (5) alternatives to legal regulation. I discuss each of these justifications below, before turning to how the regulatory response shifts when large numbers of small-scale activities occur.

De minimis character: Small-scale activities are, by their very definition, small. Each occurrence contributes only a small amount to the overall amount of the activity, and correspondingly, a minimal amount to any social "bads" caused by the activity.[22] Consequently, the regulation of small-scale actors raises what has been termed a "one percent" problem.[23] In a "one percent" problem, each individual actor contributes an incrementally *de minimis* amount to the aggregate levels of a particular activity.[24] For example, an individual commuter is just one of many thousands – or hundreds of thousands – of people engaged in driving every day. While there are recognized social "bads" caused by solo commuting – from traffic congestion to increased emissions – each individual's contribution to the overall levels of those problems is minimal. As a result, "one percent" actors are often exempted from regulation: not only do cognitive biases make it difficult to "evaluat[e] and mak[e] use of very low-value probabilities,"[25] – such as the

---

[18] *See* Aarti Shahani, *In Battle Between Uber and Lyft, Focus Is on Drivers*, 89.3 KPCC (Jan. 18, 2016), www.scpr.org/news/2016/01/18/56919/in-battle-between-lyft-and-uber-focus-is-on-driver/.

[19] *Id.* (noting the companies' different mottos reflect underlying differences between Uber and Lyft).

[20] *About Create Airbnb*, Airbnb, https://create.airbnb.com/en/about.

[21] Natasha Singer, *Twisting Words to Make 'Sharing' Apps Seem Selfless*, N.Y. Times (Aug. 8, 2015), www.nytimes.com/2015/08/09/technology/twisting-words-to-make-sharing-apps-seem-selfless.html?_r=0 (quoting Erin McKean, a lexicographer). As noted above, the term "sharing economy" itself is a contested one. *See* Zale, *supra* note 7 at 525–28 (discussing scholarly and media debates over the term).

[22] An exception to the *de minimis* justification for regulatory leniency is where *de minimis* activity poses a risk of serious harm, even if the likelihood of harm occurring is low; in such circumstances, even small-scale activity is likely to be regulated.

[23] Kevin M. Stack and Michael P. Vandenbergh, *The One Percent Problem*, 111 Colum. L. Rev. 1385, 1393 (2011).

[24] Zale, *supra* note * at 960–61.

[25] Stack and Vandenbergh, *supra* note 23 at 1398 (citing studies showing that "individuals are unresponsive to changes in probability magnitudes of 1 in 100,000, 1 in 1 million, and 1 in 10 million and also insensitive to the differences between risks of 1 in 650, 1 in 6,300, and 1 in 68,000.").

impact of each individual driver's actions on overall emissions or congestion – there is also a human "tendency to treat very small percentages and probabilities as if they were zero."[26]

Privacy and Autonomy: Regulatory leniency toward small-scale activities is also often deemed appropriate given concerns about intrusions into autonomy, privacy, and intimacy. Government regulation of noncommercial or personal activity is often viewed more skeptically than regulation of commercial activity (generally defined as involving monetary gain).[27] This is particularly true when activities take place in private, personal places – especially the home.[28] In addition, when regulation targets an activity where "unrestricted individual choice has been (or is perceived to have been) the norm," autonomy concerns may result in regulatory leniency.[29] Thus, if small-scale activities are noncommercial, they are more likely to be treated with a light regulatory touch. And even when small-scale activity is commercial, it still may receive regulatory deference if it occurs in a personal space, such as the home, or if it involves an activity where personal choice is a strong or longstanding norm.

Enforcement Costs: When the cost of enforcing regulations against an actor would exceed the benefits, then regulation is not considered an efficient response.[30] Regulation of small-scale actors raises particular concerns because enforcement costs may be significant and the benefits relatively minor. For government regulators with limited resources, it is often more cost efficient to bypass smaller actors and focus on larger ones, since larger actors account for a larger volume of the regulated activity and thus are more likely to incur violations.[31]

Fairness: In addition to efficiency, fairness is considered an important governance goal.[32] Thus, even where a particular regulation is efficient from a welfare-maximizing perspective, if the regulation produces what are perceived as unfair outcomes, then regulation may be adjusted. Small-scale activities often raise such fairness concerns. For example, small businesses receive

---

[26] *Id.* at 1399–1400 ("studies show there are circumstances in which individuals read the 'gist' of the low-probability risk as amounting to 'essentially nil,' and thus not worth effort (or payment) to prevent.").

[27] *See* Zale, *supra* note 7, at 522–24 (discussing examples of the commercial/noncommercial dichotomy in a range of legal contexts).

[28] *See, e.g.,* Katrina Fischer Kuh, *When Government Intrudes: Regulating Individual Behaviors that Harm the Environment,* 61 Duke L.J. 1111, 1168–74 (2012) (discussing the "significance of home" in substantive due process cases).

[29] Holly Doremus, *Biodiversity and the Challenge of Saving the Ordinary,* 38 Idaho L. Rev. 325, 346 (2002). While privacy and autonomy concerns may limit the direct regulation of small-scale activities, regulation often indirectly targets those activities. *See* Craig N. Oren, *Getting Commuters Out of Their Cars: What Went Wrong?,* 17 Stan. Envtl. L.J. 141, 148–49 (1998) (discussing how fuel efficiency standards that vehicle manufacturers must comply with indirectly regulate the emissions produced by individual drivers).

[30] *See generally* Alfred E. Kahn, *The Economics of Regulation: Principles and Institutions* (1988).

[31] *See* Richard J. Pierce, Jr., *Small Is Not Beautiful: The Case Against Special Regulatory Treatment of Small Firms,* 50 Admin. L. Rev. 537, 561 (1998). ("No regulatory agency has investigative and enforcement resources sufficient to ensure anything approaching comprehensive compliance with its rules. OSHA, for instance, can inspect less than one percent of the worksites for which it has regulatory responsibility in a given year. Agencies allocate their scarce compliance and enforcement resources disproportionately to large firms.")

[32] Richard H. Fallon, Jr., *Should We All Be Welfare Economists?,* 101 Mich. L. Rev. 979, 1000 (2003) (citing Thomas Nagel, *Equality and Partiality* 10–11 (1991), discussing a conception of fairness as being drawn from "an 'impersonal standpoint' from which each of us must recognize that, objectively speaking, we are no more important than anyone else").

exemptions or reduced regulatory requirements in a number of legal contexts. This regulatory leniency is often justified on the grounds that compliance with one-size-fits-all regulation would impose disproportionately higher costs on small firms (because they do not benefit from the economies of scale of large firms) and thus pose a greater risk of such firms being driven out of business. Even if such an outcome is economically efficient, it may nonetheless be perceived as unfair, and thus governance regimes may be adjusted to reduce the regulatory burdens on smaller-scale actors.[33]

Alternatives to Formal Regulation: In addition to law, non-legal tools – such as norms, markets, and architecture – can also shape and constrain behavior.[34] Small-scale activities that involve individual behavior may be particularly susceptible to regulation through norms, since norms are typically enforced through social sanctions and impose reputational costs on those who violate the norms.[35] Norms are also often well-suited to small-scale activities, since norms have been shown to be most effective when parties are relatively homogenous, have repeated interactions, and their overall numbers are relatively small.[36]

Although regulators may treat small-scale activities with leniency for the reasons discussed above, the governance response tends to shift as the amount of small-scale activity increases, due to cumulative impacts. Whereas small-scale activities may have only *de minimis* negative impacts when considered in isolation, when repeated by many individuals, the aggregate of these activities can have more significant negative effects.

The problem of negative cumulative impacts can be seen across a range of legal contexts, from corporate law to employment law to environmental law.[37] For example, environmental scholars have recognized that massive problems such as climate change, water pollution, and sprawl are attributable not to any single actor, but rather the result of incremental, small-scale actions by millions of people.[38] Although each individual action may be *de minimis* – produced by a "one percent" actor – the aggregate effects of the activity can make it impossible to achieve a particular social goal unless the individual activity is regulated.[39] Thus, regulators may need to modify the initial rules applying to individual, small-scale actions to account for these negative aggregate effects.[40]

---

[33] *See* C. Steven Bradford, *Does Size Matter? An Economic Analysis of Small Business Exemptions from Regulation*, 8 J. Small & Emerging Bus. L. 1, 25 (2004) ("If the total cost of applying a regulation to small firms or small transactions exceeds the total benefit, those firms or transactions should be exempted from the regulation in the absence of any transaction costs associated with the exemption. Thus, absent transaction costs, size-based exemptions can be efficient. [However,] exemptions do have transaction costs, and those transaction costs complicate the analysis, making it less likely that any particular small business exemption is efficient." (emphasis omitted)).

[34] *See* Lawrence Lessig, *The New Chicago School*, 27 J. Legal Stud. 661, 661–63 (1998) (identifying these constraints on behavior outside legal regulation).

[35] *See, e.g.,* Richard H. McAdams, *The Origin, Development, and Regulation of Norms*, 96 Mich. L. Rev. 338, 355 (1997) (articulating an "esteem theory" of norms; "the desire for esteem creates a norm … [And] norm violators [are punished] by withholding from them the esteem they seek").

[36] Ann E. Carlson, *Recycling Norms*, 89 Calif. L. Rev. 1231, 1245–47 (2001).

[37] *See* J. B. Ruhl and James Salzman, *Climate Change, Dead Zones, and Massive Problems in the Administrative State: A Guide for Whittling Away*, 98 Calif. L. Rev. 59, 92–93 (2010) (discussing how the concept of cumulative impacts or cumulative effects has influenced legal doctrine in these and other areas).

[38] *Id.* at 65.

[39] *Id.* at 92; *see also* Stack and Vandenbergh, *supra* note 23, at 1388.

[40] *Id.* at 1397 ("No one stands for treating trifles as anything but. The key is to see that defining something as a trifle depends on an assessment of the surrounding landscape").

III THE CASE FOR A REGULATORY RESPONSE TO SCALE IN THE SHARING ECONOMY

Section I demonstrated how scale is a key feature of the sharing economy. Section II unpacked the implications of scale for various regulatory models. Using scale as a lens, this section develops the case for a regulatory response to the sharing economy on three grounds. First, the large number of small-scale home-sharing and ride-hailing transactions can have negative cumulative impacts and externalities not fully borne by parties to the transaction. Second, the misfit between existing laws and the sharing economy's network orchestrator model is producing regulatory fractures, which threaten to undermine civil rights protections and other important policy goals. Finally, the traditional justifications for regulatory leniency for small-scale activities are not fully applicable to the networked, peer-to-peer model of the sharing economy.

A Negative Cumulative Impacts

Large numbers of small-scale activities are crucial to the success of the sharing economy: network effects depend on there being enough drivers for all the passengers who want rides and enough passengers for all the drivers who want fares. For platforms like Airbnb and Uber, the more small-scale the activity, the better. But while network orchestrators may benefit from network effects as the network expands and the number of individual transactions increases, the large-scale occurrence of small-scale activities can have a range of negative cumulative impacts.

A complete discussion of negative cumulative impacts in all sectors of the sharing economy is beyond the scope of this chapter, but home-sharing offers a snapshot of how individually *de minimis* activities can have negative cumulative impacts.[41] While the chances of any one home-sharing transaction causing significant noise, safety, traffic, or parking issues may be low, when thousands of home-sharing transactions are taking place in a particular city or neighborhood, the potential for these types of problem is amplified. Transitory home-sharing guests, who may be unfamiliar with – or simply not care about – legal rules such as parking restrictions or informal norms such as noise considerations, may disrupt residential neighborhoods or resident-occupied buildings. Formerly residential neighborhoods may essentially be de facto rezoned to mixed-use zones as residences are used more intensively for commercial activity.[42]

Large numbers of home-sharing transactions can also result in negative cumulative impacts in the long-term rental market. As increasing numbers of tenants under long-term leases rent out their apartments on home-sharing platforms like Airbnb, landlords wanting to capture the higher rents for short-term rentals themselves may be incentivized to take units out of the long-term rental market and move them into the more profitable short-term rental market. Even landlords who do not remove their rental units from the long-term rental market may raise rents in an attempt to capture short-term rental revenue they assume their tenants will be engaging in – legally or not. As a result, there is the potential for long-term rental housing supply to go down, and rental costs to go up – for everyone, not just those who operate as Airbnb hosts.[43]

---

[41] For a discussion of the negative cumulative impacts of ride-hailing, *see* Zale, *supra* note * at 988–89.

[42] While mixed uses may potentially constitute a long-term positive from a planning perspective, in the shorter term, they are likely to be perceived as a negative outcome by residents who purchased property in what they believed was a residential neighborhood.

[43] Evidence to date on the impacts of home-sharing on long-term rental markets is limited. One study found a significant reduction in long-term rental units in Los Angeles, while another found no impact in Seattle. *See* Roy Samaan,

Negative cumulative impacts may also result from the increased burdens on public infra-structure and other public services if home-sharing activities are not subject to the taxes or fees that apply to other short-term accommodations, such as hotels and traditional B&Bs.[44] While the failure to pay taxes on a single home-sharing transaction may have no discernable effect on a city's budget, the loss of tax revenue from thousands of home-sharing transactions may result in budget shortfalls, which must be made up either through higher taxes on residents or lowered level of services and infrastructure maintenance.[45]

While not all of the negative cumulative impacts discussed above will necessarily occur in every jurisdiction, and there will be localized variation in how significant such impacts are, by recognizing how the large-scale occurrence of small-scale activities can result in negative cumulative impacts, policymakers can adjust regulations as needed to account for the aggregate effects.

B Regulatory Fractures

The particular arrangement of scale in the sharing economy is also threatening to undermine a range of civil rights and other laws due to the misfit between existing regulations and new modes of activity, producing what Saskia Sassen has termed regulatory fractures.[46] In the context of the sharing economy, these regulatory fractures are occurring because numerous regulations, from local zoning codes to state employment laws to federal civil rights laws, do not map neatly onto the sharing economy's three-sided network orchestrator model. When regulated activity involves the traditional two-party model of industry–consumers or employer–employees, existing regulations have functioned well enough. But when applied to the sharing economy's three-sided model, regulations may break down.

For example, the Americans with Disabilities Act ("ADA") requires "reasonable modifications" in the provision of public accommodations to make such accommodations accessible to the disabled.[47] Commercial enterprises, such as hotels and taxis, are considered public accommo-dation under the ADA and must comply with its accessibility requirements, which is typically accomplished by ensuring that a specified percentage of drivers have accessible vehicles or a specified number of hotel rooms are accessible.[48] But applying the ADA to ride-hailing or home-sharing activities raises legal questions as well as practical difficulties. Is Uber or Airbnb providing

---

Airbnb, Rising Rent, and the Housing Crisis in Los Angeles, LAANE 3, 16 (Mar. 2015), www.laane.org/wp-content/uploads/2015/03/AirBnB-Final.pdf (finding that about seven thousand rental units had been removed from the Los Angeles long-term rental market for short-term rentals during the time Airbnb had been operating in the city); *Airbnb and the City of Seattle*, Airbnb 3 (Dec. 2015), https://1zxiwovqxooryvpz3ikczauf-wpengine.netdna-ssl.com/wp-content/uploads/2016/08/AirbnbandtheCityofSeattle.pdf. For a discussion of the impacts of Airbnb in the New York City real estate market, *see* Peter Coles et al., this volume.

[44] While Airbnb previously refused to collect such taxes via its platform, the company has changed tack and is now collecting taxes in a growing number of jurisdictions.

[45] Even if home-sharing transactions are subject to taxes and fees, whether such revenue is ultimately directed toward infrastructure and other public goods impacted by home-sharing activity will depend on the particular legal constraints imposed on the use of such revenue and decisions by elected officials about how to use such revenue.

[46] Sassen, *supra* note 5, at 2291.

[47] 42 U.S.C. §§12182 (2012).

[48] *See* Zale, *supra* note *, at 992 (discussing ADA accommodations in the context of short-term accommodation and point-to-point transportation).

public accommodation? Normally, private homes or personal vehicles are not covered under the ADA, but in the sharing economy, these assets are being used for commercial purposes and made available to the public in ways similar to other public accommodations, like hotels and taxis. However, unlike hotels or taxi companies, Uber and Airbnb do not own the fleet of vehicles or inventory of rooms at issue, and thus they cannot comply with the ADA in the same manner as hotels and taxi companies do. But applying the ADA directly to the individual hosts or drivers who use their car or home partly for personal use and partly for commercial activities raises its own set of difficulties. While these regulatory challenges are not intractable, they illustrate how the ADA, like other existing regulations, needs to adapt to the sharing economy's three-sided model.[49]

The regulatory misfit between existing governance models and the sharing economy is also evident when one considers the challenges of enforcement. For example, ensuring that a hotel has all of the necessary permits to operate is relatively straightforward: in any given jurisdiction, there are generally a known and limited number of hotels that are subject to permitting requirements and inspections. In contrast, it is a near-impossible task for regulators to ensure that homesharing hosts have necessary permits because regulators often have no idea who is actually engaged in such activity.[50] While companies like Airbnb collect precisely the data that can provide this information, to date, Airbnb and other platforms have largely resisted sharing this data with regulators.[51] Cities have thus been forced to rely on municipal enforcement departments with small staffs and limited budgets to engage in sporadic, complaint-driven enforcement.[52]

While some may argue that such regulatory misfits are the natural consequence of innovation, the innovative methods in which the sharing economy is delivering goods and services should not obscure the fact that the underlying activities are ones that we have important public policy

---

[49] *See, e.g.,* Charlotte Garden and Nancy Leong, this volume (discussing the applicability of anti-discrimination laws to the sharing economy).

[50] *See* Lawrence Lessig, *Code Version 2.0* 39 (2006) (noting that to regulate effectively, a regulator needs to know "Who did what, where?").

[51] Section 230 of the Communications Decency Act poses a potential obstacle to regulators seeking data from platforms needed to enforce local regulations. See 47 U.S.C. § 230(c)(1) (2012) (preempting any state or local law that imposes liability on "interactive computer service[s]," for the publication or speech of another "information content provider"). For example, when San Francisco amended its home-sharing ordinance to require that platforms not collect fees for listings that lack valid registration numbers, Airbnb sued, claiming the local ordinance was preempted by Section 230. *See* Zale, *supra* note * at 1001–03 (discussing Section 230 and San Francisco's and Airbnb's competing arguments regarding its preemption of the city's home-sharing regulations). Airbnb and San Francisco settled in May 2017. *See* Kate Benner, *Airbnb Settles Lawsuit with its Hometown, San Francisco,* N.Y. Times (May 1, 2017), www .nytimes.com/2017/05/01/technology/airbnb-san-francisco-settle-registration-lawsuit.html?_r=0 (discussing how under the settlement, Airbnb agreed to provide the city with host information and to deactivate invalid listings when notified by the city).

[52] *See, e.g.,* Phillip Matier and Andrew Ross, *"No Way of Enforcing" Airbnb Law, S.F. Planning Memo Says,* S.F. Chron. (Mar. 22, 2015), www.sfchronicle.com/bayarea/matier-ross/article/No-way-ofenforcing-Airbnb-law-S-F-planning-6151592.php. (discussing the San Francisco Planning Department's determination that the city's short-term rental law was "unworkable," due to the company's refusal to provide access to the data on home-sharing activity needed to enforce the regulation); *see also* Rob Walker, *Airbnb Pits Neighbor Against Neighbor in Tourist-Friendly New Orleans,* N.Y. Times (Mar. 5, 2016), www.nytimes.com/2016/03/06/business/airbnb-pits-neighbor-against-neighbor-in-tourist-friendly-new-orleans.html (describing the New Orleans mayor's acknowledgment that enforcement of that city's "short-term rental law has been 'lax and difficult.' Listings on home-sharing platforms do not reveal specific names and addresses, and identifying and building cases against violators would involve considerable time and money, city officials say").

reasons for regulating. As home-sharing and ride-hailing become increasingly large sectors of the accommodation and transportation markets, and companies like Airbnb and Uber become de facto regulators[53] of spare housing capacity, quasi-public transportation, and massive amounts of data, regulatory models will need to adapt.

C Responding to Justifications for Regulatory Leniency

As discussed in Section II, regulatory leniency for small-scale activity can be justified on a number of grounds. However, none of these justifications is fully applicable to the sharing economy's networked peer-to-peer model.

First, while each stand-alone home-sharing or ride-hailing transaction is *de minimis*, the potential cumulative impacts of these activities are not.[54] As discussed above, the aggregate impacts of these activities can produce a range of significant negative consequences, from the loss of long-term rental housing to increased burdens on public services and infrastructure. When small-scale actors comprise the bulk of the activity producing a particular social "bad," then the regulatory calculus should be recalibrated.[55]

Second, privacy and autonomy concerns are significantly diminished because the "sharing-for-a-fee" activities taking place within the sharing economy fall squarely within the definition of commercial activities.[56] Furthermore, although commercial activity may still implicate privacy concerns, particularly when it takes place in personal spaces, the simple fact that a residence or private vehicle is involved does not automatically entitle the activity to regulatory immunity on privacy grounds.[57] For example, vehicle owners must comply with registration and insurance requirements, and those working out of their home must comply with tax and employment laws, health and safety codes, and zoning laws.[58]

Third, while enforcement costs are a significant concern if cities have to monitor and enforce regulations against large numbers of individuals – particularly when cities lack access to the data necessary to determine whether individuals are engaged in the regulated activities – enforcement costs can be lowered by taking advantage of the sharing economy's network orchestrator

---

[53] The term "de facto regulators" refers to private entities that have a significant stake in a particular market and whose decisions with regard to that market function like public regulation. *See* Daniel Schwarcz and Steven L. Schwarcz, *Regulating Systemic Risk in Insurance*, 81 U. Chi. L. Rev. 1569, 1616 (2014) (discussing private ratings agencies as the de facto regulators of the reinsurance industry).

[54] In addition, even on a stand-alone basis, certain small-scale activities in the sharing economy have the potential for significant harms, weakening the justification for regulatory leniency further. For example, ride-hailing involves a personal interaction in a stranger's vehicle; while the likelihood of accidents or assaults may be rare, because of the risk of serious harm, the case for regulatory leniency on the basis of the activity's *de minimis* nature is further weakened.

[55] *See* Stack and Vandenbergh, *supra* note 23, at 1396 ("What drives these exemptions [for small-scale activities] is the relative cost of compliance and the relatively small scope of the activities subject to the exemptions. But this cost–benefit calculation should shift depending on the proportion of activities that fall within the exemptions").

[56] While some sharing economy platforms, such as Couchsurfing, do not involve a monetary exchange between parties, the vast majority of sharing economy activities do involve monetary exchanges and would be considered commercial, even if users also have other motivations (such as community-building). *See* Zale, *supra* note 7 at 523 (discussing the characteristics of commercial versus noncommercial activity).

[57] This is not to say there are no privacy concerns raised by short-term rentals. If I rent out my entire unit on Airbnb, and it is my personal residence that I otherwise live in, there are more privacy concerns than with a hotel room. But the question is not whether there are *any* privacy concerns; it is whether privacy concerns are so significant as to justify exemptions from regulations intending to achieve other important public policies.

[58] *See, e.g.*, Nicole Stelle Garnett, *On Castles and Commerce: Zoning Law and the Home-Business Dilemma*, 42 Wm. & Mary L. Rev. 1191, 1195 (2001) (discussing laws applicable to home businesses).

model and the role of the platform. By re-focusing regulatory efforts on a single actor, the platform, which not only facilitates small-scale transactions but also aggregates data about those transactions, it becomes possible to design regulations to utilize this data to lower enforcement costs. In the home-sharing context, for example, rather than trying to determine if the thousands of short-term rental hosts in a city each have obtained the necessary permit to engage in the activity – an almost Sisyphean task – regulators can focus on the platforms and require that they include permit numbers on listings posted on their sites.[59]

Fourth, fairness concerns about disproportionate burdens on small-scale actors having to comply with one-size-fits-all regulation can be addressed by adopting governance approaches that are proportional to the regulated activity or that focus on platforms as aggregators of small-scale activity. For example, while one-size-fits-all regulations may be appropriate for some aspects of the sharing economy – such as background checks for ride-hailing drivers – other aspects – such as home-sharing permit fees or tax obligations – may be better addressed through tiered regulation so as not to disproportionately impact small-scale actors. Similarly, accessibility requirements under the ADA may be satisfied by requiring that platforms charge a small fee on every transaction, which is used to fund accessible transportation or accommodation options, rather than imposing requirements on individual drivers or hosts to make accessibility modifications to their personal home or car.[60]

Finally, while non-legal alternatives may be able to constrain the behavior of small-scale actors in the sharing economy, such alternatives, on their own, are unlikely to fully address negative cumulative impacts and regulatory fractures. For example, norms have been shown to fail to take hold when there are "[l]arge numbers of people, [with] little economic incentive to act, and [a] lack of homogeneity":[61] precisely the scenario in the sharing economy. Similarly, architecture or market-based responses may be only a partial solution. For example, two-way rating systems are often cited as a highly effective non-legal mechanism for regulating behavior in the sharing economy.[62] However, even where two-way ratings effectively constrain some aspects of users' behavior, such as cleanliness of a car or house, they do not address behavior that may be more troubling from a public safety perspective. For example, a friendly Airbnb host with a clean house may receive five-star ratings, but if she has failed to install smoke detectors, the platform's rating system is unlikely to address this concern.[63]

---

[59] The Communications Decency Act may pose challenges to co-regulatory approaches, but it may not provide blanket immunity to companies seeking to avoid co-regulatory responsibilities. *See* Zale, *supra* note * at 1001–03 (discussing potential challenges raised by Section 230 of the Act to regulating platforms).

[60] *See Cities, the Sharing Economy, and What's Next,* National League of Cities 17 (2015), www.nlc.org/sites/default/files/2017-01/Report%20%20%20Cities%20the%20Sharing%20Economy%20and%20Whats%20final.pdf (discussing how Washington, D.C., Chicago and Seattle have enacted similar regulations).

[61] *See* Carlson, *supra* note 37, at 1235–36.

[62] *See* Arun Sundararajan, *Trusting the "Sharing Economy" to Regulate Itself,* N.Y. Times (Mar. 13, 2014), https://economix.blogs.nytimes.com/2014/03/03/trusting-the-sharing-economy-to-regulate-itself/?_r=2.

[63] Furthermore, regulation of behavior by mechanisms other than formal legal regulation often lacks the transparency and democratic processes (such as judicial review) of formal legal regulation. *See* Jane K. Winn, *The Secession of the Successful: The Rise of Amazon as Private Global Consumer Protection Regulator,* 58 Ariz. L. Rev. 193, 196 (2016) (discussing such concerns in the context of Amazon's de facto privatized consumer protection regulations). For example, because two-way reviews skew positive, the effect of just one negative review – for what may have been a mistake or misunderstanding – may have disproportional consequences, such as the removal of a driver from a ride-hailing platform without notice or opportunity for a hearing. See David Streitfeld, "Ratings Now Cut Both Ways, So Don't Sass Your Uber Driver," N.Y. Times (Jan. 30, 2015), www.nytimes.com/2015/01/31/technology/companies-are-rating-customers.html (noting concerns from scholars about inaccurate two-way ratings potentially leading us into to a "disinformation economy").

Kellen Zale

CONCLUSION

The sharing economy has produced a situation where small-scale activities that once fit the criteria for regulatory leniency are occurring in numbers that suggest a need to recalibrate regulatory approaches. Governance mechanisms such as co-regulation and cooperative models, discussed elsewhere in this volume, demonstrate how regulation can adapt to the sharing economy.[64] Recalibrating regulation to better fit the scale of activities in the sharing economy can help ensure that the sharing economy continues to produce economic opportunities and socially beneficial activities, while also accounting for the negative cumulative impacts and regulatory fractures that it can produce.

---

[64] *See* Zale, *supra* note * at 1004–11 (discussing how such governance mechanism might work in the context of home-sharing and ride-hailing); *see also* Bryant Cannon and Hanna Chung, this volume.

4

Sharing Economy and Social Innovation

Aurélien Acquier and Valentina Carbone

INTRODUCTION

The sharing economy encompasses a wide diversity of entrepreneurial initiatives in terms of their legal form of business organization, value creation logics, technological resources, and ideological roots.[1] What sharing economy entrepreneurs have in common is that they seek to optimize under-used resources. And most of them claim to be transforming society and promoting some form of societal promise in their business model: improving access to products and services by disrupting the revenues of big business, building social ties, extending the lifespan of objects, encouraging recycling, etc. In response to these promises, two opposing visions clash among expert and academic observers. On the one hand, "supporters" of the sharing economy describe it as a movement of reform and activism, which constitutes a breeding ground for new forms of solidarity and innovation in the area of political and organizational governance.[2] They see the sharing economy as an opportunity for individual emancipation and environmental progress, in opposition to the hierarchical power of traditional economic institutions such as large firms – the heirs of the second industrial revolution.[3] On the other hand, a growing group of opponents denounce this idealized vision as a form of mystification.[4] They criticize the sharing economy and the rise of peer-to-peer platforms for being a "low cost" access economy,[5] based on business models that destabilize employment relations,[6] promote a hidden neoliberal agenda,[7] and undermine the very concepts of enterprise and salaried employment.[8]

---

[1] A. Acquier, T. Daudigeos, and J. Pinkse, *Promises and Paradoxes of the Sharing Economy: An Organizing Framework*, 125 Tech. Forecasting & Soc. Change 1–10 (2017); A. Sundararajan, *The Sharing Economy: The End of Employment and the Rise of Crowd-Based Capitalism* (2016).

[2] M. Bauwens, The Political Economy of Peer Production, C-Theory (2005), https://journals.uvic.ca/index.php/ctheory/article/view/14464/5306; F. Laloux *Reinventing Organizations* (2014); Sundararajan, *supra* note 1.

[3] OuiShare, *Société collaborative: La fin des hiérarchies* (D. Filippova ed., 2015); Bauwens, *supra* note 2.

[4] T. Slee, *What's Yours is Mine: Against the Sharing Economy* (2016).

[5] F. Bardhi, and G. M. Eckhardt, *Access-Based Consumption: The Case of Car Sharing*, 39(4) J. Consumer Res. 881–98 (2012).

[6] T. Scholz (ed.), *Digital Labor: The Internet as Playground and Factory* (2012); A. Casilli, *Venture Labor| How Venture Labor Sheds Light on the Digital Platform Economy*, 11 Intl. J. Comm. 4 (2017).

[7] C. J. Martin, *The Sharing Economy: A Pathway to Sustainability or a Nightmarish Form of Neoliberal Capitalism?* 121 Ecological Econ. 149–59 (2016); D. Murillo, H. Buckland, and E. Val, *When the Sharing Economy Becomes Neoliberalism on Steroids: Unravelling the Controversies*, 125 Tech. Forecasting and Social Change 66–76 (2017).

[8] G. Davis, *Managed by the Markets: How Finance Reshaped America* 328 (2009); P. Fleming, *The Human Capital Hoax: Work, Debt and Insecurity in the Era of Uberization*, 38(5) Org. Stud. 691–709 (2017).

These opposing positions are all the more difficult to reconcile as they are based on vastly diverging – and sometimes irreconcilable – visions and definitions of the sharing economy itself.[9] In this chapter, we wish to move away from such extreme positions. Given the internal complexity and heterogeneity of the field, we believe that it is impossible to resolve these debates for the sharing economy as a whole. Therefore, we will conduct our analysis at a more granular level, based on a typology of business models in the sharing economy,[10] and examine how each type of initiative is related to specific mechanisms of value creation, scaling potential, and social innovation issues.

Empirically, this chapter is based on field research conducted in 2015 and 2016 on a sample of 30 sharing initiatives in France and other European countries, in the material goods sector. Our sample encompasses a wide variety of initiatives and logics, ranging from platforms for swapping, lending, selling, or gifting goods to digital modeling and fabrication workshops or "fab labs." We interviewed founders and stakeholders at each initiative, exploring business model configurations and sustainability impacts. In this chapter, we also refer to other well-known sharing economy initiatives to present our framework.

The chapter is structured as follows. In the first section, we introduce four ideal types of initiative based on their mechanisms of value creation and distribution, as well as their social innovation promises (Section I). We then underline the importance of making a sharp distinction between promises and actual impacts, as each ideal type may have vastly diverging growth potential (Section II). In this section, we differentiate between three situations: initiatives driven by social innovation with limited scaling potential (II.A); market-driven initiatives with much higher scaling potential but uncertain social innovation impacts (II.B); and hybrid organizational arrangements (II.C), which may combine high growth potential and societal value creation, but have to cope with complex managerial challenges in terms of legitimacy and mission drift.

Given the variety of organizational arrangements and value creation logics in the sharing economy, we argue that the relationship between promises and impacts is far from linear, homogeneous, and straightforward. Finally, while the sharing economy may not necessarily lead to social innovation, it nevertheless offers opportunities and organizational models that may be used to promote social innovation projects. This opens the way for political decisions: it is up to governments, academic institutions, and social actors to play an active role in shaping the sharing economy according to innovative visions and "valuable" societal projects.

I THE SHARING ECONOMY: FROM BUSINESS MODELS TO SOCIAL PROMISES

The business model concept refers to the process whereby an organization creates, delivers, and captures value with its customers, distribution channels, and specific partners, based on its value proposition and revenue streams.[11] Research on business models mainly focuses on 1) the way firms create value; and 2) the way this value is captured and shared within the firm's ecosystem.[12]

---

[9] Acquier, Daudigeos, and Pinkse, *supra* note 1, for a discussion of contradictions among sharing economy definitions and approaches.

[10] Acquier A., V. Carbone, and D. Massé, *Framing the sharing economy: a business model perspective* (2016), 32nd EGOS Colloquium, Naples, July 7–9.

[11] A. Osterwalder and Y. Pigneur, *Business Model Generation: A Handbook for Visionaries, Game Changers, and Challengers* (2010).

[12] C. Bowman and V. Ambrosini, *Value Creation Versus Value Capture: Towards a Coherent Definition of Value in Strategy*, 11(1) Brit. J. Mgmt. 1–15 (2000).

These two dimensions prove to be particularly relevant in describing the diversity of sharing economy initiatives.

A *Value Creation Mechanisms: From P2P Intermediation to Resource Pooling*

We distinguish two key value creation mechanisms in the sharing economy. Some initiatives create value by connecting peers and intermediating between them via a commercial or non-profit digital platform.[13] This includes peer-to-peer (P2P) platforms such as Airbnb (profit driven) or Couchsurfing (nonprofit). Other initiatives create value by setting up specific mechanisms to create a common pool of resources that would otherwise be inaccessible (because unavailable or unaffordable) to a segment of users. They enable wider access to resources through the sharing of knowledge, skills, services, or technical infrastructure.[14] Initiatives such as Wikipedia (common pool of knowledge freely accessible to all) or access services such as Zipcar (short-term car rentals) fall into this category.

These two value creation mechanisms are not mutually exclusive. They should be considered as two extremes of a single continuum which may sometimes be combined and hybridized.[15] Fab labs or hacker-space initiatives are an illustration of such a hybrid form. Their purpose is to provide access to a pool of resources (workshops, machines, expertise, etc.) to facilitate do-it-yourself (DIY) activities by individuals. They also foster the formation of user networks and bring together people with complementary skills.[16]

B *Value Capture and Distribution Mechanisms*

Traditionally focused on the internal processes of the firm, the thinking on business models has gradually integrated the importance of sharing value among the firm, users,[17] and/or society, causing new perspectives to emerge on how the value created by a firm is shared in its eco-system.[18] In the sharing economy, initiatives generally fall into two main configurations in terms of how they create and capture value:

1) One set of initiatives subscribes to a for-profit logic, monetizing their services and generating profits.[19] Incidentally, this configuration has given rise to numerous debates on the scope of the sharing economy and whether or not monetary transactions and for-profit exchanges represent "true" sharing or "pseudo-sharing" (Belk, 2014).[20] Value capture mechanisms are varied. They may be direct, as when the customer pays a fee or commission

---

[13] R. Belk, Z. Arsel, D. Bajde, J. Deschênes, E. Fisher, M. L. Gall-Ely, ... B. Urien, *Giving, Sharing, Consuming: Connecting Consumer Behaviors*, 39 Advances in Consumer Res. 684–85 (2011).

[14] R. Botsman and R. Rogers, *What's Mine Is Yours: How Collaborative Consumption Is Changing the Way We Live* (2010); L. Gansky, *The Mesh: Why the Future of Business Is Sharing* (reprint ed., 2012).

[15] J. Germann Molz, *CouchSurfing and Network Hospitality: "It's Not Just About the Furniture,"* 1(3) Hospitality & Soc., 215–25 (2012).

[16] C. Kohtala, and C. Bosqué, *The Story of MIT-Fablab Norway: Community Embedding of Peer Production*, 5 J. Peer Production (2014); A. Toombs, S. Bardzell, and J. Bardzell, *Becoming Makers: Hackerspace Member Habits, Values, and Identities*, 5 J. Peer Production (2014).

[17] R. L. Priem, *A Consumer Perspective on Value Creation*, 32(1) Acad. Mgmt. Rev. 219–35 (2007).

[18] M. Yunus, B. Moingeon, and L. Lehmann-Ortega, *Building Social Business Models: Lessons from the Grameen Experience*, 43(2–3) Long Range Plan. 308–25 (2010); M. E. Porter and M. R. Kramer, *The Link Between Competitive Advantage and Corporate Social Responsibility*, 84(12) Harv. Bus. Rev. 78–92 (2006).

[19] D. J. Teece, *Business Models, Business Strategy and Innovation*, 43(2–3) Long Range Plan. 172–94 (2010).

[20] R. Belk, *You Are What You Can Access: Sharing and Collaborative Consumption Online*, 67(8) J. Bus. Res. 1595–600 (2014).

for accessing services, or indirect, as when a third party – in two-sided markets – finances the service provided to the consumer. This may involve selling advertising space or monetizing user-generated data on the online platform, which would enable free access to services for users (such as Google, Facebook, etc.).

2) In contrast, some initiatives define themselves as "limited profit" or "nonprofit" ventures.[21] Unlike most high-tech start-ups, they capture a limited part of the value created and pursue a clear mission to distribute this value in their extended ecosystem.[22] This category mainly includes nonprofit initiatives. There may be monetary transactions between users and the platform, or donations and financial support to maximize the social impact of the initiative, as in the case of the Wikimedia Foundation.[23]

These two mechanisms may be combined, and constitute a continuum. At one extreme, there are for-profit initiatives that capture a large part of the value created and, at the other extreme, nonprofits that aim to democratize resources (for example, Wikipedia, whose aim is to democratize knowledge) by distributing most of the value created within their ecosystem.[24]

C *Four Types of Initiative in the Sharing Economy*

By mapping the value creation mechanisms (horizontal axis) and value distribution mechanisms (vertical axis), we distinguish four types of business model, which we refer to as *Commoners*, *Mission-Driven Platforms*, *Shared Infrastructure Providers*, and *Matchmakers* (see Figure 4.1).

1 *Commoners*

"Commoners" create and provide free access to public goods by pooling resources and skills in order to make them available to as many people as possible and to spur the emergence of alternative and non-market values, such as open knowledge, free and open access, or do-it-yourself (DIY). Value is created by and for the community or the initiative's ecosystem. While their ideology is strongly rooted in the digital culture, these initiatives are found in both the digital and physical worlds. Two examples illustrate this type of initiative. The "fab lab" (fabrication laboratory) movement emerged in the late 1990s, spearheaded by Neil Gershenfeld, a professor at MIT, who sought to make digital production tools available to everybody so they could fabricate "almost anything." Fab labs are open to the public and contain all sorts of production tools, particularly computer-controlled machines/tools (3D printers, etc.) for the design and production of various objects. In addition to fab labs that fit the MIT definition, numerous spaces have appeared with similar objectives and names, such as hackerspaces and makerspaces. As of October 2017, there were nearly 1,200 fab labs around the world.[25]

Initiatives such as iFixit (a US private company founded in 2003) or Comment Réparer (a French nonprofit equivalent started in 2011) are examples of Commoners in the digital world. They replicate the logic promoted by Wikipedia, the largest and most popular encyclopedia in the world, with 12.5 billion page views per month and more than 38 million articles available.[26] These online repair platforms build online communities of individuals searching for or offering

---

[21] C. Seelos and J. Mair, *Profitable Business Models and Market Creation in the Context of Deep Poverty: A Strategic View*, 21(4) Acad. Mgmt. Perspectives 49–63 (2007).

[22] Germann Molz, *supra* note 15.

[23] D. Jemielniak, *Common Knowledge?: An Ethnography of Wikipedia* 312 (2014).

[24] J. B. Schor, E. T. Walker, C. W. Lee, P. Parigi, and K. Cook, *On the Sharing Economy*, 14(1) Contexts 12–19 (2015).

[25] *Labs*, FabLabs, www.fablabs.io/labs.

[26] Jemielniak, *supra* note 23.

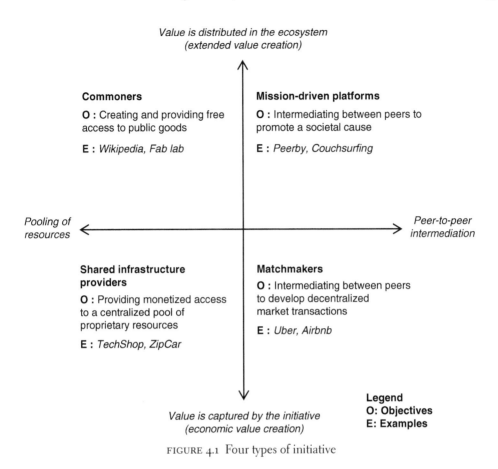

Value is distributed in the ecosystem
(extended value creation)

Commoners

O : Creating and providing free access to public goods

E : *Wikipedia, Fab lab*

Mission-driven platforms

O : Intermediating between peers to promote a societal cause

E : *Peerby, Couchsurfing*

Pooling of resources ← → Peer-to-peer intermediation

Shared infrastructure providers

O : Providing monetized access to a centralized pool of proprietary resources

E : *TechShop, ZipCar*

Matchmakers

O : Intermediating between peers to develop decentralized market transactions

E : *Uber, Airbnb*

Value is captured by the initiative
(economic value creation)

Legend
O: Objectives
E: Examples

FIGURE 4.1 Four types of initiative

help and ideas on how to repair various items. These decentralized interactions are brought together on the website, which also oversees an editorial process to develop free repair guides, written by community members and made accessible to all. Both initiatives explicitly promote their project as a way to fight against waste (in particular e-waste) and planned obsolescence, and to boost the circular economy.

These Commoners' initiatives are imbued with an alternative ideology of repair, a DIY mentality, and a "maker" culture,[27] promoting emancipation from large private organizations and struggling against planned obsolescence. They see knowledge as a common good, accessible to all, and naturally draw on a culture of exchange and gifting rather than the monetization of relations. Learning is at the heart of the thinking and values of Commoners' spaces. In fab labs, for example, non-specialists should be able to adapt the space to their own needs. Such spaces should be sufficiently versatile to allow users to adjust, repair, model, or repurpose a vast range of products.

Concern for the environment may be an explicit, founding principle, as is the case for iFixit, and is manifested in its repair work and waste reduction objectives. The initiative is also fighting for a redefinition of the concept of ownership that would introduce the "right to repair." For fab labs and makerspaces, the environmental vision is not necessarily fundamental, nor is its impact measured, even though the tools provided may be used in projects with an environmental purpose.

[27] C. Anderson, *Makers: The New Industrial Revolution* (2014).

2 Mission-Driven Platforms

"Mission-driven platforms" intermediate between peers through a digital platform to support a societal cause. Like Commoners, they pursue a mission to transform society through the initiative by facilitating new practices of consumption, exchange, and relationships. The cause and values that initially motivated the founders constitute the purpose of the initiative, which grows along with the volume of resources that are shared through the platform. These initiatives may take the form of websites whose aim is to reduce waste through an increased circulation of goods, and by promoting gifting or mutual aid among neighbors. They are based on certain values: gifting, lending, and fighting against mass-consumption or planned obsolescence. Other initiatives also pursue the aim of creating social links and increasing solidarity among "neighbors" to build communities and foster exchanges and mutual aid outside the platform (cf. Peuplade in France[28] or Shareyourmeal in the Netherlands). The legal status of these initiatives ranges from nonprofit association to "simplified joint stock company" (limited liability company). In the sphere of material goods, Mission-driven platforms can be illustrated by two types of initiative:

1) One type of platform enables private individuals to lend each other material goods. An example is the Dutch platform Peerby, founded in 2013, through which users can offer to lend or ask to borrow or rent objects from other users in the same geographic area. According to the platform, there is about an 85 percent chance of finding the sought-after object free of charge within 30 minutes. In 2016, with 15 employees, this start-up had more than 100,000 users in the Netherlands, Belgium, London, and Berlin and had raised 2.2 million dollars in crowdfunding to pursue its growth, particularly in the United States.

2) Other types of platform are focused on gifting and re-use of old items. An example is Recupe.net, a French initiative that enables individuals to give and/or receive objects, with the dual aims of fighting waste and fostering social ties among peers. Specializing in intermediation in the practice of gifting, this website attained a daily average of 15,000 visitors soon after its launch in 2001.

Mission-driven platforms are conceived as tools to promote a societal project. They fully acknowledge their social activism, which is not necessarily political in nature. Various societal causes are pursued in the initiatives we studied. Some of them fight against planned obsolescence, which is considered a negative side effect of consumerism. Through different practices, such as swapping and gifting objects, these platforms aim to increase the useful life of objects by facilitating lending/gifting when an object is underutilized by its owner. Other initiatives, such as Co-recyclage,[29] seek to reduce waste by repurposing objects when they reach the end-of-life stage. The recirculation of underused goods is therefore emerging as a way of transforming waste into resources. Some sharing initiatives have developed a set of promises on their platform which seek, through gifting and lending, to revive the social ties in an apartment building, a neighborhood, a town, or even within companies.

3 Shared Infrastructure Providers

"Shared infrastructure providers" are for-profit initiatives that monetize access to a strategic proprietary resource. Operating on a membership fee or pay-per-use basis, shared infrastructure providers earn a profit and gain power from a proprietary infrastructure that individuals and

---

[28] www.peuplade.fr is a network of voluntary and free mutual assistance between neighbors.
[29] http://co-recyclage.com.

professionals use to realize their projects. They create economic value through a service provider logic. An illustration of this type of initiative is TechShop, a chain of digital fabrication workshops created in 2006 in California, which offers an array of dedicated machines, tools, and equipment for object fabrication. TechShops are large spaces for DIYers, inventors, artists, and entrepreneurs who do not have their own workshops, equipment, or sometimes even the skills needed to realize their projects. Other similar initiatives tend to reproduce the same logic. They take two main forms:

1) Collaborative spaces for individuals that resemble a "gym" for DIYers. These spaces vary in size and are oriented toward classes for private individuals or the sharing of skills and technical infrastructure for professionals. For example, a collaborative production space called l'Etablisienne[30] opened in Paris in 2011 and specializes in woodworking and creative activities involving wood. In 2015, l'Etablisienne had more than 2,000 members who go to the work space fairly regularly to use its specialized tools.

2) Productive or collaborative spaces for professionals that act as an accelerator for start-ups, artisans, or self-employed professionals. An example of this type is ICI Montreuil,[31] a collaborative production space that opened in 2013 in a Paris suburb. The space brings together 165 residents and 365 users, made up in equal numbers of artisans, artist-designers, and digital start-ups.

The social promises of these initiatives are somewhat similar to those of the Commoners. Some of these initiatives may indeed be thought of as instruments for spurring cultural and entrepreneurial dynamism across a region. In this case, public actors may be central stakeholders in the initiative, supporting it with resources, or even getting involved in its governance. This is the case of Montreuil city council and Est Ensemble – an urban agglomeration east of Paris – who are official partners of "Ici Montreuil," a collective interest cooperative company.

4 *Matchmakers*

"Matchmakers" are the most visible and controversial initiatives in the sharing economy. These are for-profit commercial platforms that bring individuals together in networks so they can exchange goods or services on a peer-to-peer basis. In the field of personal transport or accommodation, examples include platforms such as Uber, Airbnb, and BlaBlaCar. Often promoting a free-market ideology and fighting against the "economic rents" of established companies, they identify a resource that is both under-exploited and of high sharing value. The platform intermediates between peers and captures part of the value created in order to make a profit from this intermediation.

In this category, peer-to-peer initiatives involved in the sharing of material goods are very diverse in terms of size, number of employees, their level of development, and market positioning. Two main types of market positioning can be distinguished: generalist and specialized platforms. Generalist platforms offer the resale or rental of a range of goods. For example, Place de la Loc[32] is a French internet platform, founded in 2013, through which private individuals can rent a diverse range of goods (cars, power drills, bicycles, etc.). The potential revenue for individuals who rent their goods to other users constitutes the core of the initiative's value proposition. Specialized platforms arrange the rental or resale of objects in a specific sector. For example,

[30] www.letablisienne.com/.
[31] www.icimontreuil.com/.
[32] www.placedelaloc.com/.

TABLE 4.1 *Overview of the four types of initiative*

	Commoners	Mission-driven platforms	Shared infrastructure providers	Matchmakers
Example of initiative	Wikipedia, fab labs	Couchsurfing, Peerby	Zipcar, TechShop	Uber, Airbnb, Vestiaire Collective
Dominant logic	Access	Bartering, swapping, gifting	Rental and access (B to C)	Resale, peer-to-peer rental (C to C)
Customer value proposition	Fostering collective learning, open access and DIY culture	Intermediating between peers to promote a societal cause	Access/service-based economy	Intermediating between peers to arrange market-based transactions
Social and environmental promises	Central (at the core of the undertaking)	Central (the very purpose of the initiative)	Peripheral (services may serve local development objectives)	Peripheral, but potentially significant impact (positive or negative externalities)

Vestiaire Collective,[33] founded in 2009, is a platform for the resale of objects "among peers" that specializes in luxury fashion items. Since its creation, this e-commerce site has enjoyed very strong growth (nearly 100 percent per year), with a very high turnover of items listed for sale. On average, 25 percent of the items posted are sold within a week. The platform reported revenue of 100 million euros in 2015, a figure that is expected to double in the next five years. The company has subsidiaries in England and Germany, as well as in America, and is planning to enter the Chinese market soon. It has 180 employees.

In general, positive environmental or social outcomes do not constitute a primary motivation for these platforms. Instead, Matchmakers are predominantly driven by managerial and economic logics. However, owing to their high growth potential, these initiatives generate significant environmental and social externalities, as attested by the mounting controversies surrounding the business models based on platform logics (cf. BlaBlaCar, Airbnb, or Uber). Matchmakers may also generate positive externalities, and use them as a legitimization tool. For example, BlaBlaCar communicates about the positive impact of car sharing on CO_2 emissions thanks to a better occupancy rate for vehicles.

Table 4.1 offers an overview of the four types of initiative, detailing the dominant logic, the customer value proposition, and the social promises that correspond to each type of initiative. This model illustrates the complex links between the sharing economy and social innovation, as each type of initiative exhibits differentiated social innovation patterns. Social innovation may either be central or peripheral to the project, and may take various forms: promoting environmental stewardship, fostering social ties or cultural transformation through new modes of participative governance in a common project, for example.

---

[33] https://fr.vestiairecollective.com/.

II DISTINGUISHING BETWEEN PROMISES AND IMPACTS

The sharing economy makes a variety of social innovation promises,[34] and encompasses a variety of business-model arrangements.[35] As Seelos and Mair have shown, one of the key barriers to social innovation stems from the failure of social innovations to scale up.[36] Consequently, to understand how social innovation unfolds in the sharing economy, it is necessary to better assess its potential impact, by considering social innovation promises in relation to the scaling potential of initiatives. In this section, we contrast three different situations: at one extreme of the spectrum, numerous reformist nonprofit initiatives are based on ambitious societal promises, but suffer from limited scalability, thus limiting their potential impact (II.A). At the other extreme, for-profit initiatives based on a platform logic enjoy much stronger scalability (thus increasing their potential impact), but have contradictory social innovation impacts, since the externalities they generate may either be positive or negative (II.B). Finally, we illustrate how some hybrid configurations offer an innovative organizational response to this situation by combining commercial, social, and environmental logics, but may be confronted with legitimacy issues and the risk of mission drift (II.C).

A *Initiatives Driven by Social Innovation with Limited Scaling Potential*

Among the four types of initiative observed, Commoners and Mission-driven platforms explicitly adopt mechanisms to share value in their ecosystem. They mainly operate on noncommercial models and have built their mission on ambitious promises for societal innovation. As their work is driven by this social mission, such initiatives hold significant potential for environmental and social innovation. However, their growth is often held back by different factors. One issue is the difficulty of raising external funding; another is the difficulty of identifying a business model that will support their growth. The search for a viable business model often constitutes a stumbling block in Commoners' initiatives. As little or no financial streams pass through the platform, Mission-driven platforms are unable to capture value. Platforms with a social mission often find it difficult and uncomfortable to capture value from users. In order to support their growth or pay the costs generated by the platform, Mission-driven platforms therefore have to come up with clever ways of creating indirect value-capture mechanisms. Coming up with a viable business model proves to be a complex and critical issue for these initiatives. In the sector of object lending, initiatives like Peerby and ShareVoisin[37] (platforms for borrowing/lending objects or mutual aid services among neighbors) are therefore seeking a revenue model that will enable them to finance their project while remaining consistent with the values of gifting and reciprocal gifting that they stand for. Peerby, for example, switched from a free borrowing service to a peer-to-peer rental service in order to develop the initiative's traffic and revenues. While it maintains a strong environmental and community logic, Peerby could be criticized for distancing itself from "true" or "pure" sharing, as it introduced monetary transactions alongside borrowing.

In addition to the difficulties brought on by the fragility of their business model, a third element, linked to the lack of financial resources, is the weakness of some critical managerial

---

[34] Acquier, Daudigeos, and Pinkse, *supra* note 1.
[35] Acquier, Carbone, and Massé, *supra* note 10; P. Munoz and B. Cohen, *Mapping Out the Sharing Economy: A Configurational Approach to Sharing Business Modeling*, 125(C) Tech. Forecasting and Soc. Change 21–37 (2017).
[36] Seelos and Mair, *supra* note 21.
[37] https://sharevoisins.fr/.

competencies, particularly in community management, both local or online communities, which need to be sufficiently dense to boost user activity on these platforms. This criterion is particularly important for platforms involved in object lending and mutual aid between neighbors; it is critical to build a dense local network in order to generate a durable level of traffic and to balance supply and demand in the same area. This is the reason why some authors claim that the sharing economy is predominantly an "urban phenomenon."[38]

For Commoners – initiatives that seek to create and pool resources in order to make them freely accessible to all (such as iFixit or fab labs) – the problem is just as complex. Given their relatively resource-heavy structure (this is particularly critical for initiatives requiring significant non-digital infrastructures such as machines and workshops), their local rootedness and their open, noncommercial ideals, developing a growth strategy is also a complex matter. They may, however, experience rapid growth through spin-offs. As fab labs do not have sufficient financial resources to multiply their collaborative spaces around the world, they have adopted a multi-local expansion strategy within the framework of a social movement that exceeds the scale of an isolated undertaking. To replicate the initiative at a multi-local level, they endeavor to formalize their values and mission and to codify their practices, making it possible for a broader movement to emerge (or to join one). For example, modeled on the original FabLab at the Massachusetts Institute of Technology, Neil Gershenfeld has developed a global network of fab labs following a charter[39] that stipulates a certain number of principles that have to be observed (openness, collaboration, open-access tools and equipment, ownership of inventions, for instance) to join the network.

Public actors, both at the national and local levels, may help create the proper ecosystem to nurture these types of initiative so they can generate positive societal impacts in line with the political projects and vision of a given territory. Governments, partnering with educational institutions (business, engineering, or design schools) and investors, could encourage cross-fertilization between social entrepreneurship and the peer-to-peer digital world through multiple actions, such as dedicated incubators, tools and policies for funding, and collaborative projects between different institutions and organizations. For example, the Barcelona Fab City project was created in 2014 as a partnership between Barcelona City Council and the Barcelona Fab Lab,[40] with the objectives of stimulating local creativity and transforming cities into productive hubs through the use of digital fabrication technologies. This stands as an emblematic case of how cities can become "Sharing Economy Participants" (see Rauch, this volume).

B *Initiatives with High Scaling Potential, and Massive but Uncertain Social Impacts*

At the other extreme, initiatives founded on a commercial logic (Matchmakers and Shared infrastructure providers) do not base their development on the pursuit of a societal cause. In general, as they are structured by a managerial and economic logic that guides their decisions, Matchmakers (platforms that intermediate between peers) seek to open new markets and create new practices. Environmental and social impacts constitute externalities of these platforms, i.e. incidental effects rather than the primary goals of the initiative.

---

[38] N. M. Davidson and J. J. Infranca, *The Sharing Economy as an Urban Phenomenon*, 34 Yale L. and Policy Rev. 215 (2015).

[39] The Fab Charter, http://fab.cba.mit.edu/about/charter/.

[40] *See* www.collaborative.city/item/barcelona-fab-city/.

For example, the resale of luxury items between peers has been the focus of several entrepreneurial initiatives that seized an opportunity to expand the scope of traditional e-commerce platforms. Incidentally, a positive environmental impact is achieved by extending the lifespan and circulation of products. These incidental impacts should not be ignored, because these initiatives have the potential for very rapid growth and may have a structuring effect on consumer practices. It is therefore essential to better evaluate the effects of these platforms in terms of consumer behavior. Recent studies call for caution, however.[41] They take a critical look at the idea that a positive environmental outcome is associated with using sharing platforms or systems based on utilization and access rather than ownership. In reality, numerous counterintuitive mechanisms may lead to the opposite outcome.

For access-based and rental services (the Shared infrastructure providers in our typology), the shift from ownership to access constitutes a profound identity transformation for the user, which may be manifested in a lack of care or responsibility for the product on the part of users.[42] For example, when JCDecaux launched the Vélib bicycle rental service in Paris, it had seriously underestimated the maintenance costs that would be generated by customers' lack of care for the new public infrastructure. As a result, potential environmental benefits may be reduced by the negligent behavior of non-owners. Furthermore, rental services may also create expectations among customers for more frequent product upgrades and renewal.

For peer-to-peer rental or resale platforms (Matchmakers), the impact of transport (especially in the exchange or resale of goods) is often neglected in the analysis. Yet in terms of logistics, decentralized systems are often less efficient from an environmental point of view. For example, driving several kilometers to complete a transaction through leboncoin.fr or Craigslist (classifieds website) may eliminate the positive environmental benefits associated with the increased lifespan of the item. Similarly, the platform's back office activities (running the digital platform) may generate environmental impacts that are often excluded from the analysis.

Other problems stem from the effect these platforms have on consumer behavior. There are "rebound effects" linked to the use of money generated or saved by swapping and reselling items.[43] By swapping their home during the summer holidays, a family saves money while doing something useful for the environment (better use of assets). However, with these savings, they may decide to travel across the globe by airplane, thus canceling out the environmental benefit.

In addition to these environmental externalities, the Matchmakers model, characterizing some of the "giants" of the sharing economy, generates numerous social externalities, potentially on a very large scale (see Zale, this volume). Matchmakers are often associated with the rapid rise of a platform economy based on organizational principles that differ radically from those of the integrated firm (see Acquier, this volume). These models have been severely criticized for masking a parasitical logic and irresponsible business models, extending harsh free-market practices into previously protected areas of our lives.[44] According to critics, the platform economy creates unregulated marketplaces and unfair competition, relying on tax avoidance and increased risks for individual users.[45] The platform economy is reconfiguring the sphere of work and the boundary between the professional and private/domestic spheres, raising issues

[41] For an overview, *see* A. Acquier, V. Carbone, and D. Demailly, *L'économie collaborative est-elle source de progrès environnemental?* (2016), https://theconversation.com/leconomie-collaborative-est-elle-source-de-progres-environnemental-61543.

[42] Bardi and Eckhardt, *supra* note 5.

[43] D. Demailly and A.-S. Novel, *The Sharing Economy – Make It Sustainable!* (2014).

[44] Slee, *supra* note 4.

[45] Martin, *supra* note 7.

in the area of labor law and social protection for new workers in the digital economy.[46] Some observers also point to the political nature of the platform economy in the governance of data and individual behaviors,[47] as revealed by debates on algorithmic governance and regulation.[48] Furthermore, peer rating systems for quality and reputation raise complex questions about the protection of personal data produced and/or collected by sharing platforms and about their commercial use. Recent cases where certain users have been excluded from platforms have also shown that there is a real risk of discrimination (racial, sex, etc.; see Countouris and Ratti; Garden and Leong; Jefferson-Jones; Schoenbaum, all this volume). Platforms have also been criticized for generating or reinforcing inequalities in terms of social, economic, and cultural capital.[49]

In view of the societal impact that may be dramatically amplified by the global scale of operations of many Matchmakers, these controversies call for regulators and public actors to take an active role in assessing the environmental and social impacts of platforms (encouraging independent studies and impact evaluations). Such a first step may then orientate public action toward encouraging positive externalities and/or regulating negative ones.

C A Third Way? Hybrid Organizations that Combine a Commercial Logic with a Societal Mission

Some initiatives exhibit a hybrid identity: by combining elements of Mission-driven and Matchmaker logics, they seek explicitly to reconcile economic and social value creation object-ives. In the field of social entrepreneurship, these hybrid organizations combine elements of a business logic with social and solidarity economy aims.[50] This is a fragile and precarious balan-cing act, however, as the growth of these initiatives raises many questions: they have to handle issues of legitimacy and positioning vis-à-vis neighboring models (more commercial or more activist) and manage tensions between the expectations of capital providers and the preserva-tion of the mission, resulting in a risk of mission drift. We illustrate these arguments with the case of La Ruche qui dit Oui! (The Food Assembly), a French-based initiative in food distribu-tion, meant to support small food producers and shorten the distance between production and consumption.

The Food Assembly arose from the meeting of three creators: a designer (Guilhem Chéron, particularly interested in alternatives to intensive agriculture) and two web developers, who contributed skills in digital development and management. Marc-David Choukroun, who now runs the business, describes the organizational model of The Food Assembly as "the creation of mini marketplaces" with the aim of developing short distribution channels for food. Founded in 2010, The Food Assembly is a local food distribution platform that brings together local farmers and consumers, and organizes them in local temporary micro-markets, called "Assemblies."

[46] J. Prassl and M. Risak, *Uber, Taskrabbit, and Co.: Platforms as Employers? Rethinking the Legal Analysis of Crowdwork*, 37(3) Comparative Labor L. & Policy J. 619 (2016); Scholz, *supra* note 6; G. Friedman, *Workers Without Employers: Shadow Corporations and the Rise of the Gig Economy*, 2(2) Rev. Keynesian Econ. 171–88 (2014).

[47] C. Benavent, *Plateformes* (2016).

[48] L. Lessig, *Code: Version 2.0* (2006); E. Morozov, *The Rise of Data and the Death of Politics*, The Observer, July 20, 2014.

[49] J. Schor, C. Fitzmaurice, L. B. Carfagna, W. Attwood-Charles, and E. D. Poteat, *Paradoxes of Openness and Distinction in the Sharing Economy*, 54 Poetics 66–81 (2016).

[50] J. Battilana and S. Dorado, *Building Sustainable Hybrid Organizations: The Case of Commercial Microfinance Organizations*, 53(6) Acad. Mgmt. J. 1419–40(2010); A. C. Pache and F. Santos, *Inside the Hybrid Organization: Selective Coupling as a Response to Competing Institutional Logics*, 56(4) Acad. Mgmt. J. 972–1001 (2013).

Each Assembly is supplied by farmers and producers situated within a 250 km radius (40 km on average) of the distribution center. Assembly hosts are independent individuals who organize the local micro-market and operate a pre-order system on the platform, bringing together producers and consumers. They are financially incentivized for this organizational work, as they receive a commission on the financial transactions that occur within their Assembly. Designed to promote direct distribution channels between production and consumption and fair prices for producers, the platform seeks to position itself as an alternative model to mass distribution and industrial agriculture. Right from the start, it has sought to diffuse its model on a large scale.

One of the remarkable strengths of The Food Assembly is its ability, from the start, to combine logics from the universe of internet start-ups with logics from the social and solidarity economy. On the one hand, it leverages the power of an initiative rooted in the digital universe and platform economy, underpinned by start-up and venture capital logics. From the beginning, it has accurately assessed the technical and organizational complexity of the undertaking as well as the financial and human resources that would be needed for the technical and functional development of the system. Orchestrating the emergence of local networks requires significant resources, specific learning, and dedicated competences. At the same time, The Food Assembly is also rooted in the social and solidarity economy: it conceived an organization with the aim of transforming agriculture via short distribution channels. This is also reflected in its original ideas on forms of governance, distribution schemes for sharing value within the ecosystem, distributing a significant share of profits to Assembly hosts (who receive an 8.35 percent commission on their Assembly's sales – equal to the company's commission) and farmers.

The issue of external legitimacy has also been a key challenge in the development of The Food Assembly. The company has been faced with significant criticism, much of which comes from the AMAP network in France (an association that supports small-scale farming). AMAP also supports local agriculture and fights against mass production, but subscribes to a more activist, associative and engaged model, which rejects the commercial logic underlying The Food Assembly. On the other hand, more traditional investors from the digital universe, who seek to maximize profit and build a dominant market position, will not necessarily be receptive to the hybrid arrangements promoted by The Food Assembly. Investors willing to support the hybrid nature of the undertaking therefore constitute a key element in its development. Founded in 2010 as a simplified joint stock company (SAS in France), the company launched the first version of its platform in September 2011. The initiative has experienced rapid growth, which it has mainly financed through various funding rounds: €1.5 million in 2012 and €8 million in 2015. Since 2014, its growth has accelerated and it is currently expanding internationally, opening new Assemblies in Belgium, the UK, Italy, Spain, and Germany. As of 2016, the company had about 100 employees and its network was made up of 1,000 Assemblies (750 in France).

This tension between noncommercial and for-profit logics is also manifested in the risk of mission drift, whereby one logic takes prevalence over the other to solve internal managerial contradictions.[51] In the effort to find profitable business models and compete with pure for-profit models, hybrid organizations in the sharing economy may increasingly drift toward a market logic as they grow, ultimately undermining their social innovation potential. For example, platforms such as BlaBlaCar (carpooling) or Peerby (peer-to-peer rental) shifted away from their initial nonprofit model to introduce platform commissions and monetary transactions among users.

---

[51] A. Ebrahim, J. Battilana and J. Mair, *The Governance of Social Enterprises: Mission Drift and Accountability Challenges in Hybrid Organizations*, 34 Res. Org. Behav. 81–100 (2014).

Much research needs to be done to understand what type of governance mechanisms and legal statuses may help sustain, over the long term, the hybrid nature of such ventures as they grow. When they are able to reconcile both market and social innovation logics, these hybrid organizations are likely to constitute exceptional configurations, combining very strong growth potential, an activist model, as well as constituting fertile ground for experimentation and innovation in the area of governance.

CONCLUSION

The sharing economy encompasses a range of extremely diverse initiatives, raising multiple controversies that tend to pitch "supporters" and "opponents" of the sharing movement fiercely against each other. In order to overcome these ostensibly irreconcilable positions, this chapter has sought to split the sphere of sharing initiatives into four subsets that allow us to better apprehend the diversity of the promises and societal innovations at the core of the sharing economy. We have also examined these promises in relation to their potential or real impact on society. This is a difficult exercise, given the young age of the initiatives, only a few of which currently possess tools to measure their societal impacts. The link between promises and impacts is revealed to be complex, heterogeneous, and non-linear.

Given these observations, how can we foster the rise of models that maximize the environmental and social potential of initiatives in the sharing economy? Today, some sharing economy projects are based on hybrid logics of social entrepreneurship, combining social and economic missions. But most of these initiatives lack specialized technical competencies and capacities for technological development, due to their limited financial resources. It therefore appears necessary to foster the emergence of social entrepreneurship initiatives in the digital realm by bridging the gap between social innovation and the world of software development and geek culture. This may be done through business incubators, financial support policies, and collaborative projects between educational institutions (schools of engineering, IT, design, and business). While the development of social or environmental innovation is neither intrinsic nor automatic in the sharing economy, it will become what public and private actors make of it. The sharing economy creates opportunities for innovation that public actors should grasp in order to generate positive outcomes for society. They should politicize the future of the sharing economy, and use it as a tool to promote development, welfare, and well-being rather than an umpteenth version of capitalist power.

Balancing Regulation and Innovation

5

Coase and the Platform Economy

Orly Lobel

INTRODUCTION

The synthesis of the internet, smartphones, sophisticated applications, and the integration of big data and algorithmic processing has given birth to new economic interactions. These innovative business models span a range of preexisting service and retail industries, including ride-sharing, short-term home and room rentals, freelancing, and lending, fueled by leading platforms such as Uber and Lyft, Airbnb, TaskRabbit, and Lending Club, respectively.[1] These new economic models are often clustered under the somewhat misleading term, the "sharing economy."[2] As a number of contributors to this volume aptly note, sharing connotes a romantic ideal of collaborative, anti-corporatist exchanges. In reality, what is termed the sharing economy marketplace is controlled by multi-billion dollar corporations with profit-minded goals that have little to do with sharing.[3] Digital platforms like Uber and Airbnb are very clearly corporate entities. Their commodity is a form of digital communication facilitating searches and transactions between providers and buyers. The digital platform market usually consists of three groups: (1) the platform; (2) end providers; and (3) end buyers.[4]

Though seemingly in line with traditional markets, platforms challenge older models of service delivery in valuable ways. Most basically, the platform lowers costs associated with matching transaction partners and the costs of the actual transaction. In turn, end users, providers, and buyers can find what they desire, be it work, rides, or a place to stay, more rapidly than ever before. With added fluidity for job seekers, increased access to untapped resources, and the enhancement of productivity to the market, the sharing economy may contribute to a rise in the global GDP, which in turn has the potential to increase wages and lessen the gap between

[1] Bernard Marr, *The Sharing Economy – What it is, Examples, and How Big Data, Platforms and Algorithms Fuel It*, Forbes, Oct. 21, 2016, www.forbes.com/sites/bernardmarr/2016/10/21/the-sharing-economy-what-it-is-examples-and-how-big-data-platforms-and-algorithms-fuel/#7c1225f17c5a.

[2] *Id.*

[3] Lauren Thomas, *Airbnb Just Closed a $1 Billion Round and Became Profitable in 2016*, CNBC, Mar. 9, 2017, 10:45 AM, www.cnbc.com/2017/03/09/airbnb-closes-1-billion-round-31-billion-valuation-profitable.html; Richard Beales, *Uber's $70 Bln Value Accrues Mainly to Customers*, Reuters, Dec. 22, 2016, 12:40 PM, www.reuters.com/article/us-uber-valuation-breakingviews-idUSKBN14B23A.

[4] FTC Staff Report, *The "Sharing" Economy: Issues Facing Platforms, Participants & Regulators*, Federal Trade Commission, Nov. 2016, www.ftc.gov/system/files/documents/reports/sharing-economy-issues-facing-platforms-participants-regulators-federal-trade-commission-staff/p151200_ftc_staff_report_on_the_sharing_economy.pdf.

earned income and the actual cost of living.[5] With the rise of the digital platform, entire industries have progressed. For example, despite the justified critique of certain Uber practices, the ride-sharing industry has increased the supply of drivers, improved the quality of services across transportation industries, including taxis, enhanced safer and more reliable ride-hailing, and even reduced drunk driving.[6] Short-term lodging has become cheaper and more available to a wider pool of customers, with greater variety in the type of lodging available, resulting in increased and prolonged traveling.[7]

Despite the apparent benefits brought about by the new sharing economy, the advent of Uber, Lyft, Airbnb, and other digital platforms as sources of income poses a range of regulatory challenges, including worker classification, safety protections, insurance standards, taxation, and licensing and permitting requirements. Attempts to fit new breeds of online service delivery into existing laws have resulted in much litigation with very few concrete answers. As United States Federal District Court Judge Chhabria stated regarding the classification of Lyft drivers, the task is often akin to "be[ing] handed a square peg and asked to choose between two round holes."[8] An immediate judicial resolution has been delayed in a number of cases that have either stalled in the courts for years,[9] been dismissed for procedural shortcomings,[10] or settled before a decision could be rendered.[11] As some commentators, including Judge Chhabria, have suggested, some of these issues may be better suited for regulatory and legislative resolution rather than litigation.[12] No matter the forum, the law must grapple with the ways in which new business models create both risks and opportunities for achieving the goals underlying our social policies. For legislatures, regulators, and courts to better address the range of questions posed by the tension between business innovation and existing laws, we must understand the logic and value, as well as the risks, created by the digital platform.

This chapter analyzes the ways in which digital platforms such as Uber and Airbnb are perfecting the stages of deal-making and lowering transaction costs. The chapter argues that – in each of the three stages of pre-deal, deal-making, and post-deal – 1) search costs; 2) bargaining and decision costs; and 3) policing and enforcement costs, may benefit from the digital platform model. Each stage depends on enhanced information and optimal matching to reduce costs. The chapter illustrates how the platforms, based on digital large-scale multisided networks and sophisticated algorithmic pricing, positively impact the relevant transaction costs at all three stages. Drawing primarily on examples from the legal challenges platforms face in the United States, the chapter then suggests that regulators must consider the opportunities that come from platform delivery as well as the possibility that certain traditional regulations have become redundant through platform innovations. The chapter thereby urges policymakers to identify

---

[5] Alexander Howard, *How Digital Platforms Like LinkedIn, Uber And TaskRabbit Are Changing The On-Demand Economy*, Huffington Post, Jan. 3, 2017, www.huffingtonpost.com/entry/online-talent-platforms_us_55a03545e4b0b8145f72ccf6?ncid=engmodushpmg00000004.

[6] FTC Staff Report, *supra* note 4.

[7] *Id.*

[8] *Cotter v. Lyft, Inc.*, 60 F. Supp. 3d 1067, 1081 (N.D. Cal. 2015).

[9] *See Ehret v. Uber Techs., Inc.*, 148 F. Supp. 3d 884, 888 (N.D. Cal. 2015) (class action alleging "representation of a 20% gratuity is false, misleading and likely to deceive members of the public"); *L.A. Taxi Coop., Inc. v. Uber Techs., Inc.*, 114 F. Supp. 3d 852 (N.D. Cal. 2015) (alleging Uber made false and misleading statements about safety).

[10] *See Greenwich Taxi, Inc. v. Uber Techs., Inc.*, 123 F. Supp. 3d 327, 336, 337, 338–40, 342, 343 (D. Conn. 2015) (insufficient and inadequate pleading on counts of false advertising, misrepresentation, false association, RICO, and CUPTA); *XYZ Two Way Radio Serv., Inc. v. Uber Techs., Inc.*, 214 F. Supp. 3d 179 (E.D.N.Y. 2016) (insufficient and inadequate pleading on counts of false advertising, Uber's "partnership" with its drivers, and tortious interference).

[11] *Cotter v. Lyft, Inc.*, No. 13-cv-04065-VC, 2017 WL 1033527, at *1 (N.D. Cal. Mar. 16, 2017).

[12] *See Cotter*, 60 F. Supp. 3d at 1081.

the areas that continue to require regulatory solutions and those issues that are better addressed by platform private ordering.

I VALUE ADDED

In 1960, Ronald Coase wrote in his seminal article about transaction costs that pervade the stages of deal-making: "operations are often extremely costly, sufficiently costly at any rate to prevent many transactions that would be carried out in a world in which the pricing system worked without cost."[13] During the three stages of pre-deal, deal-making, and post-deal, transaction costs include search costs, bargaining, and decision costs, and, finally, policing and enforcement costs.[14] To reduce these costs, each stage depends on obtaining information. The digital platform has the potential to increase access to information by the application of advanced technology to every aspect of the deal. It thereby impacts the relevant transaction costs at all three stages. As the platform grows, efficiency grows as well. In systemic ways, the market perfects itself.

In my article *The Law of the Platform*, I develop a novel taxonomy of ten distinct principles of the platform that together combine to reduce transaction costs:[15]

1) *Uber-scale*: The platform connects strangers on a global scale. It creates multisided networks of unprecedented size, increasing the availability of both supply and demand.

2) *Resurrection of Dead Capital*: The platform adds otherwise idle assets and resources to the market: physical products, skill, knowledge, and human labor.

3) *Tailoring the Transactional Unit*: The digital platform slices the resources it sells into smaller units, dividing up supply and demand into micro modalities: short-term rentals, an hour's access to a car or lawnmower, a few minutes of personal assistance or delivery. The technology facilitates the smaller exchanges that would have previously never existed due to prohibitive deal-making costs. By opening up the market to micro modalities, dormant human capital is now mobilized as a market participant operating at competitive costs.[16]

4) *Commodification of Everything*: The meteoric advent of the digital platform has meant that "the share of sharing is growing exponentially, but sharing is not free."[17] Most exchanges are based on the price of renting, trading, servicing, driving, and lending for a competitive fee, making the once-common practice of offering a friend a lift to the airport practically unheard of, and likely met with the thought, "Why couldn't she just call an Uber?" Commodifying every transaction, similarly to the rise in scale of end users, increases supply, such that from a Coasean perspective, costs are reduced as supply appears to be infinite.

5) *Deal Customization*: Services and resources offered on the platform are not only offered in micro modalities, but the features of the offered deal can be combined and aggregated to offer optimal customization to fit individual needs with unprecedented specificity. Need a ride right now? Call an Uber. Can't afford to ride on your own? Not a problem – just hop in an uberPool and share the cost of your ride with others going to your destination. Want a one-day house that accommodates your entire extended family plus dog, includes

13 Ronald Coase, *The Problem of Social Cost*, 3 J. of Law and Econ. 15 (1960).
14 Carl J. Dahlman, *The Problem of Externality*, 22 J. of Law and Econ. 1, 148 (1979).
15 Orly Lobel, *The Law of the Platform*, 101 Minn. L. Rev. 87, 87 (2016).
16 Yochai Benkler, *The Wealth of Networks: How Social Production Transforms Markets and Freedom* 100 (2006).
17 Lobel, *supra* note 15.

a pool, but no stairs? You are likely to find it on Airbnb. Want an office space twice a week for three coworkers, including two hours of access to an administrative assistant? Shared work spaces like LiquidSpace will provide that deal. The menu of options has become wider without undermining the facility of transacting by several online clicks.

6) *Access Over Ownership*: The platform aids a shift from a consumption mindset of property to one of access. This shift reduces transaction costs by mitigating the stakes of the deal. For example, buying a car is a far weightier decision than hailing a ride. The mindset of access also fuels usage and accelerates the circulation of resources in the market.

7) *Overhead Reduction*: The platform relies more on digital technology than brick-and-mortar offices and employees to intermediate the deal. Technological and economic innovations adopted by digital companies reduce expenses compared to their offline counterparts, and in turn, platform companies charge a relatively small percentage for their intermediation relative to their traditional brick-and-mortar counterpart. Still, as will be further discussed below, the question of costs is endogenous to the question of regulatory responsibility as well as the viability of a competitive market.

8) *Reduced Barriers to Entry*: Startup costs to digitally compete are low, primarily because of the low intermediation costs noted above. An online marketplace mostly requires a domain name and an app, dissolving some of the traditional maintenance costs. At the same time, as Kenneth Bamberger and I analyze in a forthcoming article, *Platform Market Power*, platforms tend to enjoy dominance once they have reached large-scale adoption due mainly to network effects and switching costs.[18]

9) *Pricing Precision*: Digital platforms rely on sophisticated pricing algorithms, which improve through data mining and artificial intelligence. Self-learning bots engage in dynamic pricing based on unprecedented amounts of information. From a Coasean perspective, the platforms reach a perfect marketing ideal: dynamic and comprehensive processing of market information to produce accurate valuation.

10) *Dynamic Feedback Systems*: Coase taught us that transaction costs are high when information asymmetries exist. Digital platforms innovate on this front by offering dynamic ratings, reviews, and cross-company information data to increase trust pre-deal and aid monitoring, policing, and enforcement post-deal. Ride-sharing consumers thus can take comfort in the knowledge that a system for flagging unfavorable drivers exists, likely creating the presumption that such drivers will be weeded out, leaving only those favorable to other passengers, and, due to their own ability to leave reviews, riders have the power post-deal to make known their complaints and to ensure that they are not again paired with the same driver against whom they have complained.

Beyond these ten features of the platform, note that platform companies also produce value by their differentiation from offline traditional exchanges. The platform economy does not simply deliver efficiently the exact same services offered before, it also constitutes new markets by accommodating and shaping users' tastes and preferences. By introducing and normalizing new types of transaction, digital platforms are providing new solutions to old problems. At the same time, these digital platform giants are in direct competition with older, traditional markets: think Uber versus traditional taxi cabs,[19] Airbnb versus the hotel industry. This in itself is key to the

---

[18] Kenneth Bamberger and Orly Lobel, *Platform Market Power*, Berkeley L. and Tech. J. (forthcoming 2018).

[19] Vanessa Katz, *Regulating the Sharing Economy*, 30 Berkeley Tech. L.J. 1066, 1092 (2015) ("[T]axi dispatch services in Boston and Chicago have pursued claims against Uber under the Lanham Act and state unfair competition laws.").

challenge of regulation: platforms act as market participants in a preexisting competitive market yet they can also be categorized as their own unique market, in which they compete only against other digital platforms: Uber versus Lyft as one example. The vast heterogeneity of goods and services offered on the platform and the innovative technologies and business models that digital platforms employ create a tension between new and old modes of service delivery. This in turn explains the ongoing legal battles that many of the leading platforms are now engaged in with both regulators and competitors trying to stand their ground within more traditional modes of operating, while the rug is seemingly being pulled from underneath their feet. As will be discussed in the next section, for regulators and adjudicators considering how to address these legal questions, understanding the value added by new platforms in reducing transaction costs can help them to analyze the places where continued regulation is needed and the places where regulations have become redundant.

II REGULATION, MEET INNOVATION

Regulation can have various purposes. From a Coasean perspective, rules and regulations are designed to reduce transaction costs and make the market more efficient.[20] But regulation can serve other goals, including the promotion of equal distribution, public safety, and health and consumer protection.[21] When policymakers face innovation in the way people transact, exchange goods, and deliver services, they must decide whether and which legal rules apply. The digital platform has been positively disruptive to traditional market models, but it is not without flaws. The global reach of platforms has presented a range of issues ripe for regulation. Some existing regulations lend themselves quite easily to direct application on the platform. Other regulations appear outdated. As with every wave of technological, social, and economic innovation, regulators must consider the continued value of various legal requirements in the face of new capabilities, opportunities, risks, preferences, and norms. Moreover, regulators must consider whether technological and economic innovation on the platform can serve the regulatory goals previously achieved by straight-up top-down rules. For example, systems of ratings and review need to be examined and compared to top-down modes of pre-deal quality disclosures and post-deal monitoring. Where regulation was enacted to correct market inefficiencies, such as asymmetric information or the high transaction costs involved in monitoring and enforcing the terms of the deal, new technologies employed on the platform may serve as a substitute for those policies.[22] When new legal forms of smart private ordering can be effectively substituted for regulation, both buyer and seller win.[23]

---

[20] Paul Stephen Dempsey, *Market Failure and Regulatory Failure as Catalysts for Political Change: The Choice Between Imperfect Regulation and Imperfect Competition*, 46 Wash. & Lee L. Rev. 1 (1989).

[21] Orly Lobel, *The Renew Deal: The Fall of Regulation and the Rise of Governance in Contemporary Legal Thought*, 89 Minn. L. Rev. 342, 415 (2004); Orly Lobel, New Governance as Regulatory Governance, in *Oxford Handbook of Governance* (David Levi-Faur ed., 2012); Cass R. Sunstein, *After the Rights Revolution: Reconceiving the Regulatory State* 84–91 (1990).

[22] Eric Goldman, Regulating Reputation, in *The Reputation Society: How Online Opinions Are Reshaping the Offline World* 51, 53 (Hassan Masum and Mark Tovey eds., 2011); *see also* Chrysanthos Dellarocas, Designing Reputation Systems for the Social Web, in *The Reputation Society: How Online Opinions Are Reshaping the Offline World* 3 (Hassan Masum and Mark Tovey eds., 2011); Liangjun You and Riyaz Sikora, *Performance of Online Reputation Mechanisms under the Influence of Different Types of Biases*, 12 Info. Sys. and e-Bus. Mgmt. 417, 418 (2014); Katz, *supra* note 19, at 1075 (arguing that reputation systems can serve as a safety measure).

[23] *See also* Arun Sundararajan, *The Sharing Economy: The End of Employment and the Rise of Crowd Based Capitalism* (2016).

On the other hand, when regulation is designed to address distributional concerns, such as equality and fairness goals, it is likely that some of the issues that pervaded offline exchanges will continue into platform relationships. The platform economy thereby offers a fresh opportunity to observe and analyze the fit between goals and actual outcomes of a range of existing laws. When laws do not promote social goals but instead protect incumbent industries against competition, the platform is clearly a welcome intervention and such anticompetitive laws should largely be deemed obsolete. We will too, at some point, if we have not already, reach a time when the platform may surpass, or become, the incumbent.[24] The paradigmatic example for this is Uber's dominance in the transportation market, which has made it difficult in some localities to demand either the private ordering of safety checks or the imposition of top-down regulatory requirements. When the market is more competitive, such consumer protections are more likely to be adopted. Thus we must lay the social groundwork for elimination of anticompetitive laws and set the stage for newcomers to find space in the market should they create a product sought by consumers now, as these issues first arise, so that we should have in place a means to deal with what will inevitably be a recurring problem of incumbent industries, whoever those incumbents should be, seeking to prohibit the entry of new competition into the marketplace.[25] The most difficult cases involve regulations that promote a range of social values requiring policymakers to tread carefully in carrying over those goals into the platform.

Innovation should also be viewed as an opportunity to unpack, and rethink, traditional regulatory categories. The platform creates hybrid classes, which means that:

> off-on categories such as consumer/business; employee/freelancer; residential/commercial are in some instances no longer viable as organizing frameworks... Unique fusions emerge as technology companies centralize some important aspects of the market transaction, for example, the methods of payment, search and review, and information and trust. Simultaneously, these companies are decentralizing other fundamental aspects of the exchange, which are controlled by users, such as pricing on the lodging apps and work hours on the transportation and cleaning service apps, aspects which determined the supply infrastructure of the business. What this means for regulators is that rather than a unified single entity which has traditionally been the object of regulation, transactions are now shaped by multiple actors, with varying capacities, interests, and needs.[26]

With these new constellation and definitional hybrids, regulators should aim to track the economic substance of the transaction, consider the Coasean costs and logic of the deal, and then examine these realities against the policy goals of the legal field in question.[27]

Consider the field of employment and labor law. The platform is often linked to the widespread rise of the gig economy – precarious work detached from a single long-term employer. Some representations of work on the platform portray this framework as empowering workers by enabling peer-to-peer exchanges without a corporation taking an unfair cut. Under this view, workers on the platform enjoy independence, choice, autonomy, and freedom to work on their

---

[24] Bamberger and Lobel, *supra* note 18; Joanna Penn and John Wihbey, *Uber, Airbnb and Consequences of the Sharing Economy: Research Roundup*, Journalist's Resource, June 3, 2016, https://journalistsresource.org/studies/economics/business/airbnb-lyft-uber-bike-share-sharing-economy-research-roundup.

[25] Harriet Taylor, *What Happened in Austin After Uber and Lyft Got Up and Left*, CNBC, Aug. 18, 2016, www.cnbc.com/2016/08/18/what-happened-in-austin-after-uber-and-lyft-got-up-and-left.html; Patrick Sisson, *Uber and Lyft Return to Austin: What's Changed, and Why It's Important*, CURBED, June 14, 2017, www.curbed.com/2017/6/14/15803138/austin-uber-lyft-transportation-ride-hailing-return.

[26] Lobel, *supra* note 15.

[27] Victor Fleischer, *Regulatory Arbitrage*, 89 Tex. L. Rev. 227, 229 (2010).

own terms and time. People providing their services on the platform are described as embodying an entrepreneurial spirit.[28] These qualities are often associated with classifying the worker as an "independent contractor" as opposed to the more protected classification of "employee."[29] Others critique the gig economy as bringing vast insecurity to the job market, thereby eroding the web of twentieth-century employment and labor law.[30] Thus, the effort to classify platform workers as either employees or independent contractors is heated and fraught with clashing normative understandings of the relevant regulatory goals. In my recent article, *The Gig Economy and the Future of Employment and Labor Law*, I proposed four paths for reform: 1) clarify and simplify the notoriously malleable "employee" classification doctrine; 2) expand certain employment protections to all workers, regardless of classification, or in other words: altogether reject worker classification; 3) create special rules for intermediate categories; and 4) disassociate certain social protections, such as health care and retirement security, from work.[31]

On the employee classification front, platform markets expose the limitations of century-long lines that separated the two classes: employees and independent contractors. As Judge Chhabria, considering the class action against Lyft regarding the classification of its drivers, suggested, the twentieth-century test to classify workers may not be appropriate to address twenty-first century issues.[32] Ironically, the test has never been without problems. It has occupied courts for over a century and the lines separating independent contractors and employees have continued to be blurred. More than that, drawing those lines has only made sense for some regulatory protections, for example overtime and leave laws but not for others, such as discrimination and whistleblowing laws. *O'Connor v. Uber Techs., Inc.*, a class action in California, contested Uber's classification of workers as independent contractors rather than employees.[33] Unsurprisingly, given the difficulty of applying the age-old common law multifactor employee classification test, the court found there was ample evidence supporting both sides of the argument.[34] Factors such as classifying driving as an occupation that requires no supervision and no special skills and that drivers provide a service that is integral to Uber's business, cut toward drivers having an employee status.[35] Factors supporting the status of drivers as independent contractors include the use of the driver's own vehicle, the driver's ability to be employed by a different third-party transportation company (one other than Uber), and contracts declaring no employment status had been created between the driver and Uber.[36] Uber markets to potential drivers by spewing slogans such as "be your own boss and earn extra cash."[37] The company makes it clear in its terms of service that workers are not employed by Uber.[38] Yet, the question of whether Uber has appropriately classified its workers as independent contractors and not employees is far from simple. The question depends on context and the specific goals of the protective laws

[28] Joao E. Gata, *The Sharing Economy, Competition, and Regulation*, Competition Pol'y Int'l, Nov. 25, 2015, www.competitionpolicyinternational.com/assets/Europe-Column-November-Full.pdf.

[29] 19 Samuel Williston, *Williston on Contracts* § 54:2 (4th ed., 2017).

[30] Robert Kuttner, *The Task Rabbit Economy*, The American Prospect, Oct. 10, 2013, http://prospect.org/article/task-rabbit-economy.

[31] Orly Lobel, *The Gig Economy & The Future of Employment and Labor Law* 51 U.S.F. L. Rev. 51 (2017).

[32] *Cotter v. Lyft, Inc.*, 60 F. Supp. 3d 1067, 1081 (N.D. Cal. 2015).

[33] 201 F. Supp. 3d 1110, 1113 (N.D. Cal. 2016).

[34] *Id.* at 1145.

[35] *Id.* at 1151, 1152–53.

[36] *Id.* at 1136, 1137, 1149.

[37] *Id.*

[38] Alexis Kramer, *Uber Driver Fight Helps Shape Sharing Economy*, Electronic Commerce and Law Report (BNA), Dec. 14, 2016.

that command classification. In the Uber case, the sides settled for a proposed $100 million, rendering no binding precedent.[39] The court noted that the traditional common law test determining employment status "evolved under an economic model very different from the new 'sharing economy.'"[40]

In the parallel case against Lyft, Judge Chhabria was tasked with deciding the same issue.[41] Judge Chhabria questioned whether California's test to classify workers was outdated, and reasoned that a reasonable jury could decide the case either way.[42] In his opinion, Judge Chhabria remarked that absent legislative intervention to create a new test for modern times, cases like this will go to juries in the future and be plagued with such ambiguity that their results will never render a remotely clear answer as different juries in different jurisdictions could easily reach incompatible outcomes.[43] The Lyft case also settled before reaching a final determination.[44]

The employment classification example reveals the importance of context in deciding how to regulate new economic models. One cannot view employment classification in strict isolation. Rather, the reason for asking the question is key to answering it. In other words, classification must be purposive: why are we inquiring about employee status – for what statutory protection, right, or duty are we posing the question? When it comes to social policies such as wage and hour protections, health and benefits, it is time for a change. These may benefit from being de-linked from the single employer model that pervaded the twentieth century. However, some policies should continue to be imposed on workplaces, and should be extended to all those who provide their labor, whether employees or independent contractors. For example, anti-discrimination laws should continue to be imposed on market models regardless of the classification of the worker. Yet other areas of law, such as risk regulation, safety, and privacy, depend on democratic solutions to ensure balance between competing social goals. As Nestor Davidson and John Infranca so amply have argued, many of the regulatory battles concerning the platform are happening at the local urban level. They show how the interactions between platforms and local governments help to restore balance between the efficiencies of digital innovations and the ongoing need to secure public goals. Excitingly, these interactions also require policymakers to become more open and rational about the policy goals underlying a myriad of regulations. Currently, initiatives around the world exist to better unify the local rules for operating platforms.[45] At the same time, as Davidson and Infranca illuminate, an important characteristic of the platform is its local variety and experimental quality. Too much uniformity imposed on its evolving forms can stifle innovation. Too much uniformity also hurts that ability to digitally tailor the deal and decrease transaction costs in all three stages: it prevents experimentation with systems that allow better search and information pre-deal; more tailored and precise negotiation of the deal the parties are interested in; and a greater variety of interactive online forums that allow post-deal monitoring and trust.

---

[39] Cyrus Farviar, *Judge Expresses Notable Concerns over Proposed $100M Settlement in Uber Case*, arsTECHNICA, June 2, 2016, 5:17 PM, http://arstechnica.com/tech-policy/2016/06/most-drivers-in-uber-labor-case-would-get-under-25-so-some-protest-settlement.

[40] *O'Connor v. Uber Techs., Inc.*, 201 F. Supp. 3d 1110, 1153 (N.D. Cal. 2016).

[41] *Cotter v. Lyft, Inc.*, 60 F. Supp. 3d 1067, 1081 (N.D. Cal. 2015).

[42] *Id.* at 1070, 1077.

[43] *Id.* at 1082.

[44] *Cotter v. Lyft, Inc.*, No. 13-cv-04065-VC, 2017 WL 1033527, at *1 (N.D. Cal. Mar. 16, 2017).

[45] Marie Mawad, *City Mayors Worldwide Forge Alliance in Response to Airbnb, Uber*, Bloomberg Technology, June 20, 2016), www.bloomberg.com/news/articles/2016-06-20/city-mayors-worldwide-forge-alliance-in-response-to-airbnb-uber.

III REGULATORS, MEET RATINGS

The current era of the digital platform is moving toward lower transaction costs by cutting out excessive bargaining time.[46] While transaction costs still exist in these platforms, as the number of transactions increases, so does efficiency. As efficiencies increase, transaction costs become smaller, and society begins to move closer to the marketplace Coase once envisioned. In his article, Coase states:

> In order to carry out a market transaction it is necessary to discover who it is that one wishes to deal with, to inform people that one wishes to deal and on what terms, to conduct negotiations leading up to a bargain, to draw up the contract, to undertake the inspection needed to make sure that the terms of the contract are being observed, and so on.[47]

To reach such efficiencies in drawing the terms of the deal, one also needs confidence and assurances about the enforcement of the deal. As Dahlman explains in expanding on Coase's analysis, "after the trade has been decided on, there will be the costs of policing and monitoring the other party to see that his obligations are carried out as determined by the terms of the contract, and of enforcing the agreement reached."[48]

Monitoring transactions has become part of the experience of the platform, and has given a sense of control to those using the platform. Incentivizing or mandating the review of one's most recent experience with a platform company has begun to create a relatively self-regulating system which customers can rely on, one that provides a level of accountability that could potentially replace regulatory oversight. An Uber driver, for example, who knows he or she is necessarily going to be rated and reviewed upon completion of an upcoming ride, is given an incentive to be timely, efficient, and safe that cannot be imposed nor paralleled by less salient statutory regulations. This is also why Coase's three stages of the deal are inevitably interrelated: ex-post reviews aid not only ex-ante trust and monitoring, but also help provide future deals with information that aids searching. Digital ratings and reviews, along with digital platforms' internal dispute resolution systems, can disincentivize and weed out fraudulent or irresponsible users, thus providing users with greater confidence in who they are contracting with – a necessary element to the carrying out of a market transaction in the Coasean view. As John Hawksworth, chief economist at PwC, put it, "modern digital communications allow sharing to happen across a global village of consumers and providers, with trust established through electronic peer reviews."[49] On the platform, services, providers, and users all track and review each other, creating a utopian (or some might say dystopian) Foucauldian panopticon. Eric Goldman has referred to this feature of online ratings as the "secondary invisible hand":

> When information is costly, reputational information can improve the operation of the invisible hand by helping consumers make better decisions about vendors. In this sense, reputational information acts like an invisible hand guiding the invisible hand … because reputational information can guide consumers to make marketplace choices that, in aggregate, effectuate the invisible hand.[50]

---

[46] *See* Katz, *supra* note 19, at 1100–1.

[47] Coase, *supra* note 13.

[48] Dahlman, *supra* note 14, at 148.

[49] Gill Carson, *Five Key Sharing Economy Sectors Could Generate 9 Billion of UK Revenues by 2025*, PWC Blogs, Aug. 15, 2014, http://pwc.blogs.com/press_room/2014/08/five-key-sharing-economy-sectors-could-generate-9-billion-of-uk-revenues-by-2025.html.

[50] Goldman, *supra* note 22, at 53; *see also* Dellarocas, supra note 22, at 3; Liangjun You and Riyaz Sikora, *Performance of Online Reputation Mechanisms under the Influence of Different Types of Biases*, 12 Info. Sys. and e-Bus. Mgmt. 417, 418 (2014).

Reliance on vast, dynamic information for each transaction may well be more efficient than one-shot regulatory screenings, such as licensing or quality control requirements.[51] The design of these systems, as two-way reciprocal assessments, allows buyers and sellers to rate each other. At the same time, it is far from a perfect system. In general, there is no control over who leaves a rating or if that rating is even true. Research has shown ratings may be biased toward positive reviews because only satisfied customers bother to leave one.[52] Some have suggested directions to increase transparency about the ratings system include showing the user's percentile ranking along with her aggregate score, reporting the number of completed transactions compared to the number of reviews, and weighing more recent transactions heavier than older ones.[53] Others suggest that platforms should take a more active role in conducting background checks of suppliers/users and offering refunds or insurance to consumers. What is important in these systems is that the longer they exist and the more users on the platform, the greater confidence users have in the ratings. Again, this promises an effective, and nearly costless, private mechanism of quality control.

At the same time, it again raises the question about platform market power, as dominant platforms will have the advantage of size and age of their network, making customers more inclined to stay with the service rather than switch to a new competitor. Moreover, at the same time that big data and the use of vast information to monitor transactions creates efficiencies, it also raises new risks concerning privacy. Kenneth Bamberger and I have raised the question of whether dominant platforms will be able to exploit market power to unfairly limit consumer choice regarding privacy protections. For example, Uber is emerging as a data-driven company, leading analysts to predict that "we are going to see the transformation of Uber into a big data company cut from the same cloth as Google, Facebook and Visa – using the wealth of information they know about me and you to deliver new services and generate revenue by selling this data to others."[54] Julie Cohen urges us to pay more attention to the ways platform businesses are reshaping the landscape of legal entitlements and obligations, for example, ownership of data, privacy rights, and the immunities provided to digital intermediaries.[55] As Cohen insightfully describes, "the uncoordinated patterns of self-interested, strategic intervention by platform firms are producing new legal-institutional formations optimized to their various projects and goals."[56]

Regulators thus have a new task of examining the ways data offers immense potential to replace traditional regulatory and enforcement mechanisms but can also create new perils and new forms of market abuse and inequities. The decision to be made, then, lies in whether policymakers and we as a society are willing to trade efficiency for privacy. In short, we must ask, determine, and decide if the ability of the platform to keep transaction costs down with the implementation of technology that, more or less, allows for self-policing is worth more than the sharing of information from, and about, us. Some may find the tradeoff of their email address being sold to generate revenue a small inconvenience, at best, when compared to the ability to hail a ride anywhere, at a moment's notice, while others may find this too intrusive. Those that find release of an email address worthwhile may find the sale of information as to when, where, and how frequently they visit certain locations to cross the line, while still others may find this a

---

[51] FTC Staff Report, *supra* note 4, at 1, 5.

[52] *Id.*

[53] *Id.*

[54] Ron Hirson, *Uber: The Big Data Company*, Forbes, Mar. 23, 2015, www.forbes.com/forbes/welcome/?toURL=www. forbes.com/sites/ronhirson/2015/03/23/uber-the-big-data-company/&refURL=&referrer.

[55] Julie Cohen, *Law for the Platform Economy*, 51 U.C. Davis L. Rev. (forthcoming 2017).

[56] *Id.*

fair trade. Thus, in deciding whether deals made between users of the platform and creators of it are "worth it" in Coasean terms, policymakers must take into account the fact that the price on privacy, unlike so many costs on the platform, is not a flat rate.

CONCLUSION

In *The Problem of Social Cost*, Ronald Coase explains that if we reduce transaction costs throughout all stages of the deal, we will move to more efficient and fair outcomes for all parties involved.[57] The higher the transaction costs, the more likely a deal will work out more advantageously for one party than another, and the more likely that that party will be the one with more resources. However, if there are lower transaction costs, and each party can monetize that which they are bargaining with, the benefits will end up relatively equal for each party.

The rise of twenty-first century digital platforms has unleashed a new market system that changes many of the practices of twentieth-century markets. This chapter has discussed how fundamental principles of the platform economy – a larger scale of supply and demand, a growing archive of information based on multisided end-user networks, an ability to granulate and micro-tailor transactions – help lower costs in each of Coase's stages of the deal. The digital platform model presents an unprecedented opportunity to get closer to achieving Coase's theoretical ideal. At the same time, questions about the regulation of platforms are complex and will largely depend on the social policy goals before us. In some contexts, such as safety regulation, the platform may be well suited for private ordering as systems of ratings and reviews become increasingly broad and deep. For other contexts, such as ensuring basic welfare conditions for gig workers, the platform may be disrupting settled expectations of the workforce and policymakers must step in to provide a supplementary system that delinks work and social welfare.[58]

[57] Coase, *supra* note 13, at 1, 15.
[58] Lobel, *supra* note 32.

6

Taxis, *Taxis*, and Governance in the Vehicle-For-Hire Industry

*Matthew D. Mitchell and Christopher Koopman**

INTRODUCTION

A regulation, in its broadest sense, is a rule of behavior that establishes order. The vehicle-for-hire industry is governed by a vast, complex, polycentric set of regulations. We make sense of these overlapping and intertwined mechanisms by highlighting two dimensions of governance:

1) The public/private dimension, which describes the degree to which regulations are backed by the threat of force.
2) The *cosmos/taxis* dimension, which describes the degree to which regulations are an emergent (*cosmos*) order or a created (*taxis*) order.

This allows us to create a taxonomy of four primary "types" of regulation (public-*taxis*, public-*cosmos*, private-*taxis*, private-*cosmos*) and evaluate each in turn.

Public-*taxis* regulations – coherent, deliberately designed, state-enforced rules – are exceedingly rare. Most state-enforced rules are emergent phenomena. That is, public-*cosmos* regulations are far more common. This explains why public regulation of the taxi industry has so often failed to achieve its stated ends. Public-*taxis* regulations, however, would have failed in a similar vein because they would be unable to account for and accommodate changes in technology, competition, and consumer preferences.

Private regulations – both the *taxis* and *cosmos* variety – serve the general public better than public regulations. In Section I, we introduce the concept of polycentric governance as a tool for understanding the vehicle-for-hire industry. In Section II, we explore distinctions between public and private regulation and in Section III we examine the distinction between *cosmos* and *taxis* regulation. In Section IV, we map out these four dimensions in the context of economic regulation and examine each in detail. In Section V we summarize our argument and assert that private governance is optimal in regulating the vehicle-for-hire industry.

I POLYCENTRIC GOVERNANCE

What governs the vehicle-for-hire industry?[1] Federal and state labor laws govern the relationship between a taxi company and its employees as well as that between a transportation network

---

[*] The authors gratefully acknowledge numerous and helpful comments from Michèle Finck and other contributors to this volume. We are responsible for any errors or omissions that remain.
[1] We focus primarily on US governance mechanisms as that is the jurisdiction with which we are the most familiar.

firm and its contractors. State and federal tax law governs the flow of capital into the industry as well as the degree of economic surplus generated by the industry. Common law governs the allocation of liability for harm, with some limitations created by state legislatures. And regulations – codified in statutes, promulgated by regulators, and enforced by agencies such as state Departments of Motor Vehicles, public utility regulators, and taxi commissions – govern entry, price, and business practices.

Government-created regulation, however, is not the only source of governance. As the late political economist, Vincent Ostrom put it:

> We need not think of "government" or "governance" as something provided by states alone. Families, voluntary associations, villages, and other forms of human association all involve some form of self-government. Rather than looking only to states, we need to give much more attention to building the kinds of basic institutional structures that enable people to find ways of relating constructively to one another and of resolving problems in their daily lives.[2]

Under this view of governance, the vehicle-for-hire industry is not exclusively governed by the rules of legislatures and regulators, but also by the rules of etiquette, the rules of economics, and the rules of private regulatory entities. It is governed, for example, by the cultural norm of tipping. It is governed by social media users who instantly and widely spread stories of good or bad service. It is governed by the terms and conditions each provider – ride-sharing and taxis alike – places on their service.

Public laws may govern the tax rates, but economic laws determine the actual allocation of tax cost among employers, employees, and customers.[3] Statutes and regulatory pronouncements may dictate maximum prices, but the laws of economics dictate when surpluses and shortages will arise. The market is also governed by customer reviews on Yelp and Google, as well as review curators such as the Better Business Bureau and Angie's List.[4] It is governed by insurance companies that reward safe drivers with lower premiums and by the voluntary practices of bond-posting and brand-maintenance. It is governed by the algorithms developed by programmers at Uber, Lyft, Via, and Gett and by the reviews of customers who use those apps.

In short, the industry is governed by a polycentric order. Michael Polanyi developed the concept of polycentricity, describing the organization of scientific inquiry as "the mutual adjustment of a large number of centres" in a complex system.[5] Vincent Ostrom, Charles Tiebout, and Robert Warren – in their study of metropolitan governance – extended the notion of polycentrism to political economy.[6] Three decades later, Ostrom summarized their definition of a polycentric order, stressing three characteristics. A polycentric order, he wrote, is a system composed of:

---

[2] Vincent Ostrom quoted in Paul Dragos Aligica and Peter J. Boettke, *Challenging Institutional Analysis and Development: The Bloomington School* 146 (2009).

[3] Public finance theory teaches us that the less-elastic side of a market bears the bulk of the tax. Since labor supply is generally less-elastic than labor demand, employees are thought to bear most of the burden of an income or payroll tax.

[4] Founded in 1912, the Better Business Bureau (BBB) is a private, nonprofit organization with over 100 local affiliated organizations in the United States and Canada. BBB-accredited businesses are vetted by the organization and must adhere to the BBB's code of business practices in order to remain in good standing. Founded in 1995, Angie's List allows users to read and publish reviews of local businesses.

[5] Michael Polanyi, *The Logic of Liberty* 140 (1951).

[6] Vincent Ostrom, Charles M. Tiebout, and Robert Warren, *The Organization of Government in Metropolitan Areas: A Theoretical Inquiry*, 55(4) Am. Pol. Sci. Rev. 831–42 (Dec. 1, 1961).

(1) many autonomous units formally independent of one another, (2) choosing to act in ways that take account of others, (3) through processes of cooperation, competition, conflict, and conflict resolution.[7]

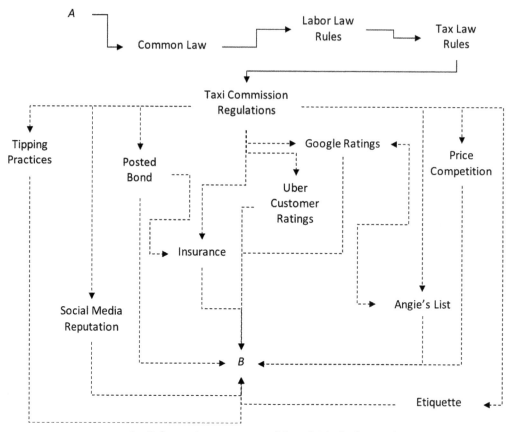

FIGURE 6.1 Polycentric governance of the vehicle-for-hire industry

The tools of systems theory help illustrate this notion.[8] Consider Figure 6.1, where *A* represents a vehicle-for-hire market at a particular point in time and *B* represents a changed state in that market. This change can represent, for example, a new configuration of prices, quantities, operators, service models, or technologies.

Various lines – dashed indicate that they are voluntary routes and solid indicate that they are mandated – connect *A* to *B*. Each node represents an autonomous governance mechanism and each route represents a path of influence. In Ostrom's words, the connections can be thought of as processes of "cooperation, competition, conflict, and conflict resolution."

This figure is, of course, a gross simplification. In reality, this polycentric system is far more complex than the web of interactions shown in Figure 6.1. Each individual platform user, for example, could be represented as a distinct node, connected to other users as well as to other nodes in the figure. There could also be many more connections between the nodes shown. Note, for example, that we have drawn a line connecting posted bonds to insurance. A firm that

7   Vincent Ostrom, Polycentricity: The Structural Basis of Self-Governing Systems, *in The Meaning of American Federalism* 223–44 (1991).
8   Kenneth E. Boulding, *General Systems Theory: The Skeleton of Science*, 2(3) Man. Sci. 197–208 (1956).

posts a larger bond may be judged a safer bet and therefore may be able to pay lower insurance premiums. We have also drawn a line connecting Angie's List to Google Ratings, with arrows on both ends of the line. These two platforms are in dynamic competition with one another so that improvements to one will likely lead to improvements in the other. In a vast and complex system such as this, the number of possible connections and permutations is astoundingly large.[9]

II THE PUBLIC–PRIVATE DIMENSION

We are accustomed to think of rules as a "top-down" phenomenon, and the way we talk about rules reinforces this conception. We say that rulers "rule," that rules come from "on high," and that we may find these rules in the "rule books." We tend to think of rules as formal pronouncements, emanating from officials with some authority to compel us to comply.

Many rules fit this description. In July of 2009, for example, then-chairman Leon Swain Jr. of the DC Taxi Commission (DCTC) issued a memorandum that created a moratorium on new independent taxicab licenses.[10] The initial order lasted 120 days but it was later extended "until further notice." Note two important features of this order. First, it was mandatory. There was no way to "exit" the order or to escape its effect, except by leaving the District of Columbia. Second, the order was enforced by the threat of force. The DCTC (now the Department of For-Hire Vehicles) is able to issue fines, suspend or revoke licenses, and impound vehicles in order to compel compliance.

The inability to exit and the implicit threat of force mark the moratorium as a "public" rule. But as we have already noted, the current vehicle-for-hire industry is *also* governed by various private mechanisms, including the most powerful private form of governance: competition.

These private forms of governance serve many of the same functions as formal, public regulations. They aim to ensure quality, to limit fraud, to yield lower prices, to ensure the performance of promises, and to correct for market failures. The simple dichotomy between "public" and "private" obscures the rich diversity of institutional arrangements. As Elinor Ostrom noted in her Nobel prize lecture:

> The classic assumptions about rational individuals facing a dichotomy of organizational forms and of goods hide the potentially productive efforts of individuals and groups to organize and solve social dilemmas such as the overharvesting of common-pool resources and the underprovision of local public goods.[11]

Put differently, some forms of private governance can have the look and feel of public governance, such as local homeowner associations (HOAs). It is true that one may exit the HOA by selling one's home. It is also true that the governance mechanism is voluntary in the sense that the agreement was freely entered into. But for many, the local HOA is a government-like authority.

Turning to the other end of the spectrum – the public sphere – some have argued that at least in the long run, governments have *some* voluntary features. In his Nobel prize lecture, for

---

[9] In a system with n nodes, the number of possible connections between nodes is $c=(n(n-1)/2$.

[10] Government of the District of Columbia Taxicab Commission, *The H-Tag Report: Final Report of the Panel on Industry: Findings and Recommendations on DCTC Policy on the Issuance of New Vehicle Licenses for Taxicabs*, Aug. 28, 2015.

[11] Elinor Ostrom, *Beyond Markets and States: Polycentric Governance of Complex Economic Systems*, 100(3) Am. Econ. Rev. 641–72 (2010).

example, James Buchanan asserted that "individuals acquiesce in the coercion of the state, of politics, only if the ultimate constitutional 'exchange' furthers their interests."[12]

Ultimately, the dichotomy between public and private rules may obscure some nuance. If public governance is characterized by the inability to exit and by the threat of coercive sanctions, then we might think of publicness as a matter of degree with higher exit costs and larger sanctions characterizing a more public regime. By this standard, the federal government – which is hard to escape – is more public than an HOA or department of for-hire vehicles. And an agency with the power to impound your vehicle is more public than one empowered to only deny the ability to operate as a cabbie.

III THE *COSMOS-TAXIS* DIMENSION

Drawing on the Greek word for "made" or "planned" order, F. A. Hayek referred to deliberately designed orders as "*taxis*" orders.[13] He contrasted *taxis* orders with what the Greeks called "*kosmos*" orders. Rather than being "made," a *cosmos* order "grows" or "emerges" from human actions. As Adam Ferguson asserted, societies occasionally "stumble upon establishments, which are indeed the result of human action, but not the execution of any human design."[14]

Taking up this theme, Adam Smith explained that he who "intends only his own gain … is in this, as in many other cases, led by an invisible hand to promote an end which was no part of his intention."[15] This notion of emergent order has been the theme of a great deal of social science. Economists, in particular, often describe the market process as an emergent order.

Both *taxis* and *cosmos* orders exist within the vehicle-for-hire industry. Chanoch Shreiber called attention to several problems with the industry, arguing that certain unique features of this market make regulation – public-*taxis* regulation, in his opinion – necessary.[16] Because drivers will "cruise" for riders, he argued that little price or quality competition exists in an unregulated industry. Riders, stuck with whatever cab happened to be nearest, could not evaluate the quality or safety of the driver and vehicle until it was too late. Drivers, moreover, were typically in possession of superior knowledge of routes, enabling them to take advantage of this information asymmetry and causing some skeptical customers to avoid cabs altogether.[17]

Though Shreiber's aim was to justify public regulation to address these problems, private entrepreneurs have profited handsomely by developing cleverly designed solutions to many of the problems identified by Shreiber.[18] Indeed, this is exactly what one would expect. For whenever a market is imperfect, entrepreneurs can profit by correcting or improving on it.[19] Today, cruising no longer limits the degree of competition in the industry because apps such as Uber and Lyft ensure that drivers are in fierce competition with one another for positive ratings from riders. The companies stop working with drivers whose scores are deemed too low and have developed

[12] James M. Buchanan, *The Constitution of Economic Policy*, 77(3) Am. Econ. Rev. 243–50 (1987).

[13] *Taxis* is pronounced tax-iss. To avoid confusion with the plural form of taxi, we will italicize *taxis* when we are referring to a planned or made order. 1 F. A. Hayek, *Law, Legislation and Liberty* Ch. 2 (1978).

[14] Adam Ferguson, *An Essay on the History of Civil Society* 205 (5th ed., 1782).

[15] Adam Smith, *The Theory of Moral Sentiments*, Part IV, Ch. 5 (1759).

[16] Chanoch Shreiber, *The Economic Reasons for Price and Entry Regulation of Taxicabs*, 9(3) J. Transport Econ. & Pol. 268–79 (1975).

[17] George A. Akerlof, *The Market for "Lemons": Quality Uncertainty and the Market Mechanism*, 84(3) Q.J. Econ. 488–500 (1970).

[18] Adam Thierer, Christopher Koopman, Anne Hobson, and Chris Kuiper, *How the Internet, the Sharing Economy & Reputation Feedback Mechanisms Solve the "Lemons Problem,"* 70 U. of Miami L. Rev. 830 (2016).

[19] Israel M. Kirzner, *Discovery and the Capitalist Process* (1985).

various mechanisms to reward good drivers. GPS technology has balanced the information asymmetry so that riders can be sure that drivers are following the best routes. Digital records and digital payment systems discourage fraud and theft. These companies have also created ratings systems that allow drivers to rate passengers, encouraging riders to be on their best behavior.

Beyond these *taxis* orders, the industry is also governed by a set of *cosmos* orders. Etiquette and certain cultural norms, for example, set boundaries on acceptable behavior and create a set of shared understandings that dictate appropriate behavior (it is polite for drivers and customers to exchange pleasantries; it is impolite to probe into one another's personal lives). One of these cultural rules – the practice of tipping – offers drivers an incentive to treat customers well. When they are allowed to operate, other emergent orders such as price and quality competition also govern the market.

As with the line between public and private, the line between *cosmos* and *taxis* is not always clear. Companies may purposely design mechanisms that leverage certain *cosmos* orders for competitive advantage. For example, Lyft has for some time integrated a tipping function into its app. This formally creates an environment that is conducive to tipping, though of course, cultural norms and other emergent phenomena will govern the practice. Still, it is not difficult to think of orders that are "more" emergent than others.

IV FOUR "TYPES" OF GOVERNANCE

We can now sketch out four "types" of orders: public-*taxis*, public-*cosmos*, private-*taxis*, and private-*cosmos*. Table 6.1 depicts these four categories, with examples of each, drawn from the vehicle-for-hire industry.

TABLE 6.1 *Four types of governance*

	Taxis	Cosmos
Public	A. No examples.	B. Federal labor law, federal tax law, DMV rules, taxi commission rules.
Private	C. Bond posting, brand-maintenance, capital markets, insurance markets, centralized or third-party reputational mechanisms (BBB), background checks, GPS monitoring of routes, algorithms to reward performance.	D. Price, quality, and dynamic competition; etiquette; social media reputation; peer-to-peer or decentralized reputational mechanisms.

A Public-Taxis Orders

Public-*taxis* governance is what comes to mind when one talks about regulation: a deliberately designed government-enforced set of rules. It is what those focused on the "public interest theory of regulation" such as Shreiber or A.C. Pigou have in mind when they call for regulations to address market failures. In so doing, they assume that voters, interest groups, legislators, and bureaucrats possess the correct information and the correct incentives to act on this information in order to craft wise rules.

Public choice economists have argued that this assumption is overly romantic.[20] Voters have strong incentives to remain ignorant of all but the most basic facts of public

---

[20] James M. Buchanan, *Public Choice: Politics Without Romance*, 19(3) Policy 13–18 (2003).

policy.[21] In some cases, we may even be governed by systematically false perceptions.[22] Special interests – gaining from public regulations – can exploit these biases by appealing to false narratives and fear-mongering.[23]

Compared with diffuse consumer groups, producer interests tend to find it easier to overcome the free-rider problem that makes all collective action difficult to organize.[24] Producer groups tend to know the technical details of their professions and are often a source of information to regulators.[25] With greater organizational ability and superior knowledge, producer groups are often able to exercise greater influence on regulations than consumer groups. They use these advantages to seek rules that limit entry, raise rivals' costs, lock in higher prices, or somehow increase demand for their products.[26]

This helps explain why the public interest theory of regulation came to be rejected as a positive description of public governance, and it performs particularly poorly as a description of taxi market regulation.[27] In fact, the industry is a favorite example for textbook writers illustrating the failure of the public interest theory of regulation.[28] By 1976, Roger Noll could report in his survey of the literature that the public interest theory of regulation was "no longer widely shared."[29]

Interestingly, adherents to the public interest theory of regulation are not the only ones who operate with the public-*taxis* type of regulation in mind. Critics of government regulation – especially those that view all or most public regulation as "captured" by industry – also seem to have the public-*taxis* model in mind.[30] "Capture theory" implies that the entire regulatory apparatus can be *seized* for the benefit of the regulated industry, and suggests that public regulations are *designed* for the purpose of creating above-normal profits (rents) for the industry.[31]

Both public interest theorists and capture theorists are wrong. No one would ever sit down and purposively design the complex, contradictory, and counterproductive set of rules that characterize public regulations. These rules are better conceived as public-*cosmos* orders, and they should give pause to anyone thinking that they can design an optimal public regulation for the sharing economy, or for any market for that matter. Any regulatory system, once designed, will quickly give way to changes that reflect particular preferences of regulators, elected officials, and interest groups.

---

[21] Anthony Downs, *An Economic Theory of Democracy* (1957).

[22] Bryan Caplan, *The Myth of the Rational Voter: Why Democracies Choose Bad Policies* (new ed., 2008).

[23] Adam Smith and Bruce Yandle, *Bootleggers and Baptists: How Economic Forces and Moral Persuasion Interact to Shape Regulatory Politics* (2014).

[24] Mancur Olson, *The Logic of Collective Action: Public Goods and the Theory of Groups, Second Printing with New Preface and Appendix* (revised ed., 1965).

[25] Ernesto Dal Bó, *Regulatory Capture: A Review*, 22(2) Oxford Rev. Econ. Pol. 203–05 (2006).

[26] George J. Stigler, *The Theory of Economic Regulation*, 2(1) Bell J. Econ. & Mgmt. Sci. 3–21 (1971).

[27] Edmund W. Kitch, Marc Isaacson, and Daniel Kasper, *The Regulation of Taxicabs in Chicago*, 14(2) J. Law & Econ. 285–350 (1971); Adrian Moore and Ted Balaker, *Do Economists Reach a Conclusion on Taxi Deregulation?* 3(1) Econ. J. Watch 109–32 (2006); Samuel Staley and Benjamin Douglas, Market Concentration and the Supply of Taxicabs in US Cities, Working Paper, DeVoe L. Moore Center, Florida State University, April 2014, http://coss.fsu.edu/dmc/sites/coss.fsu.edu.dmc/files/Staley_Douglas_APEETaxiConcentration_Ver2.pdf.

[28] *See, e.g.*, Alfred Kahn, *The Economics of Regulation: Principles and Institutions* (1988).

[29] Roger G. Noll, *Government Administrative Behavior and Private Sector Response: A Multidisciplinary Survey*, Social Science Working Paper, Pasadena, CA: California Institute of Technology, 1976.

[30] *See, e.g.*, David B. Truman, *The Governmental Process: Political Interests and Public Opinion* (1951); Marver H. Bernstein, *Regulating Business by Independent Commission*, 31 Indiana L.J. 160 (1955).

[31] Gordon Tullock, *The Welfare Costs of Tariffs, Monopolies, and Theft*, 5(3) W. Econ. J. [Economic Inquiry] 224–232 (1967).

B *Public-Cosmos Orders*

Instead of thinking of regulation as the product of perfect information, regulation should be understood as *emerging* from political exchange between different groups over time. In this dynamic process, public regulations come to serve neither consumers nor producers. There are six reasons why public regulation should be thought of as an emergent phenomenon:

1) In order to obtain a rent, one interest group may need to logroll with another and agree to support *their* regulatory privilege.[32] In the case of the vehicle-for-hire industry, one industry group such as luxury limousines may need to support the interests of another such as taxis.

2) Special interests may need to offer costly concessions to powerful or politically sympathetic consumer groups. In exchange for their regulated monopoly, for example, policymakers might require a regulated industry to agree to serve a costly community or to charge a particular set of customers a rate that is less than revenue-maximizing.[33] If interest groups were able to capture the process entirely, they wouldn't bother with these sorts of concessions.

3) Policymakers may be required to disguise regulatory privileges as public-interest regulation. This means that the transfers are accomplished in a comparatively inefficient way. If taxi interests could design the system on their own, they'd simply have legislators write them taxpayer-financed checks each year.

4) Changes in the market erode the value of regulatory privilege. Though taxi medallions limited the supply of taxis and supported above-normal profits for a time, the value of these rents was eventually capitalized into the value of the medallions. Would-be monopolists had to pay dearly – over $1 million – for the right to earn above-normal profits. So, net of these costs, their returns were actually normal.[34] Again, no taxi company would actually design a regulation like this.

5) Entrepreneurs find margins along which to compete and whittle away the above-normal profits of regulatory privilege. This necessitates further regulation. One rule leads to another. Alfred Kahn described this well in the context of airline regulation: each attempt to regulate the industry created an artificial stimulus to compete along some other margin, which led to further regulation, which created additional stimuli to compete along other margins. "Each time the dyke springs a leak," Kahn explained, "plug it with one of your fingers."[35]

6) Multiple overlapping public regulators often govern the market, and each has the power to limit or exclude access to the market. With limited ability to coordinate, each fails to fully account for its effect on the others. This leads to over-restriction in what is known as a tragedy of the anticommons. The first four nodes after A in Figure 6.1 – arranged in a series to indicate that these mechanisms of governance cannot be avoided – represent such an anticommons.[36]

---

[32] Gordon Tullock, *Problems of Majority Voting*, 67 J. Pol. Econ. 571–79 (1959); James M. Buchanan and Gordon Tullock, *The Calculus of Consent: Logical Foundations of Constitutional Democracy* (1962); William H. Riker, *The Theory of Political Coalitions* (1984).

[33] Richard A. Posner, *Taxation by Regulation*, 2(1) Bell J. Econ. 22–50 (1971).

[34] Gordon Tullock, *The Transitional Gains Trap*, 6(2) Bell J. Econ. 671–78 (1975).

[35] Quoted in Thomas K. McCraw, *Prophets of Regulation* 272 (1984).

[36] The concept was originally developed by Heller and formally modeled by Buchanan and Yoon. *See* Michael Heller, *The Tragedy of the Anticommons: Property in the Transition from Marx to Markets*, 111 Harv. L. Rev. 621 (1998); James M. Buchanan and Yong Yoon, *Symmetric Tragedies: Commons and Anticommons*, 43(1) J.L. & Econ. 1–13 (2000); Matthew Mitchell and Thomas Stratmann, *A Tragedy of the Anticommons: Local Option Taxation and Cell Phone Tax Bills*, 165(3) Pub. Choice 171–91 (2015).

The end result is a patchwork of highly-restrictive rules – what Richard Wagner has referred to as "entangled political economy" – that is in neither the general interest nor the producer interest.[37] It is a *cosmos* order because it emerges through a process of political exchange and because it evolves over time as different actors – regulators, policymakers, and interest groups – tweak it. But, unfortunately, it is a perverse *cosmos* order.

This helps explain why public regulation of taxis has become a textbook example of bad regulation. Many public-*cosmos* orders in the vehicle-for-hire industry are supposed to overcome information asymmetries, which can lead to a breakdown in the vehicle-for-hire market. As George Akerlof argued in his research on the market for used cars, such information breakdowns may require "government intervention," or public-*cosmos* orders, to increase the welfare of all parties.[38] These public regulations, however, have consistently failed in the long run for one of two reasons (or some combination). First, as we explain above, these public-*cosmos* orders inevitably end up failing to represent either the general interest or the producer interest.

Second, public-*cosmos* orders tend to create stasis within the industry. That is, public-*cosmos* regulations have a tendency to mandate processes and procedures that cannot evolve with technology and consumer preferences. Those who called for public regulation of the vehicle-for-hire industry could not predict the degree to which trust-based reputational mechanisms would continue to overcome information asymmetries nor the degree to which entrepreneurs would outperform formal government mechanisms.[39] A large degree of the disruption in the vehicle-for-hire industry is the result of platforms such as Uber and Lyft providing better solutions to old problems that were unavailable to traditional taxis.

C *Private-Taxis Orders*

Markets are a dynamic – or evolutionary – process.[40] Standards, tools, and mechanisms deemed efficient today will be supplanted by newer, more efficient means tomorrow. This is one reason why private orders outperform public orders. And the vehicle-for-hire industry provides perhaps the best example of the virtues of private governance.

Over the past three decades, the internet, and various reputational mechanisms developed by entrepreneurs, have reduced the cost of acquiring information and resolved much of Akerlof's "lemons problem." As Adam Thierer and his coauthors explain:

> [E]very perceived information problem also creates an incentive for the entrepreneur to discover new ways to create profit opportunities. By continually updating information and experimenting through trial and error, the entrepreneur discovers more efficient means of promoting human interaction and facilitating exchange.[41]

Private-*taxis* mechanisms are deliberately designed by entrepreneurs to address perceived problems. Examples of such private-*taxis* orders include brand maintenance, centralized or third-party reputational mechanisms (e.g., BBB), background checks, GPS monitoring of routes, and algorithmic rules. These mechanisms encourage trust and facilitate exchange by gathering much of the information that a consumer might wish to gather before deciding which service

---

[37] Richard E. Wagner, *Politics as a Peculiar Business: Insights from a Theory of Entangled Political Economy* (2016).
[38] Akerlof, *supra* note 17.
[39] For a fuller discussion of this *see* Thierer et al., *supra* note 18, at 836–40.
[40] *See* Israel M. Kirzner, *Competition and Entrepreneurship* 155 (1973); *see also* Armen Alchian, *Uncertainty, Evolution, and Economic Theory*, 58 J. Pol. Econ. 211, 212–21 (1950).
[41] Thierer et al., *supra* note 18, at 849 (internal citations removed).

to select. These mechanisms also regulate behavior by ensuring that bad actors cannot leverage information asymmetries to harm others (i.e., stealing from passengers or driving recklessly).

Private-*taxis* orders tend to be less perverse than public-*cosmos* orders because they are less likely to be gamed given the competitive nature of the market process. Given the ease of exit, as consumers realize a platform is no longer fulfilling their needs, they can turn elsewhere. This fact is constantly driving these designed mechanisms to become better, and whenever a platform violates consumers' trust there is another waiting to take its place.[42]

Moreover, consumers may use a platform because they trust the platform without actually trusting those with whom they are interacting on it. Take, for example, eBay's money-back guarantee.[43] This promise does not necessarily increase a buyer's trust in the seller, but it does increase the likelihood that a buyer will purchase what the seller is listing, allowing them to trust the transaction.[44] Likewise, many of the mechanisms used by ride-sharing platforms, and sharing economy platforms in general, are not so much facilitating trust between users. In other cases, users come to trust that much of the hard work of vetting whom to exchange with and whom to avoid has been done for them.[45]

In order to keep potentially bad actors from using the app to harm others, platforms such as Uber and Lyft perform criminal and driving background checks, ensure drivers have valid licenses, lay out basic safety standards for vehicles, and require that drivers be adequately insured. During drives, Uber and Lyft continually monitor quality by tracking drivers using GPS.

Unlike public-*cosmos*, private-*taxis* arrangements are constantly improved as technology improves. Each of these private-*taxis* orders, directed at both producers and consumers, acts as a regulatory measure. Each is driven by entrepreneurial alertness to consumer needs that have gone unmet (or have only been met in unsatisfactory ways), and will evolve and respond not only to changes in technology, but to consumer preferences and technical feasibility.

For example, Uber has piloted what it calls a Real-Time ID Check program.[46] While using the app, drivers are asked to take a selfie before they accept rides. Uber then uses Microsoft's Cognitive Services to instantly compare the selfie to the photos that Uber has on file. If the two photos don't match, the account is temporarily blocked while Uber resolves the situation. This ensures that passengers are picked up by the person who is supposed to be driving and that driver accounts are protected from theft.

Deliberately designed screening mechanisms may also be used to ensure good behavior by consumers. Turo, a car-sharing service, will screen potential car renters for major issues in their driving record (e.g., driving under the influence, reckless driving), and will bar potential users based on the results.[47] In fact, Turo relies on another third-party platform that creates unique "auto insurance scores" to estimate the relative risk of each individual driver.[48]

---

[42] For an example of this, see the "#deleteuber" campaign. Mike Isaac, *Uber Board Stands by Travis Kalanick as It Reveals Plans to Repair Its Image*, NY Times, Mar. 21, 2017, www.nytimes.com/2017/03/21/technology/uber-board-stands-by-travis-kalanick.html; see also reports of a corresponding spike in Lyft users during this same period. Madison Malone Kircher, *How Much Did #DeleteUber Actually Help Lyft?*, New York Magazine, Apr. 27, 2017, http://nymag.com/selectall/2017/04/lyft-user-numbers-spiked-after-delete-uber-campaign.html.

[43] *eBay Money Back Guarantee*, eBay, http://pages.ebay.com/help/policies/money-back-guarantee.html#MBG.

[44] *See* Thierer et al., *supra* note 18, at 858–63.

[45] *Id.* at 859.

[46] *Selfies and Security*, Uber, www.uber.com/ms-MY/blog/ipoh/selfies-and-security/.

[47] Turo Support, *What Are the Eligibility Requirements?*, Turo, https://support.turo.com/hc/en-us/articles/203991060-whatare-the-eligibility-requirements.

[48] Turo Support, *What is an auto insurance score?*, Turo, https://support.turo.com/hc/en-us/articles/220443588-What-is-an-auto-insurance-score-.

As effective as these private-*taxis* orders can be, however, they remain wholly dependent on the information available to entrepreneurs and their ability to process it effectively and design solutions to perceived problems.

D Private-Cosmos Orders

As we noted above, private-*taxis* orders may facilitate trust and encourage exchange, building trust among individuals or at least in their interactions. But private-*taxis* orders do not fully capture the ability of individuals to gather, process, share, and ultimately act on information. Instead, they rely on the alertness and ability of individual entrepreneurs. Private-*cosmos* orders go beyond the platforms themselves and leverage the dispersed knowledge of producers and consumers. In a market economy, a *cosmos* order manifests itself in a number of ways:

1) In a competitive market, shortages encourage entrepreneurs to raise prices while surpluses encourage them to reduce prices, causing the market to tend toward the "optimal" equilibrium in which price (and therefore marginal benefit) equals marginal cost.[49]

2) The price system serves as an important coordinating mechanism, allowing millions of disparate individuals to act on widely dispersed bits of information, including the subjective preferences of others; this permits each of us to coordinate with countless strangers, fitting our plans together even without a central planner.[50]

3) Over the long run, as markets grow larger, individuals and firms are able to grow more specialized and this in turn increases their productivity.[51]

4) The lure of monopoly profit keeps firms innovating and thinking of new ways to differentiate themselves from their competitors while the discipline of competition restrains their prices.[52]

Social media have facilitated the rise of another form of private-*cosmos* order. Individuals – whether a party to a particular transaction or not – are able to communicate approval or disapproval more easily and more rapidly than ever before. This has also made organizations (both corporations and governments) more responsive to consumer and citizen demands.[53] The #DeleteUber campaign and the social media response to United Airlines incidents in 2017 are two examples of this type of private-*cosmos* order.[54]

Ratings and reviews are another example of private-*cosmos* orders, although in this case the orders have a *taxis* element since entrepreneurs purposively design and often curate the ratings that emerge through producer and consumer interaction. Ratings systems have been a hallmark of the internet since at least the rise of eBay and Amazon. In addition to the assurances made by eBay, which we discussed above, trust between buyers and sellers is facilitated by the ability to rate and review one another after the transaction. This allows users to understand, in some detail, how those with whom they exchange have behaved in the past.

---

[49] Vernon L. Smith, *An Experimental Study of Competitive Market Behavior*, 70(2) J. Pol. Econ. 111–37 (1962).

[50] F. A. Hayek, *The Use of Knowledge in Society*, 35(4) Am. Econ. Rev. 519–30 (1945).

[51] 1 and 2 Adam Smith, *An Inquiry into the Nature and Causes of the Wealth of Nations* Book 1, Ch. 1 (Glasgow ed., 1776).

[52] Kirzner, *supra* note 19; Israel M. Kirzner, *Entrepreneurial Discovery and the Competitive Market Process: An Austrian Approach*, 35(1) J. Econ. Lit. 60–85 (1997).

[53] Thierer et al., *supra* note 18, at 864–65.

[54] Mike Isaac, *What You Need to Know About #DeleteUber*, NY Times, Jan. 31, 2017, www.nytimes.com/2017/01/31/business/delete-uber.html; Julia Zorthian, *'Boycott United': Twitter Users Outraged After Man Forcibly Removed from Flight*, Fortune, Apr. 10, 2017, http://fortune.com/2017/04/10/boycott-united-airlines/.

Private-*cosmos* orders are a fundamental piece of most sharing economy platforms, and these companies have come to heavily rely on them. Ride-sharing companies, for example, employ extensive rating systems. Both drivers and passengers rate each other after every ride, and these ratings are used to determine future exchanges. Companies may choose to no longer work with low-rated drivers, drivers may choose to avoid picking up low-rated passengers, and companies may choose to avoid matching drivers and passengers who have rated one another poorly in the past.

Platforms are also beginning to encourage direct communication between users. This is facilitating greater levels of cooperation between users, building trust on a peer-to-peer basis, and leading to the emergence of more effective private-*cosmos* orders. As Elinor Ostrom explained:

> From [the] theoretical perspective, face-to-face communication should make no difference in the outcomes achieved in social dilemmas. Yet, consistent, strong, and replicable findings are that substantial increases in the levels of cooperation are achieved when individuals are allowed to communicate face to face.[55]

Car-sharing platform Turo stumbled upon this realization several years ago:

> When the company first started, they had membership-card readers installed in every owner's car. Renters could unlock and start a car by swiping their membership card, thus eliminating the need for the car owner to be present. But it soon became clear to [Turo] that, in order to grow efficiently, they would have to abandon having card readers installed in every car. Instead, renters and owners met face to face to hand off the keys. The human connection led to gains for both parties: Owners made fewer damage claims and both renters and owners reported higher satisfaction ratings. As the CEO of [Turo], Andre Haddad, stated, "People strike up a conversation and realize they have something in common, which boosts trust and makes people feel accountable. They're going to have to return this car to that person and look them in the eye."[56]

For the same reasons, Airbnb, Uber, Lyft, and many other platforms require users to have a clear profile photo displayed with their accounts. But having access to such information, while a necessary condition, is not sufficient. This private-*taxis* order must be supplemented with private-*cosmos* practices. Cliff Lampe, a professor at the University of Michigan's School of Information, has noted that these mechanisms – acquiring, sharing, and acting on information – help establish new social norms. He states that "[b]y providing feedback about behavior, penalizing negative actions, signaling desired outcome, and rewarding users, reputation and recommender systems are providing socializing functions and becoming valuable tools for organizing online environments."[57] In short, ratings and reviews teach and enforce social norms within these platforms. As Lampe notes, "[B]y providing information about users, rating systems can act as 'cues' or 'signals' in online communities, allowing users to reach common ground about each other and facilitating social interaction."[58]

Private-*cosmos* orders fill in many of the nooks and crannies left by private-*taxis* orders. Platforms such as Uber and Lyft set general standards about appropriate behavior during rides while user reviews can communicate clearly what is and is not acceptable in certain specific

---

[55] Elinor Ostrom, *A Behavioral Approach to the Rational Choice Theory of Collective Action: Presidential Address, American Political Science Association, 1997*, 92 Am. Pol. Sci. Rev. 1, 6 (1998).

[56] *See, e.g.,* Jason Tanz, *How Airbnb and Lyft Finally Got Americans to Trust Each Other,* WIRED, Apr. 23, 2014, 6:30 AM, www.wired.com/2014/04/trustin-the-share-economy. *See also* Thierer et al., *supra* note 18, at 866–67.

[57] Cliff Lampe, The Role of Reputation Systems in Managing Online Communities, *in The Reputation Society: How Online Opinions are Reshaping The Offline World,* 77 (Hassan Masum and Mark Tovey eds., 2011).

[58] *Id.* at 81.

contexts. The platforms could not possibly do this, even if they tried. What might be appropriate interactions in New York City may be far from appropriate in Cincinnati, Ohio.

Moreover, these private-*cosmos* mechanisms may also provide strong signals to platforms about what types of regulatory steps ought to become intergrated into their private-*taxis* mechanisms. Uber, for example, has integrated a "compliments" feature to allow passengers to provide positive reinforcement by providing a specific compliment to drivers.[59]

There are other ways to integrate private-*cosmos* orders into private-*taxis* mechanisms. For example, Airbnb realized that properties with professional, verified photos are booked 2.5 times more often than those without such photos.[60] Renters, they found, were more likely to book listings that had not only better pictures but externally verified pictures (that is, pictures that were verified to be of the particular listing). Users on the platform were signaling what they preferred, and Airbnb listened.

For all of the merits of private-*cosmos* orders, there are some problems facing such reputational mechanisms. They may be gamed, manipulated, or hijacked. Some fear that relying on such mechanisms may exacerbate racial divides by making discrimination easier.[61] Many of these problems, however, are being resolved through competition between platforms.[62]

V OPTIMAL GOVERNANCE

Although deliberately designed public regulation is likely the first thing that comes to mind when one hears the word "regulation," it is actually exceedingly rare. Most public regulation is not deliberately designed, but has evolved over a long period of time, resulting in a patchwork of rules that too often fail to serve the public.

Private regulation, on the other hand, is often overlooked and has a number of virtues. First, private orders permit institutional diversity and competition. While multiple, overlapping public orders create a tragedy of the anticommons, multiple, overlapping private orders permit users to opt in and out of different governance mechanisms. This means that these mechanisms are forced to evolve and improve to compete with one another. It also means that the governance mechanisms can make better use of local knowledge and can be calibrated to the tastes and preferences of local users. In the case of private-*taxis* orders, entrepreneurs can profit by correcting the mistakes of poor governance. Because these mechanisms do not govern the whole of the market, the risks of poor governance are relatively contained.

The decentralized nature of private-*cosmos* orders makes them ideal for rapidly changing markets. Private-*taxis* orders, overlaying the private-*cosmos* orders, can overcome issues unresolved through direct, peer-to-peer interaction by allowing entrepreneurs to find such shortcomings and correct them.

---

[59] Mike Truong, *Introducing Compliment*, Uber, Nov. 21, 2016, https://newsroom.uber.com/compliments/.

[60] *Airbnb Free Photography: Celebrating 13,000 Verified Properties & Worldwide Launch*, Airbnb, Oct. 6, 2011, http://blog.atairbnb.com/airbnb-photography-celebrating-13000-verified.

[61] *See, e.g.*, Nancy Leong, *The Sharing Economy Has a Race Problem*, Salon, Nov. 2, 2014, www.salon.com/2014/11/02/the_sharing_economy_has_a_race_problem; Greg Harman, *The Sharing Economy Is Not as Open as You Might Think*, Guardian, Nov. 12, 2014, www.theguardian.com/sustainable-business/2014/nov/12/algorithms-race-discrimination-uber-lyft-airbnb-peer.

[62] For a fuller discussion, *see* Thierer et al., *supra* note 18, at 870–73.

7

Competition Law (and Its Limits) in the Sharing Economy

Niamh Dunne

INTRODUCTION

This contribution considers the potential application of competition law – specifically, the "antitrust" rules governing anticompetitive unilateral or coordinated conduct – within the sharing economy. The emergence of a vibrant, innovative, and successful sharing economy marketplace is, from one perspective, a paradigmatic example of dynamic and effective competition: *precisely* the type of activity that antitrust aims to foster and protect. Yet concerns exist that the competitive forces generated by and taking place within the sharing economy are inherently unfair and thus illegitimate; and that the success of its business models may result in market power and anticompetitive behavior. The chapter accordingly considers the extent to which competition law might and should apply to constrain ostensibly anticompetitive conduct within these markets.

Although the term "sharing economy" refers to an almost unendingly wide spectrum of business models and activities, the sector is marked by recurrent characteristics that condition competitive forces, and thus the potential application of competition law. First, the underlying economic rationale is underutilization of durable goods or other assets, which generates excess capacity that can be rented out.[1] Sharing economy businesses bring new products, assets, and suppliers into the market, using technology to reduce transaction costs that otherwise inhibit marketization.[2] The so-called "gig economy" extends this logic to man-hours, providing individuals with (not uncontentious) opportunities for flexible working.[3] Thus, sharing economy businesses expand the size of the marketplace, by including providers and customers who would not otherwise participate; but also increase competition, by attracting customers from conventional providers.[4] Second, sharing economy firms present archetypal examples of "disruptive" innovation,[5] which

---

[1] John J. Horton and Richard J. Zeckhauser, *Owning, Using and Renting: Some Simple Economics of the "Sharing Economy,"* HKS Faculty Research Working Paper Series RWP16-007, 6 (2016).

[2] David Stallibrass and John F. Fingleton, *Regulation, Innovation and Growth: Why Peer-to-Peer Businesses Should be Supported*, 7 JECLAP 414, 415 (2016); Federal Trade Commission (FTC),*The "Sharing Economy." Issues Facing Platforms, Participants & Regulators*, An FTC Staff Report, 21–23, Nov. 2016.

[3] Nathan Heller, *Is the Gig Economy Working?*, The New Yorker, May 15, 2017, www.newyorker.com/magazine/2017/05/15/is-the-gig-economy-working.

[4] Stallibrass and Fingleton, *supra* note 2, at 415.

[5] OECD, *Hearing on Disruptive Innovation, Issues Paper*, DAF/COMP(2015)3, 2 (2015).

originates outside a value network and displaces it.[6] It is thus akin to Schumpeter's description of competition as "creative destruction"[7]: disrupted products or business models may ultimately be forced from the market. Third, the innovations that underpin the sharing economy are rooted in the internet and mobile technologies.[8] Firms operate as electronic platforms in multisided markets, offering intermediation services that enable exchange between peers.[9] The "two-sided" nature of such activities has significant implications for applying, and finding violation of, antitrust.[10] Finally, sharing economy firms frequently conflict with regulatory regimes that control and limit the activities of competitors, resulting in recurrent critiques that such competition is inherently "unfair." All of which results in a market structure where competition tends to be vibrant, fast-moving, innovative, and cutthroat, particularly in terms of asymmetries with established business models and providers.

The primary focus of this chapter is the competition rules within the Treaty on the Functioning of the European Union (TFEU), namely Articles 101 and 102. The analysis that follows is nevertheless intended to be more broadly applicable to antitrust regimes, particularly given the dearth of case law in most jurisdictions. Reference is made to US antitrust provisions – §§1 and 2, Sherman Act – where appropriate. Sections I and II examine the potential application of the prohibitions against anticompetitive unilateral conduct and anticompetitive coordinated conduct, respectively, within the sharing economy. Section III subsequently considers the notion of unfair competition and the limits of antitrust more generally, exploring reasons both for the abundance of apparent competition problems and the relative ineffectiveness of competition law in this context.

I UNILATERAL CONDUCT UNDER COMPETITION LAW

Given the distinctive conditions of competition within the sharing economy, what scope exists for applying competition law? Our starting assumption is that the sector accommodates a wide spectrum of business models, which vary in potential market impact and implications for antitrust: from genuine "sharing" models to those which permit providers to make profits; from platforms that dictate *inter alia* prices that providers may charge to those which merely facilitate otherwise freestanding transactions; and from platforms involving renting of assets to exchange of labor to both.

Article 102 of the TFEU prohibits "[a]ny abuse by one or more undertakings of a dominant position within the internal market." The central idea is that dominant undertakings – roughly, firms possessing durable significant market power[11] – have a particular ability to harm competition,[12] and thus have a concomitant "special responsibility" not to subvert the competition process.[13] To establish breach, three elements must be satisfied: dominance; abusive conduct; and absence of legitimate justification. Article 102 is largely equivalent to §2, Sherman Act, which

---

[6] Alexandre de Streel and Pierre Larouche, *Disruptive Innovation and Competition Policy Enforcement*, OECD Global Competition Forum, DAF/COMP/GF(2015)7, 2 (2015).

[7] FTC, *supra* note 2, at 10.

[8] Stephen P. King, *Sharing Economy: What Challenges for Competition Law?*, 6 JECLAP 729, 729 (2015); Guy Lougher and Sammy Kalmanowicz, *EU Competition Law in the Sharing Economy*, 7 JECLAP 87, 87–88 (2016).

[9] Lougher and Kalmanowicz, *supra* note 8, at 89.

[10] *Id.* at 91–93.

[11] Commission, *Guidance on the Commission's enforcement priorities in applying Article 82 of the EC Treaty to abusive exclusionary conduct by dominant undertakings* (OJ C45/7, 24.2.2009), paras. 9–12.

[12] C-85/76 *Hoffmann-La Roche* EU:C:1979:36.

[13] C-322/81 *Michelin (I)* EU:C:1983:313, para. 57.

prohibits monopolization of trade, although the market share threshold for applying Article 102 is lower, bringing it potentially into play in a broader range of scenarios.

The concept of dominance refers to "a position of economic strength enjoyed by an undertaking which ... [gives] it the power to behave to an appreciable extent independently of its competitors, customers and ultimately of its consumers."[14] Establishing dominance is a two-stage process: definition of the relevant market, followed by assessment of existing competitive constraints. Dominance is a threshold concept, insofar as only abusive behavior by dominant undertakings is prohibited: unilateral behavior by undertakings without market power is unproblematic, at least under competition law.

The purpose of market definition is to identify and define the boundaries of competition between firms.[15] Markets are defined in terms of product and geographic dimensions.[16] Demand substitution – the range of products viewed as substitutes by customers – is the primary source of competitive constraint of relevance.[17] Conventionally, this is assessed through a "hypothetical monopolist" or SSNIP test, which considers the impact on consumer behavior of a small but significant non-transitory increase in the price of a product.[18] It is well recognized, however, that such tools are of more limited use in two-sided markets, given that a price change on one side may have feedback effects on other sides.[19]

Applying these principles to the sharing economy, several observations can be made. First, the complexity of the exercise is evident: not merely because of the two-sided nature of activities, but also because of the broad array of differing services and business models that it encompasses.[20]

Second, four sets of relevant players are affected: the platform intermediary, affiliated service providers, service users, and, more obliquely, "traditional" operators who compete with and may ultimately be displaced by new providers.[21] The question thus arises as to whether sharing economy platforms disclose one or more relevant markets. Lougher and Kalmanowicz, noting that activities normally involve one party on each side, argue that platforms are active on a single market for two-sided intermediation, rather than separate markets for each side of the underlying commercial activity.[22] This comparatively narrow approach suggests that platforms compete with other platforms providing comparable services – that Uber competes with Lyft, for instance – but do not extend beyond the sharing economy. Given the digital, and largely borderless, nature of intermediation activities, potentially an expansive geographic market could be envisaged, albeit with regional variations to take account of language requirements and so on.[23] Distinct from the platform, there would exist a separate market for the supply of services intermediated by the platform; here, providers almost certainly compete with traditional providers offering equivalent services.[24]

---

[14] 27/76 *United Brands* EU:C:1978:22, para. 65.

[15] Commission, *Notice on the Definition of the Relevant Market for the purposes of Community Competition Law* (OJ C372/5, 9.12.1997) para. 2.

[16] *Id.* at paras. 7–9.

[17] *Id.* at para. 13.

[18] *Id.* at para. 15.

[19] OECD, *Disruptive Innovation*, DAF/COMP(2015)3 at 24.

[20] Francesco Russo and Maria Luisa Stasi, *Defining the Relevant Market in the Sharing Economy*, 5(2) Internet Pol. Rev. (June 2016), DOI: 10.14763/2016.2.418.

[21] Lougher and Kalmanowicz, *supra* note 8, at 89–90; *see also* FTC, *supra* note 2, at 18.

[22] Lougher and Kalmanowicz, *supra* note 8, at 92.

[23] *Id.* at 93–94.

[24] *Id.* at 94.

The decision in *Uber Spain*, however, raises questions about whether sharing economy platforms can be dissociated from the tangible services underpinning their activities.[25] The approach of Advocate General Szpunar, followed by the Court of Justice, is particularly instructive.[26] Arguing that Uber constitutes a transport as opposed to an information services provider, he distinguished its business model from "mere intermediary" platforms, such as those which facilitate hotel or flight bookings. With mere intermediaries, service providers (hotels, airlines etc.) function independently, using the platform simply as another way to access consumers; providers set their own terms and conditions of service, including price; and platforms offer consumers a choice between different providers with distinct offerings.[27] Conversely, Uber drivers pursue an economic activity that exists solely because of its platform,[28] which is presented to customers as a single transport service,[29] and where Uber "exerts control over the key conditions governing the supply of transport made within that context."[30] The supply of transport services thus gives Uber's intermediary activities economic meaning,[31] and therefore Uber should be viewed as a transport services provider – even if immediate ride services are provided on its behalf by affiliated drivers as subcontractors.[32] The Court itself adopted the "decisive influence" criterion, well established in the context of the single economic entity doctrine within EU competition law,[33] to govern this determination: that is, the fact that Uber exercises decisive influence over the conditions under which transport services are provided by affiliated drivers.[34] Moreover, the approach in *Uber Spain* notably differs from the Commission's *Agenda for the Collaborative Economy*, which emphasized ownership of assets as an indicator of participation in services markets.[35]

Although pertaining directly to Uber's business model, the Opinion provides food for thought for sharing economy platforms generally. Translated to the market definition exercise, it suggests that, in some circumstances, the "relevant market" might be the broader underlying services market, rather than a niche intermediation market.[36] Specifically, sharing economy platforms transform what would, typically, be otherwise economically unviable activities into feasible, profitable services. Often, platforms effectively "create" the final product at issue to a far greater extent than, say, booking websites,[37] and thus cannot be considered as "mere" intermediaries. Yet few platforms are as prescriptive as Uber regarding the terms and conditions under which service providers operate, or present consumers with such an emphatically undifferentiated product offering.[38] The dearth of precedent considering this point suggests that both possibilities should be examined.

The question of whether the relevant market is narrow or broad is important insofar as it may prove determinative of whether a platform is held dominant. The primary purpose of market

---

[25] C-434/15 *Asociación Profesional Elite Taxi* v. *Uber Systems Spain* EU:C:2017:981.

[26] Opinion in C-434/15 *Asociación Profesional Elite Taxi* ("*Uber Spain Opinion*") EU:C:2017:364.

[27] *Id.*, paras. 57–60.

[28] *Id.*, para. 56. An approach also endorsed by the Court in *Uber Spain*, para. 39.

[29] *Id.*, para. 53.

[30] *Id.*, para. 72.

[31] *Id.*, para. 64.

[32] *Id.*, paras. 54–55.

[33] *See, e.g.*, C-97/08 P *Akzo Nobel and Others* v. *Commission* EU:C:2009:536.

[34] *Uber Spain, supra* note 26, at para. 39.

[35] COM(2016)356 final at 6.

[36] *See,* similarly, Vera Demary, *Competition in the Sharing Economy*, IW Policy Paper 19/2015, 13.

[37] *See,* similarly, Vassilis Hatzopoulos and Sofia Roma, *Caring for Sharing? The Collaborative Economy under EU Law*, 54 CML Rev. 81, 95 (2017).

[38] On antitrust implications of Uber's business model, *see* Julian Nowag, *The UBER-Cartel? Uber between Labour and Competition Law*, LundLawCompWP 1/2016, and Jan Kupcik, *Why Does Uber Violate European Competition Laws?*, 37 ECLR 469 (2016).

definition is to enable calculation of market shares,[39] which function as an initial proxy for market power. Under EU law, a share of 50 percent or above creates a rebuttable presumption of dominance,[40] while shares below 40 percent are "not likely" to sustain dominance.[41] The threshold within US antitrust is higher: while a 90 percent share is sufficient to constitute a monopoly, a share of 65 percent is "doubtful."[42] The relative positions of rivals are also relevant.[43] The broader the underlying market – for instance, the market for all passenger taxis and other cabs within a region, as opposed to the market for intermediation services for cabs and riders – the less likely a single platform may dominate. The two-sided nature of platform activities may, however, render market shares alone less meaningful.[44]

While market shares give a picture of existing competition, competitive constraints sufficient to deny dominance may arise from credible threats of expansion by current competitors or entry by new ones, or countervailing buyer power.[45] Since capacity constraints are unlikely given the digital context, expansion might involve the launch of an existing platform in new markets: for instance, Lyft's claimed plans to expand beyond the United States. New entry involves constructing a platform from scratch. Though digital in nature, the most innovative and thus disruptive aspect of many sharing economy platforms is their novel business model as opposed to cutting-edge technology. In contrast to earlier cases like *Microsoft*,[46] where rivals argued that access to the dominant firm's technological "know-how" was indispensable to compete, here the technology at issue appears to be rarely so difficult to replicate or essential to successful participation. A different conclusion might be reached, however, if a platform benefits from significant data collection and associated learning effects related to consumer preferences.[47] Nevertheless, arguably it is relatively straightforward for potential entrants to build a new platform that largely replicates the functions of and thus competes with existing platforms; whereas difficulties may be more likely to arise in persuading users to switch to competing platforms.

Commentators accordingly focus on the potential for sharing economy platforms to generate network effects, so that the utility of individual users increases as others join.[48] Although considered a positive externality, network effects might generate market power for favored platforms and thus dominance, which could diminish consumer welfare in the longer term.[49] The presence of network effects played an important role in persuading the Commission that Google, for instance, held a dominant position in its recent infringement decision.[50] It would be foolhardy to assume, however, that the mere existence of network effects equals dominance.[51] In particular, switching costs between sharing economy platforms appear to be comparatively low, although not zero.[52] There is anecdotal evidence of "backlash" against some prominent platforms – most notably Uber – which suggests that any market power generated

[39] *Market Definition Notice, supra* note 15, at paras. 53–55.
[40] C-62/86 *AKZO* EU:C:1991:286, para. 60.
[41] *Enforcement Priorities, supra* note 11, at para. 14.
[42] *United States v. Aluminum Co. of America*, 148 F.2d 416, 424 (2d Cir. 1945).
[43] *Enforcement Priorities, supra* note 11, at para. 13.
[44] Lougher and Kalmanowicz, *supra* note 8, at 97.
[45] *Enforcement Priorities, supra* note 11, at para. 12.
[46] T-201/04 *Microsoft* EU:T:2007:289.
[47] Lougher and Kalmanowicz, *supra* note 8, at 96.
[48] King, *supra* note 8, at 730–32.
[49] King, *supra* note 8, at 731.
[50] Commission, *Antitrust: Commission Fines Google €2.42 Billion for Abusing Dominance as Search Engine by Giving Illegal Advantage to Own Comparison Shopping Service*, June 27, 2017.
[51] OECD, *The Digital Economy* 8–9 (2012).
[52] Demary, *supra* note 36, at 11.

in the sharing economy may be relatively volatile.[53] Multi-homing, whereby suppliers and/or users participate in more than one platform, similarly lessens the ability of platforms to exercise market power,[54] amounting to a form of countervailing buyer power.[55] Moreover, the presence of network effects is considered less problematic in two-sided markets, insofar as interdependence between suppliers and customers further curtails the power of platforms.[56] Even with the narrowest market definition possible, skepticism has accordingly been expressed about whether dominance is likely to arise in the sharing economy.[57]

It is worth noting, however, an apparent incipient trend toward merger of platform economy firms with more traditional bricks-and-mortar enterprises, such as the combination of Amazon/Whole Foods.[58] The 2017 acquisition of "odd job" platform TaskRabbit by retailer IKEA presents a prominent example in the context of the sharing economy.[59] Even absent horizontal overlaps, such consolidation has the potential to increase market power in digital segments where vertical or conglomerate effects arise.[60] Additionally, the presence of dominance in a non-digital segment may be sufficient to trigger scrutiny of the merged entity's activities within the sharing economy, insofar as dominance and abuse may occur in distinct markets.[61]

Where dominance exists, Article 102 becomes potentially applicable, but is not automatically breached.[62] Instead, the provision prohibits only *abuse* of market power, meaning conduct "which, through recourse to methods different from those which condition normal competition … has the effect of hindering the maintenance of the degree of competition still existing in the market or the growth of that competition."[63] It is at this juncture that our assessment becomes more speculative.

Article 102 prohibits two categories of abuse: exploitative and exclusionary activity. Exploitative abuses arise where dominant firms take advantage of consumers directly, for instance through excessively high prices. Despite being the "textbook" example of monopoly behavior, antitrust enforcement against exploitative behavior has long been disfavored within the EU, albeit with recent signs of greater receptiveness.[64] Though claims of "exploitation" in a different sense are not uncommon in relation to sharing economy platforms, particularly involving the gig economy,[65] exploitative theories of antitrust harm are unlikely to find traction. First, in many business models, the platform does not set the underlying prices charged by providers to

---

[53] See, e.g., Leslie Hook and Mamta Badkar, *Lyft Downloads Surpass Uber on Anti-Trump Backlash*, Fin. Times, Jan. 31, 2017, www.ft.com/content/4d3e0ac2-e73c-11e6-967b-c88452263daf.

[54] King, *supra* note 8, at 732.

[55] FTC, *supra* note 2, at 26.

[56] Lougher and Kalmanowicz, *supra* note 8, at 98.

[57] FTC, *supra* note 2, at 26–28.

[58] *See* Statement of FTC's Acting Director of the Bureau of Competition on the Agency's Review of Amazon.com, Inc.'s Acquisition of Whole Foods Market Inc., published Aug. 23, 2017.

[59] See, e.g., Tiffany Hsu, *Ikea Enters 'Gig Economy' by Acquiring TaskRabbit*, NY Times, Sept. 28, 2017, www.nytimes .com/2017/09/28/business/ikea-taskrabbit.html.

[60] See, e.g., European Commission, *Guidelines on the Assessment of Non-Horizontal Mergers under the Council Regulation on the Control of Concentrations Between Undertakings* (OJ C265/6, 18.10.2008).

[61] Case T-83/91 *Tetra Pak v. Commission* EU:T:1994:246.

[62] *Michelin (I)*, *supra* note 13, at para. 10.

[63] *Hoffmann-La Roche*, *supra* note 12, at para. 91.

[64] Speech of Commissioner Vestager, *Protecting Consumers from Exploitation*, Chillin' Competition Conference, Brussels, Nov. 21, 2016.

[65] Satyajit Das, *The Sharing Economy Creates a Dickensian World for Workers – It Masks a Dark Problem in the Labour Market*, The Independent, Feb. 12, 2017, www.independent.co.uk/voices/sharing-economy-gig-economy-uber-airbnb-workers-rights-a7575856.html.

consumers, but rather charges a fixed or percentage rate of commission to either or both – a less compelling prospect for any excessive pricing claim.

Second, the nature of the sharing economy means that final consumers are likely both to be comparatively price sensitive, and to have relatively close substitutes available – whether inside or outside the sharing economy – should the dominant undertaking engage in, for instance, price-gouging. Indeed, it might even be argued that the sharing economy is precisely the sort of market – free from regulatory and other barriers to open competition – where high prices are unproblematic insofar as such markets "should, in principle, be able to self-correct in the short to medium term."[66] Even the most notorious example of deliberate high pricing – namely, Uber's surge-pricing model – is unlikely to amount to an excessive price as it arguably represents precisely the "competitive" price:[67] the price which matches supply with demand most effect-ively.[68] Moreover, the inherently sporadic nature of surge-pricing, which affects only a subset of journeys, may struggle to satisfy the recently articulated requirement that excessive pricing practices must be both "significant and persistent" – as opposed to "temporary or episodic" – to constitute an abuse of dominance.[69]

An interesting counter-suggestion, however, is that the *indirect* cost of services within the digital economy – particularly the surrender of valuable personal data – comprises a form of excessive pricing.[70] A theoretical possibility that might apply to certain sharing economy business models, this concept arguably received a boost with recognition in recent merger practice that privacy-related concerns are a factor of quality.[71] Yet it remains a speculative and, arguably, dubious theory of harm.

For service providers, an excessive price involves, in effect, the platform operator taking an unfair cut of earnings via the platform. Although this raises broader social concerns where providers occupy a position of vulnerability, the antitrust implications are unclear. The two-sided nature of intermediation markets may legitimate a higher price for providers where this balances demand between both sides of the platform[72] – and, moreover, may benefit final con-sumers directly through lower prices. Moreover, particularly where significant network effects exist, it may be challenging to establish that the price is excessive insofar as it "bears no reason-able relationship to the economic value of the product supplied":[73] given the gains arising from association with a "must-use" platform, it may be difficult to conclude that the relationship between benefit conferred and consideration demanded is disproportionate.[74]

Turning to exclusionary abuses, these concern dominant firm conduct which "impair[s] effective competition by foreclosing their competitors in an anti-competitive way, thus having an adverse impact on consumer welfare."[75] Various categories of abuse are established, including predatory pricing, exclusive dealing, refusals to deal, and tying/bundling – although as the

---

[66] Opinion in C-177/16 *Autortiesību un komunicēšanās konsultāciju aģentūra – Latvijas Autoru apvienība* EU:C:2017:286, para. 48.

[67] *Id.* at paras. 17 & 106.

[68] King, *supra* note 8, at 731; Hatzopoulos and Roma, *supra* note 37, at 111–12.

[69] C-177/16 *Autortiesību un komunicēšanās konsultāciju aģentūra – Latvijas Autoru apvienība* EU:C:2017:689, paras. 56 & 61.

[70] Michal Gal and Daniel L. Rubinfeld, *The Hidden Costs of Free Goods: Implications for Antitrust Enforcement*, 80 Antitrust L.J. 521 (2016).

[71] Case M-8124 – *Microsoft/LinkedIn* (Dec. 6, 2016).

[72] King, *supra* note 8, at 731–32.

[73] *United Brands, supra* note 14, at para. 250.

[74] Opinion in C-52/07 *Kanal 5* EU:C:2008:491, para. 39; also FTC, *supra* note 2, at 27.

[75] *Enforcement Priorities, supra* note 11, at para. 19.

Google case illustrated, the categories of prohibited behavior are not fixed rigidly.[76] Indeed, arguably in that instance the digital context both prompted and merited the ambitious theory of harm pursued, a perspective that may have ramifications for application of Article 102 within the sharing economy.

Several prospective abuses have been noted. Single homing obligations might amount to exclusive dealing, denying rival platforms a sufficient user base to generate the necessary economies of scale.[77] Other contracts that reference rivals, such as "most-favored-nation" clauses, might similarly have the effect of foreclosing competition.[78] Platforms might use algorithms and data collection to raise rivals' costs; for instance, by identifying providers that multi-home and offering them inducements to favor the dominant platform.[79] Where a platform acquires "essential facility" status – a possibility, though not a likelihood – the operator may be required to provide access to intermediation on reasonable terms.[80] More controversial would be scenarios where rival intermediaries seek to gain access to aspects of the platform infrastructure,[81] perhaps successful technology or data mined from users.[82] Conversely, the principal objection to sharing economy platforms for traditional providers – their propensity to undercut on price – is unlikely to find purchase as a theory of harm. While sustained *below*-cost pricing is illegal,[83] taking advantage of a lower cost base emphatically is not. Moreover, in many instances the bulk of any final purchase price is determined by service providers. Even if the latter is below some nominal measure of the provider's cost, it may be difficult to attribute "predatory" behavior to the platform operator.

Finally, in the perhaps unlikely event that *prima facie* abusive conduct is established, it remains open to defendants to justify their behavior by demonstrating the conduct is objectively necessary to achieve a legitimate aim or produces efficiencies which outweigh anticompetitive effects.[84] The mere fact, however, that an undertaking seeks to "meet competition" (with the subtext, perhaps, of defeating such competition) is not a valid justification:[85] to the extent that a platform acquires dominance, its "special responsibility"[86] should, in theory, inhibit it from engaging in the sort of aggressively competitive behavior that has marked the sharing economy to date.

II COORDINATED ANTICOMPETITIVE CONDUCT

Non-dominant firms fall within antitrust regulation only where they engage in anticompetitive coordination. The relevant EU law provision is Article 101(1), prohibiting "all agreements between undertakings, decisions by associations of undertakings and concerted practices … which have as their object or effect the prevention, restriction or distortion of competition." An exemption is nonetheless provided by Article 101(3) for arrangements fulfilling various

---

[76] *See id.*

[77] King, *supra* note 8, at 732.

[78] *Id.* at 733; *see generally* Pinar Akman *A Competition Law Assessment of Platform Most-Favoured-Customer Clauses*, 12 J. Competition L. & Econ. 781, 823–31 (2016).

[79] *See e.g.,* Herrera Anchustegui and Julian Nowag, *How the Uber & Lyft Case Provides an Impetus to Re-Examine Buyer Power in the World of Big Data and Algorithms*, LundComp Working Paper No.01/2017.

[80] Lougher and Kalmanowicz, *supra* note 8, at 100.

[81] An analogy can be drawn with C-418/01 *IMS Health* EU:C:2004:257.

[82] Lougher and Kalmanowicz, *supra* note 8, at 100.

[83] C-202/07 *France Telecom* EU:C:2009:214.

[84] *Enforcement Priorities, supra* note 11, at paras. 28–31.

[85] *France Telecom, supra* note 83.

[86] *See supra* note 13.

efficiency-focused criteria. The equivalent prohibition under US law is §1, Sherman Act, similarly proscribing "[e]very contract, combination in the form of trust or otherwise, or conspiracy, in restraint of trade."

Cartels are well recognized as the "supreme evil" of antitrust.[87] Should a hard-core cartel arise within a sharing economy market – involving, for instance, price-fixing or market-sharing between ostensibly independent platform intermediaries – the categorical rule against cartels is unlikely to have distinctive application. It seems uncontroversial that such behavior would breach Article 101(1) without recourse to Article 101(3), and constitute a *per se* violation of §1, Sherman Act. Outside the speculative realm of cartels arising *between* discrete sharing economy operators, how might anticompetitive coordination arise *within* sharing economy business models? Three possibilities arise: sharing economy platforms as a conduit for hub-and-spoke cartel activity; a means to effect non-cartel horizontal coordination; and a source of vertical restraints.

The central premise of each is dependent upon conceptualizing platforms as comprising "agreements between undertakings" within Article 101(1). The concept of an undertaking encompasses "every entity engaged in an economic activity,"[88] meaning "any activity consisting in offering goods and services on a given market."[89] As final consumers cannot constitute undertakings, our focus is the relationship between platforms and service providers. A defining feature of the sharing economy is that it drastically reduces the minimum efficient size of the "firm," which can become less than a single person (e.g. the homeowner who rents a room occasionally).[90] Yet the mere fact that a provider is a single individual, perhaps working part-time, is insufficient to preclude characterization as an undertaking.[91] Indeed, it is unnecessary that the entity concerned charges fees: "[t]he basic test is … whether the entity in question is engaged in an activity which could, at least in principle, be carried on by a private undertaking in order to make profits."[92] This expansive criterion suggests that even "true" sharing might fall within the definition of economic activity where such activities compete with those of for-profit providers.

Two exceptions present themselves. The first is where service providers constitute "agents" of the platform (or "principal"), so agent and principal comprise a single undertaking.[93] EU law lays down a demanding test for agency, however, requiring the agent to incur no more than a negligible proportion of the financial and commercial risks of a business.[94] Applying this criterion to most sharing economy businesses, where service providers are effectively in business for their own benefit – albeit often presenting to consumers as a component of the platform – it seems unlikely that genuine agency will arise.

The second involves providers that, though nominally independent contractors, occupy positions of such vulnerability, subservience, and proximity to the platform that they are effectively "false self-employed."[95] Such a claim arose in *FNV*, where the Court of Justice accepted that a service provider loses its status as an undertaking, "if he does not determine independently his own conduct on the market, but is entirely dependent on his principal … and operates as an auxiliary within the principal's undertaking."[96] Regardless of the provider's status under

---

[87] *Verizon Communications* v. *Trinko*, 540 U.S. 398 (2004).

[88] C-41/90 *Höfner* EU:C:1991:161, para. 21.

[89] C-218/00 *Cisal* EU:C:2002:36, para. 23.

[90] Stallibrass and Fingleton, *supra* note 2, at 414.

[91] C-413/13 *FNV Kunsten Informatie en Media* EU:C:2014:2411, para. 27.

[92] Opinion in C-67/96 *Albany* EU:C:1999:430, para. 311.

[93] C-217/05 *CEEES* EU:C:2006:784, paras. 38–42.

[94] *Id.* at para. 46.

[95] *FNV*, *supra* note 91, at para. 31.

[96] *Id.* at para. 33.

national law, where any ostensible independence is "merely notional," he cannot constitute a separate undertaking.[97] Equivalent arguments have been raised in other contexts relating to the gig economy, including efforts to subject Uber to employment protection legislation.[98] The core question, however, is whether providers enjoy greater independence and flexibility than employees in an equivalent role[99] – a relatively low threshold that could bring large swathes of the sharing economy within Article 101.

If providers constitute undertakings, any restrictive coordination potentially infringes Article 101. Here, it is useful to consider the approaches discussed in *Meyer v. Kalanick*,[100] a US antitrust lawsuit in which it was alleged that Uber and its drivers have breached §1, Sherman Act through a *horizontal* conspiracy regarding Uber's "surge-pricing" feature, alongside *vertical* price restraints akin to resale price maintenance (RPM).

The first and most egregious way a platform might generate anticompetitive coordination is as a hub-and-spoke mechanism for cartel coordination among providers. Hub-and-spoke cartels involve, broadly, horizontal collusion effected indirectly between competitors through flows of information via a common trading partner.[101] Under this theory of harm, the platform functions as "cartel facilitator,"[102] so that ostensibly vertical contacts comprise, in reality, horizontal concertation between rival providers. An example is *Apple E-Books*, where a series of vertical negotiations between an online platform operator and book publishers were found to have horizontal implications, insofar as the platform operator kept each publisher informed of the status of negotiations with rivals.[103] It is unnecessary for providers to agree precise terms of coordination; a concerted practice is sufficient, namely where undertakings knowingly substitute practical cooperation for the risks of competition.[104]

Three recent cases assist in developing this theory. In *ETURAS*,[105] a travel-booking platform informed travel agencies by email of a platform-wide policy to reduce maximum retail discounts. The Court confirmed that mere receipt of the message could demonstrate horizontal concertation where: the agencies were aware of its contents and could be regarded as having tacitly assented; they had subsequently engaged in anticompetitive conduct; and a relationship of cause and effect could be established.[106] Absent tacit assent, however, mere involvement in the platform was insufficient to establish coordination, which had to be demonstrated by other evidence.[107] Accordingly, participation in an online platform that imposes restrictions intended to suppress competition between providers can constitute indirect coordination between providers, but only where the latter knew of the restriction and acted accordingly. The Court moreover emphasized the highly fact-specific nature of this assessment.

---

[97] *Id.* at para. 35.

[98] *Uber Spain* Opinion, *supra* note 26, at para. 54.

[99] *FNV*, *supra* note 91, at para. 37.

[100] No. 1:2015cv09796, Doc.37, Motion to Dismiss (S.D.N.Y. 2016). On foot of arguments that the plaintiff is bound to resolve its claims via arbitration under Uber's terms and conditions of service, the case has been remanded back to the district court to determine whether Uber waived its right to compel arbitration by engaging in the initial litigation: *see Meyer v. Uber Technologies, Inc.*, No. 16–2750 (2d Cir. 2017), judgment of Aug. 17, 2017.

[101] Okeoghene Odudu, *Indirect Information Exchange: The Constituent Elements of Hub and Spoke Collusion*, 7 Euro. Competition J. 205 (2011).

[102] Opinion in C-74/14 *ETURAS* EU:C:2015:493, para. 42.

[103] Case COMP/AT.39847 – E-Books (OJ C73/17, 13.3.2013).

[104] C-8/08 *T-Mobile* EU:C:2009:343, para. 26.

[105] C-74/14 *ETURAS* EU:C:2016:42.

[106] *Id.*, paras. 42 & 44.

[107] *Id.*, para.45.

Within the sharing economy, however, such logic fails to capture the significant power imbalance between typically small, amateur service providers and often large, profitable platforms. Vertical agreements are generally contracts of adhesion, the terms of which providers have little ability to influence. Assessing coordination primarily from the standpoint of ostensible horizontal rivals therefore risks misunderstanding market dynamics. In *ETURAS*, Advocate General Szpunar argued that where an illicit initiative is communicated by a third party – for instance, a platform operator – the resulting restriction might be attributable solely to the unilateral behavior of that undertaking where both the initiative and its implementation are attributable to the third party acting in its autonomous interest.[108] Instead, such conduct ought to be examined as a vertical restraint, or under Article 102.

This approach receives support in *VM Remonts*, involving bid-rigging effected through an independent consultant who prepared tender submissions on behalf of several undertakings, sharing commercially sensitive information in doing so. The Court held that a competitor could not be found to have participated in horizontal coordination if it was wholly unaware that the consultant would use its information in this manner. Instead, it was necessary to demonstrate either that the defendant had directed the consultant to act anticompetitively, that it knew of ongoing anticompetitive conduct and intended to contribute to the unlawful outcome, or that it could have reasonably foreseen such conduct and was prepared to take the risk.[109] Accordingly, horizontal cooperation through a vertical conduit requires awareness and acceptance by service providers of the fact that they are, in effect, coordinating with competitors. Applied to sharing economy platforms, this implies that providers must do more than simply sign up to terms and conditions of use imposed by operators. Establishing coordination requires understanding and tacit consent to the fact that such terms and conditions extend beyond the relationship with the platform operator; additionally, there should be evidence of awareness of the ramifications for relations with competing providers.

Even where *horizontal* coordination is established, the *vertical* dimension remains relevant. Where the platform operator functions as cartel facilitator, even if not active on the market concerned, it can be held to have participated in the cartel and thus liable under Article 101(1).[110] To do so, it is necessary to establish that the operator was aware of the downstream cartel activity or could have reasonably foreseen the possibility, and that it intended to contribute to the realization of the anticompetitive plan.[111] In *AC-Treuhand*, this was satisfied where the defendant, with full knowledge, provided administrative services – organizing meetings, collecting data – "the very purpose" of which were to further the cartel.[112] In *YIRD*, the Commission similarly found facilitation by a broker which acted as the conduit by which banks engaged in horizontal manipulation of financial benchmarks.[113] Thus, if a platform operator knowingly facilitates anticompetitive horizontal coordination, it is liable as if it itself participated in the cartel.

The preceding analysis was premised on the assumption that coordination discloses some restriction of competition. Article 101(1), like §1, Sherman Act, emphatically does not catch all contractual restrictions; instead, it is necessary to demonstrate that the coordination has either the object or effect of restricting competition.

---

[108] Opinion in *ETURAS*, *supra* note 105, at para. 73.
[109] C-542/14 *VM Remonts* EU:C:2016:578, paras. 30–33.
[110] C-194/14 *AC-Treuhand* EU:C:2015:717.
[111] *Id.*, para. 30.
[112] *Id.*, paras. 37–38.
[113] Case AT.39861–*Yen Interest Rate Derivatives* (C(2015)432 final).

"Object" restrictions encompass forms of coordination that "reveal a sufficient degree of harm to competition that it may be found that there is no need to examine their effects."[114] Horizontal price-fixing or market-sharing are paradigmatic examples;[115] for instance, a price-fixing conspiracy is alleged in *Meyer*. A distinction must be made, however, between cartel and non-cartel coordination, as not every horizontal restraint constitutes a cartel as such. Cartels almost invariably occur in secret; generate no countervailing efficiencies; and are intended solely to exploit consumers. Cartels can arise in the context of otherwise legitimate coordination, like participation in a platform; but are typically considered separately from beneficial cooperation that accompanies hard-core anticompetitive behavior.[116] Evidence that a platform functions as a cartel facilitation mechanism – alleged in *ETURAS*, for instance – would almost inevitably be condemned under both Article 101 and §1, Sherman Act.

Yet platforms may involve horizontal cooperation, and even limitations of competition, that are not unambiguously anticompetitive. Where a restraint – whether concerning prices, services provided, or customers served – is indispensable or highly advantageous to the functioning of a platform, Article 101 provides ways to legitimate such coordination.

First, a distinction is drawn between mere restrictions of competition and coordination that harms competition, with only the latter suitable for peremptory prohibition as object restrictions.[117] Second, while such conduct may nonetheless have restrictive effect, this requires a nuanced counterfactual assessment of coordination in its economic and legal context.[118] Here, the two-sided nature of sharing economy markets is relevant. The fact that coordination generates benefits for one side of a multisided platform does not preclude application of Article 101(1) where disproportionate disadvantages arise on the other.[119] Yet, against this is the argument that, absent coordination, the product concerned might not exist, meaning that competition (and consumer welfare) overall would reduce.[120] Third, the ancillary restraints doctrine exempts individual restraints within otherwise pro-competitive arrangements, where the restrictive clause is objectively necessary to implement the overall commercial activity.[121] A demanding test is applied, however: it must be impossible to dissociate the restriction from the overall coordination or carry on the activity in its absence, while the restriction must be proportionate to the pro-competitive objectives.[122] Finally, *prima facie* restrictive coordination might be saved by countervailing efficiencies under Article 101(3). Defendants must demonstrate that four cumulative criteria are satisfied, including measureable economic benefits, a fair share of which accrue to consumers.[123] Given the significant welfare-enhancing effects of the development of the sharing economy, there is a clear case for an "affirmative" application of Article 101(3).[124]

Beyond the uncertain possibility of horizontal coordination, platform models comprise numerous vertical agreements potentially within Article 101. Although the object/effects

---

[114] C-67/13 *CB* EU:C:2014:2204, para. 49.

[115] *Id.*, para. 51.

[116] *See, e.g.*, COMP/39.579 – *Consumer Detergents* (OJ C193/14, 2.7.2011).

[117] *CB, supra* note 114, at paras. 69–75.

[118] C-345/14 *Maxima* EU:C:2015:784, para. 26.

[119] C-382/12 *MasterCard* EU:C:2014:2201.

[120] For instance, *Asda* v. *MasterCard* [2017] EWHC 93 (Comm).

[121] *MasterCard, supra* note 119, at paras. 89–90.

[122] *Id.* at paras. 90–91.

[123] *Guidelines on the Application of Article 81(3) of the Treaty*, Commission (OJ C101/97, 27.4.2004).

[124] David Bailey, *Reinvigorating the Role of Article 101(3) under Regulation 1/2003*, 81 Antitrust L.J. 111 (2016).

distinction holds,[125] object restraints are found less readily.[126] The principal object restriction of relevance is RPM, which might arise where a platform operator determines prices charged by service providers, at least where providers cannot depart from and/or dip below the platform price.[127] The conceptual objection to construing platform-determined prices as RPM concerns the two-sided nature of platforms: unlike conventional scenarios whereby for example a supplier exercises control over prices for products it manufactures, platform operators do not produce services supplied via platforms, meaning no resale is involved. Instead, they merely set terms and conditions for access to intermediation services, which may involve standardized pricing. Yet this argument encounters difficulty given the resolute language of *Binon*, which held that "provisions which fix the prices to be observed in contracts with third parties constitute, of themselves, a restriction of competition."[128] This formulation renders suspect any vertical agreement that determines the price for consumers, regardless of whether the latter transaction occurs with the platform or the provider directly. The reflexive object approach to RPM has received sustained criticism, while *Maxima* casts doubt on whether vertical price-fixing should be treated as equivalent to its horizontal counterpart.[129] *Prima facie* restrictive RPM might nonetheless be exempted under Article 101(3), although efficiency justifications foreseen by the Commission link acceptability to time-limited application.[130]

Outside the "object box," platform models encounter difficulty where the cumulative effect of vertical agreements is an appreciable contribution to foreclosure of a relevant market, whether an upstream market for intermediation or downstream market for the service itself.[131] The key to any successful sharing economy platform is a "thick" market involving many competing providers,[132] necessitating numerous parallel agreements with providers. Consequently, many vertical restraints commonplace in other markets – exclusive customer allocation, exclusive supply or appointment of a single or limited number of providers in a specific territory – are unlikely to arise as they make little sense. Yet, where platforms acquire market power, even if remaining below the level required for dominance,[133] potentially problematic restraints can be identified. A single homing obligation resembles single branding, with the potential to foreclose competition from competing platforms or soften competition between providers on the same platform.[134] Tying requirements, which arise where providers who purchase one product (e.g. intermediation) must purchase another (e.g. insurance), might function as single branding of the tied product.[135] Finally, most-favored nation clauses have potentially restrictive effect under Article 101(1) alongside Article 102.[136] To hold vertical restraints restrictive by effect, it is nevertheless necessary to conduct a comprehensive counterfactual analysis of the agreements in their market context, with, again, the possibility of saving arrangements under the ancillary restraints doctrine or Article 101(3).

---

[125] C-56/64 *Consten and Grundig* EU:C:1966:41.
[126] *Maxima, supra* note 118, at para. 21.
[127] *Guidelines on Vertical Restraints*, Commission (OJ C130/1, 19.5.2010), para.223.
[128] 243/83 *Binon* EU:C:1985:284, para. 44.
[129] *Maxima, supra* note 119, at paras. 19–21.
[130] *Guidelines on Vertical Restraints, supra* note 129, at para. 225.
[131] *Maxima, supra* note 119, at paras. 25–31.
[132] FTC, *supra* note 2, at 20.
[133] *Guidelines on Vertical Restraints, supra* note 129, at para. 6.
[134] *Id.* at para. 130.
[135] *Id.* at para. 214.
[136] King, *supra* note 8, at 732–33.

III THE LIMITS OF ANTITRUST IN THE SHARING ECONOMY

The preceding discussion demonstrated that, although antitrust can conceivably be applied to the market behavior of entities within the sharing economy, whether singly or in concert, many of the ostensible competition problems that might arise are not well suited to scrutiny and supervision from this perspective. In the final section, we consider this apparent paradox: if the sharing economy presents multiple examples of allegedly "unfair" competitive practices, why is this not a "competition issue" in antitrust terms?

The positive contribution of the development of the sharing economy toward overall competition and consumer welfare is well recognized.[137] Yet its emergence has generated negative impacts for two sets of players in particular: established providers displaced by innovative entrants; and certain categories of new providers vulnerable to alleged exploitation by powerful platform intermediaries. Moreover, these negative impacts are, at least in part, directly attributable to the success of sharing economy platforms as two-sided business models: attracting large numbers of customers from conventional providers, while simultaneously attracting high numbers of service providers, each with little bargaining power. Yet although claims of unfair competition often come with a distinctly human face – the taxi driver who has lost their livelihood, the cycle-courier earning less than minimum wage – "[n]ot every case of unfairness is a matter for competition law."[138] From an antitrust perspective such ostensibly negative results may nonetheless be compatible as "aggressive, yet healthy and permissible, competition."[139] Thus, "protection under EU competition rules is afforded to the competitive process as such, and not, for example, to competitors … competition law aims, in the final analysis, to enhance efficiency."[140]

Our discussion thus far has identified various means by which the sharing economy succeeds in enhancing efficiency in a manner consistent with both letter and spirit of competition law. From the outset, we noted that a core feature of the sharing economy is increased utilization of potentially valuable productive capacity that might otherwise be lost to society. By providing the means to realize this productive potential and include its benefits within the wider economy, the sharing economy at its most basic reduces societal waste.[141] Moreover, because the sharing economy – at least in theory – is premised upon inclusion of existing assets that represent sunk costs (e.g. the drill purchased for sporadic occasions of DIY), fixed costs attributable to alternative uses (e.g. the spare bedroom within an apartment rented primarily as a private home), or where there are limited opportunity costs (e.g. the Uber driver who would otherwise receive nothing for their free time), service providers may be both able and willing to offer services to consumers at lower prices than comparable conventional providers, who must contend with higher overheads and/or envisage a higher rate of remuneration or return on capital employed. From a consumer welfare perspective, particularly measured in terms of allocative efficiency, this is highly beneficial: lower prices, and greater consumer choice. It can readily be seen how this market model might be deemed "unfair" by providers, whether within or without the sharing economy, who would ideally wish to earn more for their efforts and/or avoid being undercut by rivals with lower cost bases. Yet such objections are difficult to envisage as a competition problem in the antitrust

---

[137] *See, e.g.*, Hatzopoulos and Roma, *supra* note 37, at 109.

[138] Speech of Commissioner Vestager, "Setting Priorities in Antitrust," GCLC, Brussels, Feb. 1, 2016.

[139] Opinion in C-413/14 *Intel*, EU:C:2016:788, para. 41.

[140] *Id.*

[141] Malthe Mikkel Munkøe, *Regulating the European Sharing Economy: State of Play and Challenges*, 52 Intereconomics 38, 39 (2017).

sense, even if stemming directly from increased competition: it is long established that so-called "ruinous competition" is not a concern of antitrust as such.[142]

More complicated, though for many commentators warranting a similar conclusion, is the question of whether asymmetric regulatory burdens might constitute an unfair advantage that merits antitrust scrutiny. Many critics of the sharing economy argue that its competitive advantage thus arises primarily, not from enhanced efficiency, but by exploiting loopholes to avoid conventional regulation:[143] from zoning laws that restrict hoteliers to expensive commercial areas, or taxicab regulations that impose high barriers to entry and prevent drivers from engaging in price competition, to more general requirements regarding liability insurance or business taxation.[144] The key distinction between this and the preceding category of concerns is that, whereas the desire to avoid competitive pressures that eat into an undertaking's profit is predominantly a *private* interest, the sorts of regulation that the sharing economy endeavors to circumvent has typically been enacted in the broader *public* interest. Two sets of objections to regulatory asymmetry may thus be raised. First, there is concern that the public policy goals that underlie much conventional regulation – whether public safety, consumer protection, non-discrimination, or environmental protection – receive insufficient protection within the sharing economy. Second, to the extent that such regulation effectively handicaps regulated entities by constraining market freedom and/or increasing costs, there may be an equality argument regarding differential state-imposed burdens on business.

The answer in many instances to the first concern is that there is less need for such top-down regulation, as the innovative business models and technologies that underpin sharing economy platforms can effectively address and protect public interest goals, providing *business* (as opposed to *regulatory*) solutions to market failure.[145] In particular, platforms rely heavily on better information provision and reputation systems, which abrogate much need for state control.[146] Yet this answer is not entirely adequate, partly because there is evidence that self-regulation is insufficient to provide effective protection for all consumers,[147] and partly because it relates only to a subset of regulatory controls, typically intended to enhance consumer protection in the face of information asymmetries.[148] Broader concerns regarding the extent to which sharing economy business models may fit with – or disrupt – regulation in the fields of labor law and taxation, for instance, remain unaddressed. Indeed, it would generally be contrary to the interests of sharing economy platforms and/or service providers to enhance obligations in these fields voluntarily, insofar as this would entail higher costs without increasing the attractiveness of the platform from a consumer perspective.

This leads to the second concern identified, in effect a fairness argument that "like traders should be treated alike" in terms of regulatory burdens, whereas at present, there is no level playing field.[149] As the competitive – and disruptive – potential of sharing economy platforms is realized, regulators face a dilemma: to extend existing regulation to new entrants in circumstances where the underlying need and thus justification for regulatory control is weaker, or to revise and pare

---

[142] *US v. Socony-Vacuum*, 310 U.S. 150 (1940).

[143] Horton and Zeckhauser, *supra* note 1, at 2.

[144] Sofia Ranchordas, *Does Sharing Mean Caring? Regulating Innovation in the Sharing Economy*, 16 Minn. J. L., Sci. & Tech. 413 (2015).

[145] Stallibrass and Fingleton, *supra* note 2, at 417.

[146] *Id.* at 417.

[147] *Id.* at 418–19; *see also* Michèle Finck, *Digital Regulation: Designing a Supranational Legal Framework for the Platform Economy*, LSE Law, Society and Economy Working Papers 15/2017, 12–15.

[148] Stallibrass and Fingleton, *supra* note 2, at 418.

[149] Lougher and Kalmanowicz, *supra* note 8, at 101.

back existing regimes with the attendant loss of supervisory power over potentially problematic market behavior. Transport for London (TfL)'s consultation on the future of private hire regulation following Uber's market entry presents an example in point. Here, contentious plans to extend existing regulation that sought, in effect, to eliminate Uber's competitive advantage over highly regulated black cabs were significantly altered in the face of concerns regarding protectionism, the stifling of competition and innovation, and ultimately, a fear that consumers would lose out.[150] Indeed, as the Competition & Markets Authority identified, many of the proposed regulations were purportedly necessary to solve potential market failures already addressed by the Uber platform (e.g. a five-minute wait requirement to ensure that customers take the correct vehicle), while others might have the counterintuitive effect of increasing Uber's existing market power (e.g. a prohibition on multi-homing by drivers).[151] Competition policy advocates are thus at pains to emphasize that an unthinking leveling-*up* of regulatory burdens is likely to have significant negative impacts for consumers, who will see access to services reduced or made more expensive.[152]

What both sets of concerns have in common, however, is that neither involves what is known within US jurisprudence as "antitrust injury,"[153] namely harm that follows a lessening of competition attributable to anticompetitive private behavior. This is not to suggest that concerns regarding, for instance, discrimination in accessing services or exploitation of vulnerable providers are invalid or of lesser priority; yet they are not such to engage competition law. Even the most visceral complaint regarding the asymmetric impact of regulation – that it makes it difficult if not impossible for conventional regulators to compete effectively – is unlikely to disclose *antitrust* injury: on the one hand, it stems primarily from state as opposed to private action; on the other, the mere fact of exit by some participants is considered unproblematic unless it strengthens the market power of remaining actors.[154]

Socially undesirable outcomes should, of course, attract the attention of regulators and other policymakers with a view to ensuring that the broader impacts of the emergence of the sharing economy are compatible with established public policy norms.[155] Here, again, the fate of Uber in London is instructive. In September 2017, TfL declined to renew Uber's private hire operator license on the basis that the company had demonstrated that it was not "fit and proper" to hold such a license.[156] Although presented by certain media outlets as a victory for black cabbies at the expense of their Uber-branded competitors,[157] TfL's decision was explicitly premised upon "a lack of corporate responsibility in relation to a number of issues which have potential *public safety and security* implications,"[158] such as reporting of alleged criminal offenses and use of software to evade regulatory scrutiny. Yet the high-profile popular and political backlash emphasized the extent to which the loss of Uber as a competitor would have immediate negative impacts for customers.[159] Subsequent developments suggest that a compromise – including significant

---

[150] Transport for London, *Private Hire Regulations Review. Part Two Consultation Report*, Mar. 2016.

[151] Competition & Markets Authority, *Response to Transport for London's Private Hire Regulations Proposals*, Dec. 2, 2015.

[152] Stallibrass and Fingleton, *supra* note 2, at 418.

[153] *Brunswick Corp.* v. *Pueblo Bowl-O-Mat*, 429 U.S. 477, 489 (1977).

[154] *Enforcement Priorities, supra* note 11, at para. 19.

[155] *See, e.g.,* Orly Lobel, *The Gig Economy & the Future of Employment and Labour Law*, 51 U.S.F. L. Rev. 51 (2017).

[156] TfL Press Release, *Licensing Decision on Uber London Limited*, Sept. 22, 2017.

[157] *See, e.g.,* Katrin Bennhold, *London's Uber Ban Raises Questions on Race and Immigration*, NY Times, October 2, 2017, www.nytimes.com/2017/10/02/world/europe/uber-london-cab.html.

[158] TfL, *supra* note 156 (emphasis added).

[159] *See, e.g.,* Patrick Greenfield, *Uber Licence Withdrawal Disproportionate, Says Theresa May*, The Guardian, Sept. 28, 2017, www.theguardian.com/technology/2017/sep/28/uber-licence-withdrawal-disproportionate-says-theresa-may.

concessions on its part to regulators – may be reached to allow Uber to continue competing in London in the longer term.[160]

Thus, the mere fact that competition from and within the sharing economy generates some very notable "losers," whose disadvantages moreover may raise almost existential questions about the nature of the society in which we live and work, is not an argument to attack the underlying competitive conduct from an antitrust perspective where it nonetheless delivers positive benefits for consumer welfare. Competition law is a powerful tool, but has a comparatively circumscribed scope of effective and thus legitimate application. Although the Commission now places greater emphasis on the contribution of competition enforcement toward a "fairer society," its focus even in this regard remains consumer-oriented, specifically the extent to which competitive pressures force businesses to reduce prices[161] – not, as discussed, typically a problem within the sharing economy. The issue of unfair competition in the sharing economy thus arguably represents one of the (many) acknowledged limits of antitrust; though this recognition in no way denies the possibility that more obviously *anti*competitive behavior might also occur here. It moreover calls into question the readiness of other regulatory frameworks to adapt and solve other social and economic problems as these arise in this context.

---

[160] *See, e.g.*, Julia Kollewe and Gwyn Topham, *Uber Apologizes after London Ban and Admits "We Got Things Wrong,"* The Guardian, Sept. 25, 2017, www.theguardian.com/business/2017/sep/25/uber-tfl-concerns-vows-keep-operating-london-licence.

[161] Speech of Commission Vestager, *Competition for a Fairer Society*, 10th Annual Global Antitrust Enforcement Symposium, Georgetown, Sept. 20, 2016.

8

Airbnb Usage across New York City Neighborhoods

Geographic Patterns and Regulatory Implications*

Peter Coles, Michael Egesdal, Ingrid Gould Ellen, Xiaodi Li, and Arun Sundararajan

INTRODUCTION

Over the last few years, as Airbnb and competing platforms have grown in popularity, the short-term rental market has attracted considerable attention in cities around the world. A core feature of most platform-based activity is a blurring of lines between personal and commercial: housing that was exclusively residential in the past is now a new form of mixed-use real estate. The rapid scaling of short-term rental activity that used to be informal has challenged a variety of existing regulatory structures, from zoning laws to housing codes and tax policies. Proponents and critics offer anecdotes to support their positions, and local governments around the world are adopting a range of regulatory responses. Yet all this is happening without rigorous empirical evidence about the geography of usage patterns, their evolution over time, or the relative profitability of long- and short-term rentals.

We add clarity to this discussion by providing new empirical evidence about actual Airbnb usage patterns in New York City and how they have varied across neighborhoods between 2011 and 2016. We combine unique census-tract level data obtained from Airbnb with neighborhood asking rent data from Zillow and administrative, census, and social media data on neighborhoods. We explore which neighborhoods are experiencing higher usage, and whether short-term rentals appear to be responding to a gap in the provision of hotel rooms. We also consider variation over time and space in the ratio of short-term to long-term rental prices, which offers insight into changing incentives and provides a signal of where the market is likely to grow moving forward.

Our findings reveal that as usage has grown over time, Airbnb listings have become more geographically dispersed, although centrality remains an important predictor of listing location. Controlling for centrality (as defined by proximity to Midtown Manhattan), lower-income districts have grown in popularity, and disproportionately feature "private room" listings (compared to "entire home" listings).

Saliently, short-term rental use is neither as extensive nor as profitable in New York City as many assume. Furthermore, the incentive for landlords to convert long-term to short-term rentals appears to have fallen over time as short-term rentals became less profitable relative to

* This study was conducted as an independent research collaboration between the authors. Ingrid Gould Ellen, Xiaodi Li, and Arun Sundararajan are not and have not been affiliated with Airbnb, and Peter Coles and Michael Egesdal are not and have not been affiliated with New York University. No consulting fees, research grants, or other payments have been made by Airbnb to the NYU authors, nor by NYU to the Airbnb authors.

long-term rentals over our time period. That said, we find notable variation across neighborhoods in the ratio of short-term to long-term rents. While short-term rental prices decline with distance to the Empire State Building, the distance gradient for short-term rents is considerably flatter than that for long-term rents.[1] In other words, the short-term market does not seem to place as high a premium on proximity to the city center as the long-term market, perhaps because short-term renters are less sensitive to commute times and value more residential neighborhoods. In addition, short-term rentals are most profitable relative to long-term rentals in lower-rent and upper-middle-income neighborhoods.

In sum, our empirical results show that as usage has expanded, both the benefits and burdens of the short-term rental market have begun to shift to a growing number of non-central neighborhoods. This spread, which is likely happening to different degrees in other cities, has attracted renewed attention to the short-term market, and calls for regulating short-term rentals have intensified. City leaders around the world have adopted a wide range of approaches. We conclude by reviewing these alternative regulatory responses. We consider both citywide as well as neighborhood-specific responses, like those recently enacted in Portland, Maine, or in New Orleans. A promising approach from an economic perspective is to impose fees that vary with intensity of usage. For instance, in Portland, Maine, short-term rental host fees increase with the number of units a given host seeks to register,[2] and a recent bill from Representatives in the Commonwealth of Massachusetts (H.3454) proposes taxes that vary with the intensity of usage of individual units.[3] Such varying fees may help discourage conversions of long-term rentals to short-term rentals and better internalize externalities that might rise with greater use. That said, overly customized approaches may be difficult to administer. Regulatory complexity itself should also be a criterion in choosing policy responses.

I BACKGROUND ON SHORT-TERM RENTAL EXTERNALITIES

As the short-term rental market has grown, so has discussion about its benefits and costs. Nevertheless, rigorous research is limited. On the one hand, short-term rentals create clear value for travelers and hosts, with median earnings from a typical Airbnb listing in New York City being $5,367 over the year prior to June 2017.[4] Since short-term rentals are more geographically dispersed than hotels, the benefits of tourism (which include the earnings of Airbnb hosts and increased economic activity for local businesses) are spreading to a greater number of largely residential neighborhoods where hotels are often not permitted.[5]

On the other hand, widespread short-term rental use of residential real estate may impose negative externalities on the surrounding neighborhood. Basic zoning laws, which separate personal and commercial uses, are predicated on the existence of such neighborhood-level externalities. There is considerable evidence that the condition and uses of individual buildings have spillover effects on other properties on the block or neighborhood.[6] While having a neighbor

---

[1] The Empire State Building is often used as a proxy for the business center of New York City.

[2] Randy Billings, *Portland's New Rules Limit Short-Term Rentals, Add Fees for Hosts*, The Portland Press Herald, Mar. 27, 2017, www.pressherald.com/2017/03/27/portland-enacts-rules-for-short-term-rentals/.

[3] For a review of the bill *see Bill H.3454, An Act Regulating and Insuring Shirt-Term Rentals*, Commonwealth of Massachusetts, https://malegislature.gov/Bills/190/H3454.

[4] *See* June Update on One Host, One Home: New York City, airbnbcitizen, June 9, 2017, https://new-york-city.airbnbcitizen.com/june-update-on-one-host-one-home-new-york-city/.

[5] For high-level statistics on Airbnb-generated spending *see The Economic Impacts of Home Sharing in Cities Around the World*, Airbnb, www.airbnb.com/economic-impact.

[6] John Y. Campbell, Stefano Giglio, and Parag Pathak, *Forced Sales and House Prices*, 101(5) Am. Econ. Rev. 2108–31 (2011); Ingrid Gould Ellen, Johanna Lacoe, and Claudia Ayanna Sharygin, *Do Foreclosures Cause Crime?* 74 J. Urban

rent their home on a short-term basis is hardly comparable to having a slaughterhouse or even a foreclosed home next door, it might have a modest spillover on nearby properties. Some newspaper articles have quoted nearby neighbors complaining about noise from short-term rentals,[7] but there is no rigorous research evidence showing that short-term renters are any noisier than long-term tenants. In fact, based on first principles, it is not clear whether increased short-term rental presence would decrease or increase property values.[8]

Another potential externality stems from short-term rentals increasing the number of unfamiliar faces in a building or neighborhood and simultaneously reducing the presence of long-term residents with a stake in the community, which can undermine the social fabric of residential neighborhoods. A recent review of concerns about short-term rentals submitted to the New South Wales Parliament in Sydney, Australia, finds some residents expressing general unease about the increasing presence of visitors in their neighborhoods.[9] Some research suggests that a lack of neighborhood cohesion can potentially heighten crime, as residents are less able (or less willing) to monitor their blocks and communities. For example, Sampson, Raudenbush, and Earls demonstrate a link between a neighborhood's crime level and its level of "collective efficacy," defined as willingness to intervene on behalf of social good, which is driven by social cohesion and trust.[10]

These externalities share a characteristic in common: their geographic scope is fairly limited. Airbnb guests in an apartment building impose minimal "unfamiliar faces" costs on residents in other neighborhoods. Similarly, noisy tourists staying in Greenwich Village short-term rentals will not disturb residents of other New York City neighborhoods. This localized effect of the externality suggests localized regulation may be socially efficient. For example, Cohen and Sundararajan highlight the potential regulatory role of "the increasingly ubiquitous co-op associations, condominium boards, and homeowners associations," arguing that these actors should play a role (and perhaps the central role) in mitigating the effects of such localized externalities, as "the guest-noise and strangers-in-the-building externalities are typically local."[11] Filippas and Horton go further and argue that noise and stranger externalities exist at the level of the building and thus short-term rental rules should be set and administered by individual buildings.[12] However, while noise and stranger externalities are likely to be local, they likely extend beyond buildings, to blocks and even neighborhoods, at least when usage reaches a certain level.

Perhaps the most commonly voiced concern about Airbnb and other short-term rental activity is that such activity may lead landlords to convert long-term rentals into short-term rentals, thereby reducing long-term housing supply in cities that are grappling with housing

Econ. 59–70 (2013); Jenny Schuetz, Vicki Been, and Ingrid Gould Ellen, *Neighborhood Effects of Concentrated Mortgage Foreclosures*, 17(4) J. Housing Econ. 306–19 (2008).

[7] Daniel Guttentag, *Airbnb: Disruptive Innovation and the Rise of an Informal Tourism Accommodation Sector*, 18(12) Current Issues in Tourism 1192–217 (2015).

[8] Airbnb hosting income may reduce the likelihood of mortgage defaults and increase owners' incentives to maintain their properties.

[9] Nicole Gurran and Peter Phibbs, *When Tourists Move In: How Should Urban Planners Respond to Airbnb?* 83(1) J. Am. Plan. Ass'n. 80–92 (2017).

[10] Robert J. Sampson, Stephen W. Raudenbush, and Felton Earls, *Neighborhoods and Violent Crime: A Multilevel Study of Collective Efficacy*, 277(5328) Sci. 918–24 (1997).

[11] Molly Cohen and Arun Sundararajan, *Self-Regulation and Innovation in the Peer-to-Peer Sharing Economy*, 82 U. Chi. L. Rev. Dialogue 116, 116–31 (2015).

[12] Apostolos Filippas and John Horton, *The Tragedy of your Upstairs Neighbors: Is the Negative Externality of Airbnb Internalized?* Working Paper (2017).

affordability.[13] This concern appears particularly prevalent in supply-constrained cities like New York and San Francisco, where increases in housing prices and rents have been outstripping gains in income. Unlike most of the externalities mentioned so far, this "pecuniary" externality may extend further, perhaps even to the entire local housing market.[14]

Robust evidence about the impact of Airbnb activity on long-term rents is limited. Many cities experiencing significant increases in long-term rental prices have also experienced population growth rates that far exceed their housing stock growth, which is often severely restricted due to regulatory barriers.[15] Rent control and rent stabilization laws may amplify the effects that unanticipated population growth has on the long-term rental rates of housing stock not subject to these laws. These confounding factors make it particularly challenging to isolate the effect of short-term rentals.

Prior analyses from both Airbnb and from city regulators to assess the relative importance of Airbnb hosting as a factor in housing costs have often focused on a central metric: if a host takes a long-term rental unit off the market and dedicates it to short-term rental activity, how many nights would they need to host to break even?[16] Our chapter contributes to this discussion and sheds light on the matter in New York City by providing a comprehensive analysis of the distribution and evolution of this ratio of short-term rental to long-term rental rates. Our findings for New York City suggest that the effect Airbnb hosting might have on changes in long-term rental prices through long-term housing stock being repurposed as short-term stock is likely to be minimal. Nevertheless, more comprehensive analyses are needed to fully understand the nature and magnitude of this pecuniary externality, as well as appropriate regulatory responses to this and the non-pecuniary externalities highlighted earlier.

II DATA

We have combined data from Airbnb, the American Community Survey (ACS), Zillow,[17] and TripAdvisor,[18] allowing us to extract unique insights about the relationship between short-term rentals, long-term rentals, hotels, and the characteristics of the neighborhoods in which these types of lodging are located. We use census tracts, which typically include about 4,000 people (living in 1,000 to 2,000 housing units), to capture neighborhoods.

---

[13] Katie Benner, *Airbnb Sues Over New Law Regulating New York Rentals*, N.Y. Times (Oct. 21, 2016), www.nytimes .com/2016/10/22/technology/new-york-passes-law-airbnb.html.

[14] As Filippas and Horton, *supra* note 12, point out, since any impact the short-term rental market might have on home values and long-term rents is a pecuniary externality, it may not necessitate government intervention because, rather than affecting market efficiency, it simply represents a transfer from one group to another. However, governments sometimes intervene in markets for reasons other than efficiency, and pecuniary externalities can have important distributional consequences. In the case of short-term rentals, pecuniary externalities may represent a transfer from long-term renters to short-term renters and property owners.

[15] Tracy Elsen, *SF's Population Is Growing Way Faster Than Its Housing Stock*, Curbed San Francisco, Feb. 4, 2015, https://sf.curbed.com/2015/2/4/9995388/sfs-population-is-growing-way-faster-than-its-housing-stock; Edward Glaeser and Joseph Gyourko, *The Economic Implications of Housing Supply*, Zell/Lurie Working Paper 802, Wharton School (2017); Joseph Gyourko and Raven Saks Molloy, Regulation and Housing Supply, 5 *Handbook of Regional and Urban Econ.* 1289–337 (2015).

[16] For Airbnb analysis, *see* Abby Lackner, Anita Roth, and Christopher Nulty, REPORT: The Airbnb Community in San Francisco, Airbnb, June 8, 2015, https://timedotcom.files.wordpress.com/2015/06/the-airbnb-community-in-sf-june-8-2015.pdf; for city regulators *see* Fred Brousseau, Julian Metcalf, and Mina Yu, *Analysis of the Impact of the Short-Term Rentals on Housing*, San Francisco City Budget and Legislative Office, May 13, 2015, www.scribd.com/ doc/265376839/City-Budget-and-Legislative-Analysis-Report-on-Short-term-Rentals.

[17] Zillow is an online real estate database company that was founded in 2006.

[18] TripAdvisor provides hotel booking as well as reviews of travel-related content.

Airbnb has provided census-tract level panel data ranging from 2011 to 2016, for "entire home," "private/shared room,"[19] and all listings, on booked listing counts, the median of average nightly earnings,[20] bedroom composition (studio percentage, one-bedroom percentage, etc.), and heavy-use (rented over 180 days/year) listing counts. We have data only for tracts with six or more Airbnb listings. Further, separate data on entire home listings and individual room listings was only provided if there were six or more listings of each type.

Some researchers use Inside Airbnb[21] data or other third party sources to analyze Airbnb usage and price patterns.[22] Others crawl the web and collect consumer-facing Airbnb data by themselves.[23] Both data sources have critical limitations. First, these approaches rely on Airbnb advertised listings rather than booked listings, which means they are not capable of determining whether an advertised listing was booked or not and are likely to overestimate bookings. For example, some advertised listings are outdated or accidentally created and have zero Airbnb booking activity. Scrapers that track updates to host calendars cannot distinguish real bookings from dates hosts block for other reasons. Second, and related, they fail to collect accurate occupancy rates. For example, Inside Airbnb combines a number of assumptions to estimate these, using the number of reviews, review rate, minimum stay length, and average stay length.[24] Third, these sources collect Airbnb asking prices rather than transaction prices. Some asking prices are far above the market price, resulting in no booking activity, and in other cases guests receive lower rates via negotiations with the host or longer-term stay (e.g., 7+ days) discounts. Using asking prices overestimates Airbnb prices and profitability, and consequently, measures of short-term rental rates.

To capture census-tract level rents, we use Zillow Rent Index data, which has been provided for each month in our study period. This dataset is constructed using Zillow's Rent Zestimates, which are generated via a hedonic model trained with public property data and rental listing info.[25] Zillow also provided data on the bedroom composition of rental listings (number of studio, number of one-bedroom, number of two-bedroom, and number of three-bedroom listings) at the census-tract level from 2011 to 2016.[26] We combine the Airbnb and Zillow data with ACS

[19] We group "private room" and "shared room" Airbnb listings, and use the term "individual room" interchangeably with "private/shared room" for brevity. Shared rooms are a tiny fraction of Airbnb listings.

[20] In order to properly compare short-term to long-term rental rates within census tracts, we must account for differing bedroom composition of Airbnb versus Zillow listings. To do this, we reweight the Airbnb rent estimates using the bedroom composition of Zillow rental listings. That is, we calculate the median rent for Airbnb listings of each bedroom type by census tract, and then weight these Airbnb bedroom-specific median rents using the borough-year bedroom composition of Zillow rental listings. We restricted our data to stays lasting fewer than 30 nights on Airbnb to construct the bedroom-specific short-term rent estimates.

[21] InsideAirbnb.com is a noncommercial source of data derived from publicly available information on Airbnb's website. It provides point-in-time information about Airbnb listings, and is not associated with Airbnb.

[22] Gurran and Phibbs, *supra* note 9; Javier Gutierrez, Juan Carlos Garcia-Palomares, Gustavo Romanillos, and Maria Henar Salas-Olmedo, *Airbnb in Tourist Cities: Comparing Spatial Patterns of Hotels and Peer-to-Peer Accommodation*, 62 Tourism Mgmt. 278–91 (2016); Venoo Kakar, Julisa Franco, Joel Voelz, and Julia Wu., Effects of Host Race Information on Airbnb Listing Prices in San Francisco, MRPA Paper No. 69974, San Francisco State University (2016).

[23] Giovanni Quattrone, Davide Proserpio, Daniele Quercia, Licia Capra, and Mirco Musolesi, Who Benefits from the Sharing Economy of Airbnb? Proceedings of the 25th International Conference on World Wide Web (2016); Georgios Zervas, Davide Proserpio, and John W. Byers, *The Rise of the Sharing Economy: Estimating the Impact of Airbnb on the Hotel Industry*, 54 J. Marketing Res. 687–705 (2017).

[24] *See* the San Francisco Model at *About Inside Airbnb*, Inside Airbnb, http://insideairbnb.com/about.html.

[25] *See A Peek Inside Our Newest Zestimate: The Rent Zestimate*, Zillow, www.zillow.com/research/a-peek-inside-our-newest-zestimate-the-rent-zestimate-1076/.

[26] Zillow rent estimates are based on listings that may not be representative of the entire rental stock, particularly in the earlier years of our sample. Zillow estimates are based on listed prices, which may be higher than transacted rents.

2011–2015 five-year average census-tract estimates of the number of housing units, the percentage of the population over 25 years of age with at least a bachelor's degree, and median household income. Additionally, we have collected location and review data of 578 New York City hotels from TripAdvisor in 2016.

To construct the ratio of short-term to long-term rents, we divide the weighted median Airbnb entire home average earnings per night by the Zillow Rent Index rent per night in each tract. This gives us an estimate of the short-term to long-term rental ratio for 534 tracts in 2016 (the tracts for which both Airbnb and Zillow Rent Index data exist), or roughly one quarter of the 2,167 New York City census tracts in our data. These contain 28,540 entire home listings with a booking in 2016, representing 88 percent of the city's booked entire home listings that year. Of these tracts, 198 are in Manhattan, 254 are in Brooklyn, and 80 are in Queens.[27]

III USAGE INTENSITY

In this section, we examine how the intensity of Airbnb usage differs across the city's census tracts and how usage patterns have changed between 2011 and 2016.

Our first finding is that *as Airbnb usage has grown, listings have become more geographically dispersed over time* (see Figure 8.1). The number of census tracts with at least one booked listing rose from 723 (33 percent of NYC census tracts) in 2011 to 1,744 (87 percent of NYC census tracts) in 2016,[28] and the percentage of booked listings that were located in Manhattan decreased from 66 percent in 2011 to 54 percent in 2016. The average distance to the Empire State Building increased from 4.8 km in 2011 to 6 km in 2016.

By 2016, booked Airbnb listings were considerably more geographically dispersed than hotels (Figure 8.2). In 2016, TripAdvisor data included information on 578 New York City hotels, which were located in 215 (or 10 percent) of the city's census tracts. While TripAdvisor's coverage may be limited, hotels are clearly located in a much smaller set of census tracts than Airbnb bookings, which in 2016 reached nearly 90 percent of the city's census tracts. Hotels also appear to be more centralized, perhaps due to the zoning rules that constrain them to be located in commercially zoned neighborhoods. Nearly two-thirds of hotels (and likely a larger percentage of hotel rooms) are located in Manhattan, as compared to 54 percent of Airbnb booked listings.

Despite the dispersion trend, centrality remains an important predictor of Airbnb listing location. In 2016, 28 percent of booked Airbnb listings were within 3 km of the Empire State Building, 46 percent were within 5 km, and 87 percent were within 10 km. Usage is heaviest in the central neighborhoods of Manhattan and Northern Brooklyn. Further, "booked entire home intensity," defined as the number of entire home listings booked at least once over the year-long time frame as a percentage of the housing stock, falls with distance from the center of Manhattan. Booked entire home intensity averages roughly 3–5 percent in neighborhoods that are within 3 km of

---

Granular transacted-price rent data are difficult to obtain, but we believe the Zillow rent dataset to be one of the most comprehensive and accurate available.

[27] The tracts for which we have rental ratio data are, on average, more central, higher income, and higher rent, relative to New York City overall. In this subset of tracts, the median across tracts of median household income (based on 2011–2015 ACS estimates) is $59,397, compared to $54,563 citywide, the median Zillow Rent Index in 2016 is $2,816, compared to $2,267 citywide, and the median distance to the Empire State Building is 6.8 km, compared to 12.9 km citywide.

[28] The number of census tracts with at least six booked Airbnb listings (the restricted sample for which we have price data) rose from 371 (17 percent of NYC census tracts) in 2011 to 937 (43 percent of NYC census tracts) in 2016.

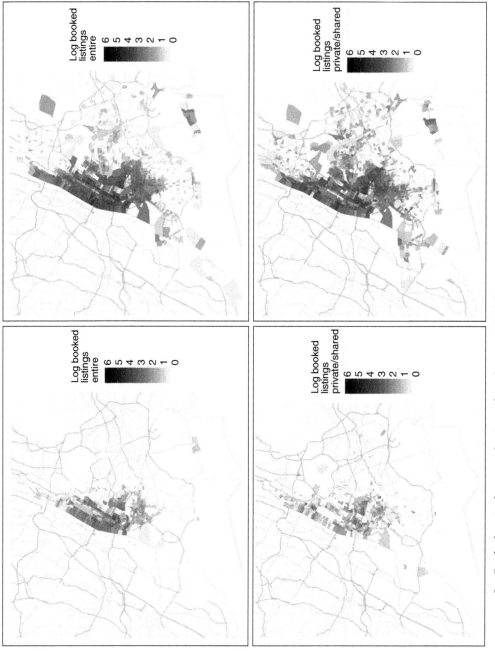

FIGURE 8.1 Booked entire home and private/shared room Airbnb listings in NYC census tracts, 2011 (left) and 2016 (right)

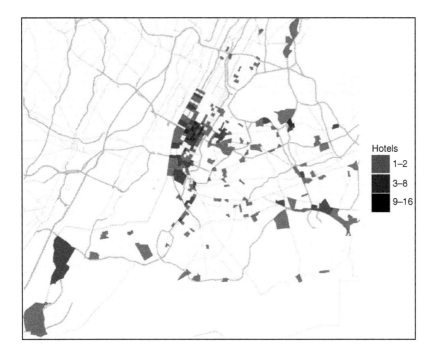

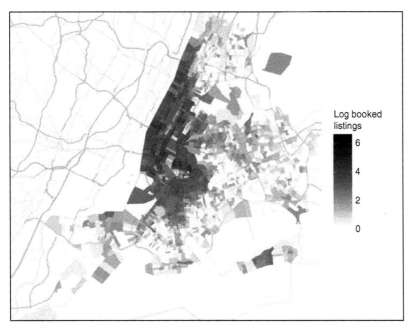

FIGURE 8.2 Hotels and Airbnb listings in NYC census tracts, 2016

the Empire State Building and drops to well under 1 percent in neighborhoods more than 10 km away (Figure 8.3).

Similarly, the share of housing units booked more than 180 nights in 2016 ranges from 0.3 percent to 0.5 percent of the housing stock in neighborhoods that are within 3 km of the Empire State Building, and drops to well under 0.1 percent in neighborhoods more than 10 km away.

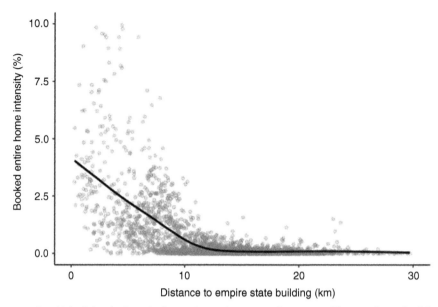

FIGURE 8.3 Airbnb booked entire home intensity versus distance to Empire State Building, 2016: Black curve represents the fit of a generalized additive model

In other words, even in central tracts, fewer than five in a thousand units are booked more than 180 nights in a year.[29]

Usage is concentrated in neighborhoods with incomes above the citywide median, but neighborhoods with somewhat lower incomes have grown in popularity. Table 8.1 illustrates neighborhood characteristics of the average Airbnb booked listing in 2011 and 2016 and shows that the average Airbnb booked listing in 2011 was in a census tract with a median household income of $82,000 in 2011, compared to $73,000 in 2016. In both years, these incomes were above the citywide household median income (which was $53,000 in the 2011–2015 ACS five-year estimates), but usage is clearly spreading to relatively lower-income areas. Similarly, the share of college graduates in the neighborhood of the average Airbnb booked listing is high relative to the share of the city as a whole (which was 35.7 percent in the 2011–2015 ACS five-year estimates), but again, it is declining over time. Finally, the average Airbnb booked listing is located in neighborhoods with a relatively large share of young adults (the share of age 25–34 in the city was 17.6 percent in the 2011–2015 ACS five-year estimates), though this proportion is declining over time.

Individual room listings have grown in number more quickly than entire home listings. In 2011, booked entire homes represented 68 percent of all booked listings, compared to 53 percent in 2016. Both types of listing grew every year during our study period.

Lower-income neighborhoods disproportionately feature individual room listings (compared to entire home listings). Figure 8.4 shows that a higher proportion of the listings in lower-income neighborhoods are individual rooms rather than full homes. In tracts with median household income less than $40,000, close to 65 percent of booked listings are individual rooms. This percentage decreases linearly with a tract's median household income, with only a quarter of

---

[29] On average, roughly 10 percent of booked Airbnb entire home listings are rented more than 180 nights per year. Note that Airbnb listings may include boutique hotels, accessory dwelling units, and other specialty listings that one might expect would be booked over 180 days per year. The dataset does not offer further detail on the nature of the listings, beyond what we describe in the Data section.

TABLE 8.1 *Listing-weighted averages of Airbnb tract characteristics in 2011 and 2016*[30]

Characteristic	2011	2016
Household income	$82,000	$73,000
Distance from Empire State Building	4.8 km	6.0 km
Share college graduates	62%	54%
Share age 25–34	27.0%	25.6%

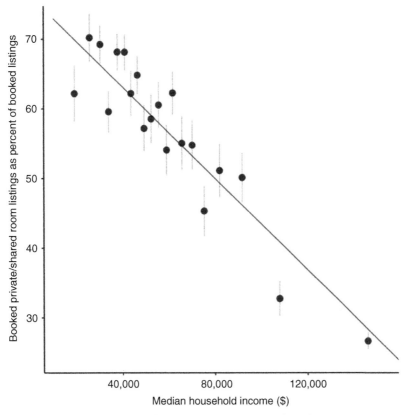

FIGURE 8.4 Median household income versus private/shared room percentage in NYC census tracts, 2016

booked listings in the highest income tracts being individual rooms. In 2016, a full 50 percent of booked individual room listings in NYC were in tracts in the bottom half of the income distribution, compared to 27 percent of booked entire home listings.[31] This suggests that hosts in lower-income areas may be more apt to share spare space in their primary residence.

The patterns described above hold up in a regression of listing intensity on neighborhood location and income (Table 8.2). For each additional kilometer from the Empire State Building, the

---

[30] Based on ACS 2011–2015 tract-level estimates.

[31] Based on 2011–2015 ACS tract-level median household income estimates, which exist for 97 percent of NYC census tracts. In 2011, 41 percent of booked individual room listings in NYC were in tracts in the bottom half of the income distribution, compared to 17 percent of booked entire home listings.

TABLE 8.2 *Regression results for Airbnb listing intensity (%) in 2016*

	All Listings	Entire Home	Private Room
	(1)	(2)	(3)
Distance to Empire State Building (km)	−0.214***	−0.110***	−0.104***
	(0.0124)	(0.00507)	(0.00957)
Median income ($1,000)	0.0415***	0.0306***	0.0109**
	(0.00579)	(0.00236)	(0.00446)
Median income square	−0.000230***	−0.000142***	−8.71e−05***
	(3.43e−05)	(1.40e−05)	(2.64e−05)
Manhattan	0.999***	0.764***	0.236
	(0.252)	(0.103)	(0.194)
Brooklyn	0.590***	0.206***	0.384***
	(0.163)	(0.0665)	(0.125)
Queens	−0.498***	−0.362***	−0.135
	(0.166)	(0.0677)	(0.128)
Constant	2.472***	0.812***	1.659***
	(0.277)	(0.113)	(0.213)
Observations	2,101	2,101	2,101
R–squared	0.264	0.429	0.106

Note: ***$p<0.01$, **$p<0.05$, *$p<0.1$

Airbnb listing intensity in a census tract drops around 0.2 percentage points. Airbnb listing intensity is significantly higher in Manhattan and Brooklyn. Compared to individual room listings, entire home listings are more concentrated in Manhattan. Controlling for centrality, usage intensity tends to be higher in neighborhoods that are higher income, though usage falls off for the very highest income neighborhoods, perhaps because households in those neighborhoods place relatively low value on the added income they can earn through the short-term market.

IV RENTS: SHORT-TERM VERSUS LONG-TERM

Some housing advocates worry that short-term rentals are displacing long-term rentals. However, we find that overall, *short-term rentals do not appear to be as profitable, relative to long-term rentals, as many assume.* In 2016, the listing-weighted average ratio of median short-term nightly rents for entire homes to estimated nightly earnings from long-term rents across the city's neighborhoods was roughly 1.7. This suggests that to match long-term rental revenue, hosts would have to have their homes booked over 216 days a year, the "break-even" number of short-term rental nights. Placed in context, as of June 2017, the median number of nights booked for a typical entire home listing in New York City was 46.[32] In fact, this revenue-based calculation may be conservative, since it assumes zero transaction costs when short-term rental hosts must manage guest reservations and clean their homes between bookings – generating costs that likely exceed those of long-term rental landlords.[33] The remainder of the section explores this relative profitability of short- to long-term rentals over time and across neighborhoods.

---

[32] *See June Update, supra* note 4.

[33] According to a calculator offered by Handy.com, a marketplace for short-term rental management services, cleaning costs for a one, two, or three bedroom unit in Manhattan are $57, $84, and $111 respectively. *See Get a Price,* Handy, www.handy.com/quotes/new?service=52 for details.

TABLE 8.3 *Listing-weighted average STR/LTR ratio (break-even nights[34]) by borough and year[35]*

	2011	2012	2013	2014	2015	2016
Manhattan	1.73	1.81	1.83	1.73	1.56	1.54
	(211)	(202)	(199)	(211)	(234)	(237)
Brooklyn	2.04	2.09	1.98	1.98	1.96	1.95
	(179)	(175)	(184)	(184)	(186)	(187)
Queens[36]	NA	NA	2.23	1.97	1.90	1.93
			(164)	(185)	(192)	(189)
NYC	1.80	1.88	1.88	1.81	1.70	1.69
	(203)	(194)	(194)	(202)	(215)	(216)

The short-term rental market became relatively less profitable between 2011 and 2016, as short-term rents remained flat, while median long-term rents rose by 19 percent in the same neighborhoods. Table 8.3 shows that across New York City, the listing-weighted average ratio of nightly short-term to long-term rents fell from 1.88 at its peak in 2012 to 1.69 in 2016 (and correspondingly, the number of nights required to outcompete the long-term rental market increased from 194 to 216). The greater stability of short-term rents is likely explained by the greater elasticity of the stock. When short-term rental demand increases, putting upward pressure on prices, residents can easily make their empty spaces available. The long-term rental supply is far less responsive to demand shifts, due to lengthy approval processes and other regulatory hurdles to housing construction, which are particularly burdensome in New York, according to the Wharton Residential Land Use Regulatory Index.

There is substantial variation across neighborhoods in relative rents. Brooklyn and Queens had listing-weighted average ratios of approximately 2 in 2016, while Manhattan had a significantly lower ratio of roughly 1.5. This implies that an apartment in Manhattan would need to be rented out an additional 50 nights in a year to outcompete the long-term rental market, compared to a similar apartment in Brooklyn or Queens. As shown in Figure 8.5, the short-term to long-term ratio is closer to 3 in a handful of outlier tracts in Central Brooklyn and Queens, suggesting that hosts would have to rent their homes for about 120 days to achieve parity with the long-term rental market.

The STR/LTR ratio is generally higher in lower-rent neighborhoods, middle-income neighborhoods, and neighborhoods outside Manhattan. In other words, the premium that long-term renters are willing to pay to live in the city's most central, highest rent neighborhoods exceeds the premium that short-term renters (visitors) are willing to pay to live in those same neighborhoods. Figure 8.6 shows how the number of break-even nights falls steadily with distance to midtown Manhattan in 2016. For example, listings in census tracts with break-even nights below 146 (rent ratio >2.5) were an average of 8.6 kilometers away from the Empire State Building in 2016, as compared to just 4 kilometers for those in tracts with break-even nights more than 243 (rent ratio <1.5). None of the census tracts with short-term to long-term rent ratios greater than 2.5 were located in Manhattan.

Figure 8.6 also shows that homes in lower-rent neighborhoods need to be rented out for fewer nights on the short-term market to break even with the long-term market. As for neighborhood

---

[34] Break-even nights=365/(STR/LTR ratio). Transaction costs are assumed to be zero.
[35] Numbers for the Bronx and Staten Island are not reported due to an insufficient sample size.
[36] Estimates are not reported for Queens in 2011 and 2012 due to an insufficient sample size (five or fewer tracts) in those years.

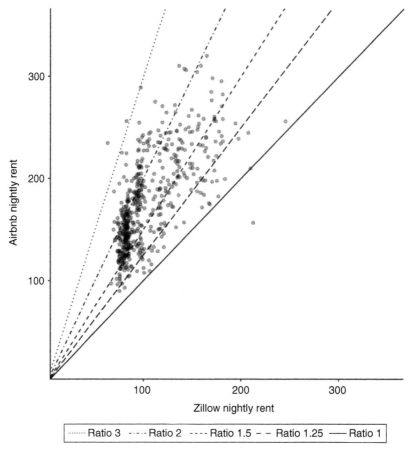

FIGURE 8.5 Nightly earnings from Airbnb entire home rents versus nightly earnings from long-term rents, census tracts, 2016

Note: Lines represent the ratio of short-term nightly rents for entire homes to nightly earnings from long-term rents.

income, the relationship between break-even nights and income is U-shaped, with the most profitable neighborhoods being those with incomes just above the citywide median.

These findings suggest that residents of less central, lower-rent, upper-middle-income neighborhoods may simultaneously have the most to gain from home-sharing, while also being at risk for dislocation by investors that may seek to remove units from the long-term rental market (Figure 8.7). However, individual rooms represent 56 percent of listings outside Manhattan – and a surprising 71 percent of listings in the Bronx – suggesting that most hosts in these neighborhoods are residents, rather than investors. And even in these neighborhoods, the risk of conversion appears to be limited, given the relative payoffs from the short-term and long-term rental markets. That said, the topic merits further research.

V REGULATORY RESPONSES

The rapid expansion of platform-based short-term rental activity has prompted cities to modernize existing regulations or adopt new ones. Drawing on economic theory as well as our empirical findings, we review options aimed at regulating short-term rental usage, which ideally serve

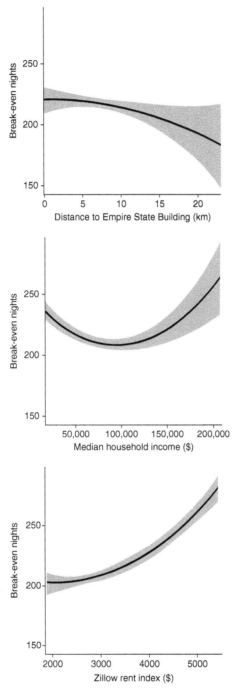

FIGURE 8.6 Break-even nights versus distance to Empire State Building, income, and rent in 2016
Note: Lines depict quadratic best fit, with standard error bands in gray. The "break-even nights" estimate is defined as 365/(short-term to long-term rental ratio); that is, the number of nights required for a unit to earn as much as it would in the long-term rental market.

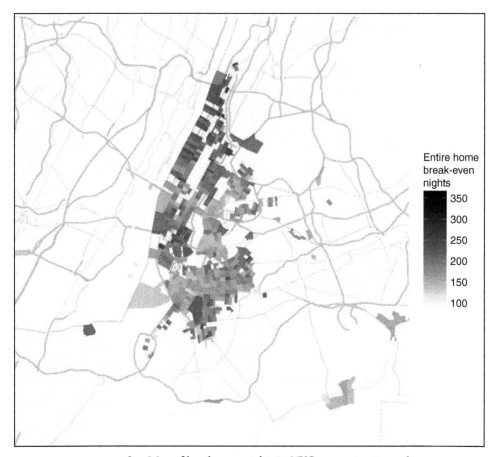

FIGURE 8.7 Map of break-even nights in NYC census tracts, 2016

the purpose of minimizing pecuniary and non-pecuniary externalities on city residents while preserving economic value. Given the significant variation we observe across neighborhoods and modes of use, we highlight the importance of approaches that address this variation. For example, since most hosts are occasional users and many rent out single rooms rather than entire homes, regulation that avoids overburdening this group is likely in order. Dedicated hosts should attract more regulatory scrutiny – perhaps more so in areas where their concentration is highest. Our empirical evidence can help guide regulations that permit economically valuable activity at levels that minimize negative spillovers.

Cities around the world have adopted a wide range of approaches to regulating short-term rentals with varied objectives. One concern is ensuring taxes are collected on short-term rental activity, with some cities requiring hosts to register and remit taxes directly to the government (e.g., San Francisco until recently) and others asking platforms like Airbnb to collect and remit taxes, as in Amsterdam, Lisbon, and London.[37] As for quality and safety concerns, most cities appear to have implicitly delegated cleanliness and hygiene issues to the platforms (whose

[37] As of September 2017, over half of Airbnb's US listings were in jurisdictions where Airbnb collects and remits taxes on behalf of hosts. This approach is a specific example of a broader philosophy of "data driven delegation" advocated in Arun Sundararajan, *What Governments Can Learn From Airbnb And the Sharing Economy*, Fortune, July 12, 2016, http://fortune.com/2016/07/12/airbnb-discrimination/; Arun Sundararajan, *The Sharing Economy: The End of Employment and the Rise of Crowd-Based Capitalism* (2016).

peer-feedback-based reputation systems can provide an effective self-regulatory solution to this issue of information asymmetry).[38] Issues of public safety are more complex, but short-term rentals are bound by standard housing and building codes, such as requirements for smoke detectors, safe electrical wiring, and clean water.[39]

In this section we assess regulatory responses that specifically address externalities tied to usage levels, as described in Section I, and primarily consider interventions governments have recently enacted. We focus on *how* the usage limits should be designed, and do not cover the important and legally complex question of *who* will enforce them.[40] We do not advocate for any single approach, given the uncertainty about the nature and magnitude of any externalities, and how these might vary across geographies. Rather, we use an economic lens, as well as our empirical findings, to lay out strengths and weaknesses of different approaches.

A Bans

Some municipalities, such as Fort Lee, New Jersey[41] or Santa Monica, California,[42] have enacted outright bans on unhosted short-term rentals. Others have imposed restrictions, either for particular types of property or for selected neighborhoods. For example, Portland, Maine, bans short-term rentals in single-family homes that are not owner-occupied, with the exception of the islands off the coast of Portland, which have a long history of vacation rentals.[43] In New Orleans, short-term rentals are banned in the French Quarter.[44] In Chicago, an alderman can propose that a precinct become a "restricted residential zone," in which short-term rentals cannot operate, and the City Council voted to approve the first restricted zone in June 2017, when the alderman of the 13th ward was able to secure valid signatures from 25 percent of registered voters in four of the Ward's 48 precincts.[45] New York City bans rentals of fewer than 30 days in buildings with three or more units if the permanent resident is not present, and imposes steep fines on illegal short-term rental units.[46]

---

[38] An extensive literature about online reputation systems has documented similar mitigating effects for problems of information asymmetry across a range of peer-to-peer marketplaces (e.g., Andrey Fradkin, Elena Grewal, and David Holtz, *The Determinants of Online Review Informativeness: Evidence from Field Experiments on Airbnb*, Working Paper (2017)). For discussion of the possible scope of reputation systems replacing government regulation, *see* Arun Sundararajan, *Why the Government Doesn't Need To Regulate the Sharing Economy*, WIRED, Oct. 22, 2012, www .wired.com/2012/10/from-airbnb-to-coursera-why-the-government-shouldnt-regulate-the-sharing-econo my/.

[39] In fact, buildings classified for transient use face stricter fire safety standards in New York City (versus those designated for permanent occupants), since transient occupants are believed to face greater risks in the event of a fire due to unfamiliarity with a building's escape routes and emergency procedures; Daniel Parcerisas and Sarah Watson, Sleeping Around: Short-term Rentals and Housing in New York City, CHPC Report, Mar. 2017), http://chpcny.org/ assets/Sleeping-Around-Final-for-Web.pdf.

[40] Cohen and Sundararajan, *supra* note 11, explain that the short-term rental digital platform should be viewed as an efficient actor to solve the negative externality caused by itself due to its tremendous potential enforcement capacities.

[41] The Fort Lee municipal laws require a minimum stay of 30 consecutive days; Christopher Lang, *N.J. Towns*, *State Government Move To Regulate Short-Term Rentals*, NorthJersey.com, Feb. 1, 2017, www.northjersey.com/story/news/ 2017/02/01/nj-towns-state-government-move-regulate-short-term-rentals/96 248564/.

[42] Santa Monica City Council bans the rental of an entire unit for less than 30 days; Sam Sanders, *Santa Monica Cracks Down on Airbnb, Bans 'Vacation Rentals' Under A Month*, NPR, May 13, 2015, www.npr.org/sections/thetwo-way/2015/ 05/13/406587575/santa-monica-cracks-down-on-airbnb-bans-vacatio n-rentals-under-a-month.

[43] Billings, *supra* note 2.

[44] Jeff Adelson, *New Orleans Begins Roll Out of Short-Term Rental Law Enforcement*, New Orleans Advocate, May 14, 2017, www.theadvocate.com/new_orleans/news/politics/article_5b428d14-38e0-11e7-8ae2-7b5409eacfab.html.

[45] Fran Spielman, *Southwest Side Alderman Is First To Declare Ward Off-Limits to Airbnb*, Chicago Sun Times, June 22, 2017, http://chicago.suntimes.com/news/southwest-side-aldermen-is-first-to-declare-ward-off-limits-to-airbnb/.

[46] We have little data on enforcement, but it is driven by complaints, as the Mayor's Office of Special Enforcement only inspected properties in response to the 311 complaints (Parcerisas and Watson, *supra* note 39). From February 2017 to

From an economic perspective, bans are generally an unnecessarily blunt and inefficient approach to addressing externalities; there is likely to be some level of short-term rental activity for which the benefits outweigh the full social costs. While eliminating the possibility of any negative externality, bans also eliminate all value that would have accrued to hosts who could have earned income, guests who would prefer to stay and spend in the banned area, and the municipality that would have received tax dollars. For example, we estimate – very roughly – that the ban on short-term rentals in buildings of three or more units in New York City, if enforced, might impact $140 million to $350 million in host income.[47]

B Caps on Number of Short-Term Rental Nights

A number of jurisdictions have adopted caps on the number of nights a host can offer their unit as a short-term rental. The motivation behind this approach is that such a cap sharply reduces the incentive for a landlord or entrepreneur to convert a long-term rental into a short-term rental, while still allowing full-time residents to share their homes.[48] For example, Japan recently passed a nationwide law imposing a 180-night cap on all short-term rental units,[49] a level that is also in place in Philadelphia.[50] London allows residents to rent out their units in the short-term market for a maximum of 90 nights per year.[51] Most caps do not apply to "hosted" stays, meaning the Airbnb host is present during the stay, as is the case with the vast majority of individual room listings.[52] For example, the 180-night cap in San Jose,[53] as well as the 90-night cap in New Orleans,[54] apply only to unhosted stays.

These regulations have the advantage of mostly affecting commercial, rather than casual users, as few permanent residents can rent their units for more than 90 nights in a year. Further, our finding that lower-income areas in New York disproportionately feature hosted, individual room stays, suggests that exempting hosted stays may have progressive distributional effects. However, the blunt nature of caps on nights also has drawbacks. Primary among these is that several classes of noncommercial units would also be impacted. One such class are Accessory Dwelling Units (ADUs), small and sometimes partial units that are attached to the primary home. In some cases,

---

April 2017, nine individuals or entities were fined a total of $65,000; *see* James Dobbins, *Making a Living With Airbnb*, N.Y. Times, Apr. 7, 2017, www.nytimes.com/2017/04/07/realestate/making-a-living-with-airbnb.html.

[47] The median entire home listing earns $5,000–6,000 over the course of a year in NYC. Since the earnings distribution is skewed to the right, we use $6,000 to $12,000 as a range for entire home average annual earnings. In 2016, there were 32,500 entire home listings with a booking in NYC, and 71 percent of NYC housing units were in buildings with three or more units, according to the ACS. To construct our estimate, we use a range of 70 percent to 90 percent for Airbnb entire home units in buildings with three or more units, understanding that this might be incorrect. Combining these ranges, we estimate that the impact on host income ranges from roughly $140 million to $350 million.

[48] Explanatory notes from the UK Deregulation Act 2015, Sections 44–45, which regulates London short-term rentals, state that: "The purpose behind the provision was to protect London's existing housing supply, for the benefit of permanent residents, by giving London boroughs greater and easier means of planning control to prevent the conversion of family homes into short term lets." *See* Deregulation Act of 2015, www.legislation.gov.uk/ukpga/2015/20/notes/division/5/46.

[49] For a review of the regulation, *see* Airstair, http://airstair.jp/minpaku_new_law/.

[50] For a review of the regulation, *see* *Short Term Home Rental*, Licenses and Inspections, City of Philadelphia, www .phila.gov/li/PDF/Limited%20Lodging%20Information%20Flyer.pdf.

[51] For a review of the regulation, *see* SimplyHospitality, http://simplyhospitality.com/short-term-lets-uk-rules-regulations/.

[52] According to Airbnb survey data from 2016, 92 percent of hosts who said that they rent a private or shared room in NYC said that they rent their primary residence, defined as the place they live in for most of the year (sample size of 348).

[53] For a review of the regulation, *see* *Memorandum*, City of San Jose, http://sanjoseca.gov/DocumentCenter/View/ 37863.

[54] Adelson, *supra* note 44.

homeowners will make the choice of whether to use this space for short-term or long-term rentals. But in many cases these units are not appropriate for long-term rentals due to the lack of a kitchen or other functionality, or because the homeowner wishes to maintain the flexibility to house visiting family members or friends.[55] Another class of noncommercial units affected are second homes, which may take the form of vacation rentals, or in cities as pied-à-terres. These spaces embody the type of space for which the sharing economy is perhaps best suited. Without short-term rentals, many of these ADUs and second homes would be left empty, and cities would have not reduced any of the pecuniary externalities the caps were intended to limit.[56]

A further drawback to the capping form of regulation is that it may be very difficult for a city to monitor "cross-platform" activity. In some cities, hosts must register their unit as a short-term rental, and Airbnb has committed to monitoring the number of nights booked to ensure hosts stay below legal limits. While a single platform may agree to monitor and limit the number of nights a unit may be listed, units may also be listed on other platforms, as well as on advertising sites like Craigslist. In this case, the city must take on the responsibility of collecting nights information from multiple platforms, matching listings between platforms, monitoring totals, and reporting information back to platforms in a timely fashion. The technical complexity of this form of regulation is itself a drawback. Worse, platforms that choose to comply with the regulation are potentially at a disadvantage to those who choose not to comply, making it competitively unfavorable for any platform to be the first to participate in joint regulation.

C Caps on Number of Short-Term Rental Units

A few cities have opted instead to allow activity but to introduce citywide or localized caps on the number of short-term rentals, often distinguishing between permanent residences and dedicated short-term rentals. The underlying assumption behind this approach is that externalities are likely to be minimal so long as tourism activity is sufficiently dispersed and dedicated short-term rentals remain a small percentage of the housing stock. For example, the City Council in Portland, Maine, recently passed a law limiting the number of non-owner-occupied units in multifamily buildings that can be registered as short-term rentals to 300 (excluding the islands), a number that is slated to be reviewed annually by the City Council.[57] The City of Nashville has adopted a cap on the number of non-owner-occupied single family short-term rental properties allowed in each census tract of Davidson County – interestingly, rather than setting a fixed cap, the cap is set as a percentage of each tract's housing stock, allowing the number of dedicated short-term rentals to grow with the housing stock.[58] The City of Chicago has targeted localized externalities by recently amending its municipal code to limit the number of units in a building that can be used as short-term rentals – regardless of owner-occupancy – to six, or a quarter of the units in a building, whichever is less.[59]

This class of regulation has the potential to be more efficient than outright bans, and, depending on implementation, a blanket cap on the number of nights on all short-term rentals. These

---

[55] Jurisdictions could address this inefficiency by treating ADU rentals as "hosted," and not subject to a cap.

[56] On the margin, short-term rentals could potentially increase the prevalence of second homes by making ownership more affordable. But banning short-term rentals is an inefficient means of limiting second homes (compared to, say, a second home tax), as it would encourage existing second homes to remain empty.

[57] Billings, *supra* note 2.

[58] For a review of the regulation, *see Short Term Rental Property*, Nashville, www.nashville.gov/Codes-Administration/Construction-and-Permits/Short-Term-Rentals.aspx.

[59] Associated Press, *Chicago Set to Begin Enforcing Tougher Short-Term Rental Laws*, Skift (Mar. 16, 2017), https://skift.com/2017/03/16/chicago-set-to-begin-enforcing-tougher-short-term-rental-laws/.

regulations commonly recognize that there are two fundamentally different types of short-term rental units – the occasionally rented permanent residence and the dedicated rental or second home – and they treat these categories differently. In doing so, they can target localized externalities and ensure that full-time short-term rentals remain a small percentage of the housing stock.

However, unit caps can also have drawbacks. They target the number of units rather than the intensity of nightly use, which may better proxy externalities related to tourism levels. For example, in Portland, Maine, the cap on registered units might mean that on some nights, there may be just a handful of short-term rentals booked, while on others there are 300 booked.[60] An analogy that highlights this possible inefficiency is limiting traffic congestion by regulating the number of cars people own rather than the number of miles they drive. Unit caps also raise the challenge of how permits should be allocated, and what the correct number of permits is. Experience from the taxi medallion world suggests that once a cap level is chosen, it can be hard to adjust, as this might require new legislation, and incumbents would likely resist increases.[61] For example, Honolulu County in Hawaii has not issued a single new short-term rental permit since 1989, despite precipitously increasing demand.[62] Finally, if permit levels are chosen across too wide a geographic region, limits would potentially bind even if there are sub-regions where higher levels of activity would be welcome.

A hybrid regulatory approach would combine night caps with unit caps. For example, a city might allow short-term rental activity in any housing unit up to a certain number of nights per year, and also issue licenses for a tolerable number of uncapped units, dependent on the housing stock, that would accommodate second homes or other dedicated rentals.

D *Regulating Activity Levels Via Taxes and Fees*

Another approach that is widely used in other contexts (ranging from traffic congestion to environmental pollution) that feature negative externalities is to charge fees or taxes on usage.[63] The principle behind this approach is that properly designed taxes allow the highest value activity to take place, but limit activity that generates the most negative externalities. The taxes generated can also be used as pecuniary transfers to agents affected more by the externalities.

Taxes and fees in short-term rentals currently take several forms. As described earlier, in most cities hosts are required to pay a transient occupancy tax (a.k.a. TOT, or hotel tax). In some cities, hosts are additionally required to pay annual registration fees to legally operate as short-term rentals. Beyond simply being a source of revenue for the city, these taxes and fees can also be an efficient lever to regulate activity levels, especially if they increase with usage and dissuade owners from converting long- to short-term rentals. For example, in Portland, Maine, registration fees increase with the number of units registered by a host.[64] Such a regime captures the principle that a host with one unit may well be renting out their primary residence (while traveling) or second home, but a host with multiple units is likely not, and will be taxed appropriately.

A challenge associated with taxes and fees is their potential for regressive distributive effects. For example, active hosts who live in more valuable homes that command higher short-term

[60] Billings, *supra* note 2.
[61] Jeff Horwitz and Chris Cumming, *Taken for a Ride*, Slate, June 6, 2012, www.slate.com/articles/business/moneybox/2012/06/taxi_medallions_how_new_york_s_terrible_taxi_system_makes_fares_higher_and_drivers_poorer_.html.
[62] Associated Press, *The Latest: Hawaii Lawmakers Mull Short-Term Rental Bills*, NewsOK (Feb. 7, 2017), http://newsok.com/article/feed/1163484.
[63] William J. Baumol, *On Taxation and the Control of Externalities*, 62(3) Am. Econ. Rev. 307–22 (1972).
[64] Billings, *supra* note 2.

rents can more easily afford a fixed registration fee, which would exclude hosts who are less active or live in socioeconomically less favorable neighborhoods or properties. One possible way to differentiate between casual and commercial hosts is to impose a *threshold*: allow hosts to rent their unit up to a threshold number of nights without paying any fee, and charge a fee that escalates with usage after that. For instance, in Philadelphia, hosts may rent out their space for up to 90 nights a year without registering with the city, but they must register and pay a fee as a "Limited Lodging Home" if they host between 91 and 180 nights, and must further secure a "Visitor Accommodations" permit if renting for more than 180 nights. This approach mitigates the regressive nature of a flat fee, which would otherwise discourage the most casual, noncommercial users of the platform. Alternatively, percentage-based taxes (like TOTs) could vary based on the intensity of usage of a particular unit. For example, Massachusetts recently proposed higher tax rates after a listing books 60 nights, which would presumably discourage conversion of long-term rentals.[65] More generally, a high tax on listings rented above a certain number of nights could be used to ensure second homes and other units that would otherwise remain empty are utilized, but other housing units are not converted into short-term rentals.

E Localized Regulation

While most jurisdictions have adopted a single, citywide set of rules, we show significant variation in the prevalence of short-term rentals together with variation in their relative profitability across New York City's neighborhoods. This variation raises the possibility of neighborhood-specific regulatory responses, like those recently enacted in Portland, Maine,[66] New Orleans,[67] or Chicago (if residents vote to support).

A flexible regulatory scheme might naturally result in different neighborhoods having different levels of regulation. For example, a citywide regime that minimally regulates casual, part-time hosts but registers, taxes, and caps the number of full-time hosts may leave some neighborhoods preferring more tourist activity, and other neighborhoods preferring less. Because of this heterogeneity across neighborhoods and their preferences, along with the observed variation in short-term rental concentrations, there is an economic argument for neighborhood-specific rules.

Neighborhoods differ in their long-term rental market characteristics, desire for economic impact and development, and preferred levels of tourism. Regulation for a community concerned about neighborhood change may not be right for a predominantly vacation rental zone. Said differently, the nature and level of externalities may depend on the neighborhood itself, hence the case for a localized response.

One form of highly localized regulation is that enacted by homeowner associations (HOAs), which might be particularly well equipped to target localized spillovers, like turnover and noise. Cohen and Sundararajan elaborate on this point:

> The existence of [HOAs] in the potential regulatory mix suggests an interesting potential division of regulatory responsibility – delegate regulatory responsibility relating to information

---

[65] Bill (H.3454) proposes to impose a 4 percent tax on earnings from "residential" listings, defined as primary residence listings rented fewer than 60 nights per year, and to impose an 8 percent tax on "commercial" listings, defined as non-primary residences or units rented more than 60 nights per year (a city or town may impose an additional local excise tax of up to 5 percent on residential listings and 10 percent on commercial listings). *See* Bill H.3454, *supra* note 3.

[66] Portland caps the number of short-term units in non-owner-occupied buildings at 300, excluding the islands; Billings, *supra* note 2.

[67] Short-term rentals are banned in the French Quarter, but legal in other neighborhoods with licenses; Adelson, *supra* note 44.

asymmetry to platforms like Airbnb (whose interests are naturally aligned with the global aggregation of information and the mitigation of adverse selection and moral hazard), and let HOAs play a key role in the regulation of local externalities, as the guest-noise and strangers-in-the-building externalities are typically local and primarily affect HOAs' membership. Homeowners and renters have a continuous, high-bandwidth relationship with their HOA; these organizations are credible, can monitor compliance, and possess robust enforcement capabilities. Buildings and communities may then naturally differentiate into "Airbnb-friendly" and "Airbnb-free," allowing future buyers and renters to self-select.[68]

However, neighborhood approaches may be less appropriate if localized externalities from the increased presence of non-residents spread to other neighborhoods and undermine quality of life in a city as a whole. They are also not appropriate if there is evidence of citywide spillovers from the removal of long-term rentals from the housing stock.

Further, localized regulations or fees could be complex to administer, could be confusing for city residents and guests, and might have concerning distributional effects.

CONCLUSION

Before crafting the most efficient and equitable responses, cities need more empirical work to understand the evolution of the short-term rental market and the nature of the externalities associated with it. We have taken a step in this direction, describing the usage patterns and relative profitability of Airbnb in New York City, across neighborhoods, and over time. Between 2011 and 2016, Airbnb spread to less central, residential neighborhoods, where short-term rentals tend to be more profitable relative to the long-term rental market. However, overall, the short-term rental market does not appear to be as profitable as many assume – even in these less central, residential neighborhoods – and it has become relatively less profitable over time. Given the limited incentives to convert housing units that we observe in the data, along with the downward trend in these incentives over time, it seems unlikely that Airbnb is currently having a major effect on the affordability of rental housing in New York City.

Using an economic lens, we reviewed the advantages and disadvantages of different regulatory approaches designed to address the externalities that may arise from the short-term rental market, including bans, caps on the number of nights, unit caps, taxes, and fees. Bans, on one end of the spectrum, eliminate the possibility of any negative externality arising from the short-term rental market, but they also eliminate all value that would have accrued to hosts and guests, as well as the municipality. On the other end of the spectrum, taxes and fees acknowledging different modes of use allow the highest value activity to take place, but limit the overall level of activity, thereby minimizing negative externalities. Allowing taxes or fees to vary with usage can serve to discourage the conversion of short-term rentals to long-term rentals, and allowing taxes and fees to vary by neighborhood ensures that a regulatory approach that makes sense for a community concerned with neighborhood change is not applied to a predominantly vacation rental zone.

In future work, we plan to research the determinants of the variation in the short-term to long-term rental ratio across neighborhoods. We also plan to consider how the relative profitability of short-term rentals may behave in a long-run equilibrium, what the level of Airbnb rental activity may be in this steady state, and what this implies about the impact of the various regulatory approaches discussed in this chapter.

---

[68] Cohen and Sundararajan, *supra* note 11, at 130–31.

9

The Novelty of TNC Regulation

Katrina M. Wyman[*]

INTRODUCTION

In *The Upstarts*, business journalist Brad Stone chronicles the development of Uber, from Garrett Camp's 2008 vision of an on-demand car service, to Uber's impact in the United States as of the end of 2016.[1] Along the way, Stone recounts some of the formative battles Uber and Lyft fought with city and state legislators and regulators.[2] Some of them saw the benefits of Uber and Lyft's innovations, but also insisted on protecting public safety.[3] Others were overly wedded to the status quo, perhaps because of longstanding ties to the traditional taxi industry.[4]

Although it is not Stone's main focus, the rise of Uber and Lyft is a story of legislative and regulatory innovation, as well as entrepreneurial chutzpah. In the past five years, but especially since 2015, pushed by Uber and Lyft, a new framework has been developed in most parts of the United States to legalize and regulate these upstarts.[5] There are important differences betweens this new framework and the approach historically used to regulate the taxi industry. While local governments historically were the main regulators of taxis, state governments have elaborated the regulatory framework governing transportation network companies (TNCs) in

[*] Thank you to Julia Kindlon, Aaron Lichter, Dana Rubin, André Smith, and Caleb Thomas for superb research assistance; to Michèle Finck, Maarit Moran, and Derek McKee for helpful comments; and to individuals in the taxi and TNC industries that provided helpful insights.

[1] Brad Stone, *The Upstarts: How Uber, Airbnb and the Killer Companies of the New Silicon Valley Are Changing the World* (2017). *See also* Adam Lashinsky, *Wild Ride: Inside Uber's Quest For World Domination* (2017).

[2] Stone, *supra* note 1, at 64, 122, 133, 163–64, 180–81, 188–92.

[3] *Id.* at 156, 202.

[4] *Id.* at 189, 193–94, 206, 312.

[5] Uber's use of lobbyists has been extensively covered in the press. *See, e.g.,* Glenn Blain and Kenneth Lovett, *Uber to Pay $98G for Underreporting N.Y. on Lobbying Expenses*, NY Daily News, June 8, 2017, www.nydailynews.com/new-york/uber-pay-98g-misleading-n-y-lobbying-expenses-article-1.3232089; Stephanie Mehta, *Meet Uber's Political Genius*, Vanity Fair, June 17, 2016, www.vanityfair.com/news/2016/06/bradley-tusk-fanduel-uber; Chris Kirkham and Tracey Lien, *Facing Regulatory Roadblocks, Uber Ramps Up Its Lobbying in California*, L.A. Times, July 26, 2015, www.latimes.com/business/la-fi-uber-california-20150726-story.html; Rosalind S. Helderman, *Uber Pressures Regulators by Mobilizing Riders and Hiring Vast Lobbying Network*, Wash. Post, Dec. 13, 2014 www.washingtonpost.com/politics/uber-pressures-regulators-by-mobilizing-riders-and-hiring-vast-lobbying-network/2014/12/13/3f43395c6-7f2a-11e4-9f38-95a187e4c1f7_story.html. Stone recounts the role of a lobbyist for Lyft in the development of the approach of the California Public Utilities Commission (CPUC) to ridesharing using nonprofessional drivers. Stone, *supra* note 1, at 200–04. Lyft and Sidecar began ridesharing in San Francisco in 2012, before Uber; CPUC was the first regulator to confront ridesharing. *Id.* at 197–200.

many parts of the United States.[6] As of the end of June 2017, 48 states have passed legislation facilitating the operations of TNCs,[7] although local governments regulate the TNCs in some of their biggest urban markets, such as New York City,[8] Washington, D.C.,[9] and Chicago.[10] Perhaps more important than the change in who is regulating is that jurisdictions are applying a much "lighter" regulatory framework to TNCs than the framework that governs the traditional taxi industry – even though both taxis and TNC vehicles compete in the same market for "point-to-point transportation."

   This chapter assesses the novelty of the regulatory regime that has been crafted for TNCs in the United States. I make three main points. First, I offer some historical context for analyzing the TNC regulatory regime in the United States. Decades before the creation of the TNCs, economists had critiqued traditional taxi regulation as antiquated and overly burdensome for the taxi industry. The old regulatory framework was ripe for change long before the TNCs arrived on the scene – and indeed their emergence was partly due to the sclerotic effect of taxi regulations on the taxi industry.[11] Second, I address the content of the regulatory regimes adopted by state and local governments for TNCs. Governments generally have adopted regulatory regimes that are broadly similar in their outlines in that they focus on public safety regulation, and omit the regulation of entry and fare levels that was central to the antiquated taxi regulatory regime. This focus on safety regulation is generally consistent with the longstanding recommendations of economists for the regulation of dispatched taxis, of which TNCs are the modern instantiation.[12] My third point concerns the limits of the regulatory innovation to date. The framework for regulating TNCs reflects the influence of the TNCs, just as the old taxi regulatory regime bore the imprint of the taxi industry. This raises the prospect that TNC regulation, like taxi regulation before it, could be sub-optimal from a broader societal perspective. It also could become a means to entrench the existing TNCs and enable them to complicate the entry of new businesses to the point-to-point transportation market.

----

[6] The term "Transportation Network Company" is commonly used in US law to refer to companies such as Uber and Lyft. CPUC is credited with coining the term; it "define[d] … a TNC as an organization … that provides prearranged transportation services for compensation using an online-enabled application (app) or platform to connect passengers with drivers using their personal vehicles." Decision Adopting Rules and Regulations to Protect Public Safety While Allowing New Entrants to the Transportation Industry, Cal. Pub. Utils. Comm'n, R. 12-02-001, 2 (2013).

[7] *Nearly Every State Requires Insurance Protections for TNC Drivers, Passengers and the Public*, Property Casualty Insurers Association of America (2017), www.pciaa.net/industry-issues/transportation-network-companies. Five of these 48 states have legislated to "address only insurance requirements for TNCs and TNC drivers." Maarit Moran et al., *Policy Implications of Transportation Network Companies: Final Report*, Texas A&M Transportation Institute: Transportation Policy Research Center 8 (2017), https://static.tti.tamu.edu/tti.tamu.edu/documents/PRC-17-70-F.pdf.

[8] New York State law preempts local regulation of TNCs, with two exceptions: New York City is not covered by the state legislation and remains allowed to regulate TNCs; and cities with populations exceeding 100,000 may refuse to allow TNCs to pick up passengers in their jurisdictions, but they may not regulate the TNCs if they allow them to operate. N.Y. Gen. Mun. Law § 182 (McKinney 2017); N.Y. Veh. & Traf. Law §§ 1691, 1692, 1693 & 1700 (McKinney 2017).

[9] D.C. Code Ann. §§ 50-301–50-332 (2017).

[10] Illinois TNC legislation establishes a regulatory floor and allows local governments to regulate more restrictively; Chicago has a TNC ordinance. 625 Ill. Comp. Stat. Ann. 57/32 (West 2017); Chicago, Ill., Municipal Code § 9-115 (Transportation Network Providers).

[11] Business journalist Adam Lashinsky has written that Travis Kalanick, one of the founders of Uber, resisted allowing Uber's short-lived Chinese operation to match riders and taxis because "For starters, Kalanick just didn't like the taxi business. Everything about Uber stood in opposition to it, most importantly what he saw as the twin pillars of taxi-industry sclerosis: fixed (low) supply of cars and set (high) prices… Simply connecting riders with taxi drivers wasn't profitable for Uber, and he had learned this the hard way in San Francisco." Lashinsky, *supra* note 1, at 193.

[12] For a nice elaboration of the point that TNCs are modern versions of dispatched taxis, *see* Eric Tucker, Uber and the Unmaking and Remaking of Taxi Capitalisms: Technology, Law and Resistance in Historical Perspective, in *Law and the "Sharing Economy": Regulating Online Market Platforms* (Derek McKee et al. eds., forthcoming).

I THE PRE-UBER STATUS QUO

According to Uber's "origins story," the company was created in response to the frustration that Garrett Camp and Travis Kalanick experienced trying to get a taxi in Paris one night in 2008.[13] In reality, this is an "after-the-fact creation myth."[14] Garrett Camp came up with "the idea of an on-demand car service"[15] before that night in Paris, because he was frustrated with the difficulty of getting a cab in San Francisco and saw the potential for smartphone technology to transform urban transportation.[16] But long before Camp identified the market opportunity in the heavily regulated San Francisco taxi industry, there was a well-developed critique of the existing taxi industry in many cities – and of the regulatory framework that governed it.

Pre-Uber, many big US cities had established local taxi industries subject to stable regulatory regimes that had not fundamentally changed in decades. These regimes often had five pillars.[17] They restricted entry into the taxi business, often by limiting the number of taxis by requiring that each one have one of a set number of taxicab licenses, frequently called medallions. These medallions were often valuable because the number of taxis in many cities was constrained to below the level of demand (at the regulated fares). Second, fares were regulated at levels that kept taxis from competing on price. Third, regulations governed the quality of taxi service, by limiting the kind and age of vehicles that could be used, requiring that drivers meet certain qualifications, and requiring insurance in the case of accidents. Fourth, in some cities there were some minimal protections for taxi drivers, although these were few and far between. Taxi drivers in many places were considered independent contractors and thus enjoyed few employment benefits.[18] Fifth, taxis were required not to discriminate, for example based on race or the destination of the passenger within city limits, although there were many complaints that taxi drivers nonetheless discriminated. In the early 2010s, a few big cities were extending universal service requirements to require that a certain percentage of taxis be accessible to persons with mobility disabilities.[19]

By the time the Uber app "went live" in San Francisco in 2010,[20] this regulatory structure and the industry that it had fostered had already been extensively critiqued by economists. The upstarts who founded and funded Uber and Lyft revolutionized the taxi business because they figured out how to use modern smartphone technology to provide more efficient point-to-point transportation, not because they were the first to perceive that the taxi industry and its regulatory framework were problematic. A canonical articulation of the economic critique of the taxi framework is a 1984 staff report from the Federal Trade Commission's Bureau of Economics.[21] The report, which drew extensively on economic scholarship, was released during the Reagan administration after the federal deregulation of the airline and other industries, and when the Federal Trade Commission was using "litigation and advocacy" to encourage local governments

---

[13] Stone, *supra* note 1, at 48 (referring to Uber's "origin myth"); Lashinsky, *supra* note 1, at 13. Stone and Lashinsky provide slightly different accounts of the origin myth. Lashinsky, *supra* note 1, at 13; Stone, *supra* note 1, at 51.

[14] Lashinsky, *supra* note 1, at 13.

[15] Stone, *supra* note 1, at 45.

[16] *Id.* at 45–47.

[17] This paragraph draws on my article *Taxi Regulation in the Age of Uber*, 20 N.Y.U. J. Legis. & Pub. Pol'y 1 (2017).

[18] *Id.* at 10 n. 19. Some traditional taxi drivers are covered by workers' compensation insurance and protected by government-mandated lease caps. *Id.* at 57–60.

[19] *Id.* at 70–71.

[20] Stone, *supra* note 1, at 57. Uber initially dispatched licensed town cars; it was not until 2013 that Uber used UberX to dispatch nonprofessional drivers. *Id.* at 204.

[21] Mark W. Frankena and Paul A. Pautler, *An Economic Analysis of Taxicab Regulation*, Federal Trade Commission, Bureau of Economics Staff Report (May 1984).

to deregulate the taxi industry.[22] The report advocated a substantial lessening of taxi regulation, at a time when a number of midsize local governments in the US were experimenting with such a policy. The report boldly stated that its "principal conclusion ... is that no persuasive economic rationale is available for some of the most important regulations" of "[t]he taxicab industry."[23] It portrayed the local experiments with deregulation in largely positive terms, although noting there had been some problems in some market segments.[24]

The 1984 report provides an accessible guide to the economics of taxi regulation – and, decades before the advent of Uber, identifies an economic rationale for some of the broad outlines of the regulatory framework that has been crafted to govern the TNCs. It finds no justification for limiting entry to the taxicab industry, and therefore recommends eliminating medallion requirements.[25] It emphasizes that restricting the number of taxis through medallion requirements constrains service because it makes it harder to get a cab during busy times, creates an artificial barrier to becoming a taxi driver because prospective drivers must obtain a medallion, and may lead to higher taxi fares.[26] Today, when people argue for limiting the number of TNC vehicles, they often do so on the basis that such vehicles contribute to traffic congestion. Frankena and Pautler dismissed the argument that limiting the number of taxis is necessary to reduce congestion. They argued that capping the number of cabs is a crude tool that "would reduce use of taxis in parts of the city and probably at times of the day for which congestion is not a serious problem," and that limiting the number of taxis might be offset by "road use by private automobiles."[27]

On the other hand, Frankena and Pautler argue that there is an economic rationale for regulating the safety of taxi service.[28] They maintain that regulations governing "vehicle safety or liability insurance coverage" are justifiable "[b]ecause it may be difficult or impossible for riders to judge some aspects of the quality of cab service."[29] They are less insistent that regulation of driver qualifications is necessary, arguing that taxi companies may have an incentive to monitor driver qualifications to maintain good reputations with customers, who may be repeat players.[30] On the other hand, they suggest that the external impacts of poor driver quality for third parties, such as pedestrians and other drivers, might justify regulating driver qualifications.[31] As I discuss below, a great deal of TNC regulation concerns the safety of TNC service, consistent with Frankena and Pautler's recommendations.

---

[22] Federal Trade Commission, *1985 Annual Report* 5 (1985), www.ftc.gov/sites/default/files/documents/reports_annual/annual-report-1985/ar1985_0.pdf; Organisation for Economic Co-operation and Development, Directorate for Financial and Enterprise Affairs, Competition Committee, *Taxi Services Regulation and Competition* 199 (2008).

[23] Frankena and Pautler, *supra* note 21, at 1.

[24] Many of these experiments were later reversed, with cities re-regulating the taxi industry. For critical assessments of the experiments with deregulation in the US taxi sector in the late 1970s and early 1980s, *see* Bruce Schaller, *Entry Controls in Taxi Regulation: Implications of U.S. and Canadian Experience for Taxi Regulation and Deregulation*, 14 Transport Pol'y 290 (2007); Price Waterhouse, *Analysis of Taxicab Deregulation & Re-Regulation*, Prepared for the International Taxicab Foundation (1993).

[25] Frankena and Pautler, *supra* note 21, at 1. The report notes the political barriers to deregulating, referring to the politics of eliminating the value of medallions, as well as transition costs. *Id.* at 124–25.

[26] *Id.* at 84–89, 93, 97–98, 104.

[27] *Id.* at 40.

[28] *Id.* at 1, 4, 38, 63, 65.

[29] *Id.* at 4; *see also id.* at 101 ("economists generally have not criticized ... regulations aimed at quality, e.g., vehicle conditions, driver qualifications, and insurance requirements").

[30] *Id.* at 56–57.

[31] *Id.* at 73, at n. 96. They are somewhat equivocal on this point, suggesting that externalities might only justify enforcing the same standards on taxis as well as other vehicles, but just more strictly. *Id.*

The report was nuanced in its recommendations concerning fare level regulation. Frankena and Pautler indicate that there is a strong rationale for fare ceilings – not the mandatory, uniform fares that many cities imposed – for cabs picking up people on the street and at cab stands at airports and other hubs, based on transaction costs. Such ceilings are needed because passengers face an informational barrier to bargaining, as they will not know when the next cab will arrive and what it will charge.[32] Bargaining also would not be easy at a cab stand given the prevailing norm of taking the first cab in the line.[33] These rationales would not justify regulating the level of fares charged by radio-dispatched cabs, historically the largest share of the taxi market in most cities,[34] and the segment which the TNCs most closely resemble because they are dispatched, albeit digitally. A passenger calling a dispatcher should have an easier time comparison shopping based on price than someone hailing a cab on the street or at a stand; the passenger can call another dispatch service if they dislike the quoted price. But, foreshadowing the argument that Uber is a natural monopoly, the report suggests that there could be economies of scale for dispatched taxi firms that might limit the number of firms that could operate profitably, and provide the active firms with market power to impose high prices.[35] However, Frankena and Pautler observe that "[t]hese economies of scale … would be more likely to cause problems of market power and inefficient resource allocation in small urban areas than in large ones. In addition, market power would not be a significant concern in areas where … good substitutes, such as public transit, exist."[36] Thus they conclude that "price competition is workable" in large cities.[37] Frankena and Pautler's reticence toward fare level regulation for dispatched taxis is worth keeping in mind, as we contemplate the virtual absence of TNC fare level regulation.

Frankena and Pautler emphasized that their conclusions that taxi regulation should be slimmed down and refocused mirrored the consensus view among economists.[38] Decades later, economists still largely favored deregulation of the taxi industry,[39] and the FTC stood by Frankena and Pautler's report as well.[40] Indeed, there were some cities where dispatched taxis were lightly regulated in general conformity with Frankena and Pautler's recommendations. For example, alongside New York City's heavily regulated yellow medallion taxis, the City, since the 1980s, has had a much more lightly regulated for-hire vehicle sector in which vehicles are dispatched and not allowed to pick up street hails or at cab stands.[41] The City never limited the number of for-hire vehicles, although it required that each vehicle affiliate with a licensed base; nor did the City set fare levels for this sector. The City, which is an extremely important US market for the TNCs, was able to use its for-hire category to license Uber and Lyft, which agreed to comply with the City's existing rules for for-hire vehicles, including the requirement that

---

[32] *Id.* at 46–52. Now that most people have smartphones, the informational obstacle to bargaining with a street hailed taxi may not be as great, because passengers – and drivers – can check on their phone when a TNC vehicle might arrive and know what it will charge.

[33] *Id.* at 50.

[34] *Id.* at 3.

[35] *Id.* at 53–56.

[36] *Id.* at 55.

[37] *Id.* at 83.

[38] *Id.* at 99.

[39] Adrian T. Moore and Ted Balaker, *Do Economists Reach a Conclusion on Taxi Deregulation?* 3 Econ. J. Watch 109, 126 (2006).

[40] *See Letter to State of Colorado Public Utilities Commission*, Federal Trade Commission, Office of Policy Planning, Bureau of Competition, Bureau of Consumer Protection, Bureau of Economics, Docket No. 13R-0009TR, March 6, 2013 at 2.

[41] Katrina M. Wyman, *Problematic Private Property: The Case of New York Taxicab Medallions*, 30 Yale J. on Reg. 133–35, 172 (2013).

drivers be licensed by the City's Taxi and Limousine Commission. Thus New York City, unlike other jurisdictions, did not need to create an entirely new regulatory framework for the TNCs.[42]

II THE TNC REGULATORY FRAMEWORK AND ITS ECONOMIC LOGIC

Flash forward to 2017. Forty-eight state legislatures have passed legislation legalizing and regulating TNCs; in some big cities, such as New York City, Washington, D.C., and Chicago, they operate under local (or a combination of local and state) regulation. The regulatory frameworks governing TNCs are broadly similar in their general outlines in that jurisdictions are mainly focusing on regulating the safety of TNC service.[43] This focus on safety is consistent with Frankena and Pautler's recommendations for regulating radio-dispatched cabs.

While many jurisdictions require that TNCs obtain a government license or a permit to operate, to my knowledge no jurisdiction explicitly limits the number of TNCs it will allow.[44] Moreover, no jurisdiction in the United States regulates the number of vehicles that a TNC can put on the road. No jurisdiction establishes the fare levels that are charged by TNCs. To the extent that jurisdictions regulate fares, they tend to be requiring disclosure by TNCs, for example by requiring that TNCs "[d]isclose fares and rates to passengers" before passengers take the trip,[45] and by requiring that TNCs provide riders with a receipt after the trip is over.[46] Only a small number of jurisdictions appear to have regulations dealing with the level of TNC fares, and these do not seem especially intrusive. A few jurisdictions limit the TNCs' ability to engage in surge pricing, for example, by restricting such pricing during emergencies[47] or requiring that customers actively consent to such pricing.[48]

The absence of entry regulation, and virtual absence of fare level regulation, is economically rational for the reasons that Frankena and Pautler argued against such regulation for radio-dispatched taxis. Limits on the number of TNC vehicles would make it harder for riders to get a vehicle, and likely increase fares and reduce service quality because they would limit

---

[42] Wyman, *supra* note 17, at 17–18; Stone, *supra* note 1, at 163–64.

[43] I base my comments on the contents of the legislation and regulations in the United States on three sources: (1) a policy brief analyzing the contents of 48 state statutes and legislation from Washington, D.C., up to date as of August 2017, prepared by the Transportation Policy Research Center at the Texas A&M Transportation Institute, *see* Moran et al., *supra* note 7; (2) a survey of 48 state statutes plus Washington, D.C., prepared for me in late 2015 and early 2016 by research assistants Aaron Lichter and André Smith, and updated in the summer and fall of 2017 by research assistants Julia Kindlon and Caleb Thomas, summarized in Summary Memorandum (Oct. 22, 2017) (on file with author); and (3) my own reading of some of the legislation and regulations passed in US jurisdictions.

[44] Moran et al., *supra* note 7, at 20 (Table 2: Policies and Regulations in State TNC Legislation as of August 2017) (36 out of 44 jurisdictions "[r]equire a TNC permit").

[45] *Id.* (41 of 44 jurisdictions require disclosure of "fares and rates to passengers"); Summary Memorandum, *supra* note 43, at 3 (39 of 49 jurisdictions require that TNCs provide fare estimate, fares, or fare calculation methods, in advance).

[46] Moran et al., *supra* note 7, at 20 (Table 2: Policies and Regulations in State TNC Legislation as of August 2017) (37 of 44 jurisdictions require TNCs to "[p]rovide electronic receipt to passengers"); Summary Memorandum, *supra* note 43, at 3 (36 of 49 jurisdictions require receipt). Georgia regulates the elements that TNCs can use to price fares. Ga. Code Ann. § 40-1-196(c) (2017); Nebraska mandates that TNCs file their rates with the state's Public Service Commission. Neb. Rev. Stat. Ann. § 75–327(2)(c) (2017).

[47] Moran et al., *supra* note 7, at 20 (Table 2: Policies and Regulations in State TNC Legislation as of August 2017) (seven states "[l]imit dynamic pricing in a state of emergency"); Summary Memorandum, *supra* note 43, at 2 (5 of 49 jurisdictions regulate dynamic pricing in emergencies). *See, e.g.*, Conn. Gen. Stat. Ann. P.A. 17–140 § 3 (4)(C) (West 2017) (TNC cannot increase price of a ride by over 2.5 times the usual price in areas subject to emergency declarations); Mass. Gen. Laws Ann. ch. 159A 1/2 § 2(e) (West 2016) (prohibiting raising "base fares" during an emergency).

[48] Moran et al., *supra* note 7, at 20 (Table 2: Policies and Regulations in State TNC Legislation as of August 2017) (four states require the disclosure of "dynamic pricing and require passenger confirmation"). *See, e.g.*, Conn. Gen. Stat. Ann. P.A. 17–140 § 3 (b) (4)(B) (West 2017).

competition. They would not reduce congestion, something that it is widely agreed would be better done through variable congestion pricing applied to all vehicles (not just taxis or TNC vehicles).[49] There is no need for fare level regulation because no TNC has the market power to dictate prices for rides; in fact, Uber is reportedly subsidizing over 50 percent of the cost of rides as it works to build scale and out-compete Lyft and traditional taxis.[50] Also, consumers can compare the prices of rides on Uber and Lyft – and substitutes for them – before they decide to use a TNC vehicle.

Most of the regulations introduced fall broadly into the category of safety regulation, which it is easy to rationalize in economic terms. Consumers want to know that the driver and car driving them are safe and that there is insurance in case of an accident, but it is costly for them to obtain information about driver and vehicle safety and to confirm insurance coverage. Such regulation also protects other drivers and pedestrians, who are not parties to the driver–passenger transaction. It also addresses cognitive failures on the part of TNC riders and drivers, who may be prone to underestimating the dangers of accidents, and unsafe vehicles and drivers.[51]

Insurance requirements are the most universal form of safety regulation of TNCs. All states that have legislation governing TNCs include insurance requirements.[52] These insurance requirements grew out of the limited provision of insurance by TNCs when they first began using nonprofessional drivers for ride-sharing in 2012/2013.[53] In March 2015, Uber, Lyft, and property and casualty insurers agreed on a model insurance bill that they then began urging state legislatures to adopt.[54] The model bill, which is reflected in much state legislation regulating TNCs, distinguishes two time periods: a first period when a driver is logged on to one or more TNC apps but does not have a passenger, and a second period, which begins when the

[49] Uber has endorsed road pricing, its term for congestion pricing. Andrew Salzberg, *Road Pricing: A Solution to Gridlock*, Medium, Mar. 30, 2017, https://medium.com/uber-under-the-hood/road-pricing-a-solution-to-gridlock-b093b3f364f2. Uber is one of the coalition partners supporting Move NY, which advocates a form of congestion pricing for New York City. *Move NY Endorsements*, Move NY, Oct. 16, 2017, https://movenewyork.wordpress.com/move-ny-endorsements/. For a recent call for congestion pricing in New York City, *see* Schaller Consulting, *Unsustainable? The Growth of App-Based Ride Services and Traffic, Travel and the Future of New York City* (2017), www.schallerconsult.com/rideservices/unsustainable.pdf.

[50] Steven Hill, *What Dara Khosrowshahi Must Do to Save Uber*, N.Y. Times, Aug. 30, 2017 (Uber is "subsidiz[ing]" at least 50 percent of every ride").

[51] Benjamin G. Edelman and Damien Geradin, *Efficiencies and Regulatory Shortcuts: How Should We Regulate Companies Like Airbnb and Uber?*, 19 Stan. Tech. L. Rev. 293, 317–18 (2016).

[52] Moran et al., *supra* note 7, at 8 ("48 states and Washington, D.C."); Summary Memorandum, *supra* note 43, at 3 (all 49 jurisdictions reviewed require the TNC or driver to have insurance). As mentioned above, a small number of states have legislation that addresses only insurance for TNCs. *Supra* note 7.

[53] Maarit Moran, *Policy Implications of Transportation Network Companies*, Texas A&M Transportation Institute: Transportation Policy Research Center 8 (2016), https://policy.tti.tamu.edu/technology/prc-report-policy-implications-of-transportation-network-companies/; Transportation Network Company Insurance Principles for Legislators and Regulators, National Association of Insurance Commissioners (2015). When Uber launched in 2010, its original business model relied on using professionally licensed drivers, and it was dispatching relatively high-end black cars. Lyft and Sidecar pioneered the use of nonprofessional drivers in 2012. Uber introduced nonprofessional drivers to its platform in 2013, after the California Public Utilities Commission legalized the use of nonprofessional drivers by Lyft and Sidecar. Stone, *supra* note 1, at 197–200, 204–05.

[54] National Association of Insurance Commissioners & The Center for Insurance Policy and Research, *Commercial Ride-Sharing*, www.naic.org/cipr_topics/topic_commercial_ride_sharing.htm; TNC Insurance Compromise Model Bill, Mar. 26, 2015, www.naic.org/documents/committees_c_sharing_econ_wg_related_tnc_insurance_compromise_bill_package.pdf; Moran, *supra* note 53, at 8–9. The National Conference of Insurance Legislators also adopted a model bill in the summer of 2015. Model Act to Regulate Insurance Requirements for Transportation Network Companies and Transportation Network Drivers, National Conference of Insurance Legislators, July 19, 2015, http://ncoil.org/wp-content/uploads/2016/04/07232015TNCModelAct.pdf. For a comparison of the model bills, *see* National Association of Insurance Commissioners & The Center for Insurance Policy and Research, *supra*.

driver accepts a ride, continues when the rider enters the vehicle, and ends when they exit.[55] The levels of required insurance are more stringent for the second period than when the driver is merely logged onto the app;[56] and the second period levels may be higher than that required of traditional taxis.[57] Insurance must be provided by the TNC, the driver, or a combination.[58]

Driver qualifications are also addressed in much of the regulation governing TNCs.[59] Traditional taxi drivers are usually licensed by government and undergo certain checks; except in a few markets, such as New York City, the bulk of TNC drivers are not required to have a specific government-issued license. Still, in most places TNC legislation and regulations establish minimal requirements for drivers before TNCs are allowed to on-board them to their platforms. For example, drivers must have a standard driver's license and personal automobile insurance, satisfy a minimum age requirement, and not have been convicted of various disqualifying criminal offenses or have more than a certain number of moving violations.[60] When Lyft and Sidecar began matching nonprofessional drivers with riders in San Francisco in 2012, they were checking drivers' criminal backgrounds but not their driving history.[61] TNC drivers now often must pass background checks.[62] The scope of these background checks has been controversial. TNCs have fiercely resisted government efforts to require that drivers be fingerprinted before being on-boarded and insisted that "name-based background check[s]" are sufficient.[63] However, in New York City, they are required to use licensed drivers who are subject to fingerprinting.[64] Also, TNCs have insisted that they want to manage the driver background checks to avoid government bureaucracy delaying on-boarding. Most state TNC legislation delegates to TNCs the task of conducting or verifying the background checks, allowing them to use third party vendors.[65]

---

[55] Moran, *supra* note 53, at 9 ("Many states, including Texas, have insurance legislation that is similar to this model"); Summary Memorandum, *supra* note 43, at 3 (48 jurisdictions use the two-period framework). Maryland seems to be an exception; its legislation specifies a single level of coverage for "while an operator is providing transportation network services." Md. Code Ann., Public Utilities § 10–405 (a)(2)(i) (2017).

[56] Under the model insurance bill, when the driver is "logged on to" an app, there must be "Primary automobile liability insurance in the amount of at least $50,000 for death and bodily injury per person, $100,000 for death and bodily injury per incident, and $25,000 for property damage" plus whatever other insurance is required for drivers under state law. When the driver is engaged in a ride there must be liability insurance of "at least $1,000,000 for death, bodily injury and property damage." TNC Insurance Compromise Model Bill, *supra* note 54, at section B.

[57] Christian Denmon, *Ride Sharing vs. Traditional Taxis, How do Insurance Injury Claims Compare?*, Huffpost, The Blog, July 7, 2014, www.huffingtonpost.com/christian-denmon/ride-sharing-vs-tradition_b_5273964.html.

[58] TNC Insurance Compromise Model Bill, *supra* note 54, at section B.

[59] Moran et al., *supra* note 7, at 20 (Table 2: Policies and Regulations in State TNC Legislation as of August 2017) (42 out of 44 jurisdictions require that drivers "[m]eet a set of driver requirements/submit an application to the TNC"); Summary Memorandum, *supra* note 43, at 4 (40 of 49 jurisdictions require some driver qualifications).

[60] Moran, *supra* note 53, at 9 ("Policies commonly require drivers to be at least a certain minimum age (18 to 21 years) and have a valid driver's license, valid vehicle registration, and proof of automobile liability insurance").

[61] Stone, *supra* note 1, at 204.

[62] Summary Memorandum, *supra* note 43, at 4 (42 jurisdictions require the TNC or a third party working for it to conduct a background check on drivers).

[63] Moran et al., *supra* note 7, at 4 ("Forty-two states and Washington, D.C., require TNCs to have a name-based background check conducted for a TNC driver before, or within a specified amount of time after, that driver is allowed to operate"). On the objections of the TNCs to fingerprinting requirements, *see, e.g., id.* at 11–12; John Kartch, *Austin's Fingerprint Regime for Uber & Lyft Will Harm Minority Drivers*, Forbes, May 12, 2016, www.forbes.com/sites/johnkartch/2016/05/12/naacp-austins-fingerprint-regime-for-uber-lyft-will-harm-minority-drivers/#2089c9021143.

[64] *New Driver Applicants*, NYC Taxi & Limousine Commission, www.nyc.gov/html/tlc/html/industry/drivers.shtml.

[65] Summary Memorandum, *supra* note 43, at 4 (42 of 49 jurisdictions require the TNC or a third party working for it to conduct a background check on drivers). Massachusetts has a dual vetting model, under which the TNCs and the state Department of Public Utilities both check drivers before they are on-boarded. Mass Gen. Laws. Ann. ch. 159A ½ § 3(d) & 4(a)&(c) (West 2017). While the text emphasizes the screening requirements for drivers, state legislation also requires TNCs to police the behavior of drivers while on the platforms. For example, TNCs are required to have

TNC regulation also commonly addresses the safety of the vehicle.[66] Many TNC vehicles are personal vehicles that are being used on the side. In contrast, traditional taxis in big cities are often special purpose vehicles that by regulation must be "hacked up" to meet various regulatory specifications, and are regularly inspected by government agencies. TNC legislation does not appear to require that vehicles be fitted in a particular way, or that they undergo a rigorous regimen of government inspections.[67]

Among the other types of consumer protections that some TNC legislation mandates are non-discrimination policies to prevent discrimination against passengers.[68] Very little TNC regulation is geared toward protecting drivers. In fact, some states seem intent on protecting TNCs from having to provide drivers with employment protections and benefits; 13 state statutes specify that TNC drivers are presumed to be independent contractors, generally provided that certain conditions are satisfied.[69]

Local regulation of TNCs is generally preempted in many states, although as mentioned above, a few states have carved out exceptions allowing major cities, such as New York City and Chicago, to regulate TNCs.[70] Like the focus on safety regulation, the shift to state regulation in many places can also be justified in economic terms. In many regions for-hire vehicles are more efficiently operated if they can pick up and drop off customers in more than one municipality. Although it was not a central theme of their report, Frankena and Pautler noted that the taxi industry suffered from being regulated by a multiplicity of small local jurisdictions. The fragmentation of regulatory authority inhibited it from operating on a wider scale, requiring cabs that dropped off in one locality to "deadhead" back to their home locality without a passenger.[71] State-level regulation allows the TNCs to operate on a geographically large scale. It also takes advantage of economies of scale in regulation by limiting the number of regulations and regulators establishing similar standards for the same industry.

III CONTINUITIES AND CONCERNS

Notwithstanding the novelty and economic rationality of aspects of the TNC regulatory framework, there are some disturbing continuities with historical taxi regulation. One is the extent to which TNC regulation, like taxi regulation before it, seems to be the product of lobbying by

---

policies prohibiting "drug and alcohol use" by their drivers. Moran et al., *supra* note 7, at 20 (Table 2: Policies and Regulations in State TNC Legislation as of August 2017) (38 of 44 jurisdictions require that TNCs "[h]ave a drug and alcohol use prohibition or policy (zero tolerance)").

[66] Moran et al., *supra* note 7, at 46 ("Twenty-three states require TNCs to complete a vehicle safety inspection or specify that the TNC is responsible for ensuring that TNC vehicles comply with a vehicle safety standard. While the wording of the requirements varies by state, TNCs are typically held to the same safety standards as private vehicles."); Summary Memorandum, *supra* note 43, at 3 (29 of 49 jurisdictions require TNC vehicles to satisfy inspection standards).

[67] Moran et al., *supra* note 7, at 20 (Table 2: Policies and Regulations in State TNC Legislation as of August 2017) (19 jurisdictions require the "display [of] a trade dress, logo, or emblem on the TNC vehicle").

[68] *Id.* at 52 ("Thirty-six states and Washington, D.C., require TNCs to adopt a non-discrimination policy").

[69] Summary Memorandum, *supra* note 43, at 4. In addition, six state statutes contain language that could be interpreted as implying that TNC drivers should be regarded as independent contractors. *Id.*; *see, e.g.*, Ok. Stat. Ann. Tit. 47, § 1011(4) (West 2017).

[70] Moran et al., *supra* note 7, at 3 ("A majority of state legislation overrules, or preempts, the local authority of cities to regulate, tax, or impose rules on TNCs"); *see also* Summary Memorandum, *supra* note 43, at 5–6 (38 of 49 jurisdictions preempt municipal regulation). States preempt local regulation to varying degrees. *See* Moran et al., *supra* note 7, at 10–11. For example, South Dakota preempts municipal regulation only of insurance for TNCs. S.D. Codified Laws § 32-40-23 (2017).

[71] Frankena and Pautler, *supra* note 21, at 91.

powerful interest groups, rather than evidence-based.[72] The TNCs, rather than the traditional taxi industry, are now likely the most powerful interest group in for-hire transportation in many jurisdictions, and they have spent large sums of money to advance their interests. This creates the possibility that TNC regulation is sub-optimal from a societal perspective.

While there is a rationale for state regulation of TNCs in many regions, there is no doubt that one reason that states are regulating in many places is that the TNCs perceived local governments as excessively influenced by the traditional taxi industry and so did an end run around them and appealed to state legislators. In Texas, for example, Uber and Lyft aggressively lobbied for state TNC legislation preempting local authority after Austin insisted on fingerprinting drivers.[73] Texas passed such legislation in the spring of 2017.[74] While accommodating the agenda of the TNCs, states have also found innovative ways of extracting revenues from the TNCs, through license or permitting fees and taxes.[75]

The TNC regulatory framework generally is a company-licensing regime that reflects the business model and interests of existing TNCs. The regime is built for large, well-capitalized companies like Uber (and to a lesser extent Lyft) that can afford to apply to state governments for a license or permit.[76] (In Colorado alone, a TNC must pay $111,250.00 annually to operate.[77]) To comply, TNCs also must have the resources to acquire fleet-wide insurance, screen (or hire another party to screen) many drivers, and satisfy the other requirements that individual states have imposed. While the app technology that undergirds Uber and Lyft may be fairly inexpensive to replicate and improve upon, building out a business that can operate legally in accordance with the existing TNC legislation and regulation will be costly, and limit the likelihood of new competitors. Also, my impression is that the ability of the traditional taxi industry to compete with the TNCs is being hampered by a tendency to legalize TNCs without significantly lightening the regulatory burden on incumbent taxis.[78] For many state legislators and regulators, it

---

[72] *Supra* note 5 (citing articles describing TNC lobbying). On the history of the taxi industry's influence on taxi regulation, *see, e.g.*, Wyman, *supra* note 41; Edmund W. Kitch et al., *The Regulation of Taxicabs in Chicago*, 14 J.L. & Econ. 285 (1971).

[73] Michael King, *Lege for Sale?, Uber and Lyft Splurge on Lobby to Deregulate Themselves*, The Austin Chronicle, Mar. 14, 2017, www.austinchronicle.com/daily/news/2017-03-14/lege-for-sale/.

[74] Alex Samuels, *Senate Sends Bill Creating Statewide Ride-hailing Regulations to Governor*, Texas Tribune, May 17, 2017, www.texastribune.org/2017/05/17/senate-tentatively-backs-measure-creating-statewide-regulations-ride-h/.

[75] *See, e.g.*, N.Y. Tax Law § 1292 (McKinney 2017) (imposing 4 percent tax on gross TNC fares for rides beginning in New York State (but not New York City) and ending in the State); N.Y. Veh. & Traf. Law § 1692(2) (McKinney 2017); *FAQ for TNC Applicants*, New York State, Department of Motor Vehicles, https://dmv.ny.gov/more-info/faq-tnc-applicants (the TNC must pay an initial license application fee of $100,000 and then $60,000 annually to renew its license).

[76] Derek McKee's contribution to this volume nicely brings out the role of government licensing in the "sharing economy." There is a historical precedent for the use of company-licensing regimes in taxi regulation. Before the advent of TNCs, some jurisdictions licensed cab companies, rather than individual cabs. Schaller, *supra* note 24, at 494; 495–96 (Table 2: Key characteristics of entry-related policies in selected cities and counties). On how licensing fees and insurance requirements may inhibit new entrants that want to compete with TNCs, *see* Matthew W. Daus, *Post-TNC Transportation Policy & Planning: Who and What Should be Regulated & How to "Level the Playing Field" with Taxicabs and For-Hire Vehicles*, University Transportation Research Center 9–10 (2016), www.utrc2.org/sites/default/files/Final-Post-TNC-Planning-Leveling-the-Playing-Field.pdf. New York City is an exception, as Uber and Lyft do not operate under company licenses. Like other actors in the for-hire sector, they are required to have licensed bases for the vehicles affiliated with them. *For-Hire Vehicles*, New York City Taxi & Limousine Commission, www.nyc.gov/html/tlc/html/industry/for_hire.shtml.

[77] Colo. Rev. Stat. Ann. § 40-10.1-606 (West 2014). Colorado's annual fee may be the highest among the states. Moran, *supra* note 53, at 8.

[78] The extent to which jurisdictions have revisited the regulation of the traditional taxi industry in light of the advent of TNCs deserves more systematic analysis. In some states, TNC legislation touches upon taxi regulation, but gestures toward changing it without actually changing it. *See, e.g.*, 80 Del. Laws 374 § 2 (2016) (Delaware Department of

may be easier to allow the traditional taxi industry to wither. The kinds of change necessary to make the taxi industry competitive may be too politically difficult to implement. Moreover, at this point, with TNCs well established in many parts of the United States, even radical changes to traditional taxi regulation might not save the taxi industry in many places.

As mentioned above, there is an economic rationale for the focus in TNC regulation on safety, but this focus– and the details of the existing safety regulation in many places – also fits nicely with the interests of TNCs. Early on, Uber opposed being regulated like traditional taxis. But Uber and Lyft quickly recognized the benefits of some regulation. Remember that in 2015, Uber and Lyft agreed with property and casualty insurers on a model insurance bill and advocated for that bill in state legislatures. Uber also developed a broader legislative package that it wanted adopted, as evidenced by the similarity of many of the state TNC statutes.[79] Some degree of regulation serves a variety of purposes for TNCs: it helps instill public trust in the industry that is essential to recruit and maintain passengers and drivers, provides regulatory certainty that may reassure the investors that the TNCs need to keep afloat while they are still losing money, fends off more burdensome regulation, and safeguards the incumbent TNCs from new competitors.

Moreover, except in a few jurisdictions such as New York City, the safety regulation of the TNCs is not especially stringent. The driver qualification requirements largely codify TNC practices, and reflect the TNCs' opposition to fingerprinting and government screening of drivers.[80] The two-period approach to insurance means that pedestrians and other drivers on the road have less insurance coverage when TNC drivers are merely logged onto the app as compared with when TNC drivers are on the way to pick up, or driving, a paying passenger. It is hard to fault policymakers for the choices that they have made because there is little empirical evidence about the costs and benefits of different levels of safety regulation for TNCs, including fingerprinting.[81] But hopefully, as more experience is gained with the sector, policymakers will be open to revisiting these choices in line with emerging evidence. Indeed some regulators already appear to be tightening up some aspects of TNC regulation.[82]

CONCLUSION

At the time of writing in the summer of 2017, there is considerable uncertainty about the future of Uber, which like Lyft, seems to still be losing large sums of money in the United States a

---

Transportation directed to recommend to General Assembly ways of leveling "'the playing field'" between TNCs and public carriers by January 15, 2017). On the other hand, there are states that seem to be willing to revisit traditional taxi regulation. *See, e.g.*, Ga. Code Ann., § 40-1-191 (West 2015) (recognizing "that it is in the public interest to provide uniform administration and parity among" TNCs and "taxi services"); 53 Pa. Cons. Stat. §57B02 (c) (2017) (directing the Philadelphia Parking Authority to reform taxi regulation).

[79] The analysis of Moran et al. nicely brings out the similar kinds of issue addressed in many state statutes. Moran et al., *supra* note 7.

[80] Business journalist Adam Lashinsky provides a lighthearted account of how easy it was for him to become an Uber driver in 2016. Lashinsky, *supra* note 1, at 161–62.

[81] Joe Fitzgerald Rodriguez, *Sweeping New Regulations Proposed for Uber, Lyft May Level Playing Field for Taxis*, San Francisco Examiner, Oct. 13, 2017, www.sfexaminer.com/more-inspections-criminal-checks-in-sweeping-new-ca-regulations-for-uber-lyft/ (referring to lack of empirical evidence about effects of fingerprinting on safety). In mandating insurance levels, some legislatures recognized that they were legislating without adequate information, and required additional study of insurance coverage. *See, e.g.*, Cal. Pub. Util. Code § 918.2 (West 2017) (California Public Utilities Commission and Department of Insurance to report on whether the insurance requirements "are appropriate to the risk of transportation network companies" by December 31, 2017 "to promote data-driven decisions on insurance requirements"); Colo. Rev. Stat. § 40.10.1-604(3)(c) (2014) (requiring Division of Insurance to study whether insurance coverage levels are appropriate).

[82] Rodriguez, *supra* note 81.

number of years after it was created. The ultimate fate of the regulatory frameworks established in the past few years to legalize and govern the TNCs is bound up with the fate of these TNCs. Having escaped the application of the antiquated taxi regulatory structure, will Uber and Lyft find a way to profitability in the United States, and entrench themselves?[83] Will new TNCs emerge, perhaps from Uber and Lyft, to take advantage of the regulatory regime that they have built? Or will Uber and Lyft be displaced by new technology and business models – such as company-owned fleets of dispatched driverless cars – that seek to construct their own regulatory regime, and leave the TNC regime to wither much as it has relegated taxi regulation to the sidelines? For all the ways that TNC regulation represents an innovative departure from traditional taxi regulation in many jurisdictions, the regulatory regime is still fundamentally reactive, because it is a response to changes in technology and business models. But the fate of the historical taxi industry emphasizes that regulatory structures themselves may influence innovation. The antiquated taxi regulatory structure protected the old taxi industry and reduced its incentive to develop new business models. It was outsiders to the industry, like Garrett Camp and Travis Kalanick, who saw the potential of smartphone technology and applied it to point-to-point transportation. Time will tell if, and how, the TNC regulatory structure influences the future course of innovation in point-to-point transportation.

---

[83] Samuels, *supra* note 74.

Framing the Regulatory Response

10

Pluralism and Regulatory Responses

Erez Aloni

INTRODUCTION

Not all activities in the platform economy are commensurate. Some nonprofessional providers perform activities infrequently and through increased excess capacity (that is, using their surplus goods, time, or skills). Conversely, specialized providers conduct other activities at a commercial pace by harnessing assets designated primarily for the exchanges. The first set of activities, which I call "work in increased use of excess capacity," generates more valuable choice to consumers and workers and often produces fewer negative externalities. The latter type of activity sometimes results, or risks resulting, in reduced choice for workers and consumers and often leads to more negative externalities than the first type. In this chapter I flesh out the differences between the two kinds of activity and argue that their dissimilarities warrant divergent regulatory responses.

Recent scholarship advancing a theory of pluralism in private law helps to show why the different activities deserve dissimilar regulatory regimes. Consequently, I build on existing literature about pluralistic theory, and develop it further, enlisting its principles to guide the regulation of the platform economy. As I explain below, pluralism charges that the state support increased choice for individuals by facilitating alternative economic and social spheres that embody diverse values. Promoting choice, however, does not mean deregulation but, rather, requires that the state establish a set of different valuable alternatives that safeguard individuals from possible free-market harms. Because work grounded in increased use of excess capacity engenders more choice for consumers and workers, pluralistic principles suggest that the state should encourage these kinds of activities by tailoring regulation to the activities in this category. By the same token, because commercial activities that are not based in increased use of excess capacity yield more negative externalities including reduced choice, lawmakers should adopt a more rigorous and protective set of regulations to restrain such harms.

In what follows, I briefly canvass the origins, development, and principles of pluralistic theory. Next, I argue that we should distinguish between activities in the platform economy, based on where they fall on a spectrum of use of excess capacity. I submit that platform-generated activities that leverage increased use of excess capacity promote valuable choice, whereas activities that gravitate toward commercial work with little or no increased use of excess capacity can decrease it. Finally, I use pluralistic theory to underpin my suggestions for the regulation of economic activities facilitated by platforms.

A note about terminology: naming the economic model at stake is a source of fierce and important debate and is not an issue of mere semantics. Because "sharing" is a misnomer, and "gig" economy describes only part of the activities that platforms facilitate (further, its use distracts attention from commercial activities that are a big part of such activities), I employ the more neutral term "platform economy."[1]

I A BRIEF INTRODUCTION TO AUTONOMY-BASED PLURALISM

The term "pluralism" has various meanings in legal academia and other academic disciplines. The version of pluralistic theory that I build on and develop here is an extension of various scholarly investigations. I refer particularly to "autonomy-based pluralism," a theoretical approach that Hanoch Dagan explicated, primarily by relying on the seminal work of Joseph Raz on the connection between autonomy and pluralism.

For Raz, personal autonomy (to distinguish from moral autonomy) is both instrumentally valuable and a constituent of well-being because it enables individuals to control, navigate, and create good lives. Alternatively, in Raz's favorite metaphor, it enables them to be the authors of their own lives. Hence, the life of an autonomous person "is, in part, of his own making."[2] When individuals can shape their own lives, their self-definition and self-realization become conceivable; this, in turn, means that they can maximize their potential.[3] Raz proposes three conditions that are necessary to exercise such personal autonomy: first, an individual must have the mental and physical capabilities required to make rational choices and carry them out; second, individuals must be independent in their choices, which means they must be free from coercion and manipulation; third, an autonomous person must have an *adequate* range of choices from which to choose.[4]

Most important to this account is the third condition. In order to lead an autonomous life, having a choice and the ability to exercise choice are not sufficient conditions for autonomy: an adequate range of choices is a requisite condition. To illustrate, a man trapped in a pit with enough food for survival has the capacity to exercise choice but not enough options to live an autonomous life.[5] Raz states, "A person is autonomous only if he has a variety of acceptable options available to him to choose from, and his life became as it is through his choice of some of these options."[6] An "adequate range" does not mean the quantity but the variety of alternatives. Many choices of the commensurate thing do not satisfy this requirement.[7]

Valuing autonomy in this sense, Raz maintains, requires adoption of moral pluralism, "the view that there are various forms and styles of life which exemplify different virtues and which are incompatible."[8] This view endorses the existence of various incompatible and valuable pursuits, relationships, and commitments that individuals can choose from as a means to exercise their autonomy. Razian pluralistic principles thus assume a meaningful range of worthwhile options

---

[1]   *See* Erez Aloni, *Pluralizing the "Sharing" Economy*, 91 Wash. L. Rev. 1397, 1406–07 (2016) (critiquing the existing definitions of the platform economic).
[2]   Joseph Raz, *The Morality of Freedom* 204 (1986).
[3]   Joseph Raz, Liberalism, Autonomy, and the Politics of Neutral Concern, *in* 7 *Midwest Studies In Philosophy* 202 (P. French, T. Uehling, and H. Wettstein eds., 1982).
[4]   Raz, *supra* note 2, at 373.
[5]   *Id.* at 373–74.
[6]   *Id.* at 204.
[7]   *Id.* at 375.
[8]   Joseph Raz, Autonomy, Toleration, and the Harm Principle, *in* Justifying Toleration: Conceptual and Historical Perspectives 155, 159 (Susan Mendus ed., 1988).

as a precondition for autonomy. Worthwhile choices do not exist if a buyer can only choose from among a hundred similar houses; an adequate choice would be among a townhouse, an urban flat, and a suburban house.

This conception of autonomy-based pluralism leads Raz to the final relevant observation: the state's role is to enable conditions that allow people to be the authors of their own lives. Hence, to ensure adequacy of choice, it is not enough that the state be committed to noninterference; rather, it is obligated to "create conditions which enable [its] subjects to enjoy greater liberty than they otherwise would."[9]

Building on the Razian conceptions of autonomy and pluralism, Dagan's recent work espouses pluralistic principles as the foundation for private-law theory.[10] His primary contributions relevant to this account are twofold. First, Dagan employs pluralistic theories other than Raz's to formulate his concepts, and he also deploys Raz's "value pluralism" to support his theory of the state's role in regulation.[11] Value pluralism is predicated on the notion that because there exists a plurality of universal values, they cannot be ranked (they are incommensurable), and there is often conflict between them.[12] For our purposes, and in a simplified version, the relevant point is that because the world is composed of plural and diverse universal values, human beings assign a variety of values to the same experiences.[13] Second, Dagan imports Raz's observations to the private-law system, arguing that only a pluralistic approach can explain private-law doctrines and institutions. No single value can or should underpin the private-law structure; only a variety of values, and the balance among them, can serve as a foundation to the entire system of private law.

These two observations merge into one coherent theory concerning the state's role in supporting private-law institutions. Accordingly, Dagan holds that pluralism is grounded in respect for diverse values, or different balances of values, and in the promotion of autonomy that can only be achieved by having adequate and meaningful choices.[14] The role of pluralistic private law "is to offer a rich repertoire of forms of human interaction."[15] While the purpose of this structural pluralistic system is to foster autonomy, the structure incorporates various values beyond autonomy. Thus, Dagan asserts, the "law should facilitate (within limits) the coexistence of various social spheres embodying different modes of valuation."[16] At the same time, facilitating diverse legal options that embed various modes of valuation is not tantamount to embodying free-market principles. As Dagan notes, "[F]acilitation is rarely exhausted by a hands-off policy and a corresponding hospitable attitude to freedom of contract. Rather, facilitation requires the law's active empowerment in providing institutional arrangements, including reliable guarantees against opportunistic behavior."[17]

Dagan's insights are relevant beyond the scope of private law. They can and should serve as guidelines for regulating matters that traditionally fall under the rubric of public law, such as housing and transportation. The state's duty, as defined by Raz, is not limited, as between private parties: it is the state's role to assure the conditions for people to flourish.

---

[9] Raz, *supra* note 2, at 18–19.

[10] *See, e.g.*, Hanoch Dagan, *Autonomy, Pluralism, and Contract Law Theory*, 76 L. & Contemp. Probs. 19 (2013).

[11] Hanoch Dagan, *Pluralism and Perfectionism in Private Law*, 112 Colum. L. Rev. 1409, 1412 (2012).

[12] George Crowder, *Liberalism and Value Pluralism* 44–56 (2002) (defining value pluralism based on four elements: (1) universal values; (2) plurality; (3) incommensurability; (4) in conflict); William A. Galston, *Liberal Pluralism: The Implications of Value Pluralism for Political Theory and Practice* 5–6 (2002).

[13] *See, e.g.*, Cass R. Sunstein, *Incommensurability and Valuation in Law*, 92 Mich. L. Rev. 779, 780 (1994).

[14] Dagan, *supra* note 11, at 1435.

[15] *Id.* at 1432.

[16] *Id.* at 1424.

[17] *Id.* at 1429.

Let us now see how pluralistic theory helps to illuminate issues concerning the platform economy and to provide general guidelines for that economy's regulation.

II THE SPECTRUM OF USE OF EXCESS CAPACITY

The platform economy expands valuable choice when it enables more activities in use of excess capacity. By "excess capacity" I mean activities that exploit the surplus of people's unused or underused time, skills, or assets to create "more capacity than the owner can herself use at once and that can thereby be monetized."[18]

Before I explain why one type of activity is choice-enhancing and the other is potentially choice-decreasing, it is important to understand the extent to which *both* activities – work in increased use of excess capacity and traditional work – are dominant in platform activity. That is, a key aspect of the platform economy, which we must take into consideration when discussing its regulations, is the distinction between exchanges based on leveraging surplus capacity and conventional exchanges that are not based on increased use of excess capacity. By failing to distinguish them, and by using terms such as "gig" or "sharing" economy, we blur the immense differences between these activities and qualify similar legal treatment for them. As stated, this is not merely semantics: platform firms often claim that their function is mainly to enable "gigs," i.e., work through increased use of excess capacity. For example, in response to a court ruling that found a New York City short-term rental, facilitated by Airbnb, illegal,[19] Airbnb stated, "It is time to fix this law and protect hosts who occasionally rent out their own homes. Eighty-seven percent of Airbnb hosts in New York list just a home they live in – they are average New Yorkers trying to make ends meet, not illegal hotels that should be subject to the 2010 law."[20] Airbnb's supporters echo this idea by arguing that "[t]he services help provide lower-cost lodging to visitors, while allowing property owners to earn returns on underused assets."[21] Similarly, in court filings Uber stated that the firm "merely provides a platform for people who own vehicles to leverage their skills and personal assets and connect with other people looking to pay for those skills and assets."[22]

Although a vast portion of the work that platforms enable comprises activities based on use of idle capacity, a large segment of that economy encompasses full-time providers who use designated capital (goods employed primarily for this purpose) or rely on their platform-economy work as their main source of income. This segment of the platform economy is large not only in terms of the number of participants and transactions but also because it yields a massive part of the platforms' revenue. Moreover, despite rhetoric emphasizing the "gig" aspect, platform firms, especially in the transportation sector, often encourage commercial use; for example, by incentivizing drivers to work over 40 hours a week.[23]

Despite data limitations regarding the types of consumers and providers in the platform economy, the data are clear about the coexistence of these two types of activities (increased excess-capacity use and conventional use without increased excess capacity) and their prominence. For

---

[18] *See* Donald J. Kochan, *I Share, Therefore It's Mine*, 51 U. Rich. L. Rev. 909, 929 (2017).

[19] *See City of New York v. Carrey*, Nos. 13006002 and 1300736 (N.Y.C. Envtl. Control Bd. May 9, 2013), www.scribd.com/document/142650911/Decision-and-Order-for-NOV-35006622J.

[20] *See Vacation Rental Site Airbnb Ruled Illegal in New York City*, Fox News, May 21, 2013, www.foxnews.com/travel/2013/05/21/airbnb-illegal-in-new-york-city.html.

[21] Andrew Moylan, *RoomScore 2016: Short-Term Rental Regulation in U.S. Cities*, R Street Policy Study No. 55, Mar. 2016, at 1, www.rstreet.org/wp-content/uploads/2016/03/RSTREET55.pdf.

[22] *Salovitz v. Uber Techs., Inc.*, No. A-14-CV-823-LY, 2014 WL 5318031, at *1 (W.D. Tex. Oct. 16, 2014).

[23] *Uber Launches Power Driver Rewards to Compete with Lyft*, Rideshare Dashboard, Mar. 10, 2016, http://ridesharedashboard.com/2016/03/10/uber-launches-power-driver-rewards-to-compete-with-lyft/; Brenton J. Malin and

example, data on short-term rental platforms consistently show how activities vary regarding the extent of underutilization by lessors. Most properties offered by Airbnb lessors capitalize on their genuinely underutilized assets, but a substantial minority use Airbnb to rent their properties commercially. A study conducted by the Penn State University School of Hospitality Management and funded by the American Hotel and Lodging Association examined activities by lessors who posted properties on Airbnb in 14 large United States metropolitan areas, from October 2014 to September 2015.[24] The study divided "hosts" (lessors) into three categories: those who offered an entire unit for a short time during the year, those who offered a unit for the entire year, and those who had two or more units on the platform. The results demonstrate that those who work with designated capital (property whose primary use is for short-term rentals), although the minority, are consistently present across all of the cities and are responsible for massive revenues for Airbnb. The study found that 2,772 full-time operators (those who made their unit or units available over 360 days a year) constitute 3.5 percent of the total lessors.[25] While this may seem like a small number, Airbnb revenue from these full-time operators was immense: in the period studied, they yielded $347,479,616 for Airbnb, or 26 percent of Airbnb's total revenue in those locations.[26] Furthermore, the study found that lessors who rented two or more units for any amount of time constituted 16.1 percent of all operators.[27] Finally, mega-operators, defined by the study as hosts who rent more than three units (for any amount of time), constituted 6.5 percent of the hosts and yielded 24.6 percent of Airbnb's revenue, or $328,299,944, in those cities during that period.[28] Data on users in other cities confirm similar results.[29]

For the transportation platforms, data do not exist on how many drivers monetize their underused private cars versus how many purchase a vehicle primarily for commercial rides. Nonetheless, several programs offered by platform transportation firms help drivers to access cars, which implies that drivers with designated vehicles are not a marginal occurrence. Uber, the largest platform transportation company, has programs enabling their drivers to rent, lease, or buy a car.[30] Uber's Xchange leasing program helps drivers with bad or no credit to lease a car,[31] without mileage restriction, and includes the maintenance of the vehicle.[32] Similarly, Lyft, Uber's main competitor, maintains the Express Drive Rental Car Program, which assists its drivers in renting a car.[33] The rental price depends on the number of hours the driver works for Lyft; the higher the number of hours worked, the cheaper the rental price.

In addition to using goods and capital, providers in the platform economy can either work full time or capitalize on their unused or underused hours. The distinction in this case is between

---

Curry Chandler, *Free to Work Anxiously: Splintering Precarity Among Drivers for Uber and Lyft*, 10 Commun. Cult. Crit. 382, 391–92 (2016).

[24] John W. O'Neill and Yuxia Ouyang, *From Air Mattresses to Unregulated Business: An Analysis of the Other Side of Airbnb*, Am. Hotel & Lodging Association (2016), www.ahla.com/sites/default/files/2016-10/Airbnb_Analysis_September_2016.pdf.

[25] *Id.* at *Key Findings*.

[26] *Id.* at *Appendix: Data Tables, Jan. 2016 Report*.

[27] *Id.* at *National Trends*.

[28] *Id.*

[29] *See* Erez Aloni, *Capturing Excess in the On-Demand Economy*, 39 U. Haw. L. Rev. 315, 324 (2017).

[30] *See Vehicle Solutions*, UBER, www.uber.com/drive/vehicle-solutions/.

[31] *See* Eric Newcomer and Olivia Zaleski, *Inside Uber's Auto-Lease Machine, Where Almost Anyone Can Get a Car*, Bloomberg, May 31, 2016, www.bloomberg.com/news/articles/2016-05-31/inside-uber-s-auto-lease-machine-where-almost-anyone-can-get-a-car.

[32] *See* Harry Campbell, *Uber Vehicle Marketplace*, Rideshare Guy, http://therideshareguy.com/uber-vehicle-marketplace/.

[33] *See Express Drive Rental Car Program*, Lyft, https://help.lyft.com/hc/en-us/articles/218196557-Express-Drive-Rental-Car-Program-#cost.

workers who use their underutilized labor or skills by working for platforms part time – selling labor-hours that are not available for their full-time job – and those who work full time for platform firms, just as incumbent employees do.

Because most platforms do not provide accurate data about their providers, we rely on alternative surveys and studies to understand the work patterns in platforms. A study by the Requests for Startups group surveyed approximately 900 workers in 78 platform firms, including Airbnb, Uber, Lyft, and TaskRabbit.[34] The authors examined the extent to which providers depend on the income they earn from platforms. If providers obtain most of their income from the platform, this is a good indication that the platform is their main source of employment. Relying partly on the platform income may indicate that it is a gig, a supplement to their main job. The survey found that 39 percent of workers rely on platform work for 25 percent of their income; 19 percent of workers surveyed earn 25–50 percent of their income from platform firms; 13 percent of workers, 50–75 percent; and 29 percent of workers, 75–100 percent.[35] Thus, in terms of use of hours, the workers in the platform economy reflect a spectrum in which some work part time, as a gig, while almost 30 percent use platforms as their primary or sole source of income. Similarly, a survey of approximately 600 Uber drivers, conducted in December 2014, found that almost 40 percent of Uber drivers had no other job; roughly 30 percent of drivers had another, full-time job; and the other 30 percent had another part-time job.[36]

In conclusion, data on the use of capital and the number of hours invested in work reveal that activities in the platform economy lie on a spectrum ranging from small gigs leveraging surplus all the way to professional providers with designated capital who work commercially through the platforms. Next, I argue that these activities produce different levels of choice and negative externalities based on the level of increased excess capacity they leverage.

III   THE PLATFORM ECONOMY AS A CHOICE-INCREASING MECHANISM

Looking through the lens of pluralistic theory, we can see that one virtue of the platform economy is that it extends valuable choices to both consumers and providers. The platform economy, de facto, enables and simplifies a set of activities, a sphere of exchanges based on transforming idle capacity (goods, capital, or time) into work. By furnishing technology that is available to many and relatively user-friendly, the platforms reduce entry barriers (e.g., expenses) to excess-maximizing transactions and ease the participation of nonprofessional providers. While work in increased use of excess capacity existed long before the emergence of platforms, the platforms make exchanges based on surplus between nonprofessional providers easier and more efficient than before.

For consumers, the platform economy creates another layer of market choice. Consumers have diverse needs, tastes, and preferences, and the platforms expand options for them. In a PwC survey, 86 percent of respondents familiar with the platforms agreed that they make life more affordable,

---

[34] Jennifer Rossa and Anne Riley Moffat, *The Workers*, Bloomberg Briefs, June 15, 2015, https://newsletters.briefs. bloomberg.com/document/4vz1acbgfrxz8uwan9/the-workers-demographics; Alison Griswold, *Young Twentysome things May Have a Leg Up in the 1099 Economy*, MoneyBox, May 22, 2015, www.slate.com/blogs/moneybox/2015/05/22/_1099_economy_workforce_report_why_twentysomethings_may_have_a_leg_up.html.

[35] *See* Rossa and Moffat, *supra* note 34.

[36] Jonathan V. Hall and Alan B. Krueger, An Analysis of the Labor Market for Uber's Driver-Partners in the United States, 10 (Princeton Univ. Indust. Relations Section, Working Paper No. 587, 2015) (describing a survey conducted by the Benenson Survey Group per Uber's request).

and 83 percent agreed that they make life more convenient and efficient. This survey confirms that the platforms satisfy different needs and preferences for consumers.[37]

Short-term rental platforms, for example, facilitate the option of staying in someone else's permanent home for a short period. In making this alternative more easily available than it was before, this option appeals to consumers who care more about price, as short-term rentals are often cheaper than hotels. This opportunity is also attractive to travelers who prefer experiencing a destination from a local resident's point of view. Conversely, other travelers may be more risk-averse and want to avoid any problem stemming from dealing with private individuals, or they prefer a hotel's scenery or cleanliness, or they care less about cost. A similar distinction applies to the transportation platform firms: they offer another layer of choice to consumers. Some passengers prefer traditional taxis, perhaps because they do not like waiting for a ride; or they perceive taxis as safer; or they want to pay cash or do not have a smartphone. Yet, others favor the lower cost of the platform rides and the technological benefit of seeing where the driver is. It is not surprising, then, that in the PwC survey, 32 percent of respondents indicated that "more choice in the marketplace" is a strong selling point for the transportation platform firms.[38] The bottom line is that, through excess-capacity enhancement, the platform economy provides more choice to consumers.

For providers, the platform economy offers the opportunity to work in a flexible structure, in small gigs, to leverage unused time or skills as a means to earn supplementary income. In other words, by reducing entry barriers into industries that once required initial monetary investment as well as some professional knowledge, the platform economy allows nonprofessional players to maximize their underused skills, from driving to cooking, to make extra income.

Flexible working hours are important to many workers across industries. Researchers at the McKinsey Global Institute examined the experience of freelancers in general (not only those working for platforms) and found that independent contractors emphasized the importance of flexibility and autonomy that this job framework offers.[39] They elaborate, "Many earners strongly prefer the autonomy and flexibility of independent work. They value being their own boss, setting their own hours to some extent, and focusing on work that interests them … The Uber driver can fit his hours around a class schedule or family priorities."[40] With regard to workers in the platform economy, they found that, in the United States, 87 percent of those workers chose this working pattern rather than resorting to it as a necessity (i.e., because they could not find a different type of job). Data provided by Uber indicate that its drivers appreciate the flexibility of their work. When drivers were asked how they decide when to work, 40 percent answered that it depends on what else is on their schedule.[41] Thus, working as a freelancer in the platform economy may increase choice for workers. Therefore, in line with pluralistic theory that individuals put different values on different aspects of life, the platform economy boosts consumer and provider choice.

---

[37] PricewaterhouseCoopers, *Consumer Intelligence Series: The Sharing Economy* 20 (2015), www.pwc.com/us/en/industry/entertainment-media/publications/consumer-intelligence-series/assets/pwc-cis-sharing-economy.pdf.

[38] *Id.*

[39] McKinsey Global Institute, *Independent Work: Choice, Necessity, and the Gig Economy* 61 (2016), www.mckinsey.com/~/media/McKinsey/Global%20Themes/Employment%20and%20Growth/Independent%20work%20Choice%20necessity%20and%20othe%20gig%20economy/Independent-Work-Choice-necessity-and-the-gig-economy-Full-report.ashx.

[40] *Id.* at 45.

[41] Amy Levin, The Driver Roadmap: Where Uber Driver-Partners Have Been, and Where They're Going, Benenson Strategy Grp. 3 (2014), https://newsroom.uber.com/wp-content/uploads/2015/01/BSG_Uber_Report.pdf.

IV THE PLATFORM ECONOMY IS ALSO A CHOICE-DECREASING MECHANISM

The platform economy can also reduce alternatives for consumers and providers. Because of the competition posed by the platforms' suppliers, some conventional services that are not platform-based are at risk of becoming scarcer. The threat to traditional services is especially imminent when platforms sanction commercial work (not using excess capacity). In that case, and without regulation that protects incumbents from unfair competition, traditional (non-platform-enabled) providers may not withstand the competition; we can already see reduction in availability of traditional services.

For instance, transportation platforms' entry into the market has led to a considerable decline in the number of taxi rides. One city that has experienced a dramatic change in the availability of taxis is Los Angeles. A report by the UCLA Labor Center found that between 2013 and 2014, taxi rides dropped by 18 percent, a total of 1.4 million fewer trips than in the previous year.[42] This number is likely larger currently because, at the time of the study, platform-operated vehicles were not allowed to pick up passengers from LAX airport, a location that constituted a large source of taxi rides – while now they can. Los Angeles's experience is typical of many US cities.[43] The resulting financial struggles have forced cab companies to fire workers, file for bankruptcy, and even close entirely, making taxi services less available to the general public in some regions.[44]

The decreased availability of traditional taxis is detrimental to consumers who feel less safe or are more likely to encounter discrimination in obtaining services, particularly individuals from minority groups. For instance, a recent study documented how African Americans had a harder time obtaining Uber and Lyft rides compared to their white counterparts.[45] This study found that in Seattle, African-American passengers had to wait longer before booking a ride via Uber, up to 35 percent longer than white passengers. In Boston, the study used passengers with African-American–sounding names and found that Uber drivers canceled rides more than twice as frequently as they canceled rides for passengers with white-sounding names. Certainly, racial discrimination by traditional taxis is a familiar, well-established fact and occurs on a regular basis.[46] However, while a host of federal and state laws discourage racial discrimination by traditional taxis,[47] the applicability of these laws to the platform-based rides, and to the firms themselves, is a more contested question.[48]

People with disabilities constitute another group that has been harmed by the disappearance or reduction of traditional taxi services. Stories abound of incidents in which Uber drivers have refused to take individuals with disabilities, either because they had service animals or used a wheelchair.[49] Indeed, the National Federation of the Blind of California filed a class-action

---

[42] Saba Waheed et al., *Ridesharing or Ridestealing? Changes in Taxi Ridership and Revenue in Los Angeles 2009–2014*, UCLA Labor Ctr. (2015), www.labor.ucla.edu/downloads/policy-brief-ridesharing-or-ridestealing/.

[43] Aloni, *supra* note 29, at 331 (describing a similar experience in Seattle and Arlington).

[44] In 2016, San Francisco's biggest taxi company filed for bankruptcy. *See In re Yellow Cab Cooperative, Inc.*, No. 3:16-bk-30063 (N.D. Cal. Jan. 22, 2016); *see also* Kate Rogers, *Uber, Lyft Put Pressure on Taxi Companies*, CNBC, Jan. 26, 2016, 1:10 PM, www.cnbc.com/2016/01/26/uber-lyft-put-pressure-on-taxi-companies.html.

[45] *See* Yanbo Ge et al., *Racial and Gender Discrimination in Transportation Network Companies* (Nat'l Bureau Econ. Research, Working Paper No. 22776, 2016), www.nber.org/papers/w22776.

[46] *See, e.g., Service Denied: Responding to Taxicab Discrimination in the District of Columbia*, The Equal Rights Ctr. (2003), https://equalrightscenter.org/wp-content/uploads/taxicab_report.pdf.

[47] Aaron Belzer and Nancy Leong, *The New Public Accommodations*, 105 Geo. L.J. 1271, 1297–98 (2017).

[48] *See, e.g.,* Brishen Rogers, *The Social Costs of Uber*, 82 U. Chi. L. Rev. Dialogue 85, 95 (2015).

[49] *See* Jason Marker, *Wheelchair Using Passenger Films Uber Driver Refusing to Pick Him Up*, Auto Blog www.autoblog.com/2017/01/10/wheelchair-using-passenger-films-uber-driver-refusing-to-pick-hi/.

lawsuit on behalf of blind Uber customers, arguing that Uber has violated the Americans with Disabilities Act; Uber replied that the Americans with Disabilities Act does not apply to them.[50] While Uber and Lyft have recently established programs to accommodate the needs of passengers who rely on wheelchairs, some aver that these services are rarely available.[51]

Finally, people who feel more vulnerable may believe that they are safer taking taxis than using platform-enabled rides. Even though there is no definitive evidence that taxis are safer than platform-facilitated rides or that many people perceive taxis as safer, multiple publicized reports in which platform drivers attacked, harassed, or refused to pick up minorities may deter some from choosing this option.[52] The firms' refusal to fingerprint their drivers, as taxi companies do, may bolster this hesitation.[53] The bottom line is that, for some people, the availability of traditional taxis is still essential because the alternative is viewed as riskier or because it is harder for them to access.

In a similar fashion, short-term rental platforms threaten the existence of valuable options in traditional accommodations, such as lower-end hotels. Competition with the short-term rental platforms has endangered less expensive hotels because the higher-end hotels are more likely than platforms to attract businesspeople and wealthier tourists. A recent study concluded that Airbnb's impact on the hotel industry in Texas is unevenly distributed because Airbnb threatens mostly lower-end hotels, making them most vulnerable to economic harm.[54] The declining options to stay in such hotels can have the most serious impact on those who cannot afford the more luxurious accommodation options or those who find it harder to book a room through the short-term housing platforms. The option of traditional hotels may be important for those who are not savvy with technology and thus cannot, or do not want to, use platforms. Other individuals may find that booking a room via a platform is more difficult due to discrimination. Researchers recently found that users with names perceived to be distinctively African American were 16 percent less likely to succeed in booking a stay than were users with identical profiles but who had names considered to be distinctively white.[55]

Finally, consumers may find that the long-term residential rental options in their own cities are decreasing as more owners convert long-term rental units to short-term rentals. This phenomenon of people who invest in apartments to transform them into short-term rentals has become widespread, as evidenced, inter alia, by websites that advise potential buyers on the cities in which this practice is most profitable.[56] Communities and local governments have responded with calls for regulations that restrain this phenomenon. Without expanding too

---

[50] *See Nat'l Fed'n of the Blind of California v. Uber Techs., Inc.,* 103 F. Supp. 3d 1073, 1082 (N.D. Cal. 2015).

[51] See Heather Kelly, *Uber's Services for the Disabled Lack Actual Cars,* CNN, http://money.cnn.com/2016/05/02/technology/uber-access/.

[52] *See* Raymond Rizzo, *Uber Driver James Henneberg is "Bothered" by the "Transgender Thing"; Refuses to be Paired with Gay Couple in Future; Admits to Lying,* E. Nashville News, Jan. 7, 2017, http://eastnashville.news/2017/01/uber-driver-james-henneberg-is-bothered-by-the-transgender-thing-refuses-to-be-paired-with-gay-couple-in-future-admits-to-lying/; Mary Emily O'Hara, *Lyft Driver Accused of Threatening Activist Monica Jones in Transphobic Post,* The Daily Dot, Feb. 28, 2016, www.dailydot.com/irl/lyft-driver-monica-jones-location-facebook/.

[53] *See, e.g.,* Heather Kelly, *Uber CEO explains why he thinks fingerprinting drivers is "unjust,"* CNNMoney, June 24, 2016, http://money.cnn.com/2016/06/23/technology/uber-travis-kalanick-ges-fingerprinting/index.html.

[54] *See* Georgios Zervas, Davide Prosperio, and John Byers, *The Rise of the Sharing Economy: Estimating the Impact of Airbnb on the Hotel Industry,* 30 Boston U. Sch. Mgmt. Research, Working Paper No. 2013–16, 2013, http://papers.ssrn.com/sol3/papers.cfm?abstract_id=2366898.

[55] *See* Benjamin Edelman, Michael Luca, and Dan Svirsky, *Racial Discrimination in the Sharing Economy: Evidence from a Field Experiment,* 1 Harv. Bus. Sch., Working Paper No. 16–069, 2016, www.hbs.edu/faculty/Publication%20Files/16-069_5c3b2b36-d9f8-4b38-9639-2175aaf9ebc9.pdf.

[56] www.airdna.co/about ("Airdna provides data and analytics to vacation rental entrepreneurs and investors").

much on this, the rise of commercial short-term rentals has exacerbated the shortage of rentals in many popular metropolitan areas and further increased rental prices. Thus, while consumers enjoy more choice in finding vacation rentals, they may face a problem securing long-term rentals in their hometown.

Importantly, the platform economy can also reduce options for workers by decreasing the number of full-time, protected employment opportunities. Workers in the platform economy are not classified "employees"; rather, their status is "independent contractor," regardless of the time or frequency they work for platform firms or the control the firms retain over them.[57] The different designation matters because the status of "employee" guarantees various employment protections, such as reimbursement of work-related expenses, overtime payment, employer contributions to unemployment insurance, and a minimum wage.[58] Indeed, one study surveyed providers in the platform economy and found that "41 percent say they prefer the security and benefits of working for a traditional company even if it might mean less flexibility."[59] Hence, another tradeoff of the platform economy: increased flexible work opportunities versus decreased availability of traditional employment.

In conclusion, the platform economy simultaneously increases and decreases options. Below, I examine what pluralistic theory teaches about this composition of choice in the market.

V ENLISTING THE PRINCIPLES OF PLURALISM TO GUIDE THE REGULATION OF THE PLATFORM ECONOMY

The platform economy enables activities that are different in their utilization of excess capacity; and based on their location on the spectrum of use, the exchanges contribute differently to the increase or the decrease in choice. Pluralism prescribes that the state support the extension of choice, which means actively endorsing the platform economy. But support does not mean an invitation to embrace a deregulation regime. The opposite is true: a truly pluralistic structure safeguards providers, consumers, and traditional options from the negative externalities that commercial-activity platforms produce. As Raz clarifies, a nonintervention approach "would undermine the chances of survival of many cherished aspects of our culture."[60] In our case, these "cherished aspects" are the conventional services that may disappear as a result of some businesses competing under different rules, while providing virtually the same products and services.

Therefore, the first principle flowing from pluralism involves capturing the distinction between activity through increased use of excess capacity and work through activity not based on increased use. Specifically, lawmakers should craft regulations that distinguish between activities based on their location along the spectrum of use of increased excess capacity. Regulations should prevent incumbent-like providers from passing as increased-excess providers as a means to evade laws governing traditional sectors.

Lawmakers can distinguish between the levels of use of increased excess capacity by examining two factors together: the frequency of supply and the infrastructure used for the transaction.

---

[57] Keith Cunningham-Parmeter, *From Amazon to Uber: Defining Employment in the Modern Economy*, 96 B.U. L. Rev. 1673, 1684–88 (2016).

[58] *See, e.g., Cotter v. Lyft, Inc.*, 60 F. Supp. 3d 1067, 1073–74 (N.D. Cal. 2015).

[59] *See* Press Release, Penn Schoen Berland, *Forty-Five Million Americans Say They Have Worked in the On-Demand Economy, While 86.5 Million Have Used It, According to New Survey*, Jan. 6, 2016, http://psbresearch.com/wp-content/uploads/2016/01/On-Demand-Economy-Release.pdf.

[60] Raz, *supra* note 2, at 162.

The frequency denotes the number of transactions the provider is involved in within a defined period. The more frequently the supplier provides the goods or services, the more likely that she is not working in increased excess capacity. The other distinguishing factor is infrastructure: whether the goods or real property are primarily designated for a commercial purpose or only intermittently converted for such use. For instance, in the platform-transportation sector, some municipalities have debated whether to allow drivers to use their "personal vehicle" rather than a designated or rental car.[61] In the short-term rental market, some municipalities have limited the number of nights that residents can lease their properties for short-term stays. The assumption is that a small number of transactions signals providers who leverage their surplus space, while those who exceed this threshold operate commercially. In San Francisco, for example, the threshold is 90 days a year.[62]

Pluralistic principles would also have the state treat each legal regime differently according to the values the regime promotes. For activities of increased use, lawmakers should endorse that innovation and its results by allowing people to leverage their goods, time, and skills. Thus, lawmakers are justified in treating each category differently. Lawmakers should, therefore, create two (or more) different regulatory regimes based on a spectrum of excess-capacity use. Activities based on increased excess capacity should be regulated lightly and tailored to casual, nonprofessional providers. Traditional work done through platforms should be governed by the same rules as those for incumbents unless a significant reason justifies a departure from such regulations.

For some critical matters, such as safety regulations, the distinctions between levels of increased excess capacity may not matter. In such matters, policymakers can reasonably insist that there is no difference between work in increased excess capacity and other work. A part-time driver can cause the same harm as one who drives regularly if she drives an unsafe vehicle or without adequate insurance. Thus, lawmakers should impose safety requirements – criminal-background checks, vehicle inspections, insurance coverage – in a way that assures public safety and reasonable allocation of risk. More generally, it means that activities in increased use of excess capacity will be subject to regulation that advances safety and prevents market failures. But the regulations of such activities, to the extent possible, should be designed in a fashion that minimizes obstacles for casual suppliers.

Except for core issues such as safety, however, the regulations of activities in increased use of excess capacity should differ from those imposed on traditional transactions (whether or not operated through platforms). Hotel tax provides an interesting test case on this point. San Francisco, like several other municipalities, created a new set of rules governing short-term rentals; it imposes on each transaction an occupancy tax (collected by Airbnb) equivalent to that levied on hotels.[63] However, regulations may reasonably set different tax rates for various transactions, based on the level of use of excess capacity, since transactions may vary in the type of visitor they attract and in their use of municipalities' infrastructures. Hotels are more likely to draw businesspeople who use amenities such as convention centers or performing-arts centers.

---

[61] *See, e.g.*, Order Instituting Rulemaking on Regulations Relating to Passenger Carriers, Ridesharing, and New Online-Enabled Transp. Servs. (Cal. P.U.C. Dec. 27, 2012), http://docs.cpuc.ca.gov/PublishedDocs/Published/G000/M040/ K862/40862944.pdf; Carolyn Said, *Uber, Lyft May Face New Rules in California*, S.F. Chronicle, April 5, 2016, www .sfchronicle.com/business/article/Uber-Lyft-may-face-new-rules-in-California-7230320.php (reporting that "The PUC is poised to allow drivers to use leased vehicles, but only if the lease is for more than four months").

[62] *See* S.F., Cal., Admin. Code § 41A.5(g)(1)(A) (2016).

[63] *See Transient Occupancy Tax (TOT) Frequently Asked Questions for Hosts, Website Companies and Merchants of Record*, Office of the Treasurer & Tax Collector, City & Cnty. of S.F., http://sftreasurer.org/tot_host_website_ merchant_faq#1.

Conversely, travelers who turn to platforms to experience a location from a resident's perspective may be less likely to use some of these infrastructures. Airbnb units offered by casual users may also be located in areas that are less touristic in nature; thus, these regions receive less revenue from hotel tax. As renting rooms or units on a short-term basis provides more business for these less-visited locations, lawmakers can incentivize people to visit these areas. Thus, unlike the path taken so far by most cities that collect hotel tax on short-term rentals by platforms, plural-istic principles justify creating a different tax rate for transactions based on casual use. Of course, such casual exchanges may use some services that are funded by hotel taxes; thus, a municipality can offer these providers a reduced tax rate (rather than cutting it altogether). Alternatively, municipalities can impose a tax equal to the regular hotel tax on short-term rentals located in the central tourist zones, while creating a reduced tax rate for short-term rentals in other zones. This should not create extra administrative burdens or confusion because, in regulated regimes, lessors typically register their units; the city can inform them of their hotel-tax rate at the time of registration.

In a similar vein, in employment situations, pluralistic principles suggest that lawmakers should treat full-time workers in the platform economy differently than they treat casual providers in that economy. The former are not substantially different from traditional employees. The platforms exert a level of control over these workers that is quite similar to employers' con-trol over traditional employees.[64] For instance, in the transportation arena, Lyft and Uber exert more control over workers who work longer hours by creating various programs that incentivize their drivers to provide more hours a week.[65] The flexibility and autonomy of the "independent contractor" framework is diminished once the driver is nudged to refuse riders. These drivers' incomes also depend heavily on the platform employer. Thus, when it comes to providers in the platform economy who may or may not be not using their increased excess capacity but, in any case, are essentially working full time (or nearly so) for an employer, they should be recognized as traditional employees for the purpose of benefits and protections. Indeed, some courts around the world have determined that Uber drivers should be classified as employees.[66]

Further, casual workers (those truly leveraging their excess capacity) should receive basic protections, as well. Pluralism calls for innovation and a variety of options. While infrequent providers are more akin to freelancers, essential norms and safeguards, such as minimum wage and overtime pay, should still apply to them. A few commentators have proposed that lawmakers create a special category, an intermediate level between employee and independent contractor, that includes basic employment protections and benefits.[67] So far, even jurisdictions that have regulated transportation platforms have not addressed the employment status of drivers. This omission leaves the final decision about employment status to the courts, which are limited in what they can do. Courts can decide whether workers are classified as employees or inde-pendent contractors but cannot create an intermediate status that incorporates the distinction between those who work in increased use of excess capacity and those who do not.

---

[64] Cunningham-Parmeter, *supra* note 57, at 1687.

[65] *See, e.g., Power Driver Bonus*, Lyft, https://help.lyft.com/hc/en-us/articles/214586477-Power-Driver-Bonus.

[66] *See, e.g.,* Reserved Judgment of the Employment Tribunal at 1, *Aslam* v. *Uber BV* [2016] IRLR 4 (U.K. Empl. Trib.) (No. 2202551/2015) (ruling that Uber drivers are "employed" as "workers" and not self-employed).

[67] *See* Seth D. Harris and Alan B. Krueger, *A Proposal for Modernizing Labor Laws for Twenty-First-Century Work: The "Independent Worker,"* Brookings Inst. 2 (2015), www.hamiltonproject.org/assets/files/modernizing_labor_laws_for_twenty_first_century_work_krueger_harris.pdf; Sarah Leberstein, *Rights on Demand: Ensuring Workplace Standards and Worker Security in the On-Demand Economy,* Nat'l Emp't Law Project, 10 (2015), www.nelp.org/content/uploads/Rights-On-Demand-Report.pdf.

In addition to creating new content, a regulatory regime designed to foster increased excess-capacity transactions must be clear and easy to follow and ought to impose minimal administrative burdens. The rules should be crafted with awareness that casual providers are micro-earners rather than sophisticated players with resources to hire legal counsel or capacity to follow complex regulations. Such design would also prevent the lost benefits that stem from evasion of the law when markets operate underground, thus reducing revenue from tax collection and putting workers and customers at risk.

In summary, pluralistic principles would separate transactions based on where they fall on the spectrum of use of increased excess capacity. They support the creation of a regime that boosts activities in monetizing idle capacity and differentiates them from exchanges that pose as using increased excess capacity but are actually akin to conventional transactions.

CONCLUSION

The platform economy introduces a promise and a risk. Its promise lies in facilitating transactions that are based on the use of increased excess capacity. In so doing, it offers another layer of choice and makes it more possible for people to be the authors of their own lives. When the platform economy functions in this way, pluralistic principles call for letting these activities flourish, with some regulation to ensure no harm to involved or third parties. But the platforms too often turn a blind eye to, or encourage, conventional commercial-work-in-disguise that is not grounded in leveraging surplus capacity. In such cases, choice for consumers, workers, and society at large can be reduced. Then, pluralistic principles call for state intervention – through regulation – to prevent multiple harms and to preserve valuable choice.

11

Finding the Right "Fit"

Matching Regulations to the Shape of the Sharing Economy

Ray Brescia

INTRODUCTION

With the advent of mobile technologies, a new kind of business model has emerged that delivers on-demand services in a range of areas. From ride sharing to errands, in-home massages to personal jets, the so-called "sharing economy" has elevated successful businesses that take this approach to rival their competitors that utilize more traditional means of delivering goods and services. Airbnb, the home-sharing platform, now has a market valuation that exceeds that of most major hotel chains. Ride-sharing giant Uber's valuation exceeds that of many of the world's largest car companies. All of this has happened in just the last ten years. This rapid growth of the sharing economy has proven a boon to the founders of these businesses, making billionaires out of intrepid entrepreneurs who have embraced the sharing economy model; has made a range of different services easy to access; has tapped into a surplus of goods and services, putting them to productive use like never before; and employed millions. But the very features of the sharing economy that make it so attractive as a business model – actors in the sharing economy adapt their business models quickly in light of and in response to new technologies, they rely on trust as an engine for economic exchange, and those exchanges are decentralized to facilitate "peer-to-peer" exchanges that are disintermediated – also make it difficult to regulate. This phenomenon challenges those who might oversee the sharing economy to balance the benefits of the sharing economy against the risk to consumers who might find themselves abused and or exploited in contexts that are rife with potential risk: i.e., in the backseat of the car of a stranger, in someone's home, or when purchasing an item from an unknown source through an online marketplace. The components of the sharing economy that make them difficult to regulate are not bugs of the system, but their core features. Yet to the extent we might seek to regulate these core features, we run the risk of stifling the very aspects of sharing economy approaches that set them apart as attractive alternatives to traditional business models. In order to continue to capitalize on the benefits of the sharing economy, regulators who wish to ensure an adequate degree of consumer protection within this growing sector of the economy need to find ways to balance innovation with regulation, experimentation with governance, and trust with oversight.

This chapter attempts to explore ways in which approaches to regulating the sharing economy might seek to identify those aspects of the sharing economy that make it unique and which are core to the benefits sharing economy models generate and match them to regulatory approaches that will serve to encourage innovation while not sacrificing consumer protection. In an effort to find a good regulatory match, I strive to identify those core features and search for regulatory models that seem to be a good "fit": i.e., models that might share these core components with the sharing economy itself. That search looks at these core features – the protean, disintermediated, and decentralized components of sharing economy models – and finds that so-called "New Governance" approaches to regulation appear most similar to the sharing economy itself.

A New Governance approach starts with the notion that law, regulation, and policy in a given regulated sphere should be crafted by a broad pool of stakeholders and decision-makers. This broad pool of participants, New Governance Theory posits, is best suited to articulate and enforce the laws, norms, and regulations in a given sphere.[1] Such an approach reflects democratic, participatory, and representative ideals, and benefits from the insights of practitioners, consumers, and regulators who may possess insights, not typically incorporated into oversight, that can help to balance the need for regulation against the benefits to be gained by innovation. It also strives to encourage experimentation through local control of regulation of the sphere that generates feedback loops that inform efforts to regulate that sphere in other communities.[2] A New Governance approach to oversight is entrepreneurial in nature, because, in the words of Orly Lobel, it "identif[ies] its customers, determin[es] their needs, and mov[es] forward to identify the best practices that would meet these needs."[3] In these ways, the "organizing principles" of New Governance approaches include "flexibility, competition, adaptability, and learning."[4]

New Governance approaches have been adopted in many contexts: in judicial processes, legislation, regulation, and administrative processes, to name just a few. As Jaime Alison Lee explains:

> Courts, for example, frequently ask litigants to negotiate their own remedies in a wide variety of cases, ranging from employment discrimination to securities regulation. The Occupational Safety & Health Administration (OSHA) emphasizes decentralized problem solving by stakeholders in urging unions and employers to design better workplace safety procedures, rather than issuing top-down rules designed by bureaucrats. Some federal agencies use the Negotiated Rulemaking Act to draft proposed regulations through direct engagement with industry actors and consumer groups, rather than following traditional, top-down notice-and-comment procedures.[5]

Using New Governance Theory, this chapter charts a course for regulatory models that can offer guidance on a regulatory regime for those sectors where sharing economy businesses are currently thriving and where they might emerge in the future.

With this approach in mind, this chapter is organized into four parts. The first three correspond to the three core features of the sharing economy: its protean nature, the fact that most sharing economy models include a degree of disintermediation in their approach, and most are decentralized. In each part, I will explore each particular feature of the sharing economy and then examine the features of traditional regulatory approaches and compare them to New Governance approaches to determine which approach aligns more consistently with each particular feature. In this way, I hope to show that, since New Governance models are more

---

[1] Representative scholarship that embodies the principles of New Governance Theory includes Ian Ayres and John Braithwaite, *Responsive Regulation: Transcending the Deregulation Debate* (1992); Michael C. Dorf, *Legal Indeterminacy and Institutional Design*, 78 N.Y.U. L. Rev. 875 (2003); Michael C. Dorf and Charles F. Sabel, *A Constitution of Democratic Experimentalism*, 98 Colum. L. Rev. 267 (1998).

[2] Dorf and Sabel, *supra* note 1, at 287–88.

[3] Orly Lobel, *The Renew Deal: The Fall of Regulation and the Rise of Governance in Contemporary Legal Thought*, 89 Minn. L. Rev. 342, 366 (2004).[3] *Id.*, at 367.

[4] *Id.*

[5] Jaime Alison Lee, *"Can You Hear Me Now?": Making Participatory Governance Work for the Poor*, 7 Harv. L. & Pol'y Rev. 405, 411 (2013) (citations omitted).

consistent with the sharing economy's features, they are a better fit as a regulatory approach. Part IV will attempt to anticipate any shortcomings that might arise were regulators to attempt to use the New Governance approaches spelled out here in their efforts to provide oversight with respect to the sharing economy.

I THE SHARING ECONOMY'S PROTEAN, EXPERIMENTAL FEATURES

Perhaps the most prominent feature of sharing economy businesses is that they are *protean*: i.e., they are evolving constantly and quickly shape-shifting in response to a range of factors. The most prominent exogenous force to which sharing economy businesses have adapted and to which they have proven adaptable is technology. Indeed, technology is what has not just driven the evolution of sharing economy businesses, it has generated them. The combination of the internet and mobile technologies has made sharing economy platforms possible. eBay and Etsy emerged in response to the internet and both have sites that are responsive to the user's means of accessing them, with accompanying mobile applications that facilitate e-commerce on the go. Uber thrives on mobile technology: i.e., the ability to hail a ride from a smartphone in the palm of one's hand while standing on a street corner. Sharing economy businesses seem to have not just embraced technology, but they have used it to disrupt entire industries. Consistent with Clayton Christensen's theories of disruptive innovation, sharing economy businesses have harnessed technology to deliver products and services that are more in line with consumer need and are delivering those products and services in a more attractive, accessible, and often more affordable fashion.[6]

But sharing economy businesses have not just responded to changes in technology and adopted technology in their delivery systems, they have also adapted to changes in the market and often deliver a product that is more consistent with customer needs. Taking the ride-hailing context as just one example, consumers in urban settings are becoming less interested in owning cars and the Uber model and others like it (e.g., Zip Car) are adapting to such customer appetites. They are doing so by offering on-demand services that do not require ownership of assets that will lie dormant when not in use yet require the owner to go through the trouble and expense of maintaining those assets by keeping them functioning for when they are needed and paying fees simply to keep them on the road and ready for use, like paying parking, registration, and insurance fees.

In addition to adapting to changes in technology and market demand, sharing economy businesses have also proven adaptable to regulation, with positive and negative consequences. On the positive side, sharing economy businesses can adapt their models to fit the regulatory approaches of different jurisdictions. Where regulators in a particular community determine that certain sharing economy services are unwanted, or that certain approaches a sharing economy business may take are unfavored, the business can supply only those services that a community desires, thus bringing a degree of innovation and benefits to those communities. For example, in certain communities, particular types of Uber rides, like those offered through "UberX" which offers lower-cost trips in lower-quality cars, have been prohibited.[7] Regulators in such communities have determined that the benefits these services might bring to the community do not

---

[6] Clayton M. Christensen, *The Innovator's Dilemma: When New Technologies Cause Great Firms to Fail*, xv (1997) (explaining the relationship between technological change, business behavior, and firm failure).

[7] For an overview of the latest regulatory challenges Uber faces, *see* Jon Henley, *Uber Clashes with Regulators in Cities around the World*, The Guardian, Sept. 29, 2017.

outweigh the negative impact they might have on incumbent providers and the overall supply of quality services offered in a particular sector. Regulators can thus make a choice about the features they wish to permit in their communities and sharing economy businesses, because they are adaptable, can transform the business model they offer in those communities. Short of an outright ban on the service, which some sharing economy businesses certainly face in some communities, the protean nature of sharing economy models often means that they can shape their offerings to meet local demands. This adaptability is one of the strengths of sharing economy models and means that sharing economy businesses can deliver services that respond to local needs.

On the negative side, the shape-shifting quality of sharing economy businesses can also mean they are difficult to regulate. Moreover, at least one sharing economy business, Uber, is alleged to have used and adapted technology to its advantage to evade regulators. Using a program called "Greyball" in several communities where its leaders knew Uber was facing scrutiny, Uber is accused of deploying this computer algorithm to try to identify when a regulator was accessing the application to try to hail a ride using the service. In those communities where it is alleged to have been used, Uber was facing significant scrutiny from regulators who were considering placing restrictions on the service or seeking to ban it outright. If the algorithm determined that a government regulator might be accessing the site so as to hail a ride and try to develop facts and build a case against Uber in the community, the Greyball program kicked in to ensure the regulator did not find an Uber car from which he or she could hail a ride.[8] Thus, the very adaptability and protean nature of sharing economy business models mean such qualities can be harnessed to try to avoid regulation or shift the manner in which services are delivered in an effort to evade detection, regulation, and oversight.

When one takes these qualities of sharing economy businesses – the adaptability, the pliability – and compares them to traditional regulatory approaches, it would seem that such approaches are not well suited to address sharing economy business models. First and foremost, by their nature, traditional forms of regulation are both static and slow to respond to change. Using traditional methods for developing oversight and regulatory regimes, elected officials must deliberate and pass laws and administrative agencies must go through deliberative processes for the issuance of regulations. These legislative and regulatory processes are often cumbersome, take time to complete, and are subject to capture by incumbents. They are also often "frozen in time" in the sense that, once passed or adopted, a law or regulation fixes a regulatory course and that course can only be changed through the commencement of the same process from the beginning. As a static form of regulation, they are often designed to address the present state of affairs and are less capable of adapting to changes to that state of affairs, again, short of recommencing the process of making new laws or issuing new regulations all over again. Traditional forms of legislation and regulation are also known as "hard law," carrying fixed, command-and-control features that can be characterized as containing strict rules that spell out in detail what is prohibited and permitted as opposed to offering standards that provide general guidance to the regulated as to the proper course of conduct in a given regulated sphere. Such hard rules are generally more difficult to draft, particularly in settings that are evolving, and can be harder to follow, particularly when innovation results in the evolution of a regulated sphere. Legislators and regulators can find it difficult to set forth hard rules that can anticipate the potential shape

---

[8] Mike Isaac, *How Uber Deceives Authorities Worldwide*, N.Y. Times, Mar. 3, 2017, www.nytimes.com/2017/03/03/technology/uber-greyball-program-evade-authorities.html.

of that sector as it evolves. For these reasons, traditional methods of regulatory oversight would seem ill suited to protean sharing economy models.

Is there an alternative, then, to traditional regulatory approaches to provide oversight of the sharing economy? New Governance approaches would seem to share many of the same qualities of sharing economy business models. Such approaches are flexible, responsive, and adaptive. They incorporate notions of "soft law" as opposed to hard: i.e., they incorporate standards that provide general guidance as opposed to strict, hard-and-fast rules that attempt to anticipate all potential situations and activities in a given sphere and offer detailed guidance on how to act within that sphere in light of pre-determined scenarios. As such, then, New Governance approaches would seem well suited to address the sectors in which sharing economy businesses are presently operating.

There is thus an apparent match between sharing economy models and New Governance Theory, at least with respect to the adaptability of sharing economy businesses and New Governance approaches. If this is the case, what are the features of a regulatory approach to the sharing economy that this apparent relationship might recommend? First, New Governance approaches prefer standards to rules, soft law to hard. Because of that, regulatory standards that set forth broad principles for compliance rather than those that attempt to anticipate every possible situation that might arise in the regulatory sphere and offer guidance on how a regulated entity should deal with it are well suited to economic arrangements that are constantly evolving in response to new technologies, new customer demands, and new community preferences. As the regulated sphere evolves so too should the regulation of that sphere.[9]

Similarly, one of the core functions of sharing economy platforms is that they serve as information conduits: they connect consumers looking for services with those services in an on-demand fashion. The more information the consumer has about the available services the better the fit between consumer need and market offerings. As such, disclosure-based regulatory approaches, which New Governance Theory tends to embrace, would seem well suited to round out the information the consumer possesses about actors within the sharing economy. Many of the most popular sharing economy platforms use a disclosure regime through their ratings systems that attempts to offer consumers information about the trustworthiness of providers on the platform. Regulators could embrace disclosure regimes by seeking to play a role in those ratings systems by auditing them, or requiring that they are placed under the control of a third-party provider, to ensure that they are not being manipulated, either by the platform, the producer, or the consumer. An example of this phenomenon is the widespread adoption of so-called "Green Building Codes," through which a neutral entity has created guidelines for sustainable architecture, which have been adopted by municipalities and incorporated into their own building codes.[10] In these ways, New Governance models can serve to strengthen the oversight regime by ensuring a disclosure-based approach is legitimate and trustworthy. Once again, since information is central to the functioning of sharing economy models in many ways, a disclosure-based regime would seem well suited to reflect the contours of the system itself.

---

[9] *See, e.g.*, Bradley C. Karkkainen, *"New Governance" in Legal Thought and in the World: Some Splitting as Antidote to Overzealous Lumping*, 89 Minn. L. Rev. 474, 474 (2004) (describing the adaptive and experimental aspects of New Governance models in response to changing conditions and new information).

[10] *See* Sarah B. Schindler, *Following Industry's LEED: Municipal Adoption of Private Green Building Standards*, 62 Fla. L. Rev. 285 (2010) (describing the privately generated Leadership in Energy and Environmental Design standards).

II THE SHARING ECONOMY'S DISINTERMEDIATED AND DEMOCRATIC FEATURES

A second critical component of the sharing economy is that it is *disintermediated*. As a result, it is both participatory, and, in some ways, democratic. Sharing economy entities connect providers of goods and services with consumers desirous of those goods or services in a direct way, cutting out the so-called "middle person," or at least minimizing the role of an intermediary to merely serving as a platform on which the commercial exchange can take place. While Uber and Airbnb are often held up as examples of the sharing economy, there are other, similar entities that also exhibit the type of disintermediation that is so central to sharing economy models. Etsy is a prime example of this platform service. Through it, artists and craftspeople who, before, had to struggle to find stores, boutiques, or galleries that might show and sell their work for a significant commission, or at a great markup, now can snap a photo of their work and sell it through the site, reaching millions of potential customers and paying a fraction of what a more traditional outlet might charge to display and sell their work. Disintermediation also happens at the oversight level, with much of the "regulation" of the sharing economy enforced through ratings mechanisms that are in the hands of consumers. A poor rating by an Uber customer or an Airbnb guest can damage the provider's reputation, driving customers from him or her, or, if that rating is bad enough, or the provider consistently receives bad ratings, he or she might lose the privilege of serving as a provider on the platform altogether. The regulatory function in sharing economy relationships is thus devolved, at least in part, to the consumer, which reflects a form of regulatory disintermediation.

In addition to lowering transaction costs – the friction that compounds along the way during the consummation of business relationships – the disintermediation available through the sharing economy has a very democratic component to it, which is a function of the gatekeeping, or lack thereof, at the entrance to the sharing economy. Most sharing economy platforms have exceedingly low barriers to entry, for both providers and consumers. These low barriers to entry mean that providers can enter a sharing economy platform to provide goods and services with few constraints and consumers can access those providers subject to few of the transaction costs typically associated with identifying and securing trusted partners for business relationships. The platform becomes a sort of social capital broker, facilitating business relationships through trust in the platform itself, a substitute for the licensing and other traditional forms of consumer protections that serve to generate – or as a stand-in for – trust.

This democratic, participatory characteristic of the sharing economy has implications for the role of law in promoting consumer protection. The trust embedded in sharing economy networks is similar to the concept of social capital, but a synthetic social capital, created not in the union halls or block parties idealized by Robert Putnam, but in the bits and bytes of the internet and mobile technologies.[11] Indeed, social capital is traditionally found in the "social networks and the ... norms of reciprocity and trustworthiness" associated with such networks.[12] Social capital generally helps to lower the whole range of transaction costs identified by Ronald Coase: i.e., partner search, information gathering, negotiation, and monitoring.[13] In sharing economy businesses models, as in social capital networks, these business functions are made a little easier. Indeed, the synthetic social capital that is embedded in sharing economy

---

[11] Robert D. Putnam, *Bowling Alone: The Collapse and Revival of American Community* (2000); *see also* James S. Coleman, *Social Capital in the Creation of Human Capital*, 94 Am. J. Soc. S95–S120 (1988).

[12] Robert D. Putnam, *E Pluribus Unum: Diversity and Community in the 21st Century: The 2006 Johan Skytte Prize Lecture*, 30 Scandinavian Pol. Stud. 137, 137 (2007).

[13] R. H. Coase, *The Nature of the Firm*, 4 ECONOMICA 386, 390–92 (1937).

networks helps facilitate peer-to-peer transactions and serves as a substitute for the type of regulation and oversight that is present in traditional market transactions. Whether such synthetic social capital creates a misplaced trust, an illusion of protection and safety, is another matter. For now, the trust evident in sharing economy transactions, a product of this synthetic social capital sharing economy networks seem to have created, is helping to facilitate sharing economy transactions in the absence of a traditional regulatory regime. But just as sharing economy models rely on trust to facilitate participation, they rely on trust itself to stand in for, or crowd out, law.[14]

The different forms in which disintermediation arises in the sharing economy has implications for the ways in which we might regulate sharing economy platforms. Indeed, the traditional form of regulation and oversight typical in market transactions bears little relationship to the disintermediated and democratic functioning of the sharing economy and the role that trust plays in that functioning. Despite the hope that lawmaking occurs through democratic processes, the typical consumer plays little role in those processes. The process of rulemaking is even less democratic. In traditional legal and regulatory regimes, despite laws that might require notice and comment, rulemaking elites, insiders, and repeat players tend to dominate legislative and rulemaking processes, leaving little room for the average consumer to play a meaningful role in them. Traditional, command-and-control-style oversight stands in direct contrast to disintermediation. Indeed, such oversight insinuates the regulator into the relationship between the regulated and the consumer in profound ways, creating significant friction in the transaction, which creates transactions costs, raising the price of doing business and increasing the ultimate cost to the consumer. Taking just one example of the costs that are imposed by regulation, barriers to entry – which might require training, licensing, and monitoring of providers – can impose a significant cost on the delivery of goods subject to such barriers. Using the legal profession to highlight this phenomenon, the expenses associated with obtaining a legal education and maintaining a law practice impose significant costs on anyone seeking to provide legal services; such costs lead to the high cost of legal services themselves, which, in turn, means many attempt to address their problems without the benefit of legal representation because the cost is prohibitive.

Contrast the legal profession with many sharing economy models. One of the benefits of the sharing economy is that the goods and services provided over sharing economy platforms are offered to consumers at incredibly competitive prices compared to those offered by providers in the traditional economy. A host on Airbnb is subject to few regulations, unlike its competitor in the hospitality industry. He or she can thus charge far less than the hotelier would charge for comparable services, or at least services the consumer considers to be "good enough." Consumers are voting with their wallets and choosing goods and services through the sharing economy at dramatic rates. Take away the cost savings by imposing barriers to entry, among other, similar legal controls that also might drive up the cost of doing business, and sharing economy businesses might lose their competitive edge. While traditional providers might cheer such developments, consumers and providers might lose out on the many valuable benefits that sharing economy platforms provide.

Given the disintermediated nature of the sharing economy, New Governance approaches share this quality, and might offer some strategies for regulating the sharing economy without sacrificing its competitive edge or the benefits it supplies. One of the key strategies embraced

---

[14] On the potential role that law can play in "crowding out" trust, *see* Larry E. Ribstein, *Law v. Trust*, 81 B.U. L. Rev. 553, 581–82 (2001).

by New Governance theorists is self-regulation.[15] Self-regulation is a type of disintermediated oversight that can be participatory and democratic. It can also foster trust. What self-regulation in the sharing economy might look like in a given sector would involve the creation of a code of conduct for that sector by which providers, and, to a certain extent, consumers, would abide. That code of conduct could be "crowdsourced": i.e., developed through a participatory process involving the coordinators of sharing economy platforms, the providers of the platform, and the consumers of the platform.[16] It could embody not just standards by which providers and consumers could guide their conduct, but offer minimal barriers to entry that are significant enough to ensure a degree of consumer protection but not so imposing that they scare off able providers or impose costs that do the same. Such self-regulatory codes of conduct, when compiled by providers and consumers alike and then adopted by such participants in the sharing economy, have a way of instilling trust, and thus do not diminish the trust that is so essential to sharing economy platforms. When one agrees to be bound by a code of conduct designed to create trustworthiness, it sends a signal that one is trustworthy at the outset, and research shows that such expressions tend to lead to one being more trustworthy.[17] Thus, by participating in the crafting of such codes and then agreeing to be bound by them, sharing economy actors can foster the trust necessary to keep the sharing economy functioning, without imposing the forms of oversight, and the transactions costs that come with them, that might stifle or eliminate the benefits the sharing economy has to offer. And those benefits are not just the low cost of many sharing economy goods and services, but also the democratic, participatory, and disintermediated characteristics of sharing economy platforms, which, themselves, are added benefits of the sharing economy itself.

Similarly, another "soft-law" approach to oversight, often embraced by New Governance, is the adoption of insurance regimes that serve as a backstop to voluntary codes of conduct. As they currently operate, some sharing economy platforms, either by preexisting law related to the service provided (as in the case of ride-hailing services), or through their own internal requirements (as in the case of Airbnb), expect providers to have insurance to guard against damages suffered by consumers at the hands of those providers when supplying goods or services through the peer-to-peer network. Sharing economy platforms can adopt insurance requirements through their codes of conduct, stating that, in order to comply with such codes, providers must possess insurance to serve as protection for consumers. As with other forms of insurance, to the extent a particular provider has a proven track record for trustworthiness, he or she should be able to maintain such insurance at a reasonable rate. Even if a platform does not wish to impose its own requirements that providers maintain an insurance policy, it can institute a disclosure mechanism that requires providers to make it clear to potential consumers whether they have insurance or do not. Such disclosure alone would send several signals to the consumer at the same time: first, that he or she has a degree of protection in the event some harm is suffered by the consumer in the transaction; second, that the provider is, to a certain extent, trustworthy: i.e., that that provider is willing to supply insurance to his or her consumers. In this way, this is the

---

[15] For a discussion of self-regulatory approaches, *see* Jason M. Solomon, *New Governance, Preemptive Self-Regulation and the Blurring of Boundaries in Regulatory Theory and Practice*, 2010 Wis. L. Rev. 591 (2010).

[16] This is consistent with the notion of "democratic experimentalism" advocated by Dorf and Sabel, *supra* note 1. For an argument for the benefits of crowdsourcing controls as superior to regulation in several contexts, *see* Richard Epstein, *The Political Economy of Crowdsourcing: Markets for Labor, Rewards, and Securities*, 82 U. Chi. L. Rev. Dialogue 35 (2015).

[17] *See e.g.*, Nina Mazar, On Amir, and Dan Ariely, *The Dishonesty of Honest People: A Theory of Self-Concept Maintenance*, 45 J. Marketing Res. 633 (2008) (revealing how subjects in a test asked to agree to a code of conduct were less likely to cheat).

sort of "trusting first move" that research into human cooperation suggests is helpful in fostering trust and spurring such cooperation.[18]

III THE SHARING ECONOMY'S DECENTRALIZED NATURE

In addition to its protean and disintermediated nature, the sharing economy is also *decentralized*. In many ways, this is a product of those first two components – the fact that the sharing economy is still evolving and diffuse, and revolves around simple, binary relationships at the lowest level of interaction: i.e., direct, peer-to-peer transactions. This is the ultimate devolution, moving from the national, to the local, to the hyper-local: from all transactions, to many transactions, to one transaction. The sharing economy's protean and disintermediated qualities allow it to tailor, customize, and fine-tune its offerings to meet the specific tastes and needs of a hyper-local market: a market of one consumer. The data obtained from those transactions, what they say about hyper-local tastes and preferences and what those tastes and preferences say, when they are aggregated, about tastes and preferences in particular markets and all markets as a whole, help to shape the services ultimately offered through the sharing economy platform. The decentralization and aggregation of information leads to experimentation and the evolution of the platforms that deliver goods and services to those hyper-local, national, and international markets.

Decentralization and experimentation (which are products of and lead to the protean nature of peer-to-peer networks) create great challenges for those who wish to regulate the sharing economy, but, at the same time, they also offer opportunities for local regulators to play a critical role in overseeing the workings of that economy. And the decentralized character of the sharing economy meshes well with New Governance approaches to the regulation, which privileges local oversight, coupled with experimentation.

Unlike traditional forms of regulation, which often emanate from centralized governmental systems, strive toward uniformity across sub-jurisdictions, are resistant to change, discount new information, and abhor experimentation, once again New Governance approaches mimic the sharing economy itself: they encourage local experimentation, are diffuse and decentralized, encourage fine-tuning of oversight to match local needs, gather information from those experiments to learn what works, and strive to translate lessons learned from the regulatory experiments into new strategies for oversight that can be taken to scale.

As described above, this experimentation would involve a dialogue between representatives of platforms, providers, consumers, and regulators. It would prefer soft-law approaches, like self-regulatory codes of conduct, backed up by insurance regimes (and the courts, as described below). Such codes could be tailored to the particular needs of local communities. And if negotiating such codes became too onerous, interest groups could collaborate to generate model codes that could be tailored to local needs or supplemented by "riders" that were a reflection of the expectations and interests of local communities. This experimentation would generate information loops that offered feedback to communities looking to adopt their own codes and could generate modification and amendment of model codes that can be disseminated for further refinement and adoption at the local level. While this may create greater transaction costs for platform providers that must negotiate in hundreds or even thousands of communities throughout the world, the benefits of such a process, like the benefits of the sharing economy itself, will result in a diffuse and decentralized regime that reflects the interests and needs of

---

[18] Carol M. Rose, *Trust in the Mirror of Betrayal*, 73 B.U. L. Rev. 531, 531 (1995). *See also* Robert Axelrod, *The Evolution of Cooperation* 13 (1984).

local markets, spurring innovation, experimentation, learning, and, in the end, trust: trust that the oversight regime is tailored to local markets and trust that sharing economy platforms and providers are cognizant and respectful of local needs.[19]

IV ANTICIPATED SHORTCOMINGS OF A NEW GOVERNANCE APPROACH TO THE SHARING ECONOMY

As outlined above, New Governance approaches, like the sharing economy itself, are flexible, participatory, and decentralized. Because they would appear to match the shape and contours of the sharing economy, they might offer useful strategies for regulating the sharing economy. There are certainly potential tradeoffs with New Governance models, models built on trust, self-regulation, and experimentation. Such tradeoffs manifest themselves most glaringly in situations where the rules imposed are not strong enough to rein in rent-seeking and predatory conduct. This section explores some of the questions raised by and potential drawbacks evident when New Governance approaches attempt to rise to the task of regulating the sharing economy.

The first question that likely emerges is whether New Governance approaches, particularly self-regulation, are strong enough to serve as a check on abusive and improper conduct. Whether it is discrimination in the delivery of ride-hailing services, or sexual misconduct in the context of housing services, the notion that self-regulation is sufficient to police such behavior is quaint at best, and dangerous and naïve at worst. Indeed, any self-regulatory regime should have outlets to remedy tortious or discriminatory conduct. And access to formal courts as the forum in which such behavior is punished would serve as a critical complement to self-regulation. Just as with the regulation of the legal profession, which, I have argued, displays features of a New Governance approach to oversight,[20] conduct is guided by a self-regulatory regime to a point; once a lawyer breaches his or her duty of care to the client, or violates his or her retainer with that client, the client has recourse to the courts, through either a legal malpractice action or prosecuting a contract claim. Oversight of the sharing economy could function in the same way. "Light touch" oversight and regulation in the first instance, backstopped by more "heavy-handed" oversight if it can be proven that the provider has breached a significant obligation to the consumer. This blended, flexible approach evokes the idea of "responsive regulation," a concept consistent with New Governance approaches.[21]

One way in which to guarantee that this muscular oversight can play a critical role in justifying self-regulation in most instances would be for sharing economy platforms to eschew the right to resolve disputes through arbitration, a much weaker form of oversight that typically resolves disputes in the shadows, away from the public eye. A critical function for judicial dispute resolution is that it helps to shape norms and sends signals to the community about such norms.[22] Admittedly, arbitration's less formal, participatory proceedings may be consistent with New Governance approaches generally. It has also become a favored forum for dispute resolution for sharing economy platforms specifically. Nevertheless, arbitration could undermine the need for a robust, dispute-resolution mechanism that is necessary to ensure an oversight

---

[19] For a discussion of new governance approaches leading to increased trust in the regulatory context, *see* Orly Lobel, *Interlocking Regulatory and industrial Relations: The Governance of Workplace Safety*, 57 Admin. L. Rev. 1071 (2005) (describing cooperative regulatory approaches in the context of worker safety).

[20] Raymond H. Brescia, *Regulating the Sharing Economy: New and Old Insights into an Oversight Regime for the Peer-to-Peer Economy*, 95 Neb. L. Rev. 87 (2016).

[21] *See, e.g.*, Ayres and Braithwaite, *supra* note 1.

[22] For a critique of non-adjudicatory dispute resolution, *see* Owen Fiss, *Against Settlement*, 93 Yale L.J. 1073 (1984).

regime is capable of policing more serious breaches of the cooperative norms a New Governance approach would seek to instill through the adoption of self-regulatory codes of conduct. Thus, arbitration does not serve the function it should serve in a New Governance regime for the sharing economy and thus should be rejected as a means of dispute resolution.

Another concern with diffuse, decentralized oversight is that well-heeled, institutional players, like some of the sharing economy platforms, could have the resources to overwhelm the regulators at the local level, marshaling economies of scale and deploying their economic power to dictate the terms of oversight even in the face of honest public servants who wish to rein in abusive conduct in the sharing economy but do not have the resources to serve as an effective counterweight to the sharing economy's behemoths. But decentralization does not have to mean deregulation. Local regulators can cooperate across jurisdictions in facilitating a dialogue about the proper contours of self-regulatory codes of conduct that can be fine-tuned and tailored to local needs. Oversight can be coordinated across jurisdictions. Devolution and local control does not require an abandonment of cooperation. Indeed, one of the purposes of local devolution is for there to be local experimentation that generates outcomes and useful metrics. Those outcomes and metrics can nourish institutional learning across jurisdictions, and examples of effective approaches can be transported, shared, and scaled in other jurisdictions, while, again, customizing those approaches to reflect local needs. This sort of dialogue and participatory process is consistent with New Governance approaches and can help chart a course toward somewhat consistent, but also locally customized, regulatory approaches that are developed in a way that offsets the political and market power that any particular sharing economy platform may enjoy and does not overburden or overwhelm local regulators.

Another fear of a self-regulatory approach is that it might crowd out more exacting regulation. Any self-regulation of the sharing economy must be serious and must be able to provide the consumer protection expected by regulators and the third-party beneficiaries of that regulation – the consumers – otherwise it will not serve its function, and regulators will not permit self-regulation to serve as the main line of defense against predatory, discriminatory, or abusive conduct. It would benefit sharing economy platforms to get ahead of this issue and suggest the adoption of self-regulatory approaches, even if they might do so as a means of avoiding the imposition of more onerous requirements. Indeed, that would be one of the main goals of embracing a self-regulatory regime. The sharing economy finds itself in a moment where the calls for extensive oversight might be forestalled by the voluntary adoption of a self-regulatory regime, at least until it is shown that such a regime is not up to the task of delivering the consumer protection that is required of regulatory oversight generally.

Another critique of a self-regulatory, standards-rather-than-rules approach is that at least some of the providers, being individuals who are not necessarily "professional" providers of goods and services and do not necessarily have any relevant training in the delivery of those goods or services, might prefer having clear guidelines (i.e., rules) that they should follow when participating in a sharing economy platform as a provider. As novices, they might want strict rules that spell out precisely the manner in which they should deliver goods and/or services over sharing economy platforms. I have two responses. First, were it the case that providers or potential providers are uncomfortable with the current level of guidance from sharing economy platforms (i.e., minimal guidance, with low barriers to entry to become a provider), we might see research that suggests that potential providers are not entering sharing economy platforms due to their desire for more guidance on how to deliver goods and services over the platform. My intuition suggests that this is not the case and I am aware of no research that suggests this. Indeed, it is more likely that intrepid providers relish the lower barriers to entry and prefer a system that does not impose onerous requirements, or even guidelines, on them. To the extent providers wanted such guidance, self-regulatory codes of conduct can provide a degree of instruction and information to providers, and additional, platform-generated assistance can offer detailed instructions to novice providers who may want to enter the market but want information on how to do so. Indeed, Airbnb already provides some degree of guidance to hosts. While it imposes almost no standards on its providers, declaring that "how you host is up to you," it offers the following, soft suggestion: "[m]ost hosts clean all the spaces a guest can use, and provide essentials like clean sheets, towels, and toilet paper."[23]

Second, one of the benefits of the lower barriers to entry is that they keep transactions costs low: there are few requirements that providers have special training, licenses, or deliver their goods or services in a particular way. The near friction-less process of becoming a provider on a sharing economy platform is probably one of the main features that attracts prospective providers to participate in the delivery of goods or services through the platform. Were stricter requirements imposed, it might increase transactions costs, raise barriers to entry, raise costs for consumers, and discourage providers from participating in the platform. In other words, it might eliminate one of the central competitive advantages sharing economy platforms hold over more traditional providers. Without that competitive advantage, which is at the heart of the sharing economy's success, the benefits that sharing economy platforms deliver – lower cost, better accessibility – will be lost, which will undermine the ability of the sharing economy to deliver the innovation and the economic benefits it generates.

CONCLUSION

This chapter has argued that three of the main characteristics of sharing economy platforms are that they are protean, disintermediated, and decentralized. As a result, traditional forms of regulation and government oversight – that are typically static, slow to adapt, anti-democratic in some ways, and centralized – are ill suited to serve in an effective, regulatory function that both delivers consumer protection while permitting for and responding to innovation in the ways in which sharing economy goods and services are delivered. In contrast, New Governance Theory offers an array of regulatory responses and approaches that seem to fit better with these characteristics of the sharing economy. Specifically, New Governance strategies favor self-regulatory models that offer standards rather than rules, endorse self-regulatory codes of conduct that are backed up by judicial authority, promote the use of insurance regimes, and encourage local experimentation. Because such approaches tend to correspond to the contours of the sharing economy itself, they might prove a better regulatory fit to serve critical consumer protection purposes, encourage innovation, and preserve the economic and societal benefits sharing economy platforms offer.

[23] *Earn Money as an AirBnB Host*, Airbnb, www.airbnb.com/host/homes?from_nav=1.

12

Licensing Regimes and Platform-Based Businesses

*Derek McKee**

INTRODUCTION

Licenses are at the center of the controversy surrounding peer-to-peer platform-based businesses. To take the most obvious example: in many jurisdictions around the world, it is illegal to drive a taxi without a special license issued by a government authority. Uber and similar transportation services often operate without such licenses. While sectoral licensing regimes for hotels and other short-term accommodations are not as ubiquitous as those for taxis, non-respect of such regimes, where they exist, has contributed to the controversy surrounding Airbnb.

Such licensing regimes have complicated debates about the appropriate form of regulation for platform-based business activities. Recognizing that such activities create risks for their users and impose costs on third parties, many policy analysts have concluded that they require regulation.[1] Commentators disagree, however, as to whether governments should regulate these businesses directly, or whether they should foster "self-regulation" by platform companies. Whichever side one takes, the presence of preexisting licensing regimes means that this debate rarely occurs under ideal conditions. Instead, when determining how the new services should be regulated, authorities must consider the applicability of older licensing regimes. In addition, they must decide what to do about the old regime: whether to maintain it in its current form, modify it, or abolish it altogether.

Licensing holds obvious attractions as a way of regulating economic activities such as those offered through peer-to-peer platforms. It is incredibly versatile, serving a variety of purposes: ensuring quality; protecting health, safety, and the environment; promoting fair business practices and employment conditions; or controlling supply so as to avoid destructive competition. Moreover, licensing is extremely powerful. Licensees can be subjected to various conditions, with revocation as the ultimate sanction for noncompliance.

* I would like to thank the editors of the handbook, as well as Katrina Wyman for comments on previous drafts. Mistakes are mine.

[1] See, e.g., the following policy reports published by governments and international organizations: *Protecting Consumers in Peer Platform Markets: Exploring the Issues*, OECD (2016), www.oecd.org/officialdocuments/publicdisplaydocumentpdf/?cote=DSTI/CP(2015)4/FINAL&docLanguage=En; *A European Agenda for the Collaborative Economy*, European Commission (2016), http://ec.europa.eu/DocsRoom/documents/16881; *The "Sharing" Economy: Issues Facing Platforms, Participants & Regulators*, United States, Federal Trade Commission, www.ftc.gov/system/files/documents/reports/sharing-economy-issues-facing-platforms-participants-regulators-federal-trade-commission-staff/p151200_ftc_staff_report_on_the_sharing_economy.pdf.

Nevertheless, licenses also have a dark side. The very power of licensing regimes has earned them suspicion from liberal critics concerned with protecting rights and freedoms.[2] Economists have drawn attention to the inefficiencies associated with licensing, notably the fact that it imposes barriers to market entry.[3] And public choice theorists, drawing together concerns about efficiency, distribution, and political legitimacy, have singled out licensing regimes for some of their sharpest critiques.[4]

Such critiques have played a prominent role in debates over the platform-based businesses associated with the "sharing economy."[5] When the new platforms and their users disregard licensing requirements, authorities must decide how rigorously they will enforce these requirements. Such decisions have sometimes been influenced, implicitly or explicitly, by judgments about the appropriateness of such regimes. Indeed, critics of licensing have often seized on the arrival of the new platforms to call for the existing regimes to be dismantled.

In practice, however, the arrival of platform-based businesses has rarely led to an outright abolition of existing licensing regimes. Instead, authorities in some jurisdictions have in fact strengthened these regimes, or rather modified them so that old and new modes of business can coexist. Both tendencies can be observed in the example of tourist accommodations in the province of Québec, Canada, which I discuss in Section III, below. Moreover, in some jurisdictions, authorities have created separate, parallel licensing regimes for the new online services, as with the legalization of "transportation network companies" in most US states and the establishment of short-term accommodation registries in cities such as Amsterdam and San Francisco. Although these parallel regimes rarely contain firm numerical quotas like some of the older regimes, supply management concerns remain relevant. This is clearly the case when it comes to smartphone-hailed transportation services in Québec, as I will also explain. These trends demonstrate that the policy concerns underlying the older licensing regimes have not gone away.

Moreover, even if authorities were to abolish licensing altogether, such a reform would not eliminate the problems associated with licensing. This is because "self-regulation" by individual platforms operates, in functional terms, as a private licensing regime. The platforms' claim to obviate public licensing rests largely on their ability to regulate providers in much the same way that governments would have done. But once this is recognized, one must also recognize that "self-regulation" by platforms is also capable of reproducing many of the pathologies typically associated with public licensing regimes, including the abusive treatment of individual licensees as well as regulatory capture. While powerfully effective, regulation by platforms may also give rise to inefficiencies, maldistributions, conflicts of interest, and arbitrariness.

The public/private distinction therefore provides an unhelpful way of determining who should be responsible for regulating platform-based businesses – through licensing or other means. Instead, a more nuanced approach is required, which will consider the possibilities as well as the pitfalls of both public and private governance, situating these in social, economic, and political context.

---

[2] *See, e.g.,* Charles A. Reich, *The New Property,* 73 Yale L. J. 733 (1964).

[3] *See, e.g.,* Shirley Svorny, Licensing. Market Entry Regulation, *in Encyclopedia of Law & Economics, Vol. III, The Regulation of Contracts* 296 (Boudewijn Bouckaert and Gerrit De Geest eds., 2000).

[4] *See, e.g.,* George J. Stigler, *The Theory of Economic Regulation,* 2 Bell J. of Econ. and Mgmt. Sci. 3 (1971).

[5] I use the term "sharing economy" in quotation marks to highlight the inaccuracy of applying this expression to commercial enterprises such as Airbnb and Uber. On the distinction between markets and sharing, *see* Yochai Benkler, *"Sharing Nicely": On Shareable Goods and the Emergence of Sharing as a Modality of Economic Production,* 114 Yale L.J. 273 (2004).

I LICENSING AS A MODE OF GOVERNANCE

Licenses are a ubiquitous feature of contemporary governance. Governments around the world issue licenses: for mundane aspects of everyday life (such as keeping a pet); for large-scale, networked economic activities (such as transportation, communication, and energy generation); and for everything in between.[6] Anthony Ogus has noted that licensing is frequently applied to professions, trades, commercial activities, products, as well as uses of land.[7] There are good reasons for the ubiquity of licensing as a governance mechanism. It is extremely powerful and versatile. Nevertheless, thanks in part to this ubiquity, licensing has earned its share of critiques.

The diverse uses of licensing make it difficult to provide a concise definition of "license." Indeed, in English-language legal scholarship, it appears that few authors have tried to do so. I have therefore adopted Pierre Issalys and Denis Lemieux's definition of a license as "a permission, often subject to conditions, given by a public authority to a natural or legal person, to carry out an act or to exercise an activity that would otherwise be illegal."[8] I have chosen this definition because it largely corresponds to commonsense understandings. It also helps to clarify these understandings and to distinguish licensing from other forms of governance. The emphasis on the fact that the underlying activity would otherwise be illegal serves to distinguish licensing from certification, which recognizes compliance with standards but is not required for the activity in question.[9] This emphasis also distinguishes licenses from other legal forms in which governments legally recognize private arrangements that would otherwise be perfectly legal (as with contracts, corporate organization, or the family).

The definition I have adopted is largely a functional one. It is indifferent to the official terminology used: licenses may appear under the guise of "permits," "authorizations," and so on. It is compatible with the fact that licenses can be administered by different kinds of authority. While licenses are generally issued by public institutions, governments may also delegate this task to private bodies (as is often the case with self-regulating professions, for example). It is also compatible with the fact that licenses can take many legal forms. In some instances, especially where they are tradable, licenses may be recognized as a form of property for some purposes.[10] In other instances, where their holders are held to strict conditions, licenses may take the form of contracts.[11] However, this definition also contains a formal element, in that it insists on a public authority as the source of the license. The "license" that an ordinary property holder grants to another person, allowing this person some use of his or her property, is therefore excluded from the definition.

The details of licensing regimes vary. Some licenses attach to a particular holder, while others are transferable. Some licenses are issued for an indefinite period; others require regular renewal. Licenses often come with conditions attached (such as the need to fulfill certain quality or safety standards). Authorities may verify compliance with these standards before issuing the license, or they may issue the license as a matter of routine, subject to the possibility of later verifications.[12]

---

[6] Glanville Williams, *Control by Licensing*, 20 Current Legal Problems 81 (1967); Richard A. Epstein, *The Permit Power Meets the Constitution*, 81 Iowa L. Rev. 407 (1995).

[7] Anthony I. Ogus, *Regulation: Legal Form and Economic Theory* 214–44 (1994).

[8] Pierre Issalys and Denis Lemieux, *L'Action gouvernementale: Précis de droit des institutions administratives* 916 (3d ed. 2009) (author's translation).

[9] Ogus, *supra* note 7 at 215.

[10] *See, e.g., Saulnier v. Royal Bank of Canada*, [2008] 3 S.C.R. 166, 2008 SCC 58.

[11] *See, e.g., Société de l'assurance automobile du Québec v. Cyr*, [2008] 1 S.C.R. 338, 2008 SCC 13.

[12] Eric Bibert and J. B. Ruhl, *The Permit Power Revisited: The Theory and Practice of Regulatory Permits in the Administrative State*, 64 Duke L.J. 133 (2014).

Licenses may be coupled with other forms of economic regulation, such as price controls. The number of licenses for an activity may be unlimited, or it may be capped (setting limits on supply). Even where licensing regimes are not subject to formal quantitative restrictions, high standards may perform an equivalent function, as in the case of London's "knowledge" requirement for taxi drivers.[13] Licenses may also be geographically bounded, giving their holder the right to exercise his or her activity only within a certain area.

Nevertheless, licenses all have one common feature, which is the possibility of suspension or revocation. This possibility gives administrative authorities leverage over license holders. It is what makes licensing an especially powerful form of governance.[14]

Public authorities use licensing regimes to pursue diverse policy objectives. Most obviously, licensing is commonly used to enforce standards for quality and safety, or to curb pollution and other unwanted side effects of economic activity. In economic terms, such standards can often be explained as responses to certain common market failures, such as information asymmetries and externalities.[15] Alternatively, licensing may be used for planning purposes, ensuring that limited resources such as land are allocated to some uses rather than others. At the same time, governments may intend such regimes to guarantee producers a certain level of revenue.[16] Governments may also couple such entry restrictions with a system of price controls, in order to ensure that consumers are able to afford the service. Licensing regimes may also require license holders to supply authorities with detailed information about their activities, and may therefore function as a mode of surveillance.[17] Finally, many authorities require license holders to pay fees, meaning that licensing can function as a means of raising revenue. These various purposes are not mutually exclusive. In practice, licensing regimes frequently serve several such goals at the same time.[18]

The use of licensing has attracted at least three lines of critique, reflecting different normative concerns. A first line of critique comes from liberal scholars concerned about the rule of law and the protection of individual rights. According to these scholars, the powerful leverage associated with suspension or revocation may give rise to arbitrariness. Indeed, the decision about whether or not to grant a license in the first place may be an occasion for abuse, enabling governments to inappropriately interfere in citizens' private lives. For example, in his famous 1964 article, Charles Reich identified licenses as one form of "government largess" that was occupying a more central social and economic role and was therefore deserving of greater legal protection.[19]

A second line of critique comes from economic analysts concerned about the inefficiencies of licensing regimes. From an economic standpoint, licenses may be understood as barriers to market entry, artificially limiting supply and therefore generating higher prices for consumers.[20] These barriers to market entry are even steeper where the number of licenses is capped and where licenses are tradable – meaning that entrants must buy their way into the market. While economic analysts acknowledge the benefits of licensing as a way of responding to certain

---

[13] Jody Rosen, *The Knowledge, London's Legendary Taxi-Driver Test, Puts Up a Fight in the Age of GPS*, NY Times, Nov. 10, 2014, www.nytimes.com/2014/11/10/t-magazine/london-taxi-test-knowledge.html.

[14] Ian Ayres and John Braithwaite, *Responsive Regulation: Transcending the Deregulation Debate* 35–36 (1992).

[15] Ogus, *supra* note 7.

[16] Williams, *supra* note 6.

[17] Mariana Valverde, *Police Science, British Style: Pub Licensing and Knowledges of Urban Disorder*, 32 Econ. and Soc'y 234 (2003).

[18] Issalys and Lemieux, *supra* note 8.

[19] Reich, *supra* note 2.

[20] *See, e.g.,* Svorny, *supra* note 3; *see also* Thomas G. Moore, *The Purposes of Licensing*, 4 J. L. & Econ. 93(1961).

market failures, they also insist on paying attention to licensing's costs, and argue that less costly alternatives are often available.[21]

A third line of critique, associated with public choice theory, incorporates these efficiency concerns and links them to concerns about distribution as well as political legitimacy. Public choice theorists have argued that economic regulation frequently serves the private interests of the regulated industry at the expense of wider public interests.[22] This critique therefore incorporates a distributive element: it is argued that regulation benefits the few at the expense of the many. Public choice theorists also argue that regulation often serves the political or bureaucratic interests of public authorities, who are more responsive to pressure from concentrated interest groups than to the general public.[23] This critique suggests that economic regulation often represents a hijacking of the democratic process. This concept of "regulatory capture" is all the more applicable in cases where the public authority formally delegates regulatory authority to the regulated industry itself. The public choice critique has been aimed at economic regulation in general, and not just licensing. Nevertheless, licensing regimes have generally served as public choice theorists' prime example of inefficient, regressive, and illegitimate regulation.

Licensing regimes are therefore associated with several familiar pathologies. Nevertheless, licenses remain in widespread use, in almost every area of social and economic life. While some scholars argue that licenses could be replaced with other forms of governance, this may be easier said than done. On one hand, the difficulty stems from the fact that licensing regimes have generated concentrations of economic interests and a resulting set of interest-group politics. Public authorities therefore do not start with a blank slate. On the other hand, the argument for abolishing licensing regimes, as made by authors such as Ogus, is often based on the assumption that such regimes have a single identifiable purpose.[24] The conceit is that one can find some other governance mechanism that would achieve that purpose more efficiently and effectively, and use it instead of licensing. But as I have pointed out, licensing regimes often serve multiple interconnected purposes. As Roderick Macdonald observed, there is rarely a straight line from the identification of a policy objective to the implementation of a legitimate, efficient, and fair way of achieving that objective. The "instruments" governments use to achieve their ends have their own internal logic and have a reciprocal effect on the ends chosen.[25]

II LICENSES AND PLATFORM-BASED BUSINESSES: A CANADIAN CASE STUDY

In the last few years, platform-based businesses associated with the "sharing economy" have clashed with licensing regimes around the world. With the help of these platforms, ordinary users (generally known as "providers") carry out economic activities for which licenses are sometimes required. Authorities have responded to this situation in different ways. On one hand, authorities have subjected platforms and providers to legal sanctions, thus reinforcing the licensing regimes. On the other hand, faced with the popularity of such services, authorities in some places have moved to exempt them from the existing licensing regimes. In doing so, however, they have often created new, parallel, licensing regimes for the new services. In this section,

---

[21] *See, e.g.,* Ogus, *supra* note 7.
[22] *See, e.g.,* Stigler, *supra* note 4.
[23] *Id.; see also* Moore, *supra* note 20.
[24] Ogus, *supra* note 7.
[25] Roderick A. Macdonald, The Swiss Army Knife of Governance, *in Designing Government: From Instruments to Governance* (Pearl Eliadis, Margaret M. Hill, and Michael Howlett eds., 2005). *See also* Lon L. Fuller, Means and Ends, *in The Principles of Social Order: Selected Essays of Lon L. Fuller* (rev'd ed., Kenneth I. Winston ed., 2001).

I illustrate these dynamics through an account of recent reforms to hotel and taxi licensing in the Canadian province of Québec, with occasional comparisons from other jurisdictions.

In Québec, as in some European jurisdictions, hotels and other "tourist accommodation establishments" are subject to a mandatory classification system. Anyone wishing to offer short-term accommodation in exchange for payment must obtain a "classification certificate" for their establishment, with a rating from zero to five stars.[26] As it is illegal to offer short-term accommodations without such a certificate, this is, in effect, a licensing regime. The Minister of Tourism has delegated responsibility for the operation of the regime to the Corporation de l'industrie touristique du Québec (CITQ), an industry association representing hotels and other establishments. The CITQ conducts regular inspections (in order to rate establishments). The Ministry of Tourism investigates cases of noncompliance, sends hosts warning letters, and may refer them to the public prosecutor's office. The certification scheme is linked to municipal zoning bylaws; one cannot obtain a certificate without the approval of one's local authorities.

When Airbnb first became popular in Québec (around 2013), critics noted that its hosts generally lacked proper classification certificates and were thus operating outside the law.[27] The hotel industry cried foul; landlords worried that tenants were subletting without their permission; housing activists expressed concern that illegal Airbnb rentals were diminishing the stock of affordable housing in Montréal and Québec City.[28] In response, the Ministry of Tourism referred a handful of cases to the public prosecutor.[29] Nevertheless, there was considerable uncertainty surrounding the application of the law, because the relevant regulation specified that one did not need a certificate to rent accommodation to tourists "on an occasional basis."[30]

In the fall of 2015, the government announced that it would amend the laws to address the arrival of Airbnb. This reform, which came into force in May 2016, dramatically increased the penalties for operating a tourist accommodation establishment without a classification certificate, with fines ranging from CDN$2,500 to CDN$100,000 (for repeat offenders).[31] It also increased the number of inspectors charged with enforcing the regime. The government initially promised to clarify the applicability of the regime to "occasional" rentals; it was rumored that the government would allow hosts without classification certificates to rent on Airbnb up to a certain number of days per year.[32] In the end, the government merely inverted the formulation in the regulation, requiring a classification certificate for anyone who offers accommodation to tourists "on a regular basis."[33] The Ministry of Tourism later issued an interpretation bulletin stating that "a regular basis" would be taken to mean more than once per year, thus exempting, for example, those who rent out their primary residence during an annual vacation or those who accommodate tourists at the time of an annual festival.[34] The Québec government's response

---

[26] Act Respecting Tourist Accommodation Establishments, CQLR c E-14.2, s 1.

[27] Nathaëlle Morissette, *Jolie chambre, ni chère ni… légale*, La Presse, 16 Mar. 2013.

[28] Isabelle Porter, *Airbnb accusé de réduire l'offre de logements*, Le Devoir, July 24, 2014.

[29] Isabelle Porter, *Québec s'en charge … mais le dernier mot va aux villes*, Le Devoir, Mar. 7, 2015. Other hosts found themselves in trouble with tax authorities for failing to declare their Airbnb income: Tristan Péloquin, *Le fisc réclame 60 000 $ à un hôte Airbnb*, La Presse, Mar. 22, 2016. Still others faced the wrath of their landlords for subletting without permission: *see, e.g.*, 9177–2541 Québec inc. c. Li, 2016 QCRDL 8129.

[30] Regulation Respecting Tourist Accommodation Establishments, RRQ c E-14.2, r 1, s 1 (previous version, in force prior to May 15, 2016).

[31] Québec, Bill 67, An Act mainly to improve the regulation of tourist accommodation and to define a new system of governance as regards international promotion, 1st Sess., 41st Leg., 2015 (first reading, Oct. 22, 2015); Act Respecting Tourist Accommodation Establishments, *supra* note 26 (version in force since May 15, 2016).

[32] Jean-Michel Genois Gagnon, *Airbnb en voie d'être légalisé au Québec*, Le Soleil, Aug. 9, 2015.

[33] Regulation Respecting Tourist Accommodation Establishments, RRQ c E-14.2, r 1, s 1.

[34] Tourisme Québec, *Guide d'interprétation de la loi et du règlement sur les établissements d'hébergement touristique*, www.tourisme.gouv.qc.ca/programmes-services/hebergement/guide-interpretation.html.

to Airbnb was therefore to reinforce the existing licensing regime, to attempt to subject Airbnb hosts to the same rules as more conventional commercial operations, albeit creating a small, vaguely defined window for informal rentals. The vagueness of this formulation became the object of considerable criticism, and the government has since expressed an intention to change the law once again, although the details of the new reform remain to be seen.[35]

The government's reform reflected a variety of policy objectives. In general, the government framed its reform as a crackdown on "illegal hotels" – thus protecting the integrity of the existing licensing regime as well as the market share of established players.[36] This concern helps explain the government's one-size-fits-all rhetoric (although the presence of a limited exception belies this rhetoric). The government also cited consumer protection concerns, and was responsive to arguments about resource allocation – a desire to limit the amount of urban space given over to tourists. Similar dynamics can be observed in other jurisdictions, such as San Francisco[37] and Amsterdam,[38] which have established new, special licensing regimes for providers of short-term accommodation. Under such regimes, short-term rentals are permitted up to a maximum number of days per year (90 days in San Francisco; 60 days in Amsterdam), evidence of a desire to contain the Airbnb phenomenon.

In the case of taxis, the clash between the platform-based business model and the existing licensing regime has been even clearer, as has been the development of new legal forms to pursue both consumer protection and resource allocation goals. Québec, like many other North American jurisdictions, uses a system in which a fixed number of taxi "permits" are available for a given geographical area (what are known elsewhere as "plates" or "medallions").[39] Although the government has stopped issuing tradable taxi permits, permits issued before November 15, 2000 are tradable and have acquired significant value.[40] Québec differs from many other North American jurisdictions, however, in that the provincial government manages the regime itself – including setting the maximum number of permits allowed in specific geographic areas – rather than delegating this function to municipalities. (In Montréal, however, a municipal arm's length agency, the Bureau du Taxi, is responsible for overseeing the day-to-day operation of the licensing regime.)

Uber began operating in Montréal in October 2013 and in Québec City in February 2015. Most of Uber's drivers operated without proper taxi permits. Uber claimed to be offering a "ride-sharing" service. But Québec's legislation is clear: except for a few limited cases, anyone transporting passengers in exchange for remuneration in Québec is offering a taxi service.[41] And it is an offense to do so without a proper permit.[42] From 2014 to 2016, provincial and municipal agencies seized hundreds of vehicles from Uber drivers for noncompliance.[43] Uber and

[35] Karl Rettino-Parazelli, *Québec promet d'en 'faire plus' pour encadrer Airbnb*, Le Devoir, Aug. 30, 2017 (discussing Airbnb's agreement to begin collecting a 3.5 percent lodging tax in Québec).

[36] Dominique Vien, *Point de presse de Mme Dominique Vien, ministre du Tourisme*, Assemblée nationale, www.assnat .qc.ca/fr/actualites-salle-presse/conferences-points-presse/ConferencePointPresse-25417.html.

[37] San Francisco Planning, *Office of Short Term Rental Registry & FAQs*, http://sf-planning.org/office-short-term-rental-registry-faqs.

[38] IAmsterdam, *Private holiday rental: What you should know*, www.iamsterdam.com/en/visiting/plan-your-trip/where-to-stay/private-holiday-rental.

[39] Act Respecting Transportation Services by Taxi, CQLR c S-6.01, s. 4.

[40] It was reported that permits for Montreal were trading at over CDN$200,000 just before the arrival of Uber: Tristan Péloquin, *La chute de la valeur des permis de taxi se confirme*, La Presse, Dec. 7, 2016.

[41] Act Respecting Transportation Services by Taxi, *supra* note 39, s. 2(3) ("transportation services by taxi").

[42] *Id.*, s. 117.

[43] Tristan Péloquin, *Saisies de véhicules Uber: le Bureau du taxi 'perplexe' devant de nombreux cas*, La Presse, Feb. 25, 2016.

its drivers also came under scrutiny from tax authorities, who raided Uber's local offices and questioned Uber's stance that its drivers' services were exempt from certain taxes.[44] Despite these legal difficulties, Uber remained popular in Québec and continued to operate.

During the same period, a number of other Canadian jurisdictions began to legalize Uber. In the province of Alberta, where taxis are largely regulated at the municipal level, the city of Edmonton established new licensing regimes for app-based drivers ("private transportation providers") as well as the platforms through which they work ("commercial private transportation provider dispatch") as of March 1, 2016.[45] These regimes, inspired by the "transportation network company" model that had spread throughout the United States, allow Uber drivers to accept passengers through their smartphone applications while reserving street hails and taxi stands for conventionally licensed taxis. (For a useful overview of these new regulatory regimes in the United States, see Katrina Wyman's chapter in this volume.) They also subject app-based drivers to background checks, vehicle inspections, and commercial insurance requirements, although the platform company oversees compliance with these conditions. Finally, they require app-based services and their drivers to pay certain licensing fees, both on an annual and on a per-ride basis. Over the course of 2015 and 2016, other cities in Alberta (notably Calgary) as well as in the province of Ontario (notably Toronto and Ottawa) adopted similar regimes.

Although the Québec government was well aware of these developments, it chose to develop a distinct regulatory model for Uber. In September 2016, the Québec government and Uber signed an "entente," legalizing Uber's services for one year on a provisional basis.[46] Under this entente, framed as a "pilot project" for the modernization of the taxi industry, Uber was granted the equivalent of 300 taxi permits, albeit measured in terms of hours rather than vehicles. Uber drivers are permitted to operate for up to a total of 50,000 hours per week. In exchange, Uber must pay the government CDN$0.90 per ride, in addition to certain other fees. If Uber's drivers are on the road for more than 50,000 hours in a given week, the per-ride fee goes up to CDN$1.10; over 100,000 hours, it becomes CDN$1.26. The entente also sets CDN$3.45 as the minimum fare for Uber rides – identical to the regulated minimum fare for conventional taxis. Uber also agrees to collect and remit certain taxes on behalf of its drivers. Uber's drivers are responsible for obtaining commercial-grade drivers' licenses; the platform is responsible for carrying out vehicle inspections and background checks on its drivers. As with the regulatory model in other North American jurisdictions, Uber drivers may only accept passengers who contact them through the app, while street hails and taxi stands are reserved for conventional taxis.

Québec's regulatory model for Uber is unusual in that it has ostensibly eschewed creating a separate state-managed licensing regime for platform-based transport services, as many other North American jurisdictions have done. Instead, at least rhetorically, Québec has clung to the notion of a unified regime. In practice, however, Québec has created an exception to this regime under the guise of experimentation. Under this experiment, Québec has delegated to Uber much of the responsibility for ensuring passenger safety and achieving other consumer protection goals. Nevertheless, by describing this arrangement as a "pilot project," Québec has insisted on its time-limited nature and reserved the right to alter it at a moment's notice. Nor has Québec been willing to entirely let go of the resource allocation aspects of its licensing regime. Its graduated per-ride fee, scaled up according to Uber drivers' road time, demonstrates

---

[44] *Uber Canada inc. c. Agence du revenu du Québec*, 2016 QCCS 2158.

[45] City of Edmonton, Bylaw 17400, Vehicle for Hire ("private transportation provider"), www.edmonton.ca/documents/Bylaws/C17400.pdf.

[46] Québec, Ministère des Transports, de la Mobilité durable et de l'Électrification des transports, *Entente*, www.transports.gouv.qc.ca/fr/salle-de-presse/nouvelles/Documents/2016-09-09/entente-uber.pdf.

a willingness to protect the market share of conventional taxis and to keep the overall market within certain boundaries.

The persistence – indeed, the renewed use – of public licensing regimes in the context of platform-based services suggests that such regimes are still seen as serving some legitimate purposes, including both consumer protection and resource allocation. The creation of exemptions or of parallel, abutting licensing regimes demonstrates an awareness of the limits of these regimes, and perhaps an attempt to overcome their pathologies. It is too early to tell whether the type of regulatory arrangements I have described in Québec will have such effects – helping to rein in the power of regulators, foster more efficient markets for services, contribute to a more equitable distribution of income, and discourage regulatory capture. Nevertheless, if the platforms' goal was to create an alternative that would obviate government licensing regimes (and overcome their pathologies), this goal has been realized only in an incomplete and fragmentary way.

III THE PLATFORMS AS PRIVATE LICENSING REGIMES

The persistence of licensing merely suggests that the concerns animating licensing are still present. It does not prove that licensing itself is useful or necessary. Indeed, the platforms' business models – as well as the arguments of some of their supporters – have often been based on the claim that "self-regulation" by individual platforms can take the place of public regulation, especially licensing regimes.[47] Such arguments imply that it would be better to eliminate public licensing regimes altogether, to finish the job. But this claim is based on the fact that the platforms operate, in some respects, as private licensing regimes. Like public licensing regimes, the platforms' strength is in their enforcement capacity – their ability to ensure compliance on the part of providers. However, the platforms may also reproduce the pathologies of public licensing regimes, including arbitrariness, inefficiency, regressive distributive effects, and conflicts of interest.

In formal terms, the platforms cannot be considered licensing regimes. It is true that, as holders of intellectual property, the platforms agree, as part of their terms of service, to grant providers with "licenses" to use their software. However, because they are considered private arrangements, based on property concepts as well as intersecting contracts, these "licenses" fall outside the definition I have adopted. Lack of access to a platform's network will not render a provider's activities illegal from the perspective of the state legal system.

Nevertheless, in functional terms, the platforms' operation resembles that of licensing regimes. Network effects create a tendency toward monopoly (or in some cases, duopoly) in certain platform-based sectors.[48] In theory, providers are free to operate independently, but in practice, they cannot operate without permission from a platform. Platforms tend to grant such permission subject to a host of conditions. They reserve the right to alter these conditions unilaterally, as well as the right to banish providers from the network. (The fact that providers can sometimes "multi-home," offering the same service through more than one network, attenuates the power of the platforms to some extent.)

---

[47] *See, e.g.*, Molly Cohen and Arun Sundararajan, *Self-Regulation and Innovation in the Peer-to-Peer Sharing Economy*, 82 U. Chi. L. Rev. Dialogue 116 (2015); Christopher Koopman, Matthew Mitchell, and Adam Thierer, *The Sharing Economy and Consumer Protection Regulation: The Case for Policy Change*, 8 J. Bus. Entrepreneurship & L. 529 (2015).

[48] K. Sabeel Rahman, *Curbing the New Corporate Power*, Boston Rev., May 4, 2015.

This set of arrangements has provided the background conditions for claims by the platforms and their supporters that they provide an effective system of "self-regulation."[49] Indeed, in these arguments, "self-regulation" is generally assumed to mean regulation of providers by individual platform companies. The leverage that platform companies are able to exert over providers, by controlling access to the networks, is seen as strong enough to ensure compliance with quality and safety standards, for example. Uber thus carries out its own vehicle inspections and background checks, and has loudly claimed that such measures obviate any such requirement by public authorities.[50]

However, in carrying out these licensing-like functions, the platforms may reproduce many of the pathologies typically associated with public licensing regimes. To begin with, the platforms may operate in an arbitrary manner. The platforms have at times loudly trumpeted their "deactivation" of providers where these providers have engaged in serious misconduct.[51] Uber and other platform-based companies have also frequently unilaterally altered providers' working conditions with little or no prior notice.[52]

Moreover, the platforms are not necessarily efficient. The platforms do not provide a perfectly seamless market; exchanges through the platforms still have transaction costs. The standards the platforms impose on providers create barriers to entry (for example, in the form of vehicle inspections and background checks) which may discourage some would-be providers. While the platforms do not impose quantitative restrictions such as those imposed by conventional taxi licensing regimes, barriers to entry remain. In some cases, as with Uber, the platform sets the price, rather than leaving it up to providers and consumers to agree on a price. There is evidence that Uber's price-setting algorithm is based on its interest in having as many drivers on the road as possible.[53] To the extent that a platform like Uber is able to achieve a degree of monopoly power in a given market, it may be in a position to extract rents (albeit likely at the expense of providers rather than consumers). Ironically, the ability to "multi-home" – to offer services through multiple platforms – likely weakens providers' bargaining power and strengthens the platforms' ability to extract rents.[54] In addition, the platforms' services produce externalities (in the form of noise, air pollution, etc.), the costs of which the platforms may fail to fully internalize. All of these phenomena represent real or potential inefficiencies. A sophisticated economic analysis would compare these inefficiencies to those generated by the publicly licensed alternatives.

---

[49] *See, e.g.,* Arun Sundararajan, *The Sharing Economy: The End of Employment and the Rise of Crowd-Based Capitalism* (2016).

[50] At one point, Uber claimed to have an "industry-leading" system of background checks; however, it abandoned this claim in response to a class action lawsuit in California: Mike Isaac, *Uber Settles Suit Over Driver Background Checks*, NY Times, Apr. 7, 2016. In Massachusetts, where lawmakers insisted on the government carrying out background checks, these turned out to be stricter than those carried out by the platforms: Adam Vaccaro and Dan Adams, *Thousands of Current Uber, Lyft Drivers Fail New Background Checks*, Boston Globe, Apr. 5, 2017.

[51] *See, e.g.,* Ann Hui, *Toronto Man Says He Was Forced To Jump Out of Moving Uber Car*, The Globe and Mail, May 26, 2015; Georgia Wilkins, *Dumped Uber Driver Pleads for Explanation*, Sydney Morning Herald, May 21, 2016. However, note that in some jurisdictions, Uber has instituted a "deactivation policy" that purports to provide some degree of transparency (and perhaps even due process) in deactivation cases: *Legal: Driver Deactivation Policy – Australia and New Zealand Only*, Uber, www.uber.com/legal/deactivation-policy/.

[52] *See, e.g.,* Alan Feuer, *Uber Drivers Up Against the App*, NY Times, Feb. 19 2016; Joel Rubin, *Lawsuit Accuses Uber of Ripping Off Drivers, Paying Them Smaller Fares than What Passengers Pay*, LA Times, Apr. 28, 2017.

[53] Noam Scheiber, *How Uber Uses Psychological Tricks to Push Its Drivers' Buttons*, NY Times, Apr. 2, 2017.

[54] *See generally* Mark Armstrong, *Competition in Two-Sided Markets*, 37 RAND J. of Econ. 668 (2006); Stephen P. King, *Sharing Economy: What Challenges for Competition Law?*, 6 J. of Eur. Competition L. & Practice 729 (2015).

Finally, the platforms are likely to operate in their own private interest rather than the public interest. Their pricing structures are designed to maximize profits, not to provide an optimal level of services. It is true that platforms tend to keep prices relatively low, and for this reason, they have remained popular with consumers. Nevertheless, the commissions taken by the platforms represent a large share of these prices. This appropriation of revenue by the platforms therefore raises distributive concerns. If governments accept the platforms as substitutes for public licensing regimes, this endorsement can be seen as a particularly extreme form of regulatory capture: the delegation of a licensing power to a private body. There are real concerns about the legitimacy of such a decision, especially when the platform established its market share by flouting existing laws (as has often been the case with Uber[55]).

CONCLUSION

Contrary to the claims of some of their boosters, platform-based businesses have not rendered public licensing regimes obsolete. With respect to licensing, governments' responses to the arrival of these platforms have varied widely. In some cases, governments have attempted to reinforce the universal application of existing licensing regimes. In other cases, as with the licensing of tourist accommodations in Québec, they have maintained existing licensing regimes while granting limited exemptions. In still other cases, they have created new, parallel licensing regimes for the platforms or their providers, or delegated licensing power to the platforms under strict conditions. (Québec's "pilot project" for the legalization of Uber, while maintaining the pretense of a single regulatory regime, is an example of the latter phenomenon.) These developments do not prove that licensing is necessary or that it is wise. But they do suggest that the objectives that have historically inspired the creation of licensing regimes – including both consumer protection and resource allocation goals – remain relevant public policy concerns. Indeed, evidence of both types of goal can be observed in new licensing regimes established for the new services.

Conversely, were governments to eliminate licensing in favor of platform-centered "self-regulation," such a reform would not necessarily avoid the problems historically associated with licensing regimes. The platforms are just as capable as any public regime – perhaps more so – of generating arbitrariness, inefficiency, regressive distributive effects, and illegitimate exercises of political power. The idea that competition will force the platforms to behave may be illusory, given that these platforms function as networks and are able to exploit network effects.

The analysis in this chapter should not be taken as a defense of the status quo. Existing licensing regimes have real problems and are susceptible of improvement. Nor should it be taken to imply that public licensing regimes are the only solution. Other regulatory models may be possible. Nevertheless, it should be taken as a warning against seductive proposals that fail to account for the social, economic, and political complexity of this regulatory challenge.

[55] Mike Isaac, *How Uber Deceives the Authorities Worldwide*, NY Times, Mar. 3, 2017, www.nytimes.com/2017/03/03/technology/uber-greyball-program-evade-authorities.html; Sam Levin, *Uber Attacked Over Pattern of Ignoring Police and Victims Before London Ban*, The Guardian, Sept. 27, 2017, www.theguardian.com/technology/2017/sep/27/uber-london-ban-sexual-assault-california-case-police.

13

Who Decides? A Framework for Fitting the Co-Regulation of Sharing Economies to the Contours of the Market

Bryant Cannon and Hanna Chung[*]

INTRODUCTION

The sharing economy continues to expand, disrupting established markets and creating new ones. Known by many names – the gig, on-demand, peer, or platform economy to name a few – the sharing economy's defining feature is the manner in which it brings to market goods and labor that are otherwise unutilized during certain time periods. For cost-conscious sellers, the new economy provides a way to share the use of goods and labor without selling ownership: monetizing the time a car sits unused in the garage or the extra time an unemployed or underemployed person may have to run errands. For frugal buyers (or those in search of convenience or choice), sharing economy enterprises offer goods and services in bite-sized units their budgets (or tastes) can stomach. This economy reflects the convergence of many different types of motivations, ranging from a waste-reducing collaborative consumption ethos to profit-seeking entrepreneurial efforts to address consumer demand for smaller units of consumption. Sharing economies animated by these principles together constitute a massive economic force that often clashes with traditional regulatory efforts.

Shared use of goods and service providers brings complicated economic relationships and dependencies. Such cooperative behavior requires well-defined rules, and discerning when and how to regulate new industries and business models can be difficult.[1] Co-regulation[2] – a method in which government and industry work together to identify, enforce, and sustain a regulatory mechanism – provides the most inclusive and information-rich framework for responding to the sharing economy's innovation and disruptive effects. But merely agreeing to share or coordinate control over market activities is not enough. We are left with many more questions: What should

---

[*] Bryant Cannon is a Deputy Attorney General in the Public Rights Division of the California Department of Justice. Hanna Chung is a Deputy Attorney General in the Criminal Division of the California Department of Justice. The views expressed in this chapter do not represent those of the California Attorney General's Office. Portions of this chapter also appear in the authors' article, Bryant Cannon and Hanna Chung, *A Framework for Designing Co-Regulation Models Well-Adapted to Technology-Facilitated Sharing Economies*, 31 Santa Clara High Tech. L.J. 23 (2015).

[1] *See* Steven C. Hackett, *Heterogeneities, Information, and Conflict Resolution: Experimental Evidence on Sharing Contracts*, 6 J. Theoretical Pol. 495, 495–97 (1994).

[2] *See, e.g.,* Tony Prosser, *Self-Regulation, Co-Regulation and the Audio-Visual Media Services Directive*, 31 J. Consumer Pol'y 99, 106 (2008); Jody Freeman, *The Private Role in Public Governance*, 75 N.Y.U. L. Rev. 543, 547–49 (2000); Edward J. Balleisen and Marc Eisner, The Promise and Pitfalls of Co-Regulation: How Governments Can Draw on Price Governance for Public Purpose, *in New Perspectives on Regulations* 127, 143–45 (David Moss and John Cisternino eds., 2009).

this sharing of responsibilities look like? Who manages what? What checks and balances should exist? Stitching this new economic patchwork onto old regulatory cloth often unravels into semantic disputes – for example, whether a sharing activity qualifies as a taxi service, a hotel, or ownership that falls under the scope of preexisting regulations. Moreover, sharing economy firms, which grew out of the self-regulatory culture of internet commerce, have often chafed against a top-down, centralized regulatory approach that favors government rulemakers.[3]

Rather than merely tweaking existing rules governing superficially similar sectors of the traditional economy to the new sharing economies – a solution that may keep government regulators on familiar territory but often results in a poor fit – decision-makers should engage in a fact-specific analysis of the particular market behaviors in order to design a regulatory garment that best fits the contours of that particular market's tendencies. Because sharing economies vary widely in the type of market activities they may involve, there is no one-size-fits-all blueprint of governance that regulators can superimpose across industries. Instead, as government and industry stakeholders debate who should govern a given market activity, they need a common decision-making framework – a generalized heuristic of how to think through the problem. In other words, they need a shared way of thinking, based on certain shared values such as effectiveness and feasibility, by which they can sort out who is better qualified to regulate a particular activity and what kinds of checks and balances should be given to the remaining stakeholders to ensure that their interests are also factored into the primary regulator's decision-making process. Therefore, in the sections that follow, rather than prescriptively identifying governance structures, we instead describe a framework for cooperative problem-solving, in which decision-makers delegate primary responsibility for handling regulatory tasks based on the relative institutional competencies of potential regulators, while establishing channels of feedback by which secondary co-regulators may exercise checks and balances on the primary regulator.[4]

I IDENTIFYING CHARACTERISTICS INHERENT IN THE SHARING ECONOMY THAT INVITE REGULATION

A logical starting point, before we consider who regulates what in a co-regulatory effort, would be to analyze why market behavior needs to be regulated in the first place. To this end, we analyze below the unique characteristics of a sharing economy and in what particular ways such characteristics may lead to market failures or externalities that require intervention.

A *How Is a Shared Economy Different from Traditional Economies?*

For the purposes of this chapter, we look at "shared economies" that fit within the following contours: (1) lenders retain permanent ownership over the good or the labor involved in the service (self-employed service providers, as opposed to service providers tied to a single employer); (2) borrowers pay for the limited use of a good or a service without purchasing exclusive ownership over the entire good or the exclusive right to the service provider's labor as an employee; and (3) facilitated by a digital market-mediating platform, allowing both the sellers' side and the buyers' side of the market to enjoy low barriers of entry, such that individuals, however

---

3   *See* Bruce L. Benson, *The Spontaneous Evolution of Cyber Law: Norms, Property Rights, Contracting, Dispute Resolution and Enforcement Without the State*, 1 J.L. Econ. & Pol'y 269, 326, 329 (2005).

4   For the purposes of this chapter, we are considering this discussion of co-regulation to apply most closely to jurisdictions where the public has easy access to information through technology, and governments have democratic accountability.

inexperienced in entrepreneurship, may easily exchange unused units of capacity with other individuals.

The presence of a digital platform distinguishes the modern sharing economy from the borrowing and lending exchanges that existed in earlier eras. Online platforms fulfill dual roles: they expand the market to include ordinary unsophisticated lenders and borrowers while countering the usual disincentives for dealing with strangers by creating risk-reducing and trust-building mechanisms such as a reputation-ratings system and an insurance net.[5] However, the characteristics inherent in sharing economies may exacerbate certain types of inefficiency. For example, borrowers in the shared economy, like consumers in any market, may underestimate their risk exposure and demand less than the optimal amount of market safeguards.[6] This is where the actors who do have long-term incentives – the marketplace platform developers and government regulators charged with protecting the public – must step in to correct the externalities and information asymmetries that yield inefficient outcomes and insufficiently protect the participants of the market.

B How the Characteristics of Sharing Economies Lead to Certain Market Inefficiencies

The confluence of low barriers to entry, inexperience, and discrete on-the-spot transactions results in an "incentives gap." The gap refers to the insufficiency of the natural incentives that inexperienced market actors – the weekend-entrepreneurs and one-time borrowers – have to self-impose an optimal level of forethought and safeguards: that is, to address failed sharing relationships, manage risk, address externalities, and build in minimum consumer protection and labor baselines in a way that maintains the long-term viability of the market.[7] As a result of this gap, sharing economies tend toward market inefficiencies in customer protection and liability allocation, labor protections, information sharing, and consideration of externalities.

1 Inefficiencies in Customer Protection and Liability Allocation

Because the spot transactions may occur at near instantaneous speed – in the click of a mouse or the tap of a smartphone screen – consumers are unlikely to think through the optimal level of safeguards they need to protect against unintended consequences. The low barriers to entry and exit result in a large number of nonprofessional participants with no ongoing obligation to remain active in the marketplace. Such participants have an incentive to supply whatever level of protection the consumers demand at the time, without looking ahead to unanticipated risks beyond the current transaction. For example, an amateur masseuse may see little harm in practicing her homegrown skill on a willing purchaser of her services – until a dissatisfied customer unexpectedly sues her for allegedly aggravating his injury. The amateur service-provider might not have thought to set ground rules governing his relationship with the customer in advance, either because he overestimated his abilities or underestimated the risks and consequences of a negative experience. Similarly, a bargain-hunting customer may accept an unlicensed masseuse because he underestimates the risk of injury and does not think to contract for liability

---

[5]   *See, e.g.,* Arun Sundararajan, *The Sharing Economy: The End of Employment and the Rise of Crowd-Based Capitalism* (2016).

[6]   Avishalom Tor, *The Fable of Entry: Bounded Rationality, Market Discipline, and Legal Policy,* 101 Mich. L. Rev. 482, 505–20, 505 n. 91 (2002).

[7]   Molly Cohen and Corey Zehngebot, *What's Old Becomes New: Regulating the Sharing Economy,* 58 Bos. B.J. 6, 7 (2014).

protections. Since the buyers and sellers are inexperienced, they are more vulnerable to optimism bias and the very human difficulty of appreciating long-term consequences.[8]

2 Inefficiencies in Labor Protection

The incentives gap may also account for non-optimal levels of labor regulation. What is "optimal" may be a subject for debate, as sharing-economy proponents may claim that precisely what makes sharing economy firms innovative and beneficial is the ability to disrupt old regulations of labor and commerce that were purely protectionist or rent-seeking. However, not all labor restrictions exist merely to privilege an entrenched class. Labor regulation may also serve to correct certain market pathologies.[9] Participants focused on short-term transactions may be willing to accept lower levels of labor protections in exchange for looser labor restrictions. However, this bargain may be suboptimal to the extent that inexperienced buyers and sellers of labor, facing little time for reflection and anticipating no long-term commercial relationship, may fall into the natural tendency to underestimate what could go wrong and at what cost. Moreover, unlike employees in traditional workplaces, people who offer labor through an online platform do not have the same relational ties and organizational structures to negotiate collective bargaining agreements[10] and there is little incentive for any one individual to expend effort in organizing her peers for collective action.[11] Finally, labor regulations may help the market correct its participants' biases undervaluing the harm to third parties, in the same way that, for example, trucking regulations cap truckers' driving hours in the interest of public safety.[12]

3 Inefficiencies in the Sharing of Reliable Market Information

The incentives gap may introduce imperfections into the feedback and trust-building mechanisms that constitute the very backbone of the shared economy. The marketplace generally benefits from honest and frequent reviews, including prompt reports of bad experiences. Consumers, incentivized by a soapbox effect and a desire for recognition in the community, post positive and negative reviews of restaurants, hotels, and companies.[13] However, even when rational human beings participate in information-sharing, misinformation may result. Specifically, (1) participants may have a tendency to underreport negative experiences;[14] (2) when some individuals intentionally spread misinformation, the community may often lack the knowledge or authority to identify it as misinformation and correct it;[15] and that (3) certain activities are so

---

[8] Christopher Koopman, Matthew Mitchell, and Adam Thierer, *The Sharing Economy and Consumer Protection Regulation: the Case for Policy Change*, 8 J. Bus. Entrepreneurship & L. 529 (2015).

[9] *See generally* Blake E. Stafford, *Riding the Line Between "Employee" and "Independent Contractor" in the Modern Sharing Economy*, 51 Wake Forest L. Rev. 1223 (2016).

[10] Gemma Newlands, Christian Fieseler, and Christoph Lutz, *Power in the Sharing Economy*, Working paper, 2017, www.researchgate.net/publication/316596585_Power_in_the_Sharing_Economy.

[11] Deepa Das Acevedo, *Regulating Employment Relationships in the Sharing Economy*, 20 Emp. Rts. & Emp. Pol'y J. 1, 14 (2016).

[12] *See, e.g., Fed. Motor Carrier Safety Admin. v. Distribution LTL Carriers Ass'n*, 374 F.3d 1209, 1218 (D.C. Cir. 2004).

[13] Abbey Stemler, *Feedback Loop Failure: Implications for the Self-Regulation of the Sharing Economy*, 18 Minn. J.L. Sci. & Tech. 673, 688 (2017).

[14] *See* Andrey Fradkin, Elena Grewal, David Holtz, and Matthew Pearson, *Reporting Bias and Reciprocity in Online Reviews: Evidence from Field Experiments on Airbnb.com*, Proceedings of the Sixteenth ACM Conference on Economics and Computation (2015), https://dl.acm.org/citation.cfm?id=2764528; Chrysanthos Dellarocas and Charles A. Wood, *The Sound of Silence in Online Feedback: Estimating Trading Risks in the Presence of Reporting Bias*, 54 Mgmt. Sci. 460, 460–76 (2008).

[15] *See* Weijia Dai, Ginger Jin, Jungmin Lee and Michael Luca, *Optimal Aggregation of Consumer Ratings: An Application to Yelp.com* (2014), www.people.hbs.edu/mluca/OptimalAggregation.pdf; Eric T. Anderson and Duncan I. Simester, *Reviews Without a Purchase: Low Ratings, Loyal Customers, and Deception*, 51 J. Marketing Res. 249 (2014).

high-risk that market participants cannot rely on the trial-and-error methods of community feed-back alone to make decisions.

4 *Externalities*

Although the failure to consider externalities can occur in any kind of market, certain attributes of sharing economies can exacerbate certain types of externality.

a *Cannibalizing the Whole-Unit Market to Enter the Piecemeal Market of the Sharing Economy*

One attribute of sharing economies is that they incentivize market participants into purchasing unused capacity for the purpose of renting them in smaller allotments. While such resource allocation often leads to more efficient use of existing resources, it can lead to inefficient allocation when instead of selling unused capacity of already owned but underused resources, sellers purchase new resources so that they can break them into piecemeal use. This trend could deplete the supply of the goods in question for buyers interested in complete ownership or control, or sellers who lose bargaining power by having to sell piecemeal.[16] Piecemeal transactions of sharing economies can disfavor the *seller* side by forcing sellers to unbundle goods and services and lower prices to the point where the cost of providing the subunit of service becomes higher without a commensurate increase in bargaining power to fight back against such costs. The gig economy may appear to promote efficiency insofar as it monetizes unused subunits of time of a full-time worker, but can cannibalize the demand for full-timers, ultimately leaving more workers scrambling to find full-time work.[17] While not all conversions of whole units into piecemeal units signal market failure, some conversions tend to function as one-way streets, resulting in market failures, where there is value being lost that is hard to recover (i.e., the market is "stickier" in one direction).

b *Disruption of Taxation and Revenue Generation for Local Communities*

Sharing economies often thrive by breaking open barriers of entry where previously only a limited number of actors could participate. Sometimes these barriers were artificial, created by governments to help generate revenue, as in the case of taxi medallions. When sharing economies provide new means of facilitating a market's supply and demand, they may disrupt not only the market but also the local government and services that depended on the revenues from that market. Whether the tax should apply to the sharing economy may depend on the reason for the tax. If the tax exists to internalize a negative externality that is common to both the sharing economy and the traditional economy, then regulators can accomplish the same ends by extending the tax to the sharing economy rather than suppressing the sharing economy. Regulators, upon noticing the demise of revenue streams from horse and buggy taxes, would not ban automobiles – they would impose a motor vehicle tax. Whatever the traditional reasons for taxing a given economic activity (e.g., compensation for usage of public resources, licensing fees for maintaining safety and quality controls, or simply a revenue stream), regulators and platform developers must work together to negotiate whether they can accomplish the same objectives by

---

[16] Daniel K. McDonald, *Is the Sharing Economy Taxing to the Traditional?*, 16 Fla. St. U. Bus. Rev. 73 (2017); Kellen Zale, *When Everything Is Small: The Regulatory Challenge of Scale in the Sharing Economy*, 53 San Diego L. Rev. 949, 985 (2016).

[17] *See* Antonio Aloisi, *Commodified Workers: A Case Study Research on Labor Law Issues Arising from a Set of "On-Demand/Gig Economy" Platforms*, 37 Comp. Lab. L. & Pol'y J. (2016); Brishen Rogers, *The Social Costs of Uber*, 82 U. Chi. L. Rev. Dialogue 85 (2015).

agreeing to functionally equivalent regulations for sharing economies. Otherwise, they may find themselves protecting an outdated and inefficient market for meeting demands.

II DETERMINING WHO IS BEST SUITED TO ADDRESS THE PROBLEM AND ENFORCE REGULATION

A co-regulatory approach challenges the assumption that the government is the primary and best-situated regulatory actor. Instead, co-regulation proceeds from the principle that regulation can be more effective when governments and market participants cooperate in determining who should regulate market behavior and how to do so. Thus, for the purposes of this chapter, we will broadly consider "co-regulation" not only when governments and market actors participate in joint institutions,[18] but also when governments and market actors cooperate to decide what areas to carve out for self-regulation or limited scenarios of state intervention, i.e., "regulated self-regulation." Even when the end result may sometimes look indistinguishable from self-regulation, co-regulation, even in its most hands-off forms, differs from pure self-regulation in that the government decides whether and under what conditions it must intervene, as an intentional policy choice to limit intervention to certain situations, in contrast to self-regulation that emerges in the absence of law.[19]

In deciding whether government regulation, self-regulation, or varying degrees of co-regulation would prove most effective in addressing certain market inefficiencies or externalities, the stakeholders should identify the market problems to which the sharing economy in question is most vulnerable. After considering the nature of the problems at issue, market participants and governing entities should evaluate their relative competencies to determine which actors are best suited to provide the information necessary for rulemaking, which actors are best suited to draw the lines for appropriate behavior in the market, and which actors are best suited to enforce these lines – whether they be government entities, the firms running the online platforms, or the buyers and sellers in the market themselves, or some combination of the above. In other words, we propose that those coming to the table adopt a common vocabulary and framework for how they will decide on who contributes what to the co-regulating process (or whether to make a deliberate decision to limit further intervention in that process, as in the case of regulated self-regulation). The scope of this chapter is to describe this common vocabulary and analytical framework for determining the best-suited actor for a regulatory step, specifically in the context of addressing potential market failures in the sharing economy; we leave to the existing literature to explain, should government entities and private firms decide to collaborate jointly as co-regulators in a formal process, what best practices exist in facilitating the co-regulation process.[20]

Once government entities or market participants come to terms with the inevitability of their coexistence, a good first step to building consensus for a course of action would be to decide, based on this common interest in building an effective solution, which actors are best positioned to provide the checks and balances to one another's actions that a laissez-faire market fails to provide. The government will generally be best positioned to establish regulatory requirements

---

[18] *See, e.g.,* Chris Ansell and Alison Gash, *Collaborative Governance in Theory and Practice*, 18 J. Pub. Admin. Research & Theory 544, 544–45 (2008); Kirk Emerson, Tina Nabatchi, and Stephen Balogh, *An Integrative Framework for Collaborative Governance*, 22 J. Pub. Admin. Research & Theory 1, 2–3 (2011).

[19] Carmen Palzer, *European Provisions for the Establishment of Co-Regulation Frameworks*, 13 Media L. & Pol'y 7, 8–9 (2003); Dennis D. Hirsch, *The Law and Policy of Online Privacy: Regulation, Self-Regulation, or Co-Regulation?*, 34 Seattle U. L. Rev. 439, 441 (2011).

[20] Ansell and Gash, *supra* note 18, at 550–63; *see also* Emerson et al., *supra* note 18, at 7–19.

in at least four areas where incentive gaps appear likely in the sharing economy – customer protection and liability allocation, labor protections, information sharing, and consideration of externalities.

For any given sharing economy industry, the online platform that facilitated the transaction may have a long-term incentive to build in mediation processes, manage expectations, or enforce some level of quality control as a part of its business model. Indeed, part of the appeal of the shared economies burgeoning online are the low transaction costs – someone else has thought of the details, so that the consumer may have instant gratification in obtaining a local good or service and the lender may have instant gratification in procuring a "taker" as soon as she offers her spare time or resources to the public.

For example, a person offering her apartment on Airbnb may check that the platform offers some level of vouching and background checks to ensure the trustworthiness of the guest, but she may not think to inquire into the property-damage insurance coverage. The apartment provider may neglect the possibility that even well-meaning, trustworthy guests may inadvertently create damage. Moreover, both the provider and the renter of the apartment may altogether ignore the effects of their transactions on third parties. In this example, the risk of inadequately protecting the consumer and the allocation of liability on the housing provider should be assessed for determining whether the parties are knowingly allocating – and accepting–risk. A market without clear attribution of risk creates uncertainty and challenges its long-term functioning.[21]

Similar to consumer protection and liability allocation, labor protections, information sharing, and certain types of externalities all constitute areas that are prone to market failure in the sharing economy context and where incentive gaps may make a strong governmental role desirable. For example, the transparency and comparative bargaining flexibility of an online marketplace of independent contractors may cause some market participants and the platforms that support them to disfavor labor regulations as overly paternalistic, and participants focused on short-term transactions may opt for the minimum level of labor protections. However, not all labor protections are purely protectionist or rent-seeking. Just as trucking regulations cap truckers' driving hours in the interest of public safety, labor regulations that limit hours, impose age limitations, or require documentation to combat labor exploitation may help correct market participants' biases undervaluing the harm to third parties or vulnerable participants with particularly weak bargaining power. As another example, where market failure affects the sources of information on which the market relies, such as when the market exhibits imperfections in the feedback and trust-building mechanisms of the online platform discussed earlier, there may be a need for stronger government intervention. Governments may also justify intervention when a market activity involves externalities, such as when the sharing economy disrupts a longstanding source of revenue that compensates the public cost of an activity or sidesteps a regulation intended to protect a public good.

Although market participants may not always welcome government intrusion, they must realize that coexistence with governments is an inevitability. Conversely, though governments may wield the jurisdictional power to legalize or ban certain activities, they must realize (if they are democratically accountable forms of government) that their coexistence with market activities that meet a deeply felt need in their community may be an inevitability as well. One shared value that may emerge out of this inevitable coexistence is the recognition that some form of intervention is necessary when there is some form of identifiable market failure. Although

---

[21] Inara Scott and Elizabeth Brown, *Redefining and Regulating the New Sharing Economy*, 19 U. Pa. J. Bus. L. 553, 572–86 (2017).

governments and sharing economy platforms may not always see eye to eye on what constitutes a market failure serious enough to need correction, this shared value could provide a common vocabulary on which to debate and ultimately justify the "legitimacy" of a mandate to regulate or to leave alone.

Then, once stakeholders decide that some form of intervention is necessary, they can facilitate cooperation by appealing to the shared value of finding the most efficient actor to do the agreed-upon intervention. For example, in areas in which stakeholders agree that the market largely runs itself, that market participants are making informed choices with low negative externalities, and that intervention is necessary only to protect against the most egregious failures, governments may take a minimal oversight role, in which they merely retain the option to intervene upon the failure of private actors to self-regulate. For example, a sharing economy platform that rents out designer party dresses may require little intervention from the government, if any. There are natural competitive incentives for sellers to provide clean, trendy dresses in good condition and refunds to maintain customer satisfaction; buyers are likely to know their own personal tastes and quality standards and are not vulnerable to chronic blind spots; the risks to poor decision-making are low; and the negative impact on third parties is negligible. Preexisting law not limited to sharing economies suffices to protect failed transactions, such as if a seller or buyer commits fraud. In such circumstances, sharing economy platforms are well positioned to serve as primary regulators in a co-regulatory environment, with the government agreeing to a minimal role and largely abstaining from regulation – a regulated self-regulation. Given the absence of market failures, there is no need for a government to cave into any pressure from more traditional market participants such as brick-and-mortar stores to regulate the activity. Given the shared values identified above, sharing economy platforms and market participants may push back on attempts to regulate by pointing out that they have little correcting benefit and serve largely protectionist purposes that disservice the consumer.

As another example, consider when a sharing platform may have access to data unavailable to government but not necessarily the market incentive to make publicly accountable decisions when left to its own devices. In one possible example of such a scenario, a shortage of long-term housing and growing frustration with soaring rent prices in San Francisco caused a public outcry against home-sharing platforms such as Airbnb. City regulators became concerned that the profitability and newfound feasibility of short-term rentals through platforms such as Airbnb would lead to investors buying up the limited long-term housing stock in the city to convert them into short-term hotels, further driving up long-term housing costs. Once stakeholders recognize the need for regulation – the public interest in intervening to correct this pattern of market behavior that may be creating negative externalities – public and private actors may come to the negotiating table, based on their shared value of efficient regulation, and come to the conclusion that Airbnb is in the best position to provide relevant data to the local government, while the local government is in the best position to determine what balance to strike in terms of urban planning needs and the public demand for housing. This model of co-regulation favors efficiency by assigning various components of the regulatory task to the actor in the best position to perform the task. Then, in exchange for data transparency, Airbnb could demand greater government decision-making transparency, demanding that the government justify its decisions based on an identifiable market failure it is trying to correct.

Appealing to common shared values also guides the co-regulatory process by providing the rules of engagement in the decision-making process. Should the reasoning justifying a regulation wear thin or the supporting data appear weak, the shared value discussed earlier – in siding against government intervention absent some kind of principled reason for intervention such as a market pathology – provides principled grounds, or a common vocabulary, for pushback. By making the reasons supporting regulation explicit, market participants gain a way to galvanize public opinion regarding the legitimacy or effectiveness of whatever regulation the government may propose and gain leverage in the co-regulating process.

Of course, other conditions may facilitate or preclude the possibility of amicable co-regulation, such as a history of trust or distrust, or the level of recognition in the industry regarding whether the industry's long-term interests are aligned with the public interest. At other times, when heightened data transparency and availability provides for more market protection, the need for government intervention shrinks.[22] Opaque pricing leading to unfair competition offers an example. More data, such as average cost for the good or service at issue or cross-platform price comparison are all data types that target the risk of unfair competition. Provision of this data allows for transparent pricing and also aligns with the interests of the platform eager to demonstrate competitive pricing or enhanced product availability.

The more serious the externalities and the potential for irrational or poorly informed choices among market participants, the greater the need for government intervention in the co-regulatory effort. However, as a sharing economy industry matures and competition stabilizes, there may be greater recognition among industry members that addressing these externalities and vulnerabilities to market failure may be in the industry's long-term interests. As industry members come into alignment to sustain the market, sharing economy platforms may form market-specific entities to undertake regulatory tasks and resolve disputes. Collaboration among market participants to create third-party review bodies may provide a neutral review and evaluation process that can limit competition failures.[23] The existence of such self-regulatory organizations may lead to less justification for government intervention, as the industry itself has provided some means for addressing the underlying problems and checking for accountability against self-dealing. Government never fully abdicates its responsibility to the public, even in such deferentially regulated self-regulation scenarios, and it should continue to oversee the process and the outcomes and be ready to intervene should the neutral bodies prove less than neutral or should a public concern remain unaddressed. The possibility of passive oversight would allow for a regulatory pathway to be exercised if an unexpected failure in the platform-led regulatory approach occurred. This could be appropriate in areas where the aspect of the technology or issue being regulated is not particularly complex or rapidly evolving and the government does not need specialized knowledge it may not otherwise possess.[24]

Where the above attributes exist, market platforms and governments are well situated to cooperate effectively and contribute their respective strengths to ensuring an efficient market with reduced opportunity for problematic failures. Where these attributes do not exist and incentive gaps are not apparent, the sharing economy industry is likely undergoing transitional phases and operating at a small scale, affecting fewer individuals and resources and with limited ability for negative public impact. As young sharing economies evolve, government may play several roles.[25] First, where industry members' interests are not aligned or where a large number of market competitors exists, governments can facilitate discussion, mobilize the public, and

---

[22] Abbey Stemler, *Regulation 2.0: The Marriage of New Governance and Lex Informatica*, 19 Vand. J. Env't. & Tech. L. 87, 102–10 (2016).

[23] Emily Hammond, *Double Deference in Administrative Law*, 116 Colum. L. Rev. 1705, 1716 (2016).

[24] Raymond H. Brescia, *Regulating the Sharing Economy: New and Old Insights into an Oversight Regime for the Peer-to-Peer Economy*, 95 Neb. L. Rev. 87, 88 (2016).

[25] Kellen Zale, *When Everything Is Small: The Regulatory Challenge of Scale in the Sharing Economy*, 53 San Diego L. Rev. 949, 960 (2016).

promote points of commonality. Second, where an issue touches key areas of ongoing competition, the government may intentionally choose to refrain from regulating in a particular area to avoid prematurely deciding a competitive market dilemma. Third, governments can fill a leadership vacuum by convening stakeholders and can incentivize the cooperation of potential key participants with the threat of more intrusive intervention or enforcement.

III SUSTAINING CO-REGULATION AND COLLABORATIVE BALANCE

Having first identified a framework for cooperative problem-solving and defining those areas where co-regulation complements the contours of the market and delegating primary responsibility for enforcing regulatory tasks based on the relative institutional competencies of potential regulators, the co-regulatory process must be sustained. The regulatory methodology should allow feedback channels by which other co-regulatory parties may exercise checks and balances on the primary regulator. In this way, co-regulatory design should allow opportunities for iteration and interaction.

A *Delegating Roles but Maintaining Checks and Balances*

After evaluating the likely market risks and areas of concerns, and assessing whether and how the government or market participants are best situated to provide regulatory controls, governmental regulators must ensure they are situated to sustain the co-regulatory dynamic. The entity that is best poised to provide adequate information should have the role of supplying the information to allow for intervention (or at least constructive interaction), while the entity that is best poised to be accountable to all interests involved, including the public interest, should be tasked with the role of using this data to arrive at a policy choice. Most, but not all of the time, the entity best situated to be the final decision-maker on how these informational and policy roles are satisfied would be the government. However, before arriving at the final decision, the entity tasked with the decision-making should transparently identify what problems it is purporting to address and how, providing means for the other actors to push back and provide a check to poorly reasoned decisions arising out of inordinate pressure from one interest group (e.g., protectionism), regulatory capture, laxity due to low prioritizing, or other regulatory failure. For example, having determined that the government is best situated to adopt a specific regulatory task, in the event that the government underregulates and allows unscrupulous platforms to cause unanticipated harm to providers or consumers, the platform leaders should have a means of coordinating and quickly detailing the deficiency in the government's regulatory approach. From a standpoint of overregulation, if a government's stringent controls deprive a platform of the ability to function, specific communication protocols and information sharing would more efficiently communicate the scope and extent of the regulatory constraints in a manner far superior to traditional lobbying practices. By contrast, in regulatory areas where the government identifies that the sharing economy platform is best situated to be the final decision-maker, the risk of self-overregulation is unlikely and governmental authorities need only be positioned to intervene as a stopgap in the event that the platforms underregulate and create unacceptable levels of risk or market inefficiencies.

As sharing economies generally reallocate unused resources to create superior market efficiencies, the application of a historic regulatory regime may be counterproductive in the co-regulatory context. Governments can play dual roles as both regulator to protect public safety and meet the goals of good regulation while also serving as a collaborator and facilitator, ushering in tech talent and jobs, promoting early adoption, measuring impacts, and making public and private assets more available for residents.[26] Governments that successfully compete for new economic growth opportunities through a receptive, collaborative attitude toward sharing-economy companies stand to gain through diversification of employment opportunities and export of their preferred governance model.[27] Intent to capitalize on this potential, many cities have launched offices to apply high technology to urban governance.[28] Yet, even in those situations where the conditions appear appropriate for permitting the platform to conduct self-regulatory activities, government must keep a watchful eye.[29]

B Prioritizing Regulatory Collaboration

Given current sharing economy dynamics, the areas of greatest unmet need lie in labor protections and third-party protections, such as using tax policy to adjust for externalities and impact on the local economy. For many sharing economies, consumer protections and regulation of deceptive speech are generally lower priority areas, as the market already has economic and reputational incentives to make reasonable judgment calls about how safe is safe enough.[30] Although manipulation of ratings, dishonest reviews, and inaccuracies do exist, industry has incentives to crack down on the most egregious manipulations and to protect speech. Moreover, state law in the United States already provides laws relating to unfair practices for those instances where industry may be complicit in distorting users' speech deceptively, minimizing the risk of complete market failure in the absence of sharing economy-specific regulation.[31] Therefore, regulators looking to coordinate regulatory efforts might determine that regulation of speech is not necessary where self-regulatory practices – either formal or through efficient trust and verification protocols – are well functioning. Co-regulation in this area need not be comprehensive or particularly intrusive and may look more like facilitating industry self-regulation, such as promoting certification to demonstrate compliance with industry best practices or obtaining informal commitments from companies to voluntarily disclose or adhere to certain reporting standards. On the other hand, where there is a vacuum of preexisting consensus, industry leadership, or natural incentives to act, the government may be the best situated to solve the problem of uncoordinated inaction in order to cultivate new or innovative economies and foster the creation of co-regulatory partners.

Co-regulatory solutions may efficiently arise as market oriented responses to widely perceived market efficiencies. Where there is convergence on outcome (this problem must be solved), if not necessarily regulatory mechanism (how do we solve this problem), finalizing the co-regulatory effort will be easier. Meaningful reform is further made easier when the market participants

---

[26] *Report on the Sharing Economy: Accessibility Based Business Models for Peer-to-Peer Markets*, Business Innovation Observatory, Eur. Comm'n 16–17 (2013), http://ec.europa.eu/enterprise/policies/innovation/policy/business-innovation-observatory/files/case-studies/12-she-accessibility-based-business-models-for-peer-to-peer-markets_en.pdf.

[27] *See Sharing Economy Advisory Network Created as Resource for Cities*, Nat'l League of Cities, Aug. 14, 2014, www.nlc.org/media-center/news-search/sharing-economy-advisory-network-created-as-resource-for-cities.

[28] *See* Bos. Mayor's Office of Urb. Mechanics, www.boston.gov/departments/new-urban-mechanics; S.F. Mayor's Office of Civic Innovation, www.innovation.sfgov.org/; Ruth Reader, *New York City Gets a Chief Technology Officer*, VentureBeat, Sept. 9, 2014, 4:15 PM, http://venturebeat.com/2014/09/09/new-york-city-gets-a-chief-technology-officer/.

[29] Ryan Calo and Alex Rosenblat, *The Taking Economy: Uber, Information, and Power*, 117 Colum. L. Rev. (forthcoming 2017), https://papers.ssrn.com/sol3/papers.cfm?abstract_id=2929643.

[30] *See* Paul Brady, *Six Tips for First-Time Airbnb Renters*, Condé Nast Traveler, Jan. 14, 2014, www.cntraveler.com/daily-traveler/2014/01/six-tips-for-first-time-airbnb-renters.

[31] *See, e.g.*, Press Release, A.G. *Schneiderman Announces Agreement With 19 Companies To Stop Writing Fake Online Reviews and Pay More Than $350,000 in Fines*, N.Y. State Office of the Att'y Gen., Sept. 23, 2014, www.ag.ny.gov/press-release/ag-schneiderman-announces-agreement-19-companies-stop-writing-fake-online-reviews-and.

have focused on an issue. This reflective prioritizing is evident in governmental focus on the liability issue. Some companies make transparency in liability allocation an important part of their business and public face. Because of high-profile accidents, particularly those occurring during "insurance gaps," sharing companies have willingly adopted increasingly progressive policies on their own.[32] What is occurring is a maturation of the market as an expectation of liability allocation is more firmly incorporated within the business models.[33] Politicians have built on the emerging trend, making explicit by law what was already fast becoming an industry practice.[34]

Against the backdrop of liability and tax problems that support strong cooperation between market platforms and government, the issue of the fair treatment of labor is the thorniest and most variable aspect of the sharing economy's maturation. Because of the fluidity of the employment relationship and the degrees to which an individual peer service or goods provider can elect to work for a sharing platform, labor protections defy uniform application. While this parallels the dialogue on proper labor protections for freelancers, the sharing economy frequently involves far less experienced labor providers (in addition to the freelancers that are also moving to services as ways of supplementing or re-orienting their income). There does not appear to be strong market or government consensus on how one should approach the regulation of labor offered through online sharing platforms, partially because the market remains highly fragmented with many subsectors and variations in services and how one shares. The user base of the sharing platforms is steadily developing an understanding for the need for labor protection regulation and this is occurring despite sharing economy corporate culture that has not generally demonstrated eagerness to rob itself of its revenue adjustable labor base.

Due to the divergent business models, types of service, and types of employee or independent service provider at stake, there is little consensus or likelihood of wholly industry-driven consensus on labor issues. This leads to a lack of clearly identifiable or credible leadership, although modest attempts to organize have occurred, whether by traditional unions (who appear currently ill-equipped to address the needs of a more independent, diffuse online base) or internally within the online communities themselves.[35] But this does not mean that government cannot intervene in this area. The intervention, however, must look more foundational, to identify areas of commonality or to build it from the ground up.

Co-regulation in this context and amid unorganized labor markets may be less like traditional lawmaking and more like community organizing: mobilizing public awareness of labor protection shortfalls, identifying and promoting potential allies or leadership in the industry or among the users, and building the groundwork for a shared culture of priorities. In short, the negotiations and the cooperation that constitute co-regulation may look very different depending on the circumstances, and it is important to be reasoned and precise on why one selects certain priorities and approaches. Whether co-regulation looks like goal-setting or legislation, convening

---

[32] Alexander B. Traum, *Sharing Risk in the Sharing Economy: Insurance Regulation in the Age of Uber*, 14 Cardozo Pub. L. Pol'y & Ethics J. 511, 523–29, 538–40 (2016).

[33] Benjamin G. Edelman and Damien Geradin, *Efficiencies and Regulatory Shortcuts: How Should We Regulate Companies Like Airbnb and Uber?*, 19 Stan. Tech. L. Rev. 293 (2016).

[34] *See* Amanda Kelly, *Chapter 389: Closing the App Gap with Insurance Requirements for Transportation Network Companies*, 46 McGeorge L. Rev. 399, 400–01 (2014).

[35] Orly Lobel, *The Gig Economy & the Future of Employment and Labor Law* (Univ. of San Diego Sch. of Law, Legal Studies Research Paper Series, Research Paper No. 16–223, Mar. 2016); Antonio Aloisi, *Commoditized Workers: Case Study Research on Labor Law Issues Arising from a Set of "On-Demand/Gig Economy" Platforms*, 37 Comp. Lab. L. & Pol'y J. 653 (2016); Independent Drivers Guild, https://drivingguild.org/; *Network for New Mutualism*, Freelancers Union, www.freelancersunion.org/network/; Gavin Kelly, *Digital Trade Unions Will Empower Tomorrow's Sharing Economy Employees*, WIRED, Jan. 12, 2017, www.wired.co.uk/article/gig-economy-digital-unions.

groups and building consensus or demanding accountability and publicizing shortcomings, or separated spheres of activity for industry and government or joint projects, government and industry leaders should assess how the natural landscape of the economies affects the need for intervention and the feasibility of their chosen method of accomplishing policy goals. Cooperation between the government and industry, though necessary because of complementary strengths and powers, is notoriously difficult, and such relationships fragile. Operating with clearly articulated reasons for each choice of approach and selection of goals will help partnerships stay the course, adhering to long-term outcomes and tailoring approaches to the more inherent attributes of sharing economies while remaining flexible enough to adjust co-regulatory relationships to the fast-moving circumstances and variations on a theme that the quick evolution of these economies presents.

14

Urban Data and the Platform City

Stephen R. Miller

I URBAN DATA AND THE PLATFORM: PAST IS PROLOGUE

Data, as well as the means of processing it to make it meaningful information or even actionable knowledge, has been at the heart of urban governance since cities began their outsized growth along the waves of industrialism in the nineteenth century. This experience with data since then instructs that the value of data is not inherent, but deeply entwined with the social constructs of those who create it, as well as how it is processed and received by the public at large. This chapter will investigate how the new rise of urban data is uniquely intertwined with the rise of the platform app, most often currently used by sharing economy companies. But before the possibilities, and dangers, of this confluence are investigated, it is worth taking a look back at the uses – for good and ill – of urban data. In many ways, the problems of the past signal a prologue to future problems with the integration of data with platforms.

Three prominent examples illustrate data's potential – and its challenges – as a tool of urban progress. First, consider how Jane Addams and volunteers of Hull House famously spent a year in the late nineteenth century collecting the nationality and wage histories of recent immigrants in a one-third-of-a-mile tract of a densely populated part of Chicago.[1] This extraordinary dataset for the time, which had little precedent, required investigators to visit "every tenement, house, and room" in the study area[2] and was carefully plotted onto colorful maps that, when published as the *Hull-House Maps and Papers* in 1895, revolutionized how people thought of immigrants by shedding light on the extraordinary poor living conditions and paltry wages new arrivals endured.[3] Data, Addams showed, can prove a valuable tool in improving the conditions of those whose suffering is too often hidden in the urban experience.

But data has had dubious uses, as well. Consider the example of the Home Owner's Loan Corporation's (HOLC) efforts, from 1935 to 1940, to map the relative credit-worthiness and risk of neighborhoods in over 250 American cities to determine their eligibility for federally backed mortgages. The resulting maps graded areas into four categories from most to least credit-worthy.

---

[1] The framework outlined in this paper is indebted to an ongoing collaboration with Professor Jamila Jefferson-Jones on future articles regarding the sharing economy and its evolution. *Residents of Hull House, Hull-House Maps and Papers: A Presentation of Nationalities and Wages in a Congested District of Chicago* 12 (Richard T. Ely ed., 1895), http://homicide.northwestern.edu/pubs/hullhouse/.

[2] *Id.* at 11.

[3] *Redlining in New Deal America*, Mapping Inequality, https://dsl.richmond.edu/panorama/redlining/#loc=14/39.7506/-84.1957&opacity=0.8&city=dayton-oh&area=D9&adimage=4/80/-121&text=intro.

The most risky areas – those for which federal mortgages would not be granted – were colored red on elaborate maps produced for every large city. The factors that resulted in such a red were several, but one that achieved dominance was "infiltration of negros" – a line on the form that had to be answered yes or no – along with the percentage of black population in the neighborhood. In addition, the form required the evaluation of "detrimental influence" to the neighborhood. One typical form, evaluating a neighborhood in Dayton, Ohio listed as such an influence, stated that the area suffered because it was an "older section of the city, negroes moving in."[4] This data, collected on thousands of neighborhoods in hundreds of American cities, had the patina of objectivity on which federal loan decisions could be made. It had a darker side to it as well: this "redlining" proved one of the most devastating methods of institutionalizing segregation by both limiting access to mortgage financing in black communities and encouraging white communities to oppose integrated communities lest whites lose access to federal mortgage lending. Data, even if collected for facially valid purposes, can have sinister uses and institutionalize prejudices.

Finally, consider the US Housing and Urban Development's massive Moving to Opportunity (MTO) study, which sought to study the neighborhood effects of concentrated poverty in 4,600 families over the decades of the 1990s and 2000s. The study had essentially two groups: one group that was offered standard affordable housing opportunities in urban areas with highly concentrated poverty, and a second group that was offered affordable housing opportunities in more affluent areas. The initial studies of MTO data, which focused on the effects of moving to more affluent areas, were underwhelming. The studies, which focused primarily on the effects on the adults that moved, showed little advantage to the new neighborhood. However, years later, a group of economists led by Raj Chetty revisited the MTO data and found that, in fact, there were tremendous neighborhood effects of living in areas of less concentrated poverty, but these positive effects accrued primarily to the long-term prospects of younger children in the families.[5] The MTO study illustrates that data requires interpretation, and the value of the data may be hidden – at first and for a long while – to even the best researchers. The question posed – such as "does the benefit of a new neighborhood accrue to the adult or the child?" – can have significant impacts on what we think the data says, and the policy determinations that result from the data.

The examples of Hull House, HOLC, and MTO provide necessary perspective as cities enter into a new epoch of technology-based decision-making that brings with it the promise to remake government, and perhaps even replace government with digitally based forms of governance. This chapter explores a particular combination of emergent urban technologies that, together, will test the capacity of cities to use data within the context of broader legal and policy frameworks reflective of cities' social norms.

The first of these three technologies is so-called "big data," which is generated through Internet of Things (IoT) smart city technologies like sensors. Such data is also generated in the background use of smartphone apps and platform-based technologies, such as Uber or Airbnb. Whether generated through sensors or the background of an app on a smartphone, an unprecedented amount of data is generated and stored, from the individual to the city level, on a daily basis. The second of the technologies is artificial intelligence, especially as characterized by "learning algorithms" that process this data with ever increasing agility the more the algorithms process data. These algorithms evaluate data with facially neutral objectivity; however, as the

---

4   *Id.*
5   Raj Chetty, Nathaniel Hendren, and Lawrence F. Katz, *The Effects of Exposure to Better Neighborhoods on Children: New Evidence from the Moving to Opportunity Experiment* (May 2015), www.nber.org/mtopublic/final/MTO_IRS_2015.pdf.

examples discussed earlier in this section make clear, facially objective analysis relies upon subjective decisions in the architecture of the algorithm itself. The third technology is the data platform, especially that subset of platforms that facilitated the rise of the sharing economy, which provide *access* to the processed data while also *generating* data of their own. In their current iterations, these sharing economy companies primarily focus on connecting market participants that might not otherwise find each other to do things like arrange a stay in a person's home or arrange a ride across town. But these platforms are angling to become much broader platforms that sell goods and services while also selling data about users that is, in turn, valuable to other businesses both on platforms and in the analog world. As noted above, platform companies like Uber are both sharing economy apps and also data generators about trips that can be sold to local governments to use in transportation planning. In this way, sharing economy platforms both utilize big data and simultaneously generate it, reinforcing the technological data cycle.

These three aspects of emerging data technologies – generation, processing, and access – will challenge existing forms of governmental regulation, offer alternative forms of data-based governance, create new technologies that replace existing industries, and create new technologies that create new industries. The future of this collection of technologies is being written now with preliminary projects in the works by almost every major city. This chapter will utilize the city-nation Singapore as an example of city-driven efforts to advance these technologies both for regulation and also to spur private investment in cities. Of all the cities in the world, Singapore has most explicitly sought to link data, AI, and sharing economy platforms for both public purposes and private growth. As a result, it signals the future of how cities around the world may further engage the next direction in these technologies.

At the same time, as cities seek to guide these technologies' futures, almost every major technology company is also investing heavily in the future of how these three technologies will fit together. This chapter will investigate several of these, including Samsung's Songdo development outside Seoul, Korea; Panasonic's Fujisawa, Japan's smart city now being replicated as the Pena Station NEXT project in Denver; Facebook's Willow Creek development; and the efforts of Sidewalk Labs (a subsidiary of Google parent company, Alphabet) to find a city that will cede all regulatory control to the company to build a community regulated solely by data. Whether driven by the public or private sector, the rules of urban data-based decision-making are being written now, and the legal and political implications will be enormous.

II MAKING MEANING AND MONEY WITH URBAN DATA

The next generation of urban data arrives with the coalescence of three technologies already in use, but still each finding their ultimate manifestation. The pace of technological development necessitates talking about each of these with some humility; indeed, these technologies have uses today that do not necessarily elide with their futures. Nonetheless, a certain general arc of the technological convergence is notable, especially for urban government, which is outlined here in its broadest form. In all cases, the platform app that is the essence of today's sharing economy plays a pivotal role in the future of how this data is integrated into urban decision-making.

A *Generating Urban Data: The Sensor and the Platform App*

The first of these technologies is the remarkable rise in *generating* urban data. The effort to make use of digital urban data is not by any means new, but several changes within the past decade have given form to what was previously more dream than reality. All levels of government have been providing access to open source data for some time. Almost every major American city has a website from which open data can be accessed, typified by such sites as San Francisco's DataSF, New York City's NYC Open Data, and Boston's Analyze Boston. Each of these sites provides access to datasets generated or owned by the respective cities; however, the open data movement has long suffered from an inability of common citizens to make sense of the massive datasets.

Cities have sought to rectify this problem in several ways. One of these is creating the relatively new position of "chief digital officer," to create citywide policies to make data more usable and "speak" to other data generated across departments.

Maybe of greater importance, cities have entered into the data generation business. Cities have always been in the data generation business to some degree; traffic movement data has arguably been among the oldest and largest of datasets maintained by major American cities, most often deployed through a "511" website and smartphone app. However, the new approach to urban data collection is on a scale never before possible largely through the advent of the "Internet of Things," or IoT, whereby relatively low-cost sensors are connected by the internet to a central location that maintains the data. Outside of the tech world, IoT deployment in urban areas is often referred to with the glossy term of "smart city" technology. Regardless of the marketing, this new effort at collecting urban data really amounts to the mass deployment of sensors collecting data that, in isolation, record what are seemingly tedious and mind-numbing facts about urban living but, when collected in aggregate, hope to provide vital information to improve city functions.

As a report by the National League of Cities detailed, smart city IoT sensors are presently available to collect data on at least the following: traffic congestion monitors that detect slowdowns and also enforce traffic rules; water and wastewater monitoring systems that detect leaks and low pressure; parking apps and kiosks that direct drivers to availability; bridge inspection systems that monitor the safety of infrastructure; self-driving cars of varying levels of autonomy, some of which are already in deployment; street lights that report when the bulbs burn out; energy monitoring systems that display energy use in real time; wide-scale deployment of drones for multiple purposes; smart inventory systems that detect when stores need to be stocked and link to traffic reports to determine best times for delivery; and widespread deployment of broadband through kiosks stationed around the city.[6] This list is merely illustrative of the wide-scale efforts of cities to deploy data to enhance – and perhaps replace – a wide swath of urban regulatory functions.

The greatest city deployment of IoT data generation may be in Singapore.[7] Having started with the launch of the Smart Nation program in late 2014, the city's deployment of sensors infiltrates virtually every sector of governmental services. A study of Singapore's smart nation program illustrated the wide variety of sensors already in use in a variety of sectors. For instance, the transportation and urban mobility sector utilizes a technology that allocates traffic green lights based on real-time traffic demands and traffic signals at neighboring intersections along major corridors.[8] All taxis in the country are equipped with GPS systems, which collectively

---

[6] *Trends in Smart City Development*, National League of Cities (2017), www.nlc.org/sites/default/files/2017-01/ Trends%20in%20Smart%20City%20Development.pdf.

[7] Jake Maxwell Watts and Newley Purnell, *Singapore Is Taking the "Smart City" to a Whole New Level*, Wall St. J., Apr. 24, 2016, www.wsj.com/articles/singapore-is-taking-the-smart-city-to-a-whole-new-level-1461550026.

[8] Inter-American Development Bank, *International Case Studies of Smart Cities: Singapore, Republic of Singapore* 20 (2016), https://publications.iadb.org/bitstream/handle/11319/7723/International-Case-Studies-of-Smart-Cities-Singapore-Republic-of-Singapore.pdf?sequence=1.

form another valuable supply of traffic data.[9] With regard to citizen safety, Singapore has already installed over 40,000 police cameras in state-owned residential buildings in which most of the population lives.[10] Other aspects of deployment include water and wastewater monitoring; emergency response; and the environment.[11] As an example of how far Singapore is taking sensor deployment, some monitors are even being tested to monitor the movements of the elderly inside their homes to ensure their continued good health.[12]

But cities are not the only ones seeking to generate data. Most of the world's major technology corporations are also seeking ways to generate, and own, urban data governance. Perhaps the first such major deployment of smart city IoT technology was in Songdo, a US$40 billion development of some 80,000 apartments, 50,000,000 square feet of office space, and 10,000,000 square feet of retail space.[13] The city was built to showcase CISCO's Smart+Connected Communities technology, which integrates data from residences, offices, and schools, and permits residents to control functions of their homes remotely. While Songdo has had some missteps, the idea of integrating technology into every aspect of commercial and residential real estate development as a means of generating data about urban life remains a major goal.

Panasonic has also entered the real estate business with several large developments that integrate their IoT devices into the development. One completed project is in Fujisawa, Japan,[14] which integrated smart sensors into every aspect of daily living. In the United States, Panasonic is currently building out an US$82 billion smart city adjacent to Denver airport. Called Peña Station NEXT, the project will include: "an innovative solar-plus-storage microgrid, smart LED street lights with video analytics and other features for community safety and parking, community Wi-Fi, electric vehicle charging stations, and autonomous electric shuttles to create a seamless mobility experience throughout the transit-oriented development to and from the rail station."[15]

Other tech companies getting into the smart city business include Sidewalk Labs. In April 2016, news leaked that Sidewalk Labs was seeking authority to build a major development with "autonomy from many city regulations, so it could build without constraints that come with things like parking or street design or utilities."[16] Similarly, Facebook is currently in plans to develop a project near its headquarters, Willow Creek, that would have 1.75 million square feet of offices, 1,500 units of housing, 125,000 square feet of retail space including a pharmacy, as well as a cultural and visitor center, that will almost certainly have some IoT component.[17]

Thus far, examples have focused primarily on the use of IoT sensors. However, smartphones, and especially many sharing economy apps, also collect substantial amounts of data that can be used by both the public and private sectors. For instance, the app Street Bump is an opt-in app first used by Boston that registers the location of potholes by registering automatically self-reporting data by phones' accelerometers.[18] Uber currently collects data on user movement even

---

[9] *Id.* at 21.

[10] *Id.* at 22.

[11] *Id.* at 22–24.

[12] *See supra* note 7.

[13] Nexcess, http://songdoibd.com/.

[14] FujisawaSST, http://fujisawasst.com/EN/.

[15] Tamara Chuang, *Denver Smart City Peña Station Next a Technological Testing Ground for Panasonic*, Denver Post, Dec. 11, 2016, www.denverpost.com/2016/12/11/pena-station-next-panasonic-smart-city/.

[16] Eliot Brown, *Alphabet's Next Big Thing: Building a 'Smart' City*, Wall St. J., Apr. 27, 2016, www.wsj.com/articles/alphabets-next-big-thing-building-a-smart-city-1461688156.

[17] George Avalos, *Facebook campus expansion includes offices, retail, grocery store, housing*, The Mercury News, July 7, 2017, www.mercurynews.com/2017/07/07/facebook-campus-expansion-includes-offices-retail-grocery-store-housing/.

[18] Phil Simon, *Potholes and Big Data: Crowdsourcing Our Way to Better Government*, WIRED, www.wired.com/insights/2014/03/potholes-big-data-crowdsourcing-way-better-government/.

while users are not utilizing the app. While users can turn this function off, most do not, which provides Uber with a vast database of user movement throughout cities. Uber is now marketing this data to urban planners in a product it calls Uber Movement, which purports to anonymize the data before selling it. However, the best transportation consultants are able to pair this data with other, typically used transportation datasets to determine trip generation that can narrow trip origination down to the cul-de-sac.[19] The collection of such data by platforms often occurs without the knowledge of users, hidden by the interface and obfuscatory user agreements that most never read.

Whether through sensors or smartphones, the collection of data by governments and corporations increases at a rapid pace. Questions abound about both the ownership, privacy, and use of that data. The broader question is what governments and corporations plan to do with that data.

B Processing Urban Data: Artificial Intelligence

As the latent potential behind the open data movement failed to materialize over the past several decades has made clear, even digital urban data alone is not that valuable. There is already far more data than is used effectively, and the creation of even more data by IoT and smartphones sharing economy apps requires an effective method of use to have meaning. It acquires value, both public and private, when it is processed and delivered in a manner that can be easily accessed in a meaningful way to citizens in the public context and consumers in the private context.

The processing of urban data increasingly falls to algorithms that utilize artificial intelligence (AI) that "learn" how to improve their performance through repetition of the assigned task. An example illustrates how cities are seeking to employ AI to process their data. The most expressly stated effort to do so is, again, in Singapore, where the city-nation has established an AI division within its National Research Foundation to process the massive amounts of data that the city-nation is collecting through its IoT sensors. In order to facilitate the use of AI, Singapore is seeking to place all of the data within a single usable interface called Virtual Singapore. From there, Singapore plans to invest $150 million in smart city AI over a five-year period with the following stated objectives:

Use AI to address major challenges that affect society and industry
AI can be used to increase traffic throughput during peak hour, for example, or to address healthcare challenges that are to come with an ageing population. Healthcare is currently both a knowledge and human-touch-intensive industry. Coupled with the progress in the digitisation of Singapore's healthcare over the years, AI could be significant applicable for safeguarding the health of Singaporeans. AI could play a big role in supporting prevention, diagnosis, treatment plans, medication management, precision medicine and drug creation. Healthcare manpower, augmented with AI tools, could better address increased healthcare demands in the future.
Invest in deep capabilities to catch the next wave of scientific innovation
These may include next-generation "explainable" AI systems exhibiting more humanlike learning abilities, as well as adjacent technologies such as computing architectures (integrating software, firmware, and hardware) and cognitive science …

---

[19] Based on an off-the-record private conversation with transit engineer at national transportation consulting firm on March 17, 2017 in Denver, Colorado.

Broaden adoption and use of AI and machine learning within industry
AI.SG will work with companies to use AI to raise productivity, create new products, and
    translate and commercialise solutions from labs to the market. NRF aims to deliver 100
    meaningful AI projects and proofs-of-concept to solve real-world problems quickly for end-
    users. There is particular potential in the sectors of finance, healthcare, and city manage-
    ment solutions, which the programme will start with.[20]

While major cities are seeking to create their own platforms that can, in turn, become the basis
for processing the data, private companies are also offering data platforms that would host such
data. Perhaps the most notable is the sharing economy company Airbnb, which is traditionally
viewed as a short-term rental company. However, Airbnb has stated that, in the not too distant
future, it foresees that less than half of its revenues will derive from short-term rentals.[21] Among
its lesser known business prospects is the long-term utilization of IoT urban data. Airbnb's entry
into this space is evidenced by Airflow, its open-sourced data management software that it gives
away for free[22] and which it is actively seeking to market to cities as a platform on which to place
data. Doing so has obvious advantages to Airbnb: data that is sorted in a way that is compatible
with its own internal processes facilitates the processing of the data in a way that can help the
company monetize that digital data.

C Accessing, Commodifying (and Creating) Urban Data: The Sharing Economy Platform

This, in turn, brings us to the third and final stage of the technologies transforming urban data: the
platforms made ubiquitous by sharing economy companies. The concept of the digital platform is
broad and arguably encompasses a host of online businesses. In the urban data context, the type
of platform that has resonance is that most closely associated with sharing economy companies.
Previous mentions of Uber, the transportation network company, and Airbnb, the short-term
rental company, have illustrated how these sharing economy companies are themselves generators
of data (Uber Movement) and platforms for the processing of data (Airflow). But the value of these
sharing economy platforms is that they provide a way to take the data generated by IoT sensors and
processed through AI, and turn it into something that can be used and mobilized both for civic
purposes and private monetization. As much as these sharing economy platforms have already
revolutionized the hotel and taxi industries, when paired with IoT urban data optimized by AI, the
potential for disruption of existing industries and creation of new industries becomes extraordinary.

One international example of how such a sharing economy company can pair with urban data
arises with the success of GrabShuttle in Singapore. Grab is the largest transportation network
company (an Uber equivalent) in Southeast Asia. In Singapore, it began operating a network of
buses that operate on two sources of data. The first is the city's real-time traffic data generated
through the IoT sensors; the second is input through a smartphone app in which users suggest
bus routes. On the basis of that information, GrabShuttle runs a series of fixed-route buses that

---

[20] *Artificial Intelligence R&D Programme*, Nat'l Research Found., Prime Minister's Office, Singapore, www.nrf.gov.sg/
    programmes/ai-sg.
[21] Katie Benner, *Airbnb Tries to Behave More Like a Hotel*, N.Y. Times, June 17, 2017, www.nytimes.com/2017/06/17/
    technology/airbnbs-hosts-professional-hotels.html ("Meantime, Airbnb has diversified its offerings by branching into
    tours and restaurant reservations. Mr. Chesky has said that these new services may someday account for more than
    half of the company's revenue. All of those may turn Airbnb into a full-service, online travel agency like Orbitz,
    making hosts a smaller part of the picture").
[22] Maxime Beauchemin, *Airflow: a workflow management platform*, Airbnb Eng'g & Data Sci. https://medium.com/
    airbnb-engineering/airflow-a-workflow-management-platform-46318b977fd8.

commuters can book on their smartphones, and also track the progress on the smartphone. Routes can change in the future on the basis of either of the data inputs – traffic information from the government sensors, or consumer demand for new routes.[23] GrabShuttle illustrates the kind of collaborative potential that could exist between government-generated data systems and private companies. Indeed, the monetization of the government data – in this case, real-time transportation data – is a goal of Singapore smart city initiatives. Cities leading the charge in municipal smart city deployment view it as a way for their cities to become the first to create the kinds of technical advancements that eventually will be deployed in cities around the world and, as a result, provide data-driven economies and knowledge-sector workforce development.

This relationship between urban data and the sharing economy could go well; it might not. In fact, the efforts of major tech companies to build smart cities from the ground up – Samsung's Songdo, Panasonic's Fujisawa and Pena Station NEXT, and Sidewalk Labs' secret project – illustrate a desire of tech firms to own the data from the moment it is generated by users. In an integrated smart city, the collection of the urban data could potentially accrue to privately owned datasets, which could then be processed through proprietary AI systems, ultimately to be deployed and marketed to individuals in the community without competition. It could be an excellent arrangement: residents may well love the services that they acquire from that company, which could potentially act as a type of digital homeowner's association making decisions about the community through the deployment of data. Just as many libertarian-minded individuals that abhor government regulation are comfortable living in gated communities with substantial private land use regulations enforced through CC&Rs, so, too, might many who are turned off by government access to data find it amenable to live in a community where a private company regulates on the basis of proprietary digital data.

As sharing economy platforms morph to encompass greater control over daily life – a prime example is the future of cars on demand that will be made possible by autonomous vehicles – they will also transform the nature of property itself. This transformation of property results from the mass intermediation of property transactions facilitated by the sharing economy platforms. Property transactions – sales and leases of real property, for instance – have long had intermediaries, such as real estate agents for residential properties and listing agents for commercial properties. What the sharing economy platforms seek to do is create an intermediary into an ever-increasing number of transactions. It is one thing to pay a real estate agent commission when purchasing a home; it is a wholly different prospect to pay a platform every time a person rents out a house on a sharing platform. Similarly, there is a difference between hiring a taxi, which has no intermediation, and using a transportation network company, which intermediates a car-for-hire transaction. In the future, with autonomous vehicles, the prospect is of payment to an intermediary platform for use of a shared car on a daily basis. These illustrations show that, with the growth of sharing economy platforms, so, too, does daily life come to require intermediation. The smooth flow of that intermediation almost certainly relies upon a steady diet of data, and AI processing of the data, to facilitate the business models that increase business opportunities and drive profits for the platforms.

III LAW AND POLICY IN THE POST-SHARING ECONOMY PLATFORM CITY

How citizens and consumers will think about the technological integration of smart city IoT data with AI and sharing economy platforms is difficult to predict, in large part because both

---

[23] *Grab Launches Shuttle Service in Collaboration with GovTech*, Channel NewsAsia, Mar. 2, 2017, www.channelnewsasia .com/news/singapore/grab-launches-shuttle-service-in-collaboration-with-govtech-8770964.

the public and private proponents of the integration cannot settle on the exact destination at which they seek to arrive. Nonetheless, the bridges between the technologies are already being built, whether through governmental programs, such as those in Singapore, or through private developments of tech companies. This section considers several parameters for how to think about the future of this technological integration, one which will be referred to in this section as the "platform city." I argue that this technological integration will transcend the current sharing economy business models – something already happening as, for instance, Airbnb is now entering the restaurant reservation space.[24] As a result, the future will not be dictated by current market sectors delineated by the first entrants of sharing economy firms, but rather, by the scope of how the platforms on which those sharing economy companies can transform themselves into integrated platforms that deliver daily solutions to consumers, many of which will integrate data-driven and AI-enhanced products.

In evaluating this future, it is important to start aspirationally, because this integration of technologies could well help to achieve some of the major governmental problems of living in complex systems. As the work of economists such as Elinor Ostrom have long noted, the management of environmental systems, including urban ecosystems, is dependent upon the right information at the right time.[25] The platform city could well start to provide access to the kind of data that cities need to manage their complex effects on their environments. Foremost among these concerns, especially in larger cities, has been the desire to work across the "silos" of departments, as illustrated by the chief resilience officer concept funded in many cities through the work of the Rockefeller Foundation in recent years. If this data proliferation is utilized to such ends, it could have dramatic effects in improving the environments of our cities as well as lowering the costs of doing so.[26]

But such aspiration immediately hits a road bump: the reality of the current deployment of the platform city is that even the municipally backed efforts are dependent and aimed at some type of commercial deployment of data. That means that there is already a bias in the types of data collected, and its deployment, which will trend toward those uses that can be monetized. Many of those commercialized uses will likely yield great value to citizens and consumers, but it becomes questionable whether data deployment that might increase the quality of life but that might not be easily monetized will ever fully materialize in the way that it might. It will probably fall to civil society and nonprofit organizations to become savvy in the utilization of platform city technologies to ensure that non-monetizable data is collected and deployed. Ensuring access to data for these civil society and nonprofit organizations that might not be able to otherwise collect the data, or pay for it from private corporations, becomes an important equitable consideration in the structure of the future integration of platforms with data and AI.

Another issue that arises with increased reliance on data as a source of governance is the "analog ghetto," or the inability of certain populations to access the platform city. This could become particularly important as more aspects of urban life switch from prioritizing owner-ship to "sharing." For instance, as autonomous vehicles become more common, those without access to the apps that call the vehicles will find themselves relegated to analog options, such as traditional taxis that are almost always more expensive. Addressing these equity issues almost certainly will demand a regulatory response or, alternatively, the work of a government to

---

[24] Kaya Yurieff, *You Can Now Book a Restaurant Reservation on Airbnb*, CNNTech.com, Sept. 20, 2017, http://money .cnn.com/2017/09/20/technology/airbnb-restaurants-booking-resy/index.html.

[25] Thomas Dietz et al., *The Struggle to Govern the Commons*, 302 Sci. 1907 (2003).

[26] *See generally* William Boyd, *Environmental Law, Big Data, and the Torrent of Singularities*, 64 UCLA L. Rev. Disc. 544 (2016).

coalesce these disparate hard-to-reach persons into a market that could be served by a digital company. For instance, many low-income communities were slow adopters of TNCs; however, cities are experimenting with subsidizing TNC rides for low-income riders to address the "last mile" dilemma. Another approach may be to simply give low-income individuals low-cost smartphones that would permit them to access the platform city.

Cities must also recognize that any turn toward data-based governance and away from analog government may mean a commitment to long-term data collection. To the extent that cities can afford such data, it will almost certainly enhance or improve decision-making. However, for cities on tight budgets, the platform city will likely prove an expensive way to do things that analog efforts could do reasonably well already. Such typically mid-sized and smaller cities will need to closely evaluate offerings of companies that purport to offer free data collection, data hosting, or data platforms that may ultimately come to complicate government efforts. For instance, such apps may all but privatize what are traditionally public goods. This occurred in San Francisco with the rise of the MonkeyParking app, which allowed individuals with street parking spaces – which are publicly owned – to sell them in real time to another individual.[27] The city sued and enjoined the app's use; however, the city has since been in the business of creating its own app that provides information about available public parking spaces – both on the street and in parking garages – that links to data sensors in each of those spaces.[28] The platform city will almost certainly lead to more such disputes between cities and private corporations, about what is public, what is private, and the relative ability to regulate or sell information. For smaller cities, entering this fray may prove expensive and may lead to potential private exploitation of public goods.

As the platform city develops, cities must also beware of how efforts at regulation may cause tension between levels of government. An example is the battle over preemption of local government regulation that is working its way through statehouses in the United States. The first thread is that local government regulation of digital firms, especially sharing economy platforms, stifles innovation and thus states must preempt city efforts. This type of preemption argument is already strong and is the basis of many preemption laws in states related to the sharing economy. The second thread, which is likely to become more popular as the platform city emerges, is that the platform city is simply too technically sophisticated for local governments to regulate. A stronger argument emerges here when there is less government control or participation in the platform city. For instance, if a tech company like Panasonic, Samsung, or Google generates the data, processes it, and deploys it for access through a platform, cities will likely run the risk that states will preempt them from enforcing regulations on such a development.

This leads to the question of whether the platform city, in the hands of a tech giant, might ultimately come to replace government with governance. There is nothing sacrosanct about local government: many company towns once existed as private enclaves without the municipal stamp. But while constitutional norms would continue to apply, a large-scale deployment of governance that is dominated by tech giants would be a remarkable reinvention of American life. While it might sound far-fetched now, Google's efforts to find a city to wholly give up land and cede regulatory control illustrates that the platform city may well, in the eyes of tech companies, be a replacement for local control as it has traditionally been viewed as government.

Of course, the most obvious concern with the platform city is what happens to privacy and whether a person can ultimately ever "turn off" the platform city. Those questions will be

---

[27] Ted Rall, *The MonkeyParking App Could Turn Us into Monsters*, L.A. Times, Jan. 15, 2015, www.latimes.com/opinion/opinion-la/la-ol-rall-monkeyparking-app-sell-parking-spot-20150114-story.html

[28] SFpark, http://sfpark.org/.

determined, ultimately, by public opinion. That public opinion may ultimately shape the trajectory of how the platform city evolves. For instance, in Singapore there is widespread trust of the government, and thus the wide-scale deployment of IoT sensors does not seem invasive. A similar deployment by the government in the United States would almost certainly meet with opposition. But what if such sensors were owned by private entities? Does it make a difference if the data sensor is owned by the City of Denver or by Panasonic? Perhaps it does, and such opinion may well shape the future public or private nature of the technology's future.

IV URBAN DATA AND THE PLATFORM'S END

Urban life and data go hand in hand. From Hull House to redlining to the neighborhood effects of poverty, the way cities are governed is linked to what we know about those lives in cities. History instructs that there is nothing inherently ethical in data; there is nothing "smart" about technology that is not directed – for good or ill – by the will of those who deploy it. The platform city, evolving as it will from today's sharing economy companies, may well be the next phase in how data is used in government. To the extent that is the case, the platform city must still answer for itself both in terms of the costs and the benefits it offers to the whole of the city: rich and poor, the old guard, and the new arrival.

It might be that this new age of data becomes something more. It might be that the platform city rivals government itself and offers an alternative means of governance that would prove more appealing than what government has to offer. It might also be that the rapid intermediation of property transactions into daily life by the evolution of today's sharing economy platforms might also cause a backlash. It might not. Much will depend upon how government, and the platforms themselves, respond to the needs of consumers and their needs as citizens.

More likely, most deployments of the platform city will prove a digitized model of the public/private partnership that became popular in urban development in the latter party of the twentieth century. In those cases, the boundaries of municipal control were breached, but cities typically received infrastructure or other benefits that they otherwise could not afford or their citizens were unwilling to fund. The approaches of Singapore seem to already lead in such a direction: municipal infrastructure for purposes of private monetization. That cooperation will almost certainly hasten the arrival of the platform city, but as with public/private partnerships in the past, will require vigilance to ensure that citizens and consumers find equal sway.

Who Should Regulate the Sharing Economy, and How?

15

The Place of the Sharing Economy

Nestor M. Davidson and John J. Infranca

INTRODUCTION

The sharing economy is grounded – situated in place – in ways that many other recent techno-logical transformations have not been. And, to a significant degree, the sharing economy is a particularly *urban* phenomenon.[1] Appreciating the place of the sharing economy sheds light not only on the nature of this phenomenon, but also on the regulatory landscape it has engendered.[2]

In what ways is the sharing economy urban? Many sharing economy firms emerged to solve problems resulting from urban density and congestion. These firms, in turn, leverage the spatial proximity, diversity, and even anonymity that mark urban places. It is difficult to imagine the rapid growth of transportation network companies (TNCs), such as Uber and Lyft, absent the thick network of providers and consumers found in cities. Similarly, while people post room shares in even the most remote places, the core of the short-term rental market flourishes in urban neighborhoods where unique amenities draw travelers. There is even an urban compo-nent to the mechanisms through which platforms foster trust, with reputation tools and ratings systems engineering around classic urban challenges of mass anonymity and a lack of strong social bonds. In these and other ways, much of the value created by sharing firms reflects their ability to effectively address urban challenges and leverage features of urban life.

The deeply urban nature of the sharing economy in turn informs the distinctive distri-bution of regulatory authority that has emerged in response to the phenomenon. Just as the sharing economy first flourished in cities, so too did the regulatory response – at least in the United States – begin at the local-government level.[3] Early on, sharing firms found themselves entangled in a myriad of local regulations across the hundreds or thousands of jurisdictions in which their users were exchanging goods and services. Many firms embraced a business

---

[1] For detailed explorations of this proposition, *see* Nestor M. Davidson and John J. Infranca, *The Sharing Economy as an Urban Phenomenon*, 34 Yale L. & Pol'y Rev. 215 (2016); Michèle Finck and Sofia Ranchordás, *Sharing and the City*, 49 Vand. J. of Transnational L. 1299 (2016); *see also* Daniel E. Rauch and David Schleicher, *Like Uber, But for Local Government Policy: The Future of Local Regulation of the Sharing Economy*, 76 Ohio St. L.J. 902 (2016); Jacob Thebault-Spieker, Loren Terveen, and Brent Hecht, *Toward a Geographic Understanding of the Sharing Economy: Systemic Biases in UberX and TaskRabbit*, 24(3) ACM Trans. Comput.-Hum. Interact. 1–40 (2017).

[2] Recognizing normative debates about nomenclature and scope, *see* Orly Lobel, this volume. This chapter takes a broad view of the sharing economy, across sectors and varieties of approaches. The chapter focuses primarily on the regulatory landscape as it is emerging in the United States, although that context holds implications for other legal systems.

[3] *See* Rauch and Schleicher, *supra* note 1, at 903–04.

strategy that involved pushing the boundaries of the local regulatory landscape while disrupting existing sectors of the local economy. As the industry has grown, the regulation of the sharing economy has become more disparate vertically, with states and national governments increasingly involved.[4]

Why did the regulation of the sharing economy largely begin in cities and why is that regulatory landscape now shifting? This is partially a story of historic contingency. Those industries within the sharing economy that initially posed the most significant regulatory challenges – ride sharing and short-term rentals – are also those whose regulation, at least in the United States, had largely devolved to the local level.[5] At the same time, sharing economy firms initially flourished in locales and sectors where regulatory regimes, for a variety of reasons (some positive, some not so much), overly constrained the supply of desired goods and services, such as taxis and housing. New entrants leveraged gaps and shortfalls in local regulation, finding opportunities for innovation.

The political economy of regulation and innovation in this sector has grown more complex as some sharing firms have circumvented local authorities and bargained for more favorable and uniform regulation at the state level. The result has been tensions not just between regulators and the regulated, but in some cases among regulators themselves as states and cities pursue different agendas. The tension between allowing space for local innovation – economic and regulatory – and establishing uniformity and oversight up the geographic scale is not unique to the sharing economy but is increasingly central to understanding the regulatory landscape.

This chapter surveys these tensions and argues for a (cautious) presumption in favor of retaining a strong role for local regulation. While legitimate concerns about local parochialism and capture bear consideration, the advantages of experimentation and the reflection of local preferences auger against overly aggressive state preemption.

Accordingly, Section I contextualizes these discussions in the place of the sharing economy, embedding them in the geography that drives both this new economy's growth and the regulatory response. Section II examines recent regulatory clashes between state and local governments, highlighting important considerations that should shape the allocation of authority moving forward. Building on those considerations, Section III concludes with the case for – and concerns about – preserving a local regulatory role in the face of a still quite rapidly changing industry.

I WHY DID THE REGULATION OF THE SHARING ECONOMY BEGIN LOCALLY?

The sharing economy implicates perennial questions regarding the allocation of authority across levels of government. In the United States, for reasons we explore in this section, regulation began at the local level and now occurs primarily at the local and state levels, with limited federal engagement. A number of factors help explain this, including the urban nature of much of the sharing economy, the localized externalities generated by sharing economy activities, historic patterns of regulation, and the distinctive political economy of the intersection of urbanism and the sharing industry.

---

[4] For further discussion of state and federal roles, *see*, in this volume, the chapters by Janice C. Griffith and Sara E. Light.

[5] To some extent personal services, such as TaskRabbit, also raised concerns about spot labor, and the sharing of goods can raise consumer law issues, but local governments have not been the primary regulators of these sectors of the sharing economy. Similarly, peer lending, another important sector of the sharing economy, has largely not engendered a local regulatory response.

A *The Sharing Economy as an Urban Phenomenon*

A significant portion of the sharing economy involves innovation firmly rooted in local – and particularly urban – geography, with an exchange of information that is highly dependent upon the spatial dimensions of the market relationships it fosters. This includes both well-known global firms that facilitate the provision of transportation (Uber, Lyft), accommodations (Airbnb), and personal services (TaskRabbit), as well as smaller firms that enable the exchange of relatively low-value items.[6] Across all these variants, the sharing economy, despite its reliance upon seemingly place-agnostic platform technology, remains profoundly place-based.

Sharing firms enlist technology to alleviate costs and frustrations of city life. TNCs enable individuals to avoid the hassles of urban car ownership. Platforms that facilitate carpools provide an affordable alternative to unreliable public transportation (albeit at the risk of increasing traffic congestion). Food delivery services save time-strapped urban workers from long hours at crowded grocery stores and the gloomy prospect of cooking in cramped kitchens. Occasionally renting out a spare room or one's whole apartment can help a cash-strapped city dweller make rent.

Urban life is not, of course, simply a series of frustrating experiences in need of solutions. As urban economists have long recognized, people are drawn to cities by the many benefits that accrue from their defining proximity and density.[7] Urban density makes moving goods, people, and ideas less expensive, fostering economic growth.[8] In the sharing economy providers of physical goods and personal services benefit, in urban areas, from the ability to more easily serve customers, resulting in greater efficiency and increasing the likelihood that potential providers and customers will find it worthwhile to participate.[9] The proximity and dense concentration of prospective buyers and sellers facilitates the rapid exchange of goods and services, and sharing technology leverages these urban characteristics.[10]

While guests and hosts matched through short-term rental platforms are unlikely to live near one another, these platforms rely on the spatial relationships they facilitate, providing users with proximity to desirable urban amenities. An Airbnb summary of its economic impact in multiple cities found that 79 percent of Airbnb travelers "want to explore a specific neighborhood" and 91 percent "want to live like a local."[11] As the company's Chief Marketing Officer noted, a crucial component of Airbnb's attractiveness to potential guests is its ability to offer housing in particular urban neighborhoods that provide a more "authentic" experience

---

[6] *See, e.g.,* Regina R. Clewlow and Gouri S. Mishra, *Disruptive Transportation: The Adoption, Utilization, and Impacts of Ride-Hailing in the United States* 28 (Inst. of Transp. Studies, Univ. of Cal., Davis, Research Report UCD-ITS-RR-17-07, 2007) (finding, based on survey of seven major US Metropolitan areas, that "[w]hile 29% of the urban population surveyed have adopted ride-hailing and use them on a regular basis, only 7% of suburban Americans in major cities use them to make trips in and around their home region").

[7] *See, e.g.,* Gilles Duranton and Diego Puga, *Micro-Foundations of Urban Agglomeration Economies,* 4 Handbook Reg. & Urb. Econs. 2063, 2065 (2004); David Schleicher, *The City as a Law and Economics Subject,* 2010 U. Ill. L. Rev. 1507, 1516 (2010). Economists describe the advantages that flow from proximity and density as agglomeration benefits, the inverse of congestion costs. *See generally* Edward L. Glaeser, *Introduction to Agglomeration Economics* (2010).

[8] Glaeser, *supra* note 7, at 140.

[9] *See* Edward L. Glaeser and Joshua D. Gottlieb, *The Wealth of Cities: Agglomeration Economies and Spatial Equilibrium in the United States,* 47 J. Econ. Lit. 983, 1001 (2009); Kristina Dervojeda et al., Eur. Comm'n, Bus. Innovation Observatory, *The Sharing Economy: Accessibility Based Business Models For Peer-To-Peer Markets* 13 (2013).

[10] Roy Sameen, *LAANE, AirBnb, Rising Rent, and the Housing Crisis in Los Angeles* 18 (2015) ("AirBnB has units listed throughout Los Angeles, but just nine of the City's 95 neighborhoods are responsible for generating 73 percent of the company's revenue").

[11] *The Economic Impacts of Home Sharing in Cities Around the World,* Airbnb, www.airbnb.com/economic-impact.

of a place than larger hotels.[12] In all of these ways, among others,[13] the sharing economy first flourished in cities and, not surprisingly, first encountered regulatory frictions in those same urban environments.

B *Localized Externalities Generate Regulatory Responses*

Having grown up in urban neighborhoods, the sharing economy has had the greatest impact – positive and negative – at the local level. The density and proximity that foster thick markets for sharing companies also magnify the local effects of these activities. By intensifying the use of existing resources and unlocking excess capacity, sharing platforms can create concentrated, localized externalities as they rapidly scale up in urban areas.[14] This kindles particularly fierce political and legal battles at the local level, where such effects are concentrated.

Conflicts over land use provide an obvious example of the kinds of localized externality that the sharing economy generates. How housing and commercial space are used has immediate effects at the neighborhood level.[15] Opposition to short-term rental platforms often stems from concerns about their localized effects, particularly on housing affordability and neighborhood character.[16] Opponents argue that platforms like Airbnb raise housing costs by reducing the supply of housing available to renters.[17] Proponents counter that sharing provides a source of revenue that may make housing more affordable for tenants and homeowners alike in high-cost areas.[18] The empirical data available to date does not clearly resolve this debate.[19] But regardless of the extent to which they are justified, concerns regarding highly localized impacts receive significant attention and play an arguably oversized role in shaping public and governmental responses.

In the transportation realm, TNCs, peer-to-peer car shares, and platform-facilitated car pools directly implicate commuting patterns, traffic, and questions of public safety at the local level. One promise of sharing is that it will reduce car usage by tapping excess personal transportation capacity. However, at least one recent study concluded that "ride-hailing is likely contributing more vehicle miles traveled (VMT) than it reduces in major cities."[20] Moreover, car pool services, coupled with fare subsidies from venture capital investment, enable TNCs to provide rides at a cost that lures individuals away from public transportation.[21]

---

[12] Dan Peltier, *Skift Global Forum: Airbnb's CMO on the Meaning of Authentic Travel Experiences*, Skift, July 14, 2015, http://skift.com/2015/07/14/skift-global-forum-2015-airbnbs-cmo-on-the-meaning -of-authentic-travel-experiences.

[13] *See* Davidson and Infranca, *supra* note 1, at 227–29; Finck and Ranchordás, *supra* note 1, at 1313–15.

[14] Kellen Zale, this volume.

[15] Lee Anne Fennell, *Agglomerama*, 2014 B.Y.U. L. Rev. 1373, 1383.

[16] David Zahniser, *Advocates are wary of Airbnb*, L.A. Times, Nov. 16, 2015, B1.

[17] *See, e.g.*, Sameen, *supra* note 10, at 19 ("AirBnB market density coincides with neighborhoods that have rents well above the citywide average… Rental pricing is based on numerous economic factors and market forces, and we do not know the exact relationship between AirBnB density and median rents"); BJH Advisors LLC, *Short Changing New York City: The Impact of Airbnb on New York City's Housing Market* (2016) (finding that geographic concentration of Airbnb listings in New York City coincides with rapid rent increases).

[18] Roberta A. Kaplan and Michael L. Nadler, *Airbnb: A Case Study in Occupancy Regulation and Taxation*, 82 U. Chi. L. Rev. Dialogue 103, 106–07 (2015).

[19] Alastair Boone, *There's New Research Behind the Contention that Airbnb Raises Rents*, CityLab, Aug. 2, 2017; Peter Coles et al., this volume; Keren Horn and Mark Merante, *Is Home Sharing Driving Up Rents? Evidence from Airbnb in Boston*, 38 J. of Housing Econ., 14, 24 (2017).

[20] Clewlow and Mishra, *supra* note 6, at 29 ("We find that 49% to 61% of ride-hailing trips would have not been made at all, or by walking, biking, or public transit").

[21] *See* Emma G. Fitzsimmons, *Subway Ridership Declines in New York. Is Uber to Blame?* N.Y. Times, Feb. 23, 2017.

Recent state legislation governing TNCs in Massachusetts nods to these localized external-ities by charging TNCs a per-ride fee, one half of which is directed to the municipality where a passenger is picked up.[22] A number of other cities, including New York, have studied the effects of TNCs on traffic congestion, air quality, and safety.[23] And San Francisco launched an investi-gation into whether Uber and Lyft – by contributing to gridlock and leading drivers to be on the road for long periods of time – constitute public nuisances.[24] These efforts highlight the heavily localized externalities of these sectors of the sharing economy.

C Historical Contingency and Regulatory Path Dependency

If the sharing economy largely developed and has had its greatest impact in cities, it should hardly be surprising that the regulators charged with managing cities have been on the front lines of responding. The fact that regulation over the activities generated by the sharing economy – lodging and urban mobility, most notably – is a local matter is partially a product of historical contingency and the path dependence of regulatory authority, but also reflects the dynamics discussed in the previous section as well as the relative competencies of local government.[25]

Taxicabs, for example, have long been regulated at the local level, where medallion systems have limited entry and fares have been fixed.[26] Cities sought to limit entry for reasons that included local concerns around traffic congestion and pollution.[27] This resulted in a heavily localized taxi industry, which historically wielded significant political power.[28] In many cities this led to a scar-city of taxis, creating demand for unlicensed "gypsy cabs,"[29] and posed challenges for passengers wishing to travel across jurisdictions. TNCs have not only challenged limits on entry and fixed fares, they have also successfully shifted the locus of regulation from local governments to the states.[30]

For short-term rentals, the traditional locus of regulation for the most closely analogous incum-bent industry, hotels, is more dispersed. Hotels are subject to local zoning and building codes, as well as health and safety regulations at the local, state, and federal levels. Unlike the taxi industry, much of the hotel industry is national and international in scope. As such the major players in competition with Airbnb are less rooted in any particular locale. In some jurisdictions, however, hotel unions have provided a local voice in opposition to short-term rentals.[31]

---

[22] 2016 Mass. Legis. Serv. Ch. 187 § 9. The other half of the 20 cents per ride fee is directed to the state Department of Transportation. *Id.*

[23] *The Downside of Ride-Hailing: More New York City Gridlock*, N.Y. Times, Mar. 6, 2017; *see also* Schaller Consulting, *Unsustainable? The Growth of App-Based Ride Services and Traffic, Travel and the Future of New York City* (Feb. 2017). Some cities have convened working groups in hopes of evaluating these local effects and crafting regulatory responses. For example, the Los Angeles City Council convened a Shared Economy Working Group tasked with ana-lyzing the sharing economy's effects, particularly in the residential sector. Los Angeles City Council File # 14–0593, https://cityclerk.lacity.org/lacityclerkconnect/index.cfm?fa=ccfi.view record&cfnumber=14-0593.

[24] *San Francisco Investigating Whether Uber, Lyft Are Public Nuisances*, Reuters, June 5, 2017. The city recently reached a compromise with Uber and Lyft, with the TNCs agreeing to comply with a per-ride tax, pending state legislation. Nuala Sawyer, *Uber and Lyft Agree to Pricey New S.F Tax*, S.F. Weekly, Aug. 1, 2018.

[25] Rauch and Schleicher, *supra* note 1, at 941–42.

[26] Katrina Miriam Wyman, *Taxi Regulation in the Age of Uber*, 20 NYU J. on Legis. & Public Pol. 1, 76 (2017).

[27] Katrina Miriam Wyman, *Problematic Private Property: The Case of New York Taxicab Medallions*, 30 Yale J. on Reg. 125, 168 (2013).

[28] Wyman, *supra* note 26 at 9, 20.

[29] Wyman, *supra* note 27 at 170–72.

[30] *See infra* Section II. Nearly every state now has some form of TNC regulation. For more detail *see Transportation Network Company (TNC) Legislation*, Texas A&M Transportation Institute, https://policy.tti.tamu.edu/technology/tnc-legislation/.

[31] Josh Dawsey, *Union Financed Fight to Block Airbnb in New York City*, Wall Street Journal, May 9, 2016.

There is an obvious relationship between historical patterns of regulation and enforcement capacity. Local governments take the lead in inspections and enforcement in the hospitality industry, particularly in the context of restaurants and food safety generally.[32] Local governments are also typically tasked with the enforcement of housing quality and safety standards. This reality may not necessitate continued local regulation, but it is likely to channel any state-level legislation, which will need to take into account the enforcement capacity (and priorities) of local governments.

D Regulatory Arbitrage

To bring the picture full circle, then, with the sharing economy inexorably entwined in city-level regulation, many firms flourished early in the development of the sector through a kind of urban "regulatory arbitrage" that, depending on your view, highlighted the shortcomings of or malevolently skirted local law.[33] The short-term rental sector, for example, thrived in the shadow of land-use regulation that tends to restrict supply, drive up costs, and segregate housing from employment and amenities.[34] Platforms that facilitate accommodation respond to these local supply constraints and spatial disconnects. And the same zoning that restricts supply strengthens the market for renters and homeowners seeking to make all or part of their dwelling available via Airbnb. By segregating uses and concentrating hotels in downtown areas away from residential neighborhoods, local zoning in the United States creates a literal space for short-term rental platforms to thrive when such neighborhoods become attractive to out-of-town visitors. Medallion systems similarly limited supply by capping the number of taxis, even in the face of increasing demand for mobility services.[35]

In the face of these constraints, many sharing firms found ways to derive economic value from avoiding regulatory constraints that apply to competitors. Firms exploited inefficiencies in urban markets, in part, by defining and structuring their operations in a manner designed to avoid unfavorable regulations.[36] Predictably, these efforts created tension as sharing economy entrants clashed with incumbent providers. Those incumbents, who historically wielded significant local political power, pushed for the first round of local regulatory responses. Sharing economy firms responded, both enlisting their growing customer base to challenge unfavorable regulation and seeking state-level preemption of unfavorable local laws. The result, on many occasions, has been a series of state–local conflicts over regulatory authority, to which we turn next.

II THE RISE OF REGULATORY CONFLICT

Sharing economy firms, in seeking state-level regulation, often find a more receptive government able and willing to displace local law. This has given rise to an increasing number of

---

[32] *See generally* Sarah B. Schindler, *Regulating the Underground: Secret Supper Clubs, Pop-up Restaurants, and the Role of Law*, 82 U. Chi. L. Rev. Online 16 (2015).

[33] In some instances these actions might be framed as what Elizabeth Pollman and Jordan Barry term "regulatory entrepreneurship" – an explicit effort "to change or shape the law." Elizabeth Pollman and Jordan M. Barry, *Regulatory Entrepreneurship*, 90 S. Cal. L. Rev. 383, 392 (2017).

[34] Edward L. Glaeser and Joseph Gyourko, *The Impact of Building Restrictions on Housing Affordability*, 9 Econ. Pol'y Rev. 21, 23 (2003).

[35] Wyman, *supra* note 27 at 171.

[36] Julia Verlaine and Jim Brunsden, *Uber Insists 'Ceci N'Est Pas un Taxi' in City of Magritte*, Bloomberg Technology, Oct. 12, 2014; David Streitfeld, *Companies Built on Sharing Balk When It Comes to Regulators*, N.Y. Times, Apr. 21, 2014.

preemption battles, with states modifying or blocking outright local regulatory efforts. These regulatory conflicts show no signs of abating. This section lays out the general landscape of such conflicts and, to illustrate the dynamics of these fights, examines the battle between the state of Texas and the city of Austin over regulation of TNCs.

A State Preemption of Local Regulation

Transportation network companies have, to date, been more effective than short-term rental platforms in obtaining state-level regulation. Currently, there are 48 states, along with the District of Columbia, with legislation regulating TNCs,[37] and, according to a recent study by the National League of Cities, at least 37 states in some way preempt local authority in this area.[38] These regulations, as Katrina Wyman has observed, focus in significant part on safety concerns, including minimum requirements for drivers.[39] In addition, much of this state legislation addresses questions of insurance coverage, frequently incorporating elements of a model bill developed by Uber, Lyft, and leading insurers.[40]

A few additional patterns have emerged in this state-level activity. Roughly half of the states explicitly preempt the field, barring local governments from any regulation of TNCs.[41] Some states are more generally enabling of the sector, allowing some local regulation, but setting baseline requirements at the state level. New York has taken the latter approach and as of April 2017 the state has allowed TNCs to operate outside of New York City, subject to a state mandate that TNCs conduct driver background checks, provide $1.25 million in liability insurance and $1.25 million in supplementary insurance for each vehicle, and impose a minimum age of 19 years for drivers.[42] This state law, however, allows individual counties and four of the state's larger cities – Buffalo, Rochester, Syracuse, and Yonkers – to decide if they want to allow ride-sharing companies to operate in their jurisdictions.[43]

State-level regulations in the transportation sector are partly justified by a desire to resolve potential coordination problems among neighboring jurisdictions within a single metropolitan area, avoiding local licensing schemes that create inefficiencies by prohibiting drivers from picking up passengers when returning from a trip outside their home jurisdiction.[44] But state-level intervention is also attributable to significant TNC lobbying efforts, spurred by opposition at the local level from the incumbent taxi industry.

There has been less preemption in the short-term rental sector of the sharing economy, but at least seven states – Arizona, Florida, New York, Utah, Idaho, Indiana, and Tennessee – have preempted or otherwise legislated at the state level, displacing all or some local regulation.[45] Indeed all of these states, except New York, flatly prohibit local bans on short-term rentals.

---

[37] For citations to these statutes *see* Appendix I to this chapter.

[38] National League of Cities, *City Rights in an Era of Preemption: A State-By-State Analysis* (2017), http://nlc.org/preemption.

[39] *See* Katrina M. Wyman, this volume.

[40] *Id.*

[41] For citations to these statutes *see* Appendix II to this chapter.

[42] N.Y. Veh. & Traf. Law §§ 1699, 1695, 1696 (McKinney, 2017).

[43] N.Y. Gen. Mun. Law § 182 (McKinney, 2017). If a county allows ridesharing, the towns and cities within that county cannot restrict ridesharing operations.

[44] Freeman Klopott, *Cuomo Seeks Statewide Uber Policy, Undercutting New York City*, Bloomberg Business, Oct. 21, 2015; Lauren Hirshon et al., Nat'l League of Cities, *Cities, The Sharing Economy and What's Next* (2015); Wyman, this volume.

[45] Ariz. Rev. Stat. §§ 9–500.39, 11–269.17 (2017); Fla. Stat. § 509.032(7) (2017); N.Y. Mult. Dwell. Law § 121 (McKinney 2017); Utah Code Ann. §§ 10-8-85.4, 17-50-338 (West 2017); Idaho Code Ann. § 67–6539 (West 2018); Ind. Code § 36-1-24-8 (2018); Tenn. Code Ann. § 66-35–102 (2018).

What accounts for these diverging paths? One explanation is that, rather than finding significant pushback from local incumbent providers, short-term rental firms often face opposition from individual residents and affordable-housing advocates. This opposition frequently targets individual bad actors, such as property owners turning multifamily buildings into illegal hotels, rather than platform companies themselves. Airbnb has responded to these criticisms by trying to distance itself from individual "hosts" with multiple listings and to curry favor with local regulators by offering to remit lodging taxes. In the TNC realm, in contrast, local opposition largely focuses on the platforms rather than individual drivers and TNCs have reacted to what they perceive as onerous local regulations (often blamed on incumbent interests) by appealing to the state government.

Another explanation is that there is a significant difference in the externalities generated by each sector, which justifies a differential apportionment of regulatory authority. Although most TNC trips are relatively short distance, they will frequently cross municipal boundaries in metropolitan areas, suggesting that a regional response (which may demand state-level intervention to implement) is more efficient. In contrast, short-term rentals, understood as an intensified use of existing housing, generate more localized externalities at the neighborhood or even block level. Short-term rentals may have some effect on citywide and perhaps even regional housing markets, but these effects are more attenuated and the benefits of uniform regulation across a metropolitan market (which is generally nonexistent in the United States for housing and land use more generally) are far less evident. Nonetheless, there may be additional costs and benefits to consider, as the discussion in the next section explains.

B *Texas Versus Austin: A Case Study in the Tension between Uniformity and Local Experimentation*

Recent developments around TNCs in Austin, Texas provide examples of both local experimentation and the threat, in the US context, of state preemption shutting down innovation. In May 2016 Uber and Lyft ceased operations in the hip, young, and technologically savvy city of Austin. Prior to departing, the companies had sponsored a ballot measure that would have reversed a local law requiring fingerprint-based background checks for drivers.[46] The measure was rejected by local voters. After the firms left the city, a number of homegrown ride-sharing apps willing to abide by the new requirements stepped in and filled the void. These included Ride Austin, a nonprofit provider that sought to direct a greater share of fares to drivers,[47] and Fasten, a company that charges a set $1 per ride surcharge, rather than a percentage fee.[48] These

---

[46]　There is debate over the safety merits of fingerprint-based background checks and complaints that such measures have a disproportionate negative impact on minorities and low-income individuals. *See* Letter from Austin Area Urban League and Austin Branch of the NAACP to Austin City Council Member Ann Kitchen, Oct. 13, 2015, www.scribd.com/doc/285911804/Letter-of-Opposition-to-Fingerprinting-Austin-s-Uber-Lyft-Drivers. We leave these criticisms of the particular merits of fingerprint-based background checks to the side to focus instead on the potential for local regulation to respond to local concerns and facilitate the development of local alternatives.

[47]　*See One Year After Fleeing Austin, Uber and Lyft Prepare a Fresh Invasion*, Wired, May 7, 2017. ("A re-entry into Austin may not go so smoothly. Many of the drivers now working with Ride Austin et al. started with Lyft and Uber. They may not want to go back: Lyft takes a 20 percent cut of the fare. Nonprofit RideAustin pays out the full amount for its standard service; Fasten takes a flat-fee commission of just under a buck per ride. Drivers tend to go where the money is, and passengers go where the drivers are.")

[48]　For discussion of Fasten, *see* Ellie Kaufman, *The Ride-Share Startup That's Competing with Uber and Lyft by Charging $1*, Fast Company, Oct. 31, 2016.

initial developments suggest that – at least in a place with an innovative technology sector – a city that imposes more rigorous regulations on sharing firms might spur development of home-grown alternatives to the large multinational firms.[49]

The Texas state legislature subsequently passed a law that preempted local control over TNCs, despite significant opposition from local officials who decried the loss of local control, particularly following the rejection of the local ballot measure.[50] The legislature expressly rejected a proposed amendment that would have permitted localities to require fingerprint background checks.[51] Austin Mayor Steve Adler reacted strongly to the state law, declaring "I'm disappointed that the legislature chose to nullify the bedrock principles of self-governance and limited government by imposing regulations on our city over the objection of Austin voters."[52]

When Uber and Lyft returned, they quickly regained significant market share and drove at least one competitor out of business.[53] Supporters of the state law championed it as a vindication of free and open markets in the face of onerous regulation and local capture.[54] However, as one commentator observed, Uber and Lyft's rapid recapture of market share is likely attributable in part to their ability to offer lower prices by subsidizing rides using their significant venture capital funding.[55] Despite this challenge at least some of the alternative platforms, including Ride Austin[56] and Fasten,[57] continue to operate in Austin.

In short, states – for their own reasons and in response to a political economy that is shifting the focus of some of the larger sharing firms to the state level – are increasingly restricting local authority over the localized impacts of the sharing economy. There are, however, reasons to be concerned about this shift.

III THE CAUTIOUS CASE FOR CONTINUING LOCALISM

There can be important reasons for state-level regulation – including establishing baseline civil rights and consumer protections, reducing inefficiencies, and tempering local-government actions that have external consequences. But there are also significant advantages to localism and decentralized experimentalism in the context of a rapidly changing industry like the sharing

---

[49] *See* Sam Levin, *"There is life after Uber": What Happens when Cities Ban the Service?*, The Guardian, Sept. 23, 2017 (discussing Uber's loss of its license to operate in London and development of local alternatives in Austin and other cities). Seoul, South Korea partially banned Uber with the goal of encouraging development of a local taxi app. *See* Neal Gorenflo, Shareable, *Why Banning Uber Makes Seoul Even More of a Sharing City*, July 25, 2014, www .shareable.net/blog/why-banning-uber-makes-seoul-even-more-of-a-sharing-city/.

[50] *Bill to regulate Uber, Lyft statewide gets green light from Texas House*, Dallas News, April 17, 2017.

[51] *Id.*

[52] *Id.*

[53] According to the CEO of Ride Austin: "In just one week – Fare, the #3 player in the market, closed up shop in Austin. Fasten dropped their rates within 3 days and quickly expanded their discount program to attempt to keep the most price sensitive riders. And at RideAustin – we saw our volumes drop by 55% in 1 week (26.4k versus 58.7k the week prior – including the ~20% seasonality drop from UT students graduating and going home). The market power of the giants is undoubtedly significant as they've gained at least 20K rides from us alone." Laura Bliss, *Why Uber Will Still Dominate*, CityLab, June 14, 2017.

[54] *See* Kimberly Reeves, *Uber's Big Win: Texas Ridesharing Rules Bill Passes Through Senate*, Austin Bus. J., May 18, 2017 (reporting that bill's Senate sponsor "said his goal was to create a minimal threshold to address safety concerns, while allowing the free market to dictate the success or failure of individual ridesharing companies").

[55] Bliss, *supra* note 53 (suggesting cities can still seek to regulate TNCs by, among other things, setting curbside limits on picking up riders, requiring vehicles to meet tailpipe standards, enforcing data-sharing mandates, or imposing congestion pricing).

[56] Ride Austin: A nonprofit rideshare built for Austin, www.rideaustin.com/.

[57] Fasten, https://fasten.com/cities.

economy[58] – and the possibility of state-level regulatory capture cannot be ignored. This section suggests a presumption in favor of a continued primary role for local regulators, while recognizing some of the inherent challenges of local parochialism.

A *The Case for a Continuing Local Role*

1 *Local Experimentalism Can Generate Regulatory Innovation Responsive to Local Conditions*

It is a worn truism that local governments are natural engines of experimentalism, and local governments in the United States are in many ways better "laboratories" than their state counterparts so valorized in the federalism literature. This is because local governments have comparative advantages in functioning – when they function well – to aggregate local preferences and channel localized information into governance.

Localist experimentalism is particularly well suited to conditions of rapid change. As Paul Diller notes, cities, at least in the United States, are structurally predisposed to innovate, given their typically unicameral legislatures and lack of supermajority requirements.[59] Moreover, local governments have been a source of particular innovation on critical policy areas, tapping into global networks of pragmatic local policymakers.[60]

For the past century one of, if not the, primary role of local governments in the United States has been addressing localized externalities and, through zoning and other forms of regulation, seeking to preserve and enhance community health, safety, and welfare.[61] Localities strike compromises among competing uses in various ways, giving rise to a diversity of communities that enable individuals to sort across and within municipalities and regions based upon their preferences.[62] Following this logic, a certain wisdom suggests that local governments are best placed to innovate in the face of the sharing economy in ways that address the interests of local citizens as providers, consumers, and concerned bystanders.[63]

2 *Local Innovation as a Check on Monopoly*

In addition, and less obviously, as the sharing economy matures and certain firms, particularly Uber, Lyft, and Airbnb, increasingly dominate their respective sectors, local governments may be uniquely situated to, in the course of encouraging innovation, simultaneously check the monopolistic tendencies of these firms.

Platform technology has allowed firms to quickly alter the dynamics of local politics.[64] Whereas historically a concentrated interest group might obtain regulatory benefits that impose

---

[58] *See* Davidson and Infranca, *supra* note 1, at 254–55; Finck and Ranchordás, *supra* note 1, at 1328–29; Rauch and Schleicher, *supra* note 1, at 938–40.

[59] *See generally* Paul A. Diller, *Why Do Cities Innovate in Public Health? Implications of Scale and Structure*, 91 Wash. U. L. Rev. 1219 (2014).

[60] *See generally* Benjamin R. Barber, *If Mayors Ruled the World: Dysfunctional Nations, Rising Cities* (2013).

[61] *C.f.* Gideon Parchomovsky and Peter Siegelman, *Cities, Property, and Positive Externalities*, 54 Wm. & Mary L. Rev. 211, 214 (2012) ("Viewed from an economic perspective, cities are all about positive and negative externalities. Cities that minimize the scope and magnitude of negative externalities and are able to produce positive externalities will have an inherent edge over localities that fail at these twin tasks.").

[62] *See generally* Charles M. Tiebout, *A Pure Theory of Local Expenditures*, 64 J. Pol. Econ. 416 (1956).

[63] Along these lines, the European Union's Committee of the Region, noting the localized externalities caused by the sharing economy, has suggested that regulation by subnational actors is most appropriate. *See* Finck and Ranchordás, *supra* note 1, at 1336.

[64] *See* Davidson and Infranca, *supra* note 1, at 273–74 (discussing how Uber mobilized users to oppose a proposed cap on drivers); Liam Dillon, *California Lawmakers Can't Figure Out What To Do with Airbnb. Here's Why*, L.A. Times,

diffuse (and often not particularly salient) costs, sharing economy firms have enlisted technology to quickly organize the thousands of diffuse individuals who experience those costs, changing the political dynamic.[65] In Austin, for example, Uber added an option called "Kitchen's Horse and Buggy" (named after the city council member who headed the committee drafting local regulations), to criticize as anachronistic proposed regulations.[66] This followed the similar "De Blasio" feature targeting New York City's mayor.

What is not entirely clear is whether this new dynamic reflects the use of technology to give voice to the broader public or instead simply the self-interested harnessing and directing of a customer base by a new concentrated interest group, the sharing economy firm, seeking regulatory benefits. Voicing the latter perspective, the targeted City Council member in Austin remarked: "These guys out in Silicon Valley like to consider themselves disrupters, but they're just another version of what we've had before: big business [types] who think they can write their own laws."[67]

Local governments have significantly more to lose from sharing economy firms dominating a given sector. If Uber begins to completely control transportation in a locality – not only driving out alternatives like taxis, liveries, and other TNCs – but also reducing public transit ridership – this may negatively affect the city's long-term capacity to provide essential services expected of local governments. Regardless of how one views these political dynamics, to the extent that one accepts or assumes there is some value in checking the growth of sharing firms that may eventually monopolize a given sector, local governments are best positioned to do so. This may seem paradoxical, given that local governments operate on a smaller scale (and hence regulate a smaller overall share of any national or global firm's business). However, as the examples of Austin, London,[68] and Seattle, Washington[69] suggest, local governments, as they craft regulations in response to local concerns, may be particularly well suited to indirectly shift the balance of power away from dominant platforms and toward local sharing economy participants.

In some localities more restrictive regulations, which larger sharing-economy firms are unwilling to comply with, may give rise to homegrown firms (at times with the promise of keeping profits local) or mission-driven platforms tailored to local needs.[70] In many instances such initiatives have been understood by their creators and supporters in explicitly place-based terms, as local efforts to improve a neighborhood or community by sharing the costs of providing a particular amenity and fostering interactions that build social capital or spur local economic development.[71] Similarly, commentators have proposed worker-owned co-ops to provide,

---

Feb. 3, 2017 (describing how Airbnb mobilized hosts to oppose a proposed bill, sending emails with link to an auto-generated letter, resulting in nearly 20,000 emails to state senators).

[65] As we write this chapter, Uber's license to operate in London has recently been revoked and an online petition in support of Uber has quickly garnered 800,000 signatures. William Booth, *How 800,000 People are Trying to Save Uber in London*, Wash. Post, Sept. 25, 2017.

[66] *See* Nellie Bowles, *"We're Just Getting Started": Inside Austin's Contentious Clash with Uber and Lyft*, The Guardian, Mar. 10, 2016.

[67] *Id.*

[68] *See* Josh Cohen, *With Uber Out, London Coalition Calls for Driver-Owned "Khan's Cars,"* NextCity, Sept. 28, 2017 (discussing proposal to "launch a new cooperatively owned, publicly regulated ride-hailing service" in London following non-renewal of Uber's operating license).

[69] *See infra* note 73 and accompanying text.

[70] *See, e.g.,* Peerby, www.peerby.com/ (enabling consumers to lend each other material goods); *cf.* Recupe.net (enabling individuals to gift and/or reuse old objects); The Food Assembly, https://thefoodassembly.com/en (enabling communities to buy fresh food directly from local producers and farmers); *see also* Aurélien Acquier and Valentina Carbone, this volume.

[71] *See* Boyd Cohen and Pablo Munoz, *Sharing Cities and Sustainable Consumption and Production: Towards an Integrated Framework*, 134 J. of Cleaner Production 87, 88 (2016) ("[W]hile the majority of recent media attention

in specific locales, apps equivalent to Uber or Lyft for local taxi drivers, along the lines of Ride Austin.[72] Rather than sending 20 or 30 percent of the cost of each ride out of the local community to the platform provider, such a co-op could use that money to undercut Uber's pricing and provide drivers with additional benefits. To the extent that cities see homegrown sharing firms as beneficial developments, their ability to encourage them will be shaped by the degree of authority they have to design regulatory strategies that reinforce aspects of the sharing economy that, at net, promote social capital or local economic development.

Rather than imposing stricter regulations on the operation of sharing firms, Seattle, Washington – a locality with relatively strong worker protections – passed a law in 2015 that would enable TNC and taxi drivers in the city to unionize and collectively bargain.[73] Such a move might serve to shift the balance of power, at least locally, between platforms and drivers.[74] Where local regulation of the sharing economy is preempted, localities still may have limited means to shape the sharing economy through non-regulatory interventions. In the transportation space, local governments have brokered agreements with TNCs to supplement public transportation by, for example, helping solve the first- and last-mile problem for commuters or providing transportation to disabled individuals.[75] Some localities enable residents to use their public transportation pass to pay for TNC travel.[76] Given the significant value sharing economy firms derive from their activity in dense urban markets,[77] those same markets, in the process of negotiating these forms of cooperation, possess the ability to broker concessions from TNCs to address local concerns or might choose to preference local firms when forming these partnerships.[78]

B Counterarguments to Local Parochialism

The case for a presumption in favor of local regulation must be a cautious one, as there are strong countervailing considerations – both pragmatic and normative. As noted, some sharing activities do implicate regional or even statewide interests.[79] There is clearly a trans-local component to the transportation sector of the sharing economy, as TNCs ferry riders across jurisdictions. Short-term rentals can also create externalities that cross jurisdictional boundaries. Housing markets

---

about the sharing economy has been focused on commercial, scalable sharing economy stalwarts like Airbnb and Uber, the historical roots of sharing in communities, and even many emerging approaches to sharing that leverage [information and communication technologies] are not even commercial endeavors.").

[72] Alex Marshall, *An Old Idea for the New App-Based Economy*, Governing, Dec. 2015.

[73] The law is currently on hold pending litigation from the US Chamber of Commerce on behalf of Uber and Lyft. Genie Johnson, *Court Blocks Seattle Law Letting Uber, Lyft Drivers Unionize*, The Associated Press, Sept. 8, 2017. Challenges to the law assert that it violates federal and state labor laws as the drivers are independent contractors and not employees and therefore not covered by the National Labor Relations Act. David Gutman, *US Chamber Sues Seattle Again, Says Uber, Lyft Taxi Drivers Can't Form Union*, Seattle Times, Mar. 10, 2017.

[74] For further discussion of how various "intermediary institutions" might shift the balance of power between TNCs and drivers, *see* John J. Infranca, *Intermediary Institutions and the Sharing Economy*, 90 Tul. L. Rev. Online. 29 (2016).

[75] *See* Erika I. Ritchie, *Laguna Beach Partners with Uber to Provide Transportation for Seniors and the Disabled – A First in the U.S.*, Orange County Register, May 10, 2017; Eric Jaffe, *Uber and Public Transit Are Trying to Get Along*, Citylab, Aug. 3 2015.

[76] Dan Bobkoff, *Uber Is Using a Tax 'Loophole' to Make Its Rides Cheaper*, Business Insider, Oct. 6 2016; Alexandra Semanova, *MTA Plans Dramatic Expansion of E-Hail Service*, Crain's New York Business, June 21, 2017.

[77] Ian Hathaway and Mark Muro, *Tracking the Gig Economy: New Numbers*, Brookings, Oct. 13 2016, www.brookings .edu/research/tracking-the-gig-economy-new-numbers/.

[78] Rauch, this volume.

[79] For a further discussion of this point, *see* Janice Griffith, this volume.

are regional in scope and if short-term rentals do, in fact, create pressures on these markets that affect affordability, they are likely to do so in a way that affects neighboring communities.

Moreover, some regulatory regimes set uniform rules that provide a floor that should be state-wide (or national), even if there can be scope for local governments to add regulatory protections. The enforcement of labor and employment law, tort law, or anti-discrimination law would seem to not depend in any significant way on the particular geography in which the regulated use occurs. Income taxes might be the same, but the assessment grows more complicated when we consider hotel taxes or user fees.

As to the democratic check on the tendencies of a handful of sharing firms to dominate their sectors, states have their own democratic legitimacy and, under most state constitutions, are empowered to take a different view of the relative merits of regulatory tradeoffs. Local parochialism and protectionism is a genuine concern and what might seem to some local governments as resisting monopoly and encouraging innovation may seem to outsiders like capture and incumbency protection.[80]

The best responses to these countervailing concerns are that they can be valid in many circumstances, but are inherently contingent. Uniformity and certainty can be a mask for a political economy that overly devalues local variation and in the clash of democratic priorities, it is still the case that local participants in the sharing economy and people most impacted by the sharing economy (for good or ill) at the local level retain the greatest stake in the regulatory response to the industry.[81] Hence the case for continued local control – on balance, if tentatively – should prevail as a default matter, particularly in the face of the continuing evolution of the industry.

CONCLUSION

The place of the sharing economy – as a regulatory matter – is likely to remain contested for the near future, as the industry evolves and lawmakers at every level reckon with the transformations wrought by the sharing economy. While that evolution continues, the recent trend of statewide preemption – for all of the advantages of uniformity and certainty – should be approached with caution. Local preferences and the ability of local governments to continue to experiment with often difficult regulatory calibration in light of local conditions has not, to say the least, yet run its course.

APPENDIX I STATE LEGISLATION REGARDING TNCS (AS OF OCTOBER 2017)

Alabama, *see* Ala. Code § 32-7C-1 to 32-7C-4 (2017); Alaska, *see* Alaska Stat. §§ 21.96.018, 28.23.010-28.23.190 (2017); Arizona, *see* Ariz. Rev. Stat. Ann. §§ 41–2138 to 41–2139.06 (2017);

---

[80] On this precise point, in relation to the battle in Austin over TNCs, *see* John Kartch, *With Governor's Signature, Uber and Lyft Return to Austin*, Forbes, May 30, 2017 (asserting that Austin's city council "imposed the type of pointless regulations that serve only to prop up entrenched taxi companies and act as a barrier to entry for those looking to earn money driving when they have time in their schedules").

[81] The sharing economy may figure differently in recurring debates regarding the vertical allocation of power for an additional reason. In significant segments of the sharing economy, many actual providers of goods and services – and certainly, so far, most consumers – are individuals operating within the same neighborhoods where they live. This is particularly true in the ride-sharing space, where both passengers and drivers are likely to live in close proximity to where a ride occurs. In the short-term rental space, consumers are likely to be out-of-towners, but the vast majority of hosts are locals renting space in their homes. Accordingly, individuals are likely to experience these regulations not only as participants in the sharing economy, but also as residents and in some cases homeowners for whom the regulations purportedly serve other interests.

Arkansas, *see* Ark. Code Ann. §§ 23-13-701 to 23-13-722 (2017); California, *see* Cal. Pub. Util. Code §§ 5430–5445.2 (West 2017); Colorado, *see* Colo. Rev. Stat. §§ 40-10.1-601 to 40-10.1-608 (2017); Connecticut, *see* 2017 Conn. Pub. Acts 140 (effective October 1, 2017); Delaware, *see* Del. Code Ann. tit. 2 §§ 1901–1922 (2017); District of Columbia, *see* 2014 D.C. Sess. L. Serv. 20–197 (West); Florida, *see* Fla. Stat. Ann. § 627.748 (West 2017); Georgia, *see* Ga. Code Ann. § 33-1-24, 40-1-190 to 40-1-200 (2017); Hawaii, *see* Haw. Rev. Stat. Ann. § 431:10C-701 to 431:10C-705 (West 2017); Idaho, *see* Idaho Code §§ 41–2517 to 41–2521, 49–3701 to 49–3715 (2017); Illinois, *see* 625 Ill. Comp. Stat. Ann. 57/10–57/34 (West 2017); Indiana, *see* Ind. Code Ann. §§ 8-2.1-19.1-1 to 8-2.1-19.1-20 (West 2017); Iowa, *see* I.C.A. §§ 321N.1- 321N.11 (West 2017); Kansas, *see* Kan. Stat. Ann. §§ 8-2701 to 8-2720 (2017); Kentucky, *see* 2015 Ky. Acts 19; Louisiana, *see* La. Stat. Ann. §§ 45:201.1-45:201.13 (2017); Maine, *see* Me. Stat. tit. 29-A §§ 1671-1677 (2017); Maryland, *see* Md. Code Ann., Pub. Util. §§ 10-401 to 10-407 (West 2017); Massachusetts, *see* Mass. Gen. Laws Ann. ch. 159A ½ (West 2017); Michigan, *see* M.C.L.A. §§ 257.2101-257.2153 (West 2017); Minnesota, *see* Minn. Stat. Ann. §65B.472 (West 2017); Mississippi, *see* Miss. Code Ann. §§ 77-8-1 to 77-8-39 (2017); Missouri, *see* Mo. Ann. Stat. §§ 387.400-387.440 (West 2017); Montana, *see* M.C.A. §§ 69-12-340 to 69-12-345 (2017); Nebraska, *see* Neb. Rev. Stat. Ann. §§ 75-323 to 75-343 (West 2017); Nevada, *see* Nev. Rev. Stat. Ann. §§ 706A.150-706A.310 (West 2017); New Hampshire, *see* N.H. Rev. Stat. Ann. §§ 376-A:1 to 376:A19 (2017); New Jersey, *see* N.J.S.A. §§ 39:5H-1 to 39:5H-27 (West 2017); New Mexico, *see* N. M. S. A. §§ 65-7-1 to 65-7-22 (2017); New York, *see* N.Y. Veh. & Traf. Law §§ 1691-1700 (McKinney 2017); North Carolina, *see* N.C.G.S. §§ 20-280.1 to 20-280.10 (2017); North Dakota, *see* N.D. Cent. Code §§ 39-34-01 to 39-34-06 (2017); Ohio, *see* Ohio Rev. Code Ann. §§ 4925.01-4925.11 (West 2017); Oklahoma, *see* Okla. Stat. tit. 47, §§ 1010-1030 (2017); Pennsylvania, *see* 66 Pa. Cons. Stat. and Cons. Stat. Ann. §§ 2601-2610 (West 2017); Rhode Island, *see* 39 R.I. Gen. Laws Ann. §§ 39-14.2-1 to 39-14.2-22 (West 2017); South Carolina, *see* S.C. Code Ann. §§ 58-23-1610 to 58-23-1720 (2017); South Dakota, *see* SDCL §§ 32-40-1 to 32-40-23 (West); Tennessee, *see* T. C. A. §§ 65-15-301 to 65-15-311 (2017); Texas, *see* Tex. Occ. Code Ann. §§ 2402.001-2402.201 (West 2017); Utah, *see* Utah Code Ann. §§ 13-51-101 to 13-51-204 (West 2017); Virginia, *see* Va. Code Ann. §§ 46.2-2099.45 to 46.2-2099.53 (2017); Washington, *see* Wa. Rev. Code. Ann. §§ 48.177.005-48.177.010 (West 2017); West Virginia, *see* W. Va. Code Ann. §§ 17-29-1 to 17-29-19 (West 2017); Wisconsin, *see* Wis. Stat. Ann. §§ 440.40-440.495 (West 2017); Wyoming, *see* Wyo. Stat. Ann §§ 31–20—101 to 31-20-111 (2017).

APPENDIX II STATE LEGISLATION THAT EXPRESSLY PREEMPTS
LOCAL TNC REGULATION (AS OF OCTOBER 2017)

Arkansas, *see* Ark. Code Ann. § 23-13-720 (2017); Colorado, *see* Colo. Rev. Stat. Ann. § 40-10.1-603 (West 2017); Delaware, *see* Del. Code Ann. tit. 2, § 1922 (2017); Florida, *see* Fla. Stat. Ann. § 627.748(15) (West 2017); Georgia, *see* Ga. Code Ann. § 40-1-191 (2017); Idaho, *see* Idaho Code § 49-3715 (2017); Indiana, *see* Ind. Code Ann. § 36-9-2-4 (West 2017); Iowa, *see* I.C.A. § 321N.11 (West 2017); Maine, *see* Me. Rev. Stat. Ann. tit. 29-A § 1677 (2017); Massachusetts, *see* Mass. Gen. Laws Ann. ch. 159A 1/2, § 10 (West 2017); Michigan, *see* M.C.L.A. § 257.2115 (West 2017); Mississippi, *see* Miss. Code Ann. § 77-8-37 (2017); Missouri, *see* Mo. ann. Stat. § 387.430 (West 2017); Montana, *see* M.C.A. § 69-12-342 (2017); New Hampshire, *see* N.H. Rev. Stat. Ann. § 376-A:17 (2017); New Jersey, *see* N.J.S.A. 39:5H-26 (West 2017); New Mexico, *see* N.M.S.A. § 65-7-18 (West 2017); North Carolina, *see* N.C.G.S. § 20-280.10 (2017); North Dakota, *see* N.D. Cent. Code § 39-34-06 (2017); Ohio, *see* Ohio Rev. Code Ann. § 4925.09 (West 2017); Oklahoma, *see* Okla. Stat. tit. 47, § 1030 (2017); Rhode Island, *see* 39 R.I. Gen. Laws § 39-14.2-18 (2017); Tennessee, *see* T. C. A. § 65-15-302 (2017); Texas, *see* Tex. Occ. Code Ann. § 2402.003 (West 2017); Virginia, *see* Va. Code Ann. § 46.2-2099.46 (2017); West Virginia, *see* W. Va. Code Ann. § 17-29-19 (West 2017); Wisconsin, *see* Wis. Stat. Ann. § 440.465 (West 2017); Wyoming, *see* Wyo. Stat. Ann. § 31-20-111 (West 2017).

16

The Role of the Federal Government in Regulating the Sharing Economy

Sarah E. Light

INTRODUCTION

The sharing economy – also known as the "platform" economy[1] among other monikers – has captured the attention of scholars, policymakers, and the public. These new forms of business organization facilitate an increasingly efficient use of resources, promote access over ownership, and have the potential to herald new forms of trust.[2] We share rides, tools, apartments, services, and land. And we also, in ways more complex than ever, share the consequences – both good and bad – of these new economic arrangements. Scholars and policymakers are beginning to grapple with how to make sense of legal responsibility in the platform economy. Legislators and regulators must determine whether existing legal rules about taxes, employment and labor law, insurance, anti-discrimination, safety, environmental protection, consumer protection, and privacy (among others) should apply to these new platforms, or whether entirely new legal categories are required.

In the transportation context, for example, ride-hailing platforms such as Uber and Lyft own no vehicles and argue that they employ no drivers, yet facilitate access to more than a million rides each day worldwide.[3] Courts and regulators are evaluating whether drivers for these platforms are "employees" or "independent contractors" for the purpose of employment and labor law.[4] Municipal and state regulatory agencies are also trying to determine whether these platforms are sufficiently similar to traditional taxi fleets for the purpose of setting safety rules on driver background checks, minimum insurance requirements, access to rides for people with

---

[1] The Oxford English Dictionary (2015) defines the term "sharing economy" as "[a]n economic system in which assets or services are shared between private individuals, either for free or for a fee, typically by means of the Internet." Because many firms that fit this definition operate in the for-profit space, rather than in the realm of gratuitous sharing, I adopt the term "platform" economy here to reflect the role of platform intermediaries that match supply with demand. *See* Orly Lobel, *The Law of the Platform*, 101 Minn. L. Rev. 87 (2016).

[2] For early discussions of how peer production has transformed the nature of firms, *see* Yochai Benkler, *Sharing Nicely*, 114 Yale L.J. 273 (2004); Yochai Benkler, *Coase's Penguin, or, Linux and the Nature of the Firm*, 112 Yale L.J. 369 (2002).

[3] *Uber Says It's Doing 1 Million Rides Per Day, 140 Million In Last Year*, Forbes Mag., Dec. 17, 2014, www.forbes.com/sites/ellenhuet/2014/12/17/uber-says-its-doing-1-million-rides-per-day-140-million-in-last-year/.

[4] Steven Davidoff Solomon, *Uber Case Highlights Outdated Worker Protection Laws*, N.Y. Times, Sept. 15, 2015; Brishen Rogers, *Employment Rights in the Platform Economy: Getting Back to Basics*, 10 Harv. L. & Pol'y Rev. 479 (2016) (summarizing this debate).

disabilities, and other matters of public concern such as anti-discrimination law.[5] Analogous legal questions have arisen for other platforms like Airbnb, for example, whether such new arrangements in hospitality and short-term home rentals should be treated like hotels for the purposes of existing tax, zoning, safety, and anti-discrimination laws.[6] As with any new business model, regulators are asking whether existing statutes and regulations can be adapted to new situations, or whether new rules are required.[7] In other words, this innovative form of business is creating policy disruption.[8]

Of course, the platform economy is not the first set of new economic arrangements to generate policy disruption.[9] Other industries have faced the rise of innovative forms of business or new technologies that have likewise created such policy disruption, when innovators exploit legal loopholes or gaps, or when there are questions as to whether existing legal rules legitimately apply.[10] In such cases of policy disruption, regulators have four primary choices – to *Block* the innovator from entering the market; to afford the innovator a *Free Pass* from existing legal rules, to the detriment of the incumbent; to apply the existing regime (*OldReg*) to the innovator, even if it is an imperfect fit; or to create an entirely new regime (*NewReg*).[11] And if the incumbent loses out with respect to its reliance interests, the issue of whether it is entitled to any form of compensation (*Buy Out*) arises as a subsidiary question.[12]

Yet before one gets to the question of what *substantive* law to apply to these platforms, there lies an antecedent question. That is, *who gets to decide* what substantive law to apply to the platform economy?[13] The application of substantive law could look very different if regulatory authority is lodged in the federal government, the states, local or municipal governments, or some combination of these. This chapter therefore examines the *federalism* implications of the rise of the platform economy, with an eye toward the role that the federal government can and should play.[14] This chapter is organized as follows. Section I offers a brief primer on federalism theory to explain why regulatory authority might best be allocated to the federal government, to the states and/or local governments, to some combination of these regulators, or to no regulators

---

[5] Katrina Wyman, *Taxi Regulation in the Age of Uber*, 20 N.Y.U. J. Legis. & Pub. Pol'y 1 (2017).

[6] Nancy Leong, *New Economy, Old Biases*, 100 Minn. L. Rev. 2153 (2016); Benjamin Edelman, Michael Luca, and Dan Svirsky, *Racial Discrimination in the Sharing Economy: Evidence from a Field Experiment*, 9 American. Econ. J. 1 (2017); Katharine Bartletter and Mitu Gulati, *Discrimination by Customers*, 102 Iowa L. Rev. 223 (2016).

[7] Elizabeth Pollman and Jordan Barry, *Regulatory Entrepreneurship*, 90 S. Cal. L. Rev. 383 (2017); Nancy Leong and Aaron Beltzer, *The New Public Accommodations*, 105 Geo. L.J. 1271 (2017).

[8] Eric Biber, Sarah E. Light, J. B. Ruhl and James Salzman, *Regulating Business Innovation as Policy Disruption: From the Model T to Airbnb*, 70 Vand. L. Rev. 1561 (2017) (offering a theory of when business or technological innovation leads to policy disruption, and a framework for policy responses).

[9] *Id.*

[10] *Id.*; *cf.* Kevin Werbach, *The Song Remains the Same: What Cyberlaw Might Teach the Next Internet Economy*, 69 Fla. L. Rev. 887 (2017); Deepa Das Acevedo, *Invisible Bosses for Invisible Workers, or Why the Sharing Economy is Minimally Disruptive*, 2017 U. Chi. L. F. 35 (2017).

[11] Biber et al., *supra* note 8.

[12] *Id.*

[13] Sarah E. Light, *Precautionary Federalism and the Sharing Economy*, 66 Emory L.J. 333 (2017).

[14] The chapter, which focuses exclusively on regulation within the United States, will not address the separation of powers question, namely which institution – the legislature, the executive, administrative agencies, or the courts, should wield that regulatory authority. Because Uber and Airbnb are two of the largest startup online platforms by valuation, and raise many of the policy issues that other platforms raise, I use those platforms (and rival Lyft), as examples here. David S. Evans and Richard Schmalensee, *The Businesses that Platforms Are Actually Disrupting*, Harv. Bus. Rev., Sept. 21, 2016, https://hbr.org/2016/09/the-businesses-that-platforms-are-actually-disrupting.

at all. Section II examines how federalism theory applies to the platform economy, arguing that both the aggregative nature of the platform economy and its local scope raise different concerns about externalities than those that might arise from manufacturing or more traditional forms of business organization – externalities and harms that motivated many existing theories about federalism. In addition, because these firms tend to challenge incumbents that are regulated at the local level, much scholarship tends to view the platform economy and its regulation as a local phenomenon. Section III argues that the federal government nonetheless has an essential role to play in at least three domains: (1) enforcement of national anti-discrimination laws;[15] (2) protection of consumers – broadly construed to include both guests and hosts on Airbnb, as well as riders and drivers of platforms like Uber or Lyft – including consumer privacy[16]; and (3) coordination of state and local experimentation, including the diffusion of policy successes.[17]

I FEDERALISM THEORY – A PRIMER

Regulatory authority can be allocated in one of four primary ways.[18] First, there can be no public regulatory regime at all. Private firms and non-governmental organizations can employ different tools to address, for example, environmental externalities through third-party certification schemes, voluntary information disclosure regimes, or private industry standards, among other forms of private governance.[19] In the absence of even such organized forms of private governance, the private sector can be left to its own devices in what some advocates call "permissionless innovation."[20] Advocates of permissionless innovation in the context of the platform economy suggest that this approach will best promote innovation without regulatory interference, and that devices like reputation ratings systems employed by the platforms can serve a quasi-governance function.[21] Advocates of private governance recognize that non-governmental organizations – for example, private insurance standards or third-party certification schemes – can serve some of the same regulatory functions as public law; however, often private governance is considered a method of filling gaps or complementing public law, rather than pure replacement.[22]

Second, regulatory authority can be left to the states without federal involvement. Rationales for allocating regulatory authority to the states include promoting policy experimentation, tailoring policies to local conditions and preferences, "matching" the smallest regulatory jurisdiction that is the locus of both positive and negative externalities associated with the activity,

[15] *Cf.* Leong and Beltzer, *supra* note 7.

[16] *Cf.* Ryan Calo and Alex Rosenblat, *The Taking Economy*, 117 Colum. L. Rev. 1623 (2017).

[17] *Cf.* Hannah Wiseman, *Regulatory Islands*, 89 N.Y.U. L. Rev. 1661 (2014); Michael C. Dorf and Charles F. Sabel, *A Constitution of Democratic Experimentalism*, 98 Colum. L. Rev. 267 (1988).

[18] Sarah E. Light, *Advisory Nonpreemption*, 95 Wash. U. L. Rev. 325, 361 (2017).

[19] Sarah E. Light and Eric W. Orts, *Parallels in Public and Private Environmental Governance*, 5 Mich. J. Envtl. & Admin. L. 1 (2015); Sarah E. Light, *The New Insider Trading: Environmental Markets within the Firm*, 34 Stan. Envtl. L.J. 3 (2015); Michael P. Vandenbergh, *Private Environmental Governance*, 99 Cornell L. Rev. 129, 133 (2013).

[20] *Cf.* Adam Thierer and Ryan Hagemann, *Removing Roadblocks to Intelligent Vehicles and Driverless Cars*, 5 Wake Forest J.L. Pol'y 339 (2015).

[21] Richard A. Epstein, *The Political Economy of Crowdsourcing: Markets for Labor, Rewards, and Securities*, 82 U. Chi. L. Rev. Dialogue 35, 36 (2015); Arun Sundararajan, *Why the Government Doesn't Need to Regulate the Sharing Economy*, WIRED (Oct. 22, 2012, 1:45 PM), www.wired.com/2012/10/from-airbnb-to-coursera-why-the-government-shouldntregulate-the-sharing-economy/. For an early, pre-platform economy account of how reputational ratings schemes can displace law enforcement, *see* Lior Strahilevitz, *"How's My Driving" For Everyone (and Everything?)*, 81 N.Y.U. L. Rev. 1699 (2006). But *see* Abbey Stemler, *Feedback Loop Failure: Implications for the Self-Regulation of the Sharing Economy*, 18 Minn. J. of L., Sci. & Tech. 673, 686–88 (2017).

[22] *See, e.g.*, Light and Orts, *supra* note 19.

and promoting good governance through participation in the democratic process.[23] Although local governments have long been viewed as a constituent part of the state, more recently, a number of scholars have argued that local governments have their own separate interests.[24]

Third, the federal government can adopt exclusive legal rules that preempt state and local government law. Federal regulatory primacy and uniform federal rules are often justified on the grounds that they promote both regulatory and manufacturing economies of scale, that they can avoid a state "race-to-the-bottom" to enact the most lax rules to attract industry, and that uniform federal rules can avoid the problem of interstate spillovers, in which states can externalize harms to neighboring states, while internalizing the benefits of the regulated activity.[25]

Fourth, the federal government and the states (and local governments) can share concurrent authority, through cooperative federalism, floor preemption, or some other approach.[26] Advocates of such "dynamic" approaches to the allocation of authority – in contrast to the exclusive "dual federalism" approaches – contend that concurrent federal/state or federal/state/local jurisdiction can promote policy experimentation while at the same time addressing concerns about interstate spillovers and promoting the national interest.[27] On this account, federalism need not be a "zero-sum" game between exclusive federal or state authority.[28]

Finally, the initial allocation of authority need not remain static. I have argued elsewhere that when addressing innovative forms of business or new technologies, the allocation of regulatory authority should be *precautionary*.[29] Just as we may not know the best policy to address such innovation, we may not know at the outset who is the optimal regulator – or whether a single, optimal regulator exists at all. Therefore, in the initial stages of innovation, where uncertainty about how the potential harms or benefits of the innovation are distributed is at its height, a dynamic allocation of concurrent jurisdiction is likely to promote regulatory and business innovation most effectively, while contributing information and knowledge about whether there is significant local variation in the harms to be regulated. As additional information develops, however, the allocation may shift toward more uniform rules.[30]

---

[23] Light, *supra* note 13, at 350–56; Henry N. Butler and Jonathan R. Macey, *Externalities and the Matching Principle: The Case for Reallocating Environmental Regulatory Authority*, 14 Yale L. & Pol'y Rev. 23, 36 (1996); Richard L. Revesz, *Rehabilitating Interstate Competition: Rethinking the "Race-to-the-Bottom" Rationale for Federal Environmental Regulation*, 67 N.Y.U. L. Rev. 1210, 1211–12 (1992); David B. Spence, *The Political Economy of Local Vetoes*, 93 Tex. L. Rev. 351, 351–52 (2014).

[24] *See, e.g.*, Nestor M. Davidson, *Cooperative Localism: Federal-Local Collaboration in an Era of State Sovereignty*, 93 Va L. Rev. 959, 995–1000 (2007); Heather K. Gerken, *Foreword: Federalism All the Way Down*, 124 Harv. L. Rev. 4, 22–23 (2010); Cristina M. Rodríguez, *The Significance of the Local in Immigration Regulation*, 106 Mich. L. Rev. 567, 568 (2008); *cf.* David J. Barron, *A Localist Critique of the New Federalism*, 51 Duke L.J. 377, 378–79 (2001).

[25] For discussions of rationales favoring federal rules, *see* Daniel C. Esty, *Revitalizing Environmental Federalism*, 95 Mich. L. Rev. 570, 570–71 (1996); David B. Spence, *Federalism, Regulatory Lags, and the Political Economy of Energy Production*, 161 U. Pa. L. Rev. 431, 477–78 (2013); Richard B. Stewart, *Pyramids of Sacrifice? Problems of Federalism in Mandating State Implementation of National Environmental Policy*, 86 Yale L.J. 1196, 1210–15 (1977).

[26] Light, *supra* note 13, at 356–60.

[27] *See, e.g.*, David E. Adelman and Kirsten H. Engel, *Adaptive Federalism: The Case Against Reallocating Environmental Regulatory Authority*, 92 Minn. L. Rev. 1796, 1798–99 (2008); William W. Buzbee, *Asymmetrical Regulation: Risk, Preemption, and the Floor/Ceiling Distinction*, 82 N.Y.U. L. Rev. 1547, 1555–56 (2007); William W. Buzbee, *Interaction's Promise: Preemption Policy Shifts, Risk Regulation, and Experimentalism Lessons*, 57 Emory L.J. 145 (2007); Ann E. Carlson, *Iterative Federalism and Climate Change*, 103 Nw. U. L. Rev. 1097, 1099–1100 (2009); Kirsten H. Engel, *Harnessing the Benefits of Dynamic Federalism in Environmental Law*, 56 Emory L.J. 159, 176–77 (2006).

[28] Erin Ryan, *Federalism and the Tug of War Within*, at xii–xiii (2012); Erin Ryan, *Negotiating Federalism*, 52 B.C. L. Rev. 1, 5 (2011).

[29] Light, *supra* note 13, at 360–65.

[30] Light, *supra* note 18.

II THE PLATFORM ECONOMY'S UNEASY FIT WITH THEORIES
OF FEDERALISM, AND THE ROLE OF LOCAL GOVERNMENT

The federalism theory summarized above tends to presume that regulators are regulating a particular kind of industrial activity; an assumption that does not necessarily hold for the platform economy. Many traditional industries – for example factories that promise jobs and tax revenues to states that wish to lure them, but also pollution that may cross beyond the state's boundaries – face a zero-sum choice about where to locate their industrial activity. This choice can arguably lead states to compete for the potential benefits of such industrial activity by adopting lax regulatory rules in a so-called "race-to-the-bottom."[31]

One major distinction between the platform economy and this traditional industrial activity is that the platform economy can simultaneously locate itself in numerous jurisdictions at little cost. By and large, any platform like Uber, Lyft, or Airbnb can enter any state or local market with little marginal cost as long as there are drivers willing to drive and hosts willing to rent out their homes.[32] This may affect whether a "race-to-the-bottom" dynamic actually occurs. Second, while some effects of the platform economy may cross state lines, often such platforms are operating at a local level. The greatest potential harms to third parties – such as interference with "quality of life" in residential neighborhoods – likewise exist at the local level. While Uber may be a global platform, in 2015, the average distance of an Uber ride was between six and seven miles.[33] Thus, in other ways, Uber is just like taxis, which have historically been "city-specific, with little cross-ownership across cities."[34] Local regulatory control operates as a kind of default because sharing platforms are competing with local incumbents providing similar services – such as taxis or hotels – which are already subject to local regulations or zoning restrictions.[35]

As a result of these dynamics, much scholarship on the platform economy has tended either to assume or expressly to prefer local regulation of these platforms.[36] While platforms like Uber and Airbnb are national or even global in nature, from the perspective of users and service providers, the scope of service provided to customers is, in general, local. As Davidson and Infranca note, the "regulatory response to these new entrants has primarily been at the municipal level."[37] The platform economy is "being shaped by zoning codes, hotel licensing regimes, taxi medallion requirements, insurance mandates, and similar distinctly local legal issues."[38] Notably, Davidson and Infranca have pointed out that the platform economy largely relies upon urban density for its "value proposition," while at the same time representing a "reaction to urban

---

[31] For debate over whether a race-to-the-bottom exists, *see* Kirsten H. Engel, *State Environmental Standard-Setting: Is There a "Race" and Is It "To the Bottom"?* 48 Hastings L.J. 271 (1997); Richard L. Revesz, *Rehabilitating Interstate Competition: Rethinking the "Race-to-the-Bottom" Rationale for Federal Environmental Regulation*, 67 N.Y.U. L. Rev. 1210 (1992).

[32] Light, *supra* note 13, at 384–85.

[33] SherpaShare, *Uber Trips Are Becoming Longer and Faster, but are they More Profitable?*, www.sherpashareblog.com/tag/uber-trip-distance/.

[34] Wyman, *supra* note 5, at 9. While individual Uber drivers may operate only in a single city, Wyman notes that Uber is a "virtual global fleet manager." *Id.* at 11 (citing Justin Jenk, *Theory Meets Practice in the Taxi Industry: Coase & Uber* 2 (Much Pers. RePEc Archive, Working Paper No. 63206, 2015)).

[35] Wyman, *supra* note 5, at 16–20, 76–77.

[36] Daniel E. Rauch and David Schleicher, *Like Uber, But for Local Government Policy: The Future of Local Regulation of the Sharing Economy*, 76 Ohio St. L.J. 901 (2015); Michèle Finck and Sofia Ranchordás, *Sharing and the City*, 49 Vand. J. of Transnat'l L. 1299, 1352–1365 (2016); Nestor M. Davidson and John J. Infranca, *The Sharing Economy as an Urban Phenomenon*, 34 Yale L. & Pol'y Rev. 215, 217 (2016); Kellen Zale, *When Everything is Small: The Regulatory Challenge of Scale in the Sharing Economy*, 53 San. Diego L. Rev. 949 (2017).

[37] Davidson and Infranca, *supra* note 36, at 217–18.

[38] *Id.*

regulatory regimes that exacerbate the frictions of urban life."[39] Such frictions include supply limits on urban amenities like taxi services or hotel rooms. Other scholars have argued that local governments can partner with platforms by subsidizing platforms to support the creation of public goods and to work with such firms to "provide traditional government services."[40] Indeed, some local governments have adopted such strategies, for example, partnering with Uber to subsidize rides that start or end at local transportation hubs.[41]

III A LEADING ROLE FOR THE FEDERAL GOVERNMENT

Despite this widespread focus on local regulatory authority, the federal government can and should play a leading role in at least three areas: (1) enforcement of national anti-discrimination laws; (2) protection of consumers, including consumer privacy; and (3) coordination of state and local experimentation, including policy diffusion. The first two represent areas of national, rather than purely local, concern, and are already the subject of strong federal laws. The third is a role that the federal government is uniquely situated to address.

A Anti-discrimination Law

First, the federal government has an essential role to play in enforcing national anti-discrimination laws and norms. Hospitality and transportation are essential components of interstate commerce – and our nation's civil rights laws were adopted to ensure that racial and other forms of discrimination would not interfere with interstate commerce.[42] Recent empirical studies have demonstrated that platforms mimic or amplify existing discrimination within society. For example, one recent study of Airbnb has demonstrated that "applications from guests with distinctively African American names are 16 percent less likely to be accepted relative to identical guests with distinctively white names."[43] Notably, the authors of this study found this effect to be widespread:

> Both African American and white hosts discriminate against African American guests; both male and female hosts discriminate; both male and female African American guests are discriminated against. Effects persist both for hosts that offer an entire property and for hosts who share the property with guests. Discrimination persists among experienced hosts, including those with multiple properties and those with many reviews. Discrimination persists and is of similar magnitude in high- and low-priced units, in diverse and homogeneous neighborhoods.[44]

This discrimination is not limited to Airbnb, but has been demonstrated in the context of transportation platforms like Uber and Lyft as well. One recent empirical study demonstrated that Uber drivers canceled rides more frequently for riders with African American sounding names

---

[39] *Id.* at 217–19.
[40] Rauch and Schleicher, *supra* note 36, at 901.
[41] Ariel Wittenberg, *Fla. City Subsidizes Uber Rides to Expand Commuting Options*, GREENWIRE (Apr. 15, 2016), www.eenews.net/greenwire/stories/1060035694/feed.
[42] Leong, *supra* note 6.
[43] Edelman et al., *supra* note 6, at 1.
[44] *Id.* at 2. However, an unpublished working paper suggests that the racial disparity is eliminated when there is a public review posted on a potential guest's Airbnb account page. Ruomeng Cui et al., *Discrimination with Incomplete Information in the Sharing Economy: Evidence from a Field Experiment* (December 8, 2016), available at https://ssrn.com/abstract=2882982.

than for other riders.[45] While each firm has undertaken steps to address this discrimination, with, for example, Airbnb hiring former Attorney General Eric Holder to conduct an internal investigation and to make recommendations to avoid discrimination in the future, these issues of national concern require a national response.[46]

Existing federal civil rights laws including Title II of the Civil Rights Act governing public accommodations,[47] the Fair Housing Act,[48] and the Americans with Disabilities Act,[49] among others, arguably apply to prohibit racial or other forms of discrimination by providers of service through the platforms – including Airbnb hosts and Uber/Lyft drivers – and potentially by the platforms themselves. However, as with many existing laws confronting business innovation, the fit is imperfect.[50] For example, Title II of the Civil Rights Act of 1964 prohibits discrimination on the basis of race, color, religion, or national origin in "public accommodations," which are defined as "any inn, hotel, motel, or other establishment which provides lodging to transient guests, other than an establishment located within a building which contains not more than five rooms for rent or hire and which is actually occupied by the provider of such establishment as his residence."[51] The general anti-discrimination provision would apply to many Airbnb listings, but a significant number may fit within the exemption. This "actually occupied" exemption was not designed with the aggregation of millions of rooms-for-hire in mind, aggregation that could have an impact on interstate commerce. Yet Airbnb is booking millions of "room-nights" annually, and could ultimately surpass traditional hotel chains on this metric.[52]

The Fair Housing Act likewise prohibits discrimination in the sale or rental of any "dwelling" on the basis of race, color, religion, sex, national origin, or family status.[53] However, the Fair Housing Act expressly exempts from its scope "any single-family house sold or rented by an owner" provided that the owner owns three or fewer houses.[54] And the Act likewise exempts "rooms or units in dwellings containing living quarters occupied or intended to be occupied by no more than four families … if the owner" actually occupies one of the living quarters as his or her residence.[55] Again, the Fair Housing Act prohibitions on discrimination may easily apply to some Airbnb listings, but some arguably fit within the exceptions, exceptions that were not drafted with the aggregation of millions of rentals in mind.

In addition, the Americans with Disabilities Act of 1990 (ADA) prohibits discrimination on the basis of disability in transportation, both by any "public accommodation," and by

---

[45] Yanbo Ge et al., *Racial and Gender Discrimination in Transportation Network Companies* 1–3, 12 (Nat'l Bureau of Econ. Research, Working Paper No. 22776, 2016), www.nber.org/papers/w22776.

[46] Abha Bhatarai, *Airbnb Hires Eric Holder to Help Company Fight Discrimination*, Wash. Post, June 16, 2016.

[47] 42 U.S.C. §2000a ("(a) All persons shall be entitled to the full and equal enjoyment of the goods, services, facilities, privileges, advantages, and accommodations of any place of public accommodation, as defined in this section, without discrimination on the ground of race, color, religion, or national origin.").

[48] 42 U.S.C. § 3601 et seq.

[49] 42 U.S.C. § 12101 et seq.

[50] Biber et al., *supra* note 8; Leong and Beltzer, *supra* note 7.

[51] 42 U.S.C. § 2000a(b) (2012).

[52] Clay Dillow, *Can Airbnb Book a Billion Nights a Year by 2025?* Fortune (Apr. 11, 2016), https://qz.com/329735/airbnb-will-soon-be-booking-more-rooms-than-the-worlds-largest-hotel-chains/.

[53] 42 U.S.C. § 3604. The Act defines "dwelling" as "any building, structure, or portion thereof which is occupied as, or designed or intended for occupancy as, a residence by one or more families." 42 U.S.C. § 3602(b). The Ninth Circuit held that "dwelling" does not include less than a full apartment or "sub-parts of a home or apartment." *Fair Housing Counc. v. Roommate.com*, LLC, 666 F.3d 1216, 1220 (9th Cir. 2012) ("There's no indication that Congress intended to interfere with personal relationships *inside* the home.") (emphasis in original).

[54] 42 U.S.C. § 3603(b) (2012).

[55] *Id.*

any private "transportation service provider," regardless of whether that provider qualifies as a public accommodation.[56] Indeed, in a recent litigation, the Department of Justice filed a statement of interest arguing that Uber has an obligation to provide reasonable accommodation for individuals with disabilities under the ADA, including an obligation to train drivers to permit blind individuals with service animals into their cars. They further argued that the ADA applies not only to "public accommodations" but also to private entities providing on-demand transportation services.[57]

The greatest legal complexities arise in determining whether these laws apply not only to the provider of the service (the host or the driver), but also to the platforms themselves.[58] In addition, there are express exemptions for certain kinds of Airbnb hosts – those who rent out space in their primary residence. To the extent that existing federal law does not currently or clearly apply to these platforms or to the services that they facilitate in the aggregate, the federal government should amend the laws, or adopt regulations to clarify that these concerns about discrimination in hospitality and transportation are federal concerns, requiring uniform laws.

B Consumer Protection

Second, the federal government has an important role to play in protecting both service providers and customers from information asymmetries between themselves and platforms. Strong consumer protection laws exist at the federal level because such concerns are arguably national in nature, and affect interstate commerce. They arise at the level of the platform because they do not necessarily vary at the local level.

Platforms collect a tremendous amount of information about consumer habits, preferences, and other data to enhance the services they provide. However, these platforms have also been known to exploit this informational advantage. A set of privacy-related concerns arose early on regarding the scope of information to which Uber had access, and the lack of controls about how that information was used or shared within the firm. For example, the press reported concerns about what Uber called "God view" – the ability to track the locations of all of its customers in ways that could reveal personal information to third parties, such as where customers had been dropped off on a Friday night.[59] Similar, more analog, concerns about such internal controls over access to information arose recently when a woman who contended that she was raped by an Uber driver in India sued Uber for sharing her personal medical information inappropriately within the firm.[60]

A recent article by Ryan Calo and Alex Rosenblat has catalogued a number of additional ways in which users of the Uber platform have reported concerns about fairness, and the manipulation or lack of transparency about information. Such concerns about the manipulation of information apply not only to riders, but also to drivers. With respect to riders, one concern is

---

[56] 42 U.S.C. § 12182(a) (2012) (prohibiting discrimination in public accommodations); 49 C.F.R. § 37.29 (2017) ("Providers of taxi service are subject to the requirements" of the ADA's transportation provisions); 42 U.S.C. § 12184 (prohibiting discrimination by transportation service providers regardless of whether they are public accommodations); Leong and Beltzer, *supra* note 7.

[57] Statement of Interest of the United States, National No. 3:14-cv-04086-NC (N.D. Cal.) (filed Dec. 23, 2014), www.ada .gov/briefs/uber_soi.pdf.

[58] Leong and Beltzer, *supra* note 7.

[59] Kashmir Hill, *"God View": Uber Allegedly Stalked Users for Party-Goers' Viewing Pleasure (Updated)*, Forbes.com (Oct. 3, 2014).

[60] Douglas MacMillan, *Rape Victim Sues Uber over Handling of Medical Records*, Wall St. J., June 15, 2017.

that "phantom cars" appear when a rider logs into the app seeking a ride.[61] The initial screen appears to show a number of vehicles in the area; however, when the rider books a ride, these multiple phantom vehicles disappear, and the actual driver – who may be farther away – appears on the app instead.[62] With respect to drivers, Calo and Rosenblat catalogue a slew of informational asymmetries that work to the detriment of drivers and the advantage of the platform. For example, Uber drivers are determined to have canceled a ride if they wait for a rider for fewer than five minutes; if they wait for five minutes or longer they are not considered to have canceled a ride. Too many cancellations (among other issues), can lead drivers to be disciplined.[63] Of course, information is crucial. While the Lyft app includes a clock that drivers can observe to determine when the requisite five minutes of wait time has elapsed, until mid-2017, the Uber app lacked access to this shared information.[64] As a result, drivers contended that they were marked as having canceled a ride when they objected that they waited the full time.[65] Yet only Uber possessed the information about what is ostensibly an objective fact – time elapsed.[66] A second example of manipulation of information is the issue of "phantom or fleeting ride requests" that flash on a driver's screen for a short period of time.[67] Uber drivers must accept a certain percentage of ride requests to receive a guaranteed hourly rate. Drivers have complained that some ride requests flash on their screen for such a brief period of time that it would be impossible to accept them; yet Uber counts such "fleeting ride requests" against drivers nonetheless.[68] Others contend that Uber's calculation of the percentage of rides accepted under-counts that percentage.[69] As with the elusive five-minute clock, however, drivers are at the mercy of Uber when it comes to information about how many rides they could have accepted, as drivers cannot track this fleeting information.[70] As Calo and Rosenblat point out, it would be a violation of the driver's services agreement to attempt to reverse-engineer the app to collect such information to defend the driver's understanding of the facts.[71]

These concerns about whether Uber is exploiting (or could exploit) informational asymmetries raise important issues of consumer protection within the jurisdiction of the Federal Trade Commission (FTC).[72] The FTC enforces Section 5(a) of the FTC Act, which prohibits unfair or deceptive acts or practices that affect commerce.[73] Such issues of deception relating to the practices described above are potentially platform-wide, rather than unique to local communities, and thus federal action and enforcement is appropriate. Indeed, in June 2015, the FTC convened a workshop on the sharing economy entitled *The "Sharing" Economy: Issues Facing Platforms, Participants, and Regulators*, and in November 2016, released its report on next steps and moving forward.[74] And in January 2017, the FTC simultaneously filed a complaint and

---

[61] Calo and Rosenblat, *supra* note 16.

[62] *Id.*

[63] *Id.*

[64] *Id.*

[65] *Id.*

[66] *Id.*

[67] *Id.*

[68] *Id.*

[69] *Id.*

[70] *Id.*

[71] *Id.*

[72] *Id.*

[73] 15 U.S.C. § 45(a) (2012).

[74] FTC, *The "Sharing" Economy: Issues Facing Platforms, Participants & Regulators* 7 (Nov. 2016), www.ftc.gov/reports/sharing-economy-issues-facing-platforms-participants-regulators-federal-trade-commission.

proposed settlement against Uber, contending that the firm had engaged in deceptive and unfair practices, including disseminating advertisements that overstated the income that Uber drivers could earn; and understating the costs and overstating the ease with which drivers could buy or lease a vehicle that they could use to drive for Uber through its "Vehicle Solutions Program."[75] Uber agreed to resolve the action for a monetary penalty of $20 million, and consented to an order restraining the firm from making misrepresentations about the potential income a driver might earn, terms and conditions of financing of vehicles by third parties, and the terms and conditions of any Vehicle Program.[76] Robust federal enforcement of consumer protection law is required because these are issues of national scope and importance; they are not limited to local jurisdictions.

C Coordination and Diffusion of Information

Finally, there is a third role for the federal government to play that transcends any substantive area of legal protection. While many scholars advocate state and local experimentation, and contend that a significant benefit of such experimentation is that "good" policies will spread to other jurisdictions, some skeptics have pointed out that there can be obstacles to such policy diffusion. For example, Hannah Wiseman has offered many examples from the environment and energy law sectors in which regulatory experimentation is difficult to catalogue, is not centrally collected, and in which different policymakers lack access to information about both other jurisdictions' policies and the success or failures of those policies.[77] In more general terms, regulatory experimentation is less valuable if state or local jurisdictions operate as "regulatory islands," isolated or disconnected from other jurisdictions such that they do not communicate their policy learning beyond their borders.[78] Michael Dorf and Charles Sabel have likewise called for the federal government to play a coordinating role in the face of state or local experimentation.[79] Thus, while they advocate the decentralization of power to state and local governments in a form of governance that they call "democratic experimentalism," they argue that the federal government can play a coordinating role to ensure the sharing of knowledge to promote benchmarking and diffusion of regulatory successes.[80]

To the extent that local governments are likely to experiment in how they regulate and interact with these platforms, the federal government can facilitate the diffusion of policies with a positive impact by providing a centralized place to gather and disseminate information about the successes and failures of local policy experimentation.

---

[75] *FTC v. Uber Technologies, Inc.*, No. 17 Civ. 0261 (N.D. Cal.), Cmplt., filed Jan. 19, 2017, ¶¶ 10–12; *FTC v. Uber Technologies, Inc.*, No. 17 Civ. 0261 (N.D. Cal.), Stipulated Order for Permanent Injunction & Monetary Judgment, filed Jan. 19, 2017.

[76] Stipulated Order, *supra* note 75. At the same time, it is worth noting that the FTC has not adopted the view that its federal jurisdiction is all-encompassing. It still recognizes a role for state and local governments. Its November 2016 Report notes that the FTC has articulated "broadly applicable principles for balancing competition policy and regulatory goals" through advocacy and comment letters to city and state governments about laws governing the collection of taxes, the preservation of neighborhoods, and provision of services to people with disabilities. FTC, *supra* note 74, at 8–9.

[77] Wiseman, *supra* note 17.

[78] *Id.*

[79] Dorf and Sabel, *supra* note 17, at 314.

[80] *Id.*

CONCLUSION

The platform economy is challenging existing legal rules at the local, state, and federal levels. In some cases, local jurisdiction over the platforms makes sense, to promote experimentation, and when the impacts are most likely to be felt at the local level. Yet there are important inter-state concerns, including to prevent discrimination and to protect platform users – both service providers and customers – for which federal governance is required. Additionally, even in the face of state or local experimentation, the federal government can play a coordinating role to ensure that policy diffusion takes place.

17

Role of State Governments in the Sharing Economy

Janice C. Griffith

INTRODUCTION

The sharing economy's complexity challenges governing bodies to regulate it in a way that does not stifle innovation, but at the same time protects the public from its potential harms. The decentralized nature of the sharing economy and the magnitude of its transactions compound the difficulty of finding answers to these provocative questions: Who should regulate it? How should it be regulated, if at all? This chapter explores the role that state governments in the United States should play to protect the public from adverse externalities that may result from sharing economy activities. Because the sharing economy affects both statewide and local interests,[1] this chapter presents guidelines for the delineation of the governance level best suited to regulate a particular sharing economy transaction.

No universal agreement has been reached as to how the sharing economy should best be defined, but consensus has formed around the concept that the sharing economy involves a digital platform that facilitates transactions between buyers and sellers of goods or services.[2] The United States Department of Commerce has defined the sharing economy as transactions between consumers and independent service providers that are "facilitated by an Internet-based platform."[3] Use of the internet, which became mainstream in the mid-to-late 1990s, enables quick and easy peer-to-peer interaction to expedite the sharing or sale of underutilized resources for which a market exists.[4] The internet has dramatically lowered transaction costs of mediated sharing by enabling the formation of a critical mass of goods and services that can be validated

---

[1]   The federal government generally has not been involved in regulating the sharing economy. *See infra* notes 31–32.

[2]   *See* Jared Meyer, *Uber-Positive: Why Americans Love the Sharing Economy* 1 (2016). The sharing economy has also been defined as "the peer-to-peer based activity of obtaining, giving, or sharing the access to goods and services, coordinated through community-based online services" (quoting Hamari, Sjöklint, and Ukkonen, "The Sharing Economy"). Niam Yaraghi and Shamika Ravi, *The Current and Future State of the Sharing Economy*, Brookings Inst. (Dec. 29, 2016), www.brookings.edu/research/the-current-and-future-state-of-the-sharing-economy/.

[3]   Rudy Telles Jr., U.S. Dept. of Commerce, *Digital Matching Firms: A New Definition in the "Sharing Economy" Space* 1 (June 3, 2016), www.esa.gov/sites/default/files/digital-matching-firms-new-definition-sharing-economy-space .pdf. Digital matching firms exhibit the following characteristics: (1) "use information technology … to facilitate peer-to-peer transactions"; (2) "rely upon user-based rating systems for quality control"; (3) grant workers flexibility in choosing their typical working hours; and (4) rely on workers to provide their own tools and assets to the extent necessary to provide a service. *Id.*

[4]   *See* Meaghan Murphy, *Cities as the Original Sharing Platform: Regulation of the New "Sharing" Economy*, 12 J. Bus. & Tech. Law 127, 128–29 (2016).

through "online reputation."[5] Technology-based platforms, such as Uber, Lyft, and Airbnb, now act as intermediary brokers who facilitate peer-to-peer transactions that match a consumer with a provider. Such digital service providers can also create payment and tax collection systems for such transactions, and they can offer marketing advice and other types of expertise.

The sharing economy has emerged in a number of different sectors. Jeremiah Owyang's Collaborative Economy Honeycomb model depicts 16 subject areas in which sharing economy transactions are occurring.[6] The Honeycomb includes several categories in which the public sector has either recently or traditionally intersected with sharing-economy-type activities, including various bike-sharing venues. The transaction types that have resulted in the most frequent clashes with state and local regulatory bodies, however, fall under the Honeycomb's "mobility services" and "space" categories. State governments are now regulating ride-sharing services, such as Uber and Lyft, which can be classified as "mobility services." Short-term rentals, including the rental of personal space in residential neighborhoods, have also generated public concern as commercial-type uses that may conflict with zoning ordinances and adversely impact surrounding properties.

The underlying business models utilized in the Honeycomb's 16 sectors have also been identified and described. Three different platform types are used frequently in the sharing economy: peer-to-peer, business-to-business, and business-to-consumer.[7] An analysis of business startups representative of the Honeycomb model resulted in the identification of five key dimensions characteristic of sharing-economy business models in addition to the type of platform used.[8] The first category, "technology," characterizes the extent to which technology is used by sharing economy participants.[9] Observations of the next category, transaction type, showed that transactions can be conducted on a market basis with price setting, as exchanges with remuneration other than cash, or free of charge.[10] In the "business approach" category, a sharing economy startup may be classified as profit driven, mission driven, or as a hybrid that is both profit and mission driven.[11] Sharing startups use resources in different ways, causing the creation of another grouping for "shared resources." They can optimize new resources, help locate a new home for resources already in use, or deploy underutilized, existing resources.[12] The fifth category, "governance model," finds a range of governance models among sharing startups from "traditional corporate structures to collaborative governance models to cooperative models."[13]

An initial question arises as to which level of governance should regulate the sharing economy. Today, a case could be made for setting the terms and conditions of this economy on the global stage because large-scale, sharing-economy platforms, such as Uber and Airbnb, operate in numerous countries. If favorable terms could be realized, these platforms most likely would prefer the uniformity in treatment that could be realized on a global scale. In a world of nation

---

[5] *See* Duncan McLaren and Julian Agyeman, *Sharing Cities* 56 (2015).

[6] Jeremiah Owyang, *Collaborative Economy Honeycomb Version 3.0*, Web-Strategist: Infographic (Mar. 10, 2016), www.web-strategist.com/blog/2016/03/10/honeycomb-3-0-the-collaborative-economy-market-expansion-sxsw/. The 16 startup areas are as follows: worker support, learning, wellness and beauty, municipal, money, goods, health, space, food, utilities, mobility services, services, logistics, vehicle sharing, corporations and organizations, and analytics and reputation. *Id.*

[7] *See* McLaren and Agyeman, *supra* note 5, at 15.

[8] Boyd Cohen, *Making Sense of the Many Business Models in the Sharing Economy*, Fast Company (Apr. 6, 2016), www.fastcompany.com/3058203/making-sense-of-the-many-business-models-in-the-sharing-economy.

[9] *Id.* The technology used can be either "tech-driven, tech-enabled, and low/no-tech." *Id.*

[10] *Id.*

[11] *Id.*

[12] *Id.*

[13] *Id.*

states, albeit a global economy, national or federal governments presently have jurisdiction over how the sharing economy can operate in their country.[14] Because the sharing economy involves transactions that affect both localities and larger regions, regulatory restrictions in the United States have been imposed on them by both municipalities and the states. This chapter explores the state regulation of the sharing economy.

State legislatures in the United States have taken an active role in formulating regulatory approaches to the sharing economy, especially in transactions relating to ride-sharing and the sharing of space on a short-term rental basis.[15] Section I of this chapter discusses the reasons why certain sectors of the sharing economy should be publicly regulated. Section II then analyzes the states' interest in regulating the sharing economy, but it also identifies local regulatory concerns. Section III presents guidelines, based in part on existing common law preemption doctrines, to determine those sharing economy transactions best left to state, as opposed to local, control. Section IV then analyzes the states' interests in the regulation of ride-sharing and short-term rentals and applies the proposed guidelines to these sharing economy activities. Section V proposes a methodology for the states' regulation of the sharing economy, discussing preferable strategic steps the states should take. Section VI argues that intrastate co-regulatory frameworks should evolve to regulate the sharing economy.

I NECESSITY TO REGULATE THE SHARING ECONOMY

The main justification for governmental regulation has simply been stated to be consumer protection.[16] Legislation may also be enacted to impose regulations designed to: (1) protect a marketplace; (2) enforce established professional standards; (3) safeguard community space and ecosystems; (4) protect scarce resources; (5) protect workers and contractors in a particular industry; (6) ensure equitable access to public accommodations; (7) generate revenue by imposing taxes on certain industries; and (8) require consumers to purchase certain goods or services such as insurance.[17] Marketplace regulations generally aim to ensure the availability of goods and services or to restrict supply to enhance a secure livelihood for certain entrepreneurs.[18] For example, the number of taxi permits may be limited to make the taxicab industry more robust and profitable.[19]

The European Commission has stated that regulatory intervention of the sharing economy is warranted for varying public interest objectives, which include protection of tourists, prevention of tax evasion, maintenance of a level playing field, protection of public safety and health and food safety, and the assurance of adequate affordable housing.[20] According to the Commission, access

---

[14] In France, for example, the national legislature has enacted a law allowing owners to enter into short-term rentals for up to four months. Loi 2014–366 du 24 mars 2014 pour l'accés au logement et un urbanisme rénové [Act 2014–366 of 24 March 2014 for Access to Housing and Renovation planning]. Journal Officiel De La Republique Française [J.O.] [Official Gazette of France]]. Mar. 26, 2014, p. 5809.

[15] *See, e.g., Short-term Home and Room Rentals for Overnight Accommodations,* Dep't. of Revenue, Wash. State, http://dor.wa.gov/Content/DoingBusiness/BusinessTypes/Industry/PersonalHomeRentals/default.aspx (referring to Wash. Rev. Code § 458-2-166); Airbnb, Inc., *In What Areas is Occupancy Tax Collection and Remittance by Airbnb Available?* www.airbnb.com/help/article/653/in-what-areas-is-occupancy-tax-collection-and-remittance-by-airbnb-available?topic=264 (listing states in which Airbnb collects and remits taxes on behalf of hosts).

[16] *See* Meyer, *supra* note 2, at 15.

[17] *See* Janelle Orsi, *Practicing Law in the Sharing Economy: Helping People Build Cooperatives, Social Enterprise, and Local Sustainable Economies* 417–19 (2012).

[18] *See id.* at 417.

[19] *See id.*

[20] European Econ. & Social Comm. & Comm. of Regions, European Comm'n, A *European Agenda for the Collaborative Economy,* 3 (June 2, 2016), www.eesc.europa.eu/resources/docs/com2016-356-final.pdf.

to markets and quality or safety safeguards must be addressed as the collaborative economy grows.[21] Even proponents of allocating responsibility to third-party platforms to self-regulate the sharing economy concede that these platforms may not always perfectly align with the public interest.[22]

Regulations generally emerge in response to public demand triggered by market failures that have led to inefficient or inequitable outcomes.[23] In the sharing economy, three common forms of market failure have been identified, namely, information asymmetry, externalities, and unprofessional providers.[24] Ride-sharing services and short-term rentals facilitated through a third-party platform are prone to these market failures. With respect to the lack of information symmetry, an Uber driver knows far more about his driving capabilities and the condition of his car than does a prospective passenger. Likewise, an Airbnb host possesses information about the cleanliness of the accommodations offered whereas a prospective guest is left to previous peer ratings for such information.

Externalities arising from sharing economy mobility services and space sharing are not difficult to ascertain. Ride-sharing leads to a greater use of automobiles in highly congested urban areas. New York City app-based ride services averaged 15 million passengers per month in fall 2016, tripling their level of service in spring 2015.[25] App-enabled short-term rentals also may produce externalities. When residents rent out their accommodations to persons contacted through web-based platforms, they introduce non-residents into the community whose behavior may not conform to established neighborhood norms. Housing that otherwise would be available for long-term rental can be taken off the market if the rate of return is greater on a short-term rental basis. Residents who rent out their homes or vacation homes most likely cannot offer their guests the type of safety and fire protection that licensed hotels provide.

The states must respond to other potential adverse externalities associated with the sharing economy. Transactions may go tax free in the sharing economy while subject to taxation otherwise. Sharing economy providers may also engage in discriminatory conduct, selectively choosing those consumers with whom they wish to engage. While the sharing economy is lauded for turning underutilized assets into fuller use, this increased utilization may cause greater harm to ecosystems than would occur with scarcer resource use.

States and local governments have also been invested heavily in the protection of laborers in the workplace. The online marketplace due to its "transparency and comparative bargaining flexibility" may justify less stringent labor regulations, but in areas involving services performed by children or minors caution is warranted.[26] Uber riders generally have been classified as independent contractors not subject to laws protecting workers.[27] Airbnb hosts, as independent

---

[21] *See id.* at 4. The European Commission, however, has not promulgated any regulations with respect to the sharing economy. *See Guidance and Policy Recommendations for the Collaborative Economy*, European Comm'n, http://ec.europa.eu/growth/single-market/services/collaborative-economy_en.

[22] Molly Cohen and Arun Sundararajan, *Self-Regulation and Innovation in the Peer-to-Peer Sharing Economy*, 82 U. Chi. L. Rev. Dialogue 116, 116–17 (2015).

[23] *See id.* at 120.

[24] *Id.* at 120–24.

[25] *Unsustainable? The Growth of App-Based Services and Traffic, Travel and the Future of New York City*, Schaller Consulting 9, Feb. 27, 2017.

[26] *See* Bryant Cannon and Hanna Chung, *A Framework for Designing Co-Regulation Models Well-Adapted to Technology-Facilitated Sharing Economy*, 31 Santa Clara High Tech. L.J. 23, 37–38 (2015).

[27] *See McGillis v. Dep't of Econ. Opportunity*, 210 So. 3d 220, 225–227 (Fla. Dist. Ct. App. 2017) (finding Uber driver not to be an employee entitled to reemployment insurance), *but see* Amie Tsang, *Uber Is Dealt a Fresh Blow in European Legal Case*, N.Y. Times (July 4, 2017), www.nytimes.com/2017/07/04/business/uber-ecj-europe-france.html (reporting on a non-binding opinion of an advocate general for the European Union's Court of Justice that Uber operations should be regulated as a taxi service in France).

providers of short-term accommodations, would also not fall within the protection of labor laws. An area perhaps more fertile for regulation would be the unequal bargaining position between the technology platform provider, such as Uber and Airbnb, and the providers or persons they match with consumers.

The sharing economy can eliminate barriers to market access in some instances. It can enable persons who might not meet licensure or other regulatory requirements to sell or share their services and assets through online transactions outside of a regulatory regime. Ensuring the quality one expects from professionals can be challenging in a sharing economy environment in which less qualified persons provide services and goods. Younger people find ride-sharing driving attractive because the cost of becoming a taxicab driver can be prohibitively expensive due to medallion and licensing requirements.[28] Ride-sharing presents a low-cost way for persons with motor vehicles to earn money.[29] Drivers who partner with Uber, in contrast to taxi drivers, typically are younger, lack previous experience as professional drivers, and work only part-time, with 50 percent working less than ten hours a week.[30] Guests in Airbnb-facilitated accommodations take risks that hotel safety and kitchen inspections can avoid.

II SHARING ECONOMY REGULATORS IN THE UNITED STATES

To date, in the United States, the states and the local governments created by them primarily regulate the sharing economy as this economy's many varied activities clearly fall within the states' constitutional realm. Because the sharing economy's primary thrust is to improve access to goods and services across the broad economy rather than within a specific industry, "blanket legislation at the federal level will almost certainly be incongruous."[31] It has been argued, however, that to the extent that the sharing economy results in the creation of monopoly platform ownership, with attendant price distortion, regulation on a national or international level is appropriate.[32] Thus, one needs to distinguish between regulations of individual service providers, such as Uber drivers, now done on a state level, from regulation of the platform itself. Irrespective of which level of government becomes the regulator, the danger exists that the industries regulated will capture the regulator and obtain favorable terms for themselves.[33]

A Constitutional Basis for State Regulation of the Sharing Economy

In the United States, the states enjoy the residuary powers not granted to the federal government. The Tenth Amendment to the United States Constitution makes clear that "powers not delegated to the United States by the Constitution … are reserved to the States respectively, or to the people."[34] In other nations, power may be shared among a national government,

---

[28] *See* Meyer, *supra* note 2, at 24–25.

[29] *See id.* at 25.

[30] *See id.* at 22–25.

[31] Cannon and Chung, *supra* note 26, at 71.

[32] *See* E. Glen Weyl and Alexander White, *Let the Best 'One' Win: Policy Lessons from the New Economics of Platforms* 22–23 (Coase-Sandor Inst. for Law and Econ., Working Paper No. 709 (2d Series), Dec. 2014), http://chicagounbound. uchicago.edu/cgi/viewcontent.cgi?article=2388&context=law_and_economics (arguing that local governments that regulate taxis should not regulate Uber because they facilitate alternative platforms in competition with Uber).

[33] *See* Eric Posner, *Why Uber Will – and Should – Be Regulated*, Slate (Jan. 5, 2015), www.slate.com/articles/news_and_ politics/view_from_chicago/2015/01/uber_surge_pricing_federal_regulation_over_taxis_and_car_ride_services.html.

[34] U.S. Const. amend. X.

regional or provincial governments, and local governments. "State" in such context might mean either the national government or a sub-territorial government with power to oversee local governments.[35]

Although the federal United States Constitution does not explicitly spell out states' powers, the United States Supreme Court recognized the so-called "police powers" of the states as early as 1829.[36] Because the United States Constitution does not prescribe any role for local governments, making no textual mention of them, the states enjoy complete discretion as to the powers they wish to delegate to any sub-territorial units.[37] Nonetheless, most state constitutions have been amended to provide for some form of protected local home rule, whether of the *imperio* or legislative type.[38]

B *Delegation of Police Powers to Local Governments*

In states granting home rule powers based on the "defined" or *imperio* model, municipalities may exercise power related to their municipal affairs, government, or property without state legislative interference.[39] Because state courts narrowly interpreted so-called "local or municipal" affairs, a number of jurisdictions adopted legislative, also known as "total unless limited," home rule.[40] This form of home rule permits a municipality to exercise power and perform functions unless the state constitution, state statutes, or the municipality's home rule charter deny same.[41] Thus, through their constitutional home rule powers or authorization from a state enabling statutes, local governments exercise powers to protect the health, safety, and welfare of their inhabitants, the so-called police powers.

In the United States, regulatory oversight often resides at the state level of government due in part to the nonexistence of regional governance and municipal fragmentation, owing to the small territorial reach of a multitude of municipalities within many metropolitan areas.[42] The relationship between states and their local governments has been structured largely on a vertical, hierarchical basis, whereas the sharing economy presents opportunities for decentralized economic transactions and development.[43] The cry for local regulation of the sharing economy has bubbled up because many of the negative externalities that can be produced by the sharing economy affect localities, including the nation's major metropolitan centers.[44]

---

[35] *See, e.g.,* S. Afr. Const., 1996, ch. 3, § 40 (1) ("In the Republic, government is constituted as national, provincial and local spheres of government which are distinctive, interdependent and interrelated.").

[36] *See Willson v. Black Bird Creek Marsh Co.,* 27 U.S. 245, 251 (1829) (ruling that measures that improve "the health of the inhabitants" undoubtedly fall within the powers reserved to the states, *id.* at 251).

[37] *See Hunter v. City of Pittsburgh,* 207 U.S. 161, 178 (1907) (opining that municipal corporations are political subdivisions of the states and that the number, duration, and nature of powers granted to them rest in the sole discretion of the states).

[38] *See generally* Daniel R. Mandelker, Judith Welch Wegner, Janice C. Griffith, Kenneth Bond, and Christopher J. Tyson, *State and Local Government in a Federal System* 89–94, 112–14 (8th ed., 2014) (describing the history and form of home rule in the United States).

[39] *Id.* at 89–90.

[40] *Id.* at 90.

[41] *Id.* at 112–13.

[42] *See* Janice C. Griffith, *Regional Governance Reconsidered,* 21 J.L. & Pol. 505, 520–21 (2005).

[43] *See* Stephen R. Miller, *Decentralized, Disruptive, and On Demand: Opportunities for Local Government in the Sharing Economy,* 77 Ohio St. L.J. 47, 49 (2016) (arguing that the sharing economy cannot be contained within local boundary lines, *id.* at 55).

[44] *See* Nestor M. Davidson and John J. Infranca, *The Sharing Economy as an Urban Phenomenon,* 34 Yale L. & Pol'y Rev. 215, 238–41 (2016) (arguing that the sharing economy should be regulated at the municipal level of governance because it generates highly localized externalities).

III GUIDELINES TO DETERMINE WHETHER THE STATES OR LOCAL GOVERNMENTS SHOULD REGULATE THE SHARING ECONOMY

A *Delineation of State Interests from Common Law Preemption Doctrines*

In determining whether the state or localities can best regulate the sharing economy, it is helpful to examine the common law implied preemption doctrines that determine whether the exercise of local power should be preempted because the state has implied that the area should be reserved for state control. In the absence of clear statutory language that expressly preempts local functions, courts frequently adjudicate claims that the state legislature has impliedly preempted a particular area for its control. The principles the judiciary has established for drawing the line between what is essentially a state matter as opposed to a local one prove useful in a similar inquiry as to what level of governance is best equipped to regulate the sharing economy.

In *imperio* jurisdictions, the state is barred from preempting matters relating to local governance or of local concern.[45] Because many public functions stem from concerns that are broader than the territorial domain of one municipality, matters of mixed state and local concern or of primary state concern greatly outnumber those of a purely local character. For example, historically one would view public security as a local concern, but with the rise of worldwide terrorism, local police departments today cooperate with both federal and state offices to increase homeland security. Thus, in *imperio* jurisdictions, state preemption may occur if the exercise of local power involves some state interests and conflicts with the thrust of a state statute or regulation.

In total unless limited home rule jurisdictions, a municipality may exercise power so long as its charter, the state constitution, or a state statute, do not prohibit same. Thus, these municipalities enjoy no protection from state preemption, but may govern until the state denies them the power to do so. The analysis here turns on whether such denial is manifested by constitutional or statutory language. Thus preemption analysis in both *imperio* and total unless limited jurisdictions may involve a resolution of whether a local activity conflicts with the state constitution, a state statute, or the municipality's charter.[46]

Irrespective of the preemption implied from conflicting state statutes and local ordinances, another type of preemption may occur as well. If a state statute comprehensively regulates a certain sector, the state may be said to occupy the field leaving no room for local regulation. In an *imperio* jurisdiction, however, purely local functions would be protected from preemption, but in any matter involving some state concerns, preemption could occur. State statutes that regulate activities potentially causing harm to the environment, for example, have been held by courts to preempt local environmental measures because the comprehensive nature of such state regulations evidences an intent to occupy the field.[47]

State courts have grappled with making clear pronouncements of when a local ordinance will be found to conflict with a state statute or regulation. One rule, the permit/prohibit rule, provides that a local enactment will be preempted if it permits what the state prohibits, or prohibits

---

[45] *See City and County of Denver v. State*, 788 P.2d 764, 767 (Colo. 1990) (ruling that, pursuant to the Colorado Constitution (based on the *imperio* model), an ordinance or charter provision relating to local matters supersedes conflicting state statutory provisions).

[46] *See Cape Motor Lodge, Inc. v. City of Cape Girardeau*, 706 S.W.2d 208, 211 (Mo. 1986) (upholding a city ordinance authorizing a cooperative city agreement with a state university because the exercise of city power did not conflict with the state constitution, state statutes, or the city charter).

[47] *See, e.g., Bd. of Supervisors v. ValAdCo*, 504 N.W.2d 267, 269 (Minn. App. 1993) (finding that the nature of the subject matter and a comprehensive state statutory scheme demonstrated a state legislative intent to preempt local enactments covering such subject matter).

what the state permits.[48] In situations, however, where a local ordinance merely supplements or more strictly regulates a matter also regulated at the state level, the permit/prohibit rule may be held not to apply even though the local enactment technically may prohibit what the state law permits.[49] On the other hand, a local ordinance that sanctions activity falling below minimum standards established by a state statute will generally be preempted as in conflict with it.[50] The permit/prohibit rule, a rather mechanical rule, has been criticized as unworkable.[51]

In lieu of reliance upon rules that could produce arbitrary results, courts frequently balance local and state interests in determining whether local activity should be cast aside by implied state preemption. In determining sharing economy jurisdictional disputes, a similar approach can be expected. In *City and County of Denver v. State*,[52] a well thought-out decision upholding a City of Denver local residency requirement for employment, the court categorized regulatory concerns as (1) matters of local concern; (2) matters of statewide concern; and (3) matters of mixed state and local concerns.[53] The court ruled that with respect to matters falling within the latter category, a charter or ordinance provision could coexist with a state statute so long as no conflict resulted.[54] When a conflict does occur in these matters of mixed state and local concerns, the state interests prevail.[55]

The *City of Denver* court admitted that it had found no particular test to determine what subject matters are local, state, or combined local and state interests.[56] Rather these types of judgment have been made on an ad hoc basis taking into consideration the relative interests of the home rule municipality and the state in regulating the contested matter at issue.[57] The court set forth several factors it considered relevant in determining whether a state interest was sufficient to justify preemption of home rule enactments, namely (1) the need for state uniformity; (2) the extraterritorial impact, if any, of the local regulation on non-residents; (3) the importance of state interests; and (4) the significance of local interests.[58] These guidelines have been recognized by other courts as well to determine whether a particular matter can best be handled by the state or conversely by a local government.[59]

Further, courts will weigh whether local regulation could result in harm to the general population due to the nature of the subject matter at issue.[60] In the *City of Denver* case, the court

---

[48] *See generally* Mandelker et al., *supra* note 38, at 128–30 (discussing state court decisions in which the prohibit/permit rule has been used).

[49] *See Miller v. Fabius Twp. Bd.*, 114 N.W.2d 205, 208–09 (Mich. 1962) (holding that a local ordinance that more narrowly restricted the permitted hours of watercraft operation activities than a state statute merely supplemented the state statute and did not conflict with it).

[50] *See, e.g., Steinberg v. Frawley*, 633 F. Supp. 548, 557 (D. Del. 1986) (holding that a state statute preempted a municipal ordinance in so far as the ordinance set lesser distance requirements for the location of adult entertainment establishments); *Overlook Terrace Mgmt. Corp. v. Rent Control Bd.*, 71 N.J. 451, 463–68 (N.J. 1976) (holding state law preempted municipal ordinance setting rents below limits set by state agency).

[51] *See* Paul Diller, *Intrastate Preemption*, 87 B.U. L. Rev. 1113, 1142–53 (2007).

[52] 788 P.2d 764 (Colo. 1990).

[53] *Id.* at 767.

[54] *Id.*

[55] *Id.*

[56] 788 P.2d at 767–68.

[57] *Id.*

[58] *Id.*

[59] *See, e.g., Beard v. Town of Salisbury*, 392 N.E.2d 832, 837 (Mass. 1979) (ruling that Town lacked power to prohibit transport of earth dug within it to points outside the Town); *In Re Pub. Serv. Elec. & Gas Co.*, 173 A.2d 233, 239 (N.J. 1961) (invalidating local requirement for underground utility lines due to need for uniformity); *City of Lorain v. Tomasic*, 391 N.E.2d 726, 728 (Ohio 1979) (invalidating ordinance that reduced state-established permissible payments of prize money because same destroyed uniformity of state statutory scheme).

[60] *See Bd. of Supervisors v. ValAdCo*, 504 N.W.2d 267, 269 (Minn. Ct. App. 1993).

thought it relevant to determine whether state action was imperative to afford protection both within and outside of the municipality.[61] For example, a municipality may ban the construction of a power plant within its confines, thereby imposing a burden upon other municipalities to meet the state's energy needs. Courts have not hesitated to invalidate local regulations that disrupt the marketplace or inequitably burden market participants, frequently finding the implied preemption of local laws that harm a segment of the business community.[62] Local rent control regulations that limit the price at which dwelling units can be rented have been struck down in several jurisdictions.[63] Some courts have also found historical considerations to be relevant in determining the outcome of a preemption issue, giving preference to the jurisdiction that has historically regulated the subject at issue.[64]

The states retain other interests in regulating the sharing economy in addition to the aforementioned concerns. Local control can lead to parochialism or exclusionary measures.[65] A local ban on certain sharing economy activities may illustrate such isolation or segregation. States also have an interest in preventing a race to the bottom in which localities lower conditions or standards in order to capture more market participants.[66] Further, states may have a clear interest in occupying a field subject to regulation due to the field's importance to the state or the perceived harm from multiple, uncoordinated regulations of it.

B Guidelines to Differentiate Between State and Local Control of the Sharing Economy

This chapter argues that the common law preemption doctrine rules discussed above provide good guiding principles as to which sharing economy transactions should be regulated by the state, as opposed to local governments. First, the weight of state and local interests should be evaluated. Should a state's interests predominate, the sharing economy matter should be regulated by the state. State hegemony will be particularly strong should local control of the sharing economy operatives (1) cause disorder due to a need for regulatory uniformity; (2) result in adverse extraterritorial impacts on other communities; (3) harm the general population or statewide interests; or (4) disrupt market integrity or efficiency. The existence of such conditions most likely will merit state regulation of a sharing economy segment.

Some difficulty may be encountered in weighing whether the local or state government occupies the best position to regulate a sharing economy sector owing to its interests in the particular field. Balancing tests have been criticized for producing uncertain results.[67] Nonetheless, a growing number of states employ a balancing test to resolve intergovernmental conflicts.[68] Given the states' dominance over local governments in the United States, the balancing of interests in situations where both strong state and local interests exist would tend to favor the state. These closely contested cases, however, could prompt the state to take an approach of joint

---

[61] *See City and County of Denver v. State*, 788 P.2d 764, 768 (Colo. 1990).

[62] *See* Diller, *supra* note 51, at 1115.

[63] *See, e.g., Old Colony Gardens, Inc.* v. *City of Stamford*, 156 A.2d 515, 516 (Conn. 1959) (holding that a general grant of police powers included in the City of Stamford's charter did not empower the City to impose rent controls); *City of Miami Beach* v. *Fleetwood Hotel, Inc.*, 261 So. 2d 801, 804 (Fla. 1972) (finding the city lacked power to enact a rent control ordinance without specific state authorization).

[64] *See City and County of Denver v. State*, 788 P.2d 764, 768 (Colo. 1990).

[65] *See* Diller, *supra* note 51, at 1132.

[66] *See id.*

[67] *See generally* Laurie Reynolds, *The Judicial Role in Intergovernmental Land Use Disputes: The Case Against Balancing*, 71 Minn. L. Rev. 611 (1987).

[68] *See* Mandelker et al., *supra* note 38, at 189.

regulation in which local interests could be protected at the local level of governance. Because the sharing economy thrives in the presence of urban density, large cities have especially strong stakeholder interests in its regulation.[69] In New York, for example, municipalities and counties with a population over 100,000 have been granted the authority to prohibit pick-ups by transportation network companies such as Uber and Lyft.[70]

IV APPLICATION OF GUIDELINES TO THE STATE'S ROLE IN REGULATING RIDE-SHARING AND SHORT-TERM RENTALS

A *State Interests in the Regulation of Ride-Sharing*

The states' interests outweigh local interests in the regulation of ride-sharing services. Transport connectivity and safety remain crucial to the states' well-being. Thus, the states have opted to license motor vehicle drivers and impose vehicle safety requirements on a statewide basis.[71] Although the taxicab industry has been regulated by municipalities, the need for uniformity in the intrastate operation of transportation systems has long been recognized. If each municipality within a metropolitan area imposed its own regulations on the use of public spaces essential for mobility, chaos would ensue. The states also have an interest in ensuring the viability of mobility services. A local ban on ride-sharing services could disrupt the ride-sharing marketplace, and it could cause unemployment, leading to a strain on social services funded by taxpayers throughout a state.[72]

Existing taxicab regulations result in inefficiencies due to the fact that drivers normally can only accept riders within the municipality in which they are licensed. Should a taxicab driver pick up a passenger desiring to travel to another jurisdiction, the driver will have to return to the municipality regulating it before taking a new rider. In a metropolitan area with a number of small-sized municipalities, this form of local regulation results in the waste of fuel and motivates drivers to reject prospective passengers who desire to travel to a destination beyond the municipality in which they hailed a taxi.

Existing municipal taxicab regulations limit market entry, regulate prices, and impose driver qualifications and vehicle safety requirements through licensing. In contrast, unregulated ride-sharing services do not face market entry barriers or price controls. The platform provider sets quality and safety standards. Although universal service requirements bind the taxicab industry, difficulties in enforcement continue to exist. Unregulated ride-sharing platforms became widely popular with consumers, in part, because they serve customers in locations underserved by taxis. Passengers typically hail a taxicab from the street without the use of a technology-based application such as ride-sharing platforms provide. The taxicab service works well primarily in places where a strong demand for mobility services creates greater service availability.

The ride-sharing platforms' disruption of the taxi industry resulted in a cry for regulatory parity. The states have enacted legislation regulating so-called transportation network companies

---

[69] *See* Michèle Finck and Sofia Ranchordás, *Sharing and the City*, 49 Vand. J. Transnat'l L. 1299, 1323 (2016).

[70] N.Y. Gen. Mun. Law § 182 (West, Westlaw current through Laws 2017, Chs. 1 to 334). In addition, an exception from the general law regulating technology network companies has been made for cities with a population of one million or more. N.Y. Veh. & Traf. Law § 1700 (3) (West, Westlaw current through Laws 2017, Chs. 1 to 334).

[71] *See, e.g.*, Ala. Code §§ 32-3-3, 32-4-2, 32-4-5, 32-5-1 (West, Westlaw current through the end of the 2017 Regular Session); Ariz. Rev. Stat. Ann. §§ 28–602(B), 28–626 (West, Westlaw current through the First Regular Session of the Fifty-Third Legislature (2017)); Colo. Rev. Stat. §§ 42-1-101, 42-1-201 to 203 (West, Westlaw current through all Laws of the First Regular Session of the 71st General Assembly (2017)).

[72] *See* Diller, *supra* note 51, at 1172.

("TNCs"), such as the digital platforms Uber and Lyft, on a statewide basis. TNCs have been actively involved in the legislative process in an attempt to protect their app-based business model, in which nonprofessional drivers, often on a part-time basis, use their own vehicles to transport passengers.[73] State legislation has imposed insurance requirements,[74] vehicle inspections,[75] and minimum qualifications for drivers.[76]

The states have an interest in the protection of passengers with limited knowledge or no knowledge of the quality of mobile service providers. Because passengers usually possess no information about the quality of the driver, the condition of the vehicle, or the reputation of the firm providing the service, they should be protected by a regulatory regime that ensures their safety. In contrast, a prospective passenger who receives transport from a ride-sharing service receives some information about the driver by the ride-sharing platform and enjoys protection to some degree due to the tracking of the geographical movement of the vehicle. In addition, the passenger has the ability to rate the driver. Although the latter protections may be insufficient to meet public safety concerns, they do provide greater protection than completely unregulated mobility services.

Although the states have a strong interest in the uniform treatment of ride-sharing services, the establishment of minimum professional driving standards, and the preservation of a marketplace for ride-sharing, local interests may also be characterized as ascendant. A municipality may desire to impose greater safety requirements for the protection of its residents than those required by legislation regulating TNCs. Taxicab licensing requirements generally entail more stringent requirements than those mandated for TNCs. Municipalities may also experience harmful externalities caused by increased mobility services in different ways. In congested, urban areas, a free rein on ride-sharing services may produce undesirable external impacts relating to traffic gridlock and increased emissions of pollutants. The environmental impact of greatly expanding mobility services through ride-sharing has yet to be determined.[77] In the past, municipalities limited the number of taxicab medallions through licensing to prevent such congestion. Local supplemental regulations may very well be in order to mitigate such adverse environmental effects. In the United States, courts have upheld supplemental local regulations that were more restrictive than state regulations covering the same area of regulatory activity provided the state law did not impliedly or expressly preempt the local law.[78] A few states permit localities to supplement statewide TNC regulation.[79]

[73] *See* Sophie Quinton, *How Should Uber Be Regulated?*, Pew Charitable Trusts: Stateline (Nov. 24, 2015), www .pewtrusts.org/en/research-and-analysis/blogs/stateline/2015/11/24/how-should-uber-be-regulated (reporting that "Uber and Lyft have lobbied hard to make sure state and local rules suit their businesses").

[74] *See, e.g.,* Cal. Pub. Util. Code §§ 5442–44 (West, Westlaw current with urgency legislation through Ch. 26, also including Chs. 28, 38, 42, 47, 50, 51, 55 and 65 of 2017 Reg. Sess.); Colo. Rev. Stat. § 40-10.1-604 (West, Westlaw current through Laws effective May 24, 2017 of the First Regular Session of the 71st General Assembly (2017)); Mass. Gen. Laws Ann. ch. 159A ½, § 2 (c) (West, Westlaw current through Ch. 20 of the 2017 1st Annual Session).

[75] *See, e.g.,* Colo. Rev. Stat. § 40-10.1-605 (1) (g)-(h) (West, Westlaw current through Laws effective May 24, 2017 of the First Regular Session of the 71st General Assembly (2017)); Mass. Gen. Laws Ann. ch. 159A ½, § 2 (f) (West, Westlaw current through Ch. 20 of the 2017 1st Annual Session).

[76] *See, e.g.,* Cal. Pub. Util. Code § 5445.2 (West, Westlaw current with urgency legislation through Ch. 26, also including Chs. 28, 38, 42, 47, 50, 51, 55 and 65 of 2017 Reg. Sess.); Colo. Rev. Stat. § 40-10.1-605 (1)(d), (3)(a)-(b), (4)(a)-(b) (West, Westlaw current through Laws effective May 24, 2017 of the First Regular Session of the 71st General Assembly (2017)); Mass. Gen. Laws Ann. ch. 159A ½, § 4 (a)-(f) (West, Westlaw current through Ch. 20 of the 2017 1st Annual Session).

[77] *See* Sarah E. Light, *Precautionary Federalism and the Sharing Economy*, 66 Emory L.J. 333, 342–43, 366–71 (2017).

[78] *See, e.g., Phantom of Brevard, Inc. v. Brevard County*, 3 So. 3d 309, 314–15 (Fla. 2008) (upholding county requirement that sellers of fireworks maintain liability insurance); *People v. McGraw*, 150 N.W. 836, 836 (Mich. 1915) (upholding local traffic regulations in recognition of "local and peculiar conditions").

[79] *See, e.g.,* 625 Ill. Comp. Stat. Ann. 57/32 (West, Westlaw current through Public Acts effective Nov. 22, 2017, through Public Acts 100–535) (barring local governments from regulating TNCs in a manner less restrictive than state law, but not prohibiting more stringent local regulation of same; La. Stat. Ann., § 45:201.3(D) (West, Westlaw current through

B State Interests in the Regulation of Short-term Rentals

The use of space triggers state and local interests that differ from those associated with mobility services. Motor vehicles regularly cross municipal borders, but land stays within municipal boundary lines. Historically, the states have delegated power over land uses to local governments, giving them a decisive stake in regulating the conditions under which home-sharing and short-term rentals occur.[80] The environmental impacts of short-term rentals also raise local concerns. Renting premises to transients on a short-term basis can produce additional noise, traffic, and nuisances in a neighborhood. Such activities can increase the demand for parking space, and guest behavior may not conform to neighborhood sensibilities. A municipality will also be concerned if its inhabitants suffer a loss of housing options due to the conversion of rental units into short-term rental use.[81] Even the preservation of neighborhood character can be at stake.

The state, however, also has interests in the regulation of short-term rentals. Tourism on a state-wide basis can be enhanced by giving tourists more options as to the type of accommodations available. The potential for new state revenue, either in the form of occupancy taxes on the short-term rentals or from the sale of goods and services to home-sharing guests cannot be overlooked from a state's perspective. Thus, either a local ban on short-term rentals or the promulgation of overly burdensome municipal regulations that stifle short-term rentals would not be consonant with a state's interests. The state, like its municipalities, will also have concerns for the safety and welfare of the short-term rental guests. The accommodations offered should be clean and provide certain protections, such as fire extinguishers, exit signs, and carbon monoxide and smoke alarms, to mitigate fire and health hazards.

A strong case can be made for uniformity in treatment of short-term rentals within a metropolitan area or within the state, especially from the digital-platform provider's perspective. Centralizing the levy and collection of taxes can increase efficiency. States have a stake in the sizable amount of revenue that can be collected through taxation of short-term rentals.[82] Taxation of such rentals at non-uniform rates may increase the burden upon those charged with collecting and remitting the taxes.[83] As of May 2017, Airbnb had 275 tax partnerships with various state and local governments pursuant to which it agreed to collect room taxes from guests.[84] Fewer partnerships would result in greater efficiency for short-term rental online platforms. Guests may also very well benefit from greater uniformity of treatment, especially if they book accommodations frequently in different locations.

The impact of electronic commerce upon the levy and collection of state and local taxes continues to raise important issues in the United States. The United States Supreme Court has

---

the 2017 Second Extraordinary Session) (providing that TNCs are not exempt "from complying with … municipal and parochial ordinances relating to the ownership, registration, and operation of automobiles in this state"); Md. Code Ann., Pub. Util. § 10–406 (West, Westlaw current through all legislation from the 2017 Regular Session of the General Assembly) (authorizing a county or a municipality to impose an assessment upon a transportation network service for use in funding transportation purposes).

[80] *See* Julian Conrad Juergensmeyer and Thomas E. Roberts, *Land Use Planning and Development Regulation Law* § 3.5 (3d ed., 2013).

[81] *See* McLaren and Agyeman, *supra* note 5, at 24 (citing a Latitude survey, in collaboration with Shareable Magazine, stating that in 2013 in San Francisco "up to 1,960 properties had been removed from the rental market for letting on Airbnb").

[82] *See Editorial: Tax, Regulate Short-term Online Rentals*, Daily Hampshire Gazette (May 23, 2017), www.gazettenet .com/Editorial-State-should-approve-legislation-taxing-short-term-online-rentals-and-giving-local-communities-regulatory-power-10255532.

[83] The ability of online platforms to use algorithms to calculate the amount of taxes levied at different rates and from different jurisdictions, however, may mitigate such burdens. *See* Aqib Aslam and Alpa Shah, *Taxation and the Peer-to-Peer Economy* 6, 26–29 (Int'l Monetary Fund, WP/17/187, Aug. 2017), www.imf.org/en/Publications/WP/Issues/2017/08/08/Taxation-and-the-Peer-to-Peer-Economy-45157 (discussing the role of the digital platform to facilitate tax administration).

[84] *See supra* note 82.

ruled that the Commerce Clause in the United States Constitution prohibits states from unduly burdening interstate commerce through the exercise of their power to tax.[85] Businesses may be subject to state taxation provided the tax: (1) applies to an activity sufficiently connected to the state to justify taxation; (2) is fairly apportioned; (3) is nondiscriminatory; and (4) is fairly related to the services provided to the taxpayer by the taxing state.[86] Before the advent of widespread online commerce, the Supreme Court ruled that the first criterion, the substantial nexus between the seller and the taxing state, required a physical presence of a retailer in a state in order for the state to mandate the retailer to collect and remit sales and use taxes.[87] In 2018, this so-called physical presence rule was declared incorrect, and the decisions placing reliance upon it were overruled.[88]

With respect to a review of possible extraterritorial effects that could stem from local control of short-term rentals, they would not appear to be sizable. Should a municipality ban or restrictively regulate short-term rentals, such action could result in increasing the number of such rentals in surrounding municipalities, thereby exacerbating the burdens such rentals place upon local residents. States have sought to prevent municipalities from avoiding their fair share of statewide burdens.[89] A state's reputation for safe tourist facilities could be eviscerated if a municipality failed to ensure that proper health and safety requirements for housing rentals were in effect and enforced. Guests could be affected by lax enforcement as well, but the impact on surrounding municipalities would not seem to be significant. Municipal restrictions upon the renting of space could also result in an increase in mortgage foreclosures for those homeowners who need to supplement their income in order to finance their mortgage loans.

Short-term rentals should involve both the states and municipalities as participants in ensuring the safety and health of short-term rental guests. Historically, states have established minimum standards for habitable dwellings through housing and building codes. Municipalities have been permitted to supplement such regulations as conditions may vary in different parts of the state, especially if one part of the state has a significantly different climate than another part of a state. Municipalities due to their local presence can readily inspect the condition of rented premises, a function they have traditionally performed. Local governments exercise land use controls through the enforcement of zoning codes and other laws, and they will continue to have a strong vested interest in the protection of property values.

V METHODOLOGY FOR THE STATES' REGULATION OF THE SHARING ECONOMY

Before a state decides to impose regulatory controls on a sharing economy participant, it should undertake certain inquiries. First, it should determine whether the sharing economy participant can self-regulate the transaction without government interference. Are the sharing economy

---

[85] *See Gwin, White & Prince Inc. v. Henneford*, 305 U.S. 434, 438–41 (1939) (ruling that a business engaged in both the local and the interstate sale and delivery of fruit was unconstitutionally burdened by a state tax on its total gross income that was no apportioned to transactions within the state, thereby subjecting interstate activity to similar taxation by other states from which intrastate activity was freed).

[86] *Complete Auto Transit, Inc. v. Brady*, 430 U.S. 274, 277–79 (1977).

[87] *See Quill Corp. v. North Dakota*, 504 U.S. 298, 312–13 (1992), *overruled by South Dakota v. Wayfair*, 585 U.S. _(2018) (ruling that interstate commerce was burdened by North Dakota's requirement that a mail order business without property or personnel in the state collect a state-imposed use tax from the business's North Dakota customers).

[88] *See South Dakota v. Wayfair*, 585 U.S._,_(2018) (upholding a South Dakota law that required out-of-state retailers with no physical presence in the state to collect and remit sales taxes on goods and services purchased from them). *See also* Eric Yauch, *News Analysis: Getting to Quill: The Path to Overturning an Outdated Supreme Court Decision*, Tax Analysts (Feb. 3, 2016), www.taxanalysts.org/content/news-analysis-getting-quill-path-overturning-outdated-supreme-court-decision.

[89] *See, e.g.*, Mass. Gen. Laws ch. 40B, §§ 20–23 (1917), https://malegislature.gov/Laws/GeneralLaws/PartI/TitleVII/Chapter40B/Section23; *Southern Burlington County v. Township of Mount Laurel*, 336 A.2d 713, 727–28 (N.J. 1975) (municipalities obligated to provide their fair share of lower-income housing needed in their region).

activities of a nature that requires the exercise of state police powers? Some collaborative activities involve personal sharing on a limited scale and should not be treated as commercial transactions, which are most likely to be subject to public regulation.[90] Other sharing activities may be placed in a gray area where it is not clear whether they fall within the realm of regulation.[91] In some instances regulations will explicitly exempt small-scale, community-based activities from their reach.[92] Sharing economy activities less likely to be regulated are those characterized as small-scale, low-impact, infrequent, cost-sharing as opposed to profit-making, and without harmful effects.[93]

Next, the type of available regulatory controls should be examined. Existing regulatory regimes have been designed for a competitive economy. Traditional regulatory approaches include registration requirements, permits, licenses, safety inspections, fines, tax payments, conditional approvals based on the performance of conditions, and input from the public in the form of notice and hearings. The sharing economy requires collaboration leaving open the possibility that the command and control type of regulations are less appropriate.[94] Clearly, at a time when the dimensions of the sharing economy are not fully understood and technology continues to provide new sharing economy opportunities, it may be appropriate for states to step back and watch how the sharing economy operates before imposing heavy-handed regulatory measures.[95]

The cost and efficiency of regulating a sharing economy field should also be evaluated. Not all sharing economy transactions should be regulated due to the difficulty of regulatory enforcement and the possible invasion of privacy interests. Because the sharing economy involves a multitude of actors, often on a part-time basis, the cost of regulating it may be prohibitive. For example, it is far easier to regulate the limited number of hotels operating in any municipality in comparison to the thousands of individuals who may be renting out part of their homes on a short-term basis. Failure to enforce regulations can engender disrespect for the law.

Should it be deemed desirable to regulate an area of the sharing economy, a decision needs to be made as to the level of governance that can best regulate it. Initial guidance for such a determination can be assisted by evaluating whether the activity primarily impacts: (1) all areas of a state; (2) state regions including metropolitan regions; or (3) localities and neighborhoods. If the impact of an activity extends beyond local jurisdictional boundary lines, a state-directed approach will be in order. This chapter further argues that a state regulatory approach should be instituted when the sharing economy transaction impinges upon strong state interests, requires uniformity in regulatory treatment, or produces harmful effects on a regional or statewide scale if left to local control.

Once the ideal regulatory body has been selected, different options may be pursued to find the optimal nature of the sharing economy regulation. For example, either minimum or high standards can be set for market entry and operations.[96] Perhaps a more hands-off approach is warranted while data is collected as to the activity's externalities. States should take care not to overregulate the sharing economy so as to destroy its viability. Burdensome ordinances

---

[90] *See* Orsi, *supra* note 17, at 420–25.

[91] *See id.*

[92] *See id.* at 424.

[93] *See id.* at 425–30.

[94] *See* Robert A. Kagan, *Adversarial Legalism: The American Way of Law* 198 (2001) (arguing that in contrast to cooperative modes of regulation, the adversarial and legalistic nature of regulatory systems in the United States results in higher legal and compliance costs and creates more alienation among regulated enterprises).

[95] The European Commission has adopted the wait-and-watch approach. *See supra* note 21.

[96] *See* Finck and Ranchordás, *supra* note 69, at 1335–51 (discussing permissive and restrictive approaches taken by cities in regulating sharing economy activities).

and regulations can eviscerate the flexibility and adaptation needed to optimize an economy based on the use of constantly changing technology. Overly stringent standards can also lead to enforcement issues when acting outside the law proves expedient.

Governmental bodies also have the option to negotiate with sharing economy entrepreneurs as to applicable regulatory standards.[97] Sometimes states may be able to nudge platform providers to engage in self-regulation.[98] Platform providers frequently have sufficient political or community support to negotiate favorable terms with their regulators.[99] Thus, care needs to be exercised to prevent unfair deal making. Different treatments of various sharing economy participants can lead to inequitable results or Equal Protection Clause[100] challenges. More widespread collaboration with diverse public and private stakeholders may also be in order to establish community standards or minimum expectations for sharing economy products and services.

State legislatures need to be better educated on the contours of the sharing economy. The desirability of local experimentation and the effects of overregulation require attention. Once a state statute specifically authorizes or regulates a particular sharing economy prototype, the field becomes legitimized, and other market participants will enter the field. The new entrants may in turn disrupt the original platform provider, or they may come to dominate the field. Thus, the consequences of state legislation should be carefully explored before enactment.

VI CO-REGULATION OF THE SHARING ECONOMY

States and local governments should cooperate and consult with each other in the regulation of the sharing economy.[101] Although existing intrastate regulatory models often involve state centralization, a consultative approach could be beneficial given the evolving scope of the sharing economy.[102] In areas where both statewide and local concerns exist, shared regulation may be in order.

Because state governments normally define the perimeters of local control, an argument has been made for regulatory coordination without hierarchy so as to realize policy objectives with fewer transaction costs and uncertainties.[103] With the emergence of cities as centers of innovation and economic growth, their consequential role in overseeing sharing economy activities should not be ignored.[104] A strong case can be made for allowing local governments to serve as laboratories in the regulation of the sharing economy because such experimentation can result in the adoption of different policies that reflect constituent needs.[105] Local control enables regulations to be more finely tailored to a municipality's needs and political preferences.[106]

---

[97] *See* Cannon and Chung, *supra* note 26, at 54 (arguing in favor of negotiated co-regulation between government and industry entities).

[98] *See* Cohen and Sundararajan, *supra* note 22, at 123–27 (describing self-regulatory organizations).

[99] *See* Bryan Lowry, *Kansas Legislature Approves Compromise that Will Return Uber to State*, Kansas City Star (May 19, 2015), www.kansascity.com/news/politics-government/article21406239.html (reporting that the state legislature enacted legislation imposing fewer restrictions on ride-sharing services after Uber terminated operations in Kansas due to more restrictive legislation).

[100] U.S. Const. amend. XIV, § 1.

[101] *See* Rick Su, *Intrastate Federalism*, 19 U. Pa. J. Const. L. 191, 226–27 (arguing that federalism can serve as a structure for resolving intrastate conflicts).

[102] *See* Michael E. Libonati, *The Law of Intergovernmental Relations: IVHS Opportunities and Constraints*, 22 Transp. L.J. 225, 244–49 (1994) (describing models of intergovernmental relations, including the centralization model, the federalism model, the consultative model, and the coordination without hierarchy model).

[103] *See id.* at 248.

[104] *See* Bruce Katz and Jennifer Bradley, *The Metropolitan Revolution: How Cities and Metros Are Fixing Our Broken Politics and Fragile Economy* 1–5 (2013).

[105] *See* Diller, *supra* note 51, at 1127–28; Finck and Ranchordás, *supra* note 69, at 1355–59.

[106] *See* Diller, *supra* note 51, at 1129.

In transactions involving physical space, the sharing economy will continue to test the desirability of creating two different regulatory regimes, one local and one statewide. Complementary regulation at both the state and local level should prove desirable because space forms a municipality's core for which self-protection will be fought.[107] Short-term rentals in particular affect the space in close proximity to their loci. Frequent complaints about Airbnb coalesce around negative externalities caused by Airbnb guests and fears that this platform decreases the supply of affordable housing and enables commercial operators to rent on a short-term basis without adherence to the safety and tax regulations applicable to hotels and other tourist facilities.[108] Likewise, ride-sharing services impact the local areas in which drivers are picking up and delivering passengers by increasing traffic and congestion.[109] It is imperative that states recognize these local impacts and either work in regulatory tandem with municipalities or empower them to adopt regulatory measures to mitigate adverse externalities caused by sharing economy transactions.

A municipality's role in facilitating infrastructure, affordable housing, and environmental protection dictates the necessity of planning and zoning measures tailored to unique local conditions. The impacts of short-term rentals upon residential neighborhoods, including increased noise, crime, and traffic and parking congestion, necessitate a new examination of land use policies and regulations.[110] The potential loss of permanent rental housing should also trigger a reexamination of existing housing policies.[111] Further studies will need to be conducted on Airbnb's actual effect upon the supply of rental housing taking into account that effects may vary depending upon local conditions.

State and local partnerships in the regulation of the sharing economy cannot succeed without a recognition of their value. Traditionally, state legislative bodies have jealously guarded their powers and exercised considerable control over local governance. When it became necessary to coordinate certain public functions on a regional scale, states opted to create single-purpose regional entities for the performance of one function only rather than establish more powerful general purpose governments entrusted to undertake multi-functions on a larger scale.[112] It is true, however, that the lack of a regional identity in many metropolitan areas and the desire for home rule have also impeded regional governance in the United States.[113]

---

[107] *See supra* notes 78 & 79 and accompanying text.

[108] *See* Stephen Sheppard and Andrew Udell, *Do Airbnb Properties Affect House Prices?*, Dep't Econ., Williams C. 4–5 (Oct. 30, 2016), http://web.williams.edu/Economics/wp/SheppardUdellAirbnbAffectHousePrices.pdf (estimating Airbnb's impact upon residential property values in New York City).

[109] *See* Regina R. Clewlow and Gouri Shankar Mishra, *Disruptive Transportation: The Adoption, Utilization, and Impacts of Ride-Hailing in the United States* 2, 11 (U.C. Davis Inst. Transp. Studies, UCD-ITS-RR-17-07, Oct. 2017), https://its.ucdavis.edu/research/publications/ (estimating that 49 percent to 61 percent of ride-hailing trips would not have been made in the absence of apps, or would have been made by walking, biking, or transit, and finding higher rates of ride-hailing utilization in cities).

[110] *See* Nicole Gurran and Peter Phibbs, *When Tourists Move In: How Should Urban Planners Respond to Airbnb?*, 83:1 J. Am. Plan. Ass'n 80, 81, 85–87, 90–91 (2017), www.tandfonline.com/doi/full/10.1080/01944363.2016.1249011 (analyzing the impacts of Airbnb in Sydney, Australia). *See also* Yu-Hua Xu, Jin-won Kim, and Lori Pennington-Gray, *Explore the Spatial Relationship between Airbnb Rental and Crime*, U. Mass. Amherst, Scholar Works@UMass Amherst (2017), http://scholarworks.umass.edu/cgi/viewcontent.cgi?article=2075&context=ttra (exploring the spatial relationship between geographical locations of Airbnb rental facilities and crime).

[111] *See* Roy Samaan, *Airbnb, Rising Rent, and the Housing Crisis in Los Angeles*, Laane, www.ftc.gov/system/files/documents/public_comments/2015/05/01166-96023.pdf (assessing the impact of Airbnb upon the Los Angeles housing market and calling for an evaluative framework to be included in any proposed short-term rental policy).

[112] *See* Richard Briffault, *Localism and Regionalism*, 48 Buff. L. Rev. 1, 4–5 (2000).

[113] *See id.* at 28–29.

State statutes that authorize state regulation of a particular sharing economy sector should explicitly lay out the areas for which supplemental control at another level of governance is permitted. For example, the state can set minimum standards to be followed while granting express authorization for the adoption of supplemental local controls where desirable. Quite often, state statutes do not delineate areas in which co-regulation can occur. More frequently, a statute will specify state control over a particular matter, but will leave open many areas in which uncertainty exists as to whether the state intended to preempt local action with respect to them. Thus, the gray area of implied preemption leads to numerous lawsuits challenging municipal authority.

Due to the uncertainty of how to regulate the sharing economy at the moment, it would be most expeditious for the states to think in terms of partnerships with their localities. Intergovernmental arrangements should be explored.[114] Such agreements could spell out local and state regulatory duties as well as make provision for regulatory flexibility and adaptation as conditions change or new data calls for a different approach.[115] In Texas, for example, a local government may enforce state limitations upon motor vehicle idling once the local government has entered into a memorandum of agreement with the Texas Commission on Environmental Quality providing for the delegation of such enforcement to it.[116]

Although the states have enacted statutes regulating ride-sharing services, such statutes mainly cover passenger protection and safety issues without addressing the environmental impacts of such services.[117] As the sharing economy emerges, other regulatory regimes will need to be institutionalized to regulate some of the negative externalities that increased ride-sharing in motor vehicles will entail. Most likely, these externalities will necessitate regulation on both a statewide and local basis.

CONCLUSION

Sharing economy transactions, occurring across broad segments of the market, call for regulatory measures geared to the underlying business models used. The states play an important role in ensuring that the quality of services and products provided meet expected norms. States must also protect resources and ecosystems that may be negatively impacted by the breadth and nature of sharing economy activities. At the same time the states need to avoid overly stringent regulations that discourage innovation and experimentation.

In determining which sharing economy transactions are better regulated at the state level of government, the chapter proposes that state and local interest be weighed. Activities that affect areas beyond municipal boundary lines will result in stronger state interests. State regulations should also prevail when local regulation can be expected to (1) cause disorder

---

[114] *See e.g.,* Tex. Comm'n on Envtl. Quality, *8-Hour Ozone Flex Program: Austin-Round Rock Metropolitan Statistical Area* 3, 5–8 (2008), www.tceq.texas.gov/assets/public/implementation/air/sip/austin/Austin-RoundRock8-HourOzoneFlexFinal.pdf (describing a voluntary program and agreement to improve air quality among the US Environmental Agency, the Texas Commission on Environmental Quality, the Central Texas Clean Air Coalition, counties, and local governments).

[115] *See* Stephen Goldsmith, *How Government Can Nurture the Nudge,* Governing (May 16, 2017), www.governing.com/blogs/bfc/col-louisville-nudge-behaviorally-informed-intervention.html (discussing the City of Louisville's nudging campaigns that pursued behavioral interventions to improve compliance with city regulations).

[116] *Vehicle Idling Restrictions,* Tex. Comm'n on Envtl. Quality, www.tceq.texas.gov/airquality/mobilesource/vehicleidling.html.

[117] *See supra* notes 74–76 and accompanying text.

due to a need for regulatory uniformity; (2) result in adverse extraterritorial impacts on other communities; (3) harm the general population or statewide interests; or (4) disrupt market integrity or efficiency. Because many sharing economy transactions will affect both state and local interests, this chapter argues that a collaborative state and municipal regulatory approach be undertaken in which supplementary local regulations are permitted when needed.

18

Local Regulation of the Sharing Economy

Daniel E. Rauch

INTRODUCTION

One striking feature of the sharing economy's rise has been the degree to which it has played out at the local government level. Around the world, the big questions of sharing economy regulation – which firms can operate and how – are often answered at City Hall rather than on Capitol Hill. But why have local governments become such important sites of sharing economy regulation? And given that cities *can* substantially regulate the sharing economy, how *should* they do so?

This short chapter offers a preliminary exploration of these questions.[1] Although many of these examples are drawn from the American legal context, this overall framework is also relevant to, and draws on, municipal governments worldwide.

Section I outlines the legal power of local governments to regulate the sharing economy – and their incentives to use this power. Here, I note that many of the most prominent "sharing economy" firms, from Lyft to AirBnB, operate in industries that have traditionally been the site of extensive municipal regulation (such as transportation or lodging). Moreover, I outline certain dynamics particular to the sharing economy – such as increased use-intensiveness, the use of nonprofessionalized workforces, and the presence of locally powerful incumbent industries – that make it all the more likely cities will engage with sharing economy regulation.

Building on this background, Section II highlights various ways local governments have used, and eventually might use, these powers to achieve important policy goals. Here, I focus in on several main strategies cities have offered: outright banning of sharing firms, attempting to regulate sharing firms using the same strategies as those used to regulate non-sharing firms, subsidizing the sharing economy (either implicitly or explicitly), using the sharing economy as an instrument of economic redistribution, and becoming sharing economy participants themselves. While this portion is primarily descriptive, to the extent I advance a predictive argument, it is that cities are deeply unlikely to adopt simplistic approaches like outright bans or total permissiveness, but instead to use a complex set of policy tools to achieve diverse policy goals. Finally, Section III offers a brief conclusion.

---

[1] Portions of this chapter are drawn from Daniel E. Rauch and David Schleicher, *Like Uber, but for Local Government Law: The Future of Local Regulation of the Sharing Economy*, 76 Ohio St. L.J. 901 (2015); and Daniel E. Rauch and David N. Schleicher, Local Regulation of the Sharing Economy, *in Who Is an Employee and Who Is the Employer?* (Kati L. Griffith and Samuel Estreicher eds., 2017).

I WHAT POWERS DO CITIES HAVE TO REGULATE THE SHARING ECONOMY, AND WHY WOULD THEY USE THEM?

The first question is what powers local governments have to regulate the sharing economy … and why they might choose to exercise such powers. To be sure, in some ways the "tool kit" of municipal regulators is not a good fit for regulating the sharing economy. In the United States, for example, cities usually have only those limited powers granted to them by state governments or state constitutions.[2] As a result, they are often without authority to regulate many of the policy areas most crucial to the sharing economy, from the legal redefinition of "independent contractors"[3] to the application of national antitrust law.[4] In some places, cities are constrained even more aggressively by state or national policies that "preempt" any municipal regulation. The state of Arizona, for example, bars municipalities from banning short-term rental firms.[5] Italy, meanwhile, has seen the imposition of a nationwide ban on Uber, irrespective of what policies a given Italian city might have chosen to adopt.[6]

And of course, even where cities have the legal authority to regulate, they may be dissuaded from doing so for practical economic reasons. After all, local governments have long been thought to compete with one another to secure economic activity.[7] This competition, in turn, constrains local sharing economy regulation (or, for that matter, any governmental unit's imposition of regulation), because if a given jurisdiction regulates too zealously, it may end up driving out sharing economy businesses that will shift their focus elsewhere in pursuit of greener (that is, less regulated) pastures.[8]

But despite these limits, the industries in which sharing economy firms participate – like taxi transport, housing, hotels, and restaurants – have long been subject to extensive local-level policymaking. Cities subsidize firms in these industries, regulate them to achieve the ends of social policy, tax them, promote them to tourists and visitors, and rely on them to help provide government services. This focus is no accident. Cities have long had both the political incentives and the legal powers to closely regulate activity in these sectors to ensure local market depth and efficient matching and to minimize effects on urban "congestion" (that is, the externalities of packing many citizens close together). At the same time, urban residents will only be willing to pay high urban property prices if cities provide access to "agglomeration gains," those benefits generated by the deep markets in goods and services that cities can provide.[9]

---

[2] *See generally* Gerald E. Frug and David Barron, *City Bound: How States Stifle Urban Innovation* (2008).

[3] *See, e.g.*, O'Connor v. Uber Techs., Inc., 82 F. Supp. 3d 1133 (N.D. Cal. 2015).

[4] *See* Mark Anderson and Max Huffman, *The Sharing Economy Meets the Sherman Act: Is Uber a Firm, a Cartel, or Something in Between?*, Colum. Bus. L. Rev. (forthcoming 2017), https://papers.ssrn.com/sol3/papers.cfm?abstract_id=2954632.

[5] Stefan Etienne, *Arizona's Governor Ducey Signs SB 1350 into Law, Prohibiting the Ban of Short-Term Rentals*, TechCrunch (May 13, 2016), https://techcrunch.com/2016/05/13/arizonas-governor-ducey-signs-sb-1350-into-law-prohibiting-the-ban-of-the-short-term-rentals/.

[6] Ben Chapman, *Uber Banned in Italy Nationwide After Court Rules App Provides Unfair Competition to Taxi Drivers*, The Independent (Apr. 11, 2015), www.independent.co.uk/news/business/news/uber-italy-ban-app-taxi-driver-unfair-competition-court-ruling-decision-trade-unions-legal-action-a7677881.html.

[7] For the classic treatment of this theme, *see* Charles M. Tiebout, *A Pure Theory of Local Expenditures*, 64 J. Pol. Econ. 416 (1956).

[8] *See, e.g.*, Biz Carson, *Uber Is Considering Leaving Seattle if Drivers Join Unions*, BusinessInsider (Mar. 24, 2017), www.businessinsider.com/uber-is-considering-leaving-seattle-if-drivers-join-unions-2017-3.

[9] *See* David Schleicher, *The City as a Law and Economic Subject*, 2010 U. Ill. L. Rev. 1507, 1558 (2010).

To see how extensive these powers are in practice, we need only consider how cities already regulate incumbent industries in key sharing sectors. Consider taxis. In New York, taxis must buy medallions before picking up riders, a source of city revenue.[10] Taxi rates are also closely controlled by the Taxi and Limousine Commission (TLC).[11] Acceptable vehicles and vehicle conditions, accessibility for those with disabilities, and payment methods are all regulated and standardized,[12] as is the behavior of taxi drivers,[13] and the TLC has the power to levy fines for violations like overcharging.[14] Meanwhile "yellow cabs" are also officially promoted as authentically "New York" experiences for tourists.[15] One can tell similar stories about the extensive, complicated relationships between city regulators and hotels, housing developers, labor providers, and restaurants.

In sum, cities often have extensive and complex powers for regulating sectors at the heart of the sharing economy. And there are compelling reasons why local governments have even stronger reasons to regulate sharing firms than their incumbent-industry counterparts.

First, sharing firms can greatly increase the "use-intensiveness" of urban resources. Much local regulation, from parking minimums to zoning law, is based on traditional assumptions on how civic resources should be used. Some homeowners constantly have guests over; most do not. Some cars are driven twelve hours a day; most are not. But the sharing economy flips many of these assumptions on their heads, leading to more intensive resource uses than originally expected.

A good example of such conflict stems from the rise of Airbnb, OneFineStay,[16] and VRBO,[17] services permitting owners and tenants to rent out rooms for short-term stays. Because many of these properties constantly have "guests," they use neighborhoods more intensively than originally planned for. The upshot is that areas once zoned as residential can become de facto commercial "hotel" districts. Because of this, neighbors to Airbnb renters have often lodged complaints under zoning, landlord–tenant, or contract law. Accordingly, it's no surprise that cities have a strong incentive to regulate such externalities by policing sharing firms.

Second, the rise of the sharing economy has enabled a massive rise in non-professional service and goods providers, a further spur toward effective urban regulation. The increased ability of "amateurs" to participate in markets like lodging and transit offers important benefits to urban economies. Adding new supply – nonprofessionals offering services alongside existing firms and workers – drives consumer prices down, and can also provide jobs to citizens looking for work.[18]

---

[10] Katrina Miriam Wyman, *Problematic Private Property: The Case of New York Taxicab Medallions*, 30 Yale J. Reg., at 125, 136–38, 148–56 (2013) (explaining how medallions function).

[11] N.Y.C. Taxi and Limousine Comm'n Rules ch. 52 at § 52-04(b)(1) (last updated Feb. 11, 2014), www.nyc.gov/html/tlc/downloads/pdf/rule_book_current_chapter_52.pdf.

[12] *See id.* at ch. 58, § 58-29–41 www.nyc.gov/html/tlc/downloads/pdf/rule_book_current_chapter_58.pdf.

[13] *Medallion Taxicab Passenger Bill of Rights*, N.Y.C. Taxicab and Limousine Comm'n (2015), www.nyc.gov/html/tlc/html/passenger/taxicab_rights.shtml.

[14] *See* N.Y.C. Taxi and Limousine Comm'n Rules, at § 54-02(e); *see also id.* at ch. 68 www.nyc.gov/html/tlc/downloads/pdf/rule_book_current_chapter_68.pdf.

[15] Phil Patton, *The Taxi as Icon*, Taxi of Tomorrow, www.nyc.gov/html/media/totweb/taxioftomorrow_taxiasicon.html ("The taxicab is a symbol of New York to millions of tourists").

[16] *See* OneFineStay, www.onefinestay.com.

[17] *See* VRBO, www.vrbo.com.

[18] *See* Ryan Lawler, *Feastly Launches an "Airbnb For Dinner" Marketplace*, TechCrunch (Apr. 21, 2014), http://techcrunch.com/2014/04/21/feastly/; *see also* John Tozzi, *It Turns Homes into Restaurants (and Tests Food Laws' Boundaries)*, Bloomberg Businessweek (July 26, 2013), www.businessweek.com/articles/2013-07-26/it-turns-homes-into-restaurants-and-tests-food-laws-boundaries; DogVacay, https://dogvacay.com.

At the same time the rise of nonprofessional service delivery can cause problems for cities.[19] Professionalized and regulated incumbents, for instance, complain of unfair competition. In the taxi industry, traditional drivers must pay for cab medallions and pass numerous city tests and requirements;[20] Lyft drivers, by contrast, can often start driving without any formal certification.[21] Likewise, traditional hotels must pay taxes and comply with extensive city regulations; Airbnb hosts, by contrast, often do not. Moreover, the sharing economy's "de-professionalization" of goods and services can create serious consumer protection concerns that cities feel compelled to address. Rentals on Airbnb do not need to meet hotel fire standards,[22] Lyft drivers frequently do not need city certification or licensure,[23] and community chefs on Josephine[24] have no obligation to follow local health regulations.

Finally, cities may be spurred to regulate the sharing economy by the desire to protect politically powerful incumbents. Many of the traditional entities most "disrupted" by the sharing economy have long been power-players in municipal politics: groups like hotel unions, taxi unions, and neighborhood preservation associations. Accordingly, cities frequently crack down on sharing firms at least partly at the behest of such groups.[25]

Taken together, these factors suggest that cities have both the legal power and the political incentive to regulate the sharing economy. The question, then, is how they might do so.

II HOW MIGHT LOCAL GOVERNMENTS REGULATE THE SHARING ECONOMY?

As the preceding discussion suggests, cities have both the power and the incentive to regulate many aspects of the sharing economy. Accordingly, at least one regulatory option – not regulating sharing firms at all – seems off the table.[26] But that said, there are still many paths cities could take.[27] This section considers five possible approaches to local-level regulation of sharing firms. These are: (1) outright bans on sharing economy firms; (2) holding sharing economy firms to similar standards as traditional economy entrants; (3) giving subsidies to sharing economy firms; (4) using the sharing economy to assist in economic redistribution and community development; and (5) becoming participants in the sharing economy.

---

[19] *See* Orly Lobel, *The Law of the Platform*, 101 Minn. Law Rev. 87, 110–11 (2015).

[20] *See* Andrea Peterson, *What It Looks Like When Taxi Drivers Protest Uber and Lyft in D.C.*, Wash. Post (Oct. 28, 2014), www.washingtonpost.com/news/the-switch/wp/2014/10/28/what-it-looks-like-when-taxi-drivers-protest-uber-and-lyft-in-d-c/.

[21] Note, however, that as some cities begin to regulate these "ride-sharing" services, some jurisdictions have begun to impose such certification requirements onto sharing economy participants as well. *See* Andy Vuong, *Colorado First to Authorize Lyft and Uber's Ridesharing Services*, Denver Post (June 5, 2014), www.denverpost.com/business/ci_25907057/colorado-first-authorize-lyft-and-ubers-ridesharing-services.

[22] Dean Baker, *Don't Buy the "Sharing Economy" Hype: Airbnb and Uber Are Facilitating Rip-Offs*, Guardian (May 27, 2014), www.theguardian.com/commentisfree/2014/may/27/airbnb-uber-taxes-regulation.

[23] *See* Bobby Kerlik, *Rivals Try to Block Uber, Lyft in Pittsburgh*, Trib Live (Aug. 2, 2014), http://triblive.com/news/allegheny/6543923-74/lyft-puc-ride#axzz3BDwh7wLz. This fact has led many states to issue ominous – if vague – warnings. *See also* Ben Popken, *States Warn of Rideshare Risks for Passengers*, NBC News (June 5, 2014), www.nbcnews.com/business/consumer/states-warn-rideshare-risks-passengers-n116736.

[24] *See* www.josephine.com/learn-more.

[25] *See, e.g.,* Caroyln Said, *Airbnb Hurts Hotels, Trade Group and Union Say*, SF Chronicle (Sept. 30, 2016), www.sfchronicle.com/business/article/Airbnb-hurts-hotels-says-trade-group-and-union-9517727.php.

[26] Notwithstanding the sometimes-libertarian rhetoric of some sharing economy business leaders. *See* Tom Slee, *The Secret Libertarianism of Uber & Airbnb*, Salon.com (Jan. 28, 2014,), www.salon.com/2014/01/28/the_big_business_behind_the_sharing_economy_partner.

[27] For an argument that "New Governance" approaches toward regulation should inform how cities (and other governmental units) regulate the sharing economy, *see* Ray Brescia, this volume.

A *Outright Bans on Sharing Firms*

Perhaps the simplest approach cities may take to regulate sharing firms is an outright ban on such operations.[28] In some places, cities might be "preempted" from taking this course by state or national governments.[29] But in the main, local governments are free to ban such firms. Sometimes, these bans are citywide, as when New Orleans, at least for a time, banned Uber.[30] In other cases, the restrictions are more limited, like the airport-specific bans on car-sharing services in Atlanta, Detroit, Boston, and Philadelphia.[31]

Advocates of this approach often point to concerns about unfair competition. The taxi industry, for example, claims Uber enjoys an unfair advantage because it need not purchase medallions or comply with consumer protection or pricing regulations.[32] Likewise, hotel and neighborhood groups argue Airbnb skirts taxes, violates lease terms, uses residentially zoned property for commercial purposes, and lacks safeguards for guests and operators.[33] And of course, to the extent it is considered a benefit, such bans do have the effect of protecting incumbent urban industries from competition.

For what it's worth, though, such bans have often proven short-lived. Instead, as discussed at length fully below, cities often seek to work with sharing firms, trading access to lucrative urban markets in exchange for accepting greater regulations. At times, this stems from the political savvy of the sharing firms themselves. By hiring top tier political talent and harnessing consumers as a powerful political base, these firms have been able to win political battles against even deeply entrenched incumbents.[34] But the success of sharing firms in eluding bans also has a great deal to do with the other tools cities can, and have, deployed to regulate them.

Perhaps, then, the greatest utility of an outright ban is less as a long-run policy and more as a bargaining chip, allowing cities to leverage a threatened prohibition in order to win buy-in for other, more balanced regulatory approaches.

---

[28] Mark J. Perry, *Minneapolis and Seattle Restrict Ride-Sharing Services Lyft and Uber as Crony Capitalism Prevails and Consumers Lose*, Am. Enter. Inst. AEI Ideas (Feb. 28, 2014), www.aei.org/publication/minneapolis-and-seattle-restrict-ride-sharing-services-lyft-and-uber-as-crony-capitalism-prevails-and-consumers-lose/.

[29] Stefan Etienne, *Arizona's Governor Ducey Signs SB 1350 into Law, Prohibiting the Ban of Short-Term Rentals*, TechCrunch (May 13, 2016), https://techcrunch.com/2016/05/13/arizonas-governor-ducey-signs-sb-1350-into-law-prohibiting-the-ban-of-short-term-rentals/; *see also* Martha Stoddard, *Nebraska Legislators Debate Bill to Ban Local Regulations of Airbnb, Other Short-Term Rentals*, Omaha World Herald (Apr. 14, 2017), www.omaha.com/news/legislature/nebraska-legislators-debate-bill-to-ban-local-regulations-of-airbnb/article_7016a212-fc93-5293-89e7-13be58b0fc4f.html.

[30] *See* Jeanie Riess, *Why New Orleans Doesn't Have Uber*, GAMBIT (Feb. 4, 2014), www.bestofneworleans.com/gambit/why-new-orleans-doesnt-have-uber/Content?oid=2307943. Eventually, though, this ban was lifted. *See New Orleans Welcomes Uber, Lyft Ride-Sharing Services as Deal Struck*, Apr. 9, 2015, www.nola.com/politics/index.ssf/2015/04/new_orleans_welcomes_uber_lyft.html.

[31] Kerry Close, *This Is Why You Can't Take an Uber Home from the Airport*, Time (Jul. 7, 2016), www.time.com/money/4396248/uber-lyft-ban-airport/.

[32] *See, e.g.*, Luz Lazo, *Cab Companies Unite Against Uber and Other Ride-Share Services*, Wash. Post (Aug. 10, 2014), www.washingtonpost.com/local/trafficandcommuting/cab-companies-unite-against-uber-and-other-ride-share-services/2014/08/10/11b23d52-1e3f-11e4-82f9-2cd6fa8da5c4_story.html.

[33] *See, e.g.*, Carolyn Said, *S.F. Planners Support, Toughen "Airbnb Law,"* S.F. Chron. (Aug. 9, 2014), www.sfgate.com/realestate/article/S-F-planners-support-toughen-Airbnb-law-5677368.php (describing criticisms of Airbnb); Bruce Watson, *Airbnb's Legal Troubles: The Tip of the Iceberg for the Sharing Economy?*, The Guardian (London) (Nov. 20, 2013), www.theguardian.com/sustainable-business/airbnb-legal-trouble-sharing-economy.

[34] *See* Davey Alba, *After Victory, AirBnB Compares Its Influence to the NRA's*, WIRED (Nov. 4, 2015), www.wired.com/2015/11/after-victory-airbnb-compares-its-influence-to-the-nras/; Christine Lagorio-Chafkin, *Resistance Is Futile*, Inc. Mag. (July–Aug. 2013), www.inc.com/magazine/201307/christine-lagorio/uber-the-car-service-explosive-growth.html. For discussions of how this strategy works, *see* Andrew Leonard, *The Sharing Economy Muscles Up*, Salon (Sept. 27, 2013), www.salon.com/2013/09/17/the_sharing_economy_muscles_up; Marcus Wohlsen, *Uber's Brilliant Strategy to Make Itself Too Big to Ban*, Wired (July 8, 2014), www.wired.com/2014/07/ubers-brilliant-strategy-to-make-itself-too-big-to-ban/.

B Traditional-Style Regulations

As noted, given political and economic realities, outright bans on sharing firms have largely proven unsustainable. By contrast, cities have more often allowed sharing firms to operate in exchange for complying with the same sorts of restriction as their incumbent-industry competitors. For example, Miami-Dade county allows firms like Airbnb to operate, but on the condition that they comply with the same "resort taxes" as traditional hotels.[35] Airbnb also agreed to comply with San Francisco's regulations requiring "hosts" to register with the city in exchange for the right to operate legally.[36] And in perhaps the most extreme example, Brussels requires home-sharing participants to comply with all regulations that hotels must meet, including a minimum number of coat hangers per guest.[37]

This approach has obvious benefits from the perspective of municipal finances and consumer protection. It can also allay concerns about unfair competition, since such policies can force sharing firms to play on an "even playing field" with more conventional, incumbent firms, like taxi companies and hotels. The challenge, though, is ensuring that such regulations do not constrain sharing firms to so great a degree that consumers and the city lose out on the more unique benefits they might offer.

C Sharing Firm Subsidies

As a further regulatory approach, cities might choose to *subsidize* sharing firms, paying them directly or indirectly in exchange for various benefits.

Why would a city take this path? An initial justification for sharing-firm subsidies is the ability of such firms to create public goods and substantial consumer and producer surplus for residents. Sharing firms can create platforms to exchange goods many people already have on hand or own for other purposes (i.e., spare bedrooms, idle cars, etc.). Once a sharing firm begins operations, there will be many sellers who can earn money without bearing substantial costs. Moreover, on the "buy" side, many goods offered by the sharing economy do not have easy substitutes (e.g. before Rent the Runway,[38] the selection of high-end clothes rentable for exactly one day was quite limited). Just as markets created by eBay and Craigslist generated new wealth from people's existing possessions, so too do sharing services offer vast consumer and producer surplus.[39]

A second benefit that might justify subsidization is that it could help "put a city on the map," in other words, lend cultural cachet that could translate into economic benefit. By analogy, today cities subsidize some amenities, like sports stadiums and art museums, partly in hopes of being seen as "world class" – or at least nationally prominent. Being "on the map" in this way

---

[35] Chabeli Herrera, *Airbnb Strikes Tax Deal with MiamiDade Mayor*, Governing (Mar. 20, 2017), www.governing.com/topics/finance/tns-airbnb-miami-dade-mayor.html.

[36] *See New York Deflates AirBnB*, The Economist (Oct. 27, 2016), www.economist.com/news/business/21709353-new-rules-may-temper-airbnb-new-york-its-future-still-looks-bright-new-york-deflates.

[37] Marilyn Haigh, *EU's "Sharing Economy" Stifled by Petty Rules on Coat Hangers to Light Bulbs*, Reuters (Sept. 26, 2016), www.reuters.com/article/us-eu-ecommerce-regulations-idUSKCN11W1SN.

[38] *See* Patricia Marx, *The Borrowers: Why Buy When You Can Rent?*, New Yorker (Jan. 31, 2011), www.newyorker.com/magazine/2011/01/31/the-borrowers (profiling the rise of high-end dress rental service Rent the Runway).

[39] *See* Ravi Bapna, Wolfgang Jank, and Galit Shmueli, *Consumer Surplus in Online Auctions*, 19 Info. Syss. Res. 400, 400 (2008); *see also* Christoph Busch, Hans Schulte-Nölke, Aneta Wiewiórowska-Domagalska, and Fryderyk Zoll, *The Rise of the Platform Economy: A New Challenge for EU Consumer Law*, 5 J. Eur. Consumer & Market L. 3 (2016), available at https://papers.ssrn.com/sol3/papers.cfm?abstract_id=2754100.

might offer two types of benefit. First, being "world class" might directly raise a city's profile for industries like tourism (though empirical support for this proposition, at least in the context of urban amenities like sports arenas, is uncertain).[40] Second, being "on the map" might make cities more attractive or exciting places to live, drawing in new residents and keeping existing ones from needing to leave for a "real city." This concern is particularly salient for younger, mobile, and well-educated workers.

Increasingly, sharing firms are important markers of "on-the-mapness." In 2014, the American Planning Association found that 67 percent of urban residents and 73 percent of the young "millennial generation" saw access to sharing services as at least somewhat important to them.[41] Echoing this, Pittsburgh's mayor opposed new regulations on ride-sharing by stating: "I will not let Pittsburgh's emerging status as a 21st-century technological hub be sacrificed by unaccountable bureaucrats clinging to the past."[42] And in 2017, members of the Anchorage, Alaska city assembly endorsed a plan to permit Uber and Lyft to operate because of an interest in appearing "forward thinking."[43]

Finally, subsidies to sharing firms offer a third benefit: reducing urban "congestion." "Congestion," as used by urban economists, refers to costs of urban density, particularly high rents, which cap a city's growth potential. The sharing economy allows property to be used more efficiently, reducing the need to devote scarce urban space to duplicative products. Further, they also may allow cities to avoid costly policies that are designed to reduce congestion.

For example, services like Airbnb can save cities space and money that might otherwise be needed for hotels and lodging by channeling guests into preexisting housing. In doing so, they can enable cities to host larger events than previously possible by providing "surge capacity" for times of peak demand. Brazil failed to build sufficient hotel rooms for the World Cup in 2014, but Airbnb and other house-sharing firms were able to shelter 20 percent of visiting fans, averting a potential crisis.[44]

In sum, reducing congestion is a positive externality that sharing firms offer cities, one that might justify subsidies even if it does not immediately appear on local balance sheets.

How might cities subsidize sharing? Sometimes, they could do so by direct ownership: cities operating proprietary sharing services of their own. This is the model already seen in urban bike shares, where cities buy and own a public fleet or hire firms to do so on their behalf.[45] Yet while bike-shares are the best-known "city-owned" sharing, they are not alone. Several cities own car fleets that, through state and federal subsidies, are rented out at subsidized rates via public

[40] Roger G. Noll and Andrew Zimbalist, The Economic Impact of Sports Teams and Facilities, *in Sports, Jobs, and Taxes: The Economic Impact of Sports Teams and Stadiums* 55, 69–70 (Roger G. Noll and Andrew Zimbalist eds., 1997).

[41] Am. Planning Ass'n, Investing in Place for Economy Growth and Competitiveness 29 (2014), www.planning.org/policy/polls/investing/pdf/pollinvestingreport.pdf.

[42] Kim Lyons, *Mayor Bill Peduto Promises Ride-Share "Fight" in Pittsburgh*, GovTech (July 3, 2014), www.govtech.com/local/Peduto-promises-ride-share-fight-in-Pittsburgh.html.

[43] Devin Kelly, *Uber and Lyft Get Anchorage Assembly's OK, but the Companies Are Awaiting State Action*, Alaska Dispatch News (Mar. 22, 2017), www.adn.com/alaska-news/anchorage/2017/03/21/assembly-allows-uber-and-lyft-in-anchorage-but-those-ride-booking-companies-are-awaiting-state-action/.

[44] Kriston Capps, *The Sharing Economy Could Drive Down the Price of Mega-Events*, Atlantic: CityLab (Sept. 29, 2014), www.citylab.com/tech/2014/09/the-sharing-economy-could-drive-down-the-price-of-mega-events/380908.

[45] The estimated cost of New York City's CitiBike, for example, was $5,000 per bike, not including fixed costs. Jersey Journal, *Jersey City Snubs North Hudson Bike-Share Program for NYC's Citi Bike System*, NJ.com (Sept. 29, 2014), www.nj.com/jjournal-news/index.ssf/2014/09/jersey_city_snubs_north_hudson.html.

car-share programs.[46] Toronto, meanwhile, operates a city-owned tool-sharing program where citizens can borrow hardware equipment in the same way they might borrow library books.[47]

Elsewhere, cities might simply use various forms of direct payments. Already, some sharing firms receive cash subsidies in exchange for expanding service: Getaround, for example, received a federal grant in return for expanding car-sharing in Portland, Oregon,[48] and has since expanded this program to include more electric vehicles for lower-income neighborhoods.[49] On this point, Summit, New Jersey, is piloting a program to subsidize Uber fares to and from the local train station in order to avoid the necessity of building new municipal parking.[50] Other cities subsidize the sharing economy through tax breaks. Multnomah County, Portland, Boston, and Chicago have all imposed lower taxes on car-sharing firms than on ordinary car rental services.[51]

Cities also might subsidize sharing firms through free or reduced-cost city services. Cities like Denver and San Francisco, for instance, have at various times offered parking to car-share users.[52] In the future, such cities might go further, requiring buildings to designate parking spaces for shared cars, or conditioning the approval of new apartments on a developer's paying for residents' car-share memberships.[53]

Finally, cities might invest in infrastructure or programs that facilitate sharing economy participation. For example, Oakland has engaged in an effort to allow citizens to use their municipal IDs as pre-paid debit cards, which in turn allows "unbanked" citizens to participate in the tech-heavy, app-based sharing economy.[54]

Of course, wherever sharing subsidies are offered, this regulatory approach might raise important normative, legal, and policy questions. The costs in public money and tilting markets in inefficient ways can, after all, be substantial. Nevertheless, as a descriptive matter, such subsidies are already here, and will likely increase in prominence in the years to come, bringing such questions to the fore.

---

[46] *See, e.g., A Bold Plan to Bring Car-Share to the Poor*, CityLab (July30, 2015), www.citylab.com/cityfixer/ 2015/07/ las-bold-plan-to-bring-car-share-to-the-poor/400031; Adam Blair and Jennifer Dotson, *Carsharing in a Small City: Ithaca Carshare's First Two Years*, N.Y. Dep't Transp. S-1 (Mar. 2011), www.dot.ny.gov/divisions/engineering/ technical-services/trans-r-and-d-repository/C-06-33%20Ithaca%20Carshare%20Final%20Report%20NYSERDA%20 Agreement%209821.pdf.

[47] Solomon Greene and John McGinty, *What if Cities Could Create a Truly Inclusive Local Sharing Economy?* Urban Institute Policy Brief (June 2016), at 5, www.urban.org/research/publication/what-if-cities-could-create-truly-inclusive-local-sharing-economy. For more on the economics of such "product sharing" approaches, *see* Saif Benjaafar, Guangwen Kong, Xiang Li, and Costas Courcoubetis, *Peer-to-Peer Product Sharing: Implications for Ownership, Usage and Social Welfare in the Sharing Economy* (Oct. 6, 2015), https://papers.ssrn.com/sol3/papers.cfm?abstract_ id=2669823.

[48] *See* Joseph Rose, *Peer-to-Peer Car-Sharing Company Getaround Ready to Launch in Portland, with Help from $1.7 Million Federal Grant*, Or. Live (Dec. 13, 2011), http://blog.oregonlive.com/commuting/2011/12/peer-to-peer_car-sharing_servi. html (discussing federal grant to car-sharing firm Getaround to open in area unserved by other such firms).

[49] Kristen Hall-Geisler, *Shared EV Access Is Expanding in Portland*, TechCrunch (Mar. 28, 2017), https://techcrunch. com/2017/03/28/shared-ev-access-is-expanding-in-portland/.

[50] Amy Cairns, *Summit Pilot Program Offering Free Uber Rides to Train Station*, New Jersey Patch (Oct. 3, 2016), www .nj.com/independentpress/index.ssf/2016/10/summit_pilot_program_offering.html.

[51] *Policies for Shareable Cities: Transportation*, Shareable (Dec. 3, 2013), www.shareable.net/blog/policies-for-shareable-cities-transportation.

[52] *Car2go Denver Parking FAQs*, Car2Go, www.car2go.com/common/data/locations/usa/denver/Denver_Parking_FAQ.pdf.

[53] Neha Bhatt, *Smarter Parking Codes to Promote Smart Growth*, Smart Growth Am. (Aug. 12, 2014), www .smartgrowthamerica.org/2014/08/12/smarter-parking-codes-to-promote-smart-growth (reviewing car-sharing parking requirements); *Car-Sharing Requirements and Guidelines*, City & County S.F. Planning Dep't, www.sf-planning .org/ index.aspx?page=2347 (last updated Oct. 6, 2015) (noting the Planning Department has the power to require developers to pay car-sharing firm membership fees).

[54] *See* Greene and McGinty, *supra* note 47, at 5.

D Regulating Against Inequality

Yet another regulatory strategy cities might pursue is requiring sharing economy firms to pledge to benefit underserved communities in exchange for market access – put differently, to impose anti-poverty exactions. At first, this might seem counterintuitive. After all, many sharing firms focus squarely on upmarket consumers (witness the take-off of UberYacht and UberCopter).[55] And at least some sharing firms, like Airbnb, have dealt with allegations that their service discriminates against some users based on their race.[56] But a closer look shows that despite these (often serious) concerns, cities might also work with sharing firms to help reduce urban inequality.

Local governments often seek to redistribute resources to poorer residents and neighborhoods by using tools other than taxes and direct spending. Sharing firms offer a potentially important vehicle for building on these efforts. Therefore, in many cases cities have good reason to harness sharing firms as instruments of redistribution and the regulation of labor policy, such as by making sharing operations conditional on providing redistributive services or on guaranteeing certain employee benefits. These measures might include requiring expanded operations in poorer areas, mandated discounts in such areas, hiring advantages for workers from disadvantaged backgrounds, or a requirement of a "living wage" and healthcare benefits for "gig" employees.

As cities take this path, they echo a long tradition of requiring anti-poverty "exactions" from firms, such as urban-property developers, seeking access to city markets. Importantly, this form of regulation may actually be welcomed by the regulated, as it may be a way to cement public support and it might be cheaper for sharing firms to comply with than other forms of local regulations. On the other hand, just as with other exactions, these policies may drive prices up, creating costs for urban consumers.

In theory, sharing services should be particularly useful for the urban poor and other marginalized groups. While such firms have been largely seen as upmarket products used mainly by yuppies, at their core sharing services allow rental access to goods that might otherwise be unaffordable, like car rides or lodging. Sharing economy services expand the number of providers, drive down the price and decrease the minimum rental time (e.g. renting a car for 30 minutes). At the same time, such firms could also allow low-income sellers to mitigate the cost of capital expenditures. Rents can be partially offset by letting rooms on Airbnb, car costs can be offset by renting on RelayRides, and so on.[57] Finally, sharing firms like TaskRabbit, Wonolo, UberX, and Lyft could provide employment opportunities for second and third jobs for unemployed or underemployed city residents.[58]

As in the context of other, more traditional regulations, this sets up a possible "trade": redistribution-minded cities may expressly or implicitly require sharing firms to serve poor

---

[55] *The Sharing Economy Brings Tycoon Lifestyles Within Reach of Some*, The Economist (Nov. 26, 2016), www .economist.com/news/business-and-finance/21710767-thanks-companies-such-netjets-getmyboat-and-thirdhomecom-merely-rich-can-upgrade.

[56] Brentin Mock, *AirBnBWhileBlack and the Legacy of* Brown vs. Board, CityLab (May 20, 2016), www.citylab.com/housing/2016/05/brown-v-board-v-airbnb/483725/. For a legal-academic analysis of this problem, *see* Nancy Leong and Aaron Belzer, *The New Public Accommodations: Race Discrimination in the Platform Economy*, 105 Georgetown L.J. 1271 (2017).

[57] Another contribution to this volume has persuasively provided an illustration of this possibility: within New York City, Airbnb listings have increasingly expanded within areas of more modest household income. *See* Peter Coles et al., Chapter 8.

[58] *See generally* Greene and McGinty, *supra* note 47. At various times, sharing firms themselves have touted this path to economic opportunity. *See, e.g.*, Airbnb: *We're Bringing "Economic Opportunity" to NYC's Black Community*, GOTHAMIST (Apr. 21, 2016), gothamist.com/2016/04/21/airbnb_data_black_nyc.php.

residents or to modify worker rights in exchange for greater regulatory approval. Such measures would allow local politicians to provide benefits to particular populations without running into the limits on tax-and-revenue raising that state law imposes on many municipalities, or the political challenges of passing an outright tax increase. In cities where it is particularly important for sharing firms to have access – that is, large and rich cities – such "trades" may be particularly attractive to firms. Moreover, providing employment and opportunities to vulnerable sub-populations could allow sharing firms to both burnish their image and gain political allies to further expand their operations.[59]

In today's sharing economy we are already seeing the beginnings of such "trades." For instance, in Uber's fight to get approval to operate in Chicago, a key issue was whether it provided cars in underserved areas (and whether it did so as well as traditional cabs).[60] Similarly, to fend off regulations by the state of New York, Airbnb has at various points advertised both how it benefits economically-stressed homeowners and how it brings tourism to places like the Bronx, which have fewer traditional hotels.[61]

In time, cities might make these deals more explicit in at least two different ways: requiring direct cash payments, or requiring in-kind benefits. On the first count, cities might condition approval for sharing services on a firm's offering help in collecting taxes from network users – an otherwise fiendishly difficult task.[62] This approach has already been used in cities like Portland, San Francisco, and Amsterdam, which impose such requirements on the Airbnb network.[63]

A more interesting possibility, though, is for redistribution-minded cities to require in-kind contributions. For instance, cities might condition approval for sharing companies on guarantees of service for poor areas. Or they might condition approval on requiring a "living wage" to "gig" employees, giving hiring advantages to workers from disadvantaged backgrounds, or reducing prices for consumers in certain areas. Cities could even ask firms to roll out new services in return for allowing their main business line to operate. For example, a city might require Lyft to operate its cut-rate "LyftLine" carpool service in exchange for the right to offer premium ride options.

E Cities as Sharing Economy Participants

Finally, whatever other regulatory strategy cities adopt, cities also have the power to act as key sharing economy participants, hiring sharing firms through government contracts or even selling "sharing" goods and services to the public.

---

[59] *See, e.g.*, Eric Jaffe, *Lyft Is Hiring a Lot of Deaf Drivers*, Atlantic: CityLab (Sept. 24, 2014), www.citylab.com/work/2014/09/lyft-is-quietly-hiring-a-lot-of-deaf-drivers/380672.

[60] Andrew MacDonald, *Uber Economic Study: Uber Serves Underserved Neighborhoods in Chicago as well as the Loop. Does Taxi?*, Uber Newsroom (Mar. 3, 2014), http://blog.uber.com/chicagoneighborhoodstudy; Ted Cox, *Uber, Taxis Clash Over Rides to Underserved Areas*, DNAinfo (Mar. 6, 2014), www.dnainfo.com/chicago/20140306/downtown/uber-taxis-clash-over-rides-underserved-areas; *See also* Matt Flegenheimer, *De Blasio Administration Dropping Plan for Uber Cap, for Now*, N.Y. Times (July 22, 2015), www.nytimes.com/2015/07/23/nyregion/de-blasio-administration-dropping-plan-for-uber-cap-for-now.html.

[61] Adrianne Jeffries and Russell Brandom, *Hey, New York: Airbnb Wants to Get You in Bed*, Verge (July 14, 2014), www.theverge.com/2014/7/14/5896785/hey-new-york-airbnb-wants-to-get-you-in-bed.

[62] John Kuo, *How Should Government Regulate the Sharing Economy?*, NerdWallet (Mar. 11, 2014), www.nerdwallet.com/blog/investing/2013/government-regulate-sharing-economy; *see* Baker, *supra* note 22.

[63] Eliot Njus, *Portland Legalizes Airbnb-Style Short Term Rentals*, OregonLive (July 30, 2014), www.oregonlive.com/front-porch/index.ssf/2014/07/portland_legalizes_airbnb-styl.html.

There is an important set of expensive goods and services that cities require – but only infrequently. Municipal employees need government-provided cars, but these cars spend most of their time sitting in garages. Cities need road-paving machines, but only when maintenance is necessary. School buildings are needed for nine hours a day but can sit largely unused for fifteen. In short, cities face precisely the types of idle-capacity dynamics that make for ideal sharing economy consumers and producers.

This has not gone unnoticed. Even today, many local governments use car-share companies to cut the cost of providing city vehicles. Boston, Houston, and Washington D.C., and even federal agencies like the General Service Administration, have contracted with ZipCar to run their car fleets as car-sharing operations among government workers.[64] Meanwhile, cities like Chicago pay for ZipCar or other car-share memberships on behalf of some city employees.[65] And for its part, San Francisco has considered abandoning its entire non-emergency fleet in favor of car sharing.[66]

But car-shares are only the beginning. A service called Munirent has emerged in Michigan and Oregon, allowing governments to share all sorts of government-owned, heavy-duty property.[67] Along similar lines, Britain's government has proposed the creation of a "sharing-economy"-style exchange for government departments to share everything from office furniture to stationery.[68]

Eventually, such sharing platforms could expand to allow cities to share employees as well, allowing cities to share the costs of not only specialized equipment but also the cost of hiring highly trained employees to operate the equipment. And in time, such platforms might expand further still, to allow the government to share goods owned by the general public (i.e., to readily rent privately owned cameras, private parking lots, or other useful property). Doing so could greatly expand the number and kinds of things the government might rent instead of buying, leading to reduced costs.

For a look at how this model might play out, consider the proposed partnership between San Francisco's Department of Emergency Preparedness and BayShare, an advocacy group funded by sharing economy firms, to deploy privately owned sharing services in response to citywide crises.[69] Or consider the Massachusetts Bay Transit Authority's partnership with Uber and Lyft aimed at providing subsidized paratransit services for elderly and disabled citizens.[70]

---

[64] The effect of this can be dramatic. Boston reduced the size of its car fleet by 50 percent. Lisa Rein, *Will the Federal Fleet be Run By Zipcar*, Wash. Post: Federal Eye (Nov. 6, 2013), www.washingtonpost.com/blogs/federal-eye/wp/2013/11/06/will-the-federal-fleet-be-run-by-zipcar; Alex Howard, *Carsharing Saves U.S. City Governments Millions in Operating Costs*, O'Reilly Radar (Apr. 10, 2012), http://radar.oreilly.com/2012/04/carsharing-through-zipcar-save.html; *Houston Electric Vehicle Fleet Car Sharing Program*, Inst. for Sustainable Communities, http://sustainablecommunitiesleadershipacademy.org/resource_files/documents/Houston-Electric-Vehicle.pdf.

[65] Michael Grass, *How Big Cities Are Saving Big Bucks with Car Sharing*, Gov't Executive (July 9, 2014), www.govexec.com/state-local/2014/07/car-sharing-chicago-zipcar-indianapolis-blueindy/88141. Indianapolis's system is perhaps the most interesting. Indianapolis's Unigov created a public–private car-sharing system of electric vehicles, which can be used by both government employees and by members of the public who join the service. *Id.*

[66] John Coté, *S.F. Supervisor Seeks to Phase Out Fleet, Use Car Sharing*, S.F. Chron. (Sept. 8, 2014), www.sfgate.com/bayarea/article/S-F-supervisor-seeks-to-phase-out-fleet-use-car-5743051.php.

[67] Colin Wood, *Munirent Brings the Sharing Economy to Government*, Gov't Tech. (Aug. 21, 2014), www.govtech.com/internet/Munirent-Brings-the-Sharing-Economy-to-Government; Ben Schiller, *Now Cities and States Can Get Involved in the Sharing Economy, Instead of Just Slowing It Down*, Fast Co.: Co.Exist (Aug. 6, 2014), www.fastcoexist.com/3033971/now-cities-and-states-can-get-involved-in-the-sharing-economy-instead-of-just-slowing-it-dow.

[68] Steve O'Hear, *Collaborative Consumption of Stationery! (and Other UK Gov Responses to Sharing Economy Report)*, TechCrunch (Mar. 19, 2015), https://techcrunch.com/2015/03/19/can-i-borrow-a-pen/.

[69] Rory Smith, *San Francisco's Mayor Lee Launches Sharing Economy Partnership for Disaster Response*, Shareable (June 12, 2013), www.shareable.net/blog/san-franciscos-mayor-lee-launches-sharing-economy-partnership-for-disaster-response.

[70] Aarian Marshall, *Good News: The Tech to Change Your Grandma's Life Is Already Here*, WIRED (Sep 26, 2016), www.wired.com/2016/09/ridesharing-paratransit-seniors/.

Relatedly, just as cities might be buyers on sharing sites, they might also choose to become sellers, mitigating the costs of large capital expenditures. The most widely discussed possibility is sharing government buildings. Cities have long made space in government buildings like schools available to private groups after hours, whether for free or for rent.[71] Listing them on popular sharing platforms might greatly expand the market for such services, generating additional municipal funds.

CONCLUSION

As the other contributions to this volume ably demonstrate, cities are far from the only meaningful sites of sharing regulation. But as this discussion suggests, cities have the power and incentive to regulate in this area – and many potentially useful strategies for doing so. In particular, as the preceding discussion suggests, local regulation of sharing firms seems quite unlikely to take a simplistic path of either total bans or of total permissiveness. To the contrary, we have seen, and will continue to see, cities deploying a wide array of policy tools and approaches in regulating the sharing economy, just as they used to regulate its "non-sharing" predecessors.

---

[71] See, e.g., *Welcome to Community Use*, Denver Pub. Schs., http://schooluse.dpsk12.ord/DPSCommunityUsePolicy.

19

The Sharing Economy and the EU

Michèle Finck[*]

INTRODUCTION

In line with the title of the present section, this chapter examines the "who" and the "how" of the regulation of the sharing economy in the European Union. Just as in other jurisdictions, the emergence of the sharing economy, in particular large online platforms, has taken European regulators by surprise. At present, uncertainty reigns not only with respect to *how* this phenomenon should be addressed but also *by whom* – that is to say whether the EU should issue regulations or leave this to the Member States. Answering these questions is no easy task.

The "who" raises important questions that go to the core of the supranational project, including the division of competences between the Union and the Member States, the application of the subsidiarity principle,[1] and the desirability of centralized versus decentralized regulation. We will see that the sharing economy is a phenomenon that touches on issues as diverse as consumer protection,[2] competition law,[3] and taxation,[4] as well as urban transportation and housing policies. Other contributions in this volume have already underlined that the question of the appropriate scale of regulatory intervention arises in many contexts, including the United States where it has been debated whether the local, state, or federal level is the appropriate scale of regulation.[5] In the EU context, as in other multi-layered systems, an added complexity is that of existing divisions of competence between various actors.[6] In light of such complexity I shall argue that a careful balance must be struck between issues that genuinely mandate a supranational response and those best left to the Member States and their local and regional authorities.

The problem of regulatory allocation in respect of the platform economy is, however, of a dual nature as it also extends to the "how" of regulation. This question is fraught with similar difficulty as the sharing economy both raises new legal questions, such as the legal classification

---

[*] I am grateful to Nestor Davidson and John Infranca for helpful comments and suggestions, and to the participants of the 2017 Handbook Workshop for inspiring discussions.
[1] Article 5(3) Treaty on European Union (TEU).
[2] See Guido Smorto, this volume.
[3] See *further* Dunne in this volume.
[4] See Katerina Pantazatou, this volume.
[5] See Nestor M. Davidson and John J. Infranca; Janice Griffith; Sarah Light; and Daniel E. Rauch in this volume.
[6] In the EU competences are, in essence, either exclusively those of the EU (such as antitrust policy), shared between the EU and the Member States (as is the case with the internal market) or left to the Member States (such as housing policies).

of a platform or a "prosumer"[7] and revisits known challenges, such as the interaction between regulation and innovation. Contrary to other chapters engaging with EU law in this volume, this contribution is not so much concerned with the substance of such regulation but rather with the procedure behind it. It will argue that existing ideals of democratic law-making should be adapted to the digital age through a polycentric process of co-regulation that can harness the advantages of digital tools for participation and enforcement while safeguarding recognized public policy objectives.

This chapter thus seeks to map how the dual challenge of regulatory allocation has played out in the European Union.[8] The analysis unfolds in four parts. I shall first address the definition of the "sharing economy" in the EU context and secondly evaluate which levels of public authority have regulatory competence in respect of the phenomenon. Thirdly, I shall examine the challenges and opportunities digital platforms present to the regulatory process itself. I will conclude by arguing that as the economy moves from a world of atoms to a world of bits, regulation must adapt and accept the need for greater techno-legal interoperability.

I THE DEFINITIONAL CHALLENGE

Before venturing on to that mapping task, the definitional challenge must first be addressed. There is, at present, no singular definition nor label of what this Handbook refers to as "the sharing economy" that attracts consensus on the European continent. Whereas the European Commission has adopted the notion of "the collaborative economy," the European Parliament has referred to the same phenomenon as "the sharing economy," and the Committee of the Regions has used both notions.[9] The European Commission has pragmatically defined the "collaborative economy" as follows:

> business models where activities are facilitated by collaborative *platforms* that create an open marketplace for the temporary usage of goods or services often provided by private individuals. The collaborative economy involves three categories of actors: (i) service providers who share assets, resources, time and/or skills – these can be private individuals offering services on an occasional basis ("peers") or service providers acting in their professional capacity ("professional service providers"); (ii) users of these; and (iii) intermediaries that connect – via an *online platform* – providers with users and that facilitate transactions between them ("collaborative platforms"). Collaborative economy transactions generally do not involve a change of ownership and can be carried out for profit or not-for-profit.[10]

This definition's emphasis on online platforms underscores that the EU is only interested in the sharing economy in so far as it pertains to the digital marketplace.[11] Platforms, in their capacity as matchmakers and gatekeepers, connect users in order to allow them to more easily make use of goods or services.[12] It is indeed through platforms that the practice of sharing, probably as

---

[7] This terminology has emerged in the sharing economy context to denote that an individual can at the same time be a producer and a consumer.

[8] This analysis takes into account developments up until the summer of 2017.

[9] *See, e.g.*, www.europarl.europa.eu/news/en/press-room/20170609IPR77014/sharing-economy-parliament-calls-for-clear-eu-guidelines.

[10] Commission Communication, *A European Agenda for the Collaborative Economy*, COM (2016) 356 final, at 2.1 (my own emphasis).

[11] This excludes more traditional forms of sharing, sometimes referred to as "true sharing." On this, *see also* Michèle Finck and Sofia Ranchordás, *Sharing and the City*, 49 Vand. J. Transnat'l L. 1299 (2016).

[12] For an argument that we should focus on platforms' gatekeeping function when evaluating sharing economy platforms, *see* Orla Lynskey, *Regulating "Platform Power*," LSE Law, Society and Economy Working Papers 1/2017.

old as human civilization itself, has been able to increase in scope and scale. To mirror the EU's focus on digital platforms, this chapter focuses solely on digital sharing economy platforms to the exclusion of offline sharing practices (such as tool libraries or offline modes of food-sharing) as well as online platforms that involve a transfer of ownership (such as Etsy or Ebay).[13]

The introductory chapter as well as various contributions to this Handbook have amply underlined the lack of consensus regarding what falls within the scope of the notion of "the sharing economy" and whether this terminology is helpful. Acknowledging this lack of definitional consensus, both in the EU and beyond, I will refer to notions such as "the sharing economy," "the platform economy," and the "collaborative economy" interchangeably. In line with the spirit of the present Handbook, the chapter adopts a wide definition, accepting a large range of phenomena to be captured by the notion according to popular usage, even those that do not involve "true sharing."[14] To mirror current EU definitions, however, only digital platforms will be considered. As a final caveat, I shall focus exclusively on the regulation of sharing economy platforms themselves, excluding the situation of providers of the underlying good or service (such as employment relations or providers' liability) as well as of the recipient of the good or service (such as consumer protection).[15] This brings us to the first of the two questions of regulatory allocation this chapter examines, that of the actor(s) who should regulate sharing economy platforms in the European Union.

II WHO SHOULD REGULATE THE SHARING ECONOMY?

At the core of contemporary regulatory debates lies, as often in the supranational context, the question of competence. Phrased differently, regulators in the EU currently struggle not only with *how* to regulate sharing economy platforms, but also *who* should regulate them: the Member States (either at national or subnational level)[16] or the European Union. This section sets out the arguments that have been voiced on both sides and concludes that there are no legal obstacles for the EU to regulate sharing economy platforms yet also takes note of the Union's current reluctance to do so as well as the argument that, given the specific characteristics of the sharing economy, regulation at smaller scales will often be preferable.[17]

The Treaties define internal market regulation as a competence shared between the Union and the Member States.[18] In the language of EU law, this means that "the Union shall act only if and in so far as the objectives of the proposed action cannot be sufficiently achieved by the Member States, either at central level or at regional and local level, but can rather, by reason of the scale or effects of the proposed action, be better achieved at Union level."[19] Given the repeated calls for a homogenous legal framework it appears that there is scope for the EU to regulate at least some aspects of the sharing economy. For example, the European Parliament has called for supranational regulation in order to eradicate regulatory gray areas, and create homogenous rules to apply throughout the EU's internal market.[20] The Commission

---

[13] In light of the Commission's observation that sharing economy models do not involve a transfer of ownership.

[14] On the desirability of a distinction between platforms in general and "true sharing" *see* Finck and Ranchordás, *supra* note 11.

[15] These questions are examined in the EU context by the contributions of Koolhoven and Smorto in this volume.

[16] Member States would, in accordance with Article 5(3) TEU, have the choice to regulate at central or subnational level.

[17] *See* further Finck and Ranchordás, *supra* note 11.

[18] Article 4(2)(a) TFEU.

[19] Article 5(3) TEU.

[20] www.europarl.europa.eu/news/en/press-room/20170609IPR77014/sharing-economy-parliament-calls-for-clear-eu-guidelines.

itself recognizes that platforms have "dramatically" changed the digital economy and play a prominent role in the EU's Digital Single Market project.[21] Indeed, in light of their transnational operation and impact, there is clearly an argument to be made that, in line with EU principles of competence division, the Union is legally competent to regulate the collaborative economy in its internal market dimension.

The related question is whether the EU considers it to be politically opportune to take such steps. The European Parliament and the Committee of the Regions have called on the Commission to "come up with a clear legal framework that ensures that fair competition principles are upheld."[22] There is, moreover, growing criticism of the Commission's laissez-faire approach. It has been argued that the most interesting aspect of the Commission's 2016 Communication on the Collaborative Economy is that "on many points it is willing to go along with the claims made by collaborative platforms that the specific characteristics of the collaborative business models allow for the application of less stringent rules than those applicable to traditional business models."[23] The Vice-President of the European Commission and the EU Commissioner for the Internal Market have further uttered criticism with respect to some Member States' moves to prohibit sharing economy practices, an issue that could be resolved through a supranational regulatory framework.[24] Indeed, in the words of the Committee of the Regions, despite the difficulty of regulating sharing economy platforms at this stage, "early action to prevent fragmentation in the first place would still be far less difficult than ex-post harmonization of 28 national frameworks and countless local and regional regulations."[25] Finally, the Commission has recognized "there is a risk that regulatory grey zones are exploited to circumvent rules designed to preserve the public interest."[26] It has as a consequence announced a monitoring framework to cover both the evolving regulatory environment and economic and business developments in the context of collaborative platforms.[27] These signs point toward the likely adoption of a EU-level regulatory framework covering at least some aspects of the platform economy in the future. Given the impact of the platform economy on the internal market as a whole, the Union appears competent to regulate sharing economy platforms, should it wish to do so.

Yet, at the same time, no such steps have been taken to date. This testifies to the lack of political consensus but also the difficulty of regulating the phenomenon. It still remains largely undetermined for instance whether platforms should be legally qualified as mere matchmakers or service providers, and any legal regime will hinge upon that classification.[28] What is more, beyond questions of labor rights and consumer protection, the collaborative economy's most controversial effects pertain to urban housing and mobility policies, an issue Member States and their subnational authorities should address. There are indeed powerful arguments that, given that many of the consequences of these new business models

---

[21] Commission Communication on Online Platforms and the Digital Single Market, *Opportunities and Challenges for Europe*, COM (2016) 288 final, 2.

[22] *Id.*

[23] Caroline Cauffman and Jan Smits, *The Sharing Economy and the Law. Food for European Lawyers*, 23 Maastricht Journal of European and Comparative Law 903, 907.

[24] D. Robinson, *Brussels Urges More Caring for Sharing Economy*, Fin. Times (May 30, 2016), www.ft.com/content/4c19a666-267f-11e6-8ba3-cdd781d02d89.

[25] *Opinion of the Committee of the Regions on the Collaborative Economy and Online Platforms: A Shared View of Cities and Regions*, ECON-VI/016, 1.

[26] European Commission, *supra* note 10, 184 final at 2.

[27] *Id.* at 15.

[28] This will be decided by the European Court of Justice in Uber Spain.

have inherently local consequences, any form of supranational regulation must not impede subnational regulators' ability to address these effects.[29] Two solutions could in this respect be envisaged. The EU could, on the one hand, issue a regulatory floor that Member States or subnational authorities could build upon, such as with respect to consumer protection. On the other hand, it is worth remembering that certain issues should not be touched by EU regulation, mirroring the specific effects of sharing practices as well as existing distributions of competence. It is in this context worth noting that the EU does not have competence when it comes to issues such as urban planning and housing policy. This leaves us with a situation of fragmented regulatory authority as the EU has competence to address sharing platforms in their transnational internal market dimension but Member States, at national or subnational level, are competent to address the collaborative economy's localized effects, an issue already addressed elsewhere.[30] I now turn to an analysis of possible forms of regulatory intervention.

III THE 'HOW' OF EU PLATFORM REGULATION

I now examine the second facet of regulatory allocation examined in this chapter, that of the actors to be involved in the regulatory process. While many aspects covered below extend to any level of public authority I focus specifically on the EU in line with the chapter's focus. This question mandates detailed attention given that in its 2016 Communication on Online Platforms, the European Commission suggested that self-regulation and co-regulation could be preferred over a traditional top-down legislative approach in the context of the collaborative economy. It put forward that "principles-based self-regulatory/co-regulatory measures, including industry tools for ensuring application of legal requirements and appropriate monitoring mechanisms" can be variants of platform regulation.[31] I briefly introduce the alternatives of top-down regulation, self-regulation, and co-regulation to suggest that the latter of these three options might be the most suitable regulatory approach given the platform economy's specific characteristics.[32]

A *Top-Down Regulation*

Top-down regulation is what typically comes to mind when thinking about regulating economic behavior: legislation. It has been defined as "regulation by the state, which is often assumed to take a particular form, that is the use of legal rules backed by criminal sanctions."[33] The EU's regulatory activity is indeed commonly associated with secondary legislation[34] crafted under the ordinary legislative procedure.[35] Conventional secondary legislation would have the advantage of creating uniformity across Member States and sharing economy platforms, thus reducing regulatory uncertainty and fragmentation across the EU.[36]

---

[29] On this *see further* Davidson and Infranca in this volume and Finck and Ranchordás, *supra* note 11.

[30] Finck and Ranchordás, *supra* note 11.

[31] European Commission, *supra* note 22, at 5.

[32] For further discussion, *see* Michèle Finck, *Digital Regulation*, Eur. L. Rev. (forthcoming, 2018).

[33] Julia Black, *Decentring Regulation: Understanding the Role of Regulation and Self-Regulation in a "Post-Regulatory" World*, 54 Current Legal Probs. 103, 105 (2001).

[34] In the EU context secondary legislation includes, as per Article 288, Treaty on the Functioning of the European Union (TFEU), regulations and directives issued by the European Union.

[35] Article 294, TFEU.

[36] On the consequences of fragmentation in the context of taxation, *see* Pantazatou in this volume.

Yet, in light of the specific characteristics of the sharing economy, we may doubt whether this is really an appropriate regulatory response.[37] First, we must take note of the stark information asymmetries between platforms and regulators. Platforms certainly have better data regarding their own operation, and likely also have better data in respect of their socioeconomic consequences. Legislating in spite of such an information gap risks stifling innovation, and thus harming platforms and the economy, making the rules created hard to enforce, and adding more regulation to an already complex regulatory framework. Moreover, the gaps in understanding these autonomous technological sharing economy platforms, for instance in respect of whether they are service providers or mere matchmakers, extend to politicians and civil servants, which burdens any regulatory exercise. Dunne has moreover shown that platforms are often hard to qualify and address under current legal frameworks so that specifically-targeted frameworks may be a more suitable response.[38] While it is true that prima facie a top-down regulatory approach appears more democratically legitimate, it is also worth recalling that it is far from unproblematic in light of capture by interest groups and closed-doors law-making in trilogues.[39] Furthermore, as highlighted below, such democratic ideals can also be embedded in a co-regulatory solution. This leads us to examine the alternatives suggested by the Commission, starting with self-regulation.

B Self-Regulation

Self-regulation is the first alternative to top-down legislation that has been suggested by the Commission. At present, sharing economy platforms are already self-regulating entities that determine the terms and conditions of their intermediary function and accordingly define online and offline standards of behavior for both providers and consumers. This confirms that technology can be a partly self-regulating force, as captured by Lessig's maxim of "code is law."[40] Up until this point, there has been no specific legislative effort at EU level to tackle the implications of the sharing economy. Member States have also by and large adopted a "wait-and-see" approach. In this context it surprises little that examples of industry self-regulation abound.[41] Some have indeed compared sharing economy platforms to governments, given that "like governments, each platform is in the business of developing policies which enable social and economic activity that is vibrant and safe."[42] Uber's Community Compact is a case in point. It regulates interactions between drivers and riders as well as issues of safety.[43] Non-respect of these standards is sanctioned by delisting from the platform.[44] A further example of self-regulation can be observed in respect of the global freelancing platform Upwork that has imposed a "minimum rate" for work contracted through the platform.[45] Beyond the "code is law" aspect of technology's regulatory potential we must further stress that technology has, for better or for worse, enormous potential to nudge individuals into adopting certain behavior. Uber, for instance, has been said to be engaged "in an extraordinary behind-the-scenes experiment in behavioral science to manipulate [its drivers] in

---

[37] For a similar observation from the American perspective *see* Brescia in this volume.
[38] *See* Dunne in this volume for an overview of competition law and platforms.
[39] Trilogues are a controversial component of the EU law-making process, consisting of informal and closed-door negotiations of secondary legislation by representatives of the Commission, Parliament, and Council.
[40] Lawrence Lessig, *Code and Other Laws of Cyberspace* (1999).
[41] These initiatives can be partly motivated by a desire to prevent future legislation.
[42] Lessig, *supra* note 41.
[43] *Id.*
[44] *Id.*
[45] www.upwork.com.

the service of its corporate growth," most notably through psychological inducements to influence when, where, and how they work.[46] Practices of this kind illustrate the need for external regulatory involvement to safeguard public policy goals such as worker and consumer protection.

Self-regulation has been defined in the EU context as "the possibility for economic operators, the social partners, non-governmental organisations or associations to adopt amongst themselves and for themselves common guidelines at European level (particularly codes of practice or sectoral agreements)."[47] The above examples highlight that it can also take the form of a firm regulating for itself, a form of isolated self-regulation that creates more risk than where this is done as a collective effort. Self-regulation can assume a number of forms as it can be mandated by public authorities or adopted voluntarily. In the context of the platform economy, self-regulation has attracted support from industry insiders[48] and Sundararajan has stressed that the trust-enforcing function of government regulation can now be fulfilled by sharing economy platforms themselves through peer-review mechanisms.[49]

Self-regulation, however, also bears risks, as highlighted above, and we should be careful about sharing economy platforms transforming into purely self-regulating oligopolies that act outside of any oversight mechanisms. This not only lacks transparency but further fails to account for the interests of actors other than the platform itself. While rating mechanisms and peer-review options are fascinating trust-enforcing mechanisms we simply do not know enough about them to allow them to replace public safeguards, so additional insight derived from behavioral psychology and management is needed.[50] Such mechanisms add value in many contexts but we also know that they are prone to bias and manipulation, and these aspects need to be further researched to determine whether they can be a stand-alone regulatory response. From the perspective of EU law, it must moreover be stressed that there is a risk that platform self-regulation breaches competition law if there is coordination between different would-be competitor platforms that limits competition between them.[51] We moreover know that self-regulation without external control is prone to failure. Despite Uber's self-imposed rules regarding sexual contact between riders and drivers it has repeatedly turned a blind eye to its drivers committing sexual offenses on riders.[52] The absence of uniform regulatory standards under self-regulatory models can moreover result in case-by-case litigation to determine applicable rules, which is undesirable for both platforms and regulators.[53] Even critics of regulation have argued that the notion that "a disembodied free market, one which does not rest upon government force, will function effectively is certainly a mistake of epic proportions, if not an anarchist myth."[54] The rejection of self-regulation as an appropriate governance technique for the collaborative economy brings us to evaluate the second alternative regulatory solution suggested by the Commission, that of co-regulation.

---

[46] www.nytimes.com/interactive/2017/04/02/technology/uber-drivers-psychological-tricks.html?_r=0.

[47] Interinstitutional Agreement on Better Law-Making (2003) OJ C 321, para. 22.

[48] Nick Grossmann, *Regulation 2.0*, www.nickgrossman.is/tag/regulation-2-0/.

[49] Arun Sundararajan, *The Sharing Economy* 138–58 (2016).

[50] The regulatory dimension of trust and reputation mechanisms is usefully discussed by Marta Cantero Gomito, *Regulation.com. Self-Regulation and Contract Governance in the Platform Economy: A Research Agenda*, 9 Eur. J. Legal Stud. 53 (2017).

[51] For a discussion, *see* Imelda Maher, *Competition Law and Transnational Private Regulatory Regimes: Marking the Cartel Boundary*, 38 J.L. & Soc'y. 119 (2011).

[52] www.theguardian.com/technology/2017/aug/13/uber-failing-to-report-sex-attacks-by-drivers-says-met-police.

[53] Edward Glaeser and Andrei Shleifer, *The Rise of the Regulatory State*, 41 J. Econ. Lit. 401, 402–03 (2003).

[54] Richard Epstein, *Can Technological Innovation Survive Government Regulation?* 36 Harv. J.L. & Pub. Pol'y. 87, 88 (2013).

C Co-Regulation

Co-regulation has been defined as a "mechanism whereby an [EU] legislative act entrusts the attainment of the objectives defined by the legislative authority to parties which are recognized in the field (such as economic operators, the social partners, non-governmental organizations, or associations)."[55] Under such a model, the EU would define objectives that are then to be achieved by entrusted non-public actors. This section illustrates that this solution, where complemented by sound safeguards, emerges as the most opportune regulatory response to regulate the collaborative economy at EU level.

Under models of co-regulation "the regulatory regime is made up of a complex interaction of general legislation and a self-regulatory body."[56] This generates collaboration between public and private bodies to regulate private activity while accounting for its particularities and safeguarding public policy objectives.[57] Acknowledging the complex interaction between the state and the market, co-regulation reflects the spirit of new governance approaches that recognize the "benefits including a broader pool of stakeholders and decision makers in the articulation, execution and evolution of policy, law, norms development, oversight and regulation."[58] Co-regulation has also been referred to as "regulated self-regulation" emphasizing the interplay between the regulator and the regulated.[59] Co-regulation is thus to be distinguished from self-regulation and indeed deregulation as public authorities are involved at all stages of the process from the definition of the legislative framework to the complex evaluation and review mechanisms.

A number of examples of sharing economy co-regulation can currently be identified in the EU. Airbnb and Amsterdam, for instance, signed a memorandum of understanding designed to "promote responsible home sharing" that introduces automated limits to ensure that entire-home listings are not shared for more than 60 days.[60] Similar models have been adopted in other European cities such as London, where their agreement encompasses a 90-day period.[61] Analogous solutions can moreover be identified in respect of fiscal policy. For example, Airbnb has assumed the task of regulating tourist tax in a number of cities, such as Lisbon and Paris.[62] Staying with the example of Airbnb, it is worth highlighting its adoption of a "Community Compact" that sets out guiding principles to develop partnerships with cities.[63] A pivotal argument for involving platforms in regulation is that many regulatory objectives can be fulfilled more efficiently with platforms' cooperation. Airbnb can simply program its algorithm to collect tourist tax whereas we know that ensuring tax compliance is a costly and burdensome task for public authorities, often yielding limited success.

In an age of de facto self-regulation, co-regulation would enable the EU to re-enter the debate to ensure that public policy objectives are achieved. Co-regulation, moreover, accounts for information asymmetries, acknowledging that platforms are data monopolies and regulators often lack

---

[55] 2003 Interinstitutional Agreement on Better Law-Making, supra note 48, at para. 18.

[56] Christopher Marsden, *Internet Co-Regulation* 46 (2011).

[57] For a perspective on co-regulation from the United States, *see* Cannon and Chung in this volume.

[58] Raymond Brescia, *Regulating the Sharing Economy: New and Old Insights into an Oversight Regime for the Peer-to-Peer Economy*, 95 Neb. L. Rev. 87, 134 (2016).

[59] *See* Wolfgang Hoffmann-Riem, Verwaltungsrechtsreform – Ansätze am Beispiel des Umweltschutzes, *in Reform des Allgemeinen Verwaltungsrechts – Grundfragen* 115, 140 (Wolfgang Hoffmann-Riem et al. eds., 1993). *See also* Wolfgang Schulz and Thorsten Held, *Regulated Self-Regulation as a Form of Modern Government* (2004).

[60] www.dutchdailynews.com/amsterdam-airbnb-announce-new-unique-agreement/.

[61] *Id.*

[62] *Id.*

[63] www.airbnbcitizen.com/the-airbnb-community-compact/.

the necessary data to make informed decisions. Involving private actors ensures that regulation is "reflexive," that is to say formulated in a way understood by the autonomous social systems it regulates.[64] Through co-regulatory solutions the interests of the objects of regulation are not eclipsed but rather form a central part of the regulatory concept. Schulz and Held have stressed that this "makes information-gathering easier, mainly because the players in the regulatory field (such as economic enterprises) are informed at first hand of ongoing developments."[65] The reality of information asymmetry is, therefore, a clear point in favor of co-regulation. Co-regulation is moreover inherently flexible. The sharing economy is made up of different platforms, and diverse transactions, involving both peers and professional providers, occur on these platforms. As technology changes and experience grows, regulation must be adapted, which highlights the value of regulatory experimentalism in this fast-changing and diverse industry.[66] Co-regulation, with its continued assessments and reports, can identify best practices and stimulate mutual learning. The Commission has indeed already encouraged public authorities to "pilot innovative regulatory approaches to verify the feasibility and sustainability of innovative solutions" in light of their complexity and changing nature.[67] Co-regulation moreover offers an ease of enforcement that cannot be achieved under top-down legislation. Collaborative platforms can, through a simple twisting of code, secure that prosumers pay taxes and comply with time limits – something regulators can only dream of. These benefits indicate that co-regulation could be a suitable approach to regulating the collaborative economy in the EU.

It is of course true that, as with anything, co-regulation comes with its own sets of risks and problems. For example, it might be easier for larger platforms to engage in this process than for smaller ones. Co-regulatory processes can, however, be complemented with additional safeguards, which ensure that there is genuine collaboration and dialogue (as opposed to a situation of self-regulation by another name). Public authorities must moreover always keep the upper hand through the possibility of abandoning the collaborative process in favor of a top-down legislative approach in cases of noncompliance, and regular review processes must be carried out objectively and independently. Just as with other regulatory techniques we must in addition be wary of regulatory capture and ensure that all relevant actors have equal voice. Two additional safeguards of vital importance, that of polycentricity and data-sharing, are examined in more detail below.

D Polycentricity and Data-Sharing as Central Components of a Co-Regulatory Approach

The traditional approach to co-regulation outlined above should be complemented by a number of features to align it specifically to the sharing economy. First, polycentricity must be a pivotal feature of any co-regulatory solution.[68] Polycentricity is a characterizing feature of new governance models that are predicated "upon a dispersal and fragmentation of authority."[69]

---

[64] Günther Teubner, Justification: Concepts, Aspects, Limits, Solutions, *in A Reader on Regulation* 406 (Robert Baldwin et al. eds., 1998) and Günther Teubner, *Law as an Autopoetic System* (1993).

[65] Schulz and Held, *supra* note 60, at 15.

[66] *See* Sofia Ranchordás, *Innovation Experimentalism in the Age of the Sharing Economy*, 19 Lewis & Clark L. Rev. 871 (2015).

[67] Communication from the Commission to the European Parliament, the Council, the European Economic and Social Committee and the Committee of the Regions Upgrading the Single Market: More Opportunities for People and Business, COM (2015), 28.10.2015.

[68] On this, *see* further Finck, *supra* note 33.

[69] Joanne Scott and David Trubek, *Mind the Gap: Law and New Approaches to Governance in the European Union*, 8 Eur. L.J. 1, 8 (2002).

Under a strict co-regulation approach, only industry and the EU would cooperate to define platform regulation. Yet, additional stakeholders should be involved for this promises superior outcomes and echoes the polycentric nature of the sharing economy itself. Under a polycentric co-regulatory approach binding rules emerge from the interaction of multiple actors. Multiple stakeholders would be consulted in a transparent fashion, from various platforms themselves (not just the operator with the highest market share) to consumers, experts, and representatives of incumbent industries. This process can be greatly facilitated by technology and the EU is indeed already relying often on online consultations to consult stakeholders on legislative plans, which could serve as inspiration to this approach.[70] This is indeed precisely what the Commission sought to achieve with its 2015 public consultation on the regulatory environment for platforms, online intermediaries, data and cloud computing, and the collaborative economy.[71] Such polycentric consultation efforts could lead to a stronger concentration of knowledge, especially valuable in contexts of information asymmetry, as knowledge is naturally dispersed across society.[72]

   The approach is further in line with the EU's 2015 Better Regulation Agenda, which promotes evidence-based regulation, including broader consultations and civic engagement.[73] This would be easy to capture given that regulatory conversations on the platform economy are already polycentric in that they are transnational, multi-sectoral, and involve actors at all levels of government from the local to the supranational.[74] Indeed, in light of the arguments introduced above, it is important that EU legislation only determines broad frameworks, leaving space for subnational authorities to determine their own response, accounting for their respective particularities, especially in relation to the very localized effects of the phenomenon.[75]

   It is worthy of special emphasis that polycentricity can be stimulated by the same technological shift that underlies the digitalized sharing economy's emergence. New digital avenues for participation and deliberation have the potential to increase networked policymaking and widen alternative spaces and forms of policy dialogues. Sharing economy platforms themselves have indeed long learned to rely on technology's civic potential. Online participation certainly isn't free from problems as it creates a cacophony of voices and raises difficult questions of legitimacy, self-selection, undue influence, and bias. Evidence mounts, however, that digital tools are having an overall positive impact on civic engagement.[76] A polycentric co-regulatory process, facilitated by technological innovation, thus appears to be preferable to self-regulation as well as top-down regulation for the reasons outlined above. The flexibility of the process further presents the notable benefit of leaving space for learning and adaptation as the technology that

---

[70] *See,* by way of example, the EU's Public Consultation on Building the European Data Economy, https://ec.europa.eu/digital-single-market/en/news/public-consultation-building-european-data-economy.

[71] European Commission, Public Consultation on the Regulatory Environment for Platforms, Online Intermediaries, Data and Cloud Computing and the Collaborative Economy (2015), https://ec.europa.eu/growth/content/public-consultation-regulatory-environment-platforms-online-intermediaries-data-and-cloud-o_en.

[72] Cass Sunstein, *Infotopia: How Many Minds Produce Knowledge* (2006); Henrik Serup Christensen, Maija Karlainen, and Laura Nurminen, *Does Crowdsourcing Legislation Increase Political Legitimacy? The Case of Avoin Ministeriö in Finland,* 7 Pol'y & Internet 25 (2015).

[73] Communication from the Commission to the European Parliament, the Council, the European Economic and Social Committee and the Committee of the Regions, "Better Regulation for Better Results – An EU Agenda," COM(2015) 215.

[74] On regulatory conversations, *see further* Julia Black, *Regulatory Conversations,* 29 J.L. & Soc'y. 163 (2002).

[75] On the status of subnational authorities in EU law, *see* Michèle Finck, *Subnational Authorities in EU Law* (2017).

[76] Shelley Boulianne, *Does Internet Use Affect Engagement? A Meta-Analysis of Research,* 26(2) Pol. Comm. 193, 205 (2009); Kevin Desouza and Aksay Bhagwatwar, *Technology-Enabled Participatory Platforms for Civic Engagement: The Case of U.S. Cities,* 21(4) J. Urban Tech. 25 (2014).

has enabled the emergence of the sharing economy is itself subject to modification.[77] Beyond accounting for polycentricity, regulating platforms through a co-regulatory approach should also provide for data-sharing.

Co-regulatory solutions in the digital economy can only work if data is shared between the regulated and the regulator. Whereas intermediaries have full knowledge of their internal operation, regulators are largely left to guess.[78] Co-regulation accordingly has to provide for some variant of data-sharing to allow regulators to acquire the necessary information and determine whether platforms enforce the given standards, subject of course to data protection standards.[79] Interesting examples have emerged in this context, such as data-sharing agreements between Milan and Airbnb.[80] However, little is known about the exact data that has been shared in this context and regulators would have to make sure that data that is shared in fact allows for a truthful assessment of whether the regulatory objectives are being achieved. Data-sharing is indeed presently self-regulated by the platform. Airbnb's "Community Compact" announces openness to data-sharing, stating that it will "provide cities with the information they need to make informed decisions about home-sharing policies."[81] The information that is revealed is relatively generic, however, including "Home Sharing Activity Reports" in cities with a significant presence that outline: the total annual economic activity generated by the Airbnb community; income earned by a "typical" host; the number of hosts having avoided eviction or foreclosure due to sharing income; the number of days a typical listing is rented on the platform and the average number of days guests stay in cities.[82]

In order to audit and review the co-regulatory process, public authorities must have access to adequate data. Numerous options exist in this respect. First, public authorities could enjoy unrestricted access to such data, which is doubtlessly the most radical option as it raises concerns of personal data protection as sophisticated methods of reverse-engineering make the total anonymization of data less likely.[83] Platforms might be equally unhappy with such radical transparency. Softer solutions can also be envisaged, including the replacement of large-scale data audits with application programming interfaces (APIs) tailored to government auditing purposes or data-sampling.[84] This chapter has thus far made the argument in favor of increased collaboration between the regulator and actors affected by regulation in the context of the collaborative economy. By way of conclusion I now reflect on how convergence between technology and regulation is not specific to the platform economy but may rather be seen as a sign of what is to come in the future.

IV TOWARD GREATER TECHNO-LEGAL CONVERGENCE

The above analysis has underscored the challenges faced when it comes to regulating new technologies. Digital platforms are transnational in their scope and effect; yet often produce consequences closely tied to the specific place in which they operate.[85] The answer of "who" should regulate the sharing economy thus yields no straightforward response and a careful

---

[77] This is underlined by the emergence of blockchains and other forms of Distributed Ledger Technology that could have a far-reaching effect on how such platforms operate.

[78] Frank Pascquale, *The Black Box Society* (2015).

[79] In the EU, this is governed by the General Data Protection Regulation.

[80] www.airbnbcitizen.com/moving-forwards-in-milan/.

[81] *Id.*

[82] *Id.*

[83] *See further* Article 29 Working Party Opinion 04/2014 on Anonymization Techniques, 0829/14/EN, 12–13.

[84] In essence, an API is a conduit that enables the flow of data between systems.

[85] *See further* Davidson and Infranca in this volume.

balance must be reached between supranational regulation accounting for the internal market objective and national and subnational actors' autonomy to define their own policies. This must of course echo the current division of competences in the Union. One of the reasons that has made it difficult to determine the supranational response to the sharing economy is precisely that it involves questions such as consumer protection[86] and also taxation[87] (which is, generally speaking, a competence left to Member States) or urban affairs and housing policy (which is equally a national competence, often exercised by subnational authorities). This fragmentation of regulatory responsibility, however, not only mirrors competence division in the Union but also the nature of the collaborative economy itself given that it is an inherently transnational phenomenon with sometimes very localized implications.

The form of proposed regulation is equally challenging to determine. Top-down legislation may for many reasons not be the most suitable technique to be applied to the digital sphere. At the same time, self-regulation risks reinforcing data monopolies and non-observance of key public policy goals. In this context, a third way, the co-regulatory solution, has been identified, a key benefit of which is its capacity to bridge the advantages of new technologies with the classical rationales of public market intervention. This, it is briefly argued by way of conclusion, hints at a need for greater techno-legal convergence in the future. In itself the idea of a polycentric co-regulatory process is far from revolutionary. It represents the idea that binding norms should be created on the basis of wide participation and consensus, and pursue objectives that work for society overall. Yet, current regulatory debates illustrate that the simple transposition of current ideals of democratic legislative processes to the digital economy in general and sharing economy platforms more specifically have proven difficult. This realization occurs at the same time as more and more criticism is directed toward a supranational legislative process unable to correspond to ideals of democracy and moreover shaped by closed-door negotiations. Sharing economy platforms are regulatory targets that have moved from the world of atoms to the world of bits, creating a wide range of difficulties but also opportunities of consultation and enforcement, as the example of tax collection by platforms underlines. At the same time, the sharing economy makes us revisit old discussions of the appropriate level of regulation, and conclude that this question remains difficult to answer in a general manner. Here, polycentric co-regulation brings a range of actors to the table to discuss regulatory issues and work together at all stages of the regulatory process, including enforcement and evaluation. While the legislator always keeps the upper hand and with that the option of issuing top-down legislation where co-regulation doesn't produce desirable results, a process like this, where designed in a genuinely open and transparent manner, could better represent ideals of representative democracy and achieve desirable outcomes.

Innovation has been a perpetual challenge for regulators as it always progresses more quickly than the regulatory process itself. Throughout history, disruptive technology has transformed industries, markets, and legal systems. Yet, while innovation has always challenged regulators it has usually affected society at a slower pace (think about the new manufacturing processes that initiated the first industrial revolution). The digital data-driven economy, however, leaves regulators very little time to learn and adapt, as evidenced by current hesitation as to what an appropriate regulatory response to a range of evolutions, spanning from digital platforms to Big Data, the Internet of Things or Distributed Ledger Technology would be.[88] Each of

---

[86] Articles 4(2)(f), 12, 114(3) and 169 TFEU and Article 38 of the Charter of Fundamental Rights of the European Union
[87] On this, *see further* Pantazatou in this volume.
[88] *See further* Michèle Finck, *Blockchain Regulation*, German L.J. (forthcoming, 2018).

these technologies bears the promise of valuable innovation, yet also carries risks that must be addressed from the early stages. Regulators, as everyone else, however, frequently struggle to fully understand these technologies, which are moreover quickly changing. While we are still trying to understand platforms as they currently operate, at the least their technological underpinnings are already subject to modification with the development of blockchains and other forms of Distributed Ledger Technology. Platforms' operation in the online world, moreover, burdens the application of legal principles fashioned for offline interactions.

In this context it is crucial to realize that technology poses not merely uncertainties and dangers for the achievement of regulatory objectives but also opportunities. Some of the early experiences with sharing economy platforms underline that public policy objectives can be coded into platforms' functioning, and may also considerably facilitate their enforcement if additional mechanisms such as data-sharing are incorporated into the regulatory process. It is likely that this trend will continue to develop in the years to come.[89] As Brescia has shown, the challenge is to identify solutions that encourage innovation while not sacrificing consumer protection.[90] What is needed are conversations between the many stakeholders affected by the sharing economy. Regulation needs to adapt to digitalization as its objectives can in part only be achieved where they are coded into the given technology and at the same time technology offers new avenues for direct participation, both by selected stakeholders and citizens in general. When used in the right way, technology furthermore offers new mechanisms of evolution and enforcement that allow regulators to evaluate a given regulatory solution's impact and technologically can equally add more transparency for citizens in this context. To determine the modalities of such techno-legal convergence, polycentric regulatory conversations are to be had between multiple stakeholders, including platforms and regulators, but also those affected such as consumers and city representatives. Where principles have been defined, regulators need to be in a position to monitor compliance, which is difficult unless they obtain access to the relevant data while data protection requirements are respected. From a regulatory perspective, technological transformation such as the development of the sharing economy thus creates not only challenges but also opportunities that can be better harnessed through a co-regulatory approach that provides for common supranational legal standards while preserving leeway for experimentation and adaptation for national and subnational regulators. As technology continues to develop at a fast pace and increasingly digitizes social norms (through AI) or codes legal agreements (through blockchain-based smart contracts) we need to rethink the relationship between technology and law. Whereas technology has always been an object of regulation it is increasingly becoming a regulatory force of its own. If we want technological innovation to continue to unfold while safeguarding long-established public policy goals and addressing shortcomings with current democratic processes, we need to find bridges between law and technology and increase their interoperability. The platform economy offers an early opportunity to test related principles and better prepare us for what is still to come.[91]

---

[89] An example would be how the EU's objectives of data protection by design and default can be incorporated into digital platforms and blockchains.

[90] *See* Brescia in this volume.

[91] For a more thorough overview of techno-legal interoperability, *see* Finck, *supra* note 89.

20

The Multi-Scalar Regulatory Challenge of the Sharing Economy from the Perspective of Platform Cooperativism and the Social and Solidarity Economy

Bronwen Morgan

INTRODUCTION

Sharing economy developments profoundly challenge settled understandings of the way local-national-international regulation interacts, but these developments are themselves deeply contested. In other words, the coherence of debates about regulating the sharing economy depend on assumptions about the emerging sharing economy, which is itself disputed. This chapter argues that it is particularly important to think through the way in which the sharing economy has become increasingly identified with what might be identified as "platform capitalism"[1] and/or the "gig economy."[2] The chapter looks at the question of multi-scalar regulation through the lens of platform cooperativism[3] and, more broadly, sharing economy initiatives rooted in discourses and practices of commons, solidarity, and community.[4]

First, I locate platform cooperativism within the second of two typologies of the contested sharing economy.[5] Second, I highlight two distinctive institutional features of the platform cooperativism and the social solidarity economy (PC/SSE) strand – novel legal forms for enterprises, and horizontal diffusion through "scaling-out" and replication. Each of these features has specific regulatory implications. I argue that, taken together, they foster a distinctive vision of multi-scalar relationships between local, national, and international dimensions of regulating the sharing economy. I draw on examples taken from different local jurisdictions in the United States, Australia, and the EU, with the aim of making a general conceptual point rather than mapping any jurisdictionally specific developments. I conclude by acknowledging some important limits to this approach to debates about regulating the sharing economy.

I TYPOLOGIES OF THE CONTESTED SHARING ECONOMY

Frenken defines the sharing economy as "the practice whereby consumers grant each other temporary access to their under-utilized physical assets."[6] Using this definition, the rise of the

---

[1] N. Srnicek, *The Challenges of Platform Capitalism: Understanding the Logic of a New Business Model*, 23 Juncture 254–57(2017); N. Srnicek, and L. De Sutter, *Platform Capitalism* (2016).

[2] O. Lobel, *The Gig Economy and the Future of Employment and Labor Law: Sharing, Share-washing, and Gigs: Who's Afraid of On-Demand Employment?* 51 U.S.F. L. Rev. 51–74 (2017).

[3] T. Scholz, *Platform Cooperativism: Challenging the Corporate Sharing Economy* (2016).

[4] P. Utting ed., *Social and Solidarity Economy Beyond the Fringe* (2015).

[5] K. Frenken, *Political Economies and Environmental Futures for the Sharing Economy*, 375 Phil. Transactions of the Royal Society A 20160367 (2017); A. R. Davies, B. Donald, M. Gray, and J. Knox-Hayes, *Sharing Economies: Moving Beyond Binaries in a Digital Age*, 10 Cambridge J. Regions, Econ. & Soc'y. 209–30 (2017).

[6] Frenken, *supra* note 5.

sharing economy can be understood as occurring at the intersection of three salient economic trends: peer-to-peer exchange, access over ownership, and circular business models. Even using this fairly narrow definition, a diverse range of future pathways for the sharing economy unfolds. Frenken articulates these pathways as three-fold: a capitalist future cumulating in monopolistic super-platforms operating on a commercial basis with a focus on maximum convenience to high volume masses of users; a state-led future that shifts taxation from labor to capital and redistributes the gains of sharing from winners to losers; and a citizen-led future based on cooperatively owned platforms under democratic control.[7]

These three options of platform capitalism, platform redistribution, and platform cooperativism are echoed and slightly expanded upon using different language in a recent report funded by the European Commission laying out a state-of-the-art literature review on the sharing economy.[8] The report distils four pathways, each of which is a potential scenario for future development of the sharing economy. The "Great Transformation," a community-led, optimistic path (green, social, and fair economic prosperity) requires no major regulatory intervention. The re-embedding of the economy happens entirely through changes in behavior and culture. Under a pathway of "Regulated Sustainability," "governments push for re-embedding through regulatory and traditional intervention to steer society toward sustainability and resolve the disempowerment and unfair effects of the sharing economy." If "Growth-oriented Globalisation" evolves, there would be no societal and cultural re-embedding, with "minimal government intervention leading to increasing inequality, social polarisation, and a negative impact on sustainability. Sharing platforms in this scenario lead to human capital specialisation and 'virtual labour migrations'." Finally, this report adds a fourth pathway not contemplated by Frenken: that of barbarization. Here, "traditional firms and work are dis-intermediated, decentralized, and parceled, to be re-intermediated through algorithms. Robots substitute work, workers perform routinized, repetitive micro-tasks. Dis-embedding and disempowerment without government intervention lead to unemployment and inequality."

While both typologies are useful, they share a notable limitation, in that they tend to push into the background the important role of the state for both market-led and citizen-led visions of a platform economy, propitiating instead assumptions regarding the "invisible hand" of the market or the "invisible hands" of communities. Frenken suggests that markets, the state, and citizens are *each* institutional leaders of *distinctive* pathways,[9] while the EC report is premised on the notion that "governments push" in a regulated sustainability scenario while other paths are either "community-led" or "have minimal government intervention."[10] Especially for the citizen-led pathways that are the particular focus of this chapter, these framings understate the important ways in which legal frameworks and government policy constitute the possibilities for collective action.

The diverse possibilities for the role of the state can be more clearly seen if we understand how the platform cooperativism trajectory of the sharing economy implicates institutionally distinct pathways of supporting laws and policies. Trebor Scholz explains platform cooperativism as putting the technological innovations of the sharing economy to work with an ownership model that adheres to democratic values and fosters solidarity between users and producers in accordance with principles that promote worker autonomy and security.[11] In this chapter

---

[7] *Id.*

[8] Davies et al., *supra* note 5.

[9] Frenken, *supra* note 5.

[10] C. Codagnone, F. Biagi, and F. Abadie, *The Passions and the Interests: Unpacking the "Sharing Economy,"* JRC Science for Policy Report. Belgium, European Commission (2016).

[11] Scholtz, *supra* note 3.

it is treated as a specific instance of a broader set of commitments to the "social and solidarity economy," which encompasses sharing economy initiatives rooted in discourses and practices of commons, solidarity, community, and open cooperativism.[12] To view sharing economy developments through the lens of platform cooperativism and the social solidarity economy will be referred as the PC/SSE approach.

The chapter articulates two important pathways implied by the PC/SSE approach: enterprise diversity and horizontal replication. For each pathway, I first describe what is entailed and then briefly chart the more detailed *regulatory* implications of these institutionally distinct alternatives. A final broader section argues that these regulatory implications converge on a multi-scalar understanding of the relationship between local, national, and international that is quite different from the standard understanding of multilevel regulation.

II PC/SSE: AN INSTITUTIONALLY DISTINCT SHARING ECONOMY?

A *Enterprise Diversity*

Enterprise diversity constitutes the first institutionally distinctive aspect of the sharing economy viewed through the lens of PC/SSE. The key aspect here is that the trajectory of the sharing economy is shaped as much by the structure and governance of the organizational legal models of sharing economy initiatives as it is by regulation of those models. Through the lens of PC/SSE, it is especially important to appreciate the role of novel legal formats for the firm that *internalize* social and environmental challenges, responding to issues that might otherwise (or also) be addressed by regulation by designing preemptive consideration of these into the legal form of the enterprise.

Scholars increasingly argue for greater attention to alternative legal models for the firm that can embed commitments to social and environmental value, as well as accountability to constituencies beyond shareholders, into the constitution of a firm.[13] These models rely on the internal governance dynamics of a firm to address the full array of societal goals. The mechanisms by which this occurs could be institutionalized via shared ownership and control, by reporting and auditing mechanisms, or by a mix of the two. There has been debate over the organizational form of sharing economy initiatives ever since the emergence of the term. Indeed, in areas like ride-sharing, which have been the fastest to "scale" commercially at a global level – as the rise of Uber attests to – there is rising enterprise diversity. Examples of this diversity are the French not-for-profit ride-sharing BlaBlaCar[14] and the Austin-based not-for-profit Rideshare,[15] as well as ride-sharing cooperatives in Buffalo that focus on low-income communities[16] and in Denver that work in partnership with unions.[17] In short, enterprise diversity is an important and

---

[12] United Nations Taskforce on the Social and Solidarity Economy, *Social and Solidarity Economy and the Challenge of Sustainable Development: A Position Paper* (2014); Utting, *supra* note 4; M. Vieta, *The New Cooperativism*, Affinities, 4 (2010).

[13] N. Boeger, *The New Corporate Movement*, Ephemera (submitted, in review); B. Morgan, J. McNeill, and I. Blomfeld, The Legal Roots of a Sustainable and Resilient Economy: New Kinds of Legal Entities, New Kinds of Lawyers, *in New Directions for Law in Australia: Essays in Contemporary Law Reform* 399 (R. Levy, M. O'Brien, S. Rice, P. Ridge, and M. Thornton eds., 2017); J. Gibson-Graham, J. Cameron, and S. Healy, *Take Back the Economy: An Ethical Guide for Transforming our Communities* (2013).

[14] N. Coca, *How BlablaCar Is Revolutionizing the Way Carpooling Now Works Around the World*, Shareable, July 31, 2017.

[15] M. Sutton, *New Ridesharing Alternatives Thrive After Uber Leaves Austin*, Shareable, July 6, 2016.

[16] J. Gottlieb, *Buffalo, N.Y., Nonprofit Launches Car Sharing Service for Low-Income People*, Gov't. Tech. (2015).

[17] M. Hansen, *What If Uber Were a Unionized, Worker-Owned Co-Op? These Denver Cabbies Are Making It Happen*, Yes! (2015).

underappreciated part of the constitutive framework of transactional law and private economic activity. What are the specific *regulatory* implications of this distinctive pathway?

B Regulatory Dimensions

The first point is conceptual: while the capacity to craft a diverse array of legal forms for private economic initiatives is to some extent the outcome of choice, enterprise diversity nonetheless remains a regulatory issue, and not (only) a question of spontaneous citizen action. The choice of a corporate form for the creation of a legal entity has long been associated with the need to maximize profit. The social desirability of this has been fiercely debated from the early historical roots of the creation of joint stock corporations right through to contemporary debates about corporate social responsibility.[18] In recent times, there has been an interesting shift to questioning the necessity of this from *within* the expert domain of company law and corporate governance experts.[19] This has opened space for more creative thinking about the social and political valence of legal entity forms. Through the activities of social entrepreneurs, legal entity form has a role to play in making concrete specific activist commitments, channeling political activism in sometimes unexpected directions. Legal form has a particular significance for the role that considerations of profit and efficiency play in creating an initiative that seeks to reimagine the link between profit, efficiency, and social and environmental benefits. Legal form is worth attending to, as it reconfigures relationships between community and market in inventive ways. Legal form can reshape standard models for the extraction of profit to eco-social questions of mutuality and reciprocity, a priority on interdependence and social relations, and a focus on "people before profit."

Inventive practices in relation to the legal form of business have flourished in the last decade. Increasingly, in countries where specific legal entity structures for social enterprise are not available, pressure is growing to adopt such models.[20] An ongoing international comparative research project is currently compiling a worldwide database to support further research on emerging or already well-established social enterprise models across 40 different countries.[21] The ICSEM project takes as a starting point the different emphases of social enterprise literature on outcomes-focused social enterprise on the one hand and democratic participation in line with longstanding cooperative traditions on the other hand. In that light, it is instructive to explore the different regulatory frameworks of two particularly noteworthy innovations in legal form in the last decade: the community interest company in the UK and the benefit corporation in the USA.

The UK introduced the Community Interest Company (CIC) structure in 2005, under the Companies (Audit, Investigations and Community Enterprise) Act 2004 (UK). The legislation provides the possibility of combining a company limited by shares that can issue dividends and be governed by paid directors, with the explicit pursuit of "community interest." There are two main mechanisms that operate to balance "profit and purpose" in this structure. First, there are

---

[18] R. Shamir, *Between Self-Regulation and the Alien Tort Claims Act: On the Contested Concept of Corporate Social Responsibility*, 38 L. & Soc'y. Rev. 635–64 (2004).

[19] S. Deakin, *The Corporation as Commons: Rethinking Property Rights, Governance and Sustainability in the Business Enterprise (2011)*, 37 Queen's L.J. 339 (2012); L. A. Stout, *The Shareholder Value Myth: How Putting Shareholders First Harms Investors, Corporations, and the Public* (2012).

[20] G. Walker, S. Hunter, P. Devine-Wright, B. Evans, and H. Fay, *Harnessing Community Energies: Explaining and Evaluating Community-Based Localism in Renewable Energy Policy in the UK*, 7 Global Envtl. Pol. 64–82 (2007).

[21] *See* ICSEM, www.iap-socent.be/icsem-project.

legislative constraints on key internal corporate governance decisions, namely caps on distribution of dividends and mandated "asset locks" in the constitution of the company. Second, the content of "community interest" is overseen by a dedicated government regulator distinct from the regulator of ordinary corporations. The Canadian state of British Columbia has a broadly similar entity structure, called a community contributions company under reforms made to the British Columbia Business Corporations Act in 2012.[22]

In the United States, the "benefit corporation" is the most popular legal entity structure for fusing profit and purpose.[23] Available since 2010 and mandating a legal duty to create general public benefit in addition to financial return, it is currently available in 34 US states and Washington D.C., including the influential Delaware jurisdiction.[24] Benefit corporations are shaped by externally focused reporting, disclosure, and transparency obligations rather than internal governance constraints. In contrast to the UK CIC format, where a government regulator supervises the content of "community interest," benefit corporations in the United States retain enterprise discretion to fill the content of the benefit they provide – as long as they report on it. There is a requirement for accredited third parties to validate, through certification, the reporting obligations of benefit corporations. However, there is a competitive market for such third-party certifiers, so the potential for discretionary interpretive power still exists, particularly relative to the UK CIC model.[25]

It is notable that the difference between these two forms embodies the dichotomy underpinning the cross-national research under way in the ICSEM project, even down to the terminology used for those forms. "Community" in the UK and Canada connotes internal process and collective identity, while "benefit" in the USA points to the fruits that result. Of course, as noted earlier, there is an overlap between the history of cooperative structures and that of social enterprise. The CIC form has received criticism for its lack of democratic practice, promoting entrepreneurial activity over accountability.[26] This view is particularly held by those rooted in the cooperative tradition of mutual and collective activity and support. Since a CIC can be seen as set up and managed by a very small group of people, it can be seen as less democratic and inclusive.[27] Seen from this perspective, the UK occupies an interesting middle position, with less emphasis on internal governance and the influence of democratic cooperativism than Europe, but more than in the USA.

Cooperatives are of course most directly relevant, in literal as well as conceptual terms, to a PC/SSE approach to the sharing economy. They are the longest-standing examples of a legal entity that builds social, democratic, and egalitarian objectives directly into the internal structure of a corporate entity. Understandings of social enterprise in mainland Europe continue to draw strongly on the influence of the cooperative tradition. Indeed, many European legal structures for social enterprise (e.g. Italy, France) require the rule of "one member, one

---

[22] S. Manwaring and A. Valentine, *Social Enterprise in Canada* (2012).

[23] There are several other structures available, vividly documented at the Social Enterprise Law Tracker, http://socentlawtracker.org.

[24] W. Davies, *20 Public Spirited Lawyers Could Change the World*, Potlatch Blog (Sept. 23, 2013), http://potlatch.typepad.com/weblog/2013/09/20-public-spirited-lawyers-could-change-the-world.html.

[25] Indeed, enforcement of the third-party certification for US benefit corporation reporting may be very patchy: UK Community Interest Company Regulator speech on 10th anniversary celebration of the CIC legislation, Bristol, UK, July 7, 2015, www.youtube.com/watch?v=kt_me_MCwbU.

[26] S. Teasdale, P. Alcock, and G. Smith, *Legislating for the Big Society? The Case of the Public Services (Social Value) Bill*, 32 Pub. Money & Mgmt. 201–08 (2012).

[27] G. Smith and S. Teasdale, *Associative Democracy and the Social Economy: Exploring the Regulatory Challenge*, 41 Econ. & Soc'y. 151–76 (2012).

vote." Notwithstanding this overlapping heritage, cooperatives are better regarded as a separate governance development from that of social enterprise, especially from the point of view of legal entity structure. This is particularly so given that there has been a recent revival of interest in and use of the form, embodied in the United Nations designating 2012 as the International Year of Cooperatives. This designation reflected revivals in diverse jurisdictions in recent decades. New secondary cooperative and representative bodies have evolved in relation to worker-owned cooperatives generally in the United States (US Federation of Worker Cooperatives) and the UK (Cooperative Enterprise Hub), as well as at European Union level,[28] particularly in relation to community-owned renewable energy cooperatives. Marcelo Vieta has described this revival as a "new cooperativism" which differs from "old cooperativism" primarily in its emphasis on multiple stakeholders, solidarity between them, and a shared return for all.[29] Instead of singling out a particular constituency such as workers or consumers, and designing corporate form around that stakeholder, new cooperativism draws on responses by working people and grassroots groups to the crisis of neoliberalism to incorporate new approaches to wealth distribution that observe sustainable development constraints, more horizontal labor relations, more egalitarian schemes for allocating surpluses and a stronger community orientation, with social objects and community development goals.[30]

The new cooperativism can be illustrated by the innovative 1992 legislation in Italy on "social cooperatives." This law also echoes some of the themes evident in social enterprise forms. The key objectives of social cooperatives in Italy under this law are the general benefit of the community and the social integration of citizens, and over 7,000 have been formed under the law.[31] The law provides for a cooperative form with legal personality and limited liability that cannot distribute more than 80 percent of its profits, limits interest payments to the bond rate and imposes an asset lock at dissolution. These constraints internalize the capacity for social goals to be given priority: "type A" cooperatives provide health, social, or educational services and "type B" social cooperatives integrate disadvantaged people[32] into the labor market.[33] The structure of the law, in effect, institutionalizes multi-stakeholder participation in governance. Various categories of stakeholder may become members, including paid employees, beneficiaries, volunteers (up to 50 percent of members), financial investors, and public institutions.[34]

Another dimension of the new cooperativism is developing at the intersection of the digital economy and cooperative traditions. Digital platforms open up the possibility of mass collaborative internal governance, even across distances: for example, Som Energia is a Spanish renewable energy cooperative that both produces and sells green energy and keeps its more than 8,000 members informed entirely through online platforms. Digital environments also create opportunities for creative ways of tracking contributions and inputs (for example, via digital currencies or virtual tokens). This has led to growing enthusiasm for the idea of "open cooperatives" that would institutionalize multi-stakeholder accountability on a perpetually responsive

---

[28] *See* www.resscoop.eu.

[29] Vieta, *supra* note 12.

[30] *Id.*; D. Stark, *The Sense of Dissonance: Accounts of Worth in Economic Life* (2011).

[31] A. Mancino and A. Thomas, *An Italian Pattern of Social Enterprise: The Social Cooperative*, 15 Nonprofit Mgmt. & Leadership 357–69 (2005).

[32] The categories of disadvantage they target may include physical and mental disability, drug and alcohol addiction, developmental disorders, and problems with the law. They do not include other factors of disadvantage such as unemployment, race, sexual orientation, or abuse.

[33] R. Laratta, *Social Cooperatives: A Model of Co-Production in the Provision of Community Services*, 10 Int'l. J. Civil Soc'y L. 9–18 (2012).

[34] In "type B" cooperatives at least 30 percent of the members must be from the disadvantaged target groups.

basis.[35] Where such experiments are animated by norms of community, sharing, and sustainability, they can also function to promote solidarity in new ways.

Finally, the influence of the cooperative tradition is also present in ways that affect the shape and structure of corporations without actually introducing a distinct novel legal entity. For example, the history of the globally influential model of Fair Trade is intertwined with that of cooperativism.[36] Developments in what Rory Ridley-Duff calls the "FairShares Model" approach to corporate governance in the UK also illustrate this.[37] FairShares provide model articles of association, as well as associated legal and technical support, to enable modification of a range of standard legal corporate structures from associations to cooperatives to companies. This approach of using internal constitutional innovation within the corporation draws on the values of multistakeholder cooperativism. The modifications institutionalize membership, voice and decision-making power not just for investors but also simultaneously for workers/labor, customers/users, and founders. Like cooperatives, the FairShares model decouples voice from financial power, and in tandem with the new cooperativism, it carefully allocates power to multiple stakeholder groups. Perhaps distinctively, it also designs in procedures for labor and user shareholders to acquire investor shares either directly or indirectly through mutualization, thus keeping the boundaries fluid between different share classes in ways that promote the creation of assets held in common.[38]

As we see from the above, legal form is important for channeling the PC/SSE approach to the sharing economy. However, in and of itself it is not sufficient. Connelly et al. explore forms of legal entities in social economy initiatives in Canada.[39] These show us that community-focused incremental change is possible but faces barriers in the form of subsidized mainstream economic activity and lack of understanding of the benefits by potential consumers. In the example, the potential for large-scale disruption to the old order is possible but requires support and policy change. This leads to the second institutionally distinctive facet of a PC/SEE vision of the sharing economy.

C *Horizontal Diffusion, Replication, and Scaling Out*

The second institutionally distinctive aspect of a PC/SSE vision of the sharing economy is its mode of diffusion. This combines inspiration from debates that have evolved over many years in the nonprofit world about how to advance systemic social innovation[40] with more local economy-focused approaches that place entrepreneurial energies at their center with a strong focus on the social and environmental benefits of such strategies.[41] The core feature of this

---

[35] M. Bauwens, J. Restakis, and D. Bollier, *Commons Transition* (2015), http://commonstransition.org/commons-transition-plans/.

[36] W. Davies and T. Mills, *Beyond the Laws of the Market: An Interview with Will Davies*, New Left Project (Aug. 28, 2014), www.newleftproject.org/index.php/site/article_comments/beyond_the_laws_of_the_market.

[37] L. Boltanski and L. Thévenot, *On Justification: Economies of Worth* (2006).

[38] R. Ridley-Duff, Internationalisation of FairShares: Where Agency Meets Structure in US and UK Company Law, *in Shaping the Corporate Landscape* Ch. 16 (N. Boeger and C. Villiers eds., 2016).

[39] S. Connelly, S. Markey, and M. Roseland, *Bridging Sustainability and the Social Economy: Achieving Community Transformation Through Local Food Initiatives*, 31 Critical Soc. Pol'y. 308–24 (2011); P. Graefe, *Whose Social Economy? Debating New State Practices in Quebec*, 21 Critical Soc. Pol'y. 35–58 (2001).

[40] M.-L. Moore, D. Riddell, and D. Vocisano, *Scaling Out, Scaling Up, Scaling Deep: Strategies of Non-profits in Advancing Systemic Social Innovation*, 58 J. Corporate Citizenship 67–84 (2015).

[41] M. Shuman, *The Local Economy Solution: How Innovative, Self-Financing "Pollinator" Enterprises Can Grow Jobs and Prosperity* (2015); J. Ramos, *Alternative futures of globalisation a socio-ecological study of the world social forum process*, PhD thesis, Queensland University of Technology (2010).

pathway is horizontal diffusion or replication of relatively small-scale local initiatives. The aim is to promote an ecology of extended relocalization that nonetheless carefully integrates selected benefits of the competitive dynamics of globalization.

Jose Ramos calls this "cosmo-localism," a pathway that yokes the "dynamic potentials of emerging globally distributed knowledge and design commons in conjunction with the emerging (high and low tech) capacity for localized production of value."[42] He argues that the "relocalization" dynamic promotes both environmental benefits (through lowered transport costs and resilience to energy crises) and social benefits (through the cultivation of community solidarity and local knowledge). The "cosmopolitan" dynamic draws on the wide array of "knowledge and design resources for a variety of critical support systems … now available in the distributed web under open licenses" and the sharply reducing cost profile of manufacturing equipment already spurring developments such as the maker movement.[43] Together, these two dynamics make possible distributed production at local levels that can be linked and coordinated almost as a form of "bottom-up" global value chain. The broader context Ramos draws on is "popular discourses articulating alternative globalization pathways: relocalization, the global network society and cosmopolitan transnational solidarity,"[44] but there are specific regulatory dimensions to this vision.[45]

D Regulatory Dimensions

It is striking that the regulatory dimension of the cosmo-localist vision draws primarily upon a more general facilitative policy environment, rather than focusing on formal general rules that regulate specific functional or sectoral interests such as labor, environment, or consumer. This is in tune with the nature of the PC/SSE approach overall, which places central reliance on novel legal models at the firm level driving a reimagined transactional economy. In such a context, regulation is more about coordination than mandate. As Ramos argues, coordinating micro-clusters of small-scale initiatives would focus on creating a "local enterprise ecosystem" supporting the sharing and exchange platforms that match resources and needs via circular "closed loop" production.[46] The building blocks of this ecosystem are policy networks, tax concessions, and capacity-building state support, as well as innovations in more rule-based functional regulatory infrastructures relating to finance, competition, and intellectual property.

The importance of policy networks is their capacity to link networks of public and private agencies that collectively support industrial upgrading and competitiveness, such as business associations, technology centers, groups of business leaders, and local government.[47] While this "upgrading" literature more usually focuses on insertion into standard global value chains premised on mainstream market competitiveness,[48] an emergent local enterprise ecosystem is

[42] J. Ramos, *Cosmo-Localism and the Futures of Material Production*, P2P Foundation (June 1, 2016), https://blog.p2pfoundation.net/cosmo-localism-futures-material-production/2016/06/01.

[43] *Id.*; *see also* M. Mclaughlin, *The Future of Mississippi's Economy: The Maker Movement*, 35 Misss. C.L. Rev. 353–64 (2017); E. J. Van Holm, *Makerspaces and Local Economic Development*, 31 Econ. Dev. Q. 164–73 (2017).

[44] Ramos, *supra* note 41.

[45] Boyd Cohen and P. Munoz, *Sharing Cities and Sustainable Consumption and Production: Towards an Integrated Framework*, 134 J. Cleaner Production 87–97 (2016).

[46] Ramos, *supra* note 42.

[47] D. Messner, *The Network Society: Economic Development and International Competitiveness as Problems of Social Governance* (1997).

[48] J. Humphrey and H. Schmitz, *How Does Insertion in Global Value Chains Affect Upgrading in Industrial Clusters?* 36 Regional Stud. 1017–27 (2002).

more attuned to the PC/SSE approach. For example, the transnational Sharing Cities Network provides mutual support to local sharing initiatives across borders, via toolkits and publications showcasing diverse methods to "activate the urban commons."[49] This kind of fairly diffuse policy network complements more nationally focused networks such as the Business Alliance for Local Living Economies in the United States.[50] Local and national governments can provide tax concessions or tax credits for social beneficial legal forms, as the UK government has done for social investment.[51] Broader mixes of fiscal, budgetary, and capacity-building state support can be designed to encourage the growth of the PC/SSE approach. These range from local government cooperative support programs such as exist in a number of US cities,[52] to state subsidies for the costs of high-tech fabrication equipment for distributed manufacturing.[53]

Certain forms of rule-based regulation can contribute to this distinctive policy environment for a PC/SSE approach to regulating the sharing economy. Crucially, these are facilitative rather than constraining, running with the grain of the "radical transactionalism" embodied by this approach and helping to reframe core market economy building blocks such as finance, competition, and intellectual property.[54] Some examples are *proactive and direct* in nature, such as the regulatory legalization of equity-based crowdfunding. This regulatory legalization is proceeding in a number of different jurisdictions cross-nationally,[55] and in some instances such as New Zealand, with minimal legal constraints. Some proactive facilitative regulatory devices, such as novel forms of intellectual property, can be catalyzed without formal legislation though benefit from its support. For example, in the context of the software underpinning platforms in technologically embedded sharing economy initiatives, "commons-based reciprocity licensing" enables mutual sharing of the capacity to use and modify the software for nonprofit entities but crafts an income stream for those entities if the software is used and modified by commercial entities.[56]

Facilitative regulation that supports a PC/SSE approach to the sharing economy also extends to more indirect regulatory innovation that is *protective-creative* in nature. In particular, this arises where the regulatory infrastructure of platform capitalism would actively stifle the development of platform cooperativism. For example, local procurement by government agencies is a powerful proactive regulatory mechanism, but existing formal legislation stemming from World Trade Organization commitments or European rules on state aid may prevent a direct use of such mechanisms.[57] While across-the-board preferences for local business are excluded, creative approaches to the broader regulatory ecosystem can foster modes of soliciting contracts that increase the probability of compliant local bids. For example, procuring agencies can use full cost triple bottom line accounting, which counts not only social and environmental outcomes of bids but also the tax dollars generated locally by contracting work (e.g. through

---

[49] www.shareable.net/sharing-cities-old; *see also* D. Mclaren and J. Agyeman, *Sharing Cities: A Case for Truly Smart and Sustainable Cities* (2015).

[50] www.livingeconomies.org; *see also* D. Korten, *Agenda for a New Economy: From Phantom Wealth to Real Wealth* (2010).

[51] M. Fountain, *DIY Social Investment*, Flip Finance (2016).

[52] C. Kerr, *Local Government Support for Cooperatives* (2015).

[53] Ramos, *supra* note 42.

[54] B. Morgan and D. Kuch, *Radical Transactionalism: Legal Consciousness, Diverse Economies, and the Sharing Economy*, 42 J. L. & Soc'y. 556–87 (2015).

[55] M. Nehme, *The Rise of Crowd Equity Funding: Where to Now?* 13 Int'l. J.L. in Context 253–276.

[56] M. Said Viera, and P. d Filippi, *Between Copyleft and Copyfarleft: Advance Reciprocity for the Commons*, 4 J. of Peer Production (2014).

[57] Christopher McCrudden, *Buying Social Justice: Equality, Government Procurement, and Legal Change* (2007).

payroll or increased consumption tax revenue).[58] Another example is creative linkages between "anchor institutions" and small-scale platform cooperative initiatives, such as efforts to finance or procure local and ecologically sustainable food through encouraging hospitals and general practitioners to issue "healthy food prescriptions" instead of, or alongside, conventional pharmaceutical prescriptions.[59]

Interestingly, the cluster of regulatory devices discussed above has some affinity with longstanding debates in political economy regarding the comparative merits and features of developmental state and regulatory state policy approaches.[60] Much of what is discussed above resonates with developmental state commitments to a set of proactive policy commitments that will nurture the conditions for industrial (in the original literature) or ecologically and socially sustainable (in this context) development. The different contexts make for different imagined outcomes as well: the regulatory approaches detailed here do not so much resemble the capital-intensive large-scale industrial cluster policy of the traditional developmental state but are much more focused on supporting and coordinating the "cosmo-local" micro-clusters discussed earlier.[61] As this scholarship evolves, the rapidly changing configuration of global comparative economic development cross-nationally may shift long-sedimented views on the incompatibility of industrial policy and free trade. This will involve building on nascent findings that the regulatory and developmental states are more synergistic than incompatible and, in particular, noting that the development of "collaborative public spaces" that provide shelter from market competition is a crucial facet of innovation.[62] PC/SSE approaches to the sharing economy, when embedded in regulatory approaches such as those canvassed in this section, are arguably an important instance of just such emergent "collaborative public spaces."

III A DISTINCTIVE MULTI-SCALAR REGULATORY VISION

These two institutionally distinctive pathways of enterprise diversity and horizontal diffusion chart a different perspective from the currently much more visible sense of a sharing economy trajectory where large standard corporations are scaling up in a competitive setting. The predominance of Uber and Airbnb tends to lead to a discussion of large-scale platforms supported by venture capital that exploit the regulatory arbitrage between different local jurisdictions to expand transnationally to oligopolistic scale. National redistributive regulation tries to push back against this, imposing duties on these entities to protect workers and consumers and the traditional tax base. This returns us to a familiar cycling between state and market which Frenken's typology discussed in the introduction would classify as "platform capitalism" versus "platform redistribution."

But this chapter has charted a different conceptual underpinning. We can draw on Simon Deakin's recent argument for viewing the corporation as an instantiation of a commons, rather than as a nexus of contracts, to provide a bridge to this different approach to the regulation of the sharing economy.[63] Deakin argues that "the firm is best seen as a collectively managed resource

---

[58] Shuman, *supra* note 41.

[59] N. Rose, *Community Food Hubs: An Economic And Social Justice Model For Regional Australia?* 26 Rural Society 225–37 (2017).

[60] N. Dubash and B. Morgan, *The Rise of the Regulatory State of the South: Infrastructure and Development in Emerging Economies* (2013).

[61] Ramos, *supra* note 42.

[62] S. Samford, *Innovation and Public Space: The Developmental Possibilities of Regulation in the Global South*, 9 Reg. & Governance 294–308 (2015).

[63] Deakin, *supra* note 19.

or 'commons' which is subject to a number of multiple, overlapping and potentially conflicting property-type claims on the part of the different constituencies or stakeholders that provide value to the firm."[64] In Deakin's argument, legal claims on a company's assets extend far beyond those of shareholders: they include enterprise liability law, duties owed under tort principles and statutory duties around health and safety, environmental quality, and consumer protection. This approach effectively reframes regulation as part of a web of "property-type" legal claims on a company's assets. All legal duties bearing on the firm, *including those emanating from regulatory frameworks external to the firm*, specify "the conditions under which various stakeholders can draw on the resources of the firm while at the same time, preserving and sustaining the firm's asset pool as a source of productive value. In this sense, he argues, the business enterprise is conceptually and practically a 'commons.'"[65]

Deakin's approach conceptually integrates "internal" corporate governance structures and "external" regulation by reference to standard forms of social regulation, which are discussed in other parts of this Handbook (see Parts 5 and 8). But what this chapter does is to extend his reframing even further. Through the PC/SSE lens, the underlying conception of regulation at stake in "regulating the sharing economy" shifts away from a set of social forces that temper an otherwise untrammeled market, and emphasizes more the notion of how an enabling state supports and runs with the grain of associative democracy.

We have actually seen this in the two principal sections of this chapter. Section I argued for a greater focus on legal models for the firm, both longstanding and novel, that instantiate shared ownership and control and internalize the pursuit of social and environmental goals into their internal constitutional procedures. As Smith and Teasdale have argued, this can extend the social economy, creating social enterprises that exhibit innovative behaviors in organizational form.[66] This approach blends the entrepreneurial and risk-taking dimensions of the sharing economy with the social character of the strictly nonprofit organizations that have previously characterized the sector. Smith and Teasdale conceptualize this explicitly in terms of legal creativity in business form creating a pathway for linking associational democracy commitments to distributive concerns around social policy. They are critical of certain legal forms for their relative lack of democratic inclusion in the governance structures mandated by regulation, suggesting that the UK CIC in particular promotes entrepreneurial activity over accountability.

However, novel formats for the firm are not the only dimension of a PC/SSE sharing economy pathway. Section II outlined a range of policy approaches that merge fiscal, regulatory, and networking strategies to support the horizontal diffusion and replication of multiple small-scale and locally embedded platform initiatives. These initiatives can extend the social economy in ways that promote shared accountability, associative democracy, and the promotion of the commons. Michel Bauwen's account of the enabling partner state conceptualizes this: in this model, the state plays an important role in investing in commons-based peer production, and the capacity for citizens and people to utilize open knowledge to empower themselves and produce for their communities. Relatedly, from a cosmo-localism perspective, the state would also support grassroots efforts to empower localized designing, making, and sharing efforts.[67]

None of this is to deny the importance of gaps and inequalities that might be produced in the development of a PC/SSE trajectory for the sharing economy. These could compromise the

---

[64] *Id.* at 381.
[65] *Id.* at 355.
[66] Smith and Teasdale, *supra* note 27.
[67] M. Bauwens and V. Kostakis, *Network Society and Future Scenarios for a Collaborative Economy* (2017).

effective achievement of democratic, social, and environmental issues both region by region and across socioeconomic lines.[68] While such issues are not addressed in this chapter, it is instructive to note that the regulatory dimensions discussed in this chapter often have bipartisan political support: benefit corporation legislation (supporting new legal models) and the Jumpstart our Business Startups (JOBS) Act 2012 in the United States (facilitating horizontal diffusion) are two good examples of this. This bipartisan support reflects shifting assumptions about whether they are "left" or "right" in nature: a shift that I would argue flows from the reframing of state/market relations that is embodied in this approach to the regulation of the sharing economy.

CONCLUSION

In the end, exploring regulation is necessary but insufficient to properly appreciate the implications of viewing the sharing economy through the lens of platform cooperativism and the social and solidarity economy. A fuller consideration would begin in two places. First, it would rethink institutional questions from much more of a long-term perspective. It is fascinating, for example, to consider the link between the issues raised here and the renaissance of interest in recent years in Karl Polanyi's account of re-embedding markets in society. An underexplored dimension of this renaissance is the way in which democratic production can contribute as much to a re-embedding counter-movement as a focus on social regulation more traditionally understood. Rather than focusing on redistributive platforms, the earlier interest of Polanyi in "corporatist systems of industrial democracy with communal property of the means of production" (Ebner, 2015 #534: 49)[69] may be in renaissance today with "new economy" developments from the collaborative, solidarity, and commons-based perspectives.

But even a longer historical perspective on the organizational dimensions of cooperative, user-owned production and the regulatory frameworks that support them, arguably misses the real "elephant in the room," which is the centrality of the growth model of economic development. Here the burgeoning literatures in political ecology and geography on degrowth and on diverse economies have much to teach us.[70] While well beyond the scope of this chapter, this literature has yet to engage in any extended way with the specificities of law and regulation.[71] Such an engagement will benefit from the first small step taken here, which conceptualizes the regulatory dimensions of the sharing economy through the lens of platform cooperativism and the social and solidarity economy. The distinctive kernel of that viewpoint is to foster understanding of how an enabling state supports and runs with the grain of associative democracy, rather than being deployed to temper an untrammeled market.

---

[68] *See* Miller in this volume.

[69] Ebner, Alexander. 2015. "The Regulation of Markets." In *Regulatory Transformations: Rethinking Economy-Society Interactions*, edited by Bettina Lange, Fiona Haines and Dania Thomas. Oxford: Hart Publishing.

[70] On degrowth *see* Giacomo D'Alisa, Federico Demaria, and Giorgos Kallis, *DeGrowth: A Vocabulary for a New Era* (2014); on diverse economies *see* Gibson-Graham et al., *supra* note 13; and N. Johanisova and E. Fraňková, Eco-Social Enterprises, *in Routledge Handbook of Ecological Economics: Nature and Society* 507 (C. L. Spash ed., 2017).

[71] But see Bronwen Morgan (2018) "The Sharing Economy" 14 *Annual Review of Law and Social Science*, www.annualreviews.org/doi/abs/10.1146/annurev-lawsocsci-101317-031201.

PART II

Addressing Specific Regulatory Concerns

Employment and Labor Law

21

Employee Classification in the United States

*Elizabeth Tippett**

INTRODUCTION

A reporter using a ride-sharing service shared a document taped to the back of her driver's headrest, entitled "The Rating System Explained."[1] The document provided that a five-star rating should apply to "mediocre, average, decent, okay" service. Four stars mean, "This driver sucks, fire him slowly; it does not mean 'average' or 'above average.' Too many of these and I [the driver] may end up homeless."[2] Three stars means "this driver sucks so bad I never want to see him again."[3] One or two stars should be reserved for dangerous driving or threats of violence.[4]

The guide served to translate the employment consequences of customer ratings, lest customers operate under the mistaken assumption that ratings are used for informational purposes only. Ride-sharing services admit that they use customer ratings to evaluate drivers. Uber's Driver Handbook states that the company "monitor[s] [drivers'] star rating as well as any complaints made by clients."[5] In its contract with drivers, Uber reserves the right to terminate drivers whose ratings "fal[l] below the applicable minimum star-rating."[6] Uber also admits to having terminated drivers in the past based on customer ratings.[7] Rival service Lyft uses a similar rating system, with "one star being 'awful' and five being 'awesome.'"[8] Lyft "automatically deactivate[s]" drivers if their average rating falls below a certain threshold, most recently, 4.6 stars out of 5.[9]

Uber and Lyft's punitive approach sounds a lot like a stringent performance rating system an employer might use with employees. Yet both services treat their drivers as independent

---

[*] Catharine Roner Reiter and Alexander Baker provided research assistance for this chapter.

[1] Caroline O'Donovan, *My Ride to Work*, Twitter (Mar. 16, 2017), https://twitter.com/ceodonovan/status/842418425695674369.

[2] *Id.*

[3] *Id.*

[4] *Id.* See also Noopur Raval and Paul Dourish, *Standing Out from the Crowd: Emotional Labor, Body Labor, and Temporal Labor in Ridesharing*, Proc. 19th ACM Conf. Comp.-Supported Cooperative Work & Soc. Computing, 5 (2016).

[5] *O'Connor v. Uber Technologies, Inc.*, 82 F. Supp.3d 1133, 1151 (N.D. Cal. 2015).

[6] *Id.*

[7] *Id.*

[8] *Cotter v. Lyft, Inc.*, 60 F. Supp.3d 1067, 1071 (N.D. Cal. 2015).

[9] *Id.* at 1082 n. 3.

contractors,[10] as do the large majority of companies in the sharing economy.[11] This chapter explores whether sharing economy workers qualify as independent contractors or employees, and whether existing US laws adequately protect these workers.

Many sharing economy workers are accurately characterized as independent contractors. However, the sharing economy presents a regulatory challenge with respect to workers on the cusp of employee status, where legal rules matter the most. For these workers, employment classification presents two related problems: noncompliance and avoidance.[12] Noncompliance can arise from willful misclassification of independent contractors by sharing companies, betting they won't be caught. In other cases, sharing companies can lawfully treat workers as independent contractors as a result of legal tests that use outdated proxies for employment status. This form of legal avoidance may give sharing companies a competitive advantage that erodes the reach of existing rules.[13]

This chapter proceeds in three parts. The first part summarizes the legal standards that govern whether a worker is classified as an independent contractor or an employee. The second part identifies the respects in which existing law facilitates noncompliance and avoidance for workers in the sharing economy. The chapter concludes with a discussion of various proposed approaches to addressing those challenges.

I LEGAL STANDARDS FOR EMPLOYEE STATUS IN THE SHARING ECONOMY

Whether a worker qualifies as an independent contractor or an employee depends upon the federal or state statute under which the employee seeks coverage.[14] Employment protections – such as the right to minimum wage and overtime,[15] anti-discrimination protections,[16] workers compensation,[17] or unemployment insurance[18] – only apply to those who qualify as "employees" under the applicable statute. Each such statute can impose a separate standard or rule for employee status. Consequently, no single test defines whether a particular individual is an employee.

US employment laws rarely impose a bright line rule differentiating independent contractors from employees. Instead, the standard tends to consist of a multifactor test that courts apply in

---

[10] *Lyft Terms of Service*, Lyft (Sept. 30, 2016), www.lyft.com/terms ("As a Driver on the Lyft Platform, you acknowledge and agree that you and Lyft are in a direct business relationship, and the relationship between the parties under this Agreement is solely that of independent contracting parties."); *see also* Justin Worland, *Uber wants to Settle a Lawsuit with Its California Drivers for Just $1 Each*, Fortune (Feb. 2, 2017), http://fortune.com/2017/02/02/uber-california-lawsuit-settlement/.

[11] Elizabeth Tippett, *Using Contract Terms to Detect Underlying Litigation Risk: An Initial Proof of Concept*, 20 Lewis & Clark L. Rev. 548, 560–62 (2016) (only one of the 25 sampled sharing companies classified workers as employees).

[12] This chapter draws upon the analysis of noncompliance and avoidance in the sharing economy set forth in Charlotte Alexander and Elizabeth Tippett, *The Hacking of Employment Law*, 82 Missouri L. Rev. 973 (2017).

[13] *Id. See also* Matthew Yglesias, *When is a Taxi Not a Taxi?*, Slate (Dec. 19, 2011), www.slate.com/articles/technology/technocracy/2011/12/uber_car_service_exposing_the_idiocy_of_american_city_taxi_regulations_.html (characterizing Uber as a "an extremely elegant use of technology to, in effect, hack the legal system"). Other commentators have described some aspects of this problem in their discussions of regulatory arbitrage. *See* Orly Lobel, *The Law of the Platform*, 101 Minn. L. Rev. 87, 92 (2016); Noah Zatz, *Does Work Have a Future if the Labor Market Does Not?*, 91 Chi-Kent L. Rev. 1081, 1093 (2016). *See also* Keith Cunningham-Parmeter, *From Amazon to Uber: Defining Employment in the Modern Economy*, 96 B.U. L. Rev. 1673, 1687 (2016).

[14] This section in large part draws from content discussed in Tippett, *supra* note 11, at 538–40.

[15] Fair Labor Standards Act, 29 U.S.C. §§ 206–207 (2012).

[16] Title VII of the Civil Rights Act, 42 U.S.C. § 2000e (2012) (defining employee).

[17] Workers' Compensation protections are defined at the state level. *See, e.g.*, O.R.S. § 656.027; *see also* McCown v. *Hones*, 353 N.C. 683 (N.C. 2001) (independent contractors not covered by workers' compensation).

[18] Coverage under unemployment insurance is defined at the state level. *See, e.g.*, O.R.S. § 657.015.

a flexible manner.[19] The most common such test, which courts apply in the absence of clear guidance in the applicable legislation, is the "control" test.[20] The control test examines the putative employer's control over the way in which the work is performed. It uses the following non-exclusive factors to assess the amount of control:

> [T]he skill required; the source of the instrumentalities and tools; the location of the work; the duration of the relationship between the parties; whether the hiring party has the right to assign additional projects to the hired party; the extent of the hired party's discretion over when and how long to work; the method of payment; the hired party's role in hiring and paying assistants; whether the work is part of the regular business of the hiring party; whether the hiring party is in business; the provision of employee benefits; and the tax treatment of the hired party.[21]

For example, in *Nationwide Mutual Co.* v. *Darden*, the Supreme Court applied the control test to assess whether an insurance agent qualified as an employee under the Employee Retirement Income Security Act (ERISA).[22] The insurance agent would have likely been considered an independent contractor because he maintained his own office at his expense, hired and paid his own staff, set his own hours, and was "free to solicit sales wherever, whenever, and from whomever he wished."[23] Because the insurance company had no day-to-day influence over the agent's activities, it exercised insufficient control to be considered his employer.

Sometimes, statutes or regulations define the term "employee" or "employ" to help courts assess whether a particular individual is covered by the statute. Many of these are variations of the control test.[24] The most important of these alternate tests is the "economic realities" test applied under the Fair Labor Standards Act ("FLSA"), the federal minimum wage and overtime statute. The FLSA defines "employ" as to "suffer or permit work."[25] Courts have interpreted this language in favor of broad coverage, using the following "economic realities" test:

1) the nature and degree of the alleged employer's control as to the manner in which the work is to be performed;
2) the alleged employee's opportunity for profit or loss depending upon his managerial skill;
3) the alleged employee's investment in equipment or materials required for his task, or his employment of workers;
4) whether the service rendered requires a special skill;
5) the degree of permanency and duration of the working relationship;
6) the extent to which the service rendered is an integral part of the alleged employer's business.[26]

The putative employer's degree of control over the performance forms part of the inquiry. However, the remainder of the test uses various other factors as proxies to asses the worker's economic dependence on the putative employer. For example, in *Secretary of Labor* v. *Lauritzen*,

---

[19] Katherine V.W. Stone, *Legal Protections for Atypical Employees: Employment Law for Workers Without Workplaces and Employees Without Employers*, 27 Berkeley J. Emp. & Labor L. 251, 260 (2006).

[20] *See Nationwide Mut. Ins. Co.* v. *Darden*, 503 U.S. 318, 322–23 (1992).

[21] *Id.* at 323–24 (internal quotations and citation omitted).

[22] *Id.*

[23] I use the term "likely" because the case was remanded to an appellate court, which signaled that Darden was unlikely to be an employee, but remanded the issue back to the district court. *See Darden* v. *Nationwide Mut. Ins. Co.*, 969 F.2d 76 (4th Cir. 1992). The district Court did not issue a subsequent written opinion.

[24] Tippett, *supra* note 11, at 556.

[25] 29 U.S.C. § 203(g) (2012).

[26] *Secretary of Labor, United States Dep't of Labor* v. *Lauritzen*, 835 F.2d 1529, 1535 (1987).

the court applied the economic realities test to assess whether migrant farmworkers harvesting cucumbers qualified as employees.[27] The farm owners exercised relatively little control over how the work was performed. Each family decided how many acres to harvest and each family member's assigned role in the harvest. The family unit's revenue (and ultimately profit) would be based on the grade of the cucumbers harvested and the overall weight of the harvest. If the test were purely a matter of control, the farmworkers arguably might not be considered employees. However, the court ultimately deemed them employees under the economic realities test because the profits did not depend on managerial skill; the work did not require special skill; and the families' investment in equipment was minimal compared to the farm's investment in land, building, equipment, and supplies.[28]

As I argued in previous research, sharing companies vary considerably in the level of control they exercise over workers, depending on the type of service they provide. Sharing companies can be broadly placed into three categories: (1) property-sharing (e.g. Airbnb); (2) property-based services (e.g. Uber); and (3) service-sharing companies (e.g. TaskRabbit, Amazon MTurk).[29]

For property-sharing companies, the service purchased by the customer is primarily exclusive (or near-exclusive) access to tangible property, like a car, an apartment, or designer clothes. Labor is incidental to the service, and primarily occurs in connection with the transfer of possession for a fixed period.[30] The risk of a misclassification claim is limited for these types of businesses primarily because comparatively little labor occurs.

By contrast, property-based services like Uber, Lyft, and Sidecar sell beneficial use of property by its owner on the customer's behalf.[31] Substantial labor is involved. Business models aside, the tasks performed by drivers are similar to those performed by taxi and delivery drivers. Both taxi and delivery companies have seen substantial misclassification litigation over the years.[32] It is therefore not surprising that sharing companies providing property-based services have seen considerable litigation over employee status.[33]

A third category – service sharing companies – involve sharing only labor. These types of services have also been characterized in the literature as "crowd work" or "crowd sourcing."[34] My earlier research suggests that these companies vary considerably in the control they exercise over workers, with few exercising high levels of apparent control.[35] However, subsequent research by

[27] *Id.*

[28] *Darden v. Nationwide Mut. Ins. Co.*, 969 F.2d 76, 77 (4th Cir. 1992).

[29] Tippett, *supra* note 11, at 553.

[30] *Id. But see* Juliet B. Schor, *Does the Sharing Economy Increase Inequality Within the Eighty Percent?: Findings from a Qualitative Study of Platform Providers*, 10 Cambridge J. Regions, Econ. & Soc'y, 23, 25 (2017) (noting the cleaning and prep work associated with hosting on Airbnb, and contrasting it with the "minimal" work involved in renting out a car on RelayRides).

[31] Tippett, *supra* note 11, at 553–54.

[32] *See generally id.* at 551; *See also Yellow Taxi Co. v. NLRB*, 721 F.2d 366, 373–74 (D.C. Cir. 1983); *Kubinec v. Top Cab Dispatch, Inc.*, No. SUCV201203082BLS1, 2014 WL 3817016, at *1, 13–15 (Mass. Super. Ct. June 25, 2014); *Yellow Cab Coop. v. Workers' Comp. Appeals Bd.*, 277 Cal. Rptr. 434, 436 (Ct. App. 1991); *Alexander v. FedEx Ground Package Sys., Inc.*, 765 F.3d 981, 989–94, 997 (9th Cir. 2014); *See also Estrada v. FedEx Ground Package Sys., Inc.*, 64 Cal. Rptr. 3d 327, 331 (Ct. App. 2007).

[33] Miriam Cherry, *Working for (Virtually) Minimum Wage: Applying the Fair Labor Standards Act in Cyberspace*, 60 Ala. L. Rev. 1077, 1078 (2009).

[34] *Id.* at 1078 (2009); *See also* Miriam Cherry, *Cyber Commodification*, 72 Md. L. Rev. 381, 445 (2012); Miriam A. Cherry, *A Taxonomy of Virtual Work*, 45 Ga. L. Rev. 951 (2011); Janine Berg, *Income Security and the On-Demand Economy: Findings and Policy Lessons from a Survey of Crowdworkers*, 37 Comp. Lab. L & Pol'y J. 543, 545 (2016); Valerio De Stefano, *The Rise of the "Just-In-Time Workforce": On-Demand Work, Crowdwork, and Labor Protection in the "Gig Economy,"* 37 Comp. Lab. L. & Pol'y J. 471, 472 (2016).

[35] Tippett, *supra* note 11 at 562.

others suggests that workers in service-sharing companies can have similar experiences to ride-sharing workers. Ilana Gershon and Melissa Cefkin noted that some service platforms "include built-in tracking systems for monitoring time-on-tasks," which workers have characterized as "big-brotherly."[36] When service-sharing companies use customer rating schemes akin to those used by Uber and Lyft,[37] workers have also described experiencing stress associated with the emotional labor of keeping customers happy.[38] As Deepa Das Acevedo observed, "platforms and customers have the power to discipline … if and when they feel like it and in essentially unpredictable or unknowable ways."[39] Workers then respond by "conforming their desires to the limits of the system" and their customers.[40]

Given the substantial variance in control that sharing companies exercise over their workers, only some sharing workers are likely misclassified as independent contractors. Thus, the overall effect of the sharing economy is not to create a new class of workers all of whom would have been treated as employees in more traditional employment arrangements. Instead, the sharing economy may ultimately erode compliance with employment laws at the margins, where innovation provides cover for noncompliance and avoidance. This chapter proceeds by describing the respects in which these marginal workers risk falling outside traditional employment law protections.

II EMPLOYMENT NONCOMPLIANCE AND AVOIDANCE IN THE SHARING ECONOMY

As Charlotte Alexander and I explore in prior research, the sharing economy involves both noncompliance and avoidance.[41] Companies may choose to misclassify workers as a result of arbitration agreements containing class action waivers, which cuts off their liability for aggregate claims. The sharing economy can also make it more difficult and complex for companies to identify control when it is exerted through software. The sharing economy further reveals certain anachronisms in existing legal tests, which assume, for example, that ownership of equipment, or flexibility in schedules, is indicative of independent contractor status. Consequently, existing rules may deem some sharing workers properly classified under existing rules, even when these proxies for independence are no longer as meaningful as they once were. Each of these sources of noncompliance and avoidance are discussed below.

---

[36] Ilana Gershon and Melissa Cefkin, *Click for Work: Rethinking Work, Rethinking Labor Through Online Work Distribution Platforms* [working paper], at *20.

[37] Deepa Das Acevedo, *Unbundling Freedom in the Sharing Economy*, 91 S.Cal. L. Rev. (forthcoming 2018) [working paper], at *18 (dog-walking service Rover can discipline workers for canceling client requests, and customers can do so through client ratings); Josh Dzieza, *The Rating Game: How Uber and Its Peers Turned Us into Horrible Bosses*, The Verge (Dec. 19, 2011), www.theverge.com/2015/10/28/9625968/rating-system-on-demand-economy-uber-olive-garden (Postmates terminates workers with a customer rating below 4.7); TaskRabbit, *Ratings and Reviews on the TaskRabbit Platform*, https://support.taskrabbit.com/hc/en-us/articles/213301766-Ratings-and-Reviews-on-the-TaskRabbit-Platform.

[38] *Id.* at *18; Schor *supra* note 30 at 26, 29 (worker described TaskRabbit as a "servant economy," another described it as "humbing"). *See also* Raval & Dourish, *supra* note 4, at 5–6 (ride sharing workers describing emotional labor).

[39] Das Acevedo, *supra* note 37 at *18.

[40] *Id.*

[41] *See* Alexander and Tippett, *supra* note 12, at 1004; *See also* Orly Lobel, *supra* note 13, at 112; Zatz, *supra* note 13, at 1086; Cunningham-Parmeter, *supra* note 13, at 1682; Benjamin Means and Joseph Seiner, *Navigating the Uber Economy*, 49 U.C. Davis L. Rev. 1511, 1517 (2016); *See generally* Brishen Rogers, *Employment Rights in the Platform Economy: Getting Back to Basics*, 10 Harv. L. & Pol'y Rev. 479 (2016).

A *Noncompliance through Arbitration Agreements*

The sharing economy has produced considerable litigation over employee status. One magazine headline declared that "the gig economy won't last because it's being sued to death."[42] In a law review article, Professor Miriam Cherry documented 14 misclassification cases against sharing companies, almost all of which were in California.[43] This level of litigation is substantial given the small number of companies operating in the sharing industry.

However, the merit of many of these cases is unknown, because a number of them have been redirected to private arbitration.[44] Many workers at sharing companies are subject to arbitration provisions. Arbitration agreements have two important effects on employment law in the sharing economy. First, arbitration is private.[45] Unlike court rulings, arbitral decisions do not form part of the public record. This crimps the development of jurisprudence on employee status in the sharing economy.

Second, arbitration agreements tend to limit the remedies available to workers. Under a series of Supreme Court decisions, most notably *AT&T* v. *Concepción*,[46] arbitration provisions can be used to preclude any form of class or collective remedy, in arbitration or in court.[47] Although workers can still pursue individual claims through arbitration, they have no viable remedy for smaller claims that can only be economically litigated on a collective basis, especially wage and hour claims.[48] In a forthcoming study of terms of service contracts for 38 sharing companies over an eight-year period,[49] around two-thirds of companies were found now to include arbitration provisions with a class action waiver.[50] Consequently, even if existing definitions of employment would have covered some portion of these workers, they are functionally unprotected as to any employee rights that depend on enforcement through aggregate litigation.

A class action lawsuit against Uber[51] typifies how arbitration provisions can limit worker remedies and influence how companies make decisions about employee classification. Both cases

---

[42] Sarah Kessler, *The Gig Economy Won't Last Because It's Being Sued to Death*, Fast Company (Feb. 17, 2015), www.fastcompany.com/3042248/the-gig-economy-wont-last-because-its-being-sued-to-death.

[43] Miriam Cherry, *Beyond Misclassification: The Digital Transformation of Work*, 37 Comp. Lab. L. & Pol'y J. 577, 584–87 (2016).

[44] In Cherry's list of 14 cases, four included motions to compel individual arbitration, three of which were granted. Cherry, *supra* note 43 at 584–87.

[45] Lewis L. Maltby, *Private Justice: Employment Arbitration and Civil Rights*, 30 Colum. Hum. Rts. L. Rev. 29, 30–32 (1998).

[46] *AT&T Mobility IIC v. Concepción*, 563 U.S. 333, 349 (2011); *See also American Exp. v. Italian Colors Restaurant*, 133 S. Ct. 2304 (2013).

[47] The Supreme Court has granted certiorari in three cases on the question of whether arbitration provisions containing class action waivers violate employee rights to engage in concerted activity under the National Labor Relations Act: *Lewis v. Epic Systems Corp.*, 823 F.3d 1147 (7th Cir. 2016), cert. granted, 137 Sup. Ct. 809 (2017); *Ernst & Young LLP v. Morris*, 834 F.3d 975 (9th Cir. 2016), cert. granted, 137 S. Ct. 809 (2017); *Murphy Oil USA, Inc.*, 361 N.L.R.B. No. 72 (2014), enforcement denied, 808 F.3d 1013 (5th Cir. 2015), cert. granted, 137 S. Ct. 809 (2017).

[48] For example, an individual claim alleging employment discrimination might be worth tens of thousands of dollars, such that a plaintiff's lawyer working on contingency might be willing to represent them in an individual arbitration. In a wage and hour claim, however, an individual worker may have only suffered hundreds of dollars in damages. That claim would not justify the expense of litigating on an individual basis, even though it would be quite lucrative in a collective or class action claim. Consequently, arbitration provisions containing a class and collective action waiver have the practical effect of cutting off remedies for certain types of worker harms.

[49] The contracts spanned the period of 2009 through 2016, although we were not able to locate the contracts for each company for every such year.

[50] Elizabeth Tippett and Bridget Schaaff, *How Concepcion and Italian Colors Affected Terms of Service Contracts in the Gig Economy*, 70 Rutgers L. Rev. 101 (2018).

[51] *Cotter v. Lyft, Inc.*, 60 F.Supp.3d 1067, 1071 (N.D. Cal. 2015); *O'Connor v. Uber Technologies, Inc.*, 82 F.Supp.3d 1133, 1151 (N.D. Cal. 2015).

were litigated in California, and the court denied the motion for summary judgment, setting them on a course for trial. The parties settled for $100 million, which was rejected by the court as insufficient.[52] The case is currently on appeal regarding whether the district court should have compelled individual arbitration.[53] According to the plaintiffs' counsel, if Uber prevails, "it is possible that the class in this case may be reduced to the few Uber drivers who opted out of arbitration (or who stopped working for Uber before the arbitration clause was first introduced in August 2013)."[54] Uber now includes an arbitration provision containing a class action waiver in its terms of service contracts. The company continues to classify its workers as independent contractors, suggesting it is not fearful of future litigation.[55]

Broadly, arbitration provisions containing class action waivers may erode working conditions for sharing economy workers over time. Sharing companies fearful of aggregate wage and hour litigation may otherwise have been hesitant to exercise substantial control over workers, lest a court deem them employees and award substantial wages and penalties. Without the deterrent of aggregate litigation, companies can indulge their preference to improve the customer experience through ever greater monitoring, control, and discipline of workers.[56]

B Control Obscured by Software

Sharing economy companies "exercise control by algorithm,"[57] also known as software rules. As Lawrence Lessig famously observed, software rules operate like physical architecture, and can constrain behavior just as legal rules do.[58] In some respects, software constrains behavior to a greater degree than legal rules because it is self-implementing.[59] Legal rules – such as antitrust rules that preclude collusion between competitors – constrain behavior by influencing the decision-making of business actors. Software rules, by contrast, operate by making certain behavior within the software impossible or extremely difficult.[60] For example, many service-sharing platforms discourage or prohibit any communications between customer and worker, lest they make arrangements for work outside of the platform (and avoid the associated commission and price structure). The messaging software for these apps is designed to detect the presence of the symbol @ – which could suggest an email address – or other language about communicating off-platform.[61] This type of software regulates behavior much more directly than a simple prohibition that operates exclusively through the user's conscience.

---

[52] Although the $100 million settlement seemed substantial, the Judge estimated that penalties in the case could have amounted to more than $1 billion. The settlement would have been divided among some 385,000 drivers. Joel Rosenblatt, *Uber's $100 Million Driver Pay Settlement Rejected by Judge*, Bloomberg Technology (Aug. 18, 2016), www.bloomberg.com/news/articles/2016-08-18/uber-s-100-million-driver-pay-settlement-is-rejected-by-judge.r.

[53] Shannon Liss-Riordan, *Uber Drivers: Read Here About an Important Lawsuit by Uber Drivers To Recover the Tips They Should Have Received and Reimbursement for Expenses*, http://uberlawsuit.com/.

[54] *Id.*

[55] Jordan Golson, *Judge Rejects Uber's $100 Million Settlement with Drivers*, The Verge (Aug. 18, 2016), www.theverge.com/2016/8/18/12545018/uber-reject-settlement-lawsuit-class-action-independent-contractor.

[56] Charlotte Garden and Nancy Leong, this volume.

[57] Alexander and Tippett, *supra* note 12 at 1008; *see also* Cherry *supra* note 43 at 597–99. See Min Kyung Lee et al., *Working with Machines: The Impact of Algorithmic and Data-Driven Management on Human Workers, in* Proceedings of the 33rd Annual ACM Conference on Human Factors in Computing Systems,1603, 1604 (2015), http://dx.doi.org/10.1145/2702123.2702548 (describing ride-sharing systems as "algorithmic management").

[58] *See* Lawrence Lessig, *Code and Other Laws of Cyberspace* 6 (1999).

[59] R. Polk Wagner, *On Software Regulation*, 78 S. Cal. L. Rev. 457, 460 (2005).

[60] James Grimmelmann, Note, *Regulation by Software*, 114 Yale L. J. 1719, 1729 (2005).

[61] The author experienced this feature while using the sharing app, Fiverr, www.fiverr.com/.

Software can thus effectuate a high level of control over workers, depending upon how the software is designed. Customer rating systems typify the challenge for regulators in assessing whether drivers are employees of the service. The touchstone for most legal tests of employment status is the amount of control that the service exercises over that worker. Applications of the control test, which I will explain in greater detail below, typically assume that control is exercised through a manager directing the putative employee's work. But in the context of the sharing economy, control is both distal and distributed. For example, control is distal because some high-level manager at headquarters sets the threshold for terminating workers based on star ratings, but it is implemented "automatically" through software. Control is distributed because the task of rating performance is assigned to customers – each of whom are fractionally responsible for determining whether a worker keeps or loses the contract with the service. Should reliance on customer ratings be treated as evidence that the service exercises little control? Or is the reservation of the right to terminate drivers based on those third-party ratings itself evidence of control? A clear-eyed assessment of the employment status of sharing economy workers requires courts, regulators, and lawmakers to think more broadly about "control" when it is exercised and enhanced through technology.

For example, Lyft monitors driver acceptance rates for ride requests – how frequently drivers reject customer pickup requests proffered by Lyft's driver/customer matching algorithms. An acceptance rate below 75 percent is considered problematic and may result in an email warning and ultimately deactivation.[62] Lyft also monitors driver cancellation decisions (rejecting a ride after accepting a request), which can also result in driver deactivation.[63] Uber, for its part, expects a dispatch acceptance rate of 80 percent.[64] By comparison, TaskRabbit does not terminate workers for poor ratings, but punishes them through its matching algorithm, offering lower quality and infrequent work to lower-rated workers.[65]

Does this represent a high or a low degree of control? It depends. First, the presence of any sort of dispatch threshold is some evidence of control. However, the matching algorithm also plays a role in worker autonomy. In this regard, it is worth comparing software to a human comparator – for example, taxi dispatchers. When taxicab operators require drivers to follow the instructions of a radio dispatcher, those drivers are often considered employees, depending on the circumstances.[66] The stated policy for a taxicab company might be that drivers must accept all dispatched jobs. However, in human interactions, there is likely room for negotiation and accommodation – the human dispatcher might accommodate a request for a break or a nap, or a skipped job with a detour to Dunkin Donuts. Human dispatchers might also note that some drivers prefer particular routes over others and attempt to accommodate those preferences as well. Human dispatch timing may also adjust for the preferences of the driver, assigning them in rapid succession to someone who wants to finish a job quickly, or more slowly to a driver that wants to wait around. Even with these accommodations, the taxi driver would likely still be considered an employee.

In applying the control test, courts will ultimately have to gauge the dispatch acceptance threshold that renders an Uber or Lyft driver comparable to a driver-employee of a taxi company. A 60 percent or an 80 percent threshold might produce a similar experience for the driver as a human dispatcher, and make the two functionally equivalent. Indeed, ethnographic

---

[62] _Cotter v. Lyft, Inc._, 60 F.Supp.3d 1067, 1071 (N.D. Cal. 2015).
[63] _Id._
[64] _O'Connor v. Uber Technologies, Inc._, 82 F.Supp.3d 1133, 1149 (N.D. Cal. 2015).
[65] Dzieza, _supra_ note 37.
[66] _Yellow Taxi Co. v. NLRB_, 721 F.2d 366, 374–79 (D.C. Cir. 1983).

research by Deepa Das Acevedo suggests that workers find algorithmic managers less oppressive than human ones.[67] On the other hand, not all algorithms are equal. One might imagine a dispatch-matching algorithm tailored to the preferences of the individual driver over time – like Netflix recommendations, or a Pandora/Spotify station. If the algorithm only presents drivers with exactly the type of rides they prefer, a 60 percent or 80 percent acceptance rate might be experienced by the driver as relatively unconstrained. Assessing control over the driver also requires an understanding of how drivers use the software. As researchers at Carnegie Mellon documented, drivers often develop clever workarounds to outsmart the dispatch algorithm when it did not suit their preferences.[68]

Software can also exert control through more subtle means. Amazon MTurk allows "requesters" (customers) to post projects at a specified rate for workers subject to certain specifications. Workers can select their preferred projects and ignore those they do not want. Many service-sharing companies operate in similar fashion, making jobs available for workers to select and complete through the platform.[69] Access to projects, however, can depend on how frequently customers reject their work. Customers can set a threshold of only making work available to those with a specified approval rate (for example, only workers whose output was accepted by the customer 90 percent of the time). While such thresholds can limit or cut off access to future work, they represent an ambiguous form of control. Sellers on eBay receive a reputational rating from customers that may influence customer decisions. The presence of the rating does not necessarily mean that eBay is exercising employer-like control over them. On the other hand, rigid quality metrics could also be consistent with a high degree of control, and is in some ways reminiscent of a cashier or call-center worker forced to churn through a certain number of transactions within a certain period of time.

Undisclosed software rules can also be perceived as oppressive by workers, and represent a marked contrast to more traditional means of disseminating workplace rules. In many cases, software rules are functionally equivalent to employer policies – which would ordinarily be set forth in an employee handbook. However, companies have no obligation to disclose the software rules that govern customer rating cutoffs, communications outside of platforms, and penalties for failing to accept work. Consequently, sharing workers may be forced to guess about the basic terms and conditions of their work. For example, Lyft apparently did not disclose the ratings-based termination threshold to workers – that fact was revealed through the deposition testimony of an executive.[70] The capricious and unknown nature of these standards can be stressful for workers. One worker at the delivery service, Postmates, reported that he was suddenly terminated by the service for late deliveries during a snowstorm.[71] As Deepa Das Aceveda observed, these workers experience "an overwhelming level of uncertainty … the only thing workers … can be sure of is the power of the platform and of the client to constrain their options in any circumstance."[72]

Thus far, courts seem to be doing a reasonably good job of identifying and evaluating control via software.[73] The Uber and Lyft decisions included detailed discussions of the respects in which expectations regarding star ratings and dispatch rejection resulted in driver discipline and

---

[67] Das Acevedo, *supra* note 37 at 13.

[68] *See* Lee et al., *supra* note 57 at 1603.

[69] Indeed, a primary complaint on some of these sites is the insufficient amount of work available. *See* Berg, *supra* note 34, at 13–14.

[70] *Cotter v. Lyft, Inc.*, 60 F.Supp.3d 1067, 1082 n.3 (N.D. Cal. 2015).

[71] Dzieza *supra* note 37.

[72] Das Acevedo, *supra* note 37 at 20.

[73] *Id.*

termination.[74] Protecting sharing economy workers heavily constrained by software will require continued judicial attention to algorithmic management as a form of control.

C Legal Proxies for Independence May Be Less Meaningful

The previously described legal tests for assessing employment status apply an anachronistic model of employee status that may be somewhat less reliable at detecting employee status in the sharing economy. The "control test" derives from a master/servant model of employment.[75] Under English common law, the master (employer) had various obligations to the servant in exchange for the servant's services.[76] Within this model, control was integral to performance.[77] A servant in the nineteenth century would not have been much use in cooking or cleaning for a household if they worked according to their own schedule and own preferences. However, the master/servant relationship was not the only pre-industrial model for completing work. As Matthew Finkin has argued, the competing pre-industrial economic relationship was mercantilism – where merchants provided raw materials to rural artisans to transform into "finished or semi-finished" products at a fixed rate (e.g. "wool, flax, cotton").[78] Finkin observes that the sharing economy more closely resembles the mercantile model. Because mercantile models involve less control, some sharing economy workers will fall out of the definition of "servant."

Some of the innovations and efficiencies of sharing economy business models happen to correspond with elements of the "control test" and "economic realities test" that favor independent contractor status. Companies in the sharing economy require workers to use their own tools and equipment, which provides a competitive advantage against competitors forced to make those capital investments.[79] It also provides the added benefit of bolstering the sharing companies' claim that their workers are independent contractors. Sharing economy companies tend not to assign workers to scheduled shifts or durations. Instead, the matching functionality of the software enables workers to participate when they choose, for the duration they choose. This too favors independent contractor status under the control test ("the extent of the hired party's discretion over when and how long to work").[80]

---

[74] *O'Connor v. Uber Technologies, Inc.*, 82 F.Supp.3d 1133, 1149–51 (N.D. Cal. 2015); *Cotter v. Lyft, Inc.*, 60 F.Supp.3d 1067, 1071 (N.D. Cal. 2015).

[75] *See Nationwide Mut. Ins. Co. v. Darden*, 503 U.S. 318, 324–25 (1992) (citing Restatement (Second) of Agency, listing "master-servant" factors); Restatement (Second) of Agency § 220 (definition of servant as "subject to the other's control or right to control" of the master, and articulating factors similar to the control test).

[76] As recounted by Jay Feinman, "American law originally adopted the rules of English law on duration of service contracts though it later departed from them in developing the at-will employment rule." Jay Feinman, *The Development of the Employment at Will Rule*, 20 Am. J. Legal Hist. 118, 118–19 (1976). Under the English rule indefinite contracts were treated as a mutual agreement to serve (and provide employment) for a one-year period. *Id.* at 120.

[77] The Restatement (Second) of Agency § 220 specifically defines control in terms of actual control, or the right to control "physical conduct in the performance of services." Restatement (Second) of Agency § 220, *supra* note 75.

[78] Matthew Finkin, *Beclouded Work, Beclouded Workers in Historical Perspective*, 37 Comp. Lab. L. & Pol'y J. 603, 607 (2016).

[79] The sharing economy departs from older business models in its reliance on the tools, equipment, and other instrumentalities of the individual worker. The central conceit of property-sharing companies is for consumers to profit from property they already own. Lisa Gansky, *The Mesh: Why the Future of Business is Sharing* 15–16 (2d ed., 2012). Likewise, property-based service companies require drivers to be able to furnish their own vehicles. For service sharing companies, workers provide their own computers, broadband connection, and work from a chosen location.

[80] To be sure, other factors common to the applicable tests favor employee status. In particular, the fact that the work is "part of the regular business" of the sharing company, and that the sharing company "is in business" favors employee status under the control test. *Darden*, 503 U.S. 318 at 324. The fact that the services represent an "integral part of the alleged employer's business" also favors employee status under the economic realities test. *Secretary of Labor,*

Furnishing tools and equipment is a factor relevant to both the control test and the economic realities test. Traditionally, furnishing one's own tools and equipment has been a reasonable indicator of an independent business. Consider, for instance, the insurance agent at issue in the *Darden* v. *Nationwide* case. The agent's own office space evidenced Nationwide's limited control over his work. The office space would likewise have been relevant under the economic realities test. In addition to evidencing reduced control, it supported his opportunity for profit or loss based on managerial skill. It also showed a substantial "investment in equipment or materials" required for the task.

Under these tests, capital investments by workers in the sharing economy would likewise be considered substantial. And to some extent, with good reason. Airbnb landlords make a substantial investment in real property, such that the income they receive seems like a bona fide profit, rather than an exchange of labor for wages. Ride-sharing drivers must own a vehicle to be eligible to drive. Indeed, some drivers treat driving as a bona fide business: one complained to former Uber CEO Travis Kalanick that he invested $98,000 in a luxury car for Uber's premium service, only to later declare bankruptcy when Uber lowered its luxury rates.[81]

Nevertheless, ownership of equipment may no longer be a reliable indicator of contractor status. While bona fide independent businesses often own and use their own equipment, many dependent workers may do so as well. Furthermore, equipment ownership as a precondition to working may simply represent a way to shift costs on workers. Labor economist David Weil has documented a larger trend toward a "fissured workplace" where large companies subcontract and franchise core parts of their businesses, and all that remains is a brand and some central HR functions and procedures.[82] Subcontracting to individual workers who are expected to operate a nominally independent business then becomes the natural extension of this subcontracting process. In other words, sharing companies are accelerating a preexisting trend. They take a share of the profits without investing in the capital, while also putting a thumb on the scale of the independent contractor inquiry.

Sharing companies also gain advantage under existing legal rules because workers select when to work, for a duration of their choosing. Workers may also have substantial control over the location of the work, depending on the service involved. Both of these factors form an explicit component of the control test ("location of the work" and "the hired party's discretion over when and how long to work"). Because the economic realities test also considers control, these facts are also relevant to that test.

Unlike investments in tools and equipment, ceding more control to workers offers them tangible benefits. The flexibility to cease work obligations at the touch of a screen, and to start back up at the worker's discretion is valuable, especially since low wage workers in more traditional sectors are subject to last-minute scheduling and strongly encouraged to offer "open availability" to their employers.[83] Indeed, sharing workers who participated in a Pew Research pool described

---

United States Dep't of Labor v. *Lauritzen*, 835 F.2d 1529,1534 (1987). However, sharing companies have these factors in common with their bricks and mortar competitors, and all would be equally disadvantaged by these factors. By contrast, ownership of tools and equipment, and the built-in worker flexibility provide a competitive advantage to sharing companies under existing rules.

[81] Eric Newcomer, *In Video, Uber CEO Argues with Driver over Falling Fares*, Bloomberg (Feb. 28, 2017), www .bloomberg.com/news/articles/2017-02-28/in-video-uber-ceo-argues-with-driver-over-falling-fares.

[82] David Weil, *The Fissured Workplace: Why Work Became So Bad for So Many and What Can Be Done to Improve It* 12 (2014). *See also* Cherry *supra* note 43 at 579 (noting that "we are currently experiencing a far-reaching digital transformation of work. The changes include the growth of automatic management and a move toward ever more precarious work").

[83] Alexander and Tippett, *supra* note 12; Cherry, *supra* note 34 at 961; De Stefano, *supra* note 34 at 32; Lobel, *supra* note 13, at 131; Charlotte Alexander, Anna Haley-Lock, and Nantiya Ruan, *Stabilizing Low-Wage Work*, 50 Harv. C.R.-CL.L. Rev. 1, 37 (2015).

flexibility as a primary motivator.[84] At the same time, many white collar employees experience flexibility that more closely resembles that of sharing economy workers – with the ability to work remotely, or use flexible schedules to complete their work outside of scheduled hours. The flexibility afforded these highly compensated workers is viewed alternately as a perk for some, and an inconvenient form of on-call status for others, but rarely presumed to erode their status as employees. Thus, while work that offers little to no flexibility may be a strong indicator of employee status, flexible work environments may be less reliable proxies for contractor status than they once were.

III REGULATORY APPROACHES TO PROTECTING WORKERS IN THE SHARING ECONOMY

Commentators offer varied suggestions for protecting workers in the sharing economy, some of which are explored elsewhere in this volume.[85] I offer a few additional suggestions, in part building upon the recommendations of others.

First, changes to existing legal rules are likely to have only limited effect if sharing companies can continue to bind workers to arbitration provisions containing class/collective action waivers. As noted, the Supreme Court is currently considering a series of cases challenging the enforceability of employee class/collective action waivers under the National Labor Relations Act.[86] Unless the Supreme Court departs from recent precedent and declares such waivers unenforceable, restoring remedies to these workers will likely require amending the 1925 Federal Arbitration Act.[87]

In terms of substantive rules, courts may want to update their application of the control test and economic realities test to deemphasize factors that may not reliably predict independent contractor status – in particular, equipment ownership and some measure of work flexibility. Similarly, Valerio De Stefano, Miriam Cherry, and Keith Cunningham-Parmeter have argued that courts should think more broadly about control, to include software-based constraints and monitoring.[88] In practice, this likely requires courts to treat software rules as employer policies,[89] and hold employers accountable for control exercised through those rules.

Other commentators recommend an approach broadly characterized as harm reduction. Rather than imposing additional costs on employers, the government might offer more benefits to workers, regardless of their employment status.[90] As Orly Lobel has argued, "regulators should prefer solutions that directly address any negative consequences that people or society may experience from the rise of the platform, rather than blanket prohibitive solutions that stymie its development."[91] The Affordable Care Act is an example of harm reduction, because it enabled individuals to purchase health insurance regardless of their employment status.[92]

---

[84] Aaron Smith, *Gig Work, Online Selling and Home Sharing*, Pew Research Center 20 (Nov. 17, 2016). *See also* Das Acevedo, supra note 37 at *11–13.

[85] *See* Charlotte Garden and Nancy Leong, Chapter 33; Miriam Cherry and Atonio Aloisi, Chapter 23; Brishen Rogers, Chapter 22, all in this volume.

[86] *See supra* note 47.

[87] Maureen A. Weston, *The Death of Class Arbitration After* Concepción?, 60 Kans. L. Rev. 767, 793 (2012).

[88] De Stefano, *supra* note 34, at 32; Cunningham-Parmeter, *supra* note 13, at 1707. *See also* Cherry, *supra* note 43 at 21.

[89] Alexander and Tippett, *supra* note 12.

[90] *Id.*

[91] Lobel, *supra* note 13, at 137.

[92] Indeed, venture capitalist Marc Andreeson argued that the sharing economy was made possible by the Affordable Care Act, because it allowed millions of people to obtain health insurance without an employer. Evan McMorris-Santoro

Paul Secunda has advocated for multi-employee retirement plans under ERISA, where those working for multiple employees could aggregate their retirement savings.[93] Secunda's model need not necessarily be based on employee status, and could be made more broadly available for sharing economy workers.

A related approach might be to extend the coverage of existing employment protections to all workers, regardless of their status as independent contractors or employees. For example, if Title VII of the Civil Rights Act were extended to include independent contractors, workers in the sharing economy would enjoy protections against discrimination regardless of their classification under existing rules. This would also reduce employer incentives to engage in regulatory arbitrage – altering the terms and conditions of the work to avoid employee status.[94]

CONCLUSION

Workers in the sharing economy are overwhelmingly classified as independent contractors. Under existing rules, some of them likely qualify as employees. However, companies have limited incentives to reclassify them due to arbitration agreements containing class action waivers, which cut off the threat of aggregate claims. Existing rules can also be somewhat misaligned with the sharing economy. Courts are expected to assess the level of control companies exercise over workers, but their task is complicated when control is exercised through software. Formerly reliable proxies for independent contractor status – such as ownership of equipment, and flexibly scheduling – may no longer be as meaningful as they once were.

As the sharing economy matures and plays a more fixed role within the landscape of employment opportunities, courts and regulators may need to adjust their approach. Such adjustments will be necessary both to ensure that sharing companies do not secure a competitive advantage from their avoidance of employment rules, and to extend a baseline level of protections to affected workers.

---

and Johana Bhuiyan, *How Obamacare Drives the Sharing Economy*, Buzzfeed News (Oct. 14, 2014), www.buzzfeed .com/evanmcsan/how-obamacare-drives-the-sharing-economy?utm_term=.tnVm10NBr#.hcZY8ydgA.

[93] Paul Secunda, *Uber Retirement*, 2017 U. Chi. Legal Forum 435, 438. https://ssrn.com/abstract=2894566.

[94] *See* discussion and citations, *supra* note 13.

22

Fissuring, Data-Driven Governance, and Platform Economy Labor Standards

Brishen Rogers

INTRODUCTION

The rise of Uber, Lyft, Deliveroo, TaskRabbit, Care.com, and other online labor intermediaries have helped to focus public attention on the high incidence of informal and precarious work in today's economy.[1] On-demand labor platforms tend to classify workers as independent contractors rather than employees, rendering them ineligible for basic rights under wage and hour, workers' compensation, collective bargaining, unemployment insurance, and anti-discrimination laws, and giving them little if any formal job security.[2] Platform economy workers have often sued, alleging misclassification and underpayment by the platforms.[3]

Whether platform economy firms are actually *undermining* labor standards compared to the status quo ante is another, more complicated, question. Silicon Valley did not invent worker misclassification, low wages, or mediocre working conditions.[4] For decades, taxi companies[5] and other logistics companies[6] have often classified drivers, lawfully or unlawfully, as independent contractors. Many day laborers and nannies who now find work on TaskRabbit or Care.com were previously employed in gray- or black-market conditions, and paid in cash.[7] And

---

[1] There seems to be no universally agreed-upon definition of "informal" work. Within labor circles it is used to indicate work that lacks formal legal entitlements of employment. Such work is often performed within micro-enterprises or by single independent contractors, though it need not be. It also tends to lack employment security or economic security. For a useful primer *see* ILO, *Unprotected Labour: What Role for Unions in the Informal Economy* (Labor Education 2002/2 No. 127) (2002).

[2] This chapter considers such issues under US law. That being said, many of the same issues have emerged in other jurisdictions. *See generally* Jeremias Prassl, *Humans as a Service* (2017); and *Economia & Lavoro* (2018) (symposium issue discussing platform economy labor standards in various European countries, Japan, Brazil, and elsewhere).

[3] *See* Elizabeth Tippett, this volume; Brishen Rogers, *Employment Rights in the Platform Economy: Getting Back to Basics*, 10 Harv. Law & Pol'y Rev. 479 (2016) (discussing Uber and Lyft misclassification suits).

[4] *See generally* David Weil, *The Fissured Workplace: Why Work Became So Bad for So Many and What Can Be Done to Improve It* (2014) (detailing incidence of worker misclassification, subcontracting, and franchising in the contemporary economy, and arguing that such practices undermine labor standards).

[5] *Yellow Cab Cooperative, Inc. v. Workers' Comp. Appeals Bd.*, 226 Cal.App.3d 1288 (1991) (cab lessees were misclassified as independent contractors, and are legally employees of cab companies, for purposes of California workers' compensation law).

[6] *Alexander v. FedEx Ground Package Sys., Inc.*, 765 F.3d 981 (9th Cir. 2014) (finding FedEx had misclassified drivers for many years).

[7] *E.g.*, National Employment Law Project, Written Statement on the Subject of Employment and Labor Protections for Day Laborers (Sept. 26, 2002); National Domestic Workers Alliance, *Key Findings, Home Economics: The Invisible and Unregulated World of Domestic Work* (2016), www.2016.domesticworkers.org/homeeconomics/key-findings (finding that 23 percent of domestic workers are paid below the state minimum wage).

Instacart,[8] Postmates,[9] and Amazon[10] are hardly the first companies to be accused of misclassifying delivery workers: grocery stores in the past have at times used subcontracted deliverymen and paid them below the minimum wage.[11]

There is nevertheless something new afoot here. Platform economy firms tend to consolidate sectors and to subject workers to data-based supervision. The effects of these developments on workers' welfare are mixed. In some instances, market consolidation can put downward pressure on wages as firms gain monopsony power. Many workers stand to lose autonomy in this transition as well. Taxi drivers who own their own medallions or companies may blanch at being under the supervision and direction of Uber or Lyft. At the same time, workers who have been working in the gray or black market may benefit from moving to a large, technologically sophisticated firm, since data gathered to supervise workers' performance can often be used to ensure compliance with wage/hour, tax, anti-discrimination, and workplace safety laws.

To better illuminate how platform firms are impacting low-wage labor markets, this chapter disaggregates two aspects of industrial organization in such markets. It maps prominent low-wage firms onto a grid which seeks to capture (a) the statutory legal entitlements enjoyed by those firms' workers, including employment status, unionization rates in their sector, and coverage by other pertinent regulations; and (b) those firms' technological and regulatory sophistication, as suggested by their market size and geographic scope. For ease of exposition, I call these axes "worker protections" and "firm size." Doing so allows us to map trajectories of change within particular sectors, and suggests possible reform strategies.

Section I, below, outlines the distinctive business model of platform economy firms, in which workers are treated as independent contractors yet subjected to close data-based supervision, and considers how both technological and institutional factors have encouraged the emergence of that model. Section II then develops the two-axis representation of low-wage firms. Section III draws out some insights, including those mentioned above.

I PLATFORM ECONOMY LABOR "INNOVATIONS"

US labor and employment laws – like similar laws in other wealthy nations – were designed in an era of industrial production, in which leading firms directly employed hundreds of thousands of workers, and in which workers tended to stay with their employer for much of their career. Those laws typically impose duties only upon direct employers, and define employment as a relationship of control.[12] When a company has the right to control how the worker carries out

---

[8] Bonnie Eslinger, *Instacart Can't Yet Ring Up $4.6M Misclassification Deal*, Law360.com (Apr. 19, 2017) (detailing settlement talks in Instacart misclassification suit).

[9] Dorothy Atkins, *Postmates' $9M Misclassification Deal Gets OK'd*, Law360.com (Sept. 1, 2017).

[10] Vin Gurrieri, *Drivers Sue Amazon, Contractors in Joint Employment Claims*, Law360.com (Nov. 3, 2016) (detailing allegations in Illinois suit that delivery drivers for Amazon's Prime Now service are misclassified as independent contractors).

[11] *See* N.Y. Atty. Gen., *Gristedes to Pay $3.2 Million in Back Wages and Fees in Deliverymen Case* (Dec. 17, 2003), https://ag.ny.gov/press-release/gristedes-pay-325-million-back-wages-and-fees-deliverymen-case.

[12] *See Nationwide Mut. Ins. Co. v. Darden*, 503 U.S. 318, 323 (1992) (common law "control test" applies to ERISA); *NLRB v. United Insurance*, 390 U.S. 254, 256 (1968) (affirming that the test for employment under the NLRA is the control test). The control test need not be applied mechanically. *See FedEx Home Delivery*, 361 N.L.R.B. No. 55 (Sep. 30, 2014) (clarifying that under NLRA, the Board should evaluate "whether the evidence tends to show that the putative independent contractor is, in fact, rendering services as part of an independent business"). *See also* Elizabeth Tippett, this volume (discussing tests for employment and independent contracting under various worker protective laws).

their work, an employment relationship exists and the company owes the worker the full pan-oply of employment duties. In contrast, a classic independent contracting relationship arises when the principal hires an independent businessperson with such specialized skills that the principal has neither the ability nor the desire to supervise.[13] As one judge put it, the "paradigm of an independent contractor" is one who sells "only expertise."[14]

Obviously, a great many work relationships fall into a gray zone, between extreme task defin-ition and very close supervision (employment) on the one hand, and the exercise of specialized skills and talents through an independent firm on the other (contracting). That has led to sub-stantial regulatory arbitrage for decades now, as leading firms have sought to avoid employment duties through various legal and organizational strategies.

The first strategy is misclassification: treating workers as independent contractors when they should be legally classified as employees. As noted above, this is quite common in the platform economy, among other delivery firms (such as FedEx), and elsewhere in the logistics sector. The second is subcontracting, in which user firms hire labor through agencies or third-party contractors. The workers have a legal employer – the contractor – but user firms may exert substantial power over their working conditions. Subcontracting is especially common in building services, agricul-ture, and hotels.[15] The third is franchising, in which large firms, especially in fast food and retail, license their trade dress and product line to independent businesses, who in turn employ line-level workers.[16] Franchisors may nevertheless retain substantial power over working conditions.[17]

All such strategies leave workers either with few rights under labor and employment laws, or with rights only against firms that in reality enjoy little to no power over their working conditions. The net result tends to be lower wages, less job security, and noncompliance with workplace safety mandates.[18] In this regard, platform economy firms' misclassification of workers is not fun-damentally new. Rather, it is the latest iteration of such long-running trends.

Platform economy firms are nevertheless different from their low-wage labor market forebears in two respects. The first relates to size and geographic scope. Cab companies, maid agencies, and temp/freelancer agencies have long acted as labor market intermediaries, referring workers to consumers for short-term discrete tasks. But such companies typically worked at the local level, not the national or even global scale achieved or contemplated by Uber, Lyft, and, per-haps soon, Upwork, TaskRabbit, or Care.com.

Such companies' rapid growth has been enabled, in large part, by advanced information tech-nology.[19] Lower communications costs, the globalization of media, mobile computing, and big

---

[13] See *Sec'y of Labor* v. *Lauritzen*, 835 F.2d 1529, 1540 (7th. Cir. 1987) (Easterbrook, J., concurring); *see also* Restatement (Second) of Agency § 220 (Am. Law Inst. 1958) (listing factors that should be used to determine whether a relationship constitutes employment).

[14] *Lauritzen*, 835 F.2d at 1545 n. 3 (Easterbrook, J., concurring).

[15] Hard data on the incidence of subcontracting is difficult to come by. But as one data point, California has identi-fied the construction, janitorial and security services, garment, and farm labor as industries with a high incidence of subcontracting, and imposed enhanced duties on firms in those sectors as a result. California Labor Code § 2810. *See generally*, Weil, *supra* note 4 at 99–121 (discussing subcontracting and its effects).

[16] *See generally* Weil, *supra* note 4 at 122–58 (discussing franchising and its effects).

[17] *Id.* at 158 (noting that franchisors still "creat[e], monitor[] and enforce[e] standards central to business strategy while ... ducking responsibility" for labor).

[18] *See generally id.*

[19] Antitrust policy may also be part of the story, as we've seen significantly greater market concentration in many sectors over the past few decades. *See, e.g.*, Lina Khan and Sandeep Vaheesan, *Market Power and Inequality: The Antitrust Counterrevolution and its Discontents*, 11 Harv. Law & Pol'y. Rev. 234 (2017) (case studies of increased market con-centration in agriculture/grocery; telecom; pharma; airlines). My sense is that technological factors predominate in explaining the growth of platform economy firms at this point, however, since so many of them are such new entrants.

data analytics make it remarkably easy for tech companies to expand to a national or even global level while still maintaining brand identity. It helps that many such firms have little real property. Uber, for example, was able to "scale" extremely rapidly, in Silicon Valley's terminology, in part because it owns no cars, no repair stations, and no massive warehouses. Like most Silicon Valley firms, its main property rights are in IP.[20]

Such firms are also different from their historic forebears in another regard: they can use advanced information technology to greatly enhance their supervisory capacities. Historically, firms that outsourced labor often did so under the table, using a middleman to achieve a particular result but not closely supervising.[21] The "sweating system" in US garment production, for example, involved jobbers hiring contractors to do production, who would in turn hire subcontractors or even let out work to individual sewers in their houses. Product specifications, piece-rates, and ex post inspections ensured labor discipline. That is still the system in the Bangladeshi ready-made garment sector, where illegal subcontracting is rampant and many firms legitimately do not know in which particular shop their clothes were made.[22] Similarly, until very recently cab companies had little real-time knowledge of what particular workers were doing.

No longer. Uber and Lyft have extensive data about workers' real-time and historical performance, and other platform economy firms could surely develop such data sources in the future given recent developments in mobile computing and similar technology.[23] Uber requires drivers to accept a certain number of fares or risk deactivation, monitors their driving speed and safety via accelerometers and other devices built into iPhones, and of course requires them to maintain a particular passenger rating.[24] Uber therefore has a clear sense of which drivers are among its best and worst, and is able to manage an enormous and constantly changing workforce with almost no direct human supervision. Other labor intermediation platforms such as Lyft, TaskRabbit, and Care.com also utilize customer ratings to ensure high-quality service, again mitigating any information asymmetries between them and workers. And Freelancer. com has implemented software that monitors users' keystrokes and even takes screenshots when they're signed in to projects in an effort to ensure that they are only billing for hours worked.[25]

---

[20] Uber's own story about its quick rise rests on the inefficiencies of the taxi sector, and the company's ability to generate and tap into network effects among drivers and passengers. The company's critics point instead to regulatory arbitrage and consumer subsidies as key. Which set of factors predominate is, in my view, far from clear. But Lyft's recent gain in the market certainly suggests that whatever network effects were supporting Uber's rise are not nearly as powerful a barrier to entry as the company might have hoped. For a summary of the company's challenging economics, *see* Alison Griswold and Akshat Rathi, *Is the Era of Cheap Uber Rides Over?* Quartz Media (Mar. 24, 2017), https://qz.com/940605/is-the-era-of-cheap-uber-rides-over/ (noting that the company "has two options for improving its margins: raising fares for riders, or increasing its take from drivers," and arguing that the latter is not possible given competition for drivers from Lyft and regulatory scrutiny relating to its labor practices).

[21] To be clear, the lack of such supervision should not and often does not immunize hiring firms from legal responsibilities toward such workers. As Alan Hyde once wryly observed, "I do not think building owners normally hire cleaning contractors and tell them to maintain the building as they see fit, in their professional discretion." Alan Hyde, *Legal Responsibility for Labour Conditions Down the Supply Chain*, in *Challenging the Legal Boundaries of Work Regulation* 83, 97 (Judy Fudge, Shae McCrystal, and Kamala Sankaran, eds., 2012).

[22] *See* Mark Anner et al., *Toward Joint-Liability in Global Supply Chains: Addressing the Root Causes of Labor Violations in International Subcontracting Networks*, 35 Comp. Lab. L. Pol'y J 1 (2013).

[23] Such practices are becoming common in the "real" economy as well. UPS, FedEx, and trucking companies, for example, use "telematics" devices to monitor drivers' delivery times, driving speed, and seatbelt usage. Jacob Goldstein, *To Increase Productivity, UPS Monitors Drivers' Every Move*, NPR (Apr. 17, 2014).

[24] *See* Elizabeth Tippett, this volume (discussing technological oversight of workers by platform firms).

[25] Liang et al., *Effects of IT-Enabled Monitoring on Labor Contracting in Online Platforms: Evidence from a Natural Experiment*, NET Institute Working Paper No. 16-01 (2016), https://papers.ssrn.com/sol3/papers.cfm?abstract_id=2844920.

Indeed, in many instances advanced information technologies may positively encourage fissuring. The reasons why are captured by "efficiency wage" theories, which arose to explain a puzzling phenomenon: why do labor markets rarely "clear" such that wages drop until unemployment approaches zero? Carl Shapiro and Joseph Stiglitz answered that firms may pay above the market wage when they find it difficult to monitor workers' performance.[26] Workers have heterogeneous skills and motivations, after all, and labor contracts are always incomplete, since workers enjoy some discretion over the manner in which tasks will be performed. An above-market wage may therefore induce loyalty and prevent shirking, particularly when coupled with the threat of unemployment.[27]

Notably, the Shapiro–Stiglitz efficiency wage model overlaps substantially with the standard Coase–Williamson theory that the firm is a means of reducing the transaction costs associated with market contracting.[28] Those include the search costs of identifying counterparties, bargaining costs of developing a suitable agreement, and monitoring costs of ensuring the other party performs. This overlap is not accidental: the Coase–Williamson theory defines firms as entities that exercise control over agents, while employment, under the law of agency, is a relationship in which a principal enjoys a right to control an agent's work.[29]

If we classify informational asymmetries among the sources of transaction costs, then firms will tend to make greater use of employment rather than market contracting when such asymmetries are high. Conversely, when information technology enables near-costless monitoring, firms will have fewer economic incentives to treat workers as employees, all else being equal.

To be clear, this is an argument about the *economics* of employment classification – not about the *law* of employment classification. Since employment laws typically seek to protect workers against harms of market ordering, it may often be *efficient* but *unlawful* for platform firms to classify workers as independent contractors. This tension between legal mandates and economic incentives has sparked extensive litigation by platform economy workers alleging that they have been misclassified as independent contractors. Numerous courts outside the United States have now sided with workers, holding that they are in fact employees.[30] Within the United States, the cases have tended to settle, but only after judicial findings that there were strong arguments in favor of employment status. In the case of Uber and Lyft, those include the platforms' right to terminate drivers at will, their requirement that drivers accept a minimum number of fares, and their very close technologically enabled supervision of drivers' performance.[31] So ambiguous definitions of employment, together with litigation costs and declining public enforcement resources, have also enabled platform economy firms' rise by encouraging worker misclassification.

---

[26] Carl Shapiro and Joseph Stiglitz, *Equilibrium Unemployment as a Worker Discipline Device*, 74 Am. Econ. Rev. 433 (1984). An alternative theory of efficiency wages holds that above-market wages reflect norms of fairness and reciprocity within the work relationship. Robert Solow, *The Labor Market as a Social Institution* (1990); George A. Akerlof, *Labor Contracts as Partial Gift Exchange*, 97 Q. J. Econ. 543 (1982).

[27] *See also* Joseph Stiglitz, *Alternative Theories of Wage Determination and Unemployment in L.D.C.'s: The Labor Turnover Model*, 88 Q. J. Econ. 194 (1974).

[28] Ronald Coase, *The Nature of the Firm*, 4 Economica 386 (1937); Oliver Williamson, *The Economics of Organization: The Transaction Cost Approach*, 87 Am. J. Sociology, 548 (1981).

[29] Restatement (Second) of Agency § 220 (1958).

[30] E.g., Ed Taylor, *Uber Drivers are Employees, Brazil Court Rules*, BNA Bloomberg (Apr. 19, 2017) (summarizing recent Brazilian Court holding that drivers are employees); Hilary Osborne, *Uber Loses Right To Classify UK Drivers as Self-Employed*, The Guardian (Oct. 28, 2016) (same, regarding a UK tribunal).

[31] *See generally O'Connor v. Uber Techs., Inc.*, 82 F. Supp. 3d 1133, 1135–36 (N.D. Cal. 2015); *Cotter v. Lyft, Inc.*, 60 F. Supp. 3d 1067 (N.D. Cal. 2015) (separate opinions finding that the question of employment status must go to a jury, and detailing facts of driver–platform relationship, many of which point in the direction of finding employment relationship). The US and UK cases are still on appeal as of late October 2017.

II TWO DIMENSIONS OF WORK ORGANIZATION AND INDUSTRIAL ORGANIZATION

Assuming platform economy firms continue to grow and thrive, what will be the net effects on worker welfare? This is ultimately a question of regulatory design. Under current laws, platform economy workers will continue to be denied decent wages and other employment-related rights. But with different regulations platform economy workers could fare better than low-wage workers have in the recent past. To explain why, it will be helpful to elaborate further on the relationship between fissuring and market consolidation in the low-wage economy today.

Figure 22.1 does so by charting two different dimensions of industrial organization. It is intended to give a rough approximation of these issues, and to inform future research.

A *Explaining the Grid*

The "worker protections" or X-axis indicates the extent to which workers for a particular firm enjoy the full panoply of legal entitlements of employment. Workers are classified as having low, medium, or high levels of protection: LWP, MWP, HWP. On the far left side are independent contractors without any formal employment rights, whether lawfully classified as contractors or not. As we move to the right, workers gain more formal legal entitlements, until the midpoint is occupied by workers who are clearly employed by whatever firm controls their work, but who are typically not unionized. Unionization and other means of worker self-representation increase

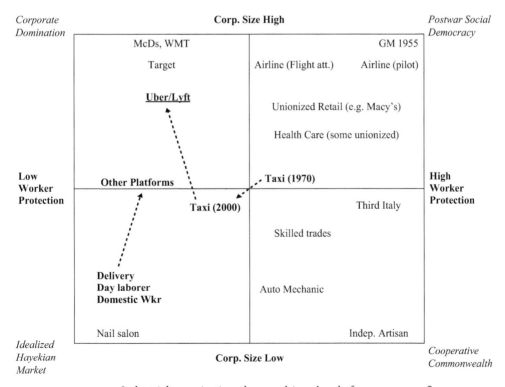

FIGURE 22.1 Industrial organization changes driven by platform economy firms

as we move right, until the far right side (HWP) is occupied by unionized workers in heavily unionized sectors, and workers such as artisans who can protect themselves through a combination of high skills and guild-type organizations.

The "corporate size" or Y-axis indicates the extent to which the firms that benefit directly from workers' labor are large, in terms of market capitalization and geographic scope. Firms can be classified on this graph as having low, moderate, or high corporate size – abbreviated below as LCS, MCS, HCS. The LCS point would be a very small independent shop or restaurant. The MCS point would be a mid-sized regional firm. HCS would be the largest firms in the country. Firm size is important here for two reasons. First, large firms tend to have significantly more capital than small ones, making it easier to satisfy a judgment against them. Second, large firms tend to be better able to utilize technological means of worker supervision.

This gives us four quadrants, each of which is represented in the contemporary American economy.[32] Quadrant 1, the top right, involves the highest level of worker protections within very large firms, epitomized by heavy industrial production carried out by unionized workers. The Big 3 automakers, the steel companies, GE, Boeing, and other such companies are here, and have been for decades. Unionized health care workers for large companies also fall here, though a bit further to the left owing to lower union density in that sector.[33]

Quadrant 2 (bottom right) is characterized by high worker protection but small firm size. Today, this corresponds to unionized craft production, particularly in smaller cities and for smaller companies. Also falling here is the "Third Italy" of small industrial districts producing high-end goods, often using artisanal methods. Workers in this system have a great deal of autonomy and high wages and benefits, because they either control the labor supply and systems of skills transfer, or because they control firms themselves. The far right-bottom corner would be occupied by individual craft producers or cottage industries.[34]

Quadrant 3 (bottom left) is characterized by low worker protection and low firm size. A substantial portion of the low-wage workforce can be found here today, being neither employed by nor proximate to a major firm. In addition to the workers listed (domestic workers, day laborers, some taxi drivers, nail salon workers), this sector would include most workers at small non-chain restaurants and stores, agricultural workers on small farms, seasonal recreational workers, and many other personal services workers such as hairdressers. It also includes many elder care and childcare workers, though those workers can also be found in Quadrant 4 (top left).[35]

Quadrant 4, finally, is characterized by low worker protection and high firm size. Walmart, Uber, and McDonalds are all in this quadrant, even though they have different legal relationships with their workers – Walmart employs store workers directly, Uber treats drivers as contractors, and McDonalds treats most fast food workers as employees of franchisees. But workers for all three firms lack full employment protections – Uber drivers and many

---

[32] Each also corresponds to an ideal-typical mode of social organization, as indicated outside the chart at the outer corner of each quadrant.

[33] This quadrant corresponds to the labor relations and economic system of postwar social democracy, in which the state intentionally empowered workers and encouraged collective bargaining – but also tolerated substantial corporate power and market concentration.

[34] This quadrant corresponds to the vision of the cooperative commonwealth envisioned by early twentieth-century labor leaders, and by some tech thinkers today who advocate worker-owned cooperatives.

[35] This quadrant corresponds to an idealized Hayekian market, in which no individual party has significant power over another.

McDonalds workers are not formally employed by those companies, and Walmart workers are not unionized.[36]

B Trends in Institutional Change

One advantage of charting industrial organization in this way is that it enables us to see multiple dimensions of change over time. The arrows on Figure 22.1 track changes spurred by the growth of Uber, TaskRabbit, Care.com, Deliveroo, Upwork, and similar online labor platforms.

For example, taxi drivers before Uber generally lacked employment rights in most US cities, since they were classified as independent contractors,[37] but they did benefit from the heavy regulations of fares and restrictions on entry in most cities. Due to the highly fragmented capital ownership structures in the sector, meanwhile, they were only moderately proximate to capital. The growth of Uber has diminished their formal protections by taking them outside local cab commissions' regulatory structures. But recent cases have also pushed the companies to grant workers more due process and other rights on the job. And Uber's displacement of taxi companies has left drivers proximate to a very large firm. Worker protection here diminishes a bit (MWP to LWP) but firm size increases (LCS to HCS).

The stories for TaskRabbit, Instacart, and Care.com, are somewhat different.[38] On the chart I have plotted them as moderately sized firms, and labeled them as "other platforms."[39]

Day laborers have long found work through word-of-mouth referrals and operated in a cash economy. Sometimes day laborers performed work for larger firms, so there is a range of positions for their work on the Y-axis; take the indicated location as a median position. Domestic workers (nannies and maids), similarly, found work through word-of-mouth, and often worked for cash. Nannies have virtually no collective power in the workplace, however, since they work in individual homes, and they are excluded from some basic federal protections such as collective bargaining rights. Maids and housecleaners had similar work dynamics, though with more clients and fewer hours per client. And as noted above, grocery delivery drivers have often worked for small subcontractors, and been paid poorly.

The rise of TaskRabbit, Care.com, and Instacart changes those dynamics. The mere fact that such workers are paid through the platform rather than in cash may be a significant improvement. And as such companies settle cases alleging misclassification, it seems likely that their

---

[36] This quadrant corresponds to a dystopian corporate/elite domination of the political economy, perhaps best captured by the saying that an economy should "pay the rich more so they'll work harder, and pay the poor less for the same reason."

[37] The pre-history here is interesting as well, and reflected on the chart. Until the late 1970s taxi drivers were unionized in many cities. *See Yellow Cab Cooperative, Inc. v. Workers' Comp. Appeals Bd.* 226 Cal.App.3d 1288 (1991) (discussing changes in industrial organization in the sector in the late 1970s).

[38] Regarding Care.com and other carework platforms, *see* Julia Ticona and Alexandra Mateescu, *Trusted Strangers: Carework Platforms' Cultural Entrepreneurship in the On-demand Economy* (draft, on file with author) (discussing carework platforms' partial formalization and commodification of the market for care).

[39] Freelancers are not represented on the chart since they tend to be much higher-skilled than Uber/Lyft drivers or workers on other platforms. My sense is that the transition to large platforms has affected freelancers quite differently depending on their human capital. More skilled workers could always command more generous wages, faster payment, and the like. Upwork and Freelancer have since consolidated the market and subjected freelancers to fairly standard contract terms, but also guaranteed payment in many instances. *See* Liang et al., *supra* note 25. So corporate size has gone up for many if not most freelancers (LCS-MCS/HCS), while their degree of protection may have stayed the same, diminished, or even increased depending on their earlier market position.

workers will receive greater employment-related benefits. For such workers, worker protection stays the same or increases marginally (LWP to MWP) but corporate size increases dramatically (LCS to HCS).

III IMPLICATIONS

Mapping work and industrial organization in this way helps illuminate a few aspects of the employment transitions being driven by platform economy firms. First, as should be clear, there is no single institutional or political-economic path to platform work, as noted above.

Second, those different paths are all embedded in, and even functions of, different ex ante institutional and legal arrangements. For example, domestic workers do not lose that much in part because they had so few protections to begin with. They have no rights to unionize under the National Labor Relations Act[40] and do not enjoy full protections under the Fair Labor Standards Act.[41] Indeed, their work is often not even recognized as work. This is an effect, in part, of our racialized and gendered political economy: domestics and agricultural workers have been disproportionately women and people of color since before the New Deal, and were excluded from the New Deal labor laws.[42] Taxi drivers did not lose many employment law protections, which they often lacked in the first place, but they did lose protections under fare regulations, safety codes, and restrictions on entry that protected them from pure market forces in the past.

Third, a key division in the private sector workforce is between those workers who are proximate to a large corporation and those who are not. This difference does not map neatly onto the more common divisions between employees and independent contractors, between formal and informal workers, or between high-skill and low-skill workers. But even if we were to extend formal employment rights to all workers, their lives would not magically improve, as over a million Walmart "associates" can attest. The number of workers who are proximate to a large firm also seems likely to be growing as an overall proportion of the workforce, or at least in the low-wage service sector, due to the growth of platforms. That may have very important implications for worker welfare, as explored below.

A *Worker Welfare and Firm Size*

Working for a large firm, whether as an employee or an independent contractor, can carry significant benefits for workers for at least three reasons.

First, large consumer-facing firms are vulnerable to moral pressure from workers and consumers in ways that smaller firms often are not. It is significantly easier to organize an online and offline campaign against a large-name brand company than it is against a small or medium-sized

---

[40] 29 U.S.C. § 152(3) (2012) (domestic workers not "employees" under NLRA).

[41] 29 U.S.C. § 213(b)(21) (2012) (many domestic workers not entitled to overtime).

[42] Indeed, there is a deeper lesson about skills, industrial structures, and workers' protections lurking here: namely that skills and industrial sector do not, on their own, determine the quadrant in which particular jobs fall. Retail workers can be found in Qs 1, 3, and 4, and perhaps even 2 if we were to include worker-owned food co-ops. Skilled craft workers can be found in Qs 1 and 2, and perhaps 3 if we count plumbers, carpenters, and similar workers hired through TaskRabbit. What about nannies? It would be strange indeed to call a successful nanny a "low-skill" worker, given the high levels of emotional intelligence, safety training, and organizational skills required for the job. In that regard, they are more like flight attendants than Uber drivers. Why do they have so little power? Not because of skills *per se*, but because of how skills intersect with the gendered and racialized political economy of labor markets. It is no accident that white men predominate in industrial and craft jobs, historically the best paid among the working class. It is also no accident that women and people of color are disproportionately represented in Qs 3–4.

taxi company, a local deli, or a local grocery chain. Public attention can be focused on those firms nationwide, often quite quickly, which can lead them to alter labor practices. In recent memory, various fast food and retail chains including Wal-Mart, Burger King, and McDonalds have agreed to pay more for produce in the wake of consumer pressure around agricultural workers' rights.[43] Similarly, while hard data is difficult to find, a great deal of anecdotal data suggests Uber's wave of bad press in 2017 has driven many consumers off the platform.[44] Some of that bad press was related to driver treatment.

Second, large firms tend to be natural targets of public regulation. Large platform firms, for example, are potentially a critical partner for tax authorities. At times they have taken on this burden in order to score public goodwill, as when Airbnb began collecting taxes directly from hosts in some cities.[45] But in other situations it may actually be a significant selling point for both workers and consumers. Improper tax treatment of domestic workers has derailed several would-be political appointees, and the effort to comply with the law has frustrated many individual families. Care.com and some other platforms may be able to deter workers and consumers from going off-platform by handling those and related issues, including unemployment insurance and workers' compensation.[46] Indeed, I suspect that this may be Care.com's main value-added; since customers tend to want the same care-giver every day or week, the market for domestic work will never be a pure spot market. But if the company can relieve the administrative burden on families and caregivers, that may solidify its market position. Similarly, if and when Uber is forced to begin treating its workers as employees, it will be able to handle tax issues at extremely low cost, and cooperate with tax authorities to ensure enforcement.

Some large platform firms would also be natural collective bargaining partners. A bargaining unit of Uber drivers could substantially raise standards in the sector, and such drivers make up a natural "community of interest," as required under US labor law, since they perform virtually identical work.[47] Indeed, where unions would need to establish a multi-employer bargaining unit to bargain with taxi companies in many cities, that is not the case for Uber, since the company itself has direct relationships with its drivers. TaskRabbit is a less clear-cut case given the diversity of jobs performed on platform, but Deliveroo and Care.com show quite similar dynamics to Uber. If delivery work and care work consolidated around those platforms, a form of collective bargaining in the sector starts to seem far more plausible.

Third, large firms often have substantial internal regulatory capacity that they use both to ensure high-quality goods or services, and to ensure legal compliance.[48] For example, large firms have especially powerful incentives to develop and promulgate sexual harassment policies, educate employees about what those policies require, and investigate complaints of sexual harassment. These duties are not limited to large firms, but smaller firms may be able to satisfy their

---

[43] Specifically, they joined the Fair Food Program, a nonprofit set up by the Coalition of Immokalee Workers to ensure brand responsibility toward tomato pickers and other workers. See www.fairfoodprogram.org/.

[44] Verge estimates that 200,000 users deleted their accounts as part of #deleteuber. *See* Nick Statt, *#DeleteUber Reportedly Led 200,000 People To Delete Their Accounts*, Verge (Feb. 2, 2017), www.theverge.com/2017/2/2/14493760/delete-uber-protest-donald-trump-accounts-deleted.

[45] *See* Airbnb fact sheet on occupancy tax, www.airbnb.com/help/article/654/what-is-occupancy-tax--do-i-need-to-collect-or-pay-it (noting that Airbnb automatically collects occupancy taxes in Portland, San Francisco, and Amsterdam).

[46] *See* Ticona and Mateescu, *supra* note 38 (discussing some ways in which carework platforms formalize carework by encouraging consumers to require documentation of work eligibility and to provide Social Security and other benefits, while encouraging providers to report all their income).

[47] *NLRB v. Catherine McAuley Health Ctr.*, 885 F.2d 341 (6th Cir. 1989).

[48] *See generally* Susan Sturm, *Second-Generation Employment Discrimination: A Structural Approach*, 101 Colum. L. Rev. 458 (2001); Cynthia Estlund, *Regoverning the Workplace: From Self-Regulation to Co-Regulation* (2010).

legal duty to deter harassment through less formal means.[49] In part as a result, large firms today tend to have large, sophisticated HR departments, and increasingly use data analytics and other forms of workplace monitoring to detect and prevent harassment.[50]

Large firms are also often better positioned than small ones to prevent discrimination. Compare here a local restaurant sector with many small players to a sector in which a couple of large chains are the predominant employers. In the former case, rooting out discriminatory hiring patterns – e.g., women as hosts and servers, men as bartenders, whites in front, Latinos in back – would require changing many firms' behavior and rooting out folkways and social practices that lead to such segregation. In the latter case, the large chains can take on much of that burden, tracking applicant flow data, establishing effective affirmative action programs, and setting a tone within the organization around such issues. In part this is a numbers issue: systemic disparate treatment or disparate impact liability can best be spotted with large datasets that can realistically be compiled only by regulators or large firms.[51]

To take another example, wage and hour compliance is required of virtually all companies, but large ones can often keep records of it automatically, while such records are often on paper or nonexistent in the jobs in Quadrants 2 and 3. Taxi drivers prior to Uber, day laborers, and nannies have often been paid in cash, off the books, often without even any record of their work. Working for a platform therefore puts a worker in view of that platform's automated timekeeping and payment software. Similarly, freelancer platforms also automatically measure workers' hours and take screen-grabs of their work as they perform it, allowing remote clients to monitor their progress. While that raises privacy issues, some platforms have instituted the practice as part of a precommitment mechanism: workers who agree to such monitoring are also guaranteed fast payment, from the platform if not the client.[52]

B *How to Impose and Enforce Employment Duties*

Of course, whether platform economy companies employ their workers or not is being fought out in courts and administrative agencies around the world. If they do not, then the duties outlined above largely do not apply. But their very use of data for human resources functions is itself a powerful argument that they should bear such duties.

For example, the degree of knowledge that Uber has regarding its drivers – and here again, it is exemplary but far from unique – is vastly greater than possessed by a garment jobber regarding its contractors.[53] Rather than getting outputs and assessing their quality, Uber knows drivers' locations, individualized work hours, work histories, current status on or off the app, and even whether they are driving safely. The same is largely true of Lyft; TaskRabbit, Deliveroo and Instacart do not seem far behind.

But precisely because firms such as Uber have such extensive knowledge about work practices, their data-driven fissuring may be easier to remedy than classic horizontal and vertical disaggregation such as the garment sector's sweating system. If Uber knows how long drivers have been

---

[49] *See, e.g., Faragher* v. *City of Boca Raton*, 118 S. Ct. 2275, 2293 (1998) (suggesting that a small employer may not need a written sexual harassment policy to avoid vicarious liability for a supervisor's hostile work environment harassment, but that a large employer almost surely would).

[50] Whether such processes actually prevent harassment is another question. *See* Noam Scheiber and Julie Creswell, *Sexual Harassment Cases Show the Ineffectiveness of Going to H.R.*, N.Y. Times, Dec 12, 2017.

[51] *Teamsters* v. *United States* 431 U.S. 324 (1977); *Hazelwood School District* v. *United States*, 433 U.S. 299 (1977).

[52] Liang et al., *supra* note 25.

[53] On a related note, the regulatory bargain Uber has struck with regulators in many states requires the company to develop knowledge about individual drivers' performance. Under that bargain, the company agrees to perform

signed into the app and taking fares, it can surely ensure they work only reasonable hours. It does not ensure reasonable hours today, of course, but that is a question of its duties under current law, not technological feasibility. One promising option here would be to revise legal definitions of employment to make clear that any firm that utilizes data to screen or monitor workers will presumptively be treated as their employer under wage/hour, collective bargaining, and discrimination laws.[54] As noted above, existing doctrine is likely broad enough to cover such work, so this reform would clarify the law rather than fundamentally changing it.

Care.com presents a different case. As noted above, their value-added may be in performing some of the classic functions of an employer, such as withholding taxes and perhaps providing collective health insurance and savings accounts. Such an entity seems entirely absent from the carework landscape today, where workers often are formally employed by individual families, with tax evasion and wage theft rampant. If Care.com could integrate its systems with workers' mobile phones or figure out other means to track hours worked, it could substantially formalize work within the sector, likely to the good.

Regulators could be even more ambitious. For example, companies could be required to disclose basic data on each worker's employment dates, wages, hours, and other activities, by social security number, directly into an Internal Revenue Service or Department of Labor database. Regulators and perhaps worker organizations could then have access to that data, and could utilize it to spot noncompliance. Or, again by compelling data disclosure from firms, regulators could develop AI-based programs to give workers a read on whether or not they have suffered wage theft, a workplace health and safety violation, or discrimination. Even the simplest example, of wage theft, gets complicated quickly, of course – any AI or regulator would need to determine when the worker was actually working versus doing personal tasks, what their hourly rate was, and whether other indicia of wage theft seem apparent. Regarding discrimination, an AI program would need either some applicant flow data for the firms at issue or data on the broader labor market and that firm's hires. Those may be difficult obstacles to overcome, but these are the sorts of publicly-minded uses of AI that we should be seeking.

CONCLUSION

Worker advocates and policymakers are concerned about the informality and low quality of work in the platform economy, and for good reason. The evidence is building that Uber and other platforms are violating employment laws and tax laws, and creating undesirable jobs. That is in part an effect of their use of fissured work, and in part the effect of their sheer size. At the same time, the move to platforms may be creating some institutional preconditions for better work, by centralizing regulatory capacity within large, sophisticated firms. Particularly if regulators encourage collective worker power through reforms to collective bargaining laws, the move to platforms could prove ultimately beneficial for low-wage workers.

---

background checks and require a certain level of insurance coverage from drivers. *See* Luz Laso, *New Regulations for Uber and Lyft Open the Door for Expansion*, Wash. Post, Feb. 21, 2015.

[54] *See, e.g.,* Brishen Rogers, Redefining Employment for the Modern Economy, American Constitution Society Issue Brief (Oct. 2016) (proposing reforms to definition of employment to address such matters).

23

A Critical Examination of a Third Employment Category for On-Demand Work

(In Comparative Perspective)

*Miriam A. Cherry and Antonio Aloisi**

INTRODUCTION

During the past five years there have been a number of lawsuits in the United States as well as in Europe challenging the employment classification of workers in the gig economy.[1] Classification of a worker as an employee is an important "gateway" to determine who receives the protections of the labor and employment laws, including the right to organize, minimum wage, and unemployment compensation, as well as other obligations such as tax treatment. In response to both litigation and widespread confusion about how gig workers should be classified, some commentators have proposed a "third" or "hybrid" category, situated between the categories of "employee" and "independent contractor." Proponents often note that creating a third category would be a novel innovation, appropriately crafted and tailored for an era of digital platform work.[2]

However, as we have noted in a previous article, such an intermediate category of worker is actually not new.[3] In this chapter we will provide snapshot summaries of five legal systems that have experimented with implementing a legal tool similar to a third category to cover non-standard workers: in Canada, Italy, Spain, Germany, and South Korea. These various legal systems have had diverse results. There has been success in some instances, and misadventure in others. We believe that examining these experiences closely will help to avoid potential problems that are beginning to surface in discussions about the third category and the gig economy.

This chapter largely will forgo the background on how platforms operate or the description of the tasks workers do, instead focusing on the classification problem.[4] After examining the

* Our appreciation to Valerio De Stefano, KU Leuven University, and Janine Berg of the International Labour Office, who have been extremely helpful with this book chapter. Many thanks to Dr. Deok Soon Hwang and Haeung Jeong of the Korea Labor Institute, Dr. Ida Dahea Lee of Seoul National University School of Law, Dr. Adrián Todolí Signes of University of Valencia and Manfred Weiss, Professor Emeritus at J.W. Goethe University, Frankfurt. Thanks for research assistance to reference librarian David Kullman and SLU Law faculty fellow Louie Spinner.

1 For a listing of the ongoing litigation surrounding the on-demand economy, *see* Miriam A. Cherry, *Beyond Misclassification: The Digital Transformation of Work*, 37 Comp. Lab. L. & Pol'y J. 577, 584–85 (2016).
2 *See, e.g.*, Vin Guerrieri, *Uber Cases Could Spur New Employee Classification*, Law360 Blog, May 6, 2016.
3 We note at the outset that this chapter owes a debt to our previous article, which explored classification issues in Canada, Italy, and Spain in greater length than we are able to in this chapter. For more on the approaches in these countries, see Miriam A. Cherry and Antonio Aloisi, *"Dependent Contractors" in the Gig Economy?: A Comparative Approach*, 66 Am. U. L. Rev. 635 (2017).
4 This topic is widely covered in the first part of this Handbook. *See also* Antonio Aloisi, *Commoditized Workers: Case Study Research on Labor Law Issues Arising from a Set of On-Demand/Gig Economy Platforms*, 37 Comp. Lab. L. & Pol'y J. 577, 653–90 (2016).

status of gig work in the United States and the calls for a third category, we turn to look at summaries of the five legal systems and their experiences with the third category. After examining how, in Italy, some employees actually lost rights because their status was downgraded into an intermediate "parasubordinate" category, we must be careful to consider the unintended consequences of creating a third category. Informed by these national case studies, we provide a review of what we might expect if a third category were to be created in the United States, and note some of the practical difficulties.

Based on the proposals for a third category as well as the country studies, we ultimately set forward a different proposal for reform. Rather than creating another category and risking further mischief around the subject of worker misclassification, we advocate that the default rule for platform work should be employee status or something resembling it closely. At the same time, we readily acknowledge that there are parts of the sharing economy that are not about labor relations or potential exploitation of workers; rather, they are about communities, innovation, and genuine sharing. The goal of our proposal is protection for those who are using platforms as their main source of income as an equivalent to professional employment, while exempting those who are using these platforms to create community values or as a way to volunteer.

I THE CLASSIFICATION PROBLEM IN THE UNITED STATES

We will begin with the United States, the jurisdiction that saw the invention of the gig economy and that, until recently, has also been the site of most classification disputes. Under US law, whether a worker is an employee or independent contractor is determined through various multifactored tests dependent on the facts of the relationship.[5] The "control" test derives from the case law and decisions on agency law, and focuses on a principal's right to control the worker. In brief we will suffice to say that some of the factors for finding employee status are whether the employer may direct the way in which the work is performed, determine the hours involved, and provide the employee with direction.[6] On the other hand, elements that lean toward independent contractor classification include high-skilled work, workers providing their own equipment, workers setting their own schedules, and getting paid per project, not per hour.[7] In an alternate test, courts examine the economic realities of the relationship to determine whether the worker is exhibiting entrepreneurial activity, or whether the worker is financially dependent upon the employer.[8] The label affixed to the relationship is a factor in the outcome, but it is certainly not dispositive.

Many commentators had hoped these disputes over worker classification would be concluded, or at least be shaped, by the wage and hour lawsuits within platform companies that have been pending in the Northern District of California. But the largest of these suits, *O'Connor v. Uber*,[9] has been in the process of settling for over a year now. Like other litigation, including the crowdwork minimum wage lawsuit *Otey* v. *Crowdflower*, the cases have been settling without

---

[5] See Katherine V.W. Stone, *Legal Protections for Atypical Employees: Employment Law for Workers without Workplaces and Employees without Employers*, 27 Berkeley J. Emp. & Lab. L. 251, 257–58 (2006) (listing factors from the cases). Oft-cited cases on this subject include *Rutherford Food Corp. v. McComb*, 331 U.S. 722, 728–29 (1947); *Ira S. Bushey & Sons, Inc. v. U.S.*, 398 F.2d 167 (2d Cir. 1968); *Nationwide Mut. Ins. Co. v. Darden*, 503 U.S. 318, 326 (1992).

[6] See, e.g., *Herman v. Express Sixty-Minutes Delivery Service, Inc.*, 161 F.3d 299 (5th Cir. 1998).

[7] See, e.g., Richard R. Carlson, *Variations on a Theme of Employment: Labor Law Regulation of Alternative Worker Relations*, 37 S. Tex. L. Rev. 661, 663 (1996).

[8] See Stone, *supra* note 5.

[9] *O'Connor v. Uber*, 3:13-cv-03826-EMC (N.D. Cal.).

providing any definite answers about whether platform workers are employees or independent contractors.[10]

II CALLS FOR CREATING A THIRD CATEGORY IN THE UNITED STATES

As litigation over worker misclassification lawsuits continues in various US jurisdictions, proponents have looked to the third category as a solution. Intuitively appealing, a third category would resolve many of the ongoing lawsuits and disputes over misclassification plaguing the on-demand sector. Many of the calls for a third category originated in Silicon Valley, with the third category virtually mirroring what is now independent contractor status.[11] Some proponents of the third category claim that such a proposal would have advantages for gig workers as well, who would at least attain some portion of the benefits that accrue to employees.

In 2015 a report written by Alan Krueger and Seth Harris, sponsored by the Hamilton Project, a subsidiary of the Brookings Institute, advocated for the creation of a third category.[12] Pursuant to this proposal, all gig economy workers would default into "independent worker" status. Under the Hamilton project proposal, such "independent workers" would gain rights to organize and bargain collectively under the National Labor Relations Act and would also gain anti-discrimination protections under Title VII. However, the Hamilton project proposal excludes payment for overtime and minimum wage arrangements. Another study has come out largely echoing the Hamilton Project proposal.[13] Meanwhile, on the political front, Senator Mark Warren of Virginia has recently begun discussing the need for legislation to address some of the issues surrounding gig-work.[14] The California Supreme Court's 2018 decision in Dynamex Operations West, Inc. v. Superior Court, which introduces the A, B, C test for workers classification moves closer to a default of employee status. Specifically, the A, B, C test puts the burden on the business to show that a worker is not an employee by proving A) the worker is free from the direction and control; B) the worker performs work outside of the usual course of the hirer's business; C) The worker is customarily engaged in an independently established trade or occupation as the work they were hired to perform for the hiring establishment. Note that Dynamex was not a gig economy case, and so the details of how the test would apply to gig workers is still undetermined.[15]

III A COMPARATIVE APPROACH

To date, the recent calls to establish a third category of "independent worker" have focused only on the present state of the gig economy. Likewise, these calls have been centered almost wholly on the

---

[10] Cherry, *supra* note 1, at 584–85.
[11] "At a recent on-demand economy event, Simon Rothman, a venture capitalist and advisor to companies like Lyft and Taskrabbit, said, "I think it's not 1099 versus W-2. I think the right answer is a third class of worker." Caroline O'Donovan, *What a New Class of Worker Could Mean for the Future of Labor*, BuzzFeed News, June 18, 2015, www.buzzfeed.com/ carolineodonovan/meet-the-new-worker-same-as-the-old-worker?utm_term=.uipR68pav#.qe99zxMmQ.
[12] Seth D. Harris and Alan B. Krueger, *A Proposal for Modernizing Labor Laws for Twenty-First-Century Work: The "Independent Worker*," The Hamilton Project, www.hamiltonproject.org/assets/files/modernizing_labor_laws_for_ twenty_first_century_work_krueger_harris.pdf.
[13] Abbey Stemler, *Betwixt and Between: Regulating the Shared Economy*, 43 Fordham Urb. L. J. 31 (2017).
[14] Mark Warner, *Asking Tough Questions About the Gig Economy*, Mark R. Warner (June 19, 2015), www.warner.senate .gov/public/index.cfm/newsclips?ContentRecord_id=9ec95aab-a96c-4dd5-8532-b45667013d2e.
[15] Dynamex Operations West, Inc. v. Superior Court, 2018 Cal. LEXIS 3152 (Cal. April 30, 2018), available at https:// urldefense.proofpoint.com/v2/url?u=http-3A__www.courts.ca.gov_opinions_documents_S222732.PDF&d=D wMGaQ&c=aqMfXOEvEJQh2iQMCb7Wy8losPnURkcqADc2guUW8IM&r=BUQebvPUw8Okclet5lJux8- bSRjbB6ywpg1D1xyqhzU&m=9Z2RASW-v5mtQd8jJJign_SxAyZZYc3E5ZJZYgo6Jpg&s=r0Aket-FMYct1ZgMT72F2 UQc30yA4Onq11UsffpNyRU&e=" www.courts.ca.gov/opinions/documents/S222732.PDF

United States, where many popular crowdwork services were created. Situating the "dependent contractor" category within an historical and global context, however, we note that other countries have already experimented with contractual forms that functionally resemble the intermediate category, with various and mixed results. We provide "snapshots" of these legal interventions below.

A Canada

Historically, Canadian law used the term "employee" as a gateway to coverage, using the binary employee/independent contractor distinction just as in the United States. As most statutory definitions of "employee" in Canadian statutes were circular and unhelpful, the starting point for most analyses was the control test that had evolved under the principle of vicarious liability for torts.

In the late 1960s and early 1970s, the doctrine around employee status took an interesting turn with the Canadian adoption of the concept of "dependent contractor." The development of the category is largely due to the efforts of leading law professor Harry Arthurs.[16] An article by Professor Arthurs noted that in the 1960s small tradespeople, artisans, plumbers, craftsmen, and the like were increasingly structuring themselves as separate business entities.[17] Yet, despite setting up shop as separate companies, and thus falling outside the traditional purview of "employees," these tradespeople had no other employees but the one worker-owner. As a matter of economic reality, Arthurs noted that these putative independent businesses were often almost wholly economically dependent on larger businesses. As such, Arthurs argued that the law did these small business people an injustice in ruling them outside of the bounds of the traditional labor relationship.[18]

The influence of Arthurs' article spread far beyond academic circles. As the court in *Fownes Construction* v. *Teamsters* noted, this was "one law review article which has had an impact on the real world."[19] Arthurs' influence was such that the concept of "dependent contractor" became established within Canadian law during the 1970s.[20] The effect was significant and beneficial in terms of bringing more workers within the scope of collective bargaining.

Ultimately, in Canada the third category of "dependent contractor" has resulted in an expansion of the definition of employee. The category was enacted to help those workers who were essentially working on their own in a position of economic dependency, thus requiring labor protections.

The labor issues around platform work have yet to be heard by a Canadian court or adjudicative body. As such, predictions are inherently uncertain. But it does seem that the "dependent contractor" category and accordingly expansive definition of "employee" will make it more likely that gig economy workers will be able to access labor protections.

B Italy

Italy's worker classification originated in the ancient Roman Law notion of *locatio operarum* (right to control the worker) and *locatio operis* (contract for a specific result).[21] This dichotomy

---

[16] Harry W. Arthurs, *The Dependent Contractor: A Case Study of the Legal Problems of Countervailing Power*, 16 U. Toronto L.J. 89 (1965).

[17] *Id.*

[18] *Id.*

[19] *Fownes Construction Co. Ltd.* v. *Teamsters*, [1974] 1 CLRBR 452 (British Columbia Labour Relations Board).

[20] *See* Michael Bendel, *The Dependent Contractor: An Unnecessary and Flawed Development in Canadian Labour Law*, 22 U. Toronto L.J. 374, 376 (1982) ("Although the notion of the dependent contractor did not surface in Canada until 1965, concern for his status had become part of the conventional wisdom on labor relations by the early 1970s. Between 1972 and 1977 seven jurisdictions in Canada adopted legislation to grant dependent contractors employee status under their labor relations legislation.").

[21] The Roman distinction was between *locatio conductio operarum*, which refers to the classic master and servant contract and implies the right to control and encompasses *respondeat superior*, and *locatio conductio conductio operis*,

was translated into the two categories of employee (in Italian, "subordinate worker") and independent contractor in the Civil Code of 1942, with those binary categories still in force today.

In addition to the *"eterodirezione"* or managerial power factor,[22] the case law has developed a spectrum of subsidiary factors that could indicate the presence of an employment relationship.[23] A judge may disregard the contractual label when the substance of the work relationship reveals legal indicia of subordination (the so-called "primacy of facts" principle).[24] These factors include: (i) the requirement that the worker follow reasonable work rules; (ii) the length of relationship; (iii) the respect of set working hours; (iv) salaried work; and (v) absence of risk of loss related to the production. None of these elements is dispositive.[25]

Italian Law 533/1973 extended some procedural protection to a tranche of self-employed workers, which would later come to be known as *"lavoratori parasubordinati"* or "quasi-subordinate" workers. Comprised of a subset of self-employed workers, these *lavoratori parasubordinati* were distinguished as those workers who were "collaborating with a principal/buyer under a continuous, coordinated and predominantly personal relationship, although not of subordinate character" ("co.co.co" by abbreviation). Four "concurrent" factors needed to be ascertained in order to denote this intermediate category: (i) cooperation; (ii) continuity and length of the relationship; (iii) functional coordination with the principal; (iv) a predominantly personal service. This measure artificially created an intermediate category.

Looking at the content of the *lavoratore parasubordinato* category, only limited rights, mostly consisting of access to the labor courts, were extended to these workers. As a subset of autonomous workers, quasi-subordinate workers were still outside the scope of the substantive labor law.[26] As a consequence, it was much cheaper to hire a quasi-subordinate worker than an employee, because employees are entitled to substantive labor rights, annual leave, sick leave, maternity leave, other employee benefits, overtime, and job security against unfair dismissal.

Undesirable effects quickly followed. Businesses increasingly began to hire workers that would previously have been classified as employees under the *lavoratore parasubordinato* category, hiding *bona fide* employment relationships in order to reduce costs and evade worker protections. Therefore, workers saw a "gradual erosion of the protections afforded to employees through jobs that are traditionally deemed to constitute master–servant relationships in the strict sense[,] progressively entering the no man's land of an inadequately defined notion."[27] Quasi-subordinate workers were seen as a low-cost alternative to stable employment relationships,

---

which was based on the production of a specific result. *See generally* William Burdik, *Principles of Roman Law and Their Relations to Modern Law* (1938); Matthew Finkin, *Introduction*, 1 Comp. Lab. L. & Pol'y J. 1 (1999–2000).

[22] Cass. 22 November 1999 no 12926, RIDL 200011633. Moreover, in order to prove a subordinate relationship, this power should imply specific and well-defined directives rather than programmatic and vague instructions, since the latter are also compatible with the independent contractor's category. Their compatibility with autonomous work is not sufficient to establish an employment relationship.

[23] Cass. sez. lav., 27/03/2000, n. 3674. "When an assessment of unambiguous elements such as the exercise of the managerial and disciplinary power is not enough to distinguish among employee and self-employed (being the presence of the two powers a safe index of subordination, while its absence is not an indisputable sign of autonomy)…"

[24] Art. 1362 of the Italian Civil Code provides that a contract must be interpreted with regard to the common intention and the behavior of the parties, and not merely to the literal meaning of its wording.

[25] Maurizio Del Conte, *Lavoro autonomo e lavoro subordinato: la volontà e gli indici di denotazione*, Orientamenti Della Giurisprudenza del Lavoro 66 (1995).

[26] Stefano Liebman, ILO Nat'l Studies, *Employment Situations and Workers' Protection*, www.ilo.org/wcmsp5/groups/public/--ed_dialogue/--dialogue/documents/genericdocument/wcms_205366.pdf; Mark Freedland and Nicola Kountouris, *The Legal Construction of Personal Work Relations* 122 n. 61 (2011) ("The emergence of the notion of parasubordinati in the Italian legal domain is traditionally linked to Law 533/1973, … which prescribed that the rules of procedure for labor litigation also apply to the 'relationship of agency, of commercial representation and other relations of collaboration materialising in a continuous and coordinated provision, predominantly personal, even if not of subordinate character.'").

[27] Liebman, *supra* note 25.

especially because "no social security contributions had to be paid in their regard by the principal, at that time."[28]

Revision truly began in 2003, when the legislature amended the content of the quasi-subordinate category with Legislative Decree No. 276/2003 (the so-called Biagi Reform). The legislature required the collaboration be linked to at least one "project" to ensure their authenticity and protect against businesses disguising employees as quasi-subordinate. Thus, a new definition emerged for quasi-subordinate workers: *"lavoro a progetto"* (i.e. project work, also "co.co.pro"). In 2012, the Italian legislature passed Law No. 92/2012 (Monti-Fornero Reform)[29] to counteract the misuse of the intermediate category by making employee status the default. Ultimately, the 2015 "Jobs Act" fundamentally eliminated the concept of project work that had its genesis in the 2003 Biagi law. The Jobs Act firmly established employee status as the default. While the quasi-subordinate category still technically exists, it is now limited in scope.[30]

For the past two decades, the quasi-subordinate category in Italy has resulted in arbitrage, struggle, and ultimately reversal. Introducing such a non-standard contract initially resulted in some employees seeing their classification status downgraded. Along with this loophole came an increase in precarious and non-standard work.

C Spain

The Spanish Workers' Act was passed in 1980, roughly ten years after Italy had engaged in major legislative reform. This law, *Estatuto de los Trabajadores*, covers only employees, defined as "those individuals who voluntarily perform their duties, in exchange for compensation, within the limits of the organization and under the directions of a natural or juridical person, referred to as employer or entrepreneur."[31] Spanish independent contractors were left to constitutional, civil, and commercial provisions of the law.[32]

The traditional binary classification between employees and independent contractors in Spain depended upon a determination of self-organization, as an exercise of contractual autonomy. Spanish case law has interpreted the definition of an employee to be a combination of two concurrent elements: (i) the exercise of managerial power (*"dirección"*); and (ii) how much autonomy the workers have.[33] Spanish legal scholars have focused on the element of "alienness" (*"ajenidad,"* also defined as "ownership by another") as a factor in determining whether an

---

[28] Ulrike Muehlberger, *Dependent Self-Employment, Workers on the Border between Employment and Self-Employment* (2007).

[29] Legge 28 giugno 2012, n. 92 – Disposizioni in materia di riforma del mercato del lavoro in una prospettiva di crescita.

[30] Article 2 of Legislative Decree No. 81/2015 (the "Jobs Act") has designed a new notion of "collaborations organised by the principal," whereby the client organizes all performance-related aspects, including above all time and site. Should this be the case, all employment statutory provisions afforded to subordinate workers apply to self-employed workers. See Antonio Aloisi, *Il lavoro "a chiamata" e le piattaforme online della "Collaborative Economy": nozioni e tipi legali in cerca di tutele/ On-Demand Work and Online Platforms in the Collaborative Economy*, 2 LLI 2421 (2016). In April 2018, the Tribunale di Torino rejected the appeal of six Foodora couriers who claimed to be employees of the platform which had dismissed them for promoting labor agitation. In particular, a daring interpretation of the article 2 of Legislative Decree 81/2015 (the article of the Jobs Act regulating collaborations organized by the client) betrays the expressed intention of the legislature, and also the text of the law. This was a wasted opportunity to apply a provision of the Jobs Act to the gig economy.

[31] Article 1.1 Ley, 8/1980, de 10 de marzo 1980: "Those persons who carry out a trade or profession for economic gain on a regular, personal and direct basis on their own account, in the absence of any supervision or direction from a third party, whether or not they employ other workers on another's account."

[32] A relatively recent one, Constitución Espanola 27 diciembre 1978.

[33] Adalberto Perulli, *Subordinate, Autonomous and Economically Dependent Work: A Comparative Analysis of Selected European Countries, in The Employment Relationship: A Comparative Overview* 173–74 (Giuseppe Casale ed., 2011); J. Lujan Alcaraz, *Introducion, El Estatuto del Trabajo Autónomo. Análisis de la Ley 20/2007, de 11 de julio*, Laborum, 2007, 20. Royal legislative decree No. 1/1995 of 24 March, through which is approved the recast text of the law on the Statute of Workers, Official Gazette, No. 75, dated 29 March 1995, pp. 9654–88.

individual is an employee. "Alienness" is a proxy for the allocation of risk, and consequently, the ownership of "the means of production and the financial benefits obtained by the company from the employee's work."[34] As with other jurisdictions, the contractual label set by the parties is not dispositive. Rather, a judicial assessment of the substance of the relationship (e.g. day-by-day arrangements) is most important.[35]

In 2007, the Spanish legislature[36] enacted a new law (Law 20/2007, July 11, *Estatuto del trabajo autónomo*, LETA, i.e. Statute for Self-Employed Workers).[37] LETA regulated all forms of self-employed or independent contractor-type of work and covered all aspects of self-employment. LETA crafted a third category of workers: *"Trabajador Autonomo Economicamente Dependiente"* (or TRADE, i.e. economically dependent self-employed worker). The TRADE was extended a fairly comprehensive package of benefits and protections that are almost as good as those given to an employee.

However, it is difficult to become a TRADE worker. The crucial component for determining whether a worker is a TRADE rests on a 75 percent threshold of economic dependency. The TRADE worker must "register" the position with the social administration agency, notify them of any changes, with the principal then verifying the information. These strict requirements are burdensome and time-consuming for both workers and businesses.[38]

Perhaps because of the extensive disclosure and heavy burden of compliance, few workers have actually become classified as TRADE.[39] Meanwhile, Spanish labor unions complained that the TRADE category was inappropriately covering what should be traditional employment relationships. With so few workers actually using this category, its usefulness is limited.

D *Germany*

Germany recognizes the categories of employees (*arbeitnehmer*) and independent workers. Although until recently there was no statutory definition of "employee," the Federal Labor Court has traditionally focused on the concepts of personal dependence and the requirement that the worker must follow instructions as to time, site, and content of services.[40] The name given in the contract is of little importance; rather, it is the substance of the relationship that is important.

A German Federal Labor Court decision about circus performers is instructive. In that case, the Court focused on the lack of control that the owners had over the performances, finding these workers to be more like independent workers.[41] Independent workers are defined in opposition to employees, with Section 84(1)(2) of the Commercial Code noting that independent

---

[34] *See* Miguel Ramón Alarcón Caracuel, Dipendenza e alienità nella discussione spagnola sul contratto di lavoro, in *Lavoro Subordinato E Dintorni. Comparazioni E Prospettive* 296 (1989); Consejo General del Poder Judicial, Trabajadores autónomos, 146 *estudio de derecho judicial* 100 (2008); Perulli, *supra* note 32.

[35] STS 29 dic. 1999 (RJ 1427/2000).

[36] *See* AA. VV. Un Estatuto Para La Promoción Y Tutela Del Trabajador Autónomo, Informe de la Comisión de Expertos, designada por el Ministerio de Trabajo y Asuntos Sociales, para la elaboración de un Estatuto del Trabajador Autónomo.

[37] Law No. 20/2007, Official Gazette, No. 166, July 12, 2007, pp. 29964–78.

[38] Mark Freedland, *Application of Labour and Employment Law Beyond the Contract of Employment*, 146 Int'l. Lab. Rev. 3 (2007).

[39] In 2012, only 9,000 TRADE contracts were signed, compared to the 400,000 forecasted. According to recent surveys by the Spanish organization *"Unión de Asociaciones de Trabajadores Autónomos y Emprendedores,"* only 2.4 percent of the workforce have one principal and consequently "were covered by the fairly extensive protections [for TRADE] afforded by the Law of 2007."

[40] *See* Wolfgang Daubler, *Working People in Germany*, 21 Comp. Lab. L. & Pol'y J. 77, 79 (1999–2000).

[41] *Zirkus P GmbH & Co. KG v. Truppe C.*, Bundesarbeitsgericht [BAG] [Federal Labor Court], Aug. 11, 2015, 9 AZR 98/14.

workers are "anybody who essentially is free in organizing his work and in determining his working time."[42]

German law also recognizes a third category of employee-like person (*arbeitnehmeraehnliche Person*). As noted by a leading commentator, employee-like persons share two common characteristics: "they are economically dependent and are in similar need of social protection."[43] German labor courts had recognized employee-like persons, and in 1974 the category was codified in Section 12a of the German Collective Bargaining Act (*Tarifvertraggesetz*). According to Section 12a, an employee-like person must perform his or her duty to (i) the benefit of a client; (ii) under service contract for a specific project; (iii) personally and largely without collaboration of subordinate employees. Importantly, the provision also states that the employee-like person works mainly for one client and relies on a single client for 50 percent of his or her income, a threshold that has much in common with the Spanish TRADE.[44]

While the definition of employee-like persons has some variation among statutes, the main characteristic seems to be economic dependence. Employee-like persons enjoy some of the protections afforded to employees, including the right to unionize and bargain collectively, parental leave, paid holidays, and safety from harassment at work.

The aim of the third category of employee-like persons was to enlarge the scope of social protections, given the organizational and economic transformations around traditional employment relationships. Will workers in the gig economy be protected as employee-like persons on the basis of this third category? A recent article by Professor Bernd Waas points out that the requirement of working for one client for 50 percent of income could prove a significant hurdle for establishing employee-like person status for gig workers.[45] But Professor Waas also invokes the possibility of joint employer doctrine as a way to connect different companies who hire the same worker to perform work on the same platform.

E South Korea

In South Korea, the employee category is defined by statute. Article 2(1) of the Korea Labor Standards Act uses the following definition: "a person, regardless of the kind of occupation, who offers labor to a business or workplace for the purpose of earning wages."[46] Other sources that elaborate upon this provision reveal that the concept of subordination is also important to making a classification determination. A 2006 Korean Supreme Court decision interpreting the Korea Labor Standards Act lists a series of factors to determine employee status. These factors include whether the employer controls the content of the work; whether the employee is subject to personnel regulations; whether the employer supervises the work; whether the employee is free to hire a subordinate to perform the work; who provides work tools; how wages and income tax are structured; and the economic situations of the parties, respectively.[47] Independent

---

[42] Manfred Weiss and M. Schmidt, *Labour Law and Industrial Relations in Germany* 45 (2008).

[43] Daubler, *supra* note 39 at 88–90.

[44] Stefanie Sorge, *German Law on Dependent Self-Employed Workers: A Comparison to the Current Situation Under Spanish Law*, 31 Comp. Lab. L. & Pol'y J. 249, 250 (2010).

[45] Bernd Waas, *Crowdwork in Germany*, in *Crowdwork – A Comparative Law Perspective* 142–86 (Bernd Waas et al. eds., 2017).

[46] Korea Labor Standards Act, Art. 2, Sec. 1, http://elaw.klri.re.kr.

[47] Decision 2004-DA-29736, Korea Supreme Court (2006). Variations of this language also appear in Jong-Hee Park, *Employment Situations and Workers Protections*, Korea Labor Institute, unpublished paper prepared for the ILO, Nov. 1999, www.ilo.org/wcmsp5/groups/public/—ed_dialogue/—dialogue/documents/genericdocument/wcms_205370.pdf.

contractor status can conversely be inferred for those who do not meet the statutory definition of employees.

Interestingly for our purposes, South Korea has had a longstanding percentage of the workforce that finds work in the informal, precarious, and casual sector. Approximately one-third of the workforce finds work in the category of irregular employment (*bijeonggyujik*).[48] According to older accounts, this large percentage of irregular workers is a result of rural to urban migration and consequent mismatches in the labor force with the jobs on offer as well as worker displacement.[49] A more recent account points to the 1997 economic crisis and the IMF bailout, in which some traditional labor protections were compromised in the name of a flexible and competitive economy.[50] As a result, more workers found themselves working in irregular employment.

Within the *bijeonggyujik*, South Korean law recognizes a category of workers known as "special-type workers." As noted by Professor Deok Soon Hwang, special-type workers are not a universal category but instead a statutorily created occupational class for purposes of extending workers' compensation coverage.[51] Specifically, Article 125 of the Korean Industrial Accident Compensation Act extends the protections of the workers' compensation laws to groups of workers in "special types of employment," so long as they provide labor service on a routine basis exclusively to a company and do not use subordinates. This seems to be a way of distinguishing those workers who are dependent and in need of protection from true entrepreneurial enterprises.

The special types of employment are enumerated in the statute and are quite specific: "insurance salesperson, visiting teachers, ready mix truck driver, golf course caddies … door to door deliverers, quick service driver … loan solicitor, credit card solicitor, and exclusive chauffeur service worker[.]"[52] This last category of chauffeur was only added in July 2016. It is difficult to justify precisely why these occupational categories, and not others, are covered; the answer lies in the politics behind union coverage in the wake of the Asian economic downturn in the late 1990s.

In 2016, the Korea Labor Institute, in connection with the International Labour Organization (ILO), organized a conference on crowdwork and the gig economy. Special sessions were held to discuss the status of gig workers in South Korea. While language barriers and translation issues have stymied market growth by gig economy companies within South Korea, the sector is continuing to grow.

While some gig workers, such as those working as drivers, might be covered as special-type workers, participants noted that other types of gig workers, such as those working to perform odd jobs or those that work only in cyberspace, would likely not be covered. Furthermore, even for the enumerated categories of special-type workers, the extent of coverage and protection is an open question. As noted above, it is far from certain if special-type workers enjoy the right to organize and the other protections extended to employees. Commentators at the ILO conference expressed concern and frustration about the precarious nature of gig work and the perceived gaps in coverage for gig workers.

---

[48] For discussion of the irregular sector, *see* Jennifer Jihye Chun, *The Struggles of Irregularly-Employed Workers in South Korea, 1992–2012*, unpublished working paper for EOIW, 2014.

[49] Ji-Whan Yun, *Unbalanced Development: The Origin of Korea's Self-Employment Problem from a Comparative Perspective*, 47 J. Dev. Stud. 786 (2011).

[50] *See* Chun, *supra* note 47.

[51] Deok Soon Hwang, *Platform Work in South Korea*, Korea Labor Institute. Translation in possession of authors. This article was published in Korean by the Korean Labor Law Institute.

[52] *Id.*

IV SUMMARY AND ASSESSMENT OF OUTCOMES

The implementation of third categories in various nations highlights both successes as well as problems. Canada's passage of legislation in the 1970s created a new category of "dependent contractors" by amending the definition of "employee" in various statutes. The practical result of the "dependent contractor" category was to expand the definition of employee and to bring more workers under the ambit of labor law protection. The end result was increased coverage and the provision of a safe harbor for workers in need of protections, based on economic dependency. The third category seems to have worked well in terms of expanding the coverage of the laws to an increasing number of workers.

From Italy's experimentation with the third category, we saw businesses trying to take advantage of a discounted status of the *parasubordinato* to evade regulations applicable to employees, such as social security contributions. The quasi-subordinate category created a loophole that actually resulted in *less* protection for workers. Through the years, the legislature attempted to adjust the category in order to provide appropriate coverage for workers. The ultimate result was confusion and, since 2015, the intermediate category has been extremely limited. Rather, workers are now presumed by default to be employees.

Spain provided an example of a legal system that adopted a third category, but only for very few workers. The law assumes that TRADE workers are predominantly working for one business; this could be a problem for platform workers who are working for multiple platforms. Looking at the causes of this very limited use of the category, it comes down to a heavy burden of requirements to be met, including the use of a strict economic threshold.

While Germany's category of employee-like persons is far less stringent and burdensome, the category still requires a 50 percent dependency threshold. This threshold may prove problematic for German crowdworkers unless they can mesh several employers together through the joint employer doctrines (where accounts across different platforms would be pooled).

Finally, South Korea has a category for special-type workers, but it is extremely narrow in scope, covering only certain types of occupational categories. The exclusivity requirement in the law may create trouble for gig workers who work for more than one platform. Further, the benefits extended to those who fall into the special-type workers category are meager. If the third type of category is too narrow, or the benefits provided too meager, the category may prove inadequate for the challenges of the on-demand economy.

A Analysis

Note that the debate over misclassification actually can be interpreted two different ways. One way to view the issue is to acknowledge that there has been legitimate confusion about forms of gig work that do not fit easily into binary distinctions. After all, gig workers have some characteristics that are common to independent contractors and yet others that are reminiscent of employees. The problem, under this view, lies with a legal test that is malleable, fact-intensive, and difficult to apply. The other way to consider the misclassification issue is to acknowledge that there has long been arbitrage of the law – illegitimate practices that lead to misclassification of what truly are employment relationships. These practices serve to hide employment relationships under the guise of "false" or "bogus" contractor situations. Note that both of these problems may exist within the same legal system.

At least in theory, establishing an intermediate category for gig work might alleviate legitimate confusion about how to apply the test to gig workers. However, if the consequences of establishing such a third category would be arbitrage and downgrading of employees to inter-mediate status, that would do nothing to eliminate bogus contractor status. In fact, adding a new category could *increase* the possibility for arbitrage. We must acknowledge that three categories create more room for mischief than two, and we can see from the Italian case that such arbitrage there became widespread in response to the adoption of the quasi-subordinate worker category.

B *Difficulties with Implementing a Third Category in the United States*

If we examine the list of benefits and protections that go along with employee status, it becomes difficult to start excluding these from the third category. What protections are completely unnecessary? One of the primary complaints of many gig workers is inadequate pay for their time, so Harris and Kreuger's suggestion that wage and hour laws could be excluded seems prob-lematic. Apart from difficulties defining the category or how it would be constituted, there are also practical difficulties. In the United States, establishing a third category over a patchwork of state and federal regulation would be complex.

While it is possible that judges and administrative bodies could shift their interpretation of the statutes so as to create a third category, it is unlikely given the way that the statutes are written. Under the current political climate it seems doubtful that a third category would be high on the legislative agenda in the United States right now. Looking beyond Congress, adding a third classification when the statutes only call for two categories would call for a vast feat of adminis-trative or judicial activism. At least at this moment, reform in this direction seems unlikely from a practical perspective.

C *Shifting Toward a Default Presumption of Employee Status*

Rather than create a new category, one way to govern the difficult classification issues is to change the default rules. Instead of having the platform choose to classify workers as inde-pendent contractors in its terms of service online and then later defend its position in lengthy, expensive, and time-consuming litigation, what if we began with a presumption that, above a certain threshold of hours, workers are employees? Then those who truly are independent businesses or self-employed would opt out of regulations based on a set of easily understood standards.

But what about the idea that the gig economy is innovative? Should platforms be given spe-cial treatment because they use new technology? Innovation has not typically been a basis for an exemption from the labor laws. The problem is distinguishing between authentic innovators, who could compete on a level playing field or who have a distinct and interesting new technology or business model, and those platforms that are profiteers who exist only to take advantage of cheap labor by undercutting the law. Hence our argument is that platforms should be normalized and treated like other employers, rather than fight over their supposed exceptionalism.

Business models that either are truly "sharing," some mix of profit and nonprofit (for example, "B" corporations),[53] or those that engage in prosumer transactions, genuinely might need room to experiment. There should be a "safe harbor" created if the work looks more like volunteerism, sharing, or the work is being undertaken for altruistic reasons or community-minded motiv-ations. More recently, the European Commission has supported this view in its Communication

---

[53] Miriam A. Cherry, *The Law and Economics of Corporate Social Responsibility and Greenwashing*, 14 U.C. Davis Bus. L. J. 281, 294 (2014).

on the "collaborative economy," distinguishing between professional providers and private individuals.[54]

There are also some instances where the provision of a service is *de minimis* (or provided so infrequently) that it does not merit employee status. For example, if someone logs into a crowdwork platform and does some proofreading for an hour a month, that user is probably not an employee. Likewise, those who participate in Lyft as a carpool on their way to work three days a week are probably not employees. We do not wish to impose burdensome legalities on users for one-off situations. Likewise, we would not want to discourage neighbors or volunteers from providing their services to others when those efforts are *truly voluntary* or used only to defray legitimate expenses, such as those who carpool from city to city in Europe through BlaBlaCar. Rather, we are more concerned with platforms that seem to be competing with, or in some instances replacing, full-time employment with on-demand precarious work.[55]

CONCLUSION

Calls for a third category in the United States reflexively appear to be an easy solution, tailor-made for the problems surfacing in the gig economy. That initial reaction, however, is tempered upon further study of the content and history of the implementation of the third category in other nations. In this chapter we examined the experiences of other nations in the hopes of learning winning strategies and avoiding problems.

In Italy, the adoption of the third category led to widespread arbitrage of the categories, with businesses moving employees into a "bogus" discounted status in the quasi-subordinate category. In Spain, the requirements for attaining the third category were burdensome enough that the third category is applicable only to a tiny number of workers. Viewed in this light, experimenting with a third category might be seen as more risky than just the "easy" or "obvious" solution as it first appears.

Rather than risking arbitrage of the categories, and the possibility that some workers will actually end up losing rights, it makes sense to think about employment status as the default rule for most gig workers, except those that may fit into a safe harbor because they are either not working very much (true "amateurs") or are engaged in volunteerism for altruistic reasons (truly "sharing"). If there is to be an intermediate category, establishing one that, like Canada's "dependent contractor," expands the scope of the employment relationship would best meet the needs of gig workers. Such a default rule or expanded definition makes sense whether we are thinking about gig workers, those in fissured workplaces, franchises, or other non-standard or contingent work arrangements.

---

[54] Communication from the Commission to the European Parliament, the Council, the European Economic and Social Committee and the Committee of the Regions, *A European Agenda for the Collaborative Economy*. On December 20, 2017, the Court of Justice of the European Union (CJEU) ruled that *UberPop* is not an information society service, but rather a transport service. In particular, the Court took the view that the service provided by the platform is more than a matching activity connecting, by means of a digital app, a nonprofessional driver with a private individual. Indeed, the provider of that intermediation service simultaneously organizes and offers urban transport services. In C-434/15 *Asociación Profesional Elite Taxi v. Uber Systems Spain* (2014) ECLI:EU:C:2017:981 the Court observed that "Uber determines at least the maximum fare by means of the eponymous application, that the company receives that amount from the client before paying part of it to the nonprofessional driver of the vehicle, and that it exercises a certain control over the quality of the vehicles, the drivers and their conduct, which can, in some circumstances, result in their exclusion."

[55] Janine Berg, *Uber, Income Security in the On-Demand Economy: Findings and Policy Lessons from a Survey of Crowdworkers*, 37 Comp. Lab. L. & Pol'y J. 543 (2016), http://papers.ssrn.com/sol3/papers.cfm?abstract_id=2740940.

24

Two Models for a Fairer Sharing Economy

Mark Graham and Mohammad Amir Anwar

INTRODUCTION

Millions of workers around the world join the so-called "sharing economy" every day to perform a variety of jobs. Most of these jobs are digitally mediated through internet-based platforms that connect buyers and sellers of goods and services. However, recent research has begun to highlight the many risks associated with jobs in the sharing economy.[1] Many such jobs are characterized by temporary contracts, long and irregular hours, and low income, and they are often unregulated. The work is highly commoditized, and a global market for this work means that many workers feel they are replaceable, with little bargaining power.[2] Workers are made to compete against each other, which drives down wages. Thus, many workers will earn below the national minimum wage of their country of location. Since many of these jobs are small "tasks," clients may have no formal or legal requirement to provide employment benefits to workers. In other words, many sharing economy work practices carry with them various forms of insecurities, and workers typically have less bargaining power than in standard labor markets. These risks are even more pronounced among workers in low- and middle-income countries, where our research is situated.

In this chapter, we discuss ways in which the sharing economy can contribute toward economic development by making its work practices fairer for workers around the world. We first argue that there is a need to reframe work practices in the sharing economy. In some cases, this will mean ensuring that platforms are seen as employers (and workers are seen as employees rather than as self-employed). Secondly, a better understanding of the important nodes in sharing economy value chains (that is, points of influence and control) can help formulate strategies involving disruption and intervention by labor so that more value is captured for and by workers. This chapter introduces and reviews two models of cooperative working that could operate in conjunction with each other to make the sharing economy fairer for workers around the world.

The first is the idea of "platform cooperatives." Worker cooperatives have been implemented in various sectors of the economy, particularly in agriculture, where they can help farmworkers

[1] T. Scholz, *Platform Cooperativism: Challenging the Corporate Sharing Economy* (2016); T. Slee, *What's Yours Is Mine: Against the Sharing Economy* (2016).

[2] M. Graham, I. Hjorth, and V. Lehdonvirta, *Digital Labour and Development: Impacts of Global Digital Labour Platforms and the Gig Economy on Worker Livelihoods*, 23 Transf. Eur. Rev. Labour Res. 135–62 (2017), doi:10.1177/1024258916687250.

overcome some of the risks of predatory capitalism (particularly high interest loans, expensive farm machinery seeds and fertilizers, casual farm labor, and low farm wages). Applying the same principles to sharing economy practices will potentially give greater control of work to workers. Such platforms can prevent a concentration of power and hence abuse by those in charge. Platforms can be run and managed by workers, instead of private firms and shareholders, thus giving workers greater powers and control over how they organize their work. Secondly, there is a need for a "Fair Work Foundation" to monitor work practices in the sharing economy. This idea is inspired by the "Fairtrade" movement in primary commodities. We suggest greater economic transparency in digital economy value chains, whereby employers/platforms are encouraged to comply with certain standards of working conditions, with a certification process for those employers who clearly abide by fair working practices at all levels of the value chain. This, we hope, will incentivize ethical working practices and reduce the risks for workers drawn into the sharing economy. Our hope is that the ideas presented in this chapter will stimulate wider debates among various stakeholders in order to encourage movement towards a fairer world of work.

I WHAT IS THE SHARING ECONOMY?

The term "sharing economy" has been used to refer to a wide range of contemporary economic practices that have emerged recently with the increasing proliferation of information and communication technologies (ICTs), such as mobile phones, computers, laptops, internet, and smartphones. Similar terms used to describe this new phenomenon include the collaborative economy, the peer-to-peer economy, the access economy, the on-demand economy, online outsourcing, the gig economy, and others.[3] The term has been subject to critique from a variety of perspectives, and tends to incorporate different meanings, such as the sustainable economy, on the one hand, or even a form of neoliberalism (particularly the casualization of labor).[4] We operationalize the sharing economy as an "assemblage," after Deleuze and Guattari and also Delanda, of multiple and heterogeneous parts (different economic practices and both state and non-state actors, for example) and their interactions with each other that enable the "whole" to function.[5] Each of these component parts can exist outside an assemblage, are autonomous and take on a certain character in the place where they are territorialized, thus making assemblages

---

[3] *See* G.M. Eckhardt and F. Bardhi, *The Sharing Economy Isn't About Sharing at All*, Harv. Bus. Rev. (2015), https://hbr.org/2015/01/the-sharing-economy-isnt-about-sharing-at-all; J. Hamari, M. Sjöklint, and A. Ukkonen, *The Sharing Economy: Why People Participate in Collaborative Consumption*, 67 J. Assoc. Inf. Sci. Technol. 2047–59 (2016), doi:10.1002/asi.23552; Scholz, *supra* note 1; J. Schor, *Debating the Sharing Economy*, 4 J. Self-Gov. Manag. Econ. 7–22 (2016); A. Taeihagh, *Crowdsourcing, Sharing Economies and Development*, 33 J. Dev. Soc. 191–222 (2017), doi:10.1177/0169796X17710072; N. van Doorn, *Platform Labor: On the Gendered and Racialized Exploitation of Low-Income Service Work in the "On-Demand" Economy*, 20 Inf. Commun. Soc. 898–914 (2017), doi:10.1080/1369118X.2017.1294194. It is a common practice to use the term "sharing economy" along with a host of other terms interchangeably in popular media and academic discourse. We use the term "sharing economy" throughout the chapter in reference to a collection of new and contemporary economic activities conducted over internet platforms. Where we use other terms, it is to highlight how that term appeared in other works and perspectives.

[4] C. J. Martin, *The Sharing Economy: A Pathway to Sustainability or a Nightmarish Form of Neoliberal Capitalism?* 121 Ecol. Econ. 149–59 (2016), doi:10.1016/j.ecolecon.2015.11.027.

[5] *See* G. Deleuze and F. Guattari, *A Thousand Plateaus* (2004); M. Delanda, *A New Philosophy of Society: Assemblage Theory and Social Complexity* (annotated ed., 2006). The absence of discussion on the role of the state in the sharing economy discourse has been largely due to the unregulated nature of these practices. We argue that it is all the more relevant to call for greater attention to be paid as to what role states can play to make the sharing economy fairer for workers.

dynamic.[6] This enables us to conceive of the sharing economy as a global assemblage of multiple economic practices and actors and also to understand the sharing economy as a subset of a larger global information economy that includes information technology hardware and software production, outsourcing, financial services, etc. Therefore, our understanding of the sharing economy includes the main platform firms such as Uber, Airbnb, Upwork, Amazon Mechanical Turk, etc. that develop and run these platforms and the technology giants such as Google, Apple, Samsung, Microsoft, Facebook, etc., whose ability to control information flows and provision of software and hardware technologies afford much needed technical support for these platforms.[7] We also include internet and financial services providers, which form a key component in the platform firms' ability to successfully operate and provide and deliver services in multiple geographical locations, thus expanding the network of sharing economy firms across the globe.[8]

Furthermore, the sharing economy is also composed of multiple sub-assemblages of various kinds of economic practices that are emerging (such as rentals, transport, gig labor, etc.). Some prominent examples include room rentals (Airbnb, Roomorama), transport and taxi services (Uber, Relayrides, Lyft, etc.), cleaning services (TaskRabbit, Handy.com, Helping.co.uk), and digital gig labor (Upwork, Amazon Mechanical Turk, Freelancer.com, etc.). Estimates by PricewaterhouseCoopers suggest that five key sharing economy activities – travel, car-sharing, finance, staffing, and music and video streaming – accounted for US$15 billion in global revenues in 2014 and is expected to grow to around US$335 billion by 2025.[9] Uber has been valued at US$70 billion,[10] which is more than Ford and GM individually, and higher than 80 percent of all companies listed on Standard and Poor's index of the 500 largest corporations.[11] Another indication of the rapid growth in sharing economy activities is the estimated 48 million people registered on various digital gig work platforms (prominent among them are Freelancer.com, Upwork, Zhubajie/Witmark, Guru, Peopleperhour, Crowdflower, Amazon Mechanical Turk).[12] Workers in different parts of the world are increasingly looking to find various types of digital work such as virtual assistance, writing jobs, transcription and translation, programming, graphic design, proofreading and editing, data entry, and the like. We are currently experiencing "a mass migration of labour without the migration of workers."[13]

The ubiquity of ICTs and data have made this possible. Silicon Valley technology companies like Uber and Airbnb have developed web applications that can be downloaded onto smartphones to connect lenders (those willing to share/rent their assets) with buyers/users (those

---

[6] Delanda, *supra* note 5.

[7] These technology giants also occupy a very powerful position in the value chains of the information economy through their intellectual property rights and patents on products and services and their ability to control information flows. Recent research is beginning to show that sharing economy firms are able to leverage their access to information much to the disadvantage of sharing economy participants; *see* R. Calo and A. Rosenblat, *The Taking Economy: Uber, Information, and Power* (2017) (SSRN Scholarly Paper No. ID 2929643).

[8] Growth of these related actors is interdependent; the case in point is that the rise of the sharing economy helps the growth of mobile payment systems. *WBS PayTech Conference: Mobile Payment Growth*, Warwick Business School (5 Feb. 2016), www.wbs.ac.uk/news/wbs-paytech-conference-mobile-payment-growth/.

[9] PricewaterhouseCoopers, *The Sharing Economy* (Aug. 15, 2014), http://pwc.blogs.com/press_room/2014/08/five-key-sharing-economy-sectors-could-generate-9-billion-of-uk-revenues-by-2025.html.

[10] Reuters, *Uber's $70 Bln Value Accrues Mainly to Customers* (2016).

[11] C. Myers, *Decoding Uber's Proposed $50B Valuation (and What It Means for You)*, Forbes (May 13, 2015), www.forbes.com/sites/chrismyers/2015/05/13/decoding-ubers-50-billion-valuation-and-what-it-means-for-you/.

[12] World Bank, *The Global Opportunity in Online Outsourcing* (2015).

[13] G. Standing, *The Corruption of Capitalism: Why Rentiers Thrive and Work Does Not Pay* (2016). *cf.* M. Graham and M. A. Anwar, *Digital Labour, in Digital Geographies* (J. Ash, R. Kitchin, and A. Leszczynski eds., forthcoming, 2018).

who want to use those assets) across different geographical locations. The result is the unlocking of the value of various unused or under-used assets by matching goods and service providers directly with customers. Proponents argue that the underlying logic is that this model eliminates intermediaries, thus reducing the cost of goods and of the provision of services.[14] However, as we shall discuss in this chapter, new forms of intermediaries are emerging in the sharing economy.

We want to stress here that many of these activities discussed above are not fundamentally different economic practices and their mechanism of provision is roughly the same, i.e., the delivery of goods and services conducted on the internet through a platform with the help of human labor. Therefore, our target of discussion is not a particular set of economic activities but rather the actual human labor forms and processes in the sharing economy. One particular aspect of this human labor that unites these activities is that most of these are small and minute "tasks" or "gigs" of different kinds to be completed by workers all around the world. Rapid penetration of the internet and mobile phones has enabled a sharp rise in the number of internet users around the world, particularly outside the OECD countries. Today, more than three-quarters of internet users live outside the European Union and North America and this trend is likely to continue.[15] Thus, there will likely be a huge number of people from low- and middle-income countries joining the sharing economy in the coming years.[16] Our focus in this chapter is on sharing economy activities in the context of labor in low- and middle-income countries, where the downsides of the sharing economy (such as economic exploitation and extraversion) tend to be more pronounced.

II LABOR-RELATED RISKS IN SHARING ECONOMY PRACTICES

Such has been the uptake of the sharing economy that some have called it a "potential new pathway to sustainability" since it allows a shift away from a culture of owning assets to a culture of sharing them.[17] For example, platforms like Uber allow individuals to pay for a ride in another person's car, rather than own a car. It is true that the sharing economy provides both economic and social benefits in the forms of temporary employment for some people, income-earning potential, social interaction, and access to resources not otherwise possible. However, there are also certain downsides to it.[18]

Platforms like Uber and Airbnb, while enabling provision of cheap and efficient services for consumers, rely for their business model on extracting value from the (private) assets of individuals shared via its platform.[19] For example, Uber retains 25 percent of the cost for each ride

---

[14] O. C. Ferrell, L. Ferrell, and K. Huggins, *Seismic Shifts in the Sharing Economy: Shaking Up Marketing Channels and Supply Chains*, 24 J. Mark. Channels 3–12 (2017), doi:10.1080/1046669X.2017.1346973.

[15] Data available from World Internet Stats. Internet World Stats, www.internetworldstats.com/stats.htm.

[16] *See* T. R. Dillahunt and A. R. Malone, *The Promise of the Sharing Economy Among Disadvantaged Communities*. Presented at the 33rd Annual CHI Conference on Human Factors in Computing Systems, CHI 2015, Association for Computing Machinery (2015), doi:10.1145/2702123.2702189; B. Dreyer, F. Lüdeke-Freund, R. Hamann, and K. Faccer, *Upsides and Downsides of the Sharing Economy: Collaborative Consumption Business Models' Stakeholder Value Impacts and Their Relationship to Context*. Technol. Forecast. Soc. Change (2017), doi:10.1016/j.techfore.2017.03.036; A. Hira, *Profile of the Sharing Economy in the Developing World: Examples of Companies Trying to Change the World*. 33 J. Dev. Soc. 244–71 (2017), doi:10.1177/0169796X17710074; C. Liem, *The Rise of the Sharing Economy in Indonesia* (2015).

[17] H. Heinrichs, *Sharing Economy: A Potential New Pathway to Sustainability*, 22 GAIA 228–31, 228 (2013).

[18] A. Malhotra and M. V. Alstyne, *The Dark Side of the Sharing Economy … and How to Lighten It*, 57 Commun. ACM 24–27 (2014).

[19] There are some free exchanges of goods and services in the sharing economy, such as Freecycle, www.freecycle.org, where people give away goods for free, or Wikipedia, a free online encyclopedia where knowledge and content is created and shared freely, for example.

a driver completes. This type of model represents a new wave of commoditization of personal assets and resources and of unlocking the value of these assets.

The rise of the sharing economy has also enabled a surge in on-demand work. As Scholz argued, the very concept of the sharing economy is not about sharing but is actually an "on-demand service economy."[20] Anyone with a smartphone and the internet can order a taxi, get food delivered to their doorstep, find someone to mind their kids at home, or get someone to deliver their weekly shopping. Those workers who are drawn into the sharing economy will often find their work being dictated by platforms. For example, Uber decides how much a trip will cost, not the driver. A driver's rating on Uber is dictated by his or her riders – who may not like the car's smell, how they drive, or that the driver talked too much (or not enough).

So, what does the sharing economy hold in the future for these new workers, from car drivers, to cycle couriers, to virtual assistants?

One of the main challenges in the contemporary world capitalist economy is that labor faces constant threats to working standards and is treated like a commodity, as has been documented since the time of Marx. As millions of people around the world compete for the same jobs on sharing economy platforms, this has the potential to further undermine a range of labor standards. For example, on Upwork, one of the largest online work platforms, workers compete against a global supply of freelancers for small jobs such as editing a CV through a bidding process. Clients list jobs on these platforms and workers then try to outbid each other for such contracts by offering a lower price or a better service. Such a scenario, where workers and clients/employers enter into a non-proximate relationship, makes monitoring and control of work difficult. Thus, platform companies rely on a user-based rating system for quality control, for efficient matching of workers and employers, and to create a mechanism for trust between providers and suppliers. These ratings and reputation scores for workers give undue advantage to clients/employers; so, while they ensure the quality of work performed on platforms, it often leaves new workers without jobs for a long time and at the mercy of clients or employers. In our ongoing work on gig workers, we have spoken to workers who had spent months trying to get their first job.[21] In order to secure it, workers often accepted extremely low wages or sometimes did free labor for the promise of high ratings that would allow them to find online work in the future.[22]

Another important problem here is that the design of online work platforms is such that labor is treated as a commodity to be bought and sold in the market. Digital gig work is often packaged up into bite-sized tasks and workers can easily be replaced.[23] If labor power is seen as a commodity to be easily bought and sold, then millions of people on online marketplaces, who are desperate for work and willing to work for low wages, carry risks themselves.[24] This creates a

---

[20] Scholz, *supra* note 1.
[21] M. Graham, S. Ojanpera, M. A. Anwar, and N. Friederici, *Digital Connectivity and African Knowledge Economies*, Questions de Communications, No. 32 (2017).
[22] *See, e.g.*, Graham et al., *supra* note 2. Along with some colleagues, we have been involved in two major projects about digital labor (Mark Graham, *Microwork and Virtual Production Networks in Sub-Saharan Africa and Southeast Asia*, Oxford Internet Institute, www.oii.ox.ac.uk/research/projects/microwork-and-virtual-production-networks/ and *Welcome to the Geonet Project*, Geonet, http://geonet.oii.ox.ac.uk/). These projects focus on several African (South Africa, Kenya, Nigeria, Ghana, and Uganda) and Asian countries (the Philippines, Malaysia, and Vietnam). We are concerned with the developmental impacts of digital gig work in the Global South, particularly from the perspective of labor. Two of the key publications from these projects are Graham et al., *supra* note 2; and M. Graham, V. Lehdonvirta, A. Wood, H. Barnard, I. Hjorth, and D. Simon, *The Risks and Rewards of Online Gig Work at the Global Margins* (2017). We are also aware that there are multiple phrases used to describe gig work. We prefer to use "digital gig work" or "gig labor" because it captures the fact that many of these work activities are treated by platforms as a temporary "gig."
[23] Graham et al., *supra* note 2.
[24] *Id.*

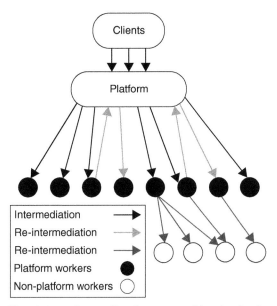

FIGURE 24.1 Heuristic understanding for types and levels of re-intermediation

downward pressure on wages and potentially renders local minimum wages or living wages less effective as workers compete against a global supply of labor to win contracts.

Furthermore, online work platforms enable new forms of platform intermediaries (Figure 24.1). During our fieldwork in African countries, and some of our previous collaborative research in both Africa and Southeast Asia, we found evidence of re-intermediation.[25] Some workers with relatively high scores tended to be offered more work from platforms than they could handle themselves. They would outsource some of their work (either through the platform or outside the platform) to someone else at a fraction of the cost and retain a large chunk of the profit. Similarly, car-rental companies are some of the biggest winners on the Uber platform, particularly in some African countries. For example, in Ghana, a big car rental transport company owns a large fleet of cars which they have registered on Uber. These cars are then rented out to prospective drivers, while the Uber payment account is kept with the owner of the rental company. This is made possible because many of these drivers do not own cars and are desperately seeking some form of paid work. Drivers pay a portion of their daily/weekly earnings to the rental company (Field Observation, Accra, April–June 2017). This kind of re-intermediation of Uber's value chain by car rental companies further reduces the value captured by drivers and has great implications for already poor and marginalized drivers/workers' lives and livelihoods. For example, many of the drivers that we spoke to told us they struggle to pay their rents for cars and have to work extremely long hours to meet their daily targets. Some drivers in Lagos we spoke to do not go home over the weekends and sleep in cars so that they can maximize their time driving customers home.

In such a scenario, what strategies do we have to ensure that workers in the sharing economy are treated fairly, earn a living wage, and have greater levels of control over their work activities? While we focus on the sharing economy in low-income contexts where our research

[25] Graham et al., *supra* note 2; V. Lehdonvirta, I. Hjorth, M. Graham, and H. Barnard, *Online Labour Markets and the Persistence of Personal Networks: Evidence From Workers in Southeast Asia*, in The Changing Nature of Work in the Twenty-First Century. Presented at the American Sociological Association Annual Meeting 2015, Chicago (2015).

is situated, it is important to point out that globally labor in the sharing economy is facing growing threats to its existence and with regards to work standards, irrespective of its location. A Deliveroo worker in London and an Uber driver in Nairobi may have different socio-economic contexts in which they work, but they both face extreme work pressure, unsociable working hours, and extremely low wages. Therefore, our discussions and suggestions below are pertinent to sharing economy labor in the global context as well as in low- and middle-income countries.

III MAKING THE SHARING ECONOMY FAIRER FOR WORKERS

One of the first steps in addressing the question of worker rights in the sharing economy is to think about reframing some of the concepts invoked in discussions of the sharing economy. We should stop treating platform companies simply as technology firms but also as transport companies, media houses, and delivery companies. For example, Uber drivers are often classed as "self-employed entrepreneurs" rather than workers. Recently in the UK, an employment court ruled that Uber drivers are not self-employed and are entitled to the national living wage, thus opening the way to further scrutiny of employment practices of platform companies and other large firms.[26]

This reframing of work in the sharing economy has the potential to build a sense of collective identity among workers and mobilize social movements,[27] which are key to determining the well-being of various social groups.[28] Here, labor unions can also play an important role in mobilizing workers (social media can be a useful tool too for organizing labor); helping them achieve class consciousness and collective identity; and highlighting the risks in sharing economy work practices. This could then also open up the possibilities for collaboration, cooperation, and collective bargaining among workers who are employed by these companies to secure better working conditions.[29]

Secondly, we need to understand important nodes in sharing economy value chains where value is created and captured, which can be disrupted by workers. For example, platform companies make effective use of technology (including big data and algorithms) to drive their platforms. Without its app or internet-based platform, Uber would not be able to match drivers with riders and remain competitive with ordinary taxi drivers. Workers do not own or control platforms and hence can be subjected to regulatory mechanisms and platform policies such as pricing, ratings, feedback, and surveillance methods, often leaving them powerless. It is true

---

[26] H. Osborne, *Uber Loses Right to Classify UK Drivers as Self-Employed*, The Guardian, Oct 28, 2016. R. Davies. *Uber loses appeal in UK employment rights case*, The Guardian, Nov 10, 2017.

[27] U. Huws and S. Dahlmann, New Forms of Work: New Occupational Identities, in *Interrogating New Economy: Restructuring Work in 21st Century* 65–92 (2010); F. Polletta and J. M. Jasper, *Collective Identity and Social Movements*, 27 Annu. Rev. Sociol. 283–305 (2001), doi:10.1146/annurev.soc.27.1.283; H. Tajfel and J. Turner, *The Social Identity Theory of Intergroup Behaviour*, in Psychology of Intergroup Relations 7–24 (S. Worchel and W. Austin eds., 1986).

[28] M. Bryan and A. Nandi, *Working Hours, Work Identity and Subjective Wellbeing* (2015); J. F. Dovidio, S. Gaertner, A. R. Pearson, and B. M. Riek, *Social Identities and Social Context: Social Attitudes and Personal Well-Being*, in Social Identification in Groups, Advances in Group Processes 231–60 (2005), doi:10.1016/S0882-6145(05)22009-X; S. A. Haslam, J. Jetten, T. Postmes, and C. Haslam, *Social Identity, Health and Well-Being: An Emerging Agenda for Applied Psychology*, 58 Appl. Psychol. 1–23 (2009), doi:10.1111/j.1464-0597.2008.00379.x.

[29] In Seattle, Washington, the city council voted in 2015 to allow Uber and Lyft drivers to unionize for better pay and working rights. However, this ordinance has been blocked pending a law suit by the US Chamber of Commerce *See Law Allowing Uber and Lyft Drivers to Unionize Temporarily Halted in Seattle*, The Guardian, Apr. 4, 2017, www.theguardian.com/technology/2017/apr/04/uber-lift-ride-sharing-union-law-seattle-judge; and www.bna.com/seattle-law-allowing-n73014463849/.

this mechanism ensures the quality of work/services, benefitting users, but it also increases punishment for workers generally. Therefore, an important question here is to think about ways in which the sharing economy works for both users and workers. One of them is for workers to have greater control over the platforms where much of the value is captured and a greater say over how these platforms are governed.

While there is no doubt that the sharing economy has become a powerful socioeconomic phenomenon, the ownership and the governance of platforms needs to be made more democratic for them to make a genuine and meaningful impact on workers' lives and livelihoods.[30] Here we outline two visions to make the sharing economy fairer for workers.

A Cooperatives for a Fairer Sharing Economy

Cooperatives have long been recognized for their role in economic development,[31] with some of the most successful ones in primary commodities such as tea, coffee, and cocoa. Cooperatives are owned and managed by their members, who therefore have an opportunity to participate in how the business is run.[32] One of the major differences between a cooperative and a privately held enterprise is this shareholding power. In a private corporate entity, the voting power is determined by the number of shares a person controls, whereas a cooperative tends to be more democratic, in that power is shared rather equally among its members. Thus, cooperatives do not allow any one person or group to concentrate power, ensuring that they remain democratic.[33]

This idea has been translated into the form of a radical movement called the "Platform Cooperativism Consortium,"[34] an international network dedicated to furthering efforts to build sustainable platform cooperatives. A platform cooperative can be defined as a member-owned platform or organization that enables the exchange of goods and services in similar fashion to already existing corporate platforms, except that it favors decentralized governance, open data, and the development of information and material commons as opposed to a corporate-style extractive model.[35] At the heart of platform cooperatives lie three principles: communal ownership, democratic governance, and transparent data. The underlying idea is that in the age of platform capitalism, there is a need to build an alternative to the extractive sharing economy that is more decentralized and democratic. Thus, platform cooperatives should leverage new technologies to create similar platforms to Uber, Airbnb, and others that promote social ownership and management of the platforms, and reframe the ideas of innovation and efficiency

---

[30] Schor, *supra* note 3.

[31] Prominent international organizations such as the International Labour Organization (ILO) and the Food and Agriculture Organization (FAO) are advocates of cooperatives. *See* FAO, *Agricultural Cooperatives are Key to Reducing Hunger and Poverty* (Oct 31, 2011), www.fao.org/news/story/en/item/93816/icode/; ILO, 2011. Cooperatives for People-Centred Rural Development, Policy Brief, International Labour Organisation, Geneva; ILO, *Cooperatives and the Sustainable Development Goals A Contribution to the Post-2015 Development Debate* (2015).

[32] The International Co-operative Alliance defines a cooperative as an autonomous association of persons united voluntarily to meet their common economic, social, and cultural needs and aspirations through a jointly-owned and democratically-controlled enterprise.

[33] T. Mazzarol, *Co-operative Enterprise: A Discussion Paper and Literature Review* (2009), www.cemi.com.au/sites/all/publications/0901-COOPS-WA-LIT-REVIEW.pdf.

[34] The Platform Cooperativism Consortium supports the development of digital/platform cooperatives through research, documentation of best practices, and the coordination of funding. The Consortium is an international network dedicated to helping efforts such as this that aim to build sustainable cooperatives. *See* The Platform Cooperativism Consortium, Platform Co-op, https://platform.coop/about/consortium.

[35] O. Silvester-Bradley, *Introducing Open 2017 – What Are Platform Co-Ops?* openDemocracy (2016), www.opendemocracy.net/open2017/introducing-open-2017-platform-co-ops.

to benefit all and not just the few.[36] Such platforms would prevent concentration of power and hence abuse by those in charge. Instead, platforms would be run and managed by workers. This would give them greater powers and control over how they want to use platforms for their own benefit. If workers can use the same technologies, data, and algorithms to design, develop, and build their own apps and manage them, then we have a greater chance of workers being able to maintain fair working conditions. Today, the movement is growing and incorporates a range of cooperative platforms that include "alternative financing models, labor brokerages for nurses, massage therapists, and cleaners, cooperatively owned online marketplaces, and data-protection platforms for patients," just to name a few.[37]

Several platform cooperatives have emerged recently in different sectors with the aim of ensuring that workers rather than shareholders have a stake in them. Such platform cooperatives are aiming to disrupt the control of big corporations over modern technologies and the socio-economic systems of our times. For example, there are several taxi apps which are built, managed, and run by drivers who own the company and share the proceeds such as Cotabo (Bologna, Italy), ATX Co-op Taxi (Texas), Green Taxi Cooperative (Colorado), The People's Ride (Michigan), and Yellow Cab Cooperative (California). Several other similar initiatives include Stocksy, a stock photo website owned and curated by photographers, and Loconomics, a platform for freelance therapists, caregivers, and cleaners who keep 100 percent of fees.[38]

In the context of sharing economy activities like taxi rides, takeaway deliveries, etc., platform cooperatives have great potential. These types of work activity (which carry with them inherent stickiness, i.e., work that can only be performed in a particular location, such as a taxi ride) cannot be outsourced to distant locations or to other countries and thus are locally contingent. Since much of the sharing economy is mediated by digital technologies, and technology is socially constructed and embedded,[39] it is critical for such types of sharing economy technologies (apps or platforms) to be designed for their local contexts. A taxi app designed in and for Los Angeles, New York, or London drivers will have greater applicability in these cities but may not necessarily be suitable for other locations such as Lagos or Kenya. Drivers in each of these locations would know more about their respective areas and places of operation, for example, what areas to avoid in the city, busy traffic times, any local incidents, etc. Thus, there is a greater utility in workers' collaboration, communication, and sharing of information toward the locally specific designs and development of the platform or the app that would suit a particular location and demographic. In such sticky-work contexts, both the buyer and seller are geographically proximate, which also ensures that local regulatory laws can easily be applied in order to protect both parties.

Platform cooperatives can also help control intermediation in the sharing economy, whereby some workers are able to get more work than others and therefore subcontract it out. Cooperatives can potentially ensure that working hours are limited in such a way that fairer distribution of work takes places among its workers. For example, a worker should be entitled to do only a certain number of hours in a week. While the details of this need to be debated, we think this could be a starting point for dialogue to curb the very practice (intermediation) the sharing economy is thought to eliminate, but instead recreates.

While platform cooperatives represent an important way to reduce some of the risks among workers in the sharing economy by transferring power into their own hands, the movement is

---

[36] Scholz, *supra* note 1.
[37] Platform Co-op, https://platform.coop/about.
[38] *How Workers Can Profit by Taking Control of Technology*, Financ. Times, Apr. 16, 2017.
[39] Donald MacKenzie and Judy Wajcman, *The Social Shaping of Technology* (2nd edition, 1999).

still in its early stages and faces some challenges relating to awareness, funding, regulation of its activities, knowledge transfer, collaboration, etc.[40] However, there are other ways through which platform cooperatives in the sharing economy can be complemented. We argue that enhancing economic transparency in production networks is key to further address harmful and unethical work practices in the emergent sharing economy.

B *Economic Transparency in Digital Economy Value Chains*

Transnational corporations (TNCs)[41] make every effort to maintain opaque production networks in order to ensure efficiency of production, gain new markets, and maintain a competitive advantage.[42] As production has become more globalized, it has become far more difficult for consumers to find out about firms' production practices taking place in distant parts of the world, and therefore to be properly informed about their products. Consumers are often not aware of the production practices behind their sports shoes or mobile phones, for example.[43] Recent reports of corporate scandals such as violation of labor laws by Apple's factories and suppliers in China,[44] the Libor scandal,[45] and the onset of financial crises with the collapse of Lehman Brothers in 2008, for example, have made the issue of transparency in global production networks[46] even more prominent.[47]

One of the main challenges in the contemporary world economy is that while we can often trace the provenance of physical goods, it is much harder to trace the provenance of informational goods or services. Consumers, therefore, lack knowledge of the sites of production and distribution, and of the way digital goods are designed or produced. In other words, consumers often have less information about value chains or the production networks of digital products or services. Someone who uses a driverless car, for instance, likely has no idea that the artificial

---

[40] A. Bigot-Verdier, L. Dessein, and T. Doennebrink, *Platform Coops Looking for the Next Steps* (2017).

[41] P. Dicken, *Global Shift : Mapping the Changing Contours of the World Economy* (6th ed., 2011).

[42] J. H. Dunning and S. M. Lundan, *Multinational Enterprises and the Global Economy* (2008).

[43] Cook's (2004) article "Follow the things" uses a multi-site ethnographic method to analyze the papaya production network that stretches from Jamaica, Hawaii, and Brazil, to the US and the UK. It attempts to inform consumers about various people and processes involved in the production of papaya, and therefore encourage them to think about important moral and ethical questions around exploitation of labor. Encouraging ethical consumption practices can enhance human development outcomes, *see* D. Kleine, A. Light, and M-J. Montero, *Signifiers of the Life We Value?: Considering Human Development, Technologies and Fair Trade from the Perspective of the Capabilities Approach*, 18(1) Inf. Technol. Dev. 42–60 (2012).

[44] G. Chamberlain, *Apple Factories Accused of Exploiting Chinese Workers*, The Guardian, Apr. 30, 2011; "*Even Worse than Foxconn": Apple Rocked by Child Labour Claims*, The Independent (Jul. 30, 2013), www.independent.co.uk/life-style/gadgets-and-tech/even-worse-than-foxconn-apple-rocked-by-child-labour-claims-8736504.html.

[45] D. Keegan, *My Thwarted Attempt to Tell of Libor Shenanigans*, Financ. Times, July 26, 2012; *The Rotten Heart of Finance*, The Economist, July 7, 2012.

[46] The 2008 financial crisis exposed the secrecy and opacity with which financial markets (and financial products such as mortgages) and actors (big investment banks, for example) have been operating since the 1990s that led to the housing markets crash in the United States in 2008; *see* Y. Sato, *Opacity in Financial Markets*, 27 Rev. Financ. Stud. 3502–46 (2014), doi:10.1093/rfs/hhu047; N. M. Coe, M. Hess, H. W. Yeung, P. Dicken, and J. Henderson, *Globalizing Regional Development: A Global Production Networks Perspective*, 29 Trans. Inst. Br. Geogr. 468–84 (2004). Its effects reverberated around the world; *see* D. Harvey, *The Enigma of Capital and the Crises of Capitalism* (2011). Subsequently, both EU and US regulators instituted several reforms to regulate financial markets and increase transparency in financial flows. For a critical commentary on these reforms *see* E. Helleiner, *The Status Quo Crisis: Global Financial Governance After the 2008 Meltdown* (2014).

[47] Transparency is a multidimensional concept that cuts across various socioeconomic, political and corporate spheres. Loosely defined, transparency deals with the access to and availability of reliable/trustworthy information at the disposal of an agent to make an informed decision. However, the concept has been the subject of extensive debate. A useful collection of essays dealing with various theoretical aspects of transparency can be found in J. Forssbaeck and L. Oxelheim, *The Oxford Handbook of Economic and Institutional Transparency* (2014). Another relevant work is by C. Ball, *What Is Transparency?* 11 Public Integr. 293–308 (2009), doi:10.2753/PIN1099-9922110400.

intelligence powering the machine was trained by warehouses full of workers in Nairobi; each a low-paid worker, categorizing trees, people, cars, and roads in order to ultimately allow a machine to be able to make those distinctions for itself. A casual user of social media will likely not know that there are offices full of content reviewers in the Philippines who ensure that uploaded pictures do not breach platform guidelines (and who are thus constantly exposed to disturbing imagery). Even a person who calls an airline to change their ticket knows little about the lives of the workers they are speaking with.[48] In the context of the sharing economy, it is ever more important that transparent production practices are maintained by platform companies, who are often dependent upon flows of data and information from one node to another. This will enable consumers to make informed decisions by being more aware of the social, political, and environmental impacts of the available products, and more importantly about the labor conditions that went into the production of information-based products.[49]

There have been various movements designed to curb exploitative labor practices, by highlighting flows of goods and values across various production networks and using consumer power to encourage firms to refrain from poor labor practices in farms and factories. Most prominent among them is the Fairtrade movement, which is largely confined to primary-sector economic activities (tea, coffee, cocoa, soya, etc.).[50] But we could similarly imagine a "Fairwork" movement to ensure that the Googles, Facebooks, Upworks, and Ubers of the world are held accountable if poor working conditions or digital sweatshops enter into their own virtual production networks.[51]

IV ENVISIONING A "FAIR WORK" FOUNDATION

Guy Standing has argued the emergence of "the precariat," a new "class-in-the-making," who lack various forms of labor-related security, hold only temporary positions, earn a precarious income, receive few (or no) benefits or social protections, lack an "occupational identity," and live with a deep existential insecurity.[52] Our own research in Africa and Asia involving interviews with around two hundred digital workers from different platforms covering a wide range of work activities (including transcribers, editors, virtual assistants, customer service agents, web developers, writers, etc.) shows that many of these workers fit the definition of "the precariat"

---

[48] Working conditions inside call and contact centres have been repeatedly found to be a lot worse than generally understood. Some key works in this regard are P. Bain, A. Watson, G. Mulvey, P. Taylor, and G. Gall, *Taylorism, Targets and the Pursuit of Quantity and Quality by Call Centre Management*, 17 New Technol. Work Employ. 170–85 (2002), doi:10.1111/1468-005X.00103; T. Hastings and D. MacKinnon, *Re-embedding Agency at the Workplace Scale: Workers and Labour Control in Glasgow Call Centres*, 49 Environ. Plan. A 104–20 (2017); P. Taylor, and P. Bain, "An Assembly Line in the Head": *Work and Employee Relations in the Call Centre*, 30 Ind. Relat. J. 101–17 (1999), doi:10.1111/1468-2338.00113; J. Woodcock, *Working the Phone: Control and Resistance in Call Centres* (2016).

[49] M. Graham and H. Haarstad, *Transparency and Development: Ethical Consumption through Web 2.0 and the Internet of Things*, 7 Inf. Technol. Int. Dev. 1–18 (2011).

[50] Fairtrade refers to the Fairtrade movement, which includes networks of different organizations under Fairtrade Labelling Organizations International (FLO), such as International Resources for Fairer Trade (IRFT), European Fair Trade Association (EFTA), Network of European Worldshops (NEWS), etc. FLO develops, designs and reviews fair trade standards, and also incorporates issues relating to tariffs, subsidies, worker rights, etc. The term Fairtrade is used to describe the certification and labeling system governed by FLO to enable consumers to make informed choices about goods produced under agreed ethical labor and environmental standards. (*See* What is Fairtrade, www .fairtrade.net/about-fairtrade/what-is-fairtrade.html).

[51] M. Graham, *Digital Transformations of Work: Digital Work & the Global Precariat*, USI – Union Solidar. Int., Mar. 30, 2016; Graham, M. and Woodcock, J. 2018. *Towards a Fairer Platform Economy: Introducing the Fairwork Foundation*. Alternate Routes. 29. 242–253.

[52] G. Standing, *The Precariat: The New Dangerous Class* (trade paperback ed., 2014).

with few notable exceptions.[53] Such workers, therefore, increasingly need an effective way to improve their working conditions.

When we use a product, a service, or even an algorithm that was brought into being using digital labor, there is no way to know whether an exhausted worker is behind it; whether they will get laid off if they become sick or get pregnant; whether they are spending 20 hours a week just searching for work; how precarious their source of income is; or whether they are being paid an unfairly low wage.[54]

Digital gig work certainly can, and should, be regulated. However, many countries are reluctant to do so. Regulators in places like the Philippines or Kenya know that if they attempt to ensure that digital work is properly regulated (by, for instance, enforcing local minimum wages), it could flow out of those countries as quickly as it flowed in. Alternatively, digital gig work could theoretically be regulated in the home countries of clients (think of, for instance, German regulators insisting that German firms must ensure certain working conditions are met – no matter where workers are based). There is, however, little political appetite for such internationally minded regulation, when regulators in the Global North already struggle to protect their own citizens.[55]

While strategies built around platform cooperatives certainly hold promise, they are also held back by a few fundamental limitations. First is the lack of capital for setting up platforms that can compete with some of the dominant ones. With crowdfunding and some form of state support, this could potentially be addressed.[56] Second is the structural problem of the massive oversupply of labor power and the intense competition for jobs on most platforms, which undermines the potential of collective bargaining power. The very existence of a huge and global pool of digitally connected workers means that even if good wages are paid to some workers, there is little to stop that work from being re-outsourced. As ever more people from low-income countries come online, we should expect this large pool of workers (in the context of an existing oversupply of labor) to act as a magnet, pulling wages and working conditions downwards.

What else, then, can be done? We argue that these are fertile conditions for strategies that demand more transparency in the global supply chains of work. While consumers of products from companies like Starbucks and Cadbury have pressured those companies into ensuring that the entire chains of production are certified as Fairtrade, users of services from companies like Apple, Microsoft, Uber, Amazon, Samsung, Upwork, Facebook, Google, etc., have no similar way of persuading those firms to behave ethically. Users currently have no idea if the workers that help to create and maintain those services are treated fairly or paid living wages. In many cases, users may be unaware that there are actual human workers behind those services. But the fact that tracing production networks of digital services and products is a challenging task should not deter us from trying.

In much the same way that the Fairtrade Foundation highlights successes and makes lead firms concerned about unethical practices in their supply chains, a "Fairwork Foundation"

---

[53] *See, e.g.*, Graham et al., *supra* note 2; and Graham et al., *supra* note 22.

[54] The following text is taken from M. Graham and J. Shaw (eds.), *Towards a Fairer Gig Economy* (2017).

[55] However, the recent decision by the London transport regulators to ban Uber in London is a case in point where governments are stepping up their pressure to ensure platform firms like Uber are more accountable. The debate, on the logic of the Uber ban and what its consequences might be, is still going on. Another similar initiative is in Québec. *See* Ashifa Kassam, *Uber Threatens to Leave Quebec in Protest at New Rules for Drivers*, The Guardia, Sept. 26, 2017. www.theguardian.com/technology/2017/sep/26/uber-threatens-leave-quebec-drivers.

[56] There are some ongoing initiatives already in this regard. *See Co-ops Can Find Finance and Members Through Crowd-Funding Platform*, Co-op. News, July 30, 2013; D. Spitzberg, *How to Crowdfund a Platform Cooperative Like a Human*, Shareable (Apr. 5, 2016), www.shareable.net/blog/how-to-crowdfund-a-platform-cooperative-like-a-human.

could have similar impacts in the realm of digital work. The specific forms that such a foundation could take is open to debate.[57] At a minimum, it would monitor and certify chains of digital work: ensuring that key standards such as fair wages and protection against non-payment are met.

Our clicks ultimately tie us to the lives and livelihoods of digital laborers in Manila or Mumbai as much as buying shoes might tie us to a Vietnamese sweatshop or buying chocolate to a Ghanaian farmer. It is therefore no longer good enough to imagine that there is nothing beyond the screen. Every click we make, every search we perform, and every photo we like reverberates around the world. We are enmeshed in complex and invisible networks of work. And with that realization comes the power to collectively make a difference. We can demand more. We can insist that everyone that we indirectly interact with in these chains of work is treated fairly and with dignity. Our actions matter; and our actions, no matter where we are and what we do, can help bring into being a fairer world of work.[58]

---

[57] Some ideas are outlined in more detail at http://fair.work and in Graham and Woodcock, *supra* note 51.

[58] The authors would like thank Alex Wood and Kat Braybrooke for their feedback on earlier drafts. This research was supported by the European Research Council under the European Union's Seventh Framework Programme for Research and Technological Development (FP/2007–2013) [ERC Grant Agreement n. 335716].

Tax Law

25

Tax Issues in the Sharing Economy

Implications for Workers

Shu-Yi Oei and Diane M. Ring

INTRODUCTION

The past several years have seen the rise of what is commonly referred to as the "sharing economy." The term generally refers to the production or distribution of goods and services by individuals through a technological platform or "app."[1] The platform seamlessly puts service providers and producers in touch with consumers of goods and services, allowing individuals to easily monetize their assets or services, often (though not invariably) by exploiting excess capacity. The types of activity done through sharing platforms vary, but common examples include renting property via platforms such as Airbnb, driving for Transportation Network Companies (TNCs) such as Uber or Lyft, performing tasks through TaskRabbit or Rover, or selling goods through a website like Etsy. While the magnitude and growth of work done on these platforms in the US economy are hard to quantify, there is some indication that it is significant. A recent Brookings study found – based on data on "nonemployer" firms in US census data – that such firms encompassed 24 million businesses in 2014, up from 15 million in 1997 and 22 million in 2007.[2] Moreover, such businesses are not limited to the US market. Many of the platforms that launched initially in the United States have expanded to other countries, and homegrown platforms have emerged in many foreign jurisdictions.

Regardless of specific numbers, what is clear is that a growing number of individuals now perform work in the sharing economy. This increase raises a number of tax and regulatory questions, including questions about the impact of sharing economy work on workers and service providers operating in this sector. One important set of questions confronting workers concerns how they are taxed, whether the tax system functions effectively with respect to this work, and relatedly, how such workers confront and ought to deal with tax compliance challenges.

---

[1]   The sector is also sometimes referred to as the "gig economy," "platform economy," or "peer-to-peer economy." *See, e.g.*, Elka Torpey and Andrew Hogan, *Working in a Gig Economy*, U.S. Department of Labor, Bureau of Labor Statistics (May 2016), www.bls.gov/careeroutlook/2016/article/what-is-the-gig-economy.htm; Shu-Yi Oei, *The Trouble with Gig Talk: Ambiguity, Choice of Narrative, and the Abetting Function of Law*, 81 Law & Contemp. Probs. 107 (2018). In this chapter, we use the term "sharing economy" to refer to the sector.

[2]   Ian Hathaway and Mark Muro, *Tracking the Gig Economy: New Numbers*, Brookings Institution (Oct. 13, 2016), www.brookings.edu/research/tracking-the-gig-economy-new-numbers/. "Nonemployer" firms are firms with at least $1,000 of gross revenues but no employees. About 86 percent of nonemployer firms are sole proprietor independent contractors. *Id.* at note 5. The authors note that not all of the growth in nonemployer firms is due to sharing economy work; it also reflects the increased use of various investment vehicles. *Id.*

In this chapter, we survey some of the key tax issues that have confronted individuals operating in the sharing economy. While our discussion focuses on the United States, these classification, documentation, and compliance challenges frequently arise in other countries. Many of the tax implications of this work stem from the threshold decision by many platforms to classify such individuals as independent contractors rather than employees. Therefore, we first discuss how the threshold classification decision affects the substantive and compliance-related tax issues faced by individuals operating in the sharing economy. We briefly summarize the doctrinal tax rules governing income taxation of sharing economy workers, discussing both the rules for income inclusion and the rules for expense tracking and taking. We then discuss some of the compliance challenges experienced by sharing economy participants in fulfilling their tax obligations, including the need to allocate expenses between business and personal use, the need to file estimated taxes, liability for self-employment taxes, and the need to track income given imperfect information reporting. The chapter then examines tax-related factors (such as lack of withholding) that may affect the labor-supply decisions of sharing economy participants. For example, we examine the potential impacts of lack of withholding and of expense estimation difficulties on how these individuals calculate their likely profit or loss from engaging in such work. Finally, we discuss possible reforms to the taxation of sharing economy participation that may help alleviate compliance challenges associated with work in this sector or may help these individuals make more informed decisions, and we explore the downsides of such reforms.

Throughout our discussion, we draw upon our previous empirical and doctrinal work concerning participants in the sharing economy as well as on the scholarship of others.[3]

This chapter focuses on tax law, but legal analysis of the sharing economy cannot be conducted exclusively on a field-by-field basis. Assessments and recommendations derived in one legal context can intentionally or unintentionally impact outcomes in other areas. This observation especially holds where the same issue, such as worker classification, arises across legal regimes. Thus, for example, a policy recommendation on workers' classification for tax purposes may find its impact extends beyond taxation to influence classification of sharing workers in other legal regimes such as labor or tort law.[4] Just because a rule may produce an appropriate outcome in the tax system does not mean that the rule similarly generates favorable policy results in other cases. As a result, some measure of caution is warranted in undertaking a predominantly field-specific analysis; the actual implementation of policy can have a more expansive effect.

---

[3] *See, e.g.,* Shu-Yi Oei and Diane M. Ring, *Can Sharing Be Taxed?*, 93 Wash. U. L. Rev. 989 (2016) [hereinafter *Can Sharing be Taxed?*]; Shu-Yi Oei and Diane M. Ring, *The Tax Lives of Uber Drivers: Evidence from Internet Discussion Forums*, 8 Colum. J. Tax L. 56 (2017) [hereinafter *The Tax Lives of Uber Drivers*]; Michèle Finck and Sofia Ranchordás, *Sharing and the City*, 49 Vand. J. Transnat'l L. 1299 (2017); Kathleen DeLaney Thomas, *Taxing the Gig Economy*, U. Pa. L. Rev. (forthcoming, 2018), https://papers.ssrn.com/sol3/papers.cfm?abstract_id=2894394; Jordan M. Barry and Paul L. Caron, *Tax Regulation, Transportation Innovation, and the Sharing Economy*, 81 Chi. L. Rev. Dialogue 69 (2015); Jordan Barry, this volume; Caroline Bruckner, Shortchanged: The Tax Compliance Challenges of Small Business Operators Driving the On-Demand Platform Economy, Kogod Tax Policy Center (May 2016), https://perma.cc/Z9J4-M49G; Miriam A. Cherry and Antonio Aloisi, this volume; Manoj Viswanathan, this volume.

[4] For example, recently proposed legislation in the Senate that purports to "clarify" the correctness of independent contractor classification of gig workers for tax purposes is likely to cement independent contractor treatment in other areas of law by endowing such classification with a default presumption of correctness. *See The New Economy Works to Guarantee Independence and Growth* (NEW GIG) *Act of 2017*, 115th Congress, 1st Session (S. 1549), www.thune .senate.gov/public/_cache/files/c9e8dda1-dbb6-4a78-8f2a-88f39c14be1e/D975731B1FE56963DD1D09F2CB8D78 CC.ott17387.pdf (proposed by Sen. John Thune, R-S.D.).

I THE THRESHOLD QUESTION OF WORKER CLASSIFICATION

The tax consequences to a sharing economy worker depend in the first instance on whether that individual is classified as an independent contractor or an employee for tax purposes.[5] The worker classification question is significant for a number of different legal areas, including state and federal labor protections.[6] Indeed, though the nuances may differ, the worker classification question has arisen in jurisdictions other than the United States and many of the basic tensions, concerns, and tradeoffs will resonate with other countries.

Resolution of the worker classification question depends on the specific legal regime and the classification test it employs.[7] Additionally, worker classification may differ from platform to platform, depending on the precise relationship between worker and platform. It is also theoretically possible that two different workers operating on the same platform might be appropriately placed in different classifications, depending on their job parameters. Classification may be more material to TNC drivers and those performing services and tasks (e.g., on TaskRabbit) than to other sharing economy participants (such as those offering property for rent on Airbnb). In short, the worker classification question is variable and complex. We summarize some of the main points, as they relate to tax, here.

If the worker is classified as an independent contractor for tax purposes, the US tax law effectively treats her as operating an independent small business as a sole proprietor. As a small business operator, she will therefore be responsible for paying self-employment taxes (social security and Medicare taxes) at a 15.3 percent rate by filing Schedule SE, but can deduct half these taxes on Form 1040, Line 27.[8] This contrasts with the tax treatment of employees: if a worker is classified as an employee, the employer will be responsible for depositing and reporting payroll taxes, and the employer is nominally responsible for half the social security and Medicare taxes.[9] Thus, the employer must not only withhold the employee's share of social security and Medicare taxes from employee wages but is also further responsible for paying an employer matching portion.[10] In theory, the same amount of employment tax would be paid to the government on behalf of a worker, and the worker would net the same after tax in either scenario (employee or independent contractor). This comparison anticipates that in shifting from employee status to independent contractor status, for example, the worker would be able to negotiate a pay increase equal to the amount of tax previously borne by the employer and now owed by the independent contractor (and deductible by that taxpayer in the process of calculating taxable income). Of course, it is possible that the economic incidence may fall on the worker in the form of lower wages.[11]

There are four further key differences between the tax treatment of employees and independent contractors. First, wages paid to employees are subject to income tax withholding by the platform-payor but amounts paid to independent contractors are not withheld but are merely subject to information reporting on Forms 1099, as described below. This means that

---

[5] There are labor law and other consequences as well to the worker's classification but this chapter will focus on tax.

[6] *See, e.g.,* V. B. Dubal, *Wage Slave or Entrepreneur?: Contesting the Dualism of Legal Worker Identities,* 105 Cal. L. Rev. 101 (2017); Benjamin Means and Joseph Seiner, *Navigating the Uber Economy,* 49 U.C. Davis L. Rev. 1511 (2016). These issues are discussed in more depth elsewhere in this volume. *See, e.g.,* Elizabeth Tippett; Brishen Rogers.

[7] *See, e.g.,* Shu-Yi Oei, *supra* note 1.

[8] I.R.C. § 1401(a), (b); I.R.C. § 164(f)(1); *Can Sharing be Taxed?, supra* note 3, at 1019–20.

[9] I.R.S. Publ'n No. 15 (*Circular E*), *Employer's Tax Guide* (2018).

[10] *Id.*

[11] *See, e.g.,* N. Gregory Mankiw, *Principles of Macroeconomics* 124 (8th ed., 2015).

those operating as independent contractors might need to file and pay estimated taxes on a quarterly basis in order to make up for the lack of withholding, and may be subject to underpayment penalties if they fail to do so.[12] Second, the federal income tax deductions available to employees are more severely restricted than those available to independent contractors. Unreimbursed expenses of employees are classified as "below the line deductions," and their deductibility is subject to limitation based on the employee's adjusted gross income.[13] Third, businesses that hire employees must pay federal unemployment insurance tax (FUTA tax). Independent contractors do not pay this tax and cannot seek unemployment benefits.[14]

Finally, in December 2017, a new provision was enacted, Section 199A, that grants a deduction of up to 20 percent of "qualified business income" to passthrough businesses (i.e. not corporations and not employees). Policy makers, taxpayers, and tax advisers are just beginning to assess the potential impact of this new deduction. With respect to sharing economy workers, it is possible that this new deduction may make independent contractor classification attractive or at least more palatable for some workers depending on their overall work and benefits situation.

There are a number of different, but related, tests for determining appropriate worker classification, depending on the legal context.[15] For tax purposes, the IRS has developed a 20-factor test for distinguishing independent contractors from employees.[16] The factors examined include behavioral control (i.e., whether the company controls what work the worker does and how she does the work) and financial control (i.e., whether the company controls the business aspects of the job, such as what tools are used and how the worker is paid) as well as the type of relationship between the company and the worker (e.g., whether there are pensions, vacations, or insurance).[17] In general, a worker will be classified as an independent contractor if the paying platform has the right to control and direct only the *result* of the work and not what and how it will be done.

As of this writing, key class action lawsuits have been brought by Uber and Lyft drivers, many of which remain unresolved.[18] Plaintiffs have confronted significant litigation risks, most pertinently the effects of binding arbitration clauses that require disputes to be settled before arbitration tribunals rather than as class actions.[19] In the meantime, many sharing economy firms have persisted in classifying their workers as independent contractors for tax and other purposes, issuing them yearly IRS Forms 1099 at tax time. As one of us has argued, the tax position taken by

---

[12] *See* I.R.C. § 6654(a), (d); *see also Tax Withholding and Estimated Tax*, I.R.S. Publ'n No. 505 (2018). According to the IRS Publication 505, taxpayers generally must pay estimated taxes for 2018 if they (1) "expect to owe at least $1,000 in tax for 2018" and (2) expect their withholding and refundable credits to be less than the smaller of "90% of the tax to be shown" on the 2018 return or "100% of the tax shown on" the 2017 tax return. *Id.* at 22.

[13] I.R.C. § 62(a)(2).

[14] *See* I.R.C. § 3301–3311.

[15] Tests applied include the common law agency test, the economic realities test, and the so-called ABC test applied by states. *See, e.g.*, Robert L. Redfearn III, *Sharing Economy Misclassification: Employees and Independent Contractors in Transportation Network Companies*, 31 Berkeley Tech. L.J. 1023 (2016); Brishen Rogers, *Employment Rights in the Platform Economy: Getting Back to Basics*, 10 Harv. L. & Pol'y Rev. 480, 487 n. 48 (2016).

[16] *See, e.g.*, Schramm v. Comm'r, 102 T.C.M. (CCH) 223 (2011); Levine v. Comm'r, T.C.M. (RIA) 2005–86 (2005); Rev. Rul. 87–41, 1987–1 C.B. 296.

[17] *Independent Contractor (Self-Employed) or Employee?*, IRS, www.irs.gov/businesses/small-businesses-self-employed/independent-contractor-self-employed-or-employee (last updated Apr. 18, 2017).

[18] *See, e.g.*, Yucesoy v. Uber Techs., Inc., No. C-15–0262 EMC, 2015 U.S. Dist. LEXIS 98515 (N.D. Cal. July 28, 2015); O'Connor v. Uber Techs., Inc., No. C-13–3826 EMC, 2015 U.S. Dist. LEXIS 116482 (N.D. Cal. Sept. 1, 2015); Del Rio v. Uber Techs., Inc., No. 15-cv-03667-EMC, 2016 U.S. Dist. LEXIS 40615 (N.D. Cal. Mar. 28, 2016); Lavitman v. Uber Techs., Inc., 32 Mass. L. Rep. 476 (2015); Cotter v. Lyft, Inc., No. 13-cv-04065-VC, 2017 U.S. Dist. LEXIS 38256 (N.D. Cal. Mar. 16, 2017) (final settlement approved); Mohamed v. Uber Technologies, Inc., 848 F.3d 1201 (9th Cir. 2016) (upholding Uber arbitration clause).

[19] On November 21, 2016, in light of a 9th Circuit decision holding that the arbitration clauses entered into by drivers were enforceable, the California District Court stayed five related litigations pending appeals. *O'Conner* v. *Uber* and related cases, *Order re Stays*, No. 3:13-cv-03826-EMC, Docket No. 769 (N.D. Cal. Nov. 21, 2016).

the sharing economy firms is clearly chosen in order to be consistent – and indeed to advance – the desired independent contractor treatment of workers in other legal areas.[20] In light of this choice by the sharing economy firms, the remainder of this discussion discusses the tax law and compliance implications that arise should sharing economy workers continue to be classified as independent contractors for tax purposes.

II THE TAX LAW OF THE SHARING ECONOMY

We have argued in prior scholarship that the doctrinal tax issues concerning taxation of the sharing economy are relatively uncontroversial. However, the law itself may be quite complex. And that complexity may pose tax compliance challenges for sharing economy participants.[21]

A Income Inclusions

The substantive income tax laws that apply to sharing economy participants are not unlike those that apply to other unincorporated sole proprietors independently operating a small business. These individuals must include amounts earned (such as gross fares, rents, and other payments) in their gross income for tax purposes.[22] They must also include in gross income any other payments received from the platform, such as driver referral bonuses in the case of TNCs, as well as tips. These receipts are includible in income for tax purposes, whether or not the worker actually receives a Form 1099 statement from the platform.

Most sharing economy participants will report income received from work performed (and deduct expenses) on Schedule C of Form 1040, Profit or Loss from Business. (In this regard, some sharing economy participants may be surprised to discover that they must file taxes just like any other individual small business entrepreneur.)[23] Those who rent out homes or apartments on a platform such as Airbnb will usually report rental income on Schedule E, Supplemental Income and Loss from real estate and other sources, or Schedule C.[24]

B Deductible Expenses

While income receipts must be included in federal gross income, workers may deduct allowable business expenses on their tax return. The key issue that is likely to arise for those operating in the sharing economy is the need to apportion expenses between business and personal use. This is because the paradigmatic sharing economy operator is likely to operate part time and on more than one platform, and thus is likely to have property – such as a car, a home, or tools – that may be used sometimes for business purposes and sometimes for personal purposes. Business-related expenses are tax deductible but personal use expenses are not.[25]

The precise rules for allocating costs between business and personal use differ depending on the context – for example, specific cost recovery rules may apply to TNC drivers driving miles

---

[20] Oei, *supra* note 1.
[21] *Can Sharing be Taxed?, supra* note 3.
[22] I.R.C. § 61.
[23] *The Tax Lives of Uber Drivers, supra* note 3, at 89–90.
[24] It is possible that the IRS may assert that some Airbnb hosts are also providing services (e.g., breakfast) and thus are subject to employment taxes. *See, e.g., 10 Tax Tips for Airbnb, HomeAway & VRBO Vacation Rentals*, Turbotax, https://turbotax.intuit.com/tax-tools/tax-tips/Self-Employment-Taxes/10-Tax-Tips-for-Airbnb--HomeAway---VRBO-Vacation-Rentals/INF29184.html (updated for tax year 2016) (raising the possibility that hosts would owe employment taxes); Aimee Picchi, *Tax Tips if You Made Money Through Airbnb*, Consumer Reports (Mar. 8, 2016) (same), www.consumerreports.org/taxes/tax-tips-if-you-made-money-through-airbnb/.
[25] I.R.C. §§ 162, 262.

for work, landlords renting out property on Airbnb that is also subject to frequent personal use, or other types of sharing economy work.

1 TNC Drivers

Those driving for TNCs may recover costs for miles driven for work. In determining how to recover such costs, TNC drivers may choose between using the actual costs method or the standard mileage method.[26] The actual costs method allows the driver to deduct the actual expenses incurred in driving for a platform. Covered expenses include: vehicle depreciation, garage rent, gas, insurance, lease payments, licensing fees, oil, parking fees, registration, repairs, tires, and tolls. If there is both business and personal use of the vehicle, then the driver must allocate these expenses between the business and personal use. This may be done based on miles driven, such that only the portion of expenses associated with work-related miles may be deducted.[27] The driver is therefore required to track the number of miles driven and to document the miles that relate to driving for a TNC.

Alternatively, the standard mileage method allows the driver to deduct a certain amount per mile driven – that rate was 54.5 cents per mile for 2018.[28] Drivers who use this method must also keep track of the miles driven for the TNC. A driver who chooses the standard mileage rate may not deduct actual expenses relating to the car (such as car lease payments, maintenance, repairs, and gasoline). However, that driver may deduct non-automobile costs (e.g., water or candy bars provided to passengers) incurred in providing the transportation service.

The important point, with respect to tax compliance, is that whether the driver uses the standard mileage rate or the actual costs method, the driver must keep track of miles driven in order to properly allocate expenses between business (deductible) and personal (non-deductible) uses. The need to accurately track business and personal expenses may raise compliance costs for those driving on TNC platforms.

2 Home-sharing

The home-sharing context presents a different but related set of issues from the TNC industry. Here, the potential application of Section 280A of the Internal Revenue Code is the primary focus for taxpayers. Section 280A limits the deductions allowable with respect to property used in part for personal use and in part for business use. If there is no personal use of the property – such as would be the case with respect to a property rented full time – then Section 280A would not apply. The sharing economy context (which often implicates excess-capacity business use of personal assets) raises the likelihood that the property being rented is of mixed use.

The Section 280A rules are complex, and are only briefly summarized here. First, as a threshold matter, a taxpayer may be able to avoid the application of Section 280A if the portion of the unit being rented qualifies as a hotel, motel, or similar establishment – even though this unit is in the taxpayer's home.[29] This exception seeks to allow taxpayers who are renting a portion of their home on a regular basis to paying customers (and who do not personally use that portion of the unit), to avoid the otherwise applicable Section 280A limits on rental expense

---

[26] *See* Treas. Reg. §1.274–5(j)(2) (2000); I.R.S. Notice 2014–79, 2014–53, I.R.B. 1001, § 3; I.R.S. News Release IR-2014–114 (Dec. 10, 2014).

[27] *See Travel, Entertainment, Gift, and Car Expenses*, I.R.S. Publ'n No. 463, 16–17 (2018).

[28] *Id.* at 16; I.R.S. News Release IR-2017–204 (Dec. 14, 2017). There are some circumstances under which the standard mileage rate cannot be used.

[29] I.R.C. § 280A(f)(1)(B).

deductions.[30] However, it seems unlikely that many properties rented through sharing economy platforms would qualify for this hotel exception.

If the taxpayer rents a dwelling unit (e.g., a house, apartment, condominium unit, mobile home, boat, etc.) and uses the property personally, but *not* as his or her "residence," then under Section 280A the taxpayer can take deductions based on the number of days rented compared to total number of days used.[31] This outcome is generally preferable to the more restrictive Section 280A deduction rules (described below) that apply to rental of units that qualify as a "residence" of the taxpayer.[32] Personal use will rise to the level of a residence if the use is for: (1) more than 14 days; or (2) 10 percent of the number of days for which the unit is rented at fair value.[33] Thus, for example, if a taxpayer owns a condominium and rents it out most of the year, but personally uses it for only five days during the year, then that use does not rise to the level of a residence, and the taxpayer should be entitled to deduct expenses under this more taxpayer-friendly rule.

If, however, the taxpayer rents a property that he or she uses in a manner that does rise to the level of a "residence," then the tax consequences depend on the number of days the property is rented. If the property is rented out for fewer than 15 days, then income need not be reported and deductions correspondingly may not be taken on the rental activity.[34] If the property is rented for 15 days or more, then the taxpayers may only take deductions based on a statutory allocation formula that is more limiting than that used for the rental of units not qualifying as a residence (but for which there has been some personal use).[35]

In short, the Section 280A rules for allocation of rental deductions are complex, and are more so in situations in which the property rented is a dwelling unit that is used as a residence. Evolving local regulation governing rental of properties on platforms such as Airbnb may increase the likelihood that taxpayers will be taxed under the Section 280A rules for rental of residences. For example, as local jurisdictions impose limits on the number of days a property may be rented on platforms such as Airbnb, the result may be more hosts renting property deemed "residential," who are then subject to the most restrictive and confusing Section 280A rules for deducting rental expenses.

3 *Other Sharing Economy Work*

Sharing economy work is not limited to home rentals and driving for TNCs. There is now an extensive array of online platforms that enable the provision of a wide variety of goods and services. Examples range from TaskRabbit[36] (assorted services) to Rover[37] (petsitting) to Fon (wifi).[38] In all of these contexts, microbusiness operators who earn income and incur related expenses must keep track of their expenses and must pay particular attention to how to distinguish between personal expenses (which are generally not deductible) and those incurred for business (which are generally deductible). To the extent that the sharing economy business model involves use of the taxpayer's home or vehicle in the provision of services, the specific rules discussed above may

---

[30] Taxpayers renting a dwelling unit (defined to include basic living accommodations such as "sleeping space, a toilet, and cooking facilities") are not covered by the hotel exception, which envisions rental of a room in the home "that is always available for short-term paying customers." *Residential Rental Property*, IRS Publ'n No. 527, 17 (2018).

[31] I.R.C. § 280A(d)(1).

[32] I.R.C. § 280A(e)(1).

[33] I.R.C. § 280A(d)(1).

[34] I.R.C. §§ 280A(c)(5), (g).

[35] I.R.C. §§ 280A(c)(5), (e)(1).

[36] www.taskrabbit.com/.

[37] www.rover.com.

[38] https://network.fon.com/.

apply. More generally, where sharing economy participants employ otherwise personal assets in the performance of platform work, the mixed character of the asset use increases the complexity of the tax analysis and correspondingly increases the compliance burden on the taxpayer.

III COMPLIANCE AND CLASSIFICATION CHALLENGES IN THE SHARING ECONOMY

As Section II demonstrates, the fundamental substantive questions of how to tax income and allow expenses from sharing economy work are generally answered by existing law. On balance, existing tax rules that apply to all trades or businesses adequately describe the taxable income and expenses of sharing economy participants. But that conclusion does not mean that the existing tax regime is simple, intuitive, or streamlined for these workers. Rather, it is likely that workers will face documentation burdens, unexpected requirements, and some confusion. In response to these problems, a number of tax reforms have been recommended, both by us and by others, to tackle the more pressing tax challenges facing sharing economy workers. This section first explores tax compliance realities that confront workers. It then considers the viability of various tax reforms and the degree to which they would solve the problems identified.

A Tax Compliance Realities for Sharing Economy Workers

To the extent sharing economy workers are classified as independent contractors (the position adopted by most platforms), they will face both documentation burdens and compliance obligations that may be entirely unfamiliar. Effectively, the tax system considers such workers to be "in business" and, as such, they are responsible for their own employment taxes, and perhaps more unexpectedly, for their own quarterly payment of estimated taxes.[39]

1 Understanding Form 1099-K

The two key items that workers must report from their sharing work are their income items and their expenses. Income is generally not difficult to determine in the abstract, but in some cases confusion over the income amount has arisen due to the documentation issued by the platform. Sharing businesses generally send a Form 1099-K to workers listing their income.[40] However, our research on TNC drivers suggests that some workers may misunderstand the numbers being reported. The Form 1099-K reported the *gross* amount generated by the worker. In the case of Uber drivers, this includes the basic fare charged to the passenger, the "safe rides" fee also charged by Uber to passengers, and the fees and commissions that Uber charges to the driver.[41] In the case of Lyft, the gross income amount on Form 1099-K includes the Lyft commission and tolls, but not certain other service fees, third-party fees, and taxes.[42] Workers are permitted to deduct the latter two amounts (the safe rides fee and Uber's cut), as these amounts are actually retained by Uber not the driver. However, there is some risk that some drivers might not understand that the Form 1099-K income number reflects the gross amount they received from Uber (inclusive of Uber's cut) and might thus fail to deduct the safe rides fee and Uber's commission before reporting their taxable income.[43] Although some drivers have sought to educate others

---

[39] *See supra* notes 8, 12 and accompanying text.
[40] For a detailed discussion of the different Forms 1099 that might apply and the issues and gaps created under current law, *see Can Sharing Be Taxed?, supra* note 3, at 1034–41.
[41] *See, e.g., How to Use your Uber 1099-K and 1099-Misc*, Stride, https://perma.cc/LGA8-JZ4U; *Uber Partner Reporting Guide*, H&R Block, https://perma.cc/6YE4-475Z.
[42] *See 2016 Tax Info for Drivers*, Lyft, https://perma.cc/BU7R-F5GM.
[43] *See The Tax Lives of Uber Drivers, supra* note 3, at 86–87.

on the correct reading of the Form 1099-K in various internet forums, the extent to which this continues to be a problem in the TNC sector and the degree to which the problem arises with other platforms and their workers remains unclear.

2 Expenses: Tracking and Documentation

A second compliance challenge concerns deductibility of expenses. Sharing economy participants whose work requires them either to use valuable personal assets in the performance of the task or to spend their own money in the performance of their services will want to deduct these costs. Beyond learning the substantive tax law detailing which expenses are deductible and how they are calculated, workers must: (1) calculate the quantity of business use versus personal use (which may involve making legal determinations regarding what counts as business use); (2) document that use; and (3) maintain records of their expenditures.

Thus, for example, TNC drivers must determine how many miles driven are for personal use, and how many are for business. This demands at the outset a legal conclusion as to what driving counts for business. The answer is easy when passengers are in the car, but is less clear when drivers are driving from home to their main pick-up location without a passenger, driving home without a passenger but with the TNC App on (evidencing willingness to pick up a fare), or running personal errands in between rides. In addition, once the threshold legal determination is made, TNC drivers must undertake the administrative task of keeping track of business versus personal miles driven. This is by no means a trivial task, given that platforms such as Uber only record miles driven with passengers in the vehicle, and do not include other miles that may potentially count as business miles, such as miles driven with the App on while looking for passengers but without an actual passenger in the car. Thus, the mileage total obtained from the TNC company understates business mileage for tax purposes, and drivers must do their own recording and documentation. In order to do this effectively, drivers have experimented with phone applications and with various electronic ledgers that help track and record mileage, but there is some uncertainty as to what types of documentation the IRS will deem acceptable.[44] Our research suggests that some drivers may not have been aware at the outset of the importance of recording mileage, or may have failed to appreciate that expense tracking and documentation is required (and that rough estimates are not acceptable).

3 Estimated and Quarterly Tax Payments

Sharing economy participants who are new to independent contractor status may also fail to realize that they likely have an obligation to file and pay estimated taxes during the year, and that their tax burden includes all components of the employment taxes. Briefly, quarterly estimated tax payments are required for taxpayers for whom amounts withheld and paid to the IRS throughout the year will be insufficient when compared with the eventual assessed tax liability.[45] Insufficient withholding becomes a possibility where the worker is self-employed and hence not subject to employer withholding – as is the case for most sharing economy workers. Although some workers may be able to avoid estimated tax filing burdens and liabilities by increasing withholding from W-2 jobs, others will not be able to avoid these obligations.

Sharing economy participants who are subject to estimated tax obligations must not only undertake the administrative burden of accurately computing and paying over such taxes. They must also make decisions about how much to set aside to meet estimated tax obligations. If they fail to meet

---

[44] *Id.* at 84–86.
[45] *See, supra* note 12; *see also Estimated Taxes*, IRS, www.irs.gov/businesses/small-businesses-self-employed/estimated-taxes (last updated Apr. 26, 2018).

estimated tax obligations, they will have to pay interest and penalties due to their failure to file. These administrative and substantive obligations may result in consumption shocks to taxpayers who may not be financially savvy enough to appropriately allocate funds and manage finances.

4 Tax Law's Impact on Labor Supply Choices of Sharing Economy Workers

Beyond compliance burdens, the structure and administration of the tax system can impact the labor decisions of sharing economy workers. Some of these impacts may result from misinformation or lack of clarity, which may raise troubling questions.

First, and perhaps most importantly, workers may experience an effect known as "spotlighting." This term captures circumstances in which workers do not accurately know the costs of undertaking sharing economy work, and therefore overestimate the net benefits of such work and risk oversupplying labor. Taxation of sharing economy work may potentially cause spotlighting on payments received from the platform for sharing economy work. For example, a TNC driver may receive these payments well in advance of having to take into account the expenses (including vehicle wear and tear) from driving and the taxes owed, which may cause her to overestimate the return on her labor. Taxation may exacerbate these effects, because tax filing (aside from estimated taxes) occurs on an annual basis, after the fact.

Another possibility is that workers may focus on average tax rates rather than marginal tax rates when deciding how much to work in the sharing economy. This may occur, for instance, where workers "just guesstimate" what their year-end tax liability is likely to be. "Guesstimating" may be a particular risk when the worker faces multiple tax rate schedules – for example, state and federal taxes – and may be compounded where the worker has more than one job, or does sharing economy work on top of a regular job. Such workers may not have a clear idea of what their eventual income bracket (and hence tax liability) is likely to be, and this may cause them to supply labor at a higher than optimal level.

In short, taxation is distortionary, and one possible margin of distortion regards how much workers decide to work. Due to the realities of the annual tax year, the lack of withholding on amounts paid to Form 1099-K workers, and the fragmented nature of work in the sharing economy, workers may be particularly likely to experience challenges in determining how much they are making and how much they should work.

The overall burden for sharing economy workers of learning to read a Form 1099-K, learning the substantive tax law governing deductions, allocating expenses between business and personal use, tracking and documenting business use and actual expenses, and managing quarterly estimated tax filings can seem significant. This assessment may be particularly true for those workers who are not familiar with taxation of small businesses (e.g., first-time independent contractors), who are pursuing sharing economy work on a part-time or short-term basis, or who earn relatively little compared to the costs of compliance (including securing competent tax return advice).

B Is Employee Classification a Tax Solution?

Is the significant administrative and compliance burden on sharing economy "micro-entrepreneurs" a problem that warrants legal reform? On the one hand, these tax compliance obligations are not new and have long been in place for self-employed individuals engaged in trade or business. Thus, it would seem that any suggestion that reform is needed ought to take into account burdens of the tax compliance regime on sole proprietors generally, not just sharing economy workers. On the other hand, there is a non-trivial risk that even if these tax compliance burdens are not excessive for self-employed individuals engaged in more traditional businesses, these burdens may not scale down appropriately for "microbusiness" individuals – that is, individuals engaged in business on a very small scale, for whom compliance burdens may outstrip any benefit to be gained from occasional platform work.

One possible way in which compliance burdens on sharing economy workers might be mitigated is if workers were classified as employees rather than independent contractors. Employee classification would result in sharing economy workers receiving Form W-2 instead of Form 1099-K, and would at least alleviate the compliance burdens associated with having to file quarterly estimated taxes and social security taxes. Employee status for sharing economy workers has been advocated by various actors, both as a conclusion of fact under existing law, and as a normatively desirable legal policy. However, the primary driver for such advocacy has been labor law and related worker protection issues, not tax law.

Yet, even if employee classification might yield labor law and worker protection benefits, it is not clear that such classification would uniformly yield positive impacts for workers with respect to tax. Three distinct points highlight the tax risks of classification as an employee.

First, documentation and compliance burdens might remain high. Take, for example, TNC drivers: assuming that after being classified as employees, drivers continued to conduct their operations as before – continuing to use their personal vehicle for driving and to incur passenger-related costs (such as insurance, water, etc.) – these taxpayers would still need to determine the business–personal split of their miles driven, appropriately record their miles, determine which costs are deductible and how, and maintain proper documentation of the outlays for which a deduction would be sought. This is the case for two reasons. First, if the employee would like to take a tax deduction for unreimbursed employee expenses, these documentation and compliance requirements remain. Second, the documentation and tracking burdens also exist if the worker is seeking reimbursement from her employer (for example, if the employer is required to bear worker expenses under certain state laws).[46] To be sure, some burdens would be lifted, in particular the obligation to file quarterly and ensuring that appropriate taxes had been paid during the course of the year, as this task would be taken on by the employer, the ride-sharing company. It is also possible that some of the salience-related effects on labor supply decisions may be improved.

Second, and related to the first point, the shift to employee status alone, without any corresponding change in the fundamental business model of TNC platforms, would mean that drivers would continue to bear significant work-related costs.[47] Not only would the tax burdens related to monitoring these costs continue, but the tax benefit from having made these outlays will disappear due to a new tax provision (Section 67(g)) enacted in December 2017. Even without this new rule, employees were more limited than independent contractors in their ability to deduct business expenses. Independent contractors must satisfy the core Section 162 test that the expense "be ordinary and necessary" in order to be deductible, and they must meet any additional limitations imposed by Section 274 (intended to help police the business/personal line and otherwise prevent abuse).[48] However, once those hurdles are met, independent contractors may deduct those expenses without further limitation.

By contrast, up through December 2017, employees who incurred identical business costs in the performance of the same function were subject to a further tax limitation. In their cases,

---

[46] *See infra* note 46.
[47] There may be some exceptions to this on a state-by-state basis, where for example, state labor law requires the employer to reimburse an employee for certain significant expenses borne by the employee. In such cases, by operation of law the employee would no longer bear such costs even though the business model had not been formally renegotiated with the employer. *See, e.g.,* Cal. Labor Code § 2802.
[48] In some circumstances, special rules may govern certain types of outlays, such as Section 195 (startup costs).

the deductions were taken "below the line," meaning that they were subject to Section 67 of the Internal Revenue Code, which allowed the deduction of expenses incurred by employees in the "trade or business of being an employee" only to the extent that these outlays (along with some others) in aggregate exceeded 2 percent of the taxpayer's adjusted gross income.[49] If those substantive tax law provisions governing employee expenses had remained in place, the shift to employee status would result in the loss of tax deductions for sharing economy workers who provide personal assets to use in their work and who incur significant unreimbursed costs in the context of their sharing economy work.[50] However, new Section 67(g) (introduced in the December 2017 tax reform) suspends any deduction of these trade or business expenses by employees for taxable years beginning before January 1, 2026. Thus, until 2026, being classified as an employee means a complete loss of tax deductions for these expenses, rather than merely a "haircut."

Third, the introduction of the new deduction in Section 199A for passthrough businesses including independent contractors (but not employees) creates a further tax wedge between the two worker classifications. Classification as an employee requires a taxpayer to sacrifice access to the new 20 percent deduction. Many sharing economy businesses clearly consider independent contractor classification for workers to be the desired classification for their business model. Many have advocated for independent contractor treatment for workers through litigation, through regulatory filings, and through the ways they talk about and market their business models.[51] Presumably, this reflects an assessment that this classification is most advantageous in terms of the business's own profitability (savings in taxes and benefits) and business risk (e.g. tort liability).

C Other Possible Fixes?

Worker reclassification aside, are there other possibilities for reform? Some commentators have suggested maybe so. Although some of the challenges raised by the sharing economy arise on the side of administration and enforcement for the taxing authority,[52] many of the key compliance and related challenges are those confronting workers. There are several possibilities for alleviating these challenges. However, there are also risks inherent in each of these possibilities. Most pertinently, each of these fixes and recommendations developed within the tax context

---

[49] I.R.C. § 67.

[50] The tax rules in place through December 2017 are captured by the following simplified example. Imagine a worker who earns $10,000 in gross income from sharing economy work and $45,000 from other employment, and spends $2,000 on qualified business expenses in the conduct of the sharing economy work. If the worker is classified as an independent contractor with respect to the sharing economy work, the $2,000 of expenses will be considered "above the line" expenses under Section 62. Such above-the-line expenses may be fully deducted in arriving at the taxpayer's "adjusted gross income," which would be $53,000, and will accordingly reduce the taxpayer's taxable income by a full $2,000. In contrast, if the worker is classified as an employee with respect to the sharing economy work, the $2,000 of employee expenses will be miscellaneous itemized deductions under Section 67 (because Section 62 excludes employee expenses), and will be disallowed to the extent they do not exceed 2 percent of the taxpayer's adjusted gross income. In this case, the worker's adjusted gross income remains at $55,000. Two percent of adjusted gross income is $1,100. Thus, the taxpayer will only be permitted to deduct $900 out of the $2,000 expenses incurred from her $55,000 of adjusted gross income. The taxpayer will not be able to deduct anywhere on her tax return the remaining $1,100 spent.

[51] Oei, *supra* note 1 (discussing sharing economy firm strategies for advocating for "gig" classification); *see also* Francine McKenna, *Uber Believes it has SEC Nod for Earnings Approach that Mirrors Business Model*, Marketwatch (Oct. 26, 2017), www.marketwatch.com/story/uber-an-early-adopter-of-new-revenue-recognition-rules-believes-it-has-secs-blessing-of-its-business-model-2017-10-25?mg=prod/accounts-mw (noting that Uber is taking the position for SEC filing purposes that its customers are the drivers, not the passengers).

[52] We discuss these and potential solutions to tax administration difficulties in *Can Sharing be Taxed?*, *supra* note 3. They will not be further discussed here.

could, if pursued, have implications for legal outcomes in other fields, and some of these effects could be costly.

For example, Congress could enact safe harbors for expense deductions (akin to the standard mileage rate currently in place for miles driven on business), to obviate the need for detailed expense allocation and tracking. One concrete proposal along these lines comes from Prof. Kathleen Thomas in the form of a "standard business deduction" for sharing economy workers, which would allow workers to deduct a certain preset amount (computed as a percentage of total gross receipts) and would eliminate the need for workers to document and track expenses throughout the year.[53] Such an approach might raise other issues, including the problem of deciding who should be eligible to take the deduction, and the level at which the deduction should be set. However, it would certainly alleviate the compliance, documentation, and expense-tracking burdens that currently confront workers engaged in microbusiness, and may make particular sense in a sector where the compliance and documentation costs might far outweigh the amounts actually earned. The bigger risk is that creating a simplified tax regime for sharing economy workers might represent a piecemeal approach to ameliorating challenges confronted by these workers at the expense of more comprehensive protections. Simplified regimes may obscure the (plausible) argument that independent contractor classification is a poor fit for sharing economy workers by allowing firms to claim that operating as an independent contractor in this sector is now "easy."

Another direct way to alleviate some worker compliance burdens is to clarify for platforms what payments need to be reported. Specifically, one challenge that has confronted a subset of sharing economy participants arises in the event the worker does not receive a Form 1099 from the platform. The rule is that even if an amount paid is not reported on Form 1099, it must still be included in the recipient's gross income. Thus, if a worker does not receive a Form 1099, she will be faced with the burden of totaling up amounts earned throughout the year for purposes of income inclusion. Nonissuance of a Form 1099 may occur, for example, in cases where the platform claims that it need not issue Form 1099 because the amount earned does not meet the appropriate threshold for Form 1099 issuance (such as the 200 transaction/$20,000 threshold under the regulations governing issuance of Form 1099-K).[54] As we have discussed in prior work, there is some ambiguity regarding whether this threshold in fact applies to sharing economy work.[55] A simple way of alleviating the compliance burden on workers would be for the IRS to clarify that issuance of a Form 1099 is required at all income levels.

Even a worker who has received a Form 1099 may be unprepared to complete her tax return accurately. As noted earlier, some workers have been confused regarding the numbers reported on the Form 1099 and have not appreciated that the numbers are gross numbers (and not net of the various platform fees and the cut owed to the platform). This confusion could be mitigated either by clearer instructions issued by the platform accompanying the Form 1099, or by redesign of the form itself by the IRS (such redesign could highlight the difference between gross and net, and better guide the worker to reporting the proper numbers in the proper places on Schedule C).

As noted above, the structures and realities of tax compliance may have impacts on the behaviors of taxpayers operating in the sharing economy. In particular, the lack of withholding on

---

[53] Thomas, *supra* note 3.
[54] *Can Sharing Be Taxed?*, *supra* note 3, at 1031–41 (discussing the Form 1099-K reporting positions taken by various platforms and the potential compliance effects of these positions).
[55] *Id.*

independent contractor payments may both increase compliance burdens on sharing economy operators and may distort their labor supply choices. A possible reform that may alleviate these effects would be to require tax withholding on certain non-employee payments. Along these lines, Professor Thomas has suggested that non-employee withholding for sharing economy workers might be imposed up front for just these reasons.[56] Such up-front wage withholding – if properly designed – would alleviate estimated tax burdens and would allow workers to more accurately understand how much of a tax burden they are likely to experience on the back end, and to make decisions accordingly. But again, the risk is that these types of piecemeal reforms in one arena (tax) may undercut movement in favor of more comprehensive protections for workers across other fields.

Finally, the importance of taxpayer education cannot be overstated. The sharing economy is an emerging sector that has drawn in many new participants. Some of these new workers might not understand that they are required to report income, or how they are supposed to report income. Others may experience confusion regarding which expenses to track, or how to track them. In prior work, we have suggested some ways in which such taxpayer education about tax compliance obligations may be accomplished. At the time of writing, the IRS, in partnership with the National Taxpayer Advocate, has launched a Sharing Economy Tax Center, a website containing resources for workers and platforms operating in the sharing economy.[57] That website includes a number of resources and links that inform those working in the sharing economy of their tax obligations and help them meet those obligations. This is a good start; however, more could be done to educate taxpayers on tax compliance obligations, even as measures are considered to alleviate these obligations.

Each of these fixes and recommendations developed within the tax context could, if pursued, have implications for legal outcomes in other fields.

CONCLUSION

The phenomenon of work in the sharing economy has generated notable discussion and debate. Much of that discussion has focused on worker protections such as collective bargaining, fragmentation of the labor market, and undercutting of traditional industries. However, tax issues also play an important part in the ultimate experience of sharing economy workers, though the role of tax has attracted relatively little notice so far. The individual who performs work in the sector through the new technology platforms will be forced to confront the realities of tax compliance and reporting in due course. Thus, the tax design choices we make may help encourage work in the sharing economy or, alternatively, may act as a brake on that sector's development. Moreover, we should expect that the design choices we make with respect to the tax treatment of sharing economy workers will inevitably have impacts on and spillovers into the labor law and broader worker protection conversation. Policymakers should therefore give serious attention to the tax system's impacts on microbusiness.

---

[56] Thomas, *supra* note 3.
[57] *Sharing Economy Tax Center*, IRS, www.irs.gov/businesses/small-businesses-self-employed/sharing-economy-tax-center (last updated Feb 2, 2018).

26

Tax Compliance and the Sharing Economy

Manoj Viswanathan

INTRODUCTION

The gig economy, also known as the "sharing" or "on-demand platform" economy, is a broad term used to describe a system in which underutilized assets or labor are matched with a consumer.[1] The economic activity of the sharing economy poses tax compliance challenges for both the federal government and state and local jurisdictions. As sharing economy asset and labor providers earn income outside of the traditional means by which the Internal Revenue Service (IRS) and local taxing authorities are accustomed, the potential for both unintentional nonpayment of income taxes and willful income tax evasion increases. The sharing economy also presents tax compliance issues beyond income tax, creating challenges with the assessment and collection of, among other things, wage, sales, occupancy, and property taxes.

This chapter describes how current tax compliance practices may not adequately address income generated by sharing economy providers, and what changes could be implemented to fairly balance the interests of both the taxing authorities and these providers. This chapter also discusses the actions local jurisdictions have already taken to regulate and tax sharing economy companies and the potential shortcomings of these actions. Although this chapter focuses on taxation in the United States, the topics discussed are of relevance across all jurisdictions in which sharing economy companies operate.

I FEDERAL INCOME TAX COMPLIANCE

The IRS obtains the bulk of its data on taxpayer income via forms submitted by payors, with a copy of these forms sent to both the IRS and the income-receiving payee. This "information reporting" by payors is statutorily obligated by the Internal Revenue Code and covers most payments made in the commercial context.[2] For example, information reporting is required for transactions involving compensation for services, interest payments, dividends, and sales by brokers, via IRS Forms W-2 and 1099-MISC, 1099-INT, 1099-DIV, and 1099-B, respectively. Comparing the information on these forms to the information submitted by taxpayers is the primary method by which the IRS ensures that taxpayers are reporting the income they receive.

---

[1] *See* Manoj Viswanathan, *Tax Compliance in a Decentralizing Economy*, 34 Ga. S. T. U. L. Rev. 283 (forthcoming, 2018); Shu-Yi Oei and Diane M. Ring, *Can Sharing Be Taxed?*, 93 Wash. U.L. Rev. 989 (2016).

[2] *See generally* I.R.C. §6041.

Notably excluded from the information reporting rules are payments made by consumers, meaning amounts paid in furtherance of a payor's personal consumption rather than as part of the payor's trade or business. For example, a tenant need not report on any IRS-mandated form the $1,000 she pays in rent to her landlord. This is true even though payments of personal consumption often constitute taxable income to the *payee* (the party receiving the payment). The landlord in the above example, for instance, must still include the $1,000 in her gross income even though the renter is not obligated to notify the IRS that she has made these payments.

Federal income tax compliance is highly dependent on the extent to which payments made by payors to payees are reported via these information returns. Because the taxpayer/payee also receives a copy of the information return, the payee knows the IRS is aware that he or she has received the reported income. As a result, information reporting dramatically increases taxpayer compliance. Salaries of employees, for example, are required to be reported to the IRS by employers on Form W-2. For these payments of compensation the misreporting percentage (the total net misreported amount divided by the sum of the amounts that should have been reported by all taxpayers) is only about 1 percent.[3] For income items subject to little or no information reporting, such as sales of business property, sole proprietor income, or rental payments, the net misreporting percentage skyrockets to over 60 percent.[4] The result is that income not reported to the IRS via an information return will likely go unreported by the taxpayer, and as a result go untaxed, whereas income documented on an information return will likely be both reported and correctly taxed.

A *Information Reporting and the Sharing Economy*

Labor and asset providers in the sharing economy are typically not treated as employees by the companies through which they earn income. Workers classified as employees are generally costlier for companies than workers classified as independent contractors. Employees often receive company perks (e.g. health insurance and retirement plans) and state and local benefits (e.g. state-mandated family leave) for which independent contractors are not eligible. Additionally, employers must pay a portion of their employees' payroll taxes. Although a company's decision to classify a worker as an employee or an independent contractor is not at the company's complete discretion, sharing economy companies' lack of managerial control over workers has emboldened these companies to deny classification of their workers as employees. As such, any income earned by labor and asset providers in the sharing economy is typically not reported on Form W-2.

Additionally, many sharing economy companies have taken the position that their providers of labor and assets are also not independent contractors. Although the earnings of independent contractors are not as tightly regulated as the wages of employees, cumulative payments to these workers greater than $600 are still reported to the IRS via Form 1099-MISC.[5] By not issuing Forms W-2 or 1099-MISC, companies such as Airbnb, Uber, TaskRabbit, and Etsy imply that their asset and labor providers are neither employees nor independent contractors. According to these companies, the true payors of these suppliers of labor and assets are the customers, with the company merely serving as an intermediary through which payments are made.[6]

Sharing economy companies often characterize themselves as "third party settlement organizations" with respect to the payments they make to their providers of labor and assets,

---

3   Internal Revenue Service, *Federal Tax Compliance Research: Tax Gap Estimates for Tax Years 2008–2010*, at 18.
4   *Id.*
5   *See generally Instructions for Form 1099-MISC.*, Internal Revenue Service (2017).
6   *See, e.g., Should I Expect to Receive a Tax Form From Airbnb?* Airbnb, www.airbnb.com/help/article/414/should-i-expect-to-receive-a-tax-form-from-airbnb and https://perma.cc/GJK8-7Z9C; *1099-K Tax Form and Your Earnings on Etsy*, Etsy, www.etsy.com/help/article/3675 and https://perma.cc/P2M9-ZWT2.

thereby precluding their issuance of Forms W-2 and 1099-MISC.[7] This characterization has important consequences for the reporting of income. Third party settlement organizations are obligated to report payments made to a specific individual via Form 1099-K only if payments to the payee exceed $20,000 *and* if the total number of transactions with the payee is greater than 200.[8] Unless a specific payee meets both of these thresholds, the IRS does not receive an information report about the payment. As a result, a service provider on TaskRabbit, for example, will most likely not have any of her payments reported to the IRS, even though these payments most likely constitute taxable income to the recipient. This outcome is common across the sharing economy. According to a 2015 survey, 61 percent of those receiving income from a sharing economy company did not receive any information return.[9]

Sharing economy companies have an incentive to resist submitting information returns on the income earned by their labor and asset providers. To the extent this income goes untaxed, the earner is effectively getting paid "under the table." As a result, the amount that sharing economy companies must pay providers of labor and assets to properly incentivize their participation in the sharing economy is lower than they would otherwise need to pay if this income was reported to, and taxed by, the IRS. Although the benefits of not reporting the income seemingly only accrues to the worker, this benefit is to some degree also captured by the sharing economy companies.

Given that these companies benefit from this lack of income reporting, it is likely that only Congressional or IRS action will catalyze these companies into submitting accurate information returns. For tax year 2016 one sharing economy company, Uber, voluntarily submitted a Form 1099-K to all drivers regardless of the income they have earned.[10] It is not immediately clear why Uber chose this more onerous reporting obligation, though scholars theorized it was to force competitors to do the same (which, as of now, they have not) and limit these competitors' pool of available drivers.[11] For tax year 2017 (and beyond, presumably) Uber modified their information reporting protocols so that only drivers earning $20,000 in payments and providing 200 trips will receive Form 1099-K.[12]

The unreported income is significant. A 2015 report commissioned by Airbnb indicated that hosts had earned over $3.2 billion, with a typical host earning an extra $7,350 annually from a single property.[13] A 2017 Airbnb report states that the municipal taxes collected by Airbnb

---

[7] Although not without ambiguity, this characterization is arguably permissible, even if not within the original intent of Congress. Erik J. Christenson and Amanda T. Kottke, *Guidance Needed to Clarify Reporting Obligations for Online Marketplaces and Peer-to-Peer Platforms*, 55 Tax Mgmt. Memorandum 243 (2014).

[8] I.R.C. §6050W(e). A third party settlement organization is defined as "the central organization which has the contractual obligation to make payments to participating payees of third party network transactions." Third party network transactions are defined as "any transaction which is settled through a third party payment network." A third party payment network is "any agreement or arrangement – (A) which involves the establishment of accounts with a central organization by a substantial number of persons who – (i) are unrelated to such organization, (ii) provide goods or services, and (iii) have agreed to settle transactions for the provision of such goods or services pursuant to such agreement or arrangement, (B) which provides for standards and mechanisms for settling such transactions, and (C) which guarantees persons providing goods or services pursuant to such agreement or arrangement that such persons will be paid for providing such goods or services." I.R.C. §6050W(d)(3).

[9] Caroline Bruckner, *Shortchanged: The Tax Compliance Challenges of Small Business Operators Driving the On-Demand Platform Economy*, Kogod Tax Policy Center, 2016.

[10] Uber, What tax documents will I receive?, *available at* https://perma.cc/2N8U-4U94 (2017).

[11] Oei and Ring, *supra* note 1 and accompanying text.

[12] Uber, What tax documents will I receive?, *available at* https://help.uber.com/h/6b3084d7-d0fa-4535-9868-8d314b3869ba and https://perma.cc/L34Y-XCTU (2018).

[13] Gene Sperling, *Airbnb: A New Resource for Middle Class Families* (2015), www.airbnbaction.com/wp-content/uploads/2015/10/Middle-Class-Economic-Report-FINAL.pdf and https://perma.cc/F7SF-SUXS.

for its 50 largest markets could exceed \$2.5 billion over the next ten years.[14] Assuming an average hotel tax rate, this represents approximately \$20 billion of revenue paid to hosts. Although these data do not indicate how much of these earnings are, in fact, reported on Form 1099-K, they do indicate that the earnings of the average host, which fall under the requirements for issuance of a 1099-K, are not reported to the IRS, and that the potential for underreporting is large.

Though the preceding example focuses solely on Airbnb, it is illustrative of the relationship between many labor and asset providers and sharing economy companies. Most labor and asset providers earn about 20 to 30 percent of their income from their sharing economy work.[15] As such, the \$20,000 and 200 transactions thresholds will likely not be satisfied for most payees. If this remains true, a significant amount of earned income will remain unreported and, absent any changes to the information reporting regime, will in many cases go untaxed.

B Addressing the Gap in Information Reporting

One solution to the information reporting issue with respect to the sharing economy is for the IRS to reduce the reporting threshold for payments under 1099-K to match the \$600 threshold of Form 1099-MISC. Even if these sharing economy companies are deemed to be "third party settlement organizations" as per Section 6050W, the \$20,000 and 200 transaction threshold simply allows too much income to go unreported. The original justification for these high thresholds, burden of compliance, is generally not persuasive given the ease by which electronic records of payments can be kept. Alternatively, if the thresholds for Form 1099-K are not reduced, Congress or the IRS could simply clarify the definition of "third party settlement organizations" for the purposes of Section 6050W and Form 1099-K to exclude sharing economy companies. The term was likely not meant to cover companies that exert the level of control that companies such as Airbnb and Lyft exert over their payees' conduct.[16] If sharing economy companies are not third party settlement organizations, there is substantial authority to suggest that these payments should be treated as payments to independent contractors, and therefore subject to the \$600 threshold mandated by Form 1099-MISC.[17]

Many of the issues associated with changes to the information reporting rules have related consequences for sharing economy workers. A more extensive discussion of these issues and their consequences is explored in Chapter 25.

C Increasing Compliance with Increased Auditing

Rather than increase the information reporting obligations of sharing economy companies, the IRS could instead ensure that the labor and asset providers receiving payments from these companies are paying all required income taxes by tailoring enforcement efforts to sharing economy companies. Given that sharing economy companies overwhelmingly make payments to labor and asset providers electronically, monitoring these payments would be technologically simple. This is especially true given that sharing economy companies typically require their labor and asset providers to submit some essential financial and identity information. TaskRabbit, for

---

[14] Gene Sperling, *Airbnb: Generating \$2.5 Billion in Potential Tax Revenue for America's Cities* (2017), www.airbnbcitizen .com/wp-content/uploads/2017/01/US-Tax-Report3.pdf and https://perma.cc/S4VF-SA7G.

[15] Caroline Bruckner, *Kogod Tax Policy Center, Shortchanged: The Tax Compliance Challenges of Small Business Operators Driving the On-Demand Platform Economy* (2016).

[16] Oei and Ring, *supra* note 1, at 1036.

[17] Christenson and Kottke, *supra* note 7.

example, requires a valid social security number, bank account, and authorization to perform a background check.[18] Uber requires a valid driver's license and proof of vehicle registration.[19] An audit of a sharing economy worker would easily reveal to the IRS the gross amount the worker has been paid. As a result, the IRS could reliably ascertain the gross earnings each asset and labor provider receives from sharing economy companies, and could then ensure that these payees are accurately reporting this income when they file their taxes.

This approach would likely, however, be politically infeasible given that it would require a dramatic increase in the audit rate for asset and labor providers. Taxpayers with adjusted gross incomes between $1 and $100,000 currently experience an audit rate of less than 1 percent.[20] Any increase in IRS enforcement actions to effectively observe payments from sharing economy workers to their asset and labor providers would require a significantly higher auditing rate. Given that the audit rate for returns with adjusted gross incomes between $500,000 and $1 million is only about 2 percent, it is likely that a significantly higher audit rate for lower-income taxpayers would be politically untenable.

D Increasing Taxpayer Awareness

Many taxpayers who earn income in the sharing economy are not willfully evading taxes when they fail to report that income on their tax returns. Unsophisticated taxpayers often believe that they do not owe taxes on income for which they do not receive information returns. In the absence of the changes described above, simply informing taxpayers of their obligation to report all earned income could have a salutary effect on tax compliance. Every payment from a sharing economy company to a labor or asset provider could be accompanied by a reminder that this payment constitutes gross income. Even though most sharing economy companies do not issue information returns to their providers of labor and assets, sharing economy companies *could* issue a reminder statement to providets in lieu of an information reporting form.

E The Role of Sharing Economy Companies in Tax Compliance

Sharing economy companies attempt to efficiently align underutilized labor and assets with a willing consumer. This endeavor requires not only using technology to align the relevant parties, but keeping meticulous data to optimize the algorithms used. The data these companies maintain about labor and asset providers could be used to monitor not only payments to the provider, but also for many other elements of effective tax compliance.[21] Airbnb keeps track of cleaning fees paid, which represent a deductible expense for Airbnb hosts. A primary expense of Uber drivers is mileage they drive, which is tracked by Uber. If the IRS had access to this information, its tax liability assessment of labor and asset providers would likely be made much easier. For those asset and labor providers voluntarily reporting and paying taxes on their sharing economy income and paying taxes as owed, this information flow from the sharing economy companies could be quite helpful.

However, as discussed earlier, it is likely that a large portion of sharing economy income is unreported, and therefore untaxed. Taxpayers not reporting income earned from their sharing

---

[18] *What Do I Need To Be a Tasker?* TaskRabbit, https://support.taskrabbit.com/hc/en-us/articles/204411070-What-do-I-need-to-be-a-Tasker- and https://perma.cc/9JVH-S3BX.

[19] *Signing Up*, Uber, https://help.uber.com/h/88b80350-8701-40c0-8493-9b21189a71ec and https://perma.cc/ZG7V-3BYA.

[20] Internal Revenue Service, *Internal Revenue Service 2016 Data Book*, 36 (2016).

[21] Oei and Ring, *supra* note 1, at 1036.

economy work would resist any increase in information flow between the sharing economy companies and the IRS. Because sharing economy companies benefit from their asset and labor providers not paying taxes on income earned, sharing economy companies will resist any required information submission that disincentivizes asset and labor providers to participate in the sharing economy.

This resistance notwithstanding, the most successful IRS initiatives to ensure tax compliance in the sharing economy will impose obligations on the sharing economy companies rather than the asset and labor providers earning this income. Enforcement targeting a concentrated set of wealthier entities is a much simpler task than monitoring a diffuse set of individuals with little income. Of course, the filing and paying of taxes ultimately falls upon individuals, but to the extent the compliance of these individuals is affected by company action, that company action should be incentivized by IRS protocols.

II STATE AND LOCAL TAX ISSUES

State and local jurisdictions levy a variety of taxes on both earners and businesses operating within their borders. In addition to an income tax, increasingly relevant to state and local jurisdictions is the extent to which both sharing economy companies as well as labor and asset providers might be subject to other taxes such as wage and payroll, occupancy, sales and use, and tangible business property taxes.

This inquiry is especially relevant when the goods and services of the sharing economy exist as untaxed substitutes for goods and services that *are* currently taxed by the state and/or locality. This differential tax treatment creates a consumer bias toward sharing economy goods and services, to the extent the untaxed sharing economy goods and services are identical to taxed goods and services in the traditional economy.

A *State Income Tax*

The majority of state and local jurisdictions levying a tax on a taxpayer's income use federal tax information in completing a state income tax return. Both New York and California, for instance, use a taxpayer's federal adjusted gross income as the starting point for assessing state tax liability. As such, the compliance issues associated with accurately reporting a taxpayer's federal income also have implications for state level taxation. Once income reporting issues are resolved at the federal level, they are effectively resolved at the state and local levels as well.

State and local governments have the potential, however, to serve as secondary information reporters for income earned by the labor and asset providers within their jurisdictions. Sharing economy companies have negotiated regulatory agreements with certain localities in order to ensure their continued operation within these jurisdictions.[22] These regulatory agreements can not only require providers of labor and assets to register their activity as a business, but can also obligate these providers to submit statements on their business activity to the local authorities. For example, San Francisco's newly formed Office of Short-Term Residential Rental Administration and Enforcement requires short-term rental hosts to submit quarterly reports on length and type of short-term rental.[23]

---

[22] Hugo Martin, *Airbnb, HomeAway Settle Rental-Registration Lawsuit Against San Francisco*, L.A. Times, May 2, 2017.
[23] *How Do I Become a Certified Host?* San Francisco Office of Short-Term Rentals, https://shorttermrentals.sfgov.org/hosting/become-certified and https://perma.cc/BNP9-BYRM.

The extent to which providers must adhere to these reporting obligations depends on the specifics of the arrangement made between the local authority and sharing economy company. These required reports could potentially obligate labor and asset providers to submit earnings statements, which could then be forwarded to the relevant state and local taxing authorities. These earnings statements would not normally be forwarded to the IRS, however, and therefore would not affect the reference point from which state income taxes are calculated. However, the disclosure of these earning statements to state authorities could motivate labor and asset providers to more readily disclose income earned on federal tax returns.[24]

State and local authorities could also potentially determine the earnings of labor and asset providers not from information submitted by the providers themselves, but from other information submitted by sharing economy companies. Airbnb, for example, currently collects occupancy taxes directly from guests and remits these funds to the city of San Francisco on hosts' behalf. If the granularity of this collection and remittance permits San Francisco to determine the occupancy taxes generated from a given property, it would be relatively straightforward to determine the approximate income a given property is generating. Because Airbnb hosts in San Francisco are obligated to register with the city, this income could easily be attributed to the correct host, assuming hosts comply with their registration obligations.

B Wage and Payroll Taxes

To the extent that labor providers in the sharing economy have income that is underreported, there will likely be an underpayment not only with the federal and state income taxes owed, but federal and, where applicable, state and local payroll taxes as well. If, for example, an Uber driver receives payment for services provided, a 15.3 percent federal self-employment tax (plus any additional amount levied by the state or locality) would apply to those earnings. The same is true for any other sharing economy participant receiving payment for labor provided. These taxes must be remitted to the taxing authority when the taxpayer files her return.

Because participants in the sharing economy are often unsophisticated taxpayers, the additional tax burden at the end of the year has the potential to create both liquidity issues and compliance challenges for these labor and asset providers. The enforcement mechanisms used by the relevant taxing authority for these wage and payroll taxes, however, are similar to those for income taxes generally, since the information reporting obligation will permit enforcement for both income and wage taxes. Properly incentivizing the reporting of federal income would likely result in an accurate statement of wage earnings. As a result, effective enforcement of income earned on the federal income side should remedy wage and payroll tax deficiencies at the local level as well.

C Occupancy Taxes

Many localities have argued that since sharing economy companies facilitating short-term rentals, such as Airbnb and Homeaway, facilitate those rentals in the same manner as hotels, these guests are obligated to pay the same occupancy taxes paid by hotel guests in the same locality. By placing the burden of collecting and remitting occupancy taxes on the sharing economy company rather than the host, localities can more easily monitor and enforce payment obligations.

---

[24] Similar to encouraging increased IRS auditing of electronic payments, this approach likely invites criticism on privacy grounds.

Such an agreement requires each sharing economy company to act as an intermediary between host and locality, but this approach is simpler than obligating (and enforcing) individual hosts to collect and remit the appropriate taxes. By placing the burden of compliance on companies with more to lose than individual hosts, localities increase their odds of compliance.

In exchange for assurance from these localities that future regulation will not preclude Airbnb's operation in these jurisdictions, Airbnb has often agreed to collect from its guests and remit on behalf of its hosts the occupancy taxes due to the locality.[25] These laws often are associated with other regulatory requirements and restrictions on the extent to which hosts are permitted to rent their properties.[26] Airbnb is currently collecting and remitting occupancy taxes in over 30 states and several municipalities. Homeaway, in contrast, simply encourages hosts to collect and remit occupancy taxes on their own.

The deal brokered between San Francisco and Airbnb is illustrative of the arrangements that sharing economy companies and municipalities are brokering in order to ensure smooth operation within certain coveted markets. The agreement between Airbnb and San Francisco arose from Airbnb's litigation over an ordinance requiring Airbnb hosts to register with the city of San Francisco. The settlement requires Airbnb to collect from guests (and remit to San Francisco) occupancy taxes identical to those charged to guests of city hotels. Airbnb hosts register with the San Francisco Office of Short-Term Rentals (which can be done directly from Airbnb's website), limit the number of unhosted reservations they accept, and make quarterly reports on rentals. Airbnb is obligated to work with the city of San Francisco to ensure that only hosts properly registered as a small business are listing their properties with Airbnb.[27]

Other companies operating in the short-term rental sector are not as tightly regulated as Airbnb. Companies such as Craigslist and Nextdoor, for instance, contain listings for temporary housing, but do not charge a fee to either the guest or the host for their services. Because no payments are routed through these sharing economy companies, requiring them to collect and remit occupancy taxes is impracticable. Even though hosts engaging in short-term rentals using these other websites are still technically governed by the same restrictions to which Airbnb and Homeaway rentals are subjected, cities cannot realistically regulate individual hosts. Only by imposing a regulatory burden on a large, centralized entity with a financial stake in the short-term rental market (such as Airbnb) and requiring the entity to report hosts in violation can a city's attempts at short-term rental enforcement become tenable.

D Sales and Use Taxes

Ascertaining whether a sharing economy company (1) meets the "substantial nexus" requirement of the U.S. Constitution and (2) is the party obligated to collect and remit sales taxes is seldom straightforward. Because there is no federal sales tax, the purchases subject to sales tax

---

[25] *In What Areas Is Occupancy Tax Collection and Remittance by Airbnb Available?* Airbnb, www.airbnb.com/help/article/653/in-what-areas-is-occupancy-tax-collection-and-remittance-by-airbnb-available and https://perma.cc/R7YQ-K3P9.

[26] In San Francisco, for example, Airbnb hosts are required to register their properties with a newly created office of short-term rentals and cannot generally host guests for more than 90 days without being present on the property. Although municipalities do not require that Airbnb be the only platform used by hosts, often the reporting requirements and other regulatory burdens are less cumbersome if Airbnb is the platform used.

[27] Katie Benner, *Airbnb Settles Lawsuit with Its Hometown, San Francisco,* N.Y. Times, at B2 (May 1, 2017), www.nytimes.com/2017/05/01/technology/airbnb-san-francisco-settle-registration-lawsuit.html. The agreements Airbnb has made in other jurisdictions differ in certain details, but generally require some form of registration with local government combined with Airbnb collecting and remitting an occupancy tax.

vary widely amongst both states and localities. Determining what is and is not subject to sales tax becomes a highly fact-dependent inquiry.

Quill, a 1992 Supreme Court case, held that a state may not require a retailer to levy a sales tax on a purchaser unless the retailer has a "substantial nexus" with the taxing state.[28] *Quill* held that this required, as a threshold matter, a physical presence within the borders of the taxing jurisdiction. In *Wayfair*, decided in 2018, the Supreme Court overruled *Quill* and held that physical presence within a taxing state is *not* a prerequisite to finding that a retailer has a "substantial nexus" with a taxing state.[29] Although *Wayfair* did not clarify precisely what activities *are* required to create a "substantial nexus," its holding unquestionably expanded the ability of states to levy sales taxes.

In the years preceding the Wayfair decision, several states enacted sales tax legislation in seeming anticipation of *Quill*'s repeal. The subject of *Wayfair* was a South Dakota statute, passed in 2016, requiring remote sellers—regardless of physical presence—with greater than $100,000 in total sales or more than 200 separate transactions to collect and remit a use tax. Other states, such as Oklahoma and Alabama, required certain out-of-state sellers to pay sales tax on their in-house purchases. Colorado legislation obligated out-of-state sellers not collecting sales taxes to notify purchasers that these taxes were not being collected, and that such a tax might be owed to the state by the purchaser.

Sharing economy companies often operate in states other than those in which they have physical offices. However, some sharing economy companies voluntarily collected and remitted sales taxes even though their obligation to do so (pre-*Quill*) was debatable. Both Uber and Lyft, for example, collected and remitted a 7 percent sales tax in Rhode Island that they likely were not obligated to pay. Airbnb has taken similar actions in Indiana, which subjects hotel stays shorter than thirty days to a sales tax rather than an occupancy tax.[30] Although *Quill* probably prevented Indiana from imposing sales taxes on Airbnb, Airbnb still voluntarily collected and remitted them to the state.[31] These companies likely viewed the collection and remittance of sales taxes as preferable to more detrimental future regulations. By aligning their financial interests with the jurisdictions within which they operate (and pay taxes), these companies incentivize jurisdictions to promote their continued operation. This strategy could still be effective post-*Wayfair*: preemptively paying taxes for which you are debatably liable could prevent future, more onerous regulation moving forward.

Sharing economy companies under less regulatory risk, such as eBay and Etsy, seem less inclined to collecting and remit sales taxes. Rather than charging or collecting sales tax, these companies give each seller the option to levy whatever sales tax they see fit.[32] Both eBay and Etsy remind sellers that sales taxes might need to be collected, and they permit sellers to charge them, however, neither eBay nor Etsy ensure the accuracy or validity of the sales taxes charged. Remittance of these sales taxes is deemed to be the burden of the seller and not the sharing economy company, a view still valid post-*Wayfair*. This approach is consistent with these companies' self-characterization as "third party settlement organizations," as discussed earlier. Because they are not selling directly to the consumer, the reasoning goes, the obligation to collect and remit sales taxes is on the sellers and not the company.

---

[28] *Quill Corp. v. North Dakota*, 504 U.S. 298 (1992).
[29] *South Dakota v. Wayfair. Inc.*, 585 U.S._(2018).
[30] State of Indiana, Department of Revenue, *Information Bulletin #41*: Sales Tax (Jan 1., 2014).
[31] Brian Eason, *Airbnb to Mayors: "We Want to Pay Taxes,"* Indianapolis Star, June 26, 2016.
[32] Etsy, How to Determine Your Sales Tax, *available at* https://www.etsy.com/seller-handbook/article/how-to-determine-your-sales-tax/22717969977; eBay, Charging Sales Tax, *available at* https://pages.ebay.com/help/pay/checkout-tax-table.html#charge.

Similar to the regulatory freedoms that San Francisco granted Airbnb in exchange for a clearly defined portion of occupancy tax revenues, certain states are seemingly willing to concede a portion of their sales tax revenue to sellers that voluntarily remit sales taxes. Alabama, for instance, allows out-of-state sellers (who might fail the "substantial nexus" test) to voluntarily collect and remit an 8 percent sales tax without having to determine any additional tax they might owe at the city and county level, reducing both the overall rate paid and the complexity associated with calculating precise rates for all localities.[33] Such a concession might entice companies to accept some payments of tax in exchange for a clearly defined regulatory position, similar to the deal Airbnb struck in San Francisco.

With these new laws states are attempting to benefit from the dramatic increase in payments made through sharing economy platforms by obligating sharing economy companies rather than individual sellers. By placing the obligation on the larger, more easily monitored company rather than on the individual seller, states can ensure greater compliance. Currently Etsy and eBay both defer to their providers of assets in determining whether or not sales tax should be collected and remitted, with neither Etsy nor eBay verifying the accuracy of their sellers' sales tax collection. Post-*Wayfair*, this obligation might instead pass to the company, allowing for greater ease of enforcement by state taxing authorities.

E Tangible Business Property Tax

Labor and asset providers in the sharing economy are often deemed to be sole proprietors of small businesses. As a consequence, some labor and asset participants might be subject to their locality's tangible business property tax. This tax, which applies to movable property used in a trade or business, is the largest tax paid by businesses on the state and local levels.[34] The tax generally requires businesses to value the tangible business property used in their business. The property subject to the tangible business property tax varies widely by jurisdiction. In San Francisco, for example, temporary use of personal use property for short-term rentals creates a tangible business property tax liability equal to 1.2 percent of the value of furniture and other movable property used in conjunction with the short-term rental.[35]

The business property tax is typically self-reported by the business proprietor. For sharing economy participants, the result is that only jurisdictions which require registration of the asset or labor provider can properly assess the business property tax. San Francisco, for example, which requires Airbnb hosts to register, can therefore easily require hosts to remit the tax. It is, however, difficult to ensure that the reported amounts are accurate. Given the generally low stakes for most participants in the sharing economy, enforcement of this tax is likely not an efficient use of local resources. For other sharing economy participants, such as the Postmates deliverer using an expensive bicycle, or the TaskRabbit Tasker using an expensive set of tools, enforcement is nearly impossible given that for these companies, there is generally no required registration.

---

[33] Chris Marr, *Online Sales Tax Case to Take Most of 2017 in Alabama*, Bloomberg BNA, Weekly State Tax Report (Dec. 16, 2016).

[34] Ferdinand Hogroian, *The State and Local Business Tax Burden: Update For Fiscal Year 2016*, 27(Nov) J. Multistate Tax'n 39 (2017).

[35] Carolyn Said, *Airbnb "Furniture Tax" Generates $120,000 for San Francisco*, S.F. Chronicle (July 21, 2016), www .sfchronicle.com/business/article/Airbnb-furniture-tax-generates-120-000-for-8399617.php. The average amount of tangible business property tax owed by each qualifying Airbnb host in San Francisco was approximately $60.

CONCLUSION

The sharing economy, by creating novel and unforeseen methods for providers of labor and assets to earn income, presents unique tax compliance challenges for federal, state, and local tax authorities. The IRS should ensure that proper information reporting is in place so that income earned is accurately reported and taxed. State and local taxing authorities should consider the extent to which they want to tax companies whose transactions are now, post-*Wayfair*, fair game. The most successful tax compliance efforts will necessarily obligate the sharing economy companies, who have more information and resources at their disposal than the labor and asset providers, who are often unsophisticated taxpayers.

27

Taxation of the Sharing Economy in the European Union

Katerina Pantazatou

INTRODUCTION

There is an inherent difficulty in writing about taxation of the sharing economy in the European Union. The reason is that, currently, there are no EU tax rules that regulate the sharing economy.[1] This results in four different conditions. First, different Member States apply different tax rules to the sharing economy. The divergence/differentiation becomes even more conspicuous as, in most cases, no Member State applies "sectoral" uniform rules in the sharing economy. Instead, different rules apply, for instance, on car-sharing or home-sharing businesses. This becomes even more problematic as, often, the enforcement of these rules depends on the visibility of these activities, allowing less popular platforms to escape taxation. The second consequence that emanates from the lack of specific EU tax rules is the need to regulate this issue both at national and supranational/EU level. This way, legal uncertainty as well as tax evasion would be minimized and predictability would be enhanced. In this context, one may wonder whether the little EU tax legislation that does exist is or could be applicable in the area of the sharing economy.

The third point relates to the spillover effect from other areas of EU law. Whether, for instance, an Uber driver qualifies as a worker or as an employee or an independent contractor will have a big impact on his tax assessment. Since no common comprehensive EU rules exist with regard to this labor law issue, it comes as no surprise that the tax treatment of the different platforms and the different platform users is largely divided among the different Member States.

Finally, the application of different taxes and tax breaks and the often poor tax enforcement and collection mechanisms from the sharing economy participants in different Member States may grant sharing economy participants a competitive advantage vis-à-vis their competitors outside the sharing economy area. This effectively different treatment may trigger other EU rules, notably EU state aid rules.

This chapter addresses all these issues. First, I provide an overview of taxation in the EU and the taxation of the sharing economy in general. Then, I turn to examine whether and if so, to what extent, secondary EU tax legislation applies in the sharing economy and how other areas of law, such as labor law, affect taxation. Following this, I briefly present some of the different initiatives of the Member States with regard to taxation of the sharing economy and the remaining challenges they face, including the potential applicability of state aid rules.

---

[1] Note, however, that progress has been made with respect to (mostly indirect) tax rules on the taxation of the digital economy and e-commerce at the EU level.

I AN OVERVIEW OF TAXATION IN THE EU

Direct taxation in the EU is, in general, a non-harmonized area. In order to harmonize direct taxation, unanimity is required at Council level,[2] and to date the divergent interests of the – currently – 28 Member States have prevented the adoption of extensive secondary legislation in this field. If one adds to this the difficulty *per se* in legislating a complicated and constantly developing area, such as the sharing economy, it comes as no surprise that no targeted EU tax legislation exists in this respect. The existing limited secondary legislation in the area of direct taxation seems to have little relevance for the sharing economy.[3] While the same unanimity requirement applies to indirect taxation,[4] it and specifically VAT legislation is much more advanced in the EU.[5] Even in this case, however, no sharing-economy-specific tax rules exist.

The fact that competence in the area of direct taxation lies with the Member States allows individual states to establish different criteria as to the definition of income and the definition of the taxable person. In addition to these essential requirements for the taxation of sharing economy actors, other important issues, such as the applicable tax rates, whether any *de minimis* rules should apply, how and when tax should be collected, what kind of exemptions and allowances are foreseen by law, and what expenses are deductible, are a matter for the Member States to decide and are, at the same time, essential tax issues that are not tackled in the EU legislation.

Not only that, but the significant variety of platforms and the many different circumstances under which someone can participate in these platforms do not allow for uniform and comprehensive tax rules within the same Member State. It is quite difficult to produce sufficiently general yet useful rules capable of applying to all the different activities and actors in the sharing economy. In the same vein, it is not unlikely that one Member State has defined the income from a sharing activity, for instance home rentals, as business income, but has not made any provision with regard to the taxation of the income from other sharing economy activities, such as car-sharing.[6]

In principle, (legal and natural) persons engaging in sharing economy activities should be subject to personal and/or corporate income tax and VAT. In addition to that and depending on the platform at issue, specific taxes like tourist tax, municipality tax, social security contributions, or license fees could be applicable.

II DIRECT TAXATION IN THE EU AND THE SHARING ECONOMY

While there are only a handful of Directives in the area of direct taxation in the EU,[7] the recent tax avoidance and tax evasion scandals seem to necessitate more harmonization in this area.[8] The European Commission has presented an ambitious package of legislation targeting

---

[2] Article 115, TFEU.

[3] Secondary legislation is defined as legislation produced by the EU institutions, notably the Council and the European Parliament, on the basis of the EU Treaties. EU secondary law derives from EU primary law, i.e., the EU Treaties. Binding secondary law instruments include EU Regulations, EU Directives, and Decisions.

[4] Article 113, TFEU.

[5] Council Dir. 2006/112/EC of 28 November 2006 on the common system of value added tax (OJ L 347, 11.12.2006).

[6] For more specific examples, see *infra* Section V.A.

[7] The Parent Subsidiary Directive (Council Dir. 2011/96/EU [recast]); the tax merger Directive (Council Dir. 2009/133/EC); the Interest & Royalty Directive (Council Dir. 2003/49/EC); the Directives relating to the administrative cooperation in the field of direct taxation (Council Dir. 2011/16/EU), as amended by Council Directives 2014/107/EU, (EU) 2015/849 and (EU) 2016/881; the Anti-Tax Abuse Directive (Council Dir. 2016/1164).

[8] In the aftermath of the "Panama papers," the leaked data that revealed among many other financial scandals also big cases of tax evasion, the "Luxembourg leaks" revealed a number of tax avoidance schemes in Luxembourg and

tax avoidance[9] – one of the main complications associated with the taxation of the sharing economy.[10]

Most of the secondary legislation in the area of direct taxation seems irrelevant or rather of no direct interest and applicability *ratione materiae*[11] for the purposes of the sharing economy.[12] While most subsidiaries of the big multinational platforms are established in the Member States under the legal form of the Limited Liability Company, it seems that they should be covered by the aforementioned Directives *ratione personae*.

The existing anti-tax avoidance package addresses the problem of tax avoidance from a corporate tax law perspective. In principle, it deals, *inter alia*, with aggressive tax planning and tax avoidance of multinational corporations such as Uber and Airbnb in their cross-border activities. Generally speaking such practices include profit shifting and/or employment of controlled foreign corporations that do not reflect any substance and do not engage in any economic activity in order to benefit from favorable tax rules. By way of example, Airbnb, as many other multinational companies operating within or outside the sharing economy, channels its European profits to its Irish subsidiary because of the very low Irish corporate income tax and transfers its losses to high corporate income tax countries. As a result Airbnb pays very little or almost no tax to all other European countries where it operates.[13] The problem is exacerbated when traditionally low income tax countries like Ireland provide multinational companies like Airbnb with tax rulings. Tax rulings are written statements or "comfort letters" issued by the national tax authorities, giving specific taxpayers clarity on how their corporate tax will be calculated, or on the use of special tax provisions such as transfer pricing arrangements. The term comprises both advance tax rulings (ATRs) and advanced pricing agreements (APAs), or any other kind of advanced confirmation given by governments to taxpayers. Besides specifying their tax due, they usually provide corporate tax breaks, raising potential state aid issues.[14]

---

elsewhere. These scandals, in addition to the BEPS project, have, allegedly, changed the political environment toward more tax transparency and have contributed to the swift adoption of the Anti-Tax Avoidance Directive.

[9] For an overview of the Package *see The Anti Tax Avoidance Package – Questions and Answers (Updated)*, European Commission, http://europa.eu/rapid/press-release_MEMO-16-2265_en.htm.

[10] *Technology Tools To Tackle Tax Evasion and Tax Fraud*, OECD Report, 7 (2017).

[11] None of the direct taxation Directives relates directly to the subject matter of the sharing economy (*ratione materiae*). What is of interest, however, is to examine whether any of the sharing economy participants is affected by the EU direct tax legal framework. In other words, whether the EU direct tax rules apply to them *ratione personae*.

[12] Most of the tax Directives have a very limited scope and applicability. The Parent Subsidiary Directive (Council Dir. 2011/96/EU [recast]) applies only to groups of companies with the purpose of eliminating double taxation and withholding taxes in dividend distributions between the qualifying parents and subsidiaries. Similarly, the Interest and Royalty Directive (Council Dir. 2003/49/EC) aims at eliminating double taxation on intra-group cross-border payments of interest and royalties. The Fiscal Merger Directive (Council Dir. 2009/133/EC) ensures that reorganizations do not trigger taxation of unrealized capital gains and are, hence, tax neutral, while the more recent Anti-Tax Avoidance Directive (ATAD 1; Council Dir. 2016/1164) lays down specific and targeted rules against tax avoidance practices that directly affect the functioning of the internal market. Finally, the Administrative Cooperation in the Field of Direct Taxation Directive (Council Dir. 2011/16/EU, as subsequently amended) concerns the (automatic) exchange of tax information among the tax authorities of different Member States.

[13] See with regard to that, the Parliamentary question *Tax Optimisation by Airbnb in Europe*, European Parliament (Dec. 18, 2015), www.europarl.europa.eu/sides/getAllAnswers.do?reference=E-2015-016006&language=EN and R. Booth and D. Newling, *Airbnb UK Tax History Questioned as Income Passes Through Ireland*, The Guardian (Dec. 19, 2016), www.theguardian.com/technology/2016/dec/19/airbnb-uk-tax-history-questioned-as-income-passes-through-ireland.

[14] By providing specific corporate tax breaks, tax rulings allow for the favorable tax treatment of some taxpayers over others. These "selective advantages" granted by state resources (or through tax allowance and tax reductions) to some companies over others are forbidden under EU law and Article 107(1) TFEU. Article 107(1) provides for a series of conditions that has to be met for the provision to apply. If sharing economy participants enjoy these kinds of tax break and are found to belong in the same market as "traditional economy" participants, they might be affected by the state aid provision. This will be examined in more detail in Section V.C.

The existing EU tax legislation would "catch" such activities if they were abusive and/or artificial or were aiming to avoid taxes by employing specific structures. So far, however, this does not seem to be the main source of revenue loss for the states from sharing economy activities.

The most common problem identified with regard to the sharing economy is the facilitation of tax evasion because of the lack of visibility of the business activity.[15] While the existing legal framework with regard to access and exchange of tax information is continuously being amended to include more and more reporting persons and data to be reported, it still does not apply to sharing economy participants in intra- or inter-Member State situations.[16] In other words, the EU legislation does not coerce a Member State to adopt legislation that will cover sharing economy participants, and as a result the existing Directives do not address the tax evasion problem at the platform or the service providers' level. This problem is not specifically identified in the Anti-Tax Avoidance Package discussed earlier. Instead, the Commission, in line with Action 1 of the BEPS project, identifies as a potential challenge the taxation of the "digital economy" altogether, which, however, suggests that "no special action [is] needed but [the EU] will monitor the situation to see if general anti-avoidance measures are enough to address digital risks."[17]

III VAT IN THE EU AND THE SHARING ECONOMY

The European Commission has acknowledged the many complications that may arise in the application of VAT in the *digital economy*.[18] While it has also identified the many challenges that arise in the context of applying the existing VAT rules in the sharing economy, it has only published two relevant Working Papers on the topic.[19] The two non-binding Working Papers provide guidelines on the application of the existing EU VAT rules to the sharing economy.

What seems to be commonly acknowledged is that the supply of goods and services provided by collaborative platforms and through the platforms by their users are, in principle, VAT taxable transactions.[20] This finding by the Commission already highlights the multi-layered transactions in the context of the sharing economy that can be subject to VAT.

As VAT applies to the provision of services and goods, one has to distinguish between the services provided by the sharing economy platforms or intermediary (for instance, Uber) to

---

[15] *Technology Tools to Tackle Tax Evasion, supra* note 10, at 7.

[16] Dir. 2011/16/EU as amended by Dir. 2014/107/EU; Dir. 2015/849; Dir. (EU) 2016/881.

[17] *See The Anti-Tax Avoidance Package – Questions and Answers (Updated)*, European Commission, Annex I, http://europa.eu/rapid/press-release_MEMO-16-2265_en.htm.

[18] The European Commission in its attempt to modernize VAT for cross-border e-commerce prepared a proposal in December 2016, a *VAT Digital Single Market Package*, European Commission, https://ec.europa.eu/taxation_customs/business/vat/digital-single-market-modernising-vat-cross-border-ecommerce_en. In the same context it has issued in the past years several non-binding documents; *see Communication from the Commission to the European Parliament, the Council and the European Economic and Social Committee on an Action Plan on VAT, Towards a single EU VAT Area – Time to Decide*, European Commission, COM(2016) 148, https://ec.europa.eu/taxation_customs/sites/taxation/files/com_2016_148_en.pdf; *Modernising VAT for Cross-Border B2C E-Commerce*, European Commission, COM(2016) 757 final, https://ec.europa.eu/taxation_customs/sites/taxation/files/com_2016_757_en.pdf.

[19] *VAT Treatment of Sharing Economy*, taxud.c.1(2015)4370160 – Working Paper No. 878, European Commission, Value Added Tax Committee (Sept. 22, 2015), https://circabc.europa.eu/sd/a/878e0591-80c9-4c58-baf3-b9fda1094338/878%20-%20VAT%20treatment%20of%20sharing%20economy.pdf. While not directly connected to the sharing economy, the Commission's Working Paper on the treatment of crowdfunding addresses similar issues to the ones arising in the context of the sharing economy; *VAT Treatment of Crowdfunding*, taxud.c.1(2015)576037 – Working Paper No. 836, European Commission, Value Added Tax Committee (Feb. 6, 2015), https://circabc.europa.eu/sd/a/c9b4bb6f-3313-4c5d-8b4c-c8bbaf0c175a/836%20-%20VAT%20treatment%20of%20Crowd%20funding.pdf.

[20] *A European Agenda for the Collaborative Economy*, Communication from the Commission, COM (2016) 356 final, 14.

the users providing their services through the platform (for instance the Uber drivers) and the provision of services by the latter to the end users (for instance, the Uber users/passengers), as facilitated by the platforms. The two types of transaction should be considered separately for VAT purposes. In this undertaking, different configurations of both types should be taken into account, notably, whether access to the platform is provided with or without consideration and/ or whether the services provided through the platform are subject to a price.[21]

Before assessing each of the transactions separately and independently for VAT purposes, the qualification of the participants as taxable persons, in accordance with the (recast) VAT Directive, has to be considered. In other words, are platform users taxable persons for purposes of the Directive?

According to the VAT Directive, the definition of a taxable person includes any person or body "who, independently, carries out in any place any economic activity, whatever the purpose or results."[22] The test the Court of Justice of the European Union (CJEU) usually applied in order to establish whether the activity at issue fulfills Art. 4(2) of the recast VAT Directive definition consists of examining whether the activity is carried out for the purpose of obtaining income on a continuing basis.[23] This criterion must be assessed on a case-by-case basis "having regard to all the circumstances of the case, which include, *inter alia*, the nature of the property concerned."[24]

The term "economic activity" has been interpreted by the Court of Justice of the European Union (CJEU) in very broad terms, considering the activity *per se* rather than its purpose or results.[25] Along these lines, the CJEU has repeatedly held that:

> [T]he fact that [the] property is suitable only for economic exploitation will normally be sufficient for a finding that its owner is exploiting it for the purposes of economic activities and, consequently, for the purpose of obtaining income on a continuing basis. By contrast, if, by reason of its nature, property is capable of being used for both economic and private purposes, all the circumstances in which it is used will have to be examined in order to determine whether it is actually being used for the purpose of obtaining income on a continuing basis.[26]

Consequently, if the property is, by reason of its nature, clearly used for the purposes of obtaining income on a continuing basis, then the economic activity will be subject to VAT. If the use of the property as a matter of fact is not clear, then a more complex factual analysis will be necessary in order to assess whether the activity is carried out for the purpose of obtaining income on a continuing basis.

Several issues arise with respect to whether sharing economy participants are, and/or should be, subject to VAT. At first sight, the judge-made "continuity" condition seems to be rebuttable

---

[21] *VAT Treatment of Sharing Economy, supra* note 19, at 3.

[22] Council Dir. 2006/112/EC, Art. 9(1). With regard to the second condition (i.e., independent performance), it may be concluded that in cases where the sharing platform can be recognized as an employer of an individual provider (for the latter, the criteria of the existence of a subordination link, the nature of work, and the presence of remuneration should be assessed pursuant to EU law), the individual provider may not be regarded as a taxable person. In such cases, only the sharing platform may be regarded as a taxable person instead – also with regard to underlying supplies of goods and services.

[23] Judgments of July 19, 2012 in *Rēdlihs*, C-263/11, EU:C:2012:497, para. 33; Judgments of June 20, 2013 in *Finanzamt Freistadt Rohrbach Urfahr*, C-219/12, EU:C:2013:413, para. 19.

[24] *Rēdlihs*, C-263/15, para. 29.

[25] Joined Cases C-354/03, C-355/03 and C-484/03 *Optigen Ltd, Fulcrum Electronics Ltd, Bond House Systems Ltd v. Commission*, ECLI:EU:C:2006:16, para. 43; Case 235/85 *Commission v. Netherlands*, ECLI:EU:C:1987:161, para. 8.

[26] *See* Case C-230/94 *Enkler* [1996] ECR I-4517, para. 27, *Rēdlihs, supra* note 23, para. 34 and *Finanzamt Freistadt Rohrbach Urfahr, supra* note 23, para. 20.

in the case of Airbnb rentals, for instance, if one shows that the purpose of renting out the property for a very short period did not aim at "obtaining income *on a continuing basis.*" Hence, in strictly literal interpretation terms, it remains unclear how someone who has rented out his apartment every August for the past five years should be assessed.

Article 12 of the VAT Directive attempts to ensure that even these service providers are subject to VAT. The provision stipulates that "Member States *may* regard as a taxable person anyone who carries out, on an *occasional basis*, a transaction relating to the activities referred to in the second subparagraph of Article 9(1) [...]" (emphasis added). While the Court has held that the mere exercise of the right of ownership and the management of the private property do not constitute economic activity[27] it has also ruled that if "the party has taken active steps to market property by mobilising resources similar to those deployed by producers, traders or persons supplying services within the meaning of Article 4(2) of the Sixth Directive, such as, in particular, the carrying out on that land of preparatory work [...] to make development possible, and the deployment of proven marketing measures," then these initiatives go beyond mere exercise of the management of the private property.[28] In other words, the "marketization" or the "advertising" of the property constitutes, in the Court's view, the distinctive element between mere exercises of the management of the private property vis-à-vis its economic exploitation.

This very broad understanding of the CJEU has led the Commission to suggest: "Given the very wide understanding of the concept of economic activity [...] it can be therefore concluded that the supplies of goods and services made through sharing economy platforms, such as driving customers to requested destinations or renting out immovable property *may* qualify as an economic activity in the sense of the VAT Directive *irrespective of whether such supplies are delivered with clear continuity or on a more occasional basis*"[29] (emphasis added).

Indeed, under these circumstances and as the Commission notes, it seems almost impossible for the sharing economy users to escape the "taxable person" definition. In the Airbnb and Uber scenarios, therefore, once someone uploads the apartment for rent or avails himself through the Uber platform to drive a customer to his destination, he becomes automatically a taxable person for VAT purposes, even if he does so on an occasional basis.[30]

The second thorny issue as to the qualification of a service provider through a sharing economy platform as a taxable person is the definition of *income*. The remuneration or "income" the service providers receive varies widely depending on the platform itself or the provider. As the Commission points out, this income could range from "recovering costs (e.g. for the personal use of a good such as in ridesharing/carsharing) to amounts comparable to business/work activities."[31] While the Commission suggests that "tax rules should follow national laws and jurisprudence, which determine from which moment an activity becomes a business activity,"[32] income is not defined in a uniform manner across the Member States. This adds to the uncertainty of the definition of what constitutes an economic activity, according to the interpretation the CJEU deploys. Accordingly, the same activity may constitute an economic activity for VAT

---

[27] Joined Cases C-180/10 and C-181/10 *Słaby and others*, ECLI:EU:C:2011:589, para. 36 and C-331/14, para. 23.

[28] Joined Cases C-180/10 and C-181/10 *Słaby and others*, paras. 39–41 and C-331/14, para. 24.

[29] *VAT Treatment of Sharing Economy*, *supra* note 19, at 6.

[30] Note here that the only possible "way-out" could be the "exempted" from VAT transactions based on the *de minimis* rules. In this vein, some Member States have established minimum annual turnover for VAT imposition (a VAT registration threshold). Belgium is such an example, whereby the Belgian Programme Law of July 1, 2016 stipulates that individuals providing sharing economy services do not have to register as VAT payers if the EUR 5,000 threshold is not exceeded.

[31] *A European Agenda for the Collaborative Economy*, *supra* note 20, at 41.

[32] *Id.*

purposes in one Member State and not in another where the remuneration at issue does not qualify as income. If one adds to this the different thresholds Member States apply by reference to what constitutes a "professional activity" vis-à-vis an "occasional" intervention of private individuals, the fulfillment of the aforementioned definition(s) becomes even more segregated.

Another difference across the different Member States relates to the exemption of "small businesses" (businesses with low annual turnover) from VAT registration.[33] This special exemption scheme applies in most EU countries but it is not compulsory. However, the VAT Directive rules do not specify whether the "small taxable persons" that participate in the sharing economy, for instance somebody who rents out his apartment occasionally, could benefit from these schemes. The one administratively burdensome option would be to treat them as "full-blown taxable persons" based on "tax points."[34] The other option would be to extend the special rules for small businesses to the "small taxpayers" in the context of the sharing economy.[35]

IV INTERDEPENDENCES WITH OTHER AREAS OF LAW IN THE EU

The lack of sharing-economy-specific tax rules both at the EU and domestic level can be further explained by the interdependence of taxation and other areas of law, such as labor law and contract law, where progress is also lacking. The attribution of the status of an independent contractor or that of a worker or that of an employee to an Uber driver, depending on the circumstances and the national legislation at issue, can have tremendous implications on the way he is taxed by the relevant Member State. For instance, under the (recast) VAT Directive a taxable person for VAT purposes is a person who performs "economic activity" independently.[36] Hence, employed and other persons bound to an employer by a contract of employment or by any other legal ties creating the relationship of employer and employee as regards working conditions, remuneration, and the employer's liability escape taxability under the EU VAT rules.

Similarly, and relevantly, there is no common understanding of the *legal status* of the platforms. The Uber case before the CJEU is demonstrative of this disarray.[37] Is Uber simply a digital platform or a (transportation) services provider?[38] While this question seems at first sight irrelevant for tax purposes, it can certainly affect taxation by (indirectly) determining the status of drivers as contractors, services providers, employees, or workers.

A similar case on the employment status of Uber drivers was decided by a UK employment tribunal.[39] The tribunal was asked whether the Uber drivers qualified as self-employed/independent contractors or workers. In defining whether the Uber drivers should be treated as contractors, the tribunal looked into whether income tax and National Insurance were deducted from their pay. Conversely, in order to determine their tax liability the "tax test" would have to look at holiday pay, sick pay, and pension rights.[40] The UK tribunal concluded that Uber drivers should

---

[33] Council Dir. 2006/112/EC, Arts. 284–87. Member States are allowed to exempt small businesses from VAT registration up to a given threshold. Usually the threshold amounts to EUR 5,000.

[34] Tax points (or "time of supply") for a transaction is the date the transaction takes place for VAT purposes. Tax points can be, for instance, the date of invoice or the day the supply took place.

[35] H. Kogels and M. van Hilten, *Never a Dull Moment*, 28 Int'l VAT Monitor, 3 (2017).

[36] Dir. 2006/112/EC on the Common System of Value Added Tax (Recast)), Arts. 9(1) and 10.

[37] *Asociación Profesional Élite Taxi v. Uber Systems Spain SL*, C-434/15, ECLI:EU:C:2017. The CJEU decided in this Grand Chamber case that the services provided by Uber are covered by services in the field of transport.

[38] AG Szpunar opined on May 11, 2017 that Uber should be treated as a transport company since the service of connecting passengers and drivers with one another by means of the smartphone application was a secondary element.

[39] *Aslam and Farrar and others v. Uber BV, Uber London Ltd and Uber Britannia Ltd* (2202550/2015), Employment Tribunal. Note that Uber has launched an appeal against the Tribunal's ruling.

[40] L. Sayliss, *Be Careful What you Wish for*, 12(178) Taxation 12, 13 (2016).

be classed as workers with access to minimum wage, sick pay, and paid holidays, although they treat themselves as self-employed for tax purposes.[41] The case highlights the "artificial" distinction between labor and tax law in the sharing economy and raises the question of whether there is a need to coordinate the interrelated policy areas.

V TAXATION OF THE SHARING ECONOMY IN THE EU: A BRIEF COMPARATIVE APPROACH

A *Different Initiatives and Challenges*

Many different trends can be discerned among the Member States with regard to the taxation of the sharing economy. Some of them are currently contemplating the adoption of specific sharing economy rules, while others are applying *mutandis mutandis* the existing legal framework to the sharing economy.[42] For the latter scenario to be successful, it would presuppose the existence of a strong network of exchange of information between the platform and the tax authorities, the platform and the services provider, as well as the platform and the end users.[43] It would also presuppose – at the national level – a clear and up-to-date definition of who is a taxable person and what constitutes income for tax purposes in the context of the sharing economy. While some Member States have already introduced such rules for *some* of the many possible sharing economy activities, some others have not followed suit. For instance, in Greece, only very recently a new provision was added to the Income Tax Code,[44] providing that income from ("Airbnb type") short-term rentals would be considered as income from immovable property and would be subject to the relevant provisions.[45] This systematization would only apply as long as the hosts do not provide any other service (with the exception of furnishing bed sheets and towels). If any other service is provided, such as breakfast, cleaning, etc., then the income received for the rental of the property would qualify as income from business activities.[46] Car-sharing-specific tax rules have not yet been enacted. The Commission in its Communication has provided for an overview of some Member States' tax initiatives targeted at the sharing economy.[47] Most of these proposed measures concentrate around providing definitions relating to the sharing economy, raising awareness concerning the tax issues that arise, facilitating the exchange of information and presenting tax relief measures for participants in the sharing economy.

Tax relief measures can be direct/intentional or indirect/unintentional. The first set encompasses tax relief measures enacted by the Member States and the second set relates to the inability (intentional or unintentional) of the Member States to collect the taxes due because of the difficulties the national tax authorities face in identifying the business activity in the sharing economy context. The latter issue is premised on the tax compliance and enforcement difficulties associated with identifying the taxpayers and taxable income as well as with under-reporting

---

[41] *Aslam and Farrar and others* v. *Uber BV, Uber London Ltd and Uber Britannia Ltd* (2202550/2015), Employment Tribunal, para. 65.

[42] According to *A European Agenda for the Collaborative Economy, supra* note 20, at 42, the Member States that build on the guidance on existing tax rules with respect to the sharing economy include Austria, Slovakia, and Lithuania.

[43] The Member States that rely on the exchange of information include the UK, France, and Finland. *Id.*

[44] The provision was added in accordance with the Law Decree 4472/2017.

[45] In this case taxation is progressive and as follows: for income of EUR 0–12,000: 15 percent; EUR 12,0001–35,000: 35 percent; and from EUR 35,001 onward: 45 percent.

[46] In this case taxation is progressive and as follows: for income of EUR 0–20,000: 22 percent; EUR 20,0001–30,000: 29 percent; EUR 30,0001–40,000: 37 percent; and from EUR 40,001 onward: 45 percent.

[47] *A European Agenda for the Collaborative Economy, supra* note 20, at 27 *et seq.*, Table 6.

by taxpayers. These possibilities for tax evasion have obliged some Member States to enhance their exchange of information systems or to facilitate and incentivize the platforms to collect the taxes due (notably VAT and tourist taxes). Some Member States have also attempted to incentivize the service providers to include their income from the sharing economy when filing their tax returns through simplified procedures or automated "pre-filled" tax declarations available to the service providers directly through the platforms.[48] In France, for example, by a law of July 2016, collaborative platforms will have to communicate to each individual providing services in the collaborative economy an annual summary of their tax situation, mentioning how and how much they have to declare to the tax authorities.[49]

A commonly cited example of a successful strategy of simplifying and streamlining tax collection is Estonia. Estonia has introduced a pilot scheme for simplified income declaration for ride-sharing services. Consequently, transactions between the driver and the customer are registered by the collaborative platform, which then only sends the data that is relevant for taxation purposes to the authorities, who will then pre-fill taxpayer tax forms. The main idea is to help taxpayers fulfill their tax obligations effectively and with minimum effort. Estonia now contemplates expanding this scheme to other types of sharing economy businesses.[50]

B Enforcement: Collection of Taxes

Besides using tax simplification and tax clarity as incentives for submitting their tax returns, another option for reducing tax evasion in the sharing economy context is premised on the collaboration between the platforms and the national tax authorities. In this case the platform at issue itself collects the relevant tax upon agreement with the national tax authorities.

This example has already been implemented in some cities in the context of Airbnb. For instance, in Amsterdam the authorities have concluded an agreement with Airbnb to collect tourist tax. Similarly, Airbnb has on several occasions partnered with local authorities around the world, including Lisbon and Paris in Europe, to collect and remit occupancy taxes.

Similarly, and with regard to VAT, the Airbnb website provides that Airbnb collects VAT in all Member States by reference to the services provided through the platform.[51] This, however, excludes the VAT the hosts (would) have to pay concerning the services they have provided to the end users. The collection of this VAT relies on the "goodwill" of the hosts. At this stage the

---

[48] It is noteworthy examining this vis-à-vis the reporting obligations in the USA. With regard to that *see* Shu-Yi Oei and D. Ring, *Can Sharing Be Taxed?* 93 Wash. U. L. Rev. 989, 1070 (2016),: "sharing businesses are […] responsible for information reporting with respect to independent contractor income. There are two primary information reporting regimes that are relevant to the sharing economy: (1) Form 1099-MISC information reporting required under I.R.C. § 6041, and (2) Form 1099-K information reporting required under I.R.C. § 6050W. […] [A]ll 'third party settlement organizations' making payments to payees in settlement of third party network transactions must report such payments on Form 1099-K if the payments to the participating payee exceed $20,000 and if there are more than 200 transactions with the participating payee. The term 'third party settlement organization' was meant to include services such as PayPal, Amazon, and Google Checkout." *Id*. at 1032–37. If the earnings of the service provider fell below this threshold, then the appropriate form to be submitted would be the Form 1099-MISC. With regard to this and the confusion about the reporting numbers in the Form 1099-K, *see also* Shu-Yi Oei and Diane Ring, this volume.

[49] *A European Agenda for the Collaborative Economy*, *supra* note 20, at 43. The Finance Act of 2016 has introduced a series of obligations to the platforms and the taxpayers in order to ensure their taxation. Specifically, the platforms are obliged to send their users' earnings directly to the relevant social security and tax administrations as of 2019. In principle, all online platforms are concerned, regardless of whether they are based in France or abroad. Hence, the tax return filled out by the platform will include information like the total gross income received by the user during the calendar year for its activities on the online platform, and a copy of it will be sent to the users.

[50] *Id.*

[51] For instance, in Greece Airbnb collects a tax rate of 5 percent VAT per night.

facilitation through Airbnb or through the tax authorities could provide an incentive for the hosts to pay VAT. Another way for Member States to force the hosts in the Airbnb example to pay VAT (and/or other taxes) is by obliging hosts who want to provide their services through the platform to sign up to a special register.[52] The problem with this solution is that it cannot monitor the frequency nor the duration of the services and, hence, it can be easily rendered ineffective.

A remedy against the possible tax evasion that may arise from the non-payment of VAT by the service providers is the collection of this VAT (also) by the relevant platform, provided, however, that the hosts have exceeded the threshold for VAT registration.[53] This way all relevant details that would define the amount to be paid by the taxpayer would already be available to the platform and the risk of tax evasion would be minimized. At the moment, no measures have been taken in this direction and it is becoming clearer that this legislative gap has caused a lot of confusion among users.[54] The collection of direct taxes poses more significant challenges. Currently it is for the Member States to ensure that effective mechanisms are in place to monitor service providers' business activities in the sharing economy and to tax them accordingly. While practically the cooperation between the platform and the national tax authorities could again be of help, it might clash with the EU data protection legal framework.[55] Hence, according to this legislation, it would most likely be against EU law for the platforms to give to the tax authorities all relevant data (for instance the name of the host, the duration of the rental, and the details of the property). It would be for the Member States to enact legislation that provides for exceptions to the rule of data protection and to ensure that these exceptions are in line with the principle of proportionality. However, in this case it would be difficult for the platform itself to collect the direct tax due. Although it has been suggested, in general, to outsource certain legislative and control functions to the platforms,[56] this recommendation would not thrive in direct taxation. While platforms are indeed "best placed to ensure compliance with the rules by their users [and] ideally positioned to ensure enforcement of service providers' legal obligations since all the information is already centralized on the platform,"[57] the assessment of the service providers' tax liability cannot take place independently from their overall tax liability, that is without taking into account the taxpayers' other income and personal and family situation.

C Competitive Advantages and Triggering of State Aid Rules?

The general trend that can be identified relates to the *effective* lower taxation many sharing economy actors enjoy. Some Member States, such as the UK, have already enacted tax relief measures especially for sharing economy actors,[58] while others indirectly and effectively allow the non-payment of several taxes.[59]

As shown in the previous section, collecting VAT and other local or sector-specific taxes poses several difficulties for many Member States. The problem is even more exacerbated, however,

---

[52] Greece, for instance, is one of the countries that adopts this system.

[53] For more details on this, *see supra* Section III.

[54] For this uncertainty see as an example the Airbnb case; VAT, Airbnb, https://community.withairbnb.com/t5/ Everything-Else/VAT/td-p/4501.

[55] Charter of Fundamental Rights of the EU, the Data Protection Directive 95/46/EC repealed by Regulation (EU) 2016/679 and Directive (EU) 2016/680, entering into force in 2018.

[56] Europe Economics, *The Cost of non-Europe in the Sharing Economy* 57 (2015).

[57] G. Vara Arribas, B. Steible, and A. De Bondt, Cost of non-Europe in the Sharing Economy: Legal Aspects, EIPA Report 65 (Feb. 2016).

[58] For a more detailed discussion of these trends and the references to the relevant documents, *see A European Agenda for the Collaborative Economy*, supra note 20, at 27 *et seq.*, Table 6.

[59] V. Hatzopoulos and S. Roma, *Caring for Sharing? The Collaborative Economy under EU Law*, 54 Common Market L. Rev. 81, 112 (2017).

in the case of direct taxes. The difficulty lies in obligating the service providers/ "prosumers" (Airbnb hosts, Uber drivers) to declare the income they have received in their tax returns. If one adds to this the fact that most Member States are currently allowing companies operating in the sharing economy, such as Uber, to avoid paying social security contributions[60] or claiming any license fees, it becomes clear that these companies enjoy tax-related and other economic advantages in comparison to other (non-sharing-economy participant) companies.[61]

These economic advantages are likely to trigger state aid rules.[62] By reducing their effective tax burden either through active tax benefits or through a poor or nonexistent collection of taxes, companies like Airbnb and Uber are placed at a competitive advantage vis-à-vis their competitors.

Despite hotel owners' and taxi drivers' complaints that they are subject to unfair competition by Airbnb and Uber with regard to taxes and other regulatory loopholes, the applicability of the state aid rules is not entirely clear. As provided in Article 107(1) TFEU and as interpreted by the Court, for state aid rules to apply the (tax) measure at issue has to be selective. The selectivity test encompasses the identification of the reference system. In other words, the examination of whether taxis and Uber or hotels and Airbnb belong in the same reference framework and can be considered in a comparable situation. If this is found to be the case, then state aid rules may be applicable, provided that all the other remaining conditions of Article 107(1) are met. There is no specific test developed by the CJEU to define the reference framework. Instead, the CJEU seeks to establish the reference framework on an ad hoc basis. This, in conjunction with some inconsistent judgments, leaves very little room for speculation as to whether sharing and non-sharing economy competitors would belong in the same reference framework.

VI REMAINING CHALLENGES

The European Commission recently published two proposals for two Council Directives on the taxation of the digital economy,[63] and one (non-binding) Commission Recommendation relating to the corporate taxation of a significant digital presence.[64] Currently, it appears that no political agreement will be reached at EU level with regard to the two proposals. These proposals came immediately after the release of the OECD interim report on the tax challenges arising from digitalization.[65] While none of these documents addresses specifically the taxation of the sharing economy, there would be significant repercussions for it. The OECD interim report

---

[60] The question relates, of course, to the definition of these service providers as independent workers, or employees. Nicola Countouris and Luca Ratti, this volume.

[61] Hatzopoulos and Roma, *supra* note 60, 112–13.

[62] State aids, or state subsidies, are forbidden in the EU. The definition of state aids is provided in Article 107(1) TFEU and reads as follows: "Save as otherwise provided in the Treaties, any aid granted by a Member State or through State resources in any form whatsoever which distorts or threatens to distort competition by favoring certain undertakings or the production of certain goods shall, in so far as it affects trade between Member States, be incompatible with the internal market." The exemptions from the general prohibition are set out in Article 107(2) and (3) TFEU. In the given context, it is interesting to note that state aids do not include only "active" state subsidies and capital injections. In contrast, they also cover tax exemptions, tax allowances, tax deductions, non-collection of taxes and in general, any kind of tax alleviation.

[63] Proposal for a Council Directive laying down rules relating to the corporate taxation of a significant digital presence, 21 March 2018, COM (2018) 147 final and Proposal for a Council Directive on the common system of a digital services tax on revenues resulting from the provision of certain digital services, 21 March 2018, COM (2018) 148 final.

[64] Commission Recommendation of 21 March 2018 relating to the corporate taxation of a significant digital presence, C(2018) 1650 final.

[65] OECD, *Tax Challenges Arising from Digitalisation – Interim Report 2018 – Inclusive Framework on BEPS* (March 2018).

notes that focus should be placed on the contractual relationships between the platforms and the service providers, as the gray zones that can be found therein could lead to the minimization of the tax liability and the tax base. The solutions in the taxation of the sharing economy, in the OECD's view, should focus a) on improving the effective taxation of activities facilitated by online platforms through improving taxpayers' education and facilitating self-reporting and through obtaining tax data about transactions facilitated through the platforms;[66] and b) on enhancing the effectiveness of tax compliance through new technologies and by reducing compliance burdens for the taxpayers through automated compliance processes.

The EU proposals focus on the digital economy and while from a contextual interpretation they appear to apply equally to all digital platforms (including sharing economy platforms) and the services they provide, a literal interpretation of the definition could provide otherwise.[67] The proposal on the corporate taxation of a significant digital presence is the suggested long-term solution by the European Commission. It aims to ensure that profits of the big digital companies are taxed where the company has a "significant digital presence," a virtual permanent establishment.[68] The interim solution, in the European Commission's view, is the introduction of a digital services tax on revenues resulting from the provision of certain digital services. These tax revenues would be collected by the Member State where the users are located. The EU proposals, thus, concentrate on ensuring that the digital (and, presumably, sharing) economy platforms are taxed sufficiently within the EU (on their profits and on their revenues respectively), without focusing on the equally problematic taxation of the service provider, i.e., the taxi driver in the Uber case or the host in the Airbnb case.

In the VAT area the Commission presented in December 2016 a package of proposed legislation on modernizing VAT for cross-border e-commerce, which, however, does not include any sharing-economy-specific rules.[69]

The main challenge remaining, even if both EU proposals are adopted is, in my opinion, compliance and enforcement. How can Member States ensure the collection of both direct and indirect taxes due? On the VAT and other taxes (such as tourist taxes) progress has been made through their collection by the platforms themselves. As explained, while this method is not comprehensive of all taxes implied nor free of pitfalls, it still ensures the collection of *some* taxes by the States.

The second challenge is identifying the taxpayers and the taxable income. This undertaking can only be successful at the service providers or "prosumers" level if effective exchange of information mechanisms are put in place. As the Commission suggests, "raising awareness on tax obligations, making tax administrators aware of collaborative business models, issuing guidance,

---

[66] This latter point could clash with data protection rules in the EU.

[67] The definitions, for instance, on what is included under "digital services" and what is not in the proposal on the corporate taxation of a significant digital presence leaves room for debate as to whether the provision of services by the sharing economy platform fall under this definition. In the press release, however, the Commission noted that the proposal would apply to digital platforms in general (including sharing economy platforms).

[68] For a company to be considered to have a significant digital presence at a Member State one or more of the following conditions must apply: a) the proportion of total revenue obtained in that tax period and resulting from the supply of those digital services to users located in that Member State in that tax period exceeds EUR 7 million; (b) the number of users of one or more of those digital services who are located in that Member State in that tax period exceeds 100,000; (c) the number of business contracts for the supply of any such digital service that are concluded in that tax period by users located in that Member State exceeds 3,000.

[69] For an overview of the package *see Digital Single Market – Modernising VAT for Cross Border e-Commerce: VAT Digital Single Package* –European Commission, Dec. 1, 2016, https://ec.europa.eu/taxation_customs/business/vat/digital-single-market-modernising-vat-cross-border-ecommerce_en.

and increasing transparency through online information can all be tools for unlocking the potential of the collaborative economy."[70]

The example of introducing thresholds that escape taxation may, indeed, incentivize service providers to report these very small tax-free amounts.[71] However, this does not solve the problem as it cannot ensure reporting in the case of higher profits.

Information sharing on the part of the platforms is the key to ensuring compliance, in particular with regard to reporting. The existing EU tax directives, however, cannot force platforms like Airbnb to give tax authorities information about their users. In contrast, the EU has very solid data protection rules enshrined either in the Charter of Fundamental Rights or in secondary legislation. Ensuring tax compliance is, thus, a domestic tax issue that must be pursued in line with the existing rules on data protection.

CONCLUSION

As discussed, the taxation of the sharing economy in the EU is not regulated at EU level, but instead at Member State level. Until recently, many Member States did not have tax-specific "sharing economy" laws, but in the light of increasing possibilities for tax evasion, they have slowly introduced relevant provisions. Hence, Member States apply different tax rules and have in place different (if any) monitoring systems in order to ensure compliance and the payment of taxes by the platforms and the service providers. In this attempt, they are often faced with challenges that emanate from the non-inclusive EU tax legislation[72] and other "legal areas" not regulated at EU level, such as labor law and the characterization of the sharing economy service providers as workers or as independent contractors. In order to mitigate these uncertainties and conflicts, the EU should take comprehensive action in the sharing economy, not necessarily by exhaustively regulating this area, but by adopting legislation that would establish general principles that could function as guidelines for all Member States. The EU put forward very recently two proposals for EU Directives that address the taxation of the *digital* economy as a whole. While it seems unlikely that political consensus will be reached with regard to these two proposals, even if they are eventually adopted they will deal with only part of the problem in the taxation of the sharing economy, notably the taxation of the profits of the platforms in the European Union. The taxation of the service providers, one of the main problems of tax evasion in the sharing economy, is, thus, yet to be resolved.

---

[70] A *European Agenda for the Collaborative Economy, supra* note 20, at 356.

[71] The UK has introduced such thresholds. The "rent a room scheme," for instance, allowed tax exemption for sharing economy participants earning up to £7,500 in a year for 2018. France introduced recently a similar measure applying to specific cases, setting the threshold at EUR 5,000 a year.

[72] See, for instance, the definition of the "taxable person" for VAT purposes in *supra* Section III.

28

Taxation and Innovation

The Sharing Economy as a Case Study

Jordan M. Barry

INTRODUCTION

New innovations in technologies and markets provide both tests and opportunities for policymakers. This chapter considers the relationship between the US federal income tax system and innovation, using the sharing economy as a focal point for analysis. It begins in Section I by considering whether, and to what extent, the tax system is well suited to encouraging innovation. Section II then takes the converse perspective, examining how innovation can be used to shed light on the tax system and can suggest ways to improve its operation and design. Surprisingly, innovation may be able to do more to advance our tax system than the tax system can to advance innovation.

I USING THE TAX SYSTEM TO ENCOURAGE INNOVATION

Is tax law a good tool for encouraging innovation? As we consider this question, it is useful to distinguish between two different types of innovation: technological innovation and transactional innovation. Technological innovation, as the name implies, refers to the development of new and improved scientific technology. Transactional innovation, in contrast, refers to different ways of transacting. Although these ideas are conceptually distinct, they are nonetheless related, as the sharing economy illustrates well: The "sharing economy" is defined by transactional innovation – people gaining access to others' assets in ways that would have been notably more difficult in earlier years. Uber and Lyft give people access to cars and drivers on a temporary, short-term, location-matched, and as-needed basis. Airbnb accomplishes a similar feat with real property; TaskRabbit connects people with labor.[1] In each of these cases, the method of transacting has become increasingly attractive as a result of new technology – specifically, information technology that helps match would-be buyers and sellers who would otherwise have difficulty connecting.[2]

---

[1] For instance, Just Park matches people with unused parking spaces and drivers looking for parking. EatWith matches people with a local host who will prepare you a home-cooked meal. GoShare, which describes itself as "Your Friend with a Truck," matches users with local truck or van owners willing to provide a variety of hauling or moving services. Streetbank lets neighbors borrow all manner of things from each other, from fondue sets to rollerblades to electric can openers. *See* JustPark, www.justpark.com/; Eat With, www.eatwith.com/; GoShare, www.goshare.co/; Streetbank, www.streetbank.com/. Other examples abound.

[2] Although technological innovation has been a key driver of the sharing economy, in general, transactional innovation need not depend on technological innovation. For example, the development of the corporation as an organizational

Because transactional innovation and technological innovation are conceptually distinguishable, it is worth considering each in turn.

A Transactional Innovation

The mechanisms through which we interact are extremely important and have far-reaching implications. A number of technology companies have concluded that changing existing transactional structures is as important to their success as developing their key technologies. For example, electric-car manufacturer Tesla has decided that changing state laws governing car sales is an essential component of its business model.[3] The Chief Technology Officer of Hyperloop One, which is attempting to make a futuristic vacuum-tube transport network that could transport passengers at over 700 miles per hour, has stated that he is more concerned about navigating the legal landscape than about developing the necessary technology.[4]

Unfortunately, transactional innovation often receives relatively little consideration from the general public and policymakers. And, to the extent that tax policymakers and regulators do think about new or unconventional ways of structuring transactions, they often do so with a skeptical eye.[5]

This is understandable once one considers the dynamics involved. It is helpful to think of transacting parties meeting over a bargaining table to hash out the terms and structure of their deal. This negotiation – be it a literal one or a metaphorical one mediated by the market or other institutions – gives the parties the opportunity to structure their deal in the way that gives them the greatest combined benefits.[6]

This is all well and good for the parties, who are at the table and thus have the chance to look after their own interests. However, any deal the parties strike will affect others as well. Notably, the US government has an interest in their transaction, as it stands to receive more or less tax revenue depending on the structure of the parties' deal.[7] For their part, the parties wish

---

form represented an important transactional innovation with far-reaching implications, but was not dependent on technological innovation *per se*.

[3] Many states prohibit car manufacturers from selling to customers directly, mandating that they sell through independent dealerships instead. Tesla is convinced that car dealerships have strong incentives to push gasoline-powered vehicles over electric ones and, as a result, it cannot succeed unless it can sell to customers directly. This has led Tesla to take on state dealership laws and, with them, locally politically powerful car dealerships. *See, e.g.*, Daniel A. Crane, *Tesla and the Car Dealers' Lobby*, Regulation, 10–14 (Summer 2014), http://object.cato.org/sites/cato.org/files/serials/files/regulation/2014/7/regulation-v37n2-3.pdf; Elizabeth Pollman and Jordan M. Barry, *Regulatory Entrepreneurship*, 90 S. Cal. L. Rev. 383, 387 (2017).

[4] Caroline O'Donovan, *Hyping the Hyperloop: How a Moonshot Technology Could Become a Reality*, BUZZFEED (Oct. 11, 2015, 6:01 AM), www.buzzfeed.com/carolineodonovan/hyping-thehyperloop-how-elon-musks-dream-could-become-a-rea#.ccRqWaX5k; *see also* Pollman and Barry, *supra* note 3, at 407–08.

[5] Jordan M. Barry and Paul Caron, *Tax Regulation, Transportation Innovation, and the Sharing Economy*, 82 U. Chi. L. Rev. Dialogue 69, 73–74 (2015).

[6] *See generally* Victor Fleischer, *Regulatory Arbitrage*, 89 Tex. L. Rev. 227 (2010); *see also* Jordan M. Barry, *On Regulatory Arbitrage*, 89 Tex. L. Rev. 69 (2011); Frank Partnoy, *Financial Derivatives and the Costs of Regulatory Arbitrage*, 22 J. Corp. L. 211 (1997).

[7] The government will often have several interests in a transaction, but this chapter focuses primarily on the government's interest as a revenue collector. *See* Fleischer, *supra* note 6, at 238 ("[C]onceptually there are three parties, not two, at the negotiating table [in tax transactions]: the buyer, the seller, and the government."). The same logic holds for state governments. One might be tempted to think that any payment by one party reduces its taxes in the same amount that its counterparty's tax bill rises, making the government indifferent to the details of the parties' transaction. There is something to this, and it is one of the reasons why arm's-length transactions are the backbone of income tax systems. *See, e.g.*, Jordan M. Barry and Victor Fleischer, *Tax and the Boundaries of the Firm*, unpublished work in progress, at 3. However, a number of issues complicate the picture. The two parties may be in different tax

to pay the government as little as possible; any dollar that the parties do not pay the government is one that the parties can divide among themselves. The incentive to reduce the amount of money that goes to the government is always there, and it drives many inventive and cutting-edge transactions.[8]

Of course, the government understands the parties' incentive to minimize their tax liability, and it crafts tax law with an eye toward encouraging compliance and discouraging transaction structures designed to avoid and evade taxes. For example, employers are required to report to the government how much they pay their individual employees in salary and must withhold and pay taxes on behalf of their employees.[9] These reporting and withholding obligations largely foreclose any opportunity for employees to avoid paying taxes by misreporting their salary income.[10] There are also rules that prevent employees and employers from avoiding these obligations.[11] Other examples abound.[12]

Taxpayers' responses to tax laws exhibit boundless creativity. This ingenuity extends to tax laws intended to constrain taxpayers' avoidance and evasion activities. As Professor Marty Ginsberg quipped, "every stick crafted to beat on the head of a taxpayer will metamorphose sooner or later into a large green snake and bite the commissioner on the hind part."[13] Nor is this creativity a new phenomenon; inventive tax avoidance schemes stretch back thousands of years.[14] In light of taxpayers' clear incentives and the historical record, when a regulator sees a new transaction structure, her first response is often skepticism, based on the concern that the new structure is motivated by the desire to avoid taxes.

Her secondary response may well be annoyance. Laws and rules designed to encourage compliance are often built based on assumptions about how the parties will interact – an employer paying a salary to an employee, a corporation paying a dividend to a shareholder, and so forth. Even if a new transaction structure is not driven by tax avoidance motives, it may still impair the operation of the tax collection system, or inconvenience regulators more generally, simply because it does not fit neatly into a transaction class that the system was designed to handle.[15]

---

brackets; the payment may not be deductible for the buyer, such as an item purchased for personal consumption; one party may be tax-exempt; the parties may have different taxable years; and so on.

[8] For instance, inversion transactions, in which a business shifts its parent corporation's legal domicile to a lower-tax nation, have been "the hottest trend in M&A" in recent years. These transactions are widely recognized as being tax-driven. *See, e.g.*, Shayndi Raice, *How Tax Inversions Became the Hottest Trend in M&A*, Wall St. J., Aug. 15, 2014, www.wsj.com/articles/how-tax-inversions-became-the-hottest-trend-in-m-a-1407240175.

[9] 26 U.S.C. §§ 3402, 6051.

[10] *See* Internal Rev. Serv., Dep't of the Treasury, *Federal Tax Compliance Research: Tax Gap Estimates for Tax Years 2008–2010* at 12 (2016), www.irs.gov/pub/irs-soi/p1415.pdf (reporting that the government collects 99 percent of income tax due on wages and salaries); Bruce Bartlett, Tax Withholding Still Controversial after 70 Years, NY Times Blog (Oct. 22, 2013), http://economix.blogs.nytimes.com/2013/10/22/tax-withholding-still-controversial-after-70-years.

[11] For instance, payments to independent contractors are generally not subject to withholding and are less likely to be subject to reporting obligations. Thus, an employer may wish to have its workers classified as independent contractors instead of employees. However, an employer cannot opt into this lighter regulatory regime simply by declaring that a worker is an independent contractor instead of an employee. Moreover, employers who misclassify their workers are subject to civil and, in certain circumstances, criminal penalties. 26 U.S.C. §§ 6041, 6674, 7204.

[12] For example, the Internal Revenue Code requires withholding on a variety of payments made to non-US taxpayers, requires disclosure of payments made in the course of business of more than $600, and treats certain contractual payments as dividend payments subject to withholding. *See* 26 U.S.C. §§ 871, 1441, 1442, 6041.

[13] *See, e.g.*, Martin D. Ginsburg, *Making the Tax Law through the Judicial Process*, 70 ABA J. 74, 76 (Mar. 1984).

[14] For example, in ancient Rome, slaves were exempt from taxes to which landowners were subjected. Some small landowners sold themselves into slavery and placed themselves under the protection of a landlord, all while continuing to farm the same lands as they had before. Bruce Bartlett, *How Excessive Government Killed Ancient Rome*, 14 Cato J. 287, 300–01 (1994).

[15] If transactions are generally a good thing – for example, if parties can usually be trusted to look out for their own interests and externalities tend to be small or positive – then the government should favor them as a policy matter. If

Viewed together, then, one can understand why, instead of encouraging transactional innovation, the government might be more likely to seek to squelch it. When the government has taken action to foster a new transactional structure, it has often done so to further some specific, identifiable government policy instead of a generalized interest in promoting innovation.[16] In other words, when the government has encouraged transactional innovation, it has often done so as a means to a particular end. Government is often a lagging actor in this realm, responding to new transaction structures after they have become popular and demonstrated some degree of useful non-tax-avoidance purpose.

B Technological Innovation

Technological innovation, in contrast to its relatively neglected cousin, receives a tremendous amount of political and policy attention. People generally favor fostering technological innovation, and tax incentives are a well-known and frequently used policy lever for encouraging desired behavior.[17] Unfortunately, it is questionable how effective this tool is in practice, especially at this moment in time.

The same dynamic described above – taxpayers using all of the tools at their disposal to reduce their tax liabilities in ways that the government did not anticipate or intend – applies with full force to tax provisions intended to foster technological innovation. This can lead to results that policymakers did not foresee or intend. For example, many members of Congress have decried violent video games, some have argued they cause mass shootings and other violent behavior, and several have introduced legislation to curb them in various ways.[18] Yet video game companies are among the greatest beneficiaries of the tax code, because they can take advantage of provisions that benefit software development, the entertainment industry, and online retail.[19] It is unlikely that Congress intended for violent video game makers to receive these benefits, but their effects are substantial; Professor Calvin Johnson has estimated that income tax laws double video game makers' profits.[20] There are numerous other examples.[21]

---

new transaction structures foster additional transactions, the government should support and encourage those new structures. If, instead, regulators discourage new structures because it makes their jobs more difficult, then this is a type of agency cost.

[16] For example, regulators sought to encourage the use of credit default swaps, on the theory that, by enabling banks to hedge credit risk, they would make banks (and thus the financial system generally) more stable. *See, e.g.*, Frank Partnoy, *Infectious Greed: How Deceit and Risk Corrupted the Financial Markets* 373–75 (2009).

[17] *See, e.g.*, United States Cong. J. Comm. on Taxation, Estimates of Fiscal Tax Expenditures for Fiscal Years 2016–2020, at 2 (2017), www.jct.gov/publications.html (noting that tax incentives "are similar to direct spending programs that function as entitlements to those who meet the established statutory criteria"); *id.* at tbl. 1 (cataloguing billions of dollars of tax incentives for "General Science, Space and Technology," among other areas); *see also* Jordan M. Barry and Bryan T. Camp, *Is the Individual Mandate Really Mandatory?* 135 Tax Notes 1633 (2012).Nor is tax the only policy tool used to create incentives for technological innovation or entrepreneurial activity. *See, e.g.*, Jordan M. Barry, *When Second Comes First: Correcting Patent's Poor Secondary Incentives Through an Optional Patent Purchase System*, 2007 Wis. L. Rev. 585; D. Gordon Smith and Darian M. Ibrahim, *Law and Entrepreneurial Opportunities*, 98 Cornell L. Rev. 1533 (2013).

[18] *See, e.g.*, Anne Broache, *Video Games in Congress' Crosshairs*, CNet.com (June 5, 2006), www.cnet.com/news/video-games-in-congress-crosshairs/; Mike Snider, *Debate Over Video-Game Violence Link Resurfaces*, USA Today (Dec. 19, 2012), www.usatoday.com/story/tech/gaming/2012/12/19/video-games-scrutinized-after-newtown/1778467/.

[19] *See, e.g.*, David Kocieniewski, *Rich Tax Breaks Bolster Makers of Video Games*, N.Y. Times (Sept. 10, 2011), www.nytimes.com/2011/09/11/technology/rich-tax-breaks-bolster-video-game-makers.html.

[20] Alexis Garcia, *Tax Breaks for Game Makers = EPIC FAIL*, Reason.com (May 6, 2014), http://reason.com/reasontv/2014/05/06/tax-breaks-for-game-makers-epic-fail.

[21] For instance, a special rule in the tax code provides that income from the sale of a patent is long-term capital gains, and therefore taxed at a reduced rate, even when the transaction would not otherwise qualify. 26 U.S.C. § 1235. Patents are the only form of intellectual property singled out for such positive treatment; copyrights are

Taxpayers' ingenuity, and the government's knowledge that it cannot predict how that ingenuity will manifest itself, favors caution when crafting special dispensations and tax benefits. Anticipating that the parties (and their lawyers, bankers, and accountants) will think of things that it did not, the government is often inclined to keep new provisions narrow, both by limiting the amount of benefits available and by forcing beneficiaries to satisfy a large number of requirements.[22] These limitations are understandable, but they also reduce the provision's efficacy as a policy tool.

This preference for narrowly circumscribed provisions is particularly problematic for new and developing industries, as their transactional structures may still be in flux. If these structures evolve in an unanticipated direction, they may fall partially or entirely outside of a provision's limited scope.[23] Thus, even a provision adopted with the express intent of helping an industry can easily miss its mark. Incumbent firms, who wish to minimize the benefits available to entrants in order to limit competition, often exacerbate the problem by intentionally reinforcing regulators' inclination toward narrowness.[24]

And, when a targeted provision does miss its mark, correcting course can be a slow and uncertain process. The wheels of the federal government turn slowly. By the time the problem gets corrected, the industry in question may no longer need the help to grow, and may have become an established, incumbent player.[25] If so, the new provision

---

even singled out for negative treatment. 26 U.S.C. § 1221(a)(3). The special rule for patents is often justified on the ground that patents are important for technological development, and that encouraging the former promotes the latter. But for years, methods for avoiding taxes were considered patentable, as a type of business method patent. Thus, the tax law encouraged the development of tax avoidance strategies that tax policymakers could not have intended to promote.

[22] It is worth noting that this concern about limiting beneficiaries also has the effect of making the tax code more complicated. For example, 26 U.S.C. § 280A, which limits deductions for business expenses tied to a person's home, runs approximately 2,200 words.

[23] For example, tax law seeks to encourage Americans to bike to work by allowing a deduction for certain bicycle commuting costs. Barry and Caron, *supra* note 5, at 77–78. Members of Congress have also made clear that they support bicycle-sharing programs. *See, e.g., Members of Congress Lead "Bike-Partisan" Campaign to Support Bike-Sharing at Conventions*, BusinessWire (July 30, 2008), www.businesswire.com/news/home/20080730005183/en/ Members-Congress-Lead-Bike-Partisan-Campaign-Support-Bike-Sharing. However, costs incurred from commuting via bike-sharing services are not deductible, presumably because Congress did not foresee the growth of bike sharing and thus did not think to include such transactions within the tightly limited scope of the bicycle commuting deduction. *See generally* IRS Office of the Chief Counsel, Letter 2013–0032 (July 26, 2013), www.irs.gov/pub/irs-wd/13–0032 .pdf; Barry & Caron, *supra* note 5, at 78–80.

[24] Barry & Caron, *supra* note 5, at 75. In a non-tax example of this, Tesla secured laws allowing it to sell cars directly to consumers in several states. However, in light of stiff resistance from existing car dealerships, these laws are quite limited. For example, New Jersey and Maryland both limit a manufacturer to four dealerships within the state. Both states' laws only apply to manufacturers that exclusively produce particular types of green vehicles. A.B. 3216, 40th Leg. (N.J. 2015); H.B. 235, 2015 Sess. (Md. 2015). Thus, even these limited exceptions are unavailable to other automotive innovators, such as Elio Motors, which has announced plans to produce a $6,800 car that gets 84 highway miles per gallon. *See* Marina Lao et al., *Direct-to-Consumer Auto Sales: It's Not Just About Tesla*, Fed. Trade Comm'n (May 11, 2015, 11:00 AM), www.ftc.gov/newsevents/blogs/competition-matters/2015/05/direct-consumer-auto-sales-its-not-just-about-tesla. New Jersey's law is also limited to manufacturers holding a specified license prior to January 1, 2014 – which essentially means only Tesla qualifies. Some other states have done the same. Todd Bishop, *Tesla Wins Battle Against Auto Dealers in Washington State, But Future Rivals Are Screwed*, GEEKWIRE (Feb. 18, 2014, 4:05 PM), www.geekwire.com/2014/tesla-wins-battle-auto-dealers-washington-state-future-rivals-screwed. *See also* Pollman and Barry, *supra* note 3, at 445–46.

[25] To take a dramatic example, Uber's valuation increased by more than a thousand times in about four years, from less than $50 million in early 2011 to more than $50 billion in mid-2015. For perspective, this put Uber's valuation near General Motors'. Suppose the legislature passed a provision in 2011 to help the then-nascent ride-hailing industry grow, but the provision did not achieve its desired ends because of poor drafting. By the time the provision was corrected, the help likely would not have been needed. Michael Arrington, *Huge Vote of Confidence: Uber Raises $11 Million from Benchmark Capital*, TechCrunch.com (Feb. 14, 2011), https://techcrunch.com/2011/02/14/huge-vote-of-confidence-uber-raises-11-million-from-benchmark-capital/; Paul R. La Monica, *Is Uber Really Worth More Than*

becomes more of a rent-seeking giveaway than a policy tool to encourage a particular result.[26]

Even assuming that these issues can be overcome, the structure of innovation in the United States has changed significantly in a way that makes tax policy a questionable lever for encouraging innovation. Before 1980, large, established corporations accounted for most US research and development activity.[27] Such companies tend to have sophisticated tax departments and thus are likely to be aware of, and responsive to, tax incentives. In such a world, tax incentives would seem a promising avenue for policymakers to deploy.

Since then, relatively small and new companies have been the primary source of growth in US private research and development activities,[28] and there is good reason to think that such companies are relatively unresponsive to tax incentives. For example, consider a group that includes many of the most prominent sharing economy companies: Silicon Valley startups. One might expect that these companies, teeming with experienced, repeat-player entrepreneurs and financiers and pursuing ambitious visions and growth plans, would be some of the country's most sophisticated small and new companies. Yet venture-backed Silicon Valley startups are almost all organized as C corporations.[29] This would seem to make little sense from a basic tax planning perspective: new companies, even those that are ultimately successful, often produce tax losses for years.[30] These losses would be a valuable tax asset for their investors, who often have high incomes and high marginal rates. But because these companies are organized as C corporations, those losses are trapped at the corporate level, where they are much less valuable.[31]

Debate continues as to exactly why this state of affairs persists.[32] The conventional wisdom is that tax is simply not a first-order concern for these companies, and the collateral consequences of tax

---

Ford and GM?, CNN Money (Oct. 27, 2015), http://money.cnn.com/2015/10/27/investing/uber-ford-gm-70-billion-valuation/index.html. The opposite is also possible; in the time that passes before the government corrects course, the industry may wither to the point that it cannot be easily revived.

[26] Of course, this is not to say that every attempt at encouraging innovation will fail, or that law must always lag behind technology. See Elizabeth Pollman, The Rise of Regulatory Affairs in Innovative Startups, in The Handbook of Law and Entrepreneurship in the United States (D. Gordon Smith and Christine Hurt eds., forthcoming, 2018). Moreover, putting rules in place to govern a new industry before that industry is established may reduce the likelihood of regulatory capture.

[27] Robert M. Hunt and Leonard I. Nakamura, The Democratization of U.S. Research and Development after 1980, at 8–9, fig. 2 (Soc'y for Econ. Dynamics, Working Paper No. 121, 2006), www.repec.org/sed2006/up.12143.1138646305 .pdf.

[28] Id. at 9; see also Michael J. Meurer, Inventors, Entrepreneurs, and Intellectual Property Law, 45 Hous. L. Rev. 1201, 1202 (2008).

[29] Joseph Bankman, The Structure of Silicon Valley Start-Ups, 41 UCLA L. Rev. 1737, 1739–40 (1994) ("At the time of initial funding, the venture capitalist will structure (or restructure) the venture. In almost all cases, the venture will be structured as a corporation."); Eric J. Allen and Sharat Raghavan, The Impact of Non-Tax Costs on the Tax Efficiency of Venture Capital Investment 21 (2011 Am. Tax. Assoc. Midyear Meeting Paper: JLTR Conference, Working Paper, 2011), http://papers.ssrn.com/sol3/papers.cfm?abstract_id=1759558 (finding that of 1,067 firms conducting IPOs from 1996–2011, only 55 had initially organized as LLCs and only 19 retained their LLC status at the time of IPO).

[30] See, e.g., Allen and Raghavan, supra note 29 (looking at 1,067 startup firms conducting IPOs from 1996 to 2011 and finding that 83.32 percent had accumulated net operating losses (NOLs) at the time of IPO; total reported accumulated NOLs were approximately $32 billion).

[31] Privately held businesses can organize themselves as partnerships or as C corporations for tax purposes, among other choices. To oversimplify, profits and losses from a partnership flow through to its partners and are included on their individual income tax returns. A partnership with net losses for the year thus gives its partners tax losses, which can offset other income they earned that year, reducing their overall tax bills. The profits and losses of a C corporation are not passed on to its shareholders and remain at the entity level. Losses in a C corporation can offset future taxable income, but that income may take years to materialize, if it ever does. Individuals also face a higher top tax rate than corporations do, making individual losses potentially more valuable.

[32] See, e.g., Bankman, supra note 29, Victor Fleischer, The Rational Exuberance of Structuring Venture Capital Start-ups, 57 Tax L. Rev. 137 (2003); Daniel S. Goldberg, Choice of Entity for a Venture Capital Start-up: The Myth

planning impair higher-priority goals, such as raising capital.[33] In other words, in their early stages, these companies ignore tax incentives because they have more important things to worry about.

But if the most sophisticated startup companies are unmoved to engage in even basic levels of tax planning, one might question whether more complicated tax incentives would be a promising policy lever in this arena.[34] And other tax incentives do seem likely to be more complicated – even if technological innovation has increasingly moved to startups, there are still many large, established companies with sizeable, well-staffed tax departments, as well as accounting firms and outside counsel with creative ideas for lowering their clients' tax burdens. Thus, as described above, any measure passed to spur innovation is potentially liable for abuse in unexpected ways, suggesting that restrictions and limitations are likely.

The Research and Experimentation tax credit illustrates this issue well. The credit is perhaps the most salient tax provision for encouraging innovation, and as such enjoys bipartisan support. It is also lengthy and complex, contains multiple limitations and exclusions, and includes approximately 30 defined terms.[35] The Treasury has issued enough regulations on the credit that it felt the need to issue a table of contents to the regulations.[36] Given the Research and Experimentation credit's intricacies, the benefits available, and the size of other challenges that startups face, there is good reason to doubt how much it encourages startups to innovate.[37]

Perhaps the strongest case for using the tax code as a policy tool to encourage technological innovation in the startup sector is that even successful startups and small companies often have serious credit or cash constraints.[38] Moreover, and relatedly, business investment in these sectors is frequently financed with (and thus limited by) reinvested profits. Viewed in this light, anything that improves these businesses' cash flow is likely to help them survive and grow. Thus, tax provisions rewarding technological innovation would have a positive effect by keeping more cash available to these companies, even if it did nothing to change their capital budgeting decisions.

However, if this is the logic justifying tax incentives to promote innovation, one wonders whether tax incentives are the right tool for the job. Given the political economy of tax lobbying alluded to above, one might worry that larger incumbent firms will shape tax incentive provisions in ways that help them and disadvantage startups. The provisions may have little effect on startups' behavior, yet result in large amounts of forgone revenue from established firms. One wonders whether a lower overall tax rate, or provisions directly aimed at new or small businesses,[39] might be a better policy tool.[40]

---

of Incorporation, 55 Tax Law. 923 (2002); Calvin H. Johnson, *Why Do Venture Capital Funds Burn Research and Development Deductions?*, 29 Va. Tax Rev. 29 (2009).

[33] *See, e.g.*, Allen and Raghavan, *supra* note 29; Fleischer, *supra* note 32, Susan C. Morse, *Startup Ltd.: Tax Planning and Initial Incorporation Location*, 14 Fla. Tax. Rev. 319 (2013); Susan C. Morse and Eric J. Allen, *Innovation and Taxation at Start-Up Firms*, 69 Tax L. Rev. 357 (2016).

[34] *See, e.g.*, Mirit Eyal-Cohen, *Down-Sizing the "Little Guy" Myth in Legal Definitions*, 98 Iowa L. Rev. 1041, 1062 (2012).

[35] 26 U.S.C. § 41. It runs approximately 6,250 words – roughly as long as a chapter in this book. Ten of its defined terms contain the word "research" and seven begin with the word "qualified."

[36] Treas. Reg. § 1.41–0. The table of contents itself runs almost a thousand words.

[37] Morse and Allen, *supra* note 33; Susan Morse, Entrepreneurship Incentives for Resource-Constrained Firms, in *The Handbook of Law and Entrepreneurship in the United States* (D. Gordon Smith and Christine Hurt eds., forthcoming, 2018).

[38] Ivo Welch, *Corporate Finance* 263–64 (4th ed., 2017); cash management can be an especially pressing issue for startups experiencing success and rapid growth; they often must pay for capacity and inventory in advance, but must wait to receive payment from customers.

[39] There are several such provisions in the tax code. *See, e.g.*, 26 U.S.C. §§ 474, 1045, 1202, 1244; *see also* Eyal-Cohen, *supra* note 34, at 1081–86.

[40] *See also* Morse, *supra* note 37.

Looking at the track records of sharing economy companies, the apparent effects of the tax system on the sector's development seem somewhat haphazard and unintentional. For example, companies can depreciate their assets for tax purposes faster than the assets actually lose value, which encourages businesses to purchase hard assets.[41] This would seem to decrease demand for sharing economy firms' products from the business sector. On the other hand, an asset owned by an individual for personal use provides deductions neither when purchased nor as its value depreciates over time.[42] This arguably makes durable goods – such as cars, bicycles, power tools, carpet shampooers, etc. – tax-disadvantaged for individuals to own, which would presumably increase consumer demand for sharing economy firms' products.[43] It seems unlikely that policymakers contemplated that they were simultaneously discouraging business-facing sharing economy companies and encouraging consumer-facing ones, much less that they intended to produce that result.

II USING INNOVATION TO ENCOURAGE THE TAX SYSTEM

Building a well-functioning regulatory regime is difficult. This section considers how innovation in general, and the sharing economy in particular, can help policymakers address two specific types of problems. First, when designing a regulatory regime, it can be challenging to design administrable rules that provide the desired results in all relevant cases. This is especially true with respect to a regime like income tax, which tries to govern the full spectrum of economic activity. Second, even when one has a clear vision of how the system should operate, interest groups undermine that vision by pushing for carve-outs, specific rules that benefit themselves at the expense of the system as a whole. Each of these carve-outs may be small, but their combined effect can be significant, ultimately producing a death by a thousand cuts. I begin with the micro-level issue of groups lobbying for tax benefits before turning to the macro-level issue of how the tax code should answer its central questions.

A Innovation and Tax Micro-Structure

There are a number of economically significant tax provisions that provide concentrated benefits to a small group, and impose costs on a much larger group, in ways that are not politically salient. Many of these provisions have been roundly criticized by tax policy experts,[44] but have nonetheless proven durable for reasons of political economy – the beneficiaries have strong incentives to push for these provisions' enactment and to keep them on the books, while each non-beneficiary (everyone else, essentially) has little incentive to resist them.

These dynamics are not unique to tax provisions. For example, occupational licensing requirements, which have grown expansively in recent decades, provide concentrated benefits to the protected industry, a relatively small group of stakeholders, while imposing costs on the

---

[41] *See* 26 U.S.C. §§ 167, 168.

[42] *See* 26 U.S.C. §§ 167, 262.

[43] On the other hand, owning durable goods provides imputed income, which is not taxed, which cuts in the opposite direction. This is probably most notable with respect to owner-occupied housing, which also comes with other tax advantages that, on net, make it tax-advantaged instead of tax dis-advantaged. *See, e.g.,* 26 U.S.C. §§ 121, 163.

[44] *See, e.g.,* Rosanne Altshuler, *The Case for Fundamental Tax Reform,* 21 Kan. J.L. & Pub. Pol'y 399 (2012); Jordan M. Barry, *The Emerging Consensus for Cutting the Corporate Income Tax Rate,* 18 Chapman L. Rev. 19, 23–24 (2014); Jane G. Gravelle, *Practical Tax Reform for a More Efficient Income Tax,* 30 Va. Tax Rev. 389 (2010).

public at large.[45] For many years, these provisions seemed to proliferate and proved difficult to root out, given the political dynamics.[46]

In recent years, however, we have seen some significant rollbacks of these types of provision. A number of these successes have been driven by "Regulatory Entrepreneurs" – companies that have made changing the law a material part of their business plans.[47] Sharing economy companies are often intermediaries that connect potential counterparties; as a result, they are generally well situated to pursue regulatory entrepreneurship strategies.[48] Some of the most prominent sharing economy companies, such as Uber, Lyft, and Airbnb, are also some of the most prominent regulatory entrepreneurs.

An example is helpful to illustrate these points. Until a few years ago, many cities required cabs to have a special government-issued license or medallion to operate. These licenses were typically in very limited supply.[49] This led to fewer cabs and reduced competition, presumably to the benefit of members of the industry and to the detriment of their customers.[50] Uber and Lyft have targeted these regimes and secured significant changes to them. As a result, Uber added almost 12,000 new for-hire cars to New York City's streets over four years.[51] For comparison, over the preceding 75 years, New York City's cab fleet increased by only 1,000 cabs in total.[52]

Because of the similarities in the political dynamics governing tax lobbying and other forms of rent-seeking, one might have some hope that regulatory entrepreneurship might provide an avenue for ameliorating this problem with our tax laws. Unfortunately, regulatory entrepreneurship is a poor fit for federal income tax policy.

First, regulatory entrepreneurs are not driven primarily by altruism or political philosophy; they are driven by profit motive.[53] Uber and Lyft, which make money by taking a cut of the fare for each ride they facilitate, had strong economic incentives to resist taxi regulations. Airbnb, which has significantly changed the laws governing short-term rentals, has a similar business model and thus similar incentives in that arena. It is somewhat difficult to imagine a company that would reap the kind of concentrated benefits from improving federal tax policy that Uber, Lyft, and Airbnb have received from changing taxi cab and short-term rental regulations.[54] It seems more likely that a company lobbying for tax policy changes will simply seek to minimize its tax liability through some sort of special industry-focused carve-out. And, because regulatory

---

[45] Jacob Goldstein, *So You Think You Can Be a Hair Braider?*, N.Y. Times Mag. (June 12, 2012), http://nyti.ms/Lm66UT.

[46] Nick Timiraos, *White House Warns States on Job-Licensing Requirements*, Wall St. J. (July 30, 2015, 7:44 AM), http://blogs.wsj.com/economics/2015/07/30/need-a-license-for-that-jobthe-white-house-warns-states-against-overdoing-it.

[47] Pollman and Barry, *supra* note 3, at 439.

[48] *See id.* at 416–17. These companies tend to be scalable, facilitating "guerilla growth" and a large number of users. Because their business is connecting people, they are well equipped to communicate with their users, a prerequisite for mobilizing them. Depending on the intermediary, users may be quite invested in its continued existence; an Uber driver, an Airbnb landlord, or a TaskRabbit Tasker may reap hundreds or even thousands of dollars a week via their interaction with the company. This can motivate users to speak up in support of the company's interests when asked to do so. Finally, intermediaries often have significant amounts of personal information about their users, such as where they live and how they use the company's product, which can help them leverage their users for the greatest political effect. *Id.*; *see also infra* notes 58 and 59 and accompanying text.

[49] *See, e.g.,* Katrina M. Wyman, this volume; Paul Stephen Dempsey, *Taxi Industry Regulation, Deregulation & Reregulation: The Paradox of Market Failure*, 24 Transp. L.J. 73, 78 (1996) (explaining that "[t]ypically, taxis are regulated at the local level, with city or county boards restricting the number of firms and number of taxis (with the issuance of medallions)" and that municipalities like New York City have strictly limited medallions, causing the price "to reach exorbitant levels").

[50] *See* Wyman, this volume.

[51] Ginia Bellafante, *Uber Makes its Pain New Yorkers' Problem*, N.Y. Times (July 24, 2015), www.nytimes.com/2015/07/26/nyregion/uber-makes-its-pain-new-yorkers-problem.html.

[52] *Id.* (describing how New York City increased from approximately 12,000 cab medallions to 13,000).

[53] Pollman and Barry, *supra* note 3, at 443.

[54] *Id.*

entrepreneurship increases companies' political power, one might predict that there will be more questionable, concentrated-benefit-providing laws in the future, not fewer.

Second, regulatory entrepreneurship tends to be a more effective strategy when targeted at state and local laws.[55] Entering a market and growing large quickly, before regulators can react definitively, has been one of regulatory entrepreneurs' most effective tactics.[56] By the time the regulators come calling, the company is hopefully "too big to ban"; it has a large network of customers and suppliers that can be mobilized as a political force on the company's behalf, giving the company leverage against the regulators.[57] For many companies, executing this type of "guerrilla growth" strategy at the national level is simply cost-prohibitive. Similarly, time is money, especially for a startup company that expects losses initially and possesses a limited "runway" of investment capital. State and local governments are often designed to move faster than the federal government, which means that legal change is achievable in a shorter period of time.[58] Moreover, the amount of resources required to have a significant political impact at the state and local level is less than at the federal level;[59] by the time a company has gotten large enough to significantly affect federal income tax policy, it may be past the point at which the tax provision in question is needed. Thus, while Uber, Airbnb, and Lyft, some of the sharing economy's most visible successes, have left multiple changed state and local laws in their wake, some of the sharing economy's most visible failures – including Aereo, Napster, Grokster, and Kazaa – failed because they lost legal battles over federal laws.[60]

B *Innovation and Tax Macro-Structure*

When the rules of a regulatory regime do not match the economic substance of the regulated activities, there will be opportunities to engage in regulatory arbitrage – for parties to change the regulatory consequences of their actions without changing the substance of what they are doing – and the regime will not accomplish its intended goals.[61] However, perfectly matching the legal consequences of every action to its substance is prohibitively difficult for a regulatory regime that covers as wide a range of activities as tax law does. Since perfection is impossible, the question then becomes how good the fit is, where the most important areas of divergence lie, and what can be done in response.

Innovation can help shed light on these questions. New developments in transacting and technology provide opportunities to examine how well a given area of regulation has identified its underlying goals and how well existing regulations are geared toward those goals. It can highlight problems that may not have been apparent previously; for example, regulations may stifle something desirable, and may do so in a way that is not obvious. Identifying these problems is a necessary prerequisite for correcting them.

Seen from this perspective, the sharing economy tells us a number of things about the US federal income tax system. There is much good news: the federal income tax is built with the purpose of taxing income, and policymakers and commentators have devoted a great deal of

---

[55] *Id.* at 418–21.

[56] *Id.* at 400–03.

[57] *Id.* at 400–06.

[58] *See, e.g.,* Paul A. Diller, *Why Do Cities Innovate in Public Health? Implications of Scale and Structure,* 91 Wash. U. L. Rev. 1219 (2013–2014).

[59] There are additional benefits to targeting state and local laws, such as the added flexibility a company has in choosing the location and timing of its battles. *See* Pollman and Barry, *supra* note 3, at 418–21.

[60] *Id.* at 422–24.

[61] Barry, *supra* note 6, at 73; Fleischer, *supra* note 6, at 229.

thought to the concept and statutory definition of income. This process has produced results that generally transplant well into new fields of economic activity, including the sharing economy. The tax code defines income expansively, embracing "all income from whatever source derived, including (but not limited to)" 15 separate enumerated items.[62] This statutory language invokes the limits of Congress's constitutional authority to tax incomes, and Treasury Regulations reinforce the statute's broad scope.[63] Thus, the questions of whether an Uber driver has income from fares, an Airbnb host has income from renting out her room, or a TaskRabbit rabbit has income from performing tasks are relatively straightforward under the income tax laws, and the answer – yes, they all have income – is what one would want and expect.[64]

Similarly, many of the rules regarding deductions are built on a well-reasoned foundation: expenses incurred for the purpose of generating income are deductible; expenses incurred for personal consumption are not. Unfortunately, when expenses are incurred for a combination of personal and business motivations, or when personal and business expenses are lumped together, it becomes difficult to maintain this clean dichotomy.

The tax code takes several approaches to the problem of mixed business and personal expenditures. In some instances, it treats mixed expenditures as either purely business-related or purely personal, based on an evaluation of various criteria.[65] In others, it attempts to tease apart the fraction of a combined economic loss attributable to business and personal activities.[66] Many of these attempts have resulted in extremely complicated rules that have given rise to simplified alternative calculation measures[67] or safe harbor provisions.[68]

By blurring the lines between assets held for personal use and for business use, the sharing economy has increased the pressure on this legal boundary. The experiences of sharing economy providers suggest that, although the rules governing expenditures with personal and business components are grounded in reasonable foundations, they are rather messy in practice. For example, as Professors Oei and Ring discuss in Chapter 25, Airbnb hosts who rent out part or all of their residences during the course of the year face a complicated mélange of rules governing the availability and magnitude of their deductions.[69] Given the increasing number of people who now function as sharing economy providers, the provisions governing deductions could benefit from some simplification.

The sharing economy has also increased the importance of distinguishing business and personal expenditures in another way. Taxpayers who are employees of someone else can generally only deduct their work-related expenses to the extent that they exceed a specified percentage of the taxpayer's income.[70] These provisions relieve some of the strain on the line dividing business and personal expenditures; many relatively small expenses that might be hard to classify are simply deemed non-deductible, ending the inquiry. However, these provisions only apply to expenses incurred by employees.[71] To date, many sharing economy providers have

---

[62] 26 U.S.C. § 61.

[63] *See* U.S. Const. Amend. XVI; Treas. Reg. §§ 1.61–1, 1.61–2, 1.61–14.

[64] *See* Shu-Yi Oei and Diane M. Ring, *Can Sharing Be Taxed?*, 93 Wash. U. L. Rev. 989 (2016).

[65] *See, e.g.*, 26 U.S.C. §§ 262(b), 280A, 280F; Treas. Reg. § 1.162–5; *Pevsner* v. *Commissioner*, 628 F.2d 467 (5th Cir. 1980). Commuting expenses are not deductible, outside of specific exemptions, while the costs of business travel are deductible. *Compare Commissioner* v. *Flowers*, 326 U.S. 465 (1946) *with* 26 U.S.C. § 162.

[66] *See, e.g.*, 26 U.S.C. § 280A.

[67] *See, e.g.*, 26 U.S.C. § 280A; Rev. Proc. 2013–13; Rev. Proc. 2010–51; IRS Notice 2016–79.

[68] *See, e.g.*, 26 U.S.C. § 183(d) (providing that, if a taxpayer's income from an activity exceeded the deductions generated by the activity in three of the past five years, the activity is presumed to have been engaged in for profit and the deductions are therefore allowable unless barred by some other provision).

[69] Shu-Yi Oei and Diane Ring, Chapter 25 this volume.

[70] *See* 26 U.S.C. §§ 62, 63, 67, 212.

[71] *See* 26 U.S.C. §§ 62, 63, 67.

not been treated as employees for tax purposes. Thus, this bar to deductibility does not apply, putting more tension on the dividing line between personal and business expenditures.

Indeed, arguably the biggest federal income tax issue that the sharing economy has raised so far has been whether service providers are independent contractors or employees.[72] Sharing economy companies have achieved tax savings by classifying service providers as independent contractors instead of employees.[73] This is perhaps the chief way in which the income tax system has grown the sharing economy. Yet, from the perspective of tax policymakers, it is not clear that this is a positive result, let alone an intended one. A significant amount of tax law's compliance structure is built on the relationship between employees and employers.[74] This both gives taxpayers incentives to avoid entering into such relationships and renders the tax system vulnerable to such relationships' decline.

Congress and the IRS have made commendable efforts to remedy the macro issues with the tax system that the sharing economy has helped highlight. Congress has enacted legislation and the IRS has issued supporting regulations designed to improve compliance with respect to payments made outside of the employer/employee relationship.[75] Congress has held hearings on issues faced by sharing economy participants and important members have made statements that the tax code should be updated to make it easier for sharing economy providers to navigate.[76] The IRS has assembled a "Sharing Economy Tax Center" with links to common topics of interest for sharing economy participants.[77] Selected topics include the distinction between an employee and an independent contractor, when expenses are deductible, and the rules governing home rentals.[78] Legislation recently introduced in the Senate would increase tax reporting on sharing economy activities and would make it easier for sharing economy participants to comply with the tax laws.[79] These are good steps, but considerable room for improvement remains.[80]

---

[72] *See* Oei and Ring, this volume.

[73] *See, e.g.*, Benjamin Means and Joseph A. Seiner, *Navigating the Uber Economy*, 49 U.C. Davis L. Rev. 1511, 1513–14 (2016) ("Employees cost more than independent contractors because businesses are responsible for, among other things, payroll taxes"); *cf.* Press Release, *Employer Costs for Employee Compensation – September 2015*, U.S. Dep't of Labor, Bureau of Labor Statistics (Dec. 9, 2015), www.bls.gov/news.release/ecec.htm (calculating that employee benefits made up more than 30 percent of employers' employee compensation costs). If the employer's tax savings from shifting its payroll tax obligations to employee self-employment tax obligations result in a higher payment to the independent contractor, the employer's savings will be reduced accordingly.

[74] *See, e.g.*, 26 U.S.C. § 3402; Internal Rev. Serv., *supra* note 10, at 10–12.

[75] *See, e.g.*, 26 U.S.C. § 6050W; 26 C.F.R. § 31.3406(b)(3)–5; 26 CFR § 1.6041–1(a); 26 CFR § 1.6041A-1(d)(4); 26 CFR § 1.6050W-1; 26 CFR § 1.6050W-2.

[76] *See, e.g.*, Amir Nasr, *The Sharing Economy and the Tax Code Don't Get Along*, Morning Consult (May 24, 2016), https://morningconsult.com/2016/05/24/sharing-economy-needs-help-via-tax-reform-tech-argues/.

[77] News Release, IRS Launches New Sharing Economy Resource Center on IRS.gov, Provides Tips for Emerging Business Area, Internal Rev. Serv., Dep't of the Treasury (Aug. 22, 2016), www.irs.gov/uac/irs-launches-new-sharing-economy-resource-center-on-irsgov.

[78] *Sharing Economy Tax Center*, Internal Rev. Serv., Dep't of the Treasury, www.irs.gov/businesses/small-businesses-self-employed/sharing-economy-tax-center.

[79] *The New Economy Works to Guarantee Independence and Growth Act of 2017* ("NEW GIG Act"), S. 1549, 115 Cong., www.thune.senate.gov/public/_cache/files/c9e8dda1-dbb6-4a78-8f2a-88f39c14be1e/D975731B1FE56963DD1D09F2C B8D78CC.ott17387.pdf, would help clarify some existing reporting obligations and would lower certain information reporting thresholds, increasing sharing economy information reporting. It also provides a safe harbor guaranteeing independent contract classification. While a clearer line between employee and independent contractor status seems a laudable goal, it is not clear whether the NEW GIG Act draws the line in the right place. *See* Diane Ring, *The Tail, the Dog, and Gig Workers*, The Surly Subgroup (July 21, 2017), https://surlysubgroup.com/2017/07/21/the-tail-the-dog-and-uber-drivers/#more-14568.

[80] *See, e.g.*, Shu-Yi Oei and Diane M. Ring, *The Tax Lives of Uber Drivers: Evidence from Internet Discussion Forums*, 8 Colum. J. Tax L. (2017).

CONCLUSION

Innovation, by its nature, is difficult to accurately predict or anticipate.[81] As a result, it is hard to tell what new developments lie beyond the horizon, how to speed them along their course, or whether our regulatory systems are well-equipped to handle them. Faced with this uncertainty, perhaps the best we can do is to look at our previous experiences with past innovations and try to generalize as best we can.

Viewed from this perspective, the interaction of tax law and the sharing economy presents a mixed picture, with bright spots, gray areas, and dark clouds. Many policymakers did not predict the growth of the sharing economy. There is little in our income tax laws that was designed to encourage its development. Nor did more general tax-incentive provisions, such as the Research and Experimentation Credit, do much to advance the sharing economy's growth. The sharing economy has exacerbated some of the existing gray areas in the tax code, including the division between independent contractors and employees. It is not yet clear whether the sharing economy will ultimately spur regulators to create greater clarity in these areas, or whether it will just add to the murk. But some areas of the tax law, such as the definition of income, have performed quite well. This suggests that these areas are indeed well-theorized and well-implemented, and that they will hold up well in the face of the next innovation – whatever it may be.

---

[81] As the saying goes, predictions are difficult, especially about the future.

Consumer Protection and Privacy Law

29

Implications for Cyber Law

Rebecca Tushnet

INTRODUCTION

As Nestor Davidson and John Infranca have written, the internet, and specifically the subset of it known as "the sharing economy," has a materiality that is vital to its functioning.[1] But the United States has Section 230 of the Communications Decency Act, an internet-specific law that provides distinct advantages to online businesses as compared to offline competitors, and courts and regulators are struggling to navigate between the Scylla of unjustified internet exceptionalism, to the detriment of ordinary consumers, and the Charybdis of suppressing the positive affordances of new online intermediaries.

Section 230, enacted when bulletin boards were important means of communicating online, prohibits treating online intermediaries as the publisher or source of content provided by another content provider (with limited exceptions related to intellectual property, US federal criminal law, and child pornography). It was drafted mainly in reaction to an early court decision that signaled that, if service providers engaged in any moderation of users' content at all, they could be liable for any defamatory or otherwise unlawful content posted by users.[2] Proponents argued that, as a result, service providers would deliberately avoid removing any user conduct, no matter how bad. To avoid this result, Section 230 immunized service providers when they did not create or contribute to the unlawful content; thus, service providers could monitor and even remove bad user content without becoming liable for leaving something up that turned out to be unlawful.[3] The only recourse in such cases would be against the actual supplier of the content, not its online disseminator.

Section 230 set up a relatively mild disparity between online and offline publishers: the print version of *The New York Times* has potential responsibility for defamatory letters to the editor it selects for print publication, subject to relevant First Amendment constraints, while it is absolutely immune for the content of comments approved for publication on its website (unless it edited them to make them defamatory). Because of the difficulty of establishing

---

[1] Nestor M. Davidson and John J. Infranca, *The Sharing Economy as an Urban Phenomenon*, 34 Yale L. & Pol'y Rev. 215 (2016).

[2] *Stratton Oakmont, Inc. v. Prodigy Services Co.*, 23 Media L. Rep. 1794, 1995 WL 323710 (N.Y. Sup 1995).

[3] "No provider or user of an interactive computer service shall be treated as the publisher or speaker of any information provided by another information content provider." 47 U.S.C § 230(c)(1) (2006). At the same time, Section 230 also precluded liability for a service provider's good-faith removal of content deemed offensive or otherwise harmful, a provision that has proved far less significant in practice.

defamation, this disparity was not substantial, and there was and remains a general consensus that the different structure of online dissemination justified the differing treatment: the print version of *The New York Times* is limited and subject to editorial review and selection before publication by its nature, whereas a nearly unlimited amount of online expression can practically be disseminated first and reviewed, if at all, only after a complaint. Congress endorsed this post-first, check-later structure with Section 230. To a more limited extent, the online service provider liability portions of the Digital Millennium Copyright Act (DMCA) did the same thing. The DMCA protected service providers from monetary liability for copyright infringement if they took down challenged content promptly after receiving a notice from the copyright owner.

Crucially, unlike the DMCA, Section 230 had no notice and takedown requirement. This difference too made sense to policymakers when the prototypical problem was defamation: it's very easy to allege defamation and hard for a service provider to evaluate whether a statement is indeed defamatory, so risk-averse intermediaries would predictably take down everything that was challenged. Thus, important political and cultural speech can easily be suppressed by a notice and takedown regime.[4]

The disparity that was merely mild as applied to traditional publishers such as *The New York Times*, however, created substantial opportunities for regulatory arbitrage when applied to other economic activities whose offline regulation was minimally constrained by the First Amendment. Short-term rentals and vehicles for hire are the key examples, though almost anything can be reimagined as part of the "sharing economy," as the cliché "Uber for X" indicates. Because of Section 230's drafting, and early judicial decisions stressing the law's breadth in response to clever plaintiffs' lawyers attempting to plead around it, it is possible for online service providers to assert Section 230 immunity well outside the core protection for dissemination of others' pure speech, even when they are profiting directly from disseminating that speech.

Consumer protection law now has significant interactions with Section 230, as regulators and courts struggle with how to react to the kinds of services unimagined 20 years ago when Section 230 was drafted. I will discuss three examples: (1) the application of standard false advertising law to claims by service providers, where the truth of the claims depends on what users actually do; (2) the updated guidelines of the Federal Trade Commission (FTC) on endorsements and testimonials, which demand that advertisers require their endorsers to disclose financial relationships with the advertisers; and (3) municipalities' use of new theories of agency to regulate entities such as Airbnb. Together, these developments show a legal system that is in some ways domesticating Section 230, limiting it in ways that preserve its core while allowing greater regulatory flexibility when a service provider is also, and perhaps more predominantly, in the business of producing something other than expression.

One might define the fundamental problem as one of "context collapse": the distinctions between speech and commerce are collapsing, as are the distinctions between public and private, work and voluntary "sharing," all of which can no longer play the same demarcating function they did for regulators in the past. But all is not lost. The legal system has other tools for dealing with new economic configurations by attributing responsibility for one entity's acts to another entity in appropriate circumstances.

---

4   Notice and takedown has notable flaws for copyright claims, and copyright claims are sometimes asserted when the notifier's real problem is disagreement with the content, but my point here is merely to note the absence of any obligation in the United States for a service provider to act in response to a claim of defamation or other non-infringing unlawful content.

I TRADITIONAL FALSE ADVERTISING CLAIMS

The easiest claims for consumer protection law to deal with are traditional advertising claims, based on what the sharing companies say about themselves and their competition. Technological innovation has historically been accompanied by deceptive practices; in a rapidly changing environment, it's not clear what is and isn't true and, perhaps more important, what regulators will and won't let businesses get away with.[5]

Courts have found claims based on false advertising by new platforms unproblematically within the scope of current consumer protection law, allowing traditional taxi services to challenge Uber's claims of greater safety, consumers to challenge similar representations that may have deceived them, and regulators to act on behalf of drivers as consumers.[6] For example, while some knowledge of how Uber's system works is necessary, a claim that Uber's default interface misleadingly shows the presence of cars nearby, inducing consumers to choose it as the fastest option, is a perfectly conventional false advertising claim.[7] A key challenge in this regard, as Ryan Calo and Alex Rosenblat indicate, is getting the right information about how platforms work to understand which of their claims and practices might be deceptive. Discovery (for lawsuits) and civil investigative demands and other administrative mechanisms (for state attorneys general) can play their usual roles here in bringing the truth to light and correcting the asymmetries of information between individual consumers and large businesses.

Traditional unfairness jurisdiction may also become increasingly relevant to platform regulation; although there is no general cause of action for competitors for "unfair" trade practices that do not violate antitrust law or some other specific law, the Federal Trade Commission, as well as a number of state attorneys general, have authority to stop generalized unfairness, and California also allows consumers to bring unfairness claims. Usually, unfairness requires showing that the practice involves substantial consumer harm that could not reasonably be avoided by the consumer and that is not outweighed by its benefits. Unfairness can be used to address concerns about privacy as a matter of consumer protection,[8] and specifically about the use of consumers' information to manipulate their choices or exploit their vulnerabilities, as in Calo and Rosenblat's example of an app that charges a person more for rides if her phone battery is low.[9]

More complicated cases arise when the truth or falsity of the platform's own claims may depend on the truth or falsity of user-provided content, implicating Section 230. At times, courts have distinguished between traditional editorial activities such as choosing which content to remove or allow – which is protected by Section 230 – and other activities. For example, Apple's editorial judgment about which apps to approve was immunized by Section 230, but its instructions to app developers that allegedly directed them to engage in several privacy-violating practices, such as instructions to avoid having users agree to a license agreement when they first launch an

---

[5] *See generally* Edward J. Balleisen, *Fraud: An American History from Barnum to Madoff* (2017).

[6] *Delux Cab v. Uber Technologies, Inc.*, 2017 WL 1354791, No. 16cv3057 (S.D. Cal. Apr. 13, 2017); *Greater Houston Transportation Company v. Uber Technologies, Inc.*, F.Supp.3d, No. 4.14–0941, 2015 WL 9660022 (S.D. Tex. Dec. 18, 2015); *L.A. Taxi Cooperative, Inc. v. Uber Technologies, Inc.*, F. Supp. 3d, 2015 WL 4397706, No. 15-cv-01257 (N.D. Cal. Jul. 17, 2015); *Ehret v. Uber Technologies, Inc.*, No. C-14-0113 (N.D. Cal. Sept. 17, 2014); Federal Trade Commission, *Uber Agrees to Pay $20 Million to Settle FTC Charges that It Recruited Drivers with Exaggerated Earnings Claims*, Press Release (Jan. 19, 2017).

[7] Ryan Calo and Alex Rosenblat, *The Taking Economy: Uber, Information, and Power*, 117 Colum. L. Rev. 1623, 1654–56 (2017) (describing the design issue).

[8] Chris Jay Hoofnagle, *Federal Trade Commission Privacy Law and Policy* (2016).

[9] Calo and Rosenblat, *supra* note 7, at 1656–57.

app, sufficed to make Apple potentially responsible for the resulting practices.[10] Likewise, eBay's claims to screen auction houses that participated in its online auctions could not create liability, because its screening was protected by Section 230, but its affirmative representations that using an auction house was "safe" and that international "floor buyers" participated in the bidding were independent of its editorial judgment and thus potentially false advertising.[11] Another court found that Section 230 did not protect the defendant's conduct when it ran a website for moving company reviews, claimed to provide accurate high-quality reviews, but actually removed positive reviews of its competitors (it was also in the moving business), and likewise removed negative reviews of its own business.[12]

Perhaps most controversially, the Ninth Circuit approved a failure-to-warn claim against a networking website for models that allegedly facilitated sexual assaults by some users against others.[13] The court ruled against the website even though a crucial cause of the plaintiff's harm was that the platform allowed the plaintiff and her attackers to post content. However, the court of appeals reasoned that the website was not being sued as a publisher, but rather as an entity that had a duty to warn because it received information about the criminal scheme from an outside source – not via postings on the website – about how models were being lured and harmed. Moreover, the duty need not be observed by screening or removing any user-provided content; a warning to users would suffice.[14] To a certain extent, this result is consistent with ordinary advertising law's treatment of omissions where the advertiser knows that the omission is material given the affirmative claims it has made (here, that the website was for talent agents to make contact with models).

Many traditional torts that might in theory be used to control intermediary behavior have been put off limits by Section 230. Pressure for statutory reform exists, and Congress recently made it easier to sue intermediaries for facilitating sexual abuse, but that appears to be the limit of federal legislative appetite for change. Further changes would inject uncertainty into online economies, including the information providers Section 230 was aimed at protecting. On a practical level, significant federal statutory reform in an age of near-paralysis in Congress is fairly unlikely. Thus, private plaintiffs and US regulators at every level of government will have to take Section 230 into account for the foreseeable future.

II ENDORSEMENTS AND TESTIMONIALS: LESSONS IN RESISTING REGULATORY ARBITRAGE FROM THE FEDERAL TRADE COMMISSION

The previous section covered old wine in new bottles: standard false advertising claims against internet-enabled businesses. Another significant type of sharing in the sharing economy is sharing experiences and opinions – sometimes merely for the joy of giving others one's opinion, but sometimes for a more tangible reward. Paid endorsements and testimonials, like false advertising, are nothing new, but their presence may be harder to detect in an environment characterized by volunteerism in promoting beloved products and no longer segmented by 30-second ads whose status as paid promotions is relatively easy to identify.

---

[10] *Opperman v. Path, Inc.*, 2014 WL 1973378, No. 13-cv-00453 (N.D. Cal. May 14, 2014).

[11] *Mazur v. eBay, Inc.*, No. C 07–3967 MHP, 2008 WL 618988, at *10 (N.D. Cal. Mar. 4, 2008).

[12] *Moving & Storage, Inc. v. Panayotov*, No. 12–12262, 2014 WL 949830 (D. Mass. Mar. 12, 2014). *See also Demetriades v. Yelp, Inc.*, 228 Cal.App.4th 294, 175 Cal.Rptr.3d 131 (Cal. Ct. App. July 24, 2014) (claims that Yelp filtered customer reviews for quality and trustworthiness were actionable as false advertising).

[13] *Doe v. Internet Brands, Inc.*, 824 F.3d 846 (9th Cir. 2016).

[14] It is unclear whether, on the merits, a duty to warn claim can succeed given the relationship between the parties, but the key here is that the Ninth Circuit denied the complete immunity from suit provided by § 230.

The sharing economy is often distinguished from platforms centered on "user-generated content" because the larger sharing economy includes the provision of physical goods and services, not just information. Manipulation of endorsements and testimonials may not be as big an issue for sharing economy intermediaries that often track actual use of their services, and can thus prevent purely fake reviews. Individual platform policies can even discourage what Airbnb, for example, calls "extortion" – tit-for-tat exchanges of something valuable in return for a good review. Key problems with sharing economy reviews include review inflation and a mismatch between what users and providers consider acceptable ratings, given the pressure to maintain a five-star rating, but very little of that has to do with undisclosed material connections between individual providers and reviewers. What the FTC's experience with endorsements and testimonials can provide broader lessons on, however, is the way in which longstanding legal tools such as the law of agency can accommodate new economic arrangements – both in terms of dealing with Section 230 and in terms of attributing legal responsibility more generally.

The FTC has taken the position that a connection between an endorser and an advertiser must be disclosed as part of the endorser's message when knowing the connection would be material to consumers.[15] Likewise, endorsers who make unsubstantiated factual claims create the risk that the advertiser may be deemed to have made the claim itself. Advertisers who pay for endorsements have to direct their endorsers to limit themselves to claims that can be substantiated or that are nonfactual opinions, and to disclose when appropriate. Advertisers have to take remedial action such as terminating the relationship if the endorsers disobey.[16] In other words, the FTC will hold advertisers, who are also certainly producing internet content of their own, responsible for what their endorsers say (or don't say). That sounds a lot like an impermissible attribution under Section 230.

But all is not lost for regulators: an internet service provider may not be held liable for content provided by another content provider, true. But what rules determine whether a content provider is "another" content provider, or is instead legally part of the same entity? A corporation cannot act except through its employees; does that mean that Section 230 mandates that a corporation can never be liable for online statements made by its employees? That seems unlikely, and to the best of my knowledge no one has ever taken the argument that far.[17] Thus, in some circumstances, background legal principles attribute the acts of one entity (an employee acting within the scope of her employment) to another (her employer). The real question, then, is whether this principle extends beyond employment – and the FTC has, understandably, taken the position that it can.[18] The common and statutory law of agency both routinely provide for a principal's liability for an agent's acts in certain non-employment contexts.[19]

---

[15] FTC Guides Concerning the Use of Endorsements and Testimonials in Advertising, 74 Fed. Reg. 53,124, 53,125 (Oct. 15, 2009) (codified at 16 C.F.R. pt. 255).

[16] FTC Endorsement Guides, at 53,139.

[17] *See Lansing* v. *Southwest Airlines Co.*, 2012 IL App (1st) 101164 (Ill. Ct. App. June 8, 2012) (§ 230 does not prohibit liability of employer for employee's acts); *Cornelius* v. *DeLuca*, 2010 WL 1709928 (D. Idaho April 26, 2010) (§ 230 does not prohibit liability of website owner for moderator's acts when acting as a site representative within the scope of the representation). *But see Miller* v. *Federal Express Corp.*, 2014 WL 1318698 (Ind. Ct. App. April 3, 2014) (§ 230 provides employer immunity for employees' use of internet provided by employer); *Delfino* v. *Agilent Technologies, Inc.*, 2006 WL 3635399 (Cal. App. Ct. Dec. 14, 2006) (§ 230 precludes liability where employee used employer's system to make threats unrelated to his employment).

[18] *E.g.*, *Federal Trade Commission* v. *Credit Bureau Center, LLC*, 235 F. Supp. 3d 1054 (N.D. Ill. 2017) (holding entity liable for acts of its online affiliates based on agency theory).

[19] *See* Restatement (Third) of Agency § 7.06 (2006) ("A principal required by contract or otherwise by law to protect another cannot avoid liability by delegating performance of the duty, whether or not the delegate is an agent."); *id.* § 7.08 cmt. b (discussing statutory bases for liability in the absence of a principal–agent relationship); *id.* § 7.01 cmt.

Consistent with this understanding, courts have found liability for internet service providers despite Section 230 when preexisting principles of agency liability justify attributing the wrongdoer's acts to the accused party.[20] Section 230 does have relevance to the law of agency: the law should preclude finding a respondeat superior or other agency relationship based on the fact that one party provides internet access or some internet service to the other, even when the second party gets payment as consideration for access. Likewise, the internet service provider's knowledge of unlawful content and failure to act, in the absence of some sort of economic relationship indicating that the speaker acts for the service provider, is insufficient. Courts have correctly rejected knowledge-based and inducement theories as ways around Section 230 for ordinary internet hosts. Being a seductive forum for unlawful content – a kind of attractive nuisance – is protected by Section 230. That kind of liability was exactly what Congress was trying to preclude. But other elements of a relationship should still be able to justify liability for others' actions.

As a result, internet service providers that invite people to share their opinions remain solidly protected by Section 230, and even traditional advertisers that host or retweet or otherwise promote truly user-generated content will generally avoid liability. However, service providers that also pay to promote their goods or services will still have to monitor their endorsers in order to comply with the FTC's rules. More broadly, however, the example of endorsements and testimonials suggests how new forms of communication and commerce online can ultimately be domesticated into existing law.

III REGULATING ECONOMIC RELATIONSHIPS

The previous section addressed new forms of promotion, where sellers might try to offload their consumer protection responsibilities onto endorsers who are not traditional ad agencies, or even onto consumers themselves, promoting to each other. Such situations do not necessarily, or even often, involve content hosted by the sellers themselves – Kim Kardashian uses Instagram, not her advertising partners' own websites, to promote those partners, as part of the very realism and intimacy that make new forms of endorsements valuable to sellers. The relationship between the seller and the endorser thus usually doesn't look very much like the platform–speaker relationship Congress sought to protect with Section 230. Sometimes, however, platforms are more deeply involved in economic transactions, creating the forum for exchanges among individuals. At first glance, this looks an awful lot like the core concern of Section 230: even if it is done for money, users are providing all the factual content that could lead other users astray, for which the platform cannot be held responsible.

In 2015, San Francisco required that hosts register their residences with the city before making them available as short-term rentals.[21] Enforcement of the registration requirement was difficult because the city lacked information about the location of short-term rentals. In an attempt to deal with the information problem, an August 2016 ordinance made it a misdemeanor to collect

---

c (2006) (recognizing that statutes may change the common law, including whether an agent is responsible for wrongful conduct and whether liability is strict).

[20] *See, e.g., FTC* v. *LeadClick Media, LLC*, 838 F.3d 158 (2d Cir. 2016) (seller (1) knew that fake news sites were common in the affiliate marketing industry and that some of its affiliates were using fake news sites, (2) approved of the use of these sites, and, (3) on occasion, provided affiliates with content to use on their fake news pages; because the seller knew of the deception and had the authority to control it, it was the provider of the unlawful content for § 230 purposes).

[21] S.F. Ordinance 218–14 (2015).

a fee for providing booking services for the rental of an unregistered unit. Booking services included "any reservation and/or payment service provided by a person or entity that facilitates a short-term rental transaction between an Owner … and a prospective tourist or transient user … for which the person or entity collects or receives … a fee in connection with the reservation and/or payment services."[22] Airbnb and similar services were covered by the ordinance because they collected fees for facilitating users' transactions.

Airbnb and another hosting platform sued, arguing that the ordinance was preempted by Section 230. The federal district court disagreed.[23] The court did not treat the platforms as publishers or speakers of the rental listings. Platforms were perfectly free to publish any listing they get from a host and to collect fees for doing so, whether the unit was lawfully registered or not. The only thing that could create liability was their own conduct: providing and collecting a fee for booking services in connection with an unregistered unit. The platforms responded that the ordinance would still have the practical effect of requiring them to monitor listings and remove posts for unregistered rentals. But the court reasoned that this was not compulsory. The platforms could make clear to users that they could only provide booking services in San Francisco for lawfully registered units. Or they could charge fees for publishing listings, rather than for facilitating transactions, which would be outside the scope of the ordinance.

The strongest argument supporting San Francisco's ordinance against a Section 230 defense is that the ordinance does not regulate the platform as a platform, but does regulate it to the extent that it takes on non-platform functions. Like the FTC, San Francisco is indifferent to whether the regulated party has any online presence of its own. An endorsee could conduct all its business in a brick and mortar store and not even have a website of its own, and if it was paying influencers online it would be subject to the recommendations of the FTC's guidelines on endorsements. So too with Airbnb and its brokering activities.

Still, a clever lawyer might find a way to use this kind of reasoning to gut Section 230. It may almost always be possible to define the defendant's conduct in some way that is independent of its role as platform. However, to the extent that regulators have to define the defendant's conduct in a platform-independent way where there are real groups also affected that are not internet service providers, there may be political constraints on the imposition of new liabilities, which itself might be a reasonable argument for allowing such doctrinal innovations.

Even as San Francisco's ordinance is regulation of traditional economic activity rather than traditional political or cultural speech, and thus is further from the intended core of Section 230 along that dimension, it is a step beyond the FTC's actions in a different way: the lack of an agency rationale. While paying someone to promote your product makes it plausible to say that their speech is "yours" for many liability purposes, making you the relevant "information content provider" as a matter of law, no principle independent of San Francisco's law itself makes Airbnb the provider (or nonprovider) of the registration number. Airbnb might be deemed an agent of the users, but the users aren't Airbnb's agents under a conventional analysis, and so it seems as if Airbnb is being punished for other content providers' failures.

Nonetheless, San Francisco's ordinance is, on its face, indifferent to whether brokers even have websites, much less whether they have websites that host content provided by other information content providers. The regulatory hook is independent of whether Airbnb is disseminating information from other content providers. It would be difficult to work around Section 230 on a major scale using this reasoning, though users of particular business models

---

[22] S.F. Ordinance 178–16 (2016).
[23] *Airbnb, Inc. v. City and County of San Francisco*, 217 F.Supp.3d 1066 (N.D. Cal. 2016).

could face regulation they do not want to face. In particular, Amazon and eBay would also lose Section 230 protection for many of their activities if state law targeted the right conduct (and if states are willing to make resellers/brokers in general subject to the relevant law).[24] Even such results would not likely threaten the core speech-protecting functions of Section 230, however, because making Amazon liable for defamatory content in the books it sells can really only be done by treating it as a publisher or otherwise relying on the fact that it is a disseminator of content. Selling content and taking a percentage of the receipts from the sale is a traditional publisher/distributor function in a way that taking a percentage of a rental price is not.[25]

One might then ask: If a state were to regulate the advertising "broker" that connects consumers to paying websites – a broker such as Google's AdWords – could it impose substantive duties on Google to monitor the websites despite Section 230? Distinctively, San Francisco is not requiring the registration number to be in the listing – it is not seeking to change or moderate the content of listings. It is seeking to change the non-expressive behavior of people who create the listings: whether they secured a registration number. Likewise, regulation of the insurance status of Uber drivers, or other regulations of sharing platforms that allow new market entrants to compete with more heavily regulated established businesses, would often escape Section 230 preemption under this analysis. That would not be true of any attempt to hold Google liable for defamation or even for false advertising by the commercial websites using AdSense to find customers. Classic products liability not based on the content of a user's statements might theoretically apply to Google as an advertising facilitator under this theory, but it is generally quite hard or impossible to hold advertising intermediaries liable in such circumstances even in the absence of Section 230.

If a regulator tried to make an internet service provider equivalent to a broker merely because it facilitated communication, however, Section 230 should continue to preempt that law. In such a case, the action triggering regulation would be exactly equivalent to the "publishing" activity Section 230 was designed to protect. Likewise, if a regulator tried to make ad-supported websites such as Facebook responsible for the non-paid content supported by advertising, the same logic would apply, as it would if someone attempted to require Google to verify the truthfulness of ad claims. Only if the entity's liability can be evaluated without looking at the content that users post online can Section 230 problems be avoided.

IV LESSONS FROM SECTION 230: INTERNET EXCEPTIONALISM ONLY GOES SO FAR

Section 230 represented an attempt to create special rules for online service providers, as compared to traditional print publishers, in order to protect the new possibilities they offered to facilitate users' speech. Section 230 has come under increasing stress as internet commerce penetrates into every area of human activity, including previously noncommercial and limited-scope "sharing." It is not particularly surprising that creative lawyers and regulators have thought of ways to get around Section 230, nor that courts have been willing to listen to their arguments as the distinction between online and offline life breaks down. After all, Congress was thinking

---

[24] *But see Milo & Gabby LLC* v. *Amazon.com, Inc.*, Fed.Appx. (Fed. Cir. 2017) (holding that Amazon was not a direct "seller" for the purposes of intellectual property law).

[25] Similarly, attempts to hold a business such as Grindr liable for its users' offline conduct are likely to founder because it is their statements to other users on the platform that can lure those other users into danger. *See Doe* v. *MySpace Inc.*, 2008 WL 2068064 (5th Cir. May 16, 2008) (rejecting a negligent supervision claim against a website operator on § 230 grounds where plaintiffs alleged sexual assault committed by users they met on the website).

about chilling speech through defamation law, not about hotel regulation, when it enacted Section 230.

The invocation of Section 230 to fight local regulation of the sharing economy also bears significant similarities to the increasing use of the First Amendment to oppose ordinary economic regulations – what some have called the Lochnerization of the First Amendment, after the famous Supreme Court case that struck down legal limits on the hours that bakers could work as a violation of workers' rights to freedom of contract. For most of the twentieth century, governments had a relatively free hand with economic regulation. But commercial transactions necessarily involve communication about the substance of the transaction, and the Supreme Court has given increasing protection to commercial speech. Thus, an economic freedom claim, when reformulated as a freedom of speech claim, has a greater chance of success, and business lawyers have used the First Amendment to fight everything from bans on credit card surcharges to minimum wage laws to the use of prize catalogs to reward smokers. When all commerce is defined as speech, the question becomes whether speech rules or commercial rules will apply – and increasingly, the answer is the former.

Similarly, as innovators attempt to disrupt conventional commercial relationships and move them all onto online platforms, businesses such as Uber and Airbnb have invoked Section 230 to protect economic relationships with their users that go far beyond facilitating speech. However, one key difference between First Amendment and Section 230 challenges is that the new First Amendment cases have arisen because of changes in politics and the judiciary that make businesses' arguments newly plausible, while Section 230 challenges have arisen because of new forms of economic organization using the internet. Section 230 defenses against sharing economy regulations certainly have political and ideological valence, but they really exist because of newly well-funded and salient business models not within the contemplation of Section 230's drafters. Notably, courts have thus far mostly resisted businesses' attempts to collapse all online platform activities into the "publishing" protected by Section 230. Regulatory arbitrage based on Section 230's internet exceptionalism has been limited, while the First Amendment constraints on economic regulation continue to expand. It remains to be seen whether these results will persist, and whether new legal distinctions between types of activity will arise to further cabin Section 230's broad reach.

30

Platform Architecture and the Brand

An Opportunity for Trademark Modernization

Sonia Katyal and Leah Chan Grinvald[*]

INTRODUCTION

If Web 1.0 was about access to information via the Internet and Web 2.0 was about the formation of the online marketplace, Web 3.0 is about the platform: the transformation of the offline marketplace, particularly the service industry, by online transactions.[1] The application of algorithmic tools to the economies of leisure, consumption, services, and manufacturing has produced a profound transformation of the service economy.[2] Even more, the movement of many of these services to cloud providers has an even greater, transnational character.[3] This move facilitates the development of a global infrastructure; as two commentators observe, the emergence of platform and cloud architecture "reconfigure globalization itself."[4]

At the same time, the definitional and regulatory complexities that accompany the emergence of platforms have posed some significant challenges for lawyers and commentators. At its simplest, a platform points to a set of "online digital arrangements whose algorithms serve to organize and structure economic and social activity."[5] This produces – and is facilitated by – a system of shared tools, technologies, and interfaces enabling decentralized innovation, but they also create a hybrid blend of market and social interactions that we have not yet seen in the digital economy.[6]

Platforms could be characterized by the particular services that they offer or the business models that they disrupt.[7] As Orly Lobel and others have explained, while the label of a "platform" is intentionally broad, it represents a myriad of new business models that disrupt previous economies of production, consumption, finance, knowledge, and education, among other

---

[*] © Sonia K. Katyal and Leah Chan Grinvald. This chapter is based on our article, *Platform Law and the Brand Enterprise*, 32 Berkeley Tech. L.J. 1135 (2017). We thank the editors for their feedback. We welcome feedback at either skatyal@berkeley.edu or lgrinvald@suffolk.edu.

[1] Orly Lobel, *The Law of the Platform*, 101 Minn. L. Rev. 87, 94 (2016).

[2] *See generally* Martin Kenney and John Zysman, *The Rise of the Platform Economy*, 32 Issues in Sci. & Tech. 61 (2016) (citing work by Stuart Feldman, Kenji Kushida, Jonathan Murray, and others).

[3] Please note that although our discussion of trademark law in this chapter has transnational impact, we only discuss US law due to space constraints.

[4] Kenney and Zysman, *supra* note 2, at 61.

[5] *Id.* at 66. For more on the definition and attributes of platforms, *see* Diane Coyle, *Making the Most of Platforms: A Policy Research Agenda*, at https://papers.ssrn.com/sol3/papers.cfm?abstract_id=2857188.

[6] Kenney and Zysman, *supra* note 2, at 67.

[7] Arun Sundararajan, *The Sharing Economy: The End of Employment and the Rise of Crowd-Based Capitalism* 77 (2016).

elements.[8] If traditional categories of business relied on the consistency of dyads like employer/ employee, seller/buyer, and producer/consumer, platform entrepreneurship exploits networks where these lines become blurred through sharing and pooling economies.[9] By lowering transaction costs through connecting consumers directly with producers, platform economies promise less waste, and a greater ability to break both supply and demand into what Lobel describes as discrete, modular units – short-term housing assistance and help with minor tasks such as furniture installation, cooking, driving, and the like.[10] "Web 3.0," Lobel argues, "is transforming the lifestyle of the masses, not only better matching a static equilibrium of supply and demand, but also generating different sets of supply and demand and reconfiguring markets."[11]

Yet these new economies usher in complex questions of both definition and regulation. Within this spectrum of views, some have expressed fear that the platform economy facilitates the avoidance of welfare-enhancing laws like long-term employment contracts, insurance, and quality control regulations.[12] As Lobel argues,

> [p]roponents romantically envision the platform as a return to the days free from corporate dominance, when interactions happened directly and intimately between individuals, when design was bottom-up and relationships were based on community rather than markets. For opponents, it is a dystopian uber-capitalist development in which every interaction becomes the basis of market exchanges, privacy and leisure are lost, and Silicon Valley style-libertarians become richer at the expense of everyone else.[13]

Central to these questions remains the ubiquity of the brand enterprise, which affects nearly every layer of platform architecture. Trademarks are central to the success of the platform economy, but few commentators have really delved into the question of how trademark law both governs – and is governed by – the emergence of these new economies. Thus, we lay out in this chapter a spectrum of trademark interactivity, identifying the emergence of two central forms of platform entrepreneurship, and then analyze how the design and architecture of these new forms ushers in new challenges and opportunities for the modernization of trademark law altogether.

Trademark law plays a central, determinative role in the success or failure of the platform enterprise. At the broadest level, first, we argue that the platform economy facilitates the emergence of what is called "macrobrands" – the rise of platform economies whose sole source of capital inheres in the value of the brand itself – the Airbnbs and Ubers of the world.[14] At the narrowest level, second, we argue that the platform economy, with its empowerment of the individual, has also facilitated a parallel emergence of the "microbrand" – the rise of discrete,

---

[8] Lobel, *supra* note 1, at 98–99.

[9] *Id.* at 100–01.

[10] *Id.* at 109–10.

[11] *Id.* at 114.

[12] *Id.* at 130–37. *See also* Nathan Heller, *Is the Gig Economy Working?*, New Yorker (May 15, 2017), www.newyorker.com/magazine/2017/05/15/is-the-gig-economy-working; Ruth Berins Collier et al., *The Regulation of Labor Platforms: The Politics of the Uber Economy* (March 2017) at 7 (working paper on file with authors) (discussing labor-related concerns in the platform economy).

[13] Lobel, *supra* note 1, at 105.

[14] Others, too, have used the macrobrand and microbrand terminology to describe similar patterns of user engagement and marketing, albeit in a non-platform context. *See, e.g.,* Jose Marti, Enrique Bigné, and Antonio Hyder, Brand Engagement, *in The Routledge Companion to the Future of Marketing* 253 (Luiz Montinho, Enrique Bigné, and Ajay K. Manrai eds., 2014) (discussing the role of each structure in reaching consumers); T. Scott Gross, *Microbranding: Build a Powerful Personal Brand & Beat Your Competition* (2002) (discussing ways to build a personal or local brand).

small enterprises made up of individual businesses, each of whom have a strong interest in utilizing the basic principles of branding and trademark protection. This interest often conflicts, as macrobrands and microbrands each have different pressures placed on them by existing trademark law. At the macrobrand level, the uncertain landscape of secondary liability incentivizes macrobrands to assert dubious claims of trademark infringement.[15] This, in turn, has had a chilling effect in some cases on the ability of microbrands to be effective entrepreneurs.[16] This conflict highlights that change is clearly needed.

Indeed, we view the platform economy as a central opportunity to modernize existing trademark law to accord with the challenges of these new business models. As we show in Sections I and II of this chapter, the interaction between the two – macrobrands and microbrands – challenges trademark law to evolve to address the new issues presented by platform economies. At the same time, however, our existing frameworks are capacious enough to meet the challenges platforms pose, underscoring the wisdom of our basic, bedrock trademark principles in the process. In Section III, we outline a host of suggestions to modernize, rather than displace, trademark law for the digital economy. While change can occur by legislation or voluntary measures, we focus specifically on the formation of statutory safe harbors and a modification of the standards for infringement in common law. As we show, these changes can both protect and encourage the vibrancy of the platform economy in an age of legal uncertainty.

I PLATFORM ARCHITECTURE AND THE RISE OF THE MACROBRAND

While much ink has been spilled in analyzing and discussing the overall effect of platform arrangements on the economy and civil rights protections, fewer pieces have addressed the central role of trademark law in the platform enterprise. Yet trademark and branding practices are implicated within nearly every element of platform architecture and entrepreneurship, raising central questions for the role of regulation. Consider an example. Parking Panda is a platform that enables users to find and secure parking spots.[17] The term "Parking Panda" itself functions as both a trademark and a brand (we will explain the difference between the two below).[18] Yet given its existence as part of the platform ecosystem, Parking Panda itself does not own the garages or the parking spaces it advertises on its platform; rather, these are owned mainly by individuals or parking companies. These companies have their own trademarks, such as "Icon Parking" or "ABM Parking Services," two large parking companies based in New York City.[19]

In the platform enterprise, trademarks function just like other trademarks in the sense that they serve informational and economic functions.[20] By enabling consumers to trust that their experience of a certain product can be consistently associated with a particular trademark, trademarks lower consumer search costs.[21] Yet trademarks play an even more central role in platform

[15] *See, e.g.,* examples discussed in Section II *infra.*
[16] For example, where platforms have complied with dubious claims of trademark infringement, they have taken down listings or products. *See, e.g.,* Section II *infra,* notes 44 and 55. This can have a serious impact on the ecosystem, and can have a deleterious impact on the long-term health of the platform economy.
[17] *See* Parking Panda, *How It Works,* www.parkingpanda.com/how-it-works (allowing advance parking reservation from computers or in real time from mobile phones).
[18] U.S. Trademark No. 4295552 ("registered mark for 'Parking Panda,' operating an online marketplace that allows drivers to find and rent parking spaces and users to rent out their parking spaces."); *See* Parking Panda, *2016 Year in Review,* www.parkingpanda.com/year-in-review.
[19] *See* Parking Panda, *Search for Parking in New York City* (images on file with authors).
[20] William M. Landes and Richard A. Posner, *Trademark Law: An Economic Perspective,* 30 J.L. & Econ. 265, 369 (1987).
[21] *Id.*

entrepreneurship because they enable consumers to identify clusters of marks with a particular platform, thereby facilitating the reduction of transaction costs that are essential to a platform's success. For example, with the Parking Panda platform, both sets of marks, the Parking Panda's and the parking companies', inform consumers that their parking experience will be similar to their previous experiences, thereby enabling purchasers to rely on their previous decisions.

Branding, too, is an essential aspect of this enterprise.[22] Brands, on one hand, incorporate a business's trademark, but instead of being primarily informational in nature, they also convey an *experience* to the consumer. Particularly in a platform ecosystem, brands tell the consumer about the other consumers who buy the product, thereby creating a community of likeminded consumers.[23] For example, although Parking Panda aims to help users "find and reserve parking," the company's mission is described as much more than just parking assistance:

> [t]hrough Parking Panda, drivers plan and commute smarter by booking guaranteed parking in advance. Parking Panda customers are empowered with the ability to search and compare thousands of parking options and prices in more than 40 cities throughout North America.[24]

Through this statement, Parking Panda attempts to create a community of "smart commuters,"[25] a consumer identity and experience, which is their "brand," while also having their related trademark, "Parking Panda." In essence, though, the platform economy has created two types of brand enterprise. At the broadest level, we have the macrobrand, and in our example, that would be Parking Panda. The value inherent in the macrobrand is the brand itself – the experience that Parking Panda is providing to its users. At the narrowest level, we have the microbrand, here, the individual parking companies that operate within the Parking Panda ecosystem. The microbrands also have value in their marks and brands, thus providing both macrobrands and microbrands with a strong interest in trademark law.

Yet the legal protection of trademarks, and by extension, brands, introduces tension into the relationship between macrobrands and microbrands. Trademark law encourages owners to provide a consistent level of quality in their products, to ensure consumer confidence and repeat purchases.[26] This is done through granting trademark owners limited exclusivity in their trademarks; for example, only one company can be known as "Parking Panda" for online parking services. In addition, trademark law rewards those owners that are active in policing their marks by granting them "strong" or even "famous" status.[27] Therefore, trademark owners are incentivized to police their marks not just against competitive infringement by others who might "pass off" their goods as those of another producer, but also against related or associative uses.[28] This has led, in some cases, to trademark overenforcement, particularly in situations where macrobrands receive takedown requests to remove allegedly infringing material that microbrands host on the platform.[29] For example, Etsy and other platforms report that a good

---

[22] *See* Deven R. Desai, *From Trademarks to Brands*, 64 Fla. L. Rev. 981, 985 (2012); Sonia K. Katyal, *Trademark Cosmopolitanism*, 47 U.C. Davis L. Rev. 875, 890 (2014); Irina D. Manta, *Branded*, 69 SMU L. Rev. 713, 734 (2016).

[23] *See* Katya Assaf, *Brand Fetishism*, 43 Conn. L. Rev. 83, 95 (2010); Deborah R. Gerhardt, *Social Media Amplify Consumer Investment in Trademarks*, 90 N.C. L. Rev. 1491, 1495 (2012).

[24] *See* Parking Panda, *About Us*, www.parkingpanda.com/company (exulting the company's goals in lofty language typically associated with a nonprofit).

[25] *Id.*

[26] Jordan Teague, *Promoting Trademark's Ends and Means through Online Contributory Liability*, 14 Vand. J. Ent. & Tech. L. 461, 465 (2012).

[27] *Id.*

[28] *Id.*

[29] *Id.* at 476.

number of takedown requests relate to questionable infringing activity, such as activity that is political in nature.[30]

Unfortunately, the doctrines governing trademarks and intermediary (mainly contributory or secondary) liability are both confusing and outdated, particularly as applied to platforms. The dominant test of contributory, or secondary, liability in the platform economy is derived from the US Supreme Court case of *Inwood Laboratories* v. *Ives Laboratories*.[31] This case addressed the question of whether manufacturers of generic drugs should be held liable for pharmacies that packaged and sold drugs under infringing packaging labels.[32] The Supreme Court held that a manufacturer and/or distributor could only be held liable for contributory infringement if it could be shown that they "intentionally induce[d] another to infringe a trademark, or if it continue[d] to supply its product to one whom it knows or has reason to know is engaging in trademark infringement."[33] Later cases have refined this standard to provide that defendants who take a "willfully blind" approach (meaning that they "suspect wrongdoing and deliberately fail to investigate") can rise to the level of contributory infringement.[34] But both elements – suspicion and failure to investigate – need to be present, because courts have held that simply failing to take precautions to limit counterfeiting, for example, does not qualify as "willful blindness."[35]

These principles have translated uncomfortably to the world of internet service providers (ISPs), which in turn creates added instability for platforms. Here, courts have generally followed a proposition advanced by the Ninth Circuit in *Lockheed Martin* v. *Network Solutions*, which held that if an ISP exercises "direct control and monitoring" over the infringing conduct, it can be held liable for secondary liability.[36] If the ISP serves as a passive "routing service," like domain name registrars, for example, which links domain names to the IP addresses of their web-hosting servers, then the ISP can be immune from claims of contributory liability.[37] If, however, the ISP is able to exercise significant control over the means of infringement, like hosting providers, search engines, or an online marketplace, then the *Inwood* test will apply.[38] If *Inwood* is deemed to apply, the inquiry explores the question of intentional inducement and whether the ISP continued to provide services to an infringer who it constructively or actually knew it was infringing.[39]

Both issues are difficult to resolve, however, particularly in the online context. Intentional inducement requires evidence of active involvement by an ISP, and this kind of "smoking gun" evidence is hard to come by.[40] The same is true for evidence of knowledge by the ISP. Even if an ISP has general knowledge that their service or site is being used to infringe, without specific knowledge of infringement, however, an ISP can generally escape liability, since there is no affirmative duty to actively prevent trademark infringement from occurring.[41]

---

[30] *See infra* notes 44 and 55.

[31] 456 U.S. 844 (1982).

[32] *Id.* at 846.

[33] *Id.* at 854.

[34] *Hard Rock Cafe Licensing Corp.* v. *Concession Servs., Inc.*, 955 F.2d 1143, 1149 (7th Cir. 1992) ("To be willfully blind, a person must suspect wrongdoing and deliberately fail to investigate").

[35] *Id.*

[36] 194 F.3d 980, 984 (9th Cir. 1999).

[37] Teague, *supra* note 26, at 471–72.

[38] *Lockheed*, 194 F.3d at 984.

[39] *Inwood*, 456 U.S. 844, 854 (1982).

[40] Rian C. Dawson, *Wiggle Room: Problems and Virtues of the Inwood Standard*, 91 Ind. L.J. 549, 564 (2016).

[41] *See Tiffany (NJ) Inc.* v. *eBay Inc.*, 600 F.3d 93, 104 (2d Cir. 2010).

Although this approach might appear predictable and uniform, it nevertheless produces unintended consequences. As one commentator has explained, because *Inwood*'s knowledge standards are so unclear, it can lead to an overreaction among platforms, leading to an over-responsiveness to trademark owners' notice and takedown requests.[42] In turn, an overactive impulse carries a disparate impact on small businesses and smaller platforms, who are often ill equipped to defend themselves against potentially false claims of contributory infringement.[43] In fact, this lack of certainty led five platform companies – Etsy, Foursquare, Kickstarter, Meetup, and Shapeways – to advocate for greater certainty in the trademark enforcement area vis-à-vis platforms.[44] The platforms note in their joint comment that: "[a] lack of statutory protections from trademark infringement claims has pushed Commenters to react to many complaints by unquestioningly removing content from their sites. Over the long term, this absence of protection will slow the growth of free expression and commerce that has been the hallmark of the Internet."[45] We will revisit the solutions that the platforms propose in Section III below.

II PLATFORM DECENTRALIZATION AND THE MICROBRAND

On the platform, everyone gets to be an entrepreneur. Scholars have written extensively about the culture of "micro-entrepreneurship," particularly in the developing world.[46] In some countries, like Bolivia, for example, individuals engage in entrepreneurial activities at three times the rate in the United States.[47] Such entrepreneurial engagement also creates opportunities for small and medium-sized businesses to market themselves more effectively, particularly since the platform economy can function as a powerful tool for digital marketing.[48] App builders can create on platforms like Android and iOS; Amazon Web Services can facilitate the formation of an ecosystem.[49] Idle time can be taken up by serving as a driver for Lyft or Uber, vacant space by renting on Airbnb. Irrespective of the specific platform, all of them direct themselves toward a single goal: encouraging everyone to contribute.[50] The most optimistic picture, then, suggests that the everyday individual can be readily transformed into an entrepreneur, able to take advantage of scheduling flexibility and able to monetize their personal and professional assets toward this goal.

In turn, the mini-entrepreneur facilitates the emergence of the microbrand. Even in digital space, platforms enable the transformation of an everyday citizen into a brand. As one study observes, "[t]he similarities between the online presentation of people and products, individuals and brands, are striking: the same interfaces and tactics apply to both, making them even more

---

[42] Teague, *supra* note 26, at 475–76.

[43] This is particularly the case after *eBay*, where the court there absolved eBay of secondary liability in large part due to its expensive "VERO" system. Smaller platforms do not have the resources to either defend themselves against the litigation eBay went through, and, more importantly, will not be able to implement a similarly expensive type of takedown system. *See id.* at 491.

[44] *See* Etsy, Foursquare, Kickstarter, Meetup, & Shapeways, *Comments in the Matter of Development of the Joint Strategic Plan for Intellectual Property Enforcement* (Oct. 16, 2015) http://extfiles.etsy.com/advocacy/Etsy_IPEC_Comment.pdf.

[45] *Id.* at 2.

[46] Karl Loo, *How the Gig Economy Could Drive Growth in Developing Countries*, Forbes (Mar. 23, 2017, 12:04PM) www.forbes.com/sites/groupthink/2017/03/23/how-the-gig-economy-could-drive-growth-in-developing-countries/#3db6d56a4a49.

[47] *Id.*

[48] *Id.*

[49] Kenney and Zysman, *supra* note 2, at 3.

[50] *Id.* at 2.

exchangeable than before."[51] Some people have lives on social media for the purposes of communication, others for the purposes of promotion, connection, and still others for the purposes of expression.[52] Yet a platform's marriage to self-branding transforms and synergizes all of these purposes into one singular purpose of micro-entrepreneurship.

Nearly every prominent platform encourages the "self-branding" of entrepreneurs, enabling ordinary citizens to essentially become corporate entities by building a consumer following. Airbnb, for example, explicitly uses language about creating a microbrand: "Your brand, or micro-brand, is what makes your listing unique and helps you stand out from the competition. Branding your listing is of utmost importance! Proper branding ensures that your listing resonates with your target market and attracts ideal guests."[53]

While at first glance it may seem that self-branding and trademark law rarely intersect, the truth is that they draw upon similar concerns regarding property, identity, and association. The endless cycle of self-branding and brand monitoring affects trademark enforcement in two primary ways. First, it may incentivize microbrands to spend significant resources of time and money to enforce their trademarks, due in part to the constantly changing brand environment they inhabit. These resources spent on brand enforcement may be wasted in some respects, as some platforms are more interested in using ratings and other reputational tools to encourage consistent quality (for example, Uber). Second, the constant pull of brand monitoring may lead macrobrands, in turn, to internalize the same range of additional costs faced by microbrands, leading, again, to trademark surveillance and overenforcement. Finally, these disparities can contribute to a widening divide between smaller and larger platforms that may have different abilities and resources to address enforcement, thus impacting the path of platform innovation.

In the context of platforms, many scholars and commentators have raised the question of whether there is a hierarchical distinction between the "platform owner" and the entrepreneurs and contractors that facilitate this economy.[54] The same question, we argue, might also be posed in the trademark arena, that is, whether our system of contributory liability, as well intended as it might be, facilitates the formation of an unequal system that extends the benefits of trademark protection and enforcement to a few, but radically undervalues the contributions of the mini entrepreneurs that characterize platform vitality. The absence of statutory safe harbors in the trademark context often has a particularly deleterious effect on smaller platforms, which may face different challenges based on their limited legal resources.[55] Many smaller platforms do not have automated systems to respond to copyright takedown notices, and therefore an attention to the diversity of platforms is especially critical in considering how to design better systems of notification and enforcement.[56]

Etsy, for example, has observed that its number of trademark-related takedown notices is greater than the copyright-related ones that it has received.[57] Because of the absence of clear safe harbors in the ISP context with respect to trademark law, Etsy and other commentators have argued that many platforms will not challenge trademark requests – even those that are questionable or even abusive – in order to avoid becoming embroiled in costly litigation.[58] Etsy offers

---

[51] José van Dijck, *You Have One "Identity": Performing the Self on Facebook and LinkedIn*, 35 Media, Culture & Soc. 199, 207 (2013).

[52] *Id.* at 211.

[53] Airbnb Guide, *Good Design is Good Business*, www.airbnbguide.com/good-design-is-good-business/.

[54] Kenney and Zysman, *supra* note 2, at 7.

[55] See Kickstarter, Makerbot, Meetup, & Shapeways, *Additional Comments in the Matter of Section 512*, Docket No. 2015–7, at 3 (Feb. 23, 2017).

[56] *See id.*, at 3–4.

[57] *Id.* at 3.

[58] *See* Etsy et al., *supra* note 44, at 3.

examples of the notices it has faced: one involving a graphic designer using the trademarked name of a television show on a set of custom party invitations; an artist using a trademarked cartoon character in a humorous oil painting; or a small business owner who repackages food packaging into purses and liquor bottles into drinking cups.[59] Even though each of these instances might be the subject of strong arguments for non-infringing uses, each of them was the subject of a takedown notice.[60]

As a recent filing concluded, "[t]he result is that a trademark claim – even one built on a weak foundation – can be an effective way to permanently quash the speech or economic activity of others."[61] In such cases, because of the complexity of trademark law, and the David versus Goliath status of the user versus the trademark owner, respectively, platforms may not even provide the user with an opportunity to challenge the assertion of infringement.[62] Here, small businesses, individual entrepreneurs, and ordinary creators might be most affected by such notices, simply because they lack the resources and channels to challenge their targeting.[63] And smaller platforms, since they may be unable to afford the legal resources required to investigate a claim, may err on the side of over-accommodation as a result.[64] Over the long term, these abusive practices can have the effect of actually undermining support for intellectual property altogether. As Etsy and others have noted, "[a] steady stream of examples of abuse can reduce the legitimacy of rightsholders as a whole in the eyes of the public, thus reducing public support for enforcement even in legitimate cases of infringement."[65]

In such cases, it is important to distinguish between abusive trademark enforcement and enforcement that seeks to execute legitimate trademark rights.[66] While the latter goal is clearly deserving of support, the former scenario – overenforcement – has a deleterious effect on startups and smaller platforms that may lack the resources to respond properly to a dispute. In such situations, the assertion of overbroad trademark rights, facilitated by an overreliance on automated systems of enforcement, may produce false positives without significant human oversight.[67] In some cases, these complaints can be sent by a rightsholder who uses these notices to undermine a competitor or to censor critical commentary.[68] For example, a recent filing noted an incident where a political action committee requested a takedown of material that parodied Hillary Clinton's campaign logo.[69] Or a similar situation where another candidate, Ben Carson, made takedown requests regarding *merchandise* that used Carson's name on merchandise relating to his candidacy.[70] Often, these claims involve a mixture of trademark and copyright claims, further muddying the waters of potential defenses.[71] The collective effect of these claims, however, limits the potential circulation of the free flow of information and ideas, further amplifying how smaller platforms become implicated in a system of overbroad (and inconsistent) regulation.

---

[59] *Id.*
[60] *Id.*
[61] *Id.*
[62] *Id.*
[63] *Id.* at 4.
[64] *Id.*
[65] *Id.*
[66] *Id.* at 5.
[67] *See* Shapeways, 2016 *Transparency Report*, at www.shapeways.com/legal/transparency/2016.
[68] *Id.*
[69] *Id.*
[70] *Id.*
[71] *Id.*

III REFORMING PLATFORM ARCHITECTURE THROUGH TRADEMARK MODERNIZATION

Platforms, then, present us with a curious paradox: as much as platforms disrupt conventional business models and challenge classic assumptions about regulation, they can also enable a rise in regulation characterized by increases in permitting, licensing, and protection.[72] In other words, the absence of law facilitates the rise of platforms, but the rise of platforms requires a regulatory system to sustain its growth. In sum, at the same time that platforms challenge established theories of the market, they also facilitate increased regulation.

The same can also be said regarding how our intellectual property system intersects with platform architecture. Particularly regarding trademark law, platforms provide us with the opportunity to look for ways to harmonize the interaction of microbrands and macrobrands while encouraging the development and protection of platform enterprises. As Rob Merges has argued in the platform context, intellectual property rights confer on their owners merely an *option* to enforce their rights.[73] This suggests that at times, the law may need to regulate the ex post policing of intellectual property enforcement in flexible and careful ways to ensure a balance between competition and regulation.[74] Drawing in part on these observations, we explore in this final part a number of ways in which trademark law can be modernized to better address the challenges presented by platform architecture. Here, acknowledging that there is no "silver bullet" to resolve these complex issues, we suggest a variety of potential improvements to the law from different angles. While change can occur through legislation or voluntary measures, our suggestions include the formation of statutory safe harbors among platforms, a "notice-and-notice" system, as well as two changes to the common law, including the application of a materiality of harm requirement and clarification of the duty to police.

A Safe Harbors

"True" statutory safe harbors are rare in trademark law.[75] By "true" we mean categories of unauthorized trademark use that are deemed to be non-infringing, or what some commentators refer to as "categorical exemptions."[76] This has likely been a conscious decision, as judges to date have been lukewarm to the idea of categorical exemptions or "bright line rules" in trademark law.[77] The reason for this is that trademark law has traditionally been context-driven, with a focus on minimizing, or avoiding altogether, consumer confusion.[78] Any attempts by judges to create shortcuts through the lengthy, time-consuming, and expensive analysis of the likelihood of confusion have been met with resistance.[79]

---

[72] Lobel, *supra* note 1, at 90.

[73] *See* Robert P. Merges, *IP Rights and Technological Platforms* 18 (Dec. 2008) (unpublished manuscript, draft on file with authors).

[74] *See id.* at 10.

[75] Except for two very narrow safe harbors for "innocent" publisher or domain name registrar. 15 U.S.C. §1114(2). *See also* William McGeveran, *Rethinking Trademark Fair Use*, 94 Iowa L. Rev. 49, 104–09 (2008) (providing a critique of the dilution safe harbor).

[76] William McGeveran, *The Trademark Fair Use Reform Act*, 90 B.U. L. Rev. 2267, 2272 (2010); Lisa P. Ramsey, *Increasing First Amendment Scrutiny of Trademark Law*, 61 SMU L. Rev. 381 (2008).

[77] McGeveran, *supra* note 76, at 2268.

[78] Leah Chan Grinvald, *Shaming Trademark Bullies*, 2011 Wis. L. Rev. 625, 658 (2011).

[79] *Compare Vornado Air Circulation Systems, Inc. v. Duracraft Corp.* 58 F.3d 1498 (10th Cir. 1995) (attempting to create a bright line rule where patents were involved) *with TrafFix Devices, Inc. v. Marketing Displays, Inc.* 532 U.S. 23, 29 (2001) (blurring the bright line rule).

However, there is a real need for such categorical exemptions in trademark law, particularly in today's world of "trademarking everything"[80] in the online world. As noted previously, some platforms themselves have argued for the need for safe harbors (as well as for a better defined system within which to operate, which we address below in our "notice-and-notice" proposal) due to the overwhelming nature of trademark infringement notices that may or may not be valid.[81] These platforms have argued that the creation of statutory safe harbors would increase accountability and public awareness, as well as encourage a greater uniformity of guiding principles to address trademark disputes in the online context.[82]

But a categorical exemption would also benefit macrobrands and microbrands in particular ways. On the macrobrand side, it would mean that platforms are no longer required to respond to every instance of perceived infringement. In addition, macrobrands would be able to provide clearer guidance to the microbrands within their ecosystem about what is and is not acceptable.[83] Since most of the trademark disputes occur extra-judicially, having clear guidelines would assist all within the platform ecosystem in deciding which claims are valid, and which involve trademark overenforcement (and perhaps even bullying).[84]

Unfortunately, though, categorical exemptions would really only work for the clear-cut cases. There are many uses of trademarks that fall in the middle and for this, we would propose a new system for trademark owners, macrobrands, and microbrands, to use in the online platform ecosystem: "notice and notice."

B "Notice and Notice"

The secondary liability standard is one of the leading causes for platform uncertainty in dealing with claims of trademark infringement, as we outlined above. Exacerbating this uncertainty is a lack of a second type of safe harbor, one that would immunize platforms and other online entities from any trademark infringing behavior by their users. The copyright "notice and take-down" has become the unintentional default regime for trademark claims (even though the law only applies to claims of copyright infringement) because copyright owners are including claims of trademark infringement within the same notice to the platforms.[85]

Although some of the platforms themselves advocate for a DMCA-like safe harbor and process, they caution that it is not as simple as replacing the term "copyright" with "trademark."[86] Due to the differences between the rights underlying copyright and trademark, we believe that a "notice and takedown" system is too blunt an instrument, as it lacks the ability to take into account the nuanced analysis that is required of claims of trademark infringement.[87] For example, while copyright law provides for a relatively discrete examination of "substantial similarity," trademark

---

[80] *See generally* Lisa P. Ramsey, *Trademarking Everything? Why Brands Should Care About Limits on Trademark Rights*, presentation at The 2015 Works-in-Progress Intellectual Property Roundtable, United States Patent and Trademark Office, Alexandria, VA (Feb. 6, 2015).

[81] *See* Etsy, et al., *supra* note 44.

[82] *See id.*

[83] Some platforms do try to provide guidance. *See, e.g.,* Etsy.com, www.etsy.com/teams/7722/discussions/discuss/13810041/.

[84] For just a sampling of scholarship on the topic of safe harbors, *see* Eric Goldman, *Deregulating Relevancy in Internet Trademark Law*, 54 Emory L.J. 507, 588–95 (2005); Ramsey, *supra* note 76, at 455–56; McGeveran, *supra* note 76, at 2303–17.

[85] *See* Etsy, et al., *supra* note 44, at 3.

[86] *Id.* at 5.

[87] Maayan Perel and Niva Elkin-Koren, *Accountability in Algorithmic Copyright Enforcement*, 19 Stan. Tech. L. Rev. 473 (2016). *See also* Teague, *supra* note 26, at 488–89.

law requires consideration of many more factors beyond similarity, including the marketing channels used, likelihood of "bridging the gap" between the goods of the defendant and the plaintiff, the defendant's intent, and evidence of actual confusion.[88] In the case of counterfeit merchandise, it becomes extremely difficult to tell whether the merchandise is actually fake or not.[89] And deferring to the plaintiff's determination opens up a host of potential problems that may facilitate abusive takedown requests, without independent examination.[90] Therefore, we suggest that the United States needs to adopt a "notice and notice" framework, borrowing from Canada's recent adoption of such a system in the copyright context.[91]

Unlike a notice and takedown format, which requires a platform to take down the infringing content upon notice, a notice and notice framework would only require the platform to forward the notice to the alleged infringer.[92] As one commentator argued, a notice and notice regime places the emphasis where it should be: on the alleged primary wrongdoer, and takes a more moderate approach to self-regulation by returning "intermediaries to their natural role as middlemen," restoring the responsibility to the courts for enforcement.[93] It also respects the privacy and expressive freedoms of end users more effectively than in a notice and takedown regime.[94]

In an ideal world, these notices from trademark owners would contain allegations of infringement for only those uses that were not within one of the categorical safe harbors as previously discussed. In such a world, then, compliance with the notice and notice framework would provide the platform with immunity from secondary liability of its users' infringement. Even in a less-than-ideal world, compliance with the notice and notice framework provides more clarity surrounding procedures, even where the alleged infringements are not valid. In particular, in the notice and notice system that we envision, the platform would not be required to take down any material. Upon receipt of the notice, the platform would simply forward onto the user the notice it received from the trademark owner. It would be up to the user to take down any material that was claimed to be infringing. Thus, the platform would be immune from any secondary liability if it ended up that the user was in fact infringing another's trademark. Beyond the scope of this chapter, but no less important, are the details of such a new system. Serious thought needs to be given to any specific proposal, as can be seen from Canada's implementation of the notice and notice regime for copyright infringement claims.[95]

---

[88] Teague, *supra* note 26, at 489.

[89] *Id.*

[90] *See* Jennifer M. Urban and Laura Quilter, *Efficient Process or Chilling Effects – Takedown Notices under Section 512 of the Digital Millennium Copyright Act*, 22 Santa Clara Computer & High Tech. L.J. 621, 694 (2006)(copyright context).

[91] *See Notice and Notice Regime*, Off. of Consumer Aff. (Jan. 20, 2015), www.ic.gc.ca/eic/site/oca-bc.nsf/eng/ca02920.html.

[92] Teague, *supra* note 26, at 488.

[93] Christina Angelopoulous and Stijn Smet, *Notice-and-Fair-Balance: How to reach a Compromise Between Fundamental Rights in European Intermediary Liability*, 8 J. of Media L. 266, 295 (2016).

[94] *Id.* It is worth noting that there is a difference in enforcement strategy between counterfeiting and trademark infringement due to the fact that counterfeiters will often simply ignore notices. The notice and notice proposal here does encompass these two different types of infringement, although recognizing that there are other approaches to handle pure counterfeiting. *See, e.g.*, Frederick Mostert and Martin Schwimmer, *Notice and Takedown*, IP Magazine 18–19 (June 2011).

[95] Canada Copyright Act, 41.25(2). *See* Claire Brownell, *Pirates in Your Neighbourhood: How New Online Copyright Infringement Laws Are Affecting Canadians One Year Later*, FP Tech Desk (Feb. 12, 2016 at 4:57 PM) http://business.financialpost.com/fp-tech-desk/pirates-in-your-neighbourhood-how-new-online-copyright-infringement-laws-are-affecting-canadians-one-year-later; Nicole Bogart, *No, You Do Not Have To Pay a 'Settlement Fee' if You Get an Illegal Download Notice*, Global Star (Jan. 13, 2017) http://globalnews.ca/news/3179760/no-you-do-not-have-to-pay-a-settlement-fee-if-you-get-an-illegal-download-notice/; Michael Geist, *Canadians Face Barrage of Misleading Copyright Demands*, Toronto Star (Jan. 9, 2015) www.thestar.com/business/tech_news/2015/01/09/canadians_face_barrage_of_misleading_copyright_demands.html.

C Common Law Changes

As changes to federal trademark legislation may be politically unpalatable or time-consuming to enact, we suggest some short-term solutions that judges could undertake now through their interpretation of the law, as many others have suggested previously.[96] The two suggestions we proffer here to add to this literature are: (1) requiring a materiality of harm; and (2) clarifying the duty to police. We believe that these two changes in the way judges approach trademark infringement cases can go a long way in mitigating some of the negative externalities that the platform architecture, as it intersects with trademark law, produces.

1 Materiality of Harm Requirement

Trademark infringement doctrine is a species of tort law. Unlike in other types of torts, missing from the infringement analysis is an examination of whether the defendant's use has, in fact, injured the plaintiff through a reduction in sales of the plaintiff's products because there was actual confusion. Although actual confusion may be assessed as part of the multifactor infringement test (the "likelihood of confusion" test), it is not required for a fact finder to determine that the test has been met.[97] This is problematic because a defendant's guilt rests on speculation of what consumers *would* think and at no time is the plaintiff required to show what consumers have *actually* done in response to the defendant's use.

We join with a line of scholars who have argued for a return to some type of materiality consideration in trademark infringement cases.[98] The practical implementation of this standard would be that the fact finders in a trademark infringement case would need to answer the question of whether a consumer would buy or perhaps pay more for a particular product based on a belief that the product was made by, or affiliated, sponsored, or endorsed by, the trademark owner.[99] If the answer is no, then the defendant's use of a mark that is either the same as or similarly confusing to the plaintiff's is not material, and therefore, causing no harm. The case would be resolved in favor of the defendant. And this would still be true even if the defendant's use was likely to cause confusion. The reintroduction of a materiality element would go a long way to rebalancing the relationship between the macrobrands and microbrands because a good deal of online trademark infringement claims deal with non-source-related confusion, such as sponsorship, affiliation, or endorsement. And with a materiality element, these claims would no longer be actionable. In addition, some platforms like Uber focus more on the rating system or other reputational tools to incentivize consistent quality of service, rather than on individual trademarks. In these cases, users of the platform likely care more about the ratings and the personal brand than they do about marks, better supporting the utility of the materiality element.

2 Clarification of the "Duty to Police"

The real driver for aggressive enforcement is the reward, as well as a lack of consequences for over-stepping the legal boundaries. Courts have taken as a probative evidence aggressive

---

[96] For a small sampling of such work, *see generally* Graeme Dinwoodie, *Developing Defenses in Trademark Law*, 13 Lewis & Clark L. Rev. 99 (2009); Gerhardt, *supra* note 23; Mark Lemley and Mark P. McKenna, *Irrelevant Confusion*, 62 Stan. L. Rev. 413 (2010); Ramsey, *supra* note 76; Alexandra J. Roberts, *Tagmarks*, 105 Cal. L. Rev. 599 (2017); Rebecca Tushnet, *Running the Gamut from A to B: Federal Trademark and False Advertising Law*, 159 U. Pa. L. Rev. 1305 (2011).

[97] 4 J. Thomas McCarthy, *McCarthy Trademarks and Unfair Competition* §23:19 (5th ed., 2018).

[98] Mark P. McKenna, *Testing Modern Trademark Law's Theory of Harm*, 95 Iowa L. Rev. 63, 70–71 (2009); Graeme W. Austin, *Tolerating Confusion about Confusion: Trademark Policies and Fair Use*, 50 Ariz. L. Rev. 157, 175 (2008); Tushnet, *supra* note 96, at 1344.

[99] Tushnet, *supra* note 96, at 1368.

enforcement strategies as proxies for a "strong" mark.[100] As one of us has argued in previous works, this aggressiveness can often cross the line into abusiveness where the parties in the dispute are imbalanced.[101] It is easy for a mark owner to slide into abusiveness, as trademark law lacks any mechanisms to hold trademark bullies accountable. There are virtually no consequences for overenforcement.[102] But the rewards are great, as a strong or famous trademark is granted a larger scope of protection.[103]

Related to our above suggestion regarding a materiality requirement, but not mutually exclusive, is the proposal that judges make concerted efforts to clarify the "duty to police" one's trademark. A number of other commentators have previously noted that this clarification is needed.[104] We agree with these commentators and further argue that what is needed is leadership from one of the circuits active in trademark law (such as the Second, Seventh, or Ninth Circuit) in judicially pronouncing that the real question "is public perception of plaintiff's mark, not a battle count of how often it has threatened to sue or in fact sued."[105] Courts must stop rewarding bad behavior. Instead of accepting the fallacy that a lack of third party use automatically equates to high levels of trademark strength or fame, as some trademark owners argue, courts should require stronger evidence of such acquired distinctiveness. This would go a long way in lowering the expectations of some trademark owners for their "reward" in over-policing their marks, thereby cutting down on the number of takedown notices sent to platforms.

CONCLUSION

The platform has challenged established theories of contributory liability at the same time as it has strengthened the need for increased regulation. We have argued that trademarks play a particular role in the design and formation of nearly every aspect of a platform, producing two discrete entities: macrobrands and microbrands. In turn, the formation, and the intersection between these two, both challenges and transforms trademark law. In order to protect the vitality and innovation of the platform ecosystem, trademark law must begin to reinvent itself in addressing contributory liability. Rather than turning to copyright law as an example of how to govern online infringement, we have argued instead for the employment of additional tools with both legislative reform and common law adjustments. By considering both, trademark law can facilitate an even greater level of growth and innovation within the platform ecosystem.

---

[100] Jessica M. Kiser, *To Bully or Not to Bully: Understanding the Role of Uncertainty in Trademark Enforcement Decisions*, 37 Colum. J.L. & Arts 211, 224–26 (2014).

[101] Leah Chan Grinvald, *Policing the Cease-and-Desist Letter*, 49 U.S.F. L. Rev. 411, 417–18 (2015).

[102] *Id.*

[103] In addition, Jessica Kiser's work in the emotional attachment to marks provides additional grounds to understand why trademark owners would want to be aggressive in their policing. *See generally* Kiser, *supra* note 100, at 73.

[104] *See* Xiyin Tang, *Against Fair Use: The Case for a Genericness Defense in Expressive Trademark Uses*, 101 Iowa L. Rev. 2021, 2063 (2016); *See* Kiser, *supra* note 100, at 73.; Stacey Dogan, *Bullying and Opportunism in Trademark and Right-of-Publicity Law*, 96 B.U. L. Rev. 1293, 1319 (2016); Kenneth L. Port, *Trademark Extortion Revisited: A Response to Vogel and Schachter*, 14 Chi.-Kent J. Intell. Prop. 217, 219 (2014); Jeremy N. Sheff, *Fear and Loathing in Trademark Enforcement*, 22 Fordham Intell. Prop. Media & Ent. L.J. 873, 877–79 (2012); Deven R. Desai and Sandra L. Rierson, *Confronting the Genericism Conundrum*, 28 Cardozo L. Rev. 1789, 1791, 1834–42 (2007).

[105] 2 J. Thomas McCarthy, *McCarthy Trademarks and Unfair Competition* § 11:91 (4th ed., 1996).

31

The "Matching" Platform and Mandatory Agency Law

*Rosalie Koolhoven**

INTRODUCTION

The European Commission has provided guidelines for the application of EU law on economic activities in the sharing – or "collaborative" – economy.[1] It is positive about the impact that open marketplaces may have on the development of a sustainable, inclusive market with lower prices.[2] There is, however, a commonly felt legal discrepancy: platforms claim that they are not liable to pay damages for contractual or delictual faults by parties in the "sharing contract." The significant influence they have on human behavior and the amount of money they make do not congruate with this point of view. The legal debate about this discrepancy generally focuses on public law systems of regulation. The question I will address in this chapter is whether such liabilities can be based on (mandatory) private law.

This question is difficult to answer in one way because each European Member State has its own national private law. Furthermore, there is a large variety of activities that fall within the notion of "the collaborative economy," such as the sharing of assets, resources, time, and skills.[3] Furthermore, this "sharing" is facilitated by a large variety of "matching" contracts.

In my opinion, there is only one way to shed light on the legal consequences of these contracts, and that is to, first of all, assess each relationship separately and divide the collaborative economy into the "matching economy" and the "sharing economy."[4] That will allow us to assess what legal framework should be applied to begin with.

Because European private law has a multi-layered structure, I shall canvass how national contract law of the European Member States complements European law, by describing forum and conflict

---

* I would like to thank Jelmer Snijder, Derek McKee, and Nestor Davidson for their comments on the draft of this chapter.

[1] European Commission, *A European Agenda for the Collaborative Economy* (Communication) COM (2016) 356 final, 3, www.eesc.europa.eu/resources/docs/com2016-356-final.pdf. (Hereafter: the EC Communication.)

[2] European Commission, *A European Agenda for the Collaborative Economy – Supporting Analysis*, COM (2016) 184 final, 5, https://ec.europa.eu/docsroom/documents/16881/attachments/3/translations/en/renditions/pdf. (Hereafter: EC Supporting Analysis.)

[3] J. Sénéchal, *The Diversity of the Services Provided by Online Platforms and the Specificity of the Counter-Performance of these Services – A Double Challenge for European and National Contract Law*, 5 J. Eur. Consumer & Market L. 39–44 (2016).

[4] EC Communication, *supra* note 1, at 3–4, n. 6. The separate assessment was one of the recommendations made in the Impulse Paper prepared in preparation of this Communication: R. Koolhoven, E. D. C. Neppelenbroek, O. E. Santamaria, and T. H. L Verdi, Analytical Paper on Liability Issues in the Short-Term Accommodation Rental Sector in Barcelona, Paris and Amsterdam (2016), http://ec.europa.eu/DocsRoom/documents/16946/attachments/1/translations.

rules. After that I address the different ways in which a selection of Member States qualify plat-form "matching" services, acting as agents, brokers, or limited payment collection agents. Qualified contracts determine whether an agent, broker, or payment collection agent is, for example, respon-sible for the (non)performance of obligations of the sharing contract to which it is generally not a party.[5] The reason lies in the fact that the quintessence of these contracts is that the service provider should pursue the interest of another.

The private law perspective shows that the protection consumers have throughout the EU varies, but is higher than assumed in the debate about public law regulation.

I MATCHING VERSUS SHARING

When speaking of the collaborative or sharing economy as one economy, we speak of too large a variety of actors governing too large a variety of services in different sectors to obtain legal clarity. There are professional users, consumer users, and platforms. Some platforms offer an online "noticeboard," whereas others only facilitate users to meet in a virtual space. Mere noticeboard platforms are to be treated differently from a platform such as Uber that is involved in the con-tract making, governance, and performance of the sharing contract. According to the opinion of Advocate-General Szpunar, Uber's matching activity and the sharing (transportation) contract are economically dependent in such a way that Uber basically offers one "composite service" of which both the contract making by electronic means and the factual transport are part.[6] Yet, not every com-mercially driven platform offers a composite service and with it a sharing service. If the matching and the sharing contract are economically independent, one finds two matching contracts (plat-form user) and one sharing contract, separated from each other and together forming a triangle.[7]

Legal obligations of a platform based on the matching contract derive from the E-Commerce Directive 2000/31/EC, complemented by specific sector regulation (transportation or accom-modation) and national contract law on matching. Matching is found in contract law in several typical forms: brokerage, where the platform is authorized and instructed to take steps which are meant to lead to, or facilitate, the conclusion of a (prospective) contract between a principal (a user) and a third party. This is linked to the second kind of matching: "agency," which means that a platform is authorized and instructed to conclude a juridical act on behalf of the principal, in such a way *that the platform is the party to the juridical act*. The Draft Common Frame of Reference (DCFR) would refer to all those engaged in both brokerage and agency activities as "agents."[8] Another kind of "matching" is done by the representative who acts on behalf of the principal, *in such a way that the principal is the party to the juridical act*. This third form is under *common law* referred to as agency as well, but in the European realm referred to as (direct) representation.[9] Notwithstanding differences in terminology, *the quintessence of these contracts*

---

5   EC Supporting Analysis, *supra* note 2, at 7.
6   Opinion of Advocate General Szpunar delivered on May 11, 2017, in case C-434/15, *Asociación Profesional Elite Taxi/ Uber Systems Spain SL*, no. 26–28, 33–34. The Court later found that the main component of the Uber service is a transport service and, accordingly, must be classified not as 'an information society service' but as 'a service in the field of transport'. C-434/15, ECJ 20 December 2017, ECLI:EU:C:2017:981.
7   C. Wendehorst, *Platform Intermediary Services and Duties under the E-Commerce Directive and the Consumer Rights Directive*, 1 J. Eur. Consumer & Market L. 30–34 (2016).
8   The DCFR is a scientific project of a large group of European private law experts, divided into Working Groups designing a "European Civil Code" based on best practices and common origins. The DCFR is not a mandatory code, but used by scientists to practice comparative law, used by judges to fill in open norms and offers a source of inspiration for legislators.
9   C. von Bar and E. M. Clive, Study Group on a European Civil Code and the Research Group on EC Private Law, *Principles, Definitions and Model Rules of European Private Law, Draft Common Frame of Reference* Art. IV.D.– 1:101, pp. 19–20 (2009). (Hereafter: DCFR.)

is that the service provider should pursue the interest of another. Understanding norms deriving from this activity could offer guidance as to what a sustainable, consumer-friendly market in which platforms play a role could look like.

A *The E-Commerce Directive 2000/31/EC Complemented?*

When assessing platform obligations, the starting point in the European Union is the E-Commerce Directive.[10] This Directive has as its objective to contribute to the proper functioning of the internal market by ensuring the free movement of information society services between Member States. The center of it is the limited liability of internet service providers for damages in the case of mere conduit, caching, and hosting.

When entering into a contract with a platform, the first question to address is whether a platform is a natural or legal person providing an information society service,[11] which is "any service normally provided for remuneration, at a distance, by electronic means and at the individual request of the recipient of services."[12]

Information society service providers are subject to a number of duties to provide information (Articles 5, 6, 10) and effective means for correcting erroneous input (Article 11). Besides these obligations they seem to profit from an exemption of liability for passing on false information or information that could lead to damages. Recently, however, it seems that the European Commission and Court reconsidered this regime for platforms that engage in matching activities.

B *Additional and Ancillary Services*

First of all, more regard is given to the fact that platforms offer additional or ancillary services nowadays beyond the scope of passing on information. The European Commission wrote that offering additional or ancillary services will not exclude the exemption for the hosting services, but that liability based on additional or ancillary services is to be assessed separately.[13] In that respect, the coordinated field of the E-Commerce Directive and its Considerations are important. The coordinated field concerns behavioral rules applicable to information society service providers, regardless of whether they are of a general nature or specifically designed for them (Article 2(h)–(i)). That means that behavioral rules are supposed to be unified by the E-Commerce Directive at the same level. Some Member States offer better rules for consumers than the European standard requires. In those cases the E-Commerce Directive gives priority to the application of the better national protection: "the Directive cannot have the result of depriving the consumer of the protection afforded to him by the mandatory rules relating to contractual obligations of the law of the Member State in which he has his habitual residence."[14]

---

[10] Directive 2000/31/EC of the European Parliament and of the Council of 8 June 2000 on certain legal aspects of information society services, in particular electronic commerce, in the internal market, (2000) Official Journal L 178/1.

[11] Article 2(a) refers to Article 1(2) of Directive 98/34/EC of 22 June 1998 laying down a procedure for the provision of information in the field of technical standards and regulations [1998] Official Journal L 204/37.

[12] Article 1(1)(b) of Directive (EU) 2015/1535 of the European Parliament and of the Council of 9 September 2015 laying down a procedure for the provision of information in the field of technical regulations and of rules on Information Society services [2015] Official Journal L 241/1.

[13] EC Communication, *supra* note 1, at 9.

[14] *See* Considerations 54 and 55 to the E-Commerce Directive.

Assessing all activities separately leads to the conclusion that agency rules apply and that they have to be respected in consumer contracts when they offer more protection.

C Active, Responsible Platforms

There are reasons as well to assume it is not only obligatory to apply mandatory consumer protection rules, but also beneficial for the fair development of the platform–user relationship to take the mandate rules and their consumer protection into account.

The liability exemption that Article 14 of the E-Commerce Directive provides is limited to passive hosting. A hosting provider is not liable for the information stored at the request of a user on condition that (a) the provider does not have actual knowledge of illegal activity or information and, as regards a claim for damages, is not aware of facts or circumstances from which the illegal activity or information is apparent; or (b) the provider, upon obtaining such knowledge or awareness, acts expeditiously to remove or to disable access to the information.

Application would lead to the conclusion that, for example, Uber is not liable for damages caused by driver X who is a sex offender, saying he is a reliable driver. But the European Court of Justice ruled in the case of *Google France/Louis Vuitton* that the exemption only applies "when [the] service provider has not played an active role of such a kind as to give it knowledge of, or control over, the data stored."[15]

When assessing the extent of control that platforms have and how they influence the users through "algorithmic management," one should conclude that some platforms play an active role instead of a passive role. Marie Jull Sørensen describes that Uber under Danish law could be liable for the damages of a passenger, if it does not remove a driver who is a sex offender from its app. The reason for that is that Uber has a "considerable degree of control" over the driver by setting all standards for both drivers and cars and because it has the vital power to exclude misbehaving drivers.[16]

It becomes clear from the mentioned opinion and decision in the *Uber* case that this might be the future of liability: in economic terms one cannot always divide the matching activity from the sharing activity. Basically, as the Advocate General and the Court opined, Uber is not an information society service provider any more, it is a transportation service provider.

Secondly, we find in the EC Communication that the European Commission encourages platforms to take responsibility for creating a platform market in which consumers are well protected. When platforms turn to ensuring the quality of transactions through the handling of complaints, insurance services, and payment collection services, reviews and identity verification, it becomes not in an economic sense, but in a factual way, unclear who is responsible for what part of the performance of a characteristic, fundamental "sharing" contract.[17]

---

[15] Joined Cases C-236/08 to C-238/08 *Google France SARL and Google Inc.* v. *Louis Vuitton* [2010] ECLI:EU:C:2010:159, no. 120 and operative part 3. Confirmed in Case C-324/09 *L'Oréal SA and Others* v. *eBay International AG and Others* [2011] ECLI:EU:C:2011:474, no. 116, 123 and operative part 6.

[16] M. J. Sørensen, *Uber – a Business Model in Search of a New Contractual Legal Frame?* 3 J. Eur. Consumer & Market L. 15–19 (2016), referring to the no-tolerance policy.

[17] Asser/Hartkamp & Sieburgh 6-III 2014/90 use the term "fundamental contract" in relation to the "ancillary contract" that "prepares" the fundamental contract. In the collaborative economy, the sharing contract is the fundamental contract and the mandate/negotiation/(indirect) representation is the ancillary contract. A. S. Hartkamp and C. H. Sieburgh, *Mr. C. Assers Handleiding tot de beoefening van het Nederlands Burgerlijk Recht. 6. Verbintenissenrecht. Deel III. Algemeen overeenkomstenrecht* (2014).

II FORUM AND APPLICABLE NATIONAL LAWS

A *Forum*

If we continue from the point of view that national contract law governs the platform–user relationship, and if a consumer-user challenges one of the platform's general terms and conditions, the first question is which court will decide and which law will be applied.

Platforms often use exclusive or non-exclusive arbitration clauses. An exclusive choice of forum will make any other forum incompetent.[18] Such forced arbitration is valid under US law,[19] but not under European consumer law. Article 6:236n Dutch CC (based on EU law) allows an arbitration clause only if the consumer has a period of one month to choose to have the conflict resolved by a court that is referred to by law.[20] Article 18 of the Brussels I bis (also called EEX II) Directive[21] states that the jurisdiction of the court of residence of the consumer is the appropriate forum.

In accordance with this, Article 6 of Uber's terms provides for an arbitration clause, respecting consumers' rights referred to in Article 18 of the Brussel I bis and – for its Amsterdam-based limited company – Article 6:236n Dutch CC. Airbnb writes in its terms under no. 37 called "Additional Clauses for Users Contracting with Airbnb Ireland": "You and we agree to submit to the non-exclusive jurisdiction of the Irish courts for resolving any dispute between the parties. […] The Dispute Resolution section shall be removed and is not applicable."[22]

Platforms that do not have an arbitration clause or forum choice will rely on the respective national procedural codes. A Dutch court will accept jurisdiction even when two parties have agreed to a specific forum. A Dutch court has jurisdiction in the case of a contract between a professional party and a consumer who has his residence in the Netherlands when the professional party engages in professional activities on Dutch territory (Article 6(d)). A national judge will also accept jurisdiction in a case that is sufficiently connected to its legal sphere.[23]

B *Applicable Law*

The law applicable to the contract between a platform and a European user is governed by Regulation (EC) No 593/2008 on the law applicable to contractual obligations.[24] This regulation is called "Rome I" and is applied to contractual obligations in civil and commercial matters. The law that is specified by Rome I shall be applied whether or not it is the law of a Member State.

If the contracting parties choose the applicable law, expressly or clearly demonstrated by the terms of the contract or the circumstances of the case, that law will apply (Article 3 (1)). Where other elements relevant to the situation at the time of the choice are located in a country other than whose law has been chosen, "the choice of the parties shall not prejudice the application of

---

[18] Court (Hof) Den Haag 15.10.2013, ECLI:NL:GHDHA:2013:3895, *Llanos Oil/Republiek Colombia*, Supreme Court (Hoge Raad) 9.2.2001, ECLI:NL:PHR:2001:AA9896, *Cogenius/Schothorst*.

[19] V. Mak, *Private Law Perspectives on Platform Services* 5(1) J. Eur. Consumer and Market L. 19 2016.

[20] *See also* C-168/05 ECLI:EU:C:2006:675 [2006] *Mostaza Claro v. Centro Móvil Milenium SL*; Court (Hof) 's-Hertogenbosch 17.03.2009, ECLI:NL:GHSHE:2009:BH6958, *JOR* 2009/310.

[21] Regulation (EU) 1215/2012 of 12 December 2012 on jurisdiction and the recognition and enforcement of judgments in civil and commercial matters (Brussels I bis) [2012] Official Journal EU 2012 L351/1.

[22] Airbnb, *Terms of Service* (last updated June 19, 2017), www.airbnb.nl/terms.

[23] J. J. Kuipers and J. Vlek, *Het Hof van Justitie en de bescherming van de handelsagent: over voorrangsregels, dwingende bepalingen en openbare orde*, 2 Nederlands Internationaal Privaatrecht 198–206 (2014).

[24] Regulation (EC) No 593/2008 of 17 June 2008 on the law applicable to contractual obligations (Rome I) [2008] Official Journal L 177/6.

provisions of the law of that other country which cannot be derogated from by agreement." That means that the mandatory law of another country will be applied. Airbnb, for example, writes that the terms will be interpreted under Irish law. When contracting with a German consumer Airbnb cannot profit from a very tolerant Irish set of rules, for instance, that infringes German mandatory consumer law. This point of view leads to the conclusion that Airbnb offers services which might collide with mandatory consumer law in the Netherlands, where it is forbidden to ask remuneration from both parties dependent of the same intermediary or broker (Article 7:425 jo. 417).

Without a choice of law clause, Article 6 points to the law of the country where the consumer has his habitual residence, which could be anywhere.

A good example of increasing awareness of the legal framework in the European Union is visible in Airbnb's change to its General Terms. As of June 19, 2017 the Terms state in 21.3:

> Terms will be interpreted in accordance with Irish law. [...] The choice of law does not impact your rights as a consumer according to the consumer protection regulations of your country of residence. If you are acting as a consumer, you agree to submit to the non-exclusive jurisdiction of the Irish courts. Judicial proceedings that you are able to bring against us arising from or in connection with these Terms may only be brought in a court located in Ireland or a court with jurisdiction in your place of residence. If Airbnb wishes to enforce any of its rights against you as a consumer, we may do so only in the courts of the jurisdiction in which you are a resident. If you are acting as a business, you agree to submit to the exclusive jurisdiction of the Irish courts.

III THE PLATFORM AS A BROKER

Even though platforms state in their general terms that they are not in any way a party to the prospective – sharing – contract, the interpretation of their activities underlies mandatory definitions as well, so-called "Legaldefinitionen."[25] Parties cannot decide which rules apply or not; certain activities are brought under certain rules.[26] These mandatory rules vary from duties of care to liability for the result and performance of the prospective contract.

To begin with the legal definition, a German case about a contract with a platform that specialized in relationships illustrates that the definition of activities and not the given name is decisive.[27] German law prohibits a person engaged in marriage brokerage to ask for remuneration (§656 German Bürgerliches Gesetzbuch: BGB). A platform offering brokerage activities for finding a partner tried to escape this rule by calling it "work" (*Werkvertrag*, §631 a.f. BGB), which also led to the application of §649 BGB: the full price is to be paid if the work is finished. The *Werkvertrag*, however, requires a continuous activity that leads to a specified result. The platform said this work was the list of 25 possible partners based on psychological analysis. The court ruled that it is misleading to use the term "work" in this situation. Instead, the contract was a "contract resembling brokerage" (*Maklervertrag ähnliches Vertragsverhältnis*).

Under Dutch law also the activities of a platform fall within the scope of brokerage. Facilitating the conclusion of a contract between two others is qualified as such: 7:425 Dutch CC.

---

[25] Busch, C., "BGB §312i" [2017] *BeckOGK*, no. 5–8; C. Busch, G. Dannemann, and H. Schulte-Nölke, *Ein neues Vertrags- und Verbraucherrecht für Online-Plattformen im Digitalen Binnenmarkt?* 12 Multimedia und Recht 787–92 (2016).

[26] Case C-149/15 *Wathelet/Garage Bietheres & Fils* ECLI:EU:C:2016:840, NJW 2017/874.

[27] OLG Hamburg 28. 8. 1985–5 U 135/84, "Partnervermittlungsvertrag als Maklervertrag," NJW 1986/325.

Under Danish law Uber, for example, would be an agent. Sørensen writes: "Uber is not just a billboard where users can post items (like in the supermarket) [...] Uber plays an active intermediary role."[28] Like in the before-mentioned DCFR, Denmark is one of the countries in which the law uses the term "agency" to refer to those who facilitate the conclusion of a (prospective) contract, as well as direct and indirect representatives.

The European Commission acknowledges that platforms offer brokerage activities and not just an open market.[29] The use of algorithms might make them look like technical innovations and might cover up the "agency perspective" that lies hidden underneath. That also leads to the realization that the agency framework does not show one European legal landscape.[30] It does explain that platform activity – which might be thought of as an unregulated innovation – can be subject to norms, which could be used to shape the future economy of "responsible platforms."[31]

A Obligations Concerning the "Prospective" Sharing Contract

Brokerage and/or agency rules in some countries lead to platform liability in the case of nonperformance of the prospective contract.[32] A court in Zeeland, the Netherlands, found a real estate broker liable against an owner for finding him a tenant that was insolvent and could not pay the rent.[33] Two other cases led to the same result.[34] One sees that liability is based on the duty of care that a broker has vis-à-vis the client.

The opinion in the Uber case suggests that liability for performance of the prospective contract can follow from the fact that the platform itself is the service provider of the prospective contract.[35]

Uber's factual service provider and matching internet service are economically connected and therefor seen as one. In Germany, before this opinion several courts had already ruled that software applications to provide passenger transport agreements should be viewed as an integral part of an overall service which involves a transport service.[36] Therefore the platform in Germany would be liable for the illegality of the provision of the transport service.[37] Also, the French Transport code (L3120-3) sets the liability regime for an intermediary vis-à-vis the execution of the transport service.

If a platform activity would be seen as agency, the Dutch CC provides in Article 3:70 that an agent can be liable for non-performance of the prospective agreement. If a host offers a beautiful

---

[28] Sørensen, *supra* note 16.

[29] T. Gillespie, *The Politics of Platforms*, 12 New Media & Soc'y 347 (2010/12); Mak, *supra* note 19; EC Supporting Analysis, *supra* note 2, at 28–30.

[30] In Germany one finds the *Vermittler*, the *Zivilmakler* (a real estate agent or broker in work), the *Handelsmakler* (in transportation), and the *Handelsvertreter* with authority only to solicit offers. Ebenroth/Boujong/Joost/Strohn (Reiner), Handelsgesetzbuch §93 2014/32–36; OLG Hamburg GRUR 2006, 788; BeckOGK/Meier, BGB §652 2017/37–41; DCFR, *supra* note 9, at 439–40.

[31] Of course the degree of liability depends on whether platforms only provide information or whether they give advice or control their users through algorithms. For example, Article IV.C.–7:104 DCFR states that the obligation of skill and care only binds advisers, not information providers.

[32] Asser/Hartkamp and Sieburgh, *supra* note 17, at *6-III* 2014/516–18; *see also* DCFR, *supra* note 9, at 454–55.

[33] Court of First Instance (Rechtbank) Zeeland-West-Brabant 29.6.2016, ECLI:NL:RBZWB:2016:3999.

[34] Court of Appeal (Gerechtshof) Amsterdam 1.3.2016, ECLI:NL:GHAMS:2–16:755, Court of Appeal (Gerechtshof) Arnhem 1.3.2011, ECLI:NL:GHARN:2011:BP9121.

[35] Opinion of Advocate General Szpunar delivered on 11 May 2017, in case C-434/15 *Asociación Profesional Elite Taxi/Uber Systems Spain SL*, no. 26–28, 33–34.

[36] Oberverwaltungsgericht Hamburg, 24.9.2014 (3 Bs 175/14); Oberverwaltungsgericht Berlin-Brandenburg, 10.4.2015 (VG 11 L 353.14).

[37] EC Supporting Analysis, *supra* note 2, at 29–30.

room on Airbnb which in practice is a basement, the platform could be liable not for performing the accommodation service itself, but for compensating for the financial loss. This of course is why platforms often write: "your relationship with [platform, *RK*] is limited to being a member and an independent, third-party contractor."

The DCFR is rather complex in this respect. Under mandate law (brokerage, agency as in indirect and direct representation are all "mandate") only the agent who acts "in accordance with the applicable provisions" is not liable for a prospective contract which turns out detrimental to the principal. Article II.–3:301 DCFR seems to cover this problem by imposing the duty to negotiate in accordance with good faith and fair dealing. For example, misrepresentation or giving promises may give rise to a right to damages.[38] This is linked to the question whether a platform guarantees a certain result of the prospective agreement or not, since a guarantee becomes the platform's obligation.[39]

In Denmark, one finds the broad concept of agency as in the DCFR to cover brokerage and other kinds of mandate. Also, liability of the agent for non-performance of the prospective contract can be established. A passenger who suffers damage from an accident may hold the platform liable for damages on the ground of joint liability with the driver or based on the brokerage rules. Sørensen also gives the example of a driver raping a passenger: if this driver is not denied access to the app and commits the same offense again, Uber could be liable when having knowledge of the first offense.[40] Sørensen explains that platform liability is connected to the expectations that the platform generates and the control that Uber has over its drivers, based on general rules of joint liability and on agency.

Different justifications are found to hold the platform liable as a broker or agent for non-performance of the sharing contract: economic connectivity, control, duty of care, guarantee, or the *causa* of the contract being the obligation to care for the interests of the client (sometimes by way of an insurance). It leads to the general thought that there are numerous reasons that justify liability of a platform for the result of the sharing contract. Of course, if the European Court of Justice in Luxembourg will follow the opinion of Advocate General Szpunar in the Uber case, liability can be based on the assumption that an active platform is actually the service provider.[41]

B *Other Obligations*

Within the matching economy one finds that, on average, over 85 percent of gross revenue generated by platforms goes to the service providers. The revenue models vary between fixed and variable commissions ranging from 1 percent to up to 20 percent for ride-sharing services.[42] Most platforms ask for a remuneration as soon as a sharing contract has come into existence and the "matching" result is achieved. Also in this respect, "remuneration" may be subject to mandatory rules when users of a platform are consumers.

German law (§652 I BGB) describes the result of matching as a concrete contract between two users. The right to be remunerated for this result still exists when one of the parties to the prospective contract cancels later on. Also under Dutch law, the broker is allowed to keep the

---

[38] DCFR, *supra* note 9, at 273, 2045–46 and 2141–45.
[39] Asser/Hartkamp and Sieburgh, *supra* note 17, at 6-III 2014/531–32.
[40] Sørensen, *supra* note 16.
[41] Busch advocates for an EU Platform Directive which could base liability on the reliance principle and on the potentially dominant role that a platform may achieve. *See* C. Busch, *The Rise of the Platform Economy: A New Challenge for EU Consumer Law?* 3 J. Eur. Consumer & Market L. 3–10 (2016).
[42] EC Supporting Analysis, *supra* note 2, at 8–9.

remuneration, which is then based on "non-performance of one of the parties to that prospective contract" (creditors' non-performance, Article 6:58 CC).[43] According to Danish law non-mandatory regulation rules about commissions state that an agent has no claim for commission or remuneration if the prospective contract is not performed, if the principal can prove that the failure to perform is not due to circumstances within the control of the principal. The third party's insolvency risk is on the agent.[44]

A problem in the area of remuneration is, however, that many "costs," such as contract costs, administration fees, and service fees are often just hidden broker fees. According to several legislators, parties who need a third party to help them on a market are in a dependent position, and easy victims for extended pricing or inappropriate contract terms. One duty in consumer contracts therefore is to be transparent. Transparent in concrete situations means informing the user beforehand of a remuneration.[45] A fluctuating percentage is not transparent. Setting a price at a very late stage – the way Airbnb does – is unfair according to the purpose of the E-Commerce rules, which is to protect users.[46] When analyzing different Member States, one finds a large variety of mandatory and non-mandatory norms – between professional and non-professional agency and sector dependent – which shows that it will not be easy for platforms to comply with all of them in one set of General Terms. Transparency, it seems, is key. I am aware that the pricing is often clear before the conclusion of the prospective contract, but users will already have registered and given personal data before that. Not being clear about what the data are used for constitutes an unfair practice. I am aware that many platforms ask only a small percentage and that many consumers might see that their accommodation via Airbnb is cheaper than a hotel, but on a large scale – the European Commission found that one out of six EU citizens uses the collaborative economy – it is about EUR 20 billion and many single transactions are opaque.[47]

Another obligation, the quintessence of service provision, is the obligation to pursue the interest of the client. This is treated as a duty to undertake proper effort or behave with the diligence of a prudent businessperson (Ccom §347, Austria), as a duty to act "in the best possible manner in accordance with the interests of the principal" under Bulgarian law and LOA §620 in Estonia. In Finland there is the obligation to ensure that the performance corresponds to the interests of the principal and a failure due to negligence of the agent makes the agent liable for any loss the principal suffers. The same norm is found in French case law (Cass.civ. 1re, 3 Jun 1997, no. 95–17111) and in the German BGB, §666 jo. 280 BGB and the Spanish Código Civil in Article 255. One finds this duty also if the agency is offered for free (Article 7:425 Dutch CC), which is a well-known strategy to scale up the platform. When operating on a large scale, the platform – which is increasingly important because it can become a monopoly – can offer its services at a higher price. This contrasts with any agent's obligation to pursue the interest of its client. In the ideological marketing we find in the sharing economy, this aspect of the *matching*

---

[43] Asser/Tjong Tjin Tai 7-IV* 2009/129; Supreme Court (Hoge Raad) 23.5.2003, ECLI:NL:HR:2003:AF4626; Bijzondere Overeenkomsten (S.Y.Th. Meijer), 2016, p. 272.

[44] DCFR, *supra* note 9, at 2079 *et seq*.

[45] Asser/Tjong Tjin Tai 7-IV* 2009/126, 134–137.

[46] G. Straetmans, *Misleading Practices, the Consumer Information Model and Consumer Protection*, 5 J. Eur. Consumer & Market L. 199–210(2016).

[47] Notice that copying common law business models like Airbnb's and Uber's are a source of inspiration that do not always transplant well into civil law. Connected to transparency are the many information duties of: Directive 2005/29/EC on Unfair Commercial Practices; Directive 2011/83/EU on Consumer Rights; Directive 93/13/EEC on Unfair Terms in Consumer Contracts. *See* D. P. Kuipers and M. A. M. L. van de Sanden, *E-Commerce Sector Inquiry*, 10 NtER 341–48 (2016).

economy and *causa* of agency is overshadowed: platforms should be seen as essentially service providers acting on behalf of their clients. In Austria, Scotland, and England this is described as a fiduciary duty; in Belgium and France as an obligation of fair dealing. In Ireland this even leads to a duty to not make a secret profit.[48]

In Dutch law pursuing one's own interest and/or plural interests without being clear about it leads to avoidability (Article 3:40 (2) Dutch CC) and a loss of the right to remuneration. Some authors are even of the opinion that it is illegal to serve two clients at the same time.[49] In the DCFR this is called a "double mandate" (IV.D.–5:102), which is allowed in consumer agency only if the agent has disclosed that information and both principals have given express consent; or the content of the prospective contract is so precisely determined in the mandate contract that there is no risk that the interests of the principal may be disregarded. Within the European Union there are differences also at the national level, declaring the double mandate, for example, inadmissible for agents – (181 German BGB) – and permissible in cases of brokerage (§654 BGB) or after having given consent. The same variety of answers exists to the question whether it is admissible to receive a double remuneration.[50]

Even though platforms might be smart and enable consumers to get cheaper services than in the "traditional" market, this does not relieve them from transparency obligations in pricing and balancing all interests at stake, nor from the duty of care that underlies each service contract that can be justified either by the extent of control, economic intertwined contracts, and the *causa* of the broker contract. There are various consequences of acting upon a double mandate: in some countries it is not allowed to seek double remuneration, in others it could lead to avoidability or to liability.

IV THE PLATFORM AS AGENT

A last point is the qualification of the platform's activity when it engages in the collection of the payment from the tenant/passenger/user on behalf of the owner/driver/service provider.

The legal basis on which Airbnb collects payments is a contractual one; it does not derive from the assignment of the claim creditor–debtor to the platform. Using a common law "limited payment collection agent" in civil law countries that adhere to a strict *numerus clausus* principle and do not accept a *trust* imposes an insolvency risk on the creditor.[51]

A *The Limited Payment Collection Agent*

In *common law* an "agent" is allowed to act on behalf of the principal either in his own name or in the name of the principal.[52] The "The Hague Convention on the Law Applicable to Agency of 14 March 1978" speaks of agency in both situations as well (Article 1). In Denmark, Ireland,

---

[48] DCFR, *supra* note 9, at 2136–39.

[49] H. C. F. Schoordijk, *De ontwerpregeling van de opdracht in het zevende boek*, 24A NJB 65–66 (1973); Groene Serie Bijzondere overeenkomsten (Van Neer-van den Broek), Art. 7:417, no. 1; A. C. van Schaick, *Volmacht* (Mon. BW B-5), no. 36–38.

[50] DCFR, *supra* note 9, at 2229–32.

[51] Some Member States, such as Germany, are even stricter and forbid unilateral pricing. In the DCFR a remuneration is not part of the mandate contract, so these restrictions also apply to free intermediation contracts.

[52] D. Busch, *Middellijke vertegenwoordiging in het Europese contractenrecht*, diss. Utrecht, 2002, at 149: common law knows a uniform agency concept. *See* H. L. E. Verhagen, *Agency in Private International Law* (1995); H. L. E. Verhagen and L. Macgregor, Agency and Representation, *in Elgar Encyclopedia of Comparative Law* 37–64 (2nd ed., J. M. Smits ed., 2012).

Scotland, and England – in terminology common law countries as opposed to civil law countries – there are regimes which also govern all sorts of agency alike. Yet, there is a distinction between "general" agents and "special" or "limited" agents. General agents carry out all the business of the principal, or all the business of a particular type. Special or limited agents carry out a particular transaction.

Some civil law systems attach different rules to the situation in which an agent acts in the name of the principal as a "direct representative" (who affects the legal position of the principal directly[53]) and an agent who acts *in his own name* (as an "indirect representative").[54] Furthermore, some systems interpret the (authorized) collection of another's debt as a juridical act governed by agency rules. Others find it a non-juridical act for which different rules apply, because "agency" would only cover juridical acts on behalf of someone else.

It is therefore hard to find one "translation" that fits all jurisdictions, but some notions are true for several legal systems.

B Bankruptcy Risk

In systems that do not recognize the *trust*, a platform collecting money in its own name leaves the creditor with a bankruptcy risk, even if the agent is under the contractual obligation to transfer the collected sum to the creditor.[55]

If there is no trust or other fiduciary framework available, the collected payment will belong to the platform's estate, as the bank account shows who is entitled to the sum of money on the bank account. If then the platform goes bankrupt, the creditor is left with a worthless claim to forward the money.[56]

Platforms operating from a "trust law" system are probably safe, but if platforms try to offer a similar activity from another market consumers are easily misled. In the Netherlands only special public law notaries and barristers – not platforms – are entitled by law to have an estate separate from their own estate.[57] However, in Estonia, for example, there is a rule that claims acquired by an agent when performing a mandate in the agent's name on account of the principal are not included in the bankruptcy estate of the agent and cannot be subject to a claim against the agent in an enforcement procedure.[58]

In short: in *common law* bankruptcy of a platform may not be a problem for the creditor, because those who keep money *in escrow* are holding this money on trust.[59] Such terms and conditions cannot have effect in all civil law systems. The point I wish to make is that consumers

---

[53] Article II.–6:102 DCFR.

[54] One finds jurisdictions with rules on representation in general, on commission, on mandate, and also jurisdictions that extend the application of benevolent intervention to indirect representation. Some distinguish between "undisclosed agency" and "mandato especial," or the *mandatário sem representação*, DCFR, *supra* note 9, at 2053–56. Dutch law, for example, has rules on direct representation based on a unilateral act and based on a contract, and distinguishes between having either the *authority* or the *duty* to *represent*. In France, this difference lies in perfect (*apparent*) and imperfect (*undisclosed*) representation. DCFR, at 447.

[55] Supreme Court (Hoge Raad) 3.2.1984, NJ 1984/752 (Slis-Stroom); Asser/Van der Grinten & Kortmann 2-I 2004/61–63.

[56] There are ways for the creditor to claim a "direct action" – against the debtor – to receive direct payment without the sum passing through the agent's estate, but this only helps before the payment was made.

[57] Supreme Court (Hoge Raad) 13.6.2003, NJ 2004/196 (ProCall/Van Dam). There is discussion because the mandate contract allows agents to collect payments in the name of both the principal/creditor and themselves, Article 7:414 (2) jo. 7:419–421 Dutch CC. Asser/Van der Grinten & Kortmann 2-I 2004/130.

[58] DCFR, *supra* note 9, at 460, 4127.

[59] Factoring is a term used for many different legal constructions that lead to similar results. Asser/Houben 7-X 2014/95; J. W. A. Biemans, *Rechtsgevolgen van stille cessie*, diss. Nijmegen; Serie Onderneming en Recht (deel 65) 2011, at 34; Asser/Bartels & Van Mierlo 3-IV 2013/359.

should be aware that platform activity is often benchmarked as "trust enhancing," whereas it may not protect the users sufficiently, and the law differs considerably from country to country.

CONCLUSION

Cheap access to services may blind consumers and regulators. They feel they are better off than in the traditional economy, which in terms of pricing might be true. However, they are not if we forget that the factual behavior of platforms makes them brokers and "indirect representatives." Brokers and representatives, agents in general, have duties to pursue the interests of their contracting parties. The quintessence of these duties is the duty of care. In the compliance of this duty, platform users are legally and morally bound. I can imagine that the platforms' business models, based on manipulating human behavior in order to extract the greatest possible commissions for the platforms themselves, rather than pursuing the interests of users, may be incompatible with such a duty.

Also, the fact that some platforms' matching activities are so strongly intertwined in the sharing contract that they are seen as one contract makes platforms responsible for the (non) performance of the sharing contract.

When considering the role of the platform as a payment collection agent, it is important to consider who bears the financial risks. I can imagine it is very unclear for users to see whether their money "safely" kept on trust actually becomes part of the platform's estate or not. Since the trust is not available in all legal systems, it remains a source of difference within Member States as to whether the collaborative economy as a whole benefits both consumers that are on the service providing (host/owner/driver) side and consumers on the receiving (guest/tenant/borrower/passenger) side.

32

The Protection of the Weaker Parties in the Platform Economy

Guido Smorto

INTRODUCTION

Known by many names – platform, sharing, peer-to-peer (p2p), collaborative economy, and so on – entirely new business models have emerged in recent years, whereby online platforms use digital technologies to connect distinct groups of users in order to facilitate transactions for the exchange of assets and services. Compared to both offline and online providers, these platforms do not act as direct suppliers, but leverage the widespread diffusion of internet and mobile technologies to operate as virtual meeting points for supply and demand, providing ancillary facilities for the smooth functioning of these markets.[1]

This dramatic shift in business organization and market structure has opened an intense debate on the persisting need for those regulatory measures that typically protect the weaker party in bilateral business-to-consumer (b2c) transactions. In the platform economy both customers and providers are said be empowered, with the former enjoying wider choice and lower prices and the latter benefiting from countless new business opportunities, while platforms make transactions safe and efficient by adopting new mechanisms to enhance trust. Widespread calls for a "level playing field" make a strong argument for reconsidering the scope of regulation and delegating regulatory responsibility to the platforms. Accordingly, the appeal of lighter rules and reliance on self-regulatory mechanisms is pervasive.[2]

This chapter calls into question these assumptions. It demonstrates that platforms make frequent use of boilerplate, architecture, and algorithms to leverage their power over users – whether customers or providers[3] – and that it is still not clear to what extent effective market-based solutions

---

[1] *Cf.* Kenneth A. Bamberger and Orly Lobel, *Platform Market Power*, 32 Berkeley Tech. L.J. 1051 (2017), Liran Einav et al., *Peer-to-Peer Markets*, 8 Ann. Rev. Econ. 615 (2016); Bertin Martens, An Economic Policy Perspective on Online Platforms, Institute for Prospective Technological Studies Digital Economy Working Paper 2016/05. JRC101501 (2016), https://ec.europa.eu/jrc/sites/jrcsh/files/JRC101501.pdf.

[2] *See generally* Adam Thierer et al., *How the Internet, the Sharing Economy, and Reputational Feedback Mechanisms Solve the "Lemons Problem,"* 70 U. Miami L. Rev. 830 (2016); Christopher Koopman et al., *The Sharing Economy and Consumer Protection Regulation: The Case for Policy Change*, 8 J. Bus. Entrepreneurship & L. 529 (2015); Molly Cohen and Arun Sundararajan, *Self-Regulation and Innovation in the Peer-to-Peer Sharing Economy*, 82 U. Chi. L. Rev. Dialogue 116 (2015); Darcy Allen and Chris Berg, *The Sharing Economy: How Over-Regulation Could Destroy an Economic Revolution* (2014).

[3] *See* Communication from the Commission to the European Parliament, the Council, the European Economic and Social Committee and the Committee of the Regions, A European Agenda for the Collaborative Economy, {WD(2016) 184 final, at 3 ("The collaborative economy involves three categories of actors: (i) service providers who share assets, resources, time and/or skills – these can be private individuals offering services on an occasional basis ('peers') or service providers acting in their professional capacity ('professional services providers'); (ii) users of these;

are emerging to tackle these issues. Section I illustrates the reasons for the alleged reduction in disparities, and it explains why such a conclusion fails to fully appreciate the many grounds to the contrary. Section II scrutinizes terms and conditions adopted by online platforms to assess whether they mirror an imbalance in the parties' rights and obligations. The chapter concludes that it is crucial to protect the weaker parties in these emerging markets, and it presents some brief recommendations.

I BARGAINING POWER IN THE PLATFORM ECONOMY

A *Assessing Empowering Processes: From the Rise of the Internet to P2P Transactions*

Protecting the weaker party has long been the main reason for external regulatory intervention in bilateral business-to-consumer (b2c) transactions, mainly justified on the weaker party's lack of ability to negotiate on an equal basis with her professional counterpart. However, with the rise of the internet and the platform economy, this need is said to be dramatically reduced.

1 *The Rise of the Internet*

A first significant change in market power to the benefit of consumers has been predicted since the beginning of the web. The main reason is commonly identified in the widening of choice, due to the removal of geographic and time constraints. The amount of available information, both from the "crowd" and from experts, and the reduction in search costs have expanded the capacity to access and to compare products and services, significantly increasing consumer surplus.[4] As a result, consumers are now considered more sophisticated and educated, and better able to make informed decisions, therefore creating more efficient incentives for firms as well. Further, consumers do not only have much more information than in the past, but they are also active players in producing it through reviews and opinions, thus intensifying the potential for individual opinions to signal dissatisfaction, influence markets, and impose effective market sanctions through both "voice" and "exit."[5]

2 *Platforms and Digital Marketplaces*

With the rise of online platforms, and the shift from contracts between a trader and a consumer to trilateral relationships with a platform acting as an intermediary, this change in power in favor of consumers is supposedly even more pronounced. Compared with internet suppliers that themselves trade goods and services, online platforms operate as third parties mediating the transaction. And since platforms' commercial success is obviously related to the quality of the marketplace, they have a compelling interest in creating a safe environment and reducing moral hazard. Further, in performing these tasks platforms can leverage an enormous amount of

---

and (iii) intermediaries that connect – via an online platform – providers with users and that facilitate transactions between them ('collaborative platforms')").

4   *See generally* Jeremy Heimans and Henry Timms, *Understanding "New Power,"* Harv. Bus. Rev., Dec. 2014, https://hbr.org/2014/12/understanding-new-power; Lauren I. Labrecque et al., *Consumer Power: Evolution in the Digital Age*, 27 J. Interactive Marketing 257 (2013); Eric Brynjolfsson et al., *Consumer Surplus in the Digital Economy: Estimating the Value of Increased Product Variety at Online Booksellers*, 49 Mgmt. Sci. 1580 (2003). With specific reference to the sharing economy, *see* Arun Sundararajan, *The Sharing Economy. The End of Employment and the Rise of Crowd-based Capitalism* (2016), at 111 ("As search engine use has become widespread, consumers have become increasingly empowered – they can make better choice with access to superior information, a larger number of markets, and up-to-date feedback and reviews on products").

5   The alternative between voice and exit has been famously stated by Albert O. Hirschman, *Exit, Voice, and Loyalty: Responses to Decline in Firms, Organizations, and States* (1970).

information and make use of a wide range of tools – ex ante screening, reputation mechanisms, and other monitoring systems – through which they can manage the marketplace, dictate rules, and sanction conducts. Hence, they not only recreate analogues to brick-and-mortar guarantees (e.g., images and videos of the product, detailed descriptions and tech specs, online chat, complaint services), but they also provide an entirely new way of signaling reliability (e.g., rating systems and trust mechanisms).[6] For these reasons, digital platforms should be deemed to have both a manifest interest, and the related tools, to address many of the market failures that commonly justify government regulation in firm-to-consumer transactions.

3 *From Professionals to Peers*

A final transformation of bargaining power in favor of customers is said to have taken place with specific regard to p2p transactions. With the transition from traditional, large-scale corporations to a "crowd" of nonprofessional "micro-entrepreneurs," disparity of bargaining power between suppliers and customers is less likely, with regard to both asymmetric information and wealth inequalities. Asymmetric information, which conventionally justifies external intervention in b2c transactions, can run in both directions when transactions occur between "peers": hosts in short-term accommodation and drivers in ride-sharing services may be as concerned as guests and riders on the reliability of the counterpart.[7] Similarly, with the massive service provision by "regular people" sharing their time and assets, those wealth disparities that typically affect firm-to-consumer transactions are much less likely, as the economic power of counterparts becomes much more even, making the relationships between nonprofessionals more equal than b2c ones.

B *Is There a Weaker Party in the Platform Economy?*

While these transformations undeniably affect both internet-enabled market structure and digital economic organizations, their effect on parties' bargaining power is far from clear. The widespread belief in an informed and empowered platform user, who is now able to transact on equal terms with her counterparts, is too one-sided. In contrast, a quite different picture emerges if other relevant factors are also taken into account.[8]

1 *New Information Asymmetries*

A first reason for a more cautious conclusion about this apparent empowerment of platform users is the enhanced capabilities of platforms to collect and use an enormous amount of data,[9]

---

[6] *See generally* Hassan Masum and Mark Tovey (eds.), *The Reputation Society: How Online Opinions are Reshaping the Offline World* (2012).

[7] *Cf.* Alex Tabarrok and Tyler Cowen, *The End of Asymmetric Information?*, Cato Unbound (Apr. 6, 2015), www.cato-unbound.org/2015/04/06/alex-tabarrok-tyler-cowen/end-asymmetric-information; Alex Tabarrok and Tyler Cowen, *Symmetric Information Won't Be Perfect*, Cato Unbound (Apr. 20, 2015), www.cato-unbound.org/2015/04/20/alex-tabarrok-tyler-cowen/symmetric-information-wont-be-perfect.

[8] *See generally* Yochai Benkler, *Degrees of Freedom, Dimensions of Power*, 145 Dœdalus 18 (2016), which discusses the shift from the original internet design of decentralized power to a concentration of power in the hands of a relatively small set of actors, at 20 ("Mobile and cloud computing, the Internet of Things, fiber transition, big data, surveillance, and behavioral marketing introduce new control points and dimensions of power into the Internet as a social-cultural-economic platform."). *Cf. also* Vasilis Kostakis and Michel Bauwens, *Network Society and Future Scenarios for a Collaborative Economy* (2014) (defining "netarchical capitalism" as the economic system that matches centralized control of a distributed infrastructure with an orientation toward the accumulation of capital).

[9] *See* Julia E. Cohen, *Law for the Platform Economy*, 51 U.C. Davis L. Rev. 133 (2017), at 145 ("Economically speaking, platforms represent both horizontal and vertical strategies for extracting the surplus value of user data"). On the growing importance of knowledge-based markets *see* Mayo Fuster Morell, Online Creation Communities Viewed

a novelty which makes the balance less clear than sometimes asserted. The collection of vast amounts of data by platforms may give rise to new information asymmetries between platform operators on the one hand and platform users on the other. Notably, this conclusion holds not only with regard to consumers vis-à-vis platforms, but more generally for all platforms' "users," whether customers or providers.

With regard to the latter, the same reputational mechanisms that are often at the center of the supposed consumer empowerment are open to gaming and other forms of exploitation, with the aim of taking advantage of the growing reliance of users.[10] User-generated content is commonly used to profile consumers, leading to both traditional market failures and increased chances to exploit cognitive vulnerabilities by means of "market manipulation."[11] Moreover, due to big data analysis, platforms enjoy an enhanced opportunity to set different offerings and to charge each customer the exact "reservation price" – the maximum price she is willing and able to pay.[12] This novelty makes price (and terms) discrimination easier and reduces the capacity for consumers to capture welfare gains enjoyed in a traditional model of static prices.[13]

With regard to the former, much relevant information is often not accessible to suppliers who provide their services via online marketplaces. Online platforms do not give sufficient information about the functioning of the algorithm and the adopted ranking criteria: they do not specify what individual factors mean and what their weight is or how they are taken into account.[14] Further, providers are often unable to assess ex ante the profitability of a transaction or to set

---

through the Analytical Framework of the Institutional Analysis and Development, in *Governing Knowledge Commons* (Brett M. Frischmann, Michael J. Madison, and Katherine J. Strandburg eds., 2014).

[10] *See* Juliet B. Schor, *Does the Sharing Economy Increase Inequality Within the Eighty Percent?: Findings from a Qualitative Study of Platform Providers*, 10 Cambridge J. Regions, Econ. & Soc'y 263 (2017) ("In general, we believe that users are likely overstating the accuracy of the ratings and reputational data on these sites."); Sonja Utz et al., *Consumers Rule: How Consumer Reviews Influence Perceived Trustworthiness of Online Stores*, 11 Elec. Comm. Res. & Apps. 49, at 54 (2012) (the separation of information and product may lead consumers to believe that the information is more objective, making the case more dangerous than old-fashioned conventional advertising).

[11] *See, e.g.,* Damian Clifford, *Citizen-Consumers in a Personalised Galaxy: Emotion Influenced Decision-Making, a True Path to the Dark Side?* (Sept. 15, 2017), CiTiP Working Paper Series, 31/2017, https://ssrn.com/abstract=3037425; Max N. Helveston, *Regulating Digital Markets*, 13 N.Y.U. J. L. & Bus. 33 (2016); Ryan Calo, *Digital Market Manipulation*, 82 Geo. Wash. L. Rev. 995 (2014). *See also* Sofia Ranchordás, *Online Reputation and the Regulation of Information Asymmetries in the Platform Economy*, Critical Analysis of Law 5(1), 127, at 146 ("In the context of the platform economy, reputational feedback does not create a scenario of perfect information. Rather, it creates the illusion thereof").

[12] On the effects of algorithms and pricing bots on competition and price discrimination *see* Salil K. Mehra, *Antitrust and the Robo-Seller: Competition in the Time of Algorithms*, 100 Minn. L. Rev. 1323 (2016); Maurice E. Stucke and Ariel Ezrachi, *How Pricing Bots Could Form Cartels and Make Things More Expensive*, Harv. Bus. Rev. (Oct. 27, 2016), https://hbr.org/2016/10/how-pricing-bots-could-form-cartels-and-make-things-more-expensive; Ariel Ezrachi and Maurice E. Stucke, *Artificial Intelligence & Collusion: When Computers Inhibit Competition*, 2017 U. Ill. L. Rev. 1775 (2017).

[13] *See, e.g.,* Saul Levmore and Frank Fagan, *The End of Bargaining in the Digital Age*, Cornell L. Rev. (forthcoming 2018), https://ssrn.com/abstract=3062794 (advocating for a requirement of uniform or transparent pricing that limits a seller's ability to price discriminate in consumer contracts). On how price discrimination can affect consumer welfare and competition, *see generally* Dirk Bergemann et al., *The Limits of Price Discrimination*, 105 Am. Econ. Rev. 921 (2015), www.aeaweb.org/articles.php?doi=10.1257/aer.20130848; Hal R. Varian, *Computer Mediated Transactions*, 100 Am. Econ. Rev. 1 (2010) (arguing that when fixed costs are high and marginal costs are low, personalized pricing will tend to increase output, consumer surplus, and welfare); Kenneth S. Corts, *Third-Degree Price Discrimination in Oligopoly: All-Out Competition and Strategic Commitment*, 29(2) RAND J. of Econ. 306 (1998), www.jstor.org/stable/2555890?seq=1#page_scan_tab_contents. *See also* UK Office of Fair Trading, The Economics of Online Personalised Pricing (2013), http://webarchive.nationalarchives.gov.uk/20140402142426/; www.oft.gov.uk/shared_oft/research/oft1488.pdf.

[14] *See* discussion *infra* Section II.

the price, being forced to accept any proposal, regardless of their preference[15] – a practice that may be especially problematic when a platform has a reason to keep prices low for competitive reasons.[16]

2 *Communication, Control, and Influence*

Another fundamental aspect in assessing bargaining power of both customers and providers vis-à-vis online platforms concerns the capacity of contracting parties to negotiate and influence the rules of the transaction and to communicate with their counterparts. Such abilities are at least questionable in the platform economy. Platforms usually impose terms of service on their user-base in a take-it-or-leave-it fashion, with no room for users to influence or amend them. These contracts are formally agreed upon even if hardly ever read, as the adhering parties typically affirm to have read terms and conditions by "clicking" an "I agree" icon.[17]

In addition, platforms make an increasing use of website architecture to constrain available information and the kind of interaction allowed among participants.[18] Empirical findings show that this closeness has led to what has been labeled a "platform churn" – an increasing turn-over, especially among providers, due to the fact that "exit" remains the only viable option when "voice" – the ability to raise concerns and negotiate contractual terms – has failed.[19]

3 *Algorithmic Governance*

Not only consent, but also enforcement is dramatically reshaped in online mass transactions. Contract terms are often implemented via algorithms, "machine rules" that create a sort of "private automatic injunction" highly resistant to legal scrutiny, and that do not take into account all those individual circumstances which may have affected a given outcome.[20] Even where redress possibilities are available, clear instructions about the operation of these mechanisms may be missing and access to justice may be restricted in practice. Foreign jurisdiction and/or foreign law are commonly applicable and internal redress mechanisms might be arranged only

---

[15] *Cf.* Alex Rosenblat and Luke Stark, *Algorithmic Labor and Information Asymmetries: A Case Study of Uber's Drivers*, 10 Int. J. Comm. 3758 (2016).

[16] There may be various reasons for keeping prices low. *See, e.g.*, David S. Evans and Richard Schmalensee, *Markets with Two-Sided Platforms*, 1 Issues in Competition Law and Policy (ABA Section of Antitrust Law), Ch. 28, 690 (2008) ("Profit-maximizing two-sided platforms may find that it is profitable overall to price the product offered on one side below average variable cost, below marginal cost, or even below zero"), https://ssrn.com/abstract=1094820. Further, platforms may also adopt a "growth first, revenue later" strategy: first lower prices until they are below the average costs of its competitors and later raise them, earning monopoly profit and recouping losses. *Cf.* Amelia Fletcher, *Predatory Pricing in Two-Sided Markets: A Brief Comment*, 3 Competition Pol'y Int'l 221 (2007).

[17] Consumers' failure to read contract terms may not be an issue when even a small proportion of consumers actually read the boilerplate, thus inducing firms to adopt efficient terms. The thesis of a margin of informed and sophisticated consumers that through their action help discipline the market for the benefit of infra-marginal consumers has been famously stated by Alan Schwartz and Louis Wilde, *Intervening on Markets on the Basis of Imperfect Information: A Legal and Economic Analysis*, 127 U. Pa. L. Rev. 630 (1979). This thesis has been criticized for resting on questionable empirical assumptions about competition and information symmetries. *See* Yannis Bakos et al., *Does Anyone Read the Fine Print? Consumer Attention to Standard-Form Contracts*, 43 J. Legal Stud. 1 (2014).

[18] *See, e.g.*, Cohen, *supra* note 9, at 155 ("The combination of asserted contractual control and technical control becomes the vehicle through which the platform imposes its own logics on the encounters that it mediates.").

[19] *See* G. Newlands et al., *Power in the Sharing Economy* (2017), at 6 ("Sharing economy platforms are facing increasing turnover among their provider base"), www.bi.edu/globalassets/forskning/h2020/power-working-paper.pdf. *Cf.* Min K. Lee et al., *Working with Machines: The Impact of Algorithmic and Data-Driven Management on Human Workers*, Proceedings of the 33rd Annual ACM Conference on Human Factors in Computing Systems 1603 (2015) (finding that providers' emails to these companies usually go without response).

[20] *Cf.* Margaret J. Radin, *The Deformation of Contract in the Information Society*, 37 Oxford J. Legal Stud. 505, (2017) at 511.

via email, without the possibility of a direct human contact and a responsible case handler.[21] While appeals for transparency of these enforcement systems via algorithm are diffuse, such an outcome is difficult to attain for machine learning algorithms, thus leaving both providers and customers without viable legal remedies.[22]

4 Market Structure

When a platform has a dominant position in the market, becoming its only point of access for providers and consumers, the dangers of an imbalance in bargaining power in favor of platforms are clearly exacerbated. Admittedly, such market structure may benefit users on both sides of the platform, as a dominant platform would display a thick market, but at the same time it poses risks of higher prices and exploitative practices, due to the complete dependency of providers and customers on the platform.

Most online marketplaces are believed to bear an ingrained tendency to monopolies and display an anticompetitive structure, often reduced to a single operator (winner-takes-all, or most). The main reason that leads us to identify the risk of dominant positions is the occurrence of indirect network externalities, so that an increase in participants of a given group raises the value of their participation for the other group of users, potentially causing overwhelming difficulties for potential entrants to collect a sufficient amount of initial customers in order to be competitive.[23] In addition to network effects, the massive acquiring of proprietary data can give a very significant competitive advantage to a single operator, as the higher the number of interactions occurring via the platform, the better the algorithm governing transactions and the underlying service.[24] In sum, the combination of network effects and data gathering may generate significant competitive advantages, so that a single platform may insulate itself from competition by creating an artificial barrier to entry, to the detriment of its user base.

---

[21] Ecorys, *Business-to-Business Relations in the Online Platform Environment.* Final Report. FWC ENTR/300/PP/2013/FC-WIFO (2017), at 29.

[22] *See generally* Frank Pasquale, *The Black Box Society. The Secret Algorithms that Control Money and Information* (2015).

[23] *See generally* Federal Trade Commission, *The "Sharing" Economy: Issues Facing Platforms, Participants and Regulators* (2016), at 26 ("Two-sided network effects may enable a large platform to become dominant and insulated from competition from smaller platforms with fewer participants"); Geoffrey G. Parker, Marshall W. Van Alstyne, and Sargeet P. Choudary, *Platform Revolution: How Networked Markets Are Transforming the Economy – and How to Make Them Work for You* (2016). *But see* Andrei Hagiu and Simon Rothman, *Network Effects Aren't Enough*, Harv. Bus. Rev., April 2016; David S. Evans and Richard Schmalensee, *Why Winner-Takes-All Thinking Doesn't Apply to the Platform Economy*, Harv. Bus. Rev, May 2016; Jonathan A. Knee, *All Platforms Are Not Equal*, MIT Sloan Mgmt. Rev., Sept. 15, 2017 (arguing that key structural attributes that drive the value of network effects in the digital domain are: the minimum market share at which the network can achieve financial breakeven; the nature and durability of the customer relationships; the extent to which the data generated by the network facilitates product and pricing optimization). With specific reference to the sharing economy, *see* Sundararajan, *supra* note 4, at 119 (arguing that the nature of two-sided network effects varies in very significant ways across different sharing economy platforms, due to the local nature of the sharing economy).

[24] *See generally* Federal Trade Commission, *Big Data: A Tool for Inclusion or Exclusion? Understanding the Issues* (2016); Autorité de la concurrence – Bundeskartellamt, *Competition Law and Data* (2016) ("The collection of data may result in entry barriers when new entrants are unable either to collect the data or to buy access to the same kind of data, in terms of volume and/or variety, as established companies"); OECD, *Data Driven Innovation for Growth and Well-Being: Interim Synthesis Report* (2014); Autoritat Catalan de la Competència, *The Data-Driven Economy. Challenges for Competition* (2016). *See also* Bruno Carballa Smichowski, *Data as a Common in the Sharing Economy: a General Policy Proposal*, CEPN Document de travail n. 2016–10 (2016), at 25 ("Most of the competition problems we detected in the sharing economy arise from the fact that platforms have private and exclusive property over the databases they create with users' information.").

II A LEGAL FRAMEWORK FOR THE PLATFORM ECONOMY

On the above basis, it is hard to conclude that the risk of disparity of bargaining power is lowered or even eradicated in the platform economy, and the often asserted reduction of inequalities fails to appreciate the persistent problem of protecting the weaker party of the transaction. In this second part, after a survey on standard form contracts adopted by the most successful platforms, an examination of the legal relationships between the different actors is conducted, in order to verify whether existing legal categories can provide effective protection, and to suggest when a regulatory intervention may be desirable.

A *Survey of Standard Form Contracts*

Compared to traditional standard form contracts, typically drafted by professional suppliers and adhered by consumers, contracts in the platform economy involve three different players: the online platforms and the "users" – both providers and users – concluding transactions through it. Each of these actors enters into legal relationship with the others, thus creating an extremely complex legal scenario. In the vast majority of cases, there is only one contract governing all transactions: terms are usually drafted by the platform and adhered by its users and, unless otherwise specified, the same clauses usually apply to service providers and customers, as both users of those services provided by the platform.

A survey of contractual agreements points to a twofold result. In the first place, contractual clauses usually provide roughly comparable rights and duties for peers, making them fully responsible for performing their obligations. Being laid down by the platform, contracts between provider and customer usually display fewer one-sided terms compared to bilateral ones, equally imposing on both parties to comply with their basic obligations. At the same time, by controlling the entire matching system, platforms exert considerable power over consumers and providers, and such power is clearly revealed in their terms and conditions, which contain many of those clauses that are typically deemed to reflect an imbalance of bargaining power between contracting parties.[25]

Unequal bargaining positions can be reflected in high prices for using platforms as well as in the terms and conditions. Contract terms usually allow platforms to make unilateral changes in contract terms, and in some cases even in the final price[26] often without prior notification and with no need to rely on a valid reason to make these modifications.[27] Lack of or very short-term prior notice about changes is usually applicable, with a presumption of acceptance of changes

---

[25] The one-sidedness of standard form contracts is generally explained as a result of informational and cognitive problems, and adverse selection. *See, e.g.*, Oren Bar-Gill, *Seduction by Plastic*, 98 Nw. U. L. Rev. 1373 (2004); Eric A. Posner, *Contract Law in the Welfare State: A Defense of the Unconscionability Doctrine, Usury Laws, and Related Limitations on the Freedom to Contract*, 24 J. Legal Stud. 283 (1995); Michael I. Meyerson, *The Efficient Consumer Form Contract: Law and Economics Meets the Real World*, 24 Ga. L. Rev. 583, 594–603 (1990); Phillipe Aghion and Benjamin Hermalin, *Legal Restrictions on Private Contracts Can Enhance Efficiency*, 6 J. L. Econ. & Org. 381 (1990).

[26] Cf. European Commission – Press release, The European Commission and EU consumer authorities are calling on Airbnb to align their terms and conditions with EU consumer rules and be transparent on their presentation of prices, Brussels, 16 July 2018, http://europa.eu/rapid/press-release_IP-18-4453_en.pdf.

[27] Airbnb Terms and Condition, § 3 ("Airbnb reserves the right, at its sole discretion, to modify the Site, Application or Services or to modify these Terms, including the Service Fees, at any time and without prior notice (…) If the modified Terms are not acceptable to you, your only recourse is to cease using the Site, Application and Services. If you do not close your Airbnb Account you will be deemed to have accepted the changes."); Uber Terms and condition, §1 ("Uber may amend the Terms from time to time. Amendments will be effective upon Uber's posting of such updated Terms at this location or in the amended policies or supplemental terms on the applicable Service(s). Your continued access or use of the Services after such posting confirms your consent to be bound by the Terms, as amended."); Etsy, Terms of Use, § 12 ("Changes to the Terms. We may update these Terms from time to time. (…) You are responsible for reviewing and becoming familiar with any changes. Your use of the Services following the changes constitutes your acceptance of the updated Terms."); BlaBlaCar, Terms & Conditions, § 13 ("BlaBlaCar reserves the

by continuation of use. Platforms appear to make extensive use of this ability, in some cases with an almost daily frequency, and this practice does not always allow users to adjust themselves to the changes completely and in time for their application.[28]

Similar provisions regard the right to terminate the contract at the discretion of the platform,[29] to suspend an account, or to delist individual products or services.[30] Despite the fact that unilateral delisting of products and suspension or termination of accounts may threaten the very existence of certain economic activities, the conditions and the procedures related to suspension and blocking of accounts and products are not transparent and often completely missing, and the lack of contractual obligations to provide an explanation makes it very difficult to substantiate a claim against these actions.[31]

Other ubiquitous clauses concern the choice of law and/or jurisdiction,[32] arbitration agreement and dispute resolution clauses, frequently in conjunction with class actions and jury

---

right to modify or suspend all or part of access to the Platform or its functionalities, at its sole discretion, temporarily or permanently."); Getaround Terms of Service ("Eligibility. We may, in our sole discretion, modify or update this Agreement from time to time, and so you should review this page periodically (…) Your continued use of the Service after any such change constitutes your acceptance of the new Terms of Service"); TaskRabbit Terms of Service, § 26 ("Company reserves the right, at its sole and absolute discretion, to change, modify, add to, supplement or delete any of the terms and conditions of this Agreement (including the Privacy Policy) and review, improve, modify or discontinue, temporarily or permanently, the TaskRabbit Platform or any content or information through the TaskRabbit Platform at any time, effective with or without prior notice and without any liability to Company.")

[28] *Cf.* Ryan Calo and Alex Rosenblat, *The Taking Economy: Uber, Information, and Power*, 117 Colum. L. Rev. 1623 (2017). *Cf. also* David Horton, *The Shadow Terms: Contract Procedure and Unilateral Amendments*, 57 UCLA L. Rev. 605 (2010) (arguing that changes to boilerplate or other contracts result in "shadow terms" of which consumers are not aware).

[29] Airbnb Terms and Conditions, §24 ("Airbnb may deactivate or delay Listings, reviews, or other Member Content, cancel any pending or confirmed Bookings, limit your use of or access to your Airbnb Account and the Site, Application or Services, temporarily or permanently revoke any special status associated with your Airbnb Account, or temporarily or permanently suspend your Airbnb Account if (i) you have breached these Terms or our Policies, including material and non-material breaches and receiving poor ratings from Hosts or Guests, or (ii) Airbnb believes in good faith that such action is reasonably necessary to protect the safety or property of Members, Airbnb or third parties, for fraud prevention, risk assessment, security or investigation purposes."); Uber Terms and condition, §1 ("Uber may immediately terminate these Terms or any Services with respect to you, or generally cease offering or deny access to the Services or any portion thereof, at any time for any reason."); Etsy, Terms of Use, § 7 ("Termination By Etsy. We may terminate or suspend your account (and any related accounts) and your access to the Services at any time, for any reason, and without advance notice."); BlaBlaCar, Terms & Conditions, § 9 ("BlaBlaCar reserves the right to terminate the T&Cs binding you with BlaBlaCar immediately and without notice."); Getaround Terms of Service ("Termination. We may terminate your participation in the Service at any time, for any reason or no reason, without explanation"); TaskRabbit Terms of Service, § 8 ("Company may terminate, limit or suspend your right to use the TaskRabbit Platform in the event that we believe that you have breached this Agreement (…) you will not be entitled to any refund of unused balance in your account (…) this Agreement will remain enforceable against you"); Lyft Terms of Service, § 16 ("Lyft may terminate this Agreement or deactivate your User account immediately in the event").

[30] Airbnb Terms and Conditions, § 7 ("Airbnb reserves the right, at any time and without prior notice, to remove or disable access to any Listing for any reason"); Uber Terms and conditions, § 4 ("Uber may, but shall not be obligated to, review, monitor, or remove User Content, at Uber's sole discretion and at any time and for any reason, without notice to you").

[31] Ecorys, *supra* note 21, at 70. (Several users have identified the danger of delisting or suspension of their activity as a major risk, suggesting that claims based upon breach of conditions are sometimes abused, be it by brand owners, by competing businesses, by customers or by unspecified third parties. Further, "A few of the interviewed business users active in e-commerce indicated to have sought compensation for the lost turnover and fees paid, but no compensation was offered by the specific platform, even in the case where suspension was a platform's mistake, which was admitted by the platform.")

[32] Airbnb Terms and Conditions, § 33 ("These Terms and your use of the Services will be interpreted in accordance with the laws of the State of California and the United States of America, without regard to its conflict-of-law provisions."); Uber Terms and Conditions, § 7 ("These Terms are governed by and construed in accordance with the laws of the State of California, U.S.A., without giving effect to any conflict of law principles."); Etsy Terms of Use, § 11 ("A.

trials waiver,[33] and price (and non-price) parity clauses.[34] Further, contracts usually contain "bundling" clauses that prescribe the use of certain auxiliary services provided by the platform (payment systems, data cloud, communications channels, and delivery services).[35]

Even more importantly, most platforms depict themselves as "networks" or "marketplaces."[36] Often coupled with exemption clauses, these definitions suggest that users are the only service

Governing Law. The Terms are governed by the laws of the State of New York, without regard to its conflict of laws rules, and the laws of the United States of America."). Last visited, Sept. 13, 2017.

[33] Airbnb Terms and Conditions, § 34 ("Any dispute, claim or controversy (…) will be settled by binding arbitration"); Uber Terms and conditions, § 2 ("You are required to resolve any claim that you may have against Uber on an individual basis in arbitration (…) This will preclude you from bringing any class, collective, or representative action against Uber, and also preclude you from participating in or recovering relief under any current or future class, collective, consolidated, or representative action brought against Uber by someone else (…) You acknowledge and agree that you and Uber are each waiving the right to a trial by jury or to participate as a plaintiff or class member in any purported class action or representative proceeding."); Etsy Terms of Use, § 11 ("B. Arbitration. You and Etsy agree that any dispute or claim arising from or relating to the Terms shall be finally settled by final and binding arbitration (…) you and Etsy are each waiving the right to trial by jury or to participate in a class action or class arbitration."); Getaround Terms of Service ("Arbitration. We each agree to resolve any claim, dispute, or controversy (…) by binding arbitration (…) All claims must be brought in the parties' individual capacity and not as a plaintiff or class member in any purported class or representative proceeding (…) you and Getaround are each waiving the right to a trial by jury or to participate in a class action, collective action, private attorney general action, or other representative proceeding of any kind."); TaskRabbit Terms of Service, § 20 ("You and company mutually agree to waive your respective rights to resolution of all claims between you (…) in a court of law by a judge or jury and agree to resolve any disputes by binding arbitration on an individual basis (…) you acknowledge and agree that you and company are each waiving the right to participate as a plaintiff or class member in any purported class action or representative proceeding"); Lyft Terms of Service, § 17 ("You and Lyft mutually agree to waive our respective rights to resolution of disputes in a court of law by a judge or jury and agree to resolve any dispute by arbitration (…) Class arbitrations and class actions are not permitted (…) All disputes and claims between us (…) shall be exclusively resolved by binding arbitration solely between you and Lyft"). It is worth noting that BlaBlaCar makes reference to the online dispute resolution platform developed by the European Commission (BlaBlaCar Terms & Conditions, § 15). In some cases, these clauses are coupled with the assignment to the platforms of the possibility to select different jurisdiction/applicable law, without at the same time recognizing this privilege to the other party. *See, e.g.,* Booking.com General Delivery Terms, § 10.6 ("Notwithstanding this Clause 10.5, nothing in this Agreement shall prevent or limit Booking.com in its right to bring or initiate any action or proceeding or seek interim injunctive relief or (specific) performance before or in any competent courts (…) the Accommodation waives its right to claim any other jurisdiction or applicable law to which it might have a right.").

[34] In such a clause the seller agrees to offer a price for a product and/or service no less favorable than that granted to other platforms. Besides displaying an imbalance of market power, these clauses can present further problems, such as creating a barrier to entry for new platforms or raising prices to the detriment of consumers. The most notable case is that concerning Booking.com, which has been addressed by Italian, French, and Swedish competition authorities. *See* European Commission press release, *Antitrust: Commission announces the launch of market tests in investigations in the online hotel booking sector by the French, Swedish and Italian competition authorities* (Dec. 15, 2014), http://europa.eu/rapid/press-release_IP-14-2661_en.htm. In the end, these authorities accepted Booking.com's commitment to address this concern. The German Bundeskartellamt prohibited Booking.com to use these clauses, www.bundeskartellamt.de/SharedDocs/Meldung/EN/Pressemitteilungen/2015/23_12_2015_Booking.com.html.

[35] *Cf.* Report of an engagement workshop hosted by the European Commission, *Business-to-Business Relationships in the Online Platforms Environment – Legal Aspects and Clarity of Terms and Conditions of Online Platforms* (Brussels, Nov. 14, 2016), http://ec.europa.eu/newsroom/document.cfm?doc_id=43829.

[36] Airbnb Terms and Conditions, § 1.1 ("The Airbnb Platform is an online marketplace that enables registered users and certain third parties who offer services (…) to publish such Host Services on the Airbnb Platform and to communicate and transact directly with Members that are seeking to book such Host Services"); TaskRabbit Terms of Service, §§ 1, 12, 17 ("The TaskRabbit Platform only enables connections between Users for the fulfillment of Tasks. Company is not responsible for the performance of Users (…) The TaskRabbit Platform is not an employment service and Company is not an employer of any User"); Lyft Terms of Service, §§ 1, 12 ("The Lyft Platform provides a marketplace where persons who seek transportation to certain destinations ("Riders") can be matched with persons driving to or through those destinations ("Drivers") (…) Lyft does not provide transportation services, and Lyft is not a transportation carrier"; "We disclaim liability for, and no warranty is made with respect to, connectivity and availability of the Lyft Platform or Services (…) We cannot guarantee that each Rider is who he or she claims to be. Please use common sense when using the Lyft Platform and Services").

providers, while platforms limit their activity (and consequent liability) to the provision of "transactional services." A conclusion that may be justified when the platform merely provides a matching system for independent agents by offering an infrastructure that facilitates the matching of supply and demand among its users, but which is clearly inappropriate when a higher degree of control and influence is exercised, thus shifting the burden of responsibility to users for issues that are outside their control, but within the control of the platform.[37]

In conclusion, while in principle platforms have contributed to making contracts governing the provision of services more even-handed,[38] the same cannot be said with regard to legal relationships between platforms and their users. Many clauses adopted by online platforms vis-à-vis their users call into question essential contractual rights, such as the availability of legal remedies or the capacity of one party to hold the other accountable for failing to comply with its obligations.[39]

B The Platform and Its Users

In the platform economy the consumer is notoriously no longer set apart from producer and seller, as the line between providers and customers is increasingly blurring. However, providers and customers still have different sets of challenges concerning platforms, and separate assessments of each position are still preferable for the purpose of this analysis.

The relationship between platforms and providers has usually been scrutinized under the lens of labor law. The vast majority of online platforms for on-demand services claim to make use of contractors hired by the job rather than workers, with a significant shift from long-term employment contracts to spot labor markets and the "gig" economy. Quite predictably, this position on worker qualification has been challenged before courts all over the world for the risk of misclassification and dodging of those legal safeguards that are usually justified when market forces do not adequately protect workers. The main question is whether those who supply services over platforms should be viewed as employees or independent contractors. The current debate revolves around the criteria that should point to one or the other direction, and on whether this sharp dichotomy should be revised in the light of the ongoing changes.[40]

---

[37] *Cf.* C-434/15 *Press and Information Asociación Profesional Elite Taxi v. Uber Systems Spain SL* (The service provided by Uber is more than an intermediation service: it must be regarded as being inherently linked to a transport service and, accordingly, must be classified as "a service in the field of transport" within the meaning of EU law). *See also* Pierre Hausemer et al., *Final Report, Exploratory Study of Consumer Issues in Online Peer-To-Peer Platforms Markets* (2017) ("The discrepancy between the platforms' level of intervention in the P2P transaction and the liability clauses in its T&Cs risks to confuse or mislead users with regard to the responsibility of the platform in case of problems with the P2P transaction"), http://ec.europa.eu/newsroom/just/item-detail.cfm?item_id=77704#_ftn4.

[38] However, in some cases platforms may have reasons to favor one group of agents of the platform. *See, e.g.*, Rosenblat and Stark, *supra* note 15, at 3765 (finding that drivers perceive Uber as favoring consumers). On the price structure in two-sided markets *see* Jean C. Rochet and J. Tirole, *Platform Competition in Two-Sided Markets*, 1 J. Eur. Econ. Assn. 990 (2003) (Platforms choose a price structure and not only a price level, thus allocating prices between the two sides of the market).

[39] *See, e.g.*, Radin, *supra* note 20, at 505 ("The technological and concomitant social features of today's information society have enabled private firms to engage in massive re-organization of legal rights in their favor"); Jack M. Balkin, *Free Speech in the Algorithmic Society: Big Data, Private Governance, and New School Speech Regulation*, 51 U.C. Davis L. Rev. 1149 (2018) ("Big Data allows new forms of manipulation and control, which private companies will attempt to legitimate and insulate from regulation"). On boilerplates, *see generally* Margaret J. Radin, *Boilerplate: The Fine Print, Vanishing Rights, and the Rule of Law* (2013); Nancy S. Kim, *Wrap Contracts* (2013); Omri Ben-Shahar (ed.), *Boilerplate. The Foundation of Market Contracts* (2007).

[40] *See* Chapter 6 of this book. The claim made by Uber that drivers are its customers (or "partners") has been rejected by American and British courts. *Cf.* *O'Connor v. Uber Technologies Inc.*, 82 F.Supp.3d 1133 (N.D. Cal. 2015); *Cotter v. Lyft Inc.*, 60 F.Supp. 3d 1067 (N.D. Cal. 2015); *Aslam v. Uber*, judgment of Oct. 28, 2016 (London Employment

While the distinction between employers and independent contractors goes beyond the scope of this chapter, a related aspect is more relevant to our analysis. When a provider is deemed an "employee," labor and employment laws apply, thus offering a protective legal framework for a category typically considered as weaker vis-à-vis her employer. By contrast, a less protective b2b legal framework is pertinent when providers are regarded as truly autonomous entrepreneurs who offer their services via online platforms.[41]

However, the risk of imbalance of contractual rights, and the consequent need to protect the weaker party of the transaction, is not ruled out in the case of independent professional providers.[42] In some instances, a well-reputed business may be able to negotiate its own contractual terms with the digital platform,[43] but this is not a realistic option in the vast majority of cases.

In addition to the clauses discussed above (*cf.* § 1.3), certain contractual terms are especially significant for service providers vis-à-vis the platform. In this regard, lack of transparency is a central concern, particularly for crucial aspects of the transaction, such as search rankings criteria, reputation systems, and dynamic pricing.[44] In fact, in many cases platforms do not provide sufficient information to service providers on how their offerings are displayed or ranked, make no clear reference to the adopted standards, and employ an extremely vague language (e.g., the meaning of criteria such as "popularity" are not clear to providers).[45] By presenting a long list of general and non-exhaustive factors, sometimes coupled with clauses which confer to platforms the ability to change placement at their sole will, platforms enjoy a significant degree of discretion.[46] And since the way offerings are listed and presented is the most relevant variable to

Tribunal) ("The notion that Uber in London is a mosaic of 30,000 small businesses linked by a common 'platform' is to our minds faintly ridiculous").

[41] The need for special rules for the protection of the weaker commercial party is a highly controversial topic. Yet, under EU law SMEs enjoy a special protection in limited cases. *See, e.g.*, Council Directive 90/314, 1990 O.J. (L 158), 59–64 (EEC); European Parliament and Council Directive 2011/7, 2011 O.J. (L 2011), 48–1 (EU). *See also* Communication from the Commission to the European Parliament, the Council, the European Economic and Social Committee and the Committee of the Regions, Online Platforms and the Digital Single Market – Opportunities and Challenges for Europe (May 25, 2016), COM (2016) 288/2.

[42] Cf. European Commission, Proposal for a Regulation of the European Parliament and of the Council on promoting fairness and transparency for business users of online intermediation services, Brussels, 26.4.2018 COM(2018) 238 final, 2018/0112 (COD). Ecorys, *supra* note 21, at IX (A total of 46 percent of business users have experienced problems and disagreements with the platforms. Among heavy users the share of those that experienced problems is significantly higher (75 percent)).

[43] On eBay "power sellers" were obtained to do "bulk listings" (to automate the listing of many products) and this enabled these sellers to negotiate lower per-listing fees from the platform. *See* Hagiu and Rothman, *supra* note 23 ("Over the years, power sellers came to dominate eBay's supply side and made it difficult for nonprofessional sellers to compete").

[44] *See* Hausemer et al., *supra* note 36, at 8 ("One of the main issues concerning the relationship between platforms and their users relates to the lack of transparency in online p2p platform rules and practices.").

[45] *Cf.* Report of an engagement workshop hosted by the European Commission "Business-to-Business Relationships in the Online Platforms Environment – Algorithms, Ranking and Transparency" (Brussels, Mar. 16, 2017), http://ec.europa.eu/information_society/newsroom/image/document/2017-12/report_on_the_workshop_16_03_2017_clean_F7EF00C2-E39F-1747-949E9C1820629D05_43830.pdf.

[46] Airbnb Terms and Conditions, § 7 ("You understand and agree that the placement or ranking of Listings in search results may depend on a variety of factors, including, but not limited to, Guest and Host preferences, ratings and/or ease of booking."); BlaBlaCar Terms & Conditions, § 4.1 ("You recognise and accept that the criteria taken into account in the classification and the order of display of your Advert among the other Adverts are at the sole discretion of BlaBlaCar."); Booking.com General Delivery Terms, § 4.1.1 ("The order in which the Accommodation is listed on the Platforms (the 'Ranking'), is determined automatically and unilaterally by Booking.com. Ranking is based on and influenced by various factors, including but not limited to the commission percentage (to be) paid by the Accommodation, the minimum availability stated by the Accommodation, the number of bookings related to the number of visits to the relevant accommodation page on the Platform (the 'Conversion'), the volume realized by the Accommodation, the ratio of cancellations, the guest review scores, the customer service history, the number and type of complaints from Guests and the on-time payment record of the Accommodation.").

explain who gets attention from customers and to determine which goods or services will be chosen,[47] this substantial flexibility enjoyed by the platform may cause considerable harm to their counterparts.[48]

This danger is increased in the case of vertical integration, when the same platform that operates as a marketplace also offers its own products. When platforms adopt these hybrid business models, the incentives of the firm as a marketplace may conflict with the incentives of the firm as a service provider: the interests of the marketplace likely prevail when a market has not tipped, but the interest of the service is likely to become more dominant once the platform is uncontested. The same applies when the platform obtains higher revenues from some providers (i.e., when the best ranked results are due to high commissions paid by the offeror).[49]

In both these instances, the platform may place its listings at the top of the ranking or providers with deeper pockets may be able to get a better ranking simply by increasing their commission, even though their service may not be as good as others. These practices are clearly detrimental to other providers, who may be forced to pay an extra fee to be competitive, but may also be harmful for consumers, who will not necessarily get to see the best or most relevant offer but instead the one with the highest commission, and likely to pay higher prices (the weight of ranking fee in relation to other criteria used by the algorithm is not clear to business users and consumers).[50] In fact, in many cases platforms fail to clearly distinguish editorial content from advertising content, thus misleading customers on whether search results are sponsored or not.[51] Thus the conflict-of-interest problem is exacerbated, especially if the platform is the only gateway to the market.

A second major issue regarding providers with respect to service providers concerns contractual restrictions on data access and use. Despite often being user-generated content, the use of this data outside platforms is frequently restricted by contractual clauses, as platforms usually affirm their exclusive ownership on user reviews and other relevant information, well beyond what is required by data protection laws.[52] This practice may artificially increase switching costs to other platforms for service providers, making them more dependent on the platform as they are unable to transfer their reputation (suffering *lock-in*),[53] thus not only restricting voice, but also curbing exit as an alternative strategy.

---

[47] *See, e.g.,* Matthew Goldman and Justin M. Rao, *Experiments as Instruments: Heterogeneous Position Effects in Sponsored Search Auctions* (Nov. 20, 2014) (Buyers are about twice as likely to click a listing in the top position as they would be if it were moved one position down), https://ssrn.com/abstract=2524688.

[48] Ecorys, *supra* note 21, at 38 ("To business users it is not clear when their ranking drops due to their own mistakes and transgressions and when it drops due to the proper functioning of the ranking algorithm.").

[49] *See, e.g.,* Booking.com General Delivery Terms, § 4.1.2 ("The Accommodation has the possibility to influence its own ranking by changing the commission percentage and availability for certain periods, and continuously improving the other factors.").

[50] *Cf.* EC Report, *supra* note 44.

[51] *Cf.* European Commission – Press release, The European Commission and EU consumer authorities are calling on Airbnb to align their terms and conditions with EU consumer rules and be transparent on their presentation of prices, Brussels, 16 July 2018, http://europa.eu/rapid/press-release_IP-18-4453_en.pdf.

[52] Airbnb Terms and Conditions, § 24 ("If you or we terminate this Agreement, we do not have an obligation to delete or return to you any of your Member Content, including but not limited to any reviews or Feedback."); Uber Terms and Conditions, § 4 ("By providing User Content to Uber, you grant Uber a worldwide, perpetual, irrevocable, transferable, royalty-free license, with the right to sublicense, to use, copy, modify, create derivative works of, distribute, publicly display, publicly perform, and otherwise exploit in any manner such User Content (…).".; Etsy Terms of Use, § 7 ("If you or Etsy terminate your account, you may lose any information associated with your account, including Your Content."); TaskRabbit Terms of Service, § 10 ("You hereby grant Company a non-exclusive, worldwide, perpetual, irrevocable, royalty-free, sublicensable (through multiple tiers) right to exercise all copyright, publicity rights, and any other rights you have in Your Information, in any media now known or not currently known in order to perform and improve upon the TaskRabbit Platform").

[53] The same result can be obtained with comparable practices, such as platform-sponsored auto-loans. *Cf.* www.uber.com/en-GB/drive/vehicle-solutions/. *See* Newlands et al., *supra* note 19, at 8 ("If providers are 'locked-in' to auto-loans for use on the platform, platforms maintain a significant power advantage").

C Peer-to-Peer Transactions

When the user providing the service is deemed to be an employee and the platform is truly the service provider, the platform is held liable to consumers for non-performance and/or damages, in accordance with "vicarious liability" and similar doctrines. In this case, the platform is the professional counterpart of the customer, and consumer law clearly applies to the provision of the underlying service, in addition to sector-specific legislation.

Moreover, when entering an online transaction via a platform, customers usually rely on both the counterpart's and the platform's reputation. The presence of an intermediary and the same fact that providers are allowed to offer their services via platform – using a logo, having an account, and so on – may suggest that a certain level of safety is assured and, in some cases, that the platform itself is the service provider. On this note, the gap between ex ante reasonable expectations and ex post costs and benefits should be taken into account,[54] and platforms should be made liable for the confusion they contribute to creating, thus going beyond adopted contract terms, also taking into account market design, especially when there is a chance of diffuse misperception of risks.[55]

In contrast, when the agent operating via a platform is the actual service provider, two alternative scenarios may occur. It is possible that the provider is a professional according to relevant law. As the lines between professionals and amateurs are blurring, more and more professionals are entering these markets over time, and many platforms are open to both professionals and occasional providers. In this case, consumer law clearly applies to the contract concluded between the professional service provider and the consumer. Such a conclusion would not only be consistent with the need to protect consumers vis-à-vis a professional, but it would further avoid creating an uneven playing field between incumbents and new entrants, which would not be justified in the light of the professional nature of both actors.

When instead the provider is not a professional, consumer protection and sector-specific legislation do not apply to the provision of the underlying service. In this case, only ordinary civil remedies may be invoked in the first place. But, while it has been affirmed that ex post remedies may be the most suited solution to encourage innovation,[56] this significant shift from ex ante requirements to an almost exclusive reliance on ex post remedies is not always desirable. The rise of a massive provision of services by nonprofessionals has significantly lowered barriers to

---

[54] *See, e.g.,* Ecorys, *supra* note 21, at 29 (Consumers are unable to differentiate who is responsible for what with regard to the online transaction and usually contact the business with which they are dealing); Mareike Möhlmann, *Digital Trust and Peer-to-Peer Collaborative Consumption Platforms: A Mediation Analysis* (July 22, 2016) (Trust in the platform has a positive effect on the trust in peers sharing on this platform), https://ssrn.com/abstract=2813367; Hausemer et al., *supra* note 35 (On the larger platforms peers are likely to be confused or misled about who is responsible when something goes wrong: platforms' practices may give the impression they assume at least partial responsibility in case of problems, but their Terms and Conditions exclude any liability. About 60 percent of peer consumers say they do not know or are not sure who is responsible when something goes wrong, what the responsibility of the platform is or if they have a right to compensation or reimbursement. About 40 percent of peer providers say they do not know or are not sure about their rights and responsibilities, and about 30 percent think they know more or less. At the same time about 85 percent of peer consumers find it important or very important that P2P platforms are clear and transparent about who is responsible when something goes wrong).

[55] *See, e.g.,* Robert H. Sloan and Richard Warner, *When Is an Algorithm Transparent?: Predictive Analytics, Privacy, and Public Policy,* https://ssrn.com/abstract=3051588 (arguing that predictive systems are transparent for consumers if they are able to readily ascertain the risks and benefits associated with the predictive systems to which they are subject); Lauren E. Willis, *Performance-Based Consumer Law,* 82 U. Chi. L. Rev. 1309 (2015) (discussing a new approach to consumer law in order to bring consumer transactions in line with consumer expectations in online transactions).

[56] Koopman et al., *supra* note 2, at 18; Adam Thierer, *Permissionless Innovation. The Continuing Case for Comprehensive Technological Innovation* (2014); Richard A. Epstein, *The War Against Airbnb,* Hoover Institution (Oct. 20, 2014), www.hoover.org/research/war-against-airbnb.

entry, as upfront legal requirements for traditional business – ex ante screenings, authorization procedures, inspections, certifications, and so on – cannot be adduced. Further, peer providers do not have an established business reputation and have made no investments in a physical commercial space. Therefore, new forms of market failures are likely to occur and the need to protect customers is a present one.[57]

In this scenario, harm-based sanctions may be a viable solution in some cases. However, they may often be lacking in effectiveness, for example when the magnitude of possible harms is likely considerable in relation to the assets of the actor, in the case of judgment-proof parties or when dangerous behaviors are difficult to observe and identify. When such risks are real ones, prevention via public enforcement may prove to work better, and to be more appealing at least for fundamental assumptions and expectations about basic safe and risk-free expectation.[58] On this note, it is important to consider that many platforms show offerings without clearly distinguishing between private individuals ('peers') and professional providers, thus misleading customers on the nature and identity of the trader. The distinction is crucial, inter alia, having implications for the applicability of consumer law.[59]

CONCLUSION

Disparity of bargaining power exists in the platform economy, even if in different forms than in bilateral b2c transactions. At the same time, it is far from clear to what extent effective market-based solutions are emerging to tackle the issue. Quite the opposite, the combining effect of boilerplate terms, platform architecture, and hidden algorithms is not only enabling a massive re-organization of legal rights in platforms' favor, but also a significant realignment of power from the legal power of the state to the private power exercised by online platforms, in many cases shielding their decisions from any meaningful external scrutiny.

As clearly mirrored in surveyed terms and conditions, platforms make frequent use of different mechanisms to leverage their power over users, by considering themselves not liable for safety standards, and allocating the burden for compliance with service regulations on the providers, and liability disproportionately falling on their users. Further, despite platforms often depicting themselves as neutral intermediaries and thus better positioned to arbitrate disputes between provider and customers, in some cases they may well have reasons to favor one type of economic agent operating via the platform, rather than acting as an objective judge, with the risk of becoming unsuitable to impartially adjudicate.

For these reasons, the often invoked, almost exclusive, reliance on market-based solutions for the platform economy is hardly justified. To be sure, platforms' self-governing capacity can definitely complement more traditional forms of regulation, and it is important to recognize platforms' remarkable ability to set up self-governing mechanisms and data-based solutions. But

---

[57] *See* Hausemer et al., *supra* note 36 (Peer consumers report frequent problems with transactions on P2P platforms. More than half (55 percent) have experienced at least one problem over the past year. The most frequent problems relate to the poor quality of goods or services, or to the goods and services not being as described. Problems with the quality of products/services appear to be almost twice as frequent in P2P markets (29 percent) as in online purchases in general (15 percent)).

[58] On the general structure of legal intervention from an efficiency perspective, *see generally* Steven M. Shavell, *Foundations of Economic Analysis of Law* (2004).

[59] Cf. European Commission – Press release, The European Commission and EU consumer authorities are calling on Airbnb to align their terms and conditions with EU consumer rules and be transparent on their presentation of prices, Brussels, 16 July 2018, http://europa.eu/rapid/press-release_IP-18-4453_en.pdf.

at the same time it is also crucial to identify the many issues platforms are unable or have no interest in dealing with.

If sometimes the case for protecting the weaker party may be addressed by existing legal frameworks – inter alia, labor and consumer law, torts, and other harm-based remedies – in other cases a regulatory intervention is surely needed. And a certain degree of preemptive regulation may be necessary in addition to ex post remedies, as a kind of backstop to the liability regime in order to assure basic health and safety conditions, which hold regardless whether or not the service is professionally provided. In this line of reasoning, the widespread appeal for a "safe harbor" for the platform economy can only be accepted if it does not imply relinquishing a meaningful external regulation, bearing in mind that "peer-to-peer" does not always mean equality of bargaining power.

Anti-discrimination Law

33

The Platform Identity Crisis

Responsibility, Discrimination, and a Functionalist Approach to Intermediaries

Charlotte Garden and Nancy Leong

INTRODUCTION

When is a car service not a car service? Perhaps when it is a " 'lead generation platform' that can be used to connect 'businesses that provide transportation' with passengers who desire rides."[1] That description, offered up by Uber in a driver-misclassification class action, is decidedly less catchy than Uber's original tagline: "everyone's private driver."

Or, alternatively, when is a company that offers short- and long-term housing rentals not a housing rental company? Maybe when that company is a "trusted community marketplace for people to list, discover, and book unique accommodations around the world ... online or from a mobile phone or tablet."[2] Thus Airbnb describes itself in a 2016 report describing its efforts to "fight discrimination and build inclusion,"[3] a response to reports of discrimination against renters of color, the hashtag #AirbnbWhileBlack trending on Twitter, and a lawsuit alleging race discrimination against not only the Airbnb host, but also Airbnb itself.

So, is Uber a lead generation platform, your private driver, or something in between? And is Airbnb a housing rental company, a community marketplace for accommodation, or a hybrid of the two?

The question is not merely one of theoretical interest. The answer turns out to be critically important for a number of unresolved legal issues: not only the question of whether drivers are actually employees instead of independent contractors, but also a number of important questions involving responsibility in the platform (sometimes called the "gig" or "sharing") economy.[4] To name a few: Are platforms responsible when affiliated workers or providers discriminate on the basis of race, sexual orientation, or another protected characteristic? What about when affiliates inflict tortious or criminal harms on customers? Or when a customer harms a worker, or damages a provider's property? And should governments regulate platform-based transactions similarly to their traditional-economy counterparts, or instead mostly leave platform enterprises – not to mention their workers and customers – to the mercies of the free market?

---

[1] *O'Connor v. Uber Techs.*, 82 F. Supp. 3d 1133, 1137 (N.D. Cal. 2015).

[2] Laura W. Murphy et al., Airbnb's Work to Fight Discrimination and Build Inclusion, Airbnb (Sept. 2016), https:// blog.atairbnb.com/wp-content/uploads/2016/09/REPORT_Airbnbs-Work-to-Fight-Discrimination-and-Build-Inclusion.pdf.

[3] *Id.* at 2.

[4] One of us has explained elsewhere why the term "platform" seems more accurate to us. Nancy Leong and Aaron Belzer, *The New Public Accommodations: Race Discrimination in the Platform Economy*, 105 Geo. L.J. 1271 (2017).

This chapter shows that leading "platform economy" enterprises like Uber and Airbnb are in the midst of an identity crisis of their own making. On one hand, they often argue that they should not be regulated like their "traditional" economy counterparts because their function is limited to facilitating transactions between customers and service providers. In other words, they are platforms that enable dyadic transactions between providers and customers, and they have little to do with the actual content of those transactions. But some platform enterprises' public personas are much different: through both their advertising and their user interfaces, these enterprises emphasize their role in exercising control over providers and customers, building community, and mediating consumer choice – in other words, the platform intercedes in and exercises control within the provider–customer relationship, as well as nurturing its own relationships with the participants in a now-triadic transaction.[5]

This chapter begins by illustrating how the platform identity crisis complicates legal disputes that arise in the context of the platform economy in two ways.[6] First, courts and agencies sometimes have difficulty deciding whether to credit platforms' public or legal representations about themselves – how do we know if a platform is just a platform, in that it merely enables dyadic relationships between others, or if it is instead an active participant in a triadic relationship? The second is more fundamental: legal disputes tend to center two participants in a platform transaction at a time – the platform and the customer; the platform and the provider; or the provider and the customer. The very structure of our adversarial system places two parties facing one another across the "v." But one innovation of many platform economy enterprises is to change the allocation of rights and responsibilities among these three parties, as compared to the allocation that tends to exist in the traditional economy. Thus, the chapter argues that in the context of the platform economy, decision-makers should begin their analysis by asking whether the platform merely facilitates a dyadic relationship, or if it instead reserves a role for itself, creating a triadic relationship. Where it creates a triadic relationship, the decision-maker should then analyze the position of the plaintiff vis-à-vis both of the other transaction participants. While we draw on a range of real-world platform economy disputes for context, these disputes and their resolution have particular implications for unresolved legal issues relating to discrimination, public accommodation, workers' rights, and the responsibility of platforms to communicate norms relating to these issues within the platform economy.

I PLATFORM IDENTITIES

There is no single, accepted definition of the "platform economy."[7] Ryan Calo and Alex Rosenblat have characterized it as a "set of practices and techniques that leverage digital architectures to facilitate trusted transactions between strangers."[8] Orly Lobel puts it slightly differently: "Platform companies adamantly endeavor to be defined first and foremost by what

---

[5]   One group of researchers has described transactions that occur within triadic relationships involving platforms, consumers, and providers as "collaborative consumption." Sabine Benoit et al., *A Triadic Framework for Collaborative Consumption (CC): Motives, Activities and Resources & Capabilities of Actors*, 79 J. Bus. Res. 219 (2017).

[6]   To be clear, these are not the *only* ways. As one of us has argued, another reason is the omnipresence of individual arbitration clauses in platform enterprises' customer and worker/provider agreements.

[7]   One of us has discussed this multiplicity in other work. *See, e.g.*, Nancy Leong and Aaron Belzer, *The New Public Accommodations: Race Discrimination in the Platform Economy*, 105 Geo. L.J. 1271 (2017).

[8]   Ryan Calo and Alex Rosenblat, *The Taking Economy: Uber Information, and Power*, 117 Colum. L. Rev. 1623, at 1634 (2017). Calo and Rosenblat use the term "sharing economy," which is often used interchangeably with the term "platform economy," as well as terms like "gig economy," "on-demand economy," "app-based economy," or "collaborative economy." *Id.*

they are not. These companies are not selling the thing itself … Rather, they are selling access to the software, the matching algorithms, and a digital system of reputation and trust between their users."[9]

Those definitions hint at one source of the platform identity crisis: platforms designers often want to create a system of trust between a vast network of strangers. And by "trust," we mean more than just generalized social reciprocity that might prompt one toward pro-social behavior like paying taxes or cleaning up after one's dog: rather, platform enterprises must facilitate a sense of immediate physical safety that will overcome natural reticence about getting into a total stranger's car or staying in their home. As one district judge put it, "For generations, parents have admonished their children not to get into cars with strangers… But in today's 'sharing economy,' that warning is an anachronism."[10] Likewise, successful platforms must instill a sense of trust that a transaction will yield an economic outcome that both parties reasonably desire and expect. In order to enter their credit card information into an app that will allow payment to a stranger, or to convince someone to drive a stranger with the expectation that drive will result in payment rather than merely a waste of time and gas, the platform has to provide both parties to the platform with a degree of economic security.

Creating both physical and economic trust requires delicate social engineering. This is particularly so given that the trust must flow between parties who often very differ along axes of socioeconomic status, racial identity, background, education, lifestyle, and many other factors. Thus, it should come as no surprise that platform economy enterprises want to exercise significant ex ante control over interactions between customers and service providers, and receive a more-or-less constant stream of feedback from customers and providers during and after the transaction.

For example, Airbnb now requires a "community commitment" from users not to engage in discrimination on the basis of "race, religion, national origin, ethnicity, disability, sex, gender identity, sexual orientation, or age," and has created a "community center" for users to share information and insights about all aspects of transacting business on Airbnb.[11] It also encourages hosts to use "empathy" and "respect" when creating their listing and interacting with guests, emphasizes the personal connections that might result from hosting,[12] and encourages both hosts and guests to use their real names and clear photographs of themselves when completing their profiles in order to "build trust." And similarly, the for-hire ride service Lyft initially encouraged passengers to begin their trip by sitting in the front seat and fist-bumping their drivers, to mimic the experience of getting a ride from a friend. When some would-be passengers declined to use the service for this reason, Lyft changed the norms by telling riders that they could choose to sit in the backseat, and that doing so would signal that they did not wish to chat with their driver during the ride.[13]

One might assume that platform enterprises would make much of their often-significant efforts at oversight. After all, trust encourages use, which leads to profits. Yet that is not the case, or at least not always the case – instead, platforms are often anxious to create the impression that they do very little beyond creating the infrastructure to allow a two-sided marketplace.

---

[9] Orly Lobel, *The Law of the Platform*, 101 Minn. L. Rev. 87, 100 (2016).
[10] *Search v. Uber Techs. Inc.*, 128 F. Supp. 3d 222, 226 (D.D.C. 2015).
[11] *General Questions About the Airbnb Community Commitment*, Airbnb, www.airbnb.com/help/article/1523/general-questions-about-the-airbnb-community-commitment.
[12] *Guide to Hosting Success*, Airbnb, http://blog.atairbnb.com/guide-to-hosting-success/.
[13] Tracy Lien, *Lyft Distances Itself from Fist Bump During Busiest Week Yet*, L.A. Times (Nov. 28, 2014), www.latimes.com/business/technology/la-fi-tn-lyft-fist-bump-20141128-story.html.

Of course, the reason for this is to minimize the exposure to regulation or legal liability that comes with exercising a high degree of oversight and control over transactions. If Uber and Lyft set too many rules for their drivers, the drivers may be held to be employees, rather than independent contractors.[14] This is probably why each company tolerates the fact that many of its workers simultaneously drive for the other company, often in back-to-back jobs, and neither requires its drivers to sign a noncompete agreement – even though the two companies are in competition for drivers. Likewise, if Airbnb asserts more control over its hosts, it may be liable for instances of discrimination in violation of public accommodation and other civil rights laws, or for torts that take place on a negligent host's property. And if Handy and TaskRabbit overclaim the amount of screening and supervision they assert over their professionals, they might be liable if a given professional damages a home or commits a crime there. Too much oversight leaves companies vulnerable to unwanted (by the company) regulation, as well as the possibility of liability through courts and administrative entities.

In short, it is sometimes advantageous for platform companies to closely monitor transactions (and to give the impression of oversight), and at other times it is advantageous for the companies to appear to be hands off in their approach to both workers and consumers. Airbnb's approach to its Community Center reveals this internal tension:

> The Community Center will be largely self-moderated, but you may also see faces from the Airbnb team around from time to time to share updates, answer tricky questions, and help keep things clean and safe.[15]

The quoted material perfectly exemplifies the heart of the platform identity crisis. The Community Center will be "largely self-moderated," because Airbnb does not want to be *too* involved in the day-to-day operation of the platform. Yet Airbnb cannot be wholly absent – if it was, then the platform's character might change, and trust among users might diminish. This is why the Airbnb team "may" be "around from time to time." The intent is clear: just enough oversight to reassure the community; not enough to allow regulation to the same degree as a bricks-and-mortar business. Yet it is difficult to walk so fine a line without creating tensions or even outright contradictions in the way platforms describe themselves.

In light of this self-created tension, how should courts treat platforms? When should they treat them as mere facilitators of transactions, rather than as intricately involved overseers of economic activity? The next two sections take up that question.

II THE PLATFORM IDENTITY CRISIS IN COURT

The platform identity crisis is often at its most acute during litigation over platform enterprises' legal obligations. For example, whether or not platform enterprises and workers are engaged in the same business – that is, whether Uber is a technology company or everyone's private driver – is relevant to whether workers are properly classified as independent contractors under both state and federal employment law. And Title II of the 1964 Civil Rights Act, which addresses discrimination by public accommodations, applies to any "establishment which provides lodging to transient guests," with the exception of certain small owner-occupied properties, while the Fair Housing Act similarly prohibits discrimination in the sale and rental of "dwellings," again

---

[14] *Cf. S. G. Borello & Sons, Inc.* v. *Department of Industrial Relations*, 769 P.2d 399, 404 (Cal. 1989) (describing an eleven-factor test used to differentiate employees from independent contractors).

[15] *What is the Airbnb Community Center?*, Airbnb, www.airbnb.com/help/article/1183/what-is-the-airbnb-community-center?topic=376.

with relatively limited exceptions for small-scale transactions. These definitions in turn raise the question of whether platforms like Airbnb themselves provide lodging, or just allow hosts to do so. Another set of legal disputes flows from the question of whether companies like Uber and Lyft are "common carriers" – that is, whether they "hold [themselves] out to the public as offering to transport freight or passengers for a fee"[16] – or whether they simply allow others to do so. The "common carrier" designation may determine the outcome of disputes where respondeat superior liability may attach – for example, when platform workers harm customers – and liability under some anti-discrimination laws prohibiting discrimination by public accommodations, which are sometimes viewed as coextensive with common carriers. And finally, similar questions can arise in public policy contexts, when platforms resist new regulations by arguing that they should not be expected to play a role in enforcing laws governing workers or providers.[17]

Yet, despite the fact that these issues are both important and recurring, lawyers, courts, and agencies seem to have difficulty figuring out how to analyze them. Two driver misclassification cases, *O'Connor* v. *Uber*, and *Cotter* v. *Lyft*, both filed in the federal district court in San Francisco, offer clear examples of this difficulty – though they are far from the only ones.

Both *O'Connor* and *Cotter* began as large class actions raising the question of whether drivers are properly classified as independent contractors under California law. And in both, the question of whether the respective enterprises, Lyft and Uber, were technology platforms or transportation providers was front and center. That is because, under California law, workers are presumptively classified as employees when they provide a service to the putative employer. Attempting to avoid that presumption, Uber argued at summary judgment in *O'Connor* that "Plaintiffs pay *Defendant* for access to leads via the Uber App and to benefit from Defendant's marketing efforts and payment processing. *Like passengers, Plaintiffs and other drivers are* customers *who receive a service from Defendant.*"[18] Similarly, Lyft described itself in *Cotter* as follows: "Lyft's business is to maintain an on-line platform, making it possible for riders and drivers to freely arrange transportation by automobile with other members of the community … The services that Lyft provides include, as part of maintaining the platform, monitoring compliance with the [terms of service] and managing access to the platform to help maintain an acceptable level of trust and safety among members of the ride-sharing community."[19] In other words, by Uber's and Lyft's telling, they are technology companies providing services to drivers, and not the other way around.

Unsurprisingly, the plaintiffs had a different account of the Uber and Lyft business models. In *Cotter*, the plaintiffs at summary judgment emphasized a statement by the company's Director of Product Marketing that the company's "mission" was "providing 'peer-to-peer service of rides,'"[20] and observed that the company "could not survive without its drivers." In addition, the plaintiffs

[16] *Black's Law Dictionary* (10th ed., 2014).

[17] This chapter is focused on US law, but similar issues are being addressed in tribunals around the world. For example, an Advocate General of the Court of Justice of the European Union has twice advised that Uber is a transport company, and not an "information society service," Opinion of AG Szpunar in Case C_434/12 Uber Spain (2017) EU:C:2017:364 and Opinion of AG Szpunar in Case C-320/16 Uber France (2017) EU:C:2017:51, and the Court of Justice agreed, C-434/15, ECJ 20 December 2017.

[18] Notice of Motion & Motion of Defendant Uber Techs., Inc., for Summary Judgment; Memorandum of Points and Authorities in Support Thereof, *O'Connor* v. *Uber Techs., Inc.,* No. 13-03826-EMC, 2014 WL 10889983 (N.D. Cal. Dec. 4, 2014).

[19] Defendant Lyft, Inc's Motion for Summary Judgment Against Plaintiffs Patrick Cotter & Alejandra Maciel, *Cotter* v. *Lyft,* 3:13-cv-04065, 2014 WL 8185397 (N.D. Cal. Dec. 22, 2014)

[20] Memorandum of Points and Authorities in Support of Plaintiffs' Motion for Summary Judgment as to Liability, *Cotter* v. *Lyft,* No. 3:13-cv-04065-VC, 2014 WL 10890008 (N.D. Cal. Dec. 1, 2014).

urged the court to consider Lyft's role in creating a market for Lyft rides. Unsurprisingly, the plaintiffs' arguments in *O'Connor* were similar to those made in *Cotter* – the two cases were brought by the same plaintiffs' lawyers – and emphasized that "it would be impossible for Uber to operate its business without the drivers, whose work constitutes the core service Uber provides to the public."[21]

The platforms' arguments failed in both *O'Connor* and *Cotter*. In *O'Connor*, the district court reasoned that "Uber engineered a software method to connect drivers with passengers, but this is merely one instrumentality used in the context of its larger business. Uber does not simply sell software; it sells rides."[22] The Court also cited Uber's own marketing materials, quoting both the "everyone's private driver" tagline and other Uber self-descriptions, including that it was the "best transportation service in San Francisco." If anything, Lyft fared worse; there, the court called its argument "obviously wrong" while relying on a raft of Lyft's own marketing materials, as well as the fact that Lyft "gives drivers detailed instructions about how to conduct themselves."[23]

O'Connor and *Cotter* are helpful examples because they progressed through the summary judgment stage, allowing the respective district judges in the two cases an opportunity to apply law to facts. But the fact that both arise under California law might make them seem idiosyncratic – one might wonder if California law is unusual in its emphasis on whether a worker is providing a service to the putative employer.[24] However, other common methods of distinguishing employees from independent contractors require a similar analysis, though not necessarily to create a presumption of employment status. For example, some state and federal employment statutes (including the National Labor Relations Act) resolve the employee or independent contractor question using the multifactor test found in the Restatement (Second) of Agency § 220, which calls for the decision-maker to consider "whether or not the one employed is engaged in a distinct occupation or business." The "economic realities" test that is used to analyze whether workers are employees for purposes of the Fair Labor Standards Act also uses multiple factors, including whether the work is "an integral part of the employer's business." And still other jurisdictions use the three-factor "ABC" test, which asks whether the service performed by the putative employee is "outside the usual course of business" for the putative employer.[25] The point here is not to catalogue every jurisdiction's approach to separating employees from independent contractors, but instead to illustrate that the question of whether platforms are in the technology business or the business of providing a particular service (or services) will be a frequently occurring question in misclassification litigation in many jurisdictions.

Nor is that question limited to the employee misclassification context. For example, in *National Federation of the Blind* v. *Uber*, the plaintiffs argued that Uber discriminated against blind passengers in violation of the federal Americans With Disabilities Act and California's Unruh Act. Uber responded by arguing in part that it could not qualify as a "place of public accommodation" because it was a "smartphone application" that "exist[ed] solely in a virtual environment," and not a "taxi service" because it did not own any cars.[26] The court rejected

---

[21] Plaintiff's Opposition to Defendant Uber Technologies, Inc.'s Motion for Summary Judgment, *O'Connor* v. *Uber Techs., Inc.*, No. CV-13-3826-EMC, 2015 WL 2456295 (N.D. Cal. Jan. 29, 2015).

[22] *O'Connor* v. *Uber Techs.*, 82 F.Supp. 3d 1133 (N.D. Cal. 2015).

[23] *Cotter v. Lyft, Cotter v. Lyft, Inc.*, 60 F. Supp. 3d 1067, 1078 (N.D. Cal. 2015).

[24] Shortly before this volume went to press, the California Supreme Court adopted a new test, known as the "ABC test" to distinguish independent contractors from employees for purposes of wage orders. *Dynamex Operations W. v. Superior Ct.*, 416 P.3d 1 (Cal. 2018). However, the O'Connor and Cotter decisions discussed in this chapter predate Dynamex, and we do not discuss that case (or the ABC standard) further.

[25] *See, e.g., Costello v. BeavEx, Inc.*, 810 F.3d 1045, 1050 (7th Cir. 2016) (discussing Illinois and Massachusetts law).

[26] Defendants' Notice of Motion and Motion to Dismiss Plaintiffs' First Amended Complaint and/or for a More Definite Statement; Memorandum of Points and Authorities in Support Thereof, *Nat'l Fed. of the Blind of Cal. v. Uber Techs., Inc.*, No. 3:14-cv-04086-NC, 2014 WL 10889967 (N.D. Cal. Dec. 3, 2014.)

Uber's motion to dismiss, citing a lack of "binding law" governing the question of whether an enterprise like Uber could qualify as a public accommodation; the case then settled. Much the same result obtained in *Doe* v. *Uber*, a tort case brought by passengers alleging that they were sexually assaulted by drivers. In that case, Uber argued that it could not be subject to common carrier liability because it was only a "broker" of transportation services; the court held that the plaintiffs had plausibly alleged that "Uber's services are available to the general public and … Uber charges customers standardized fees for car rides."[27]

Examples arise outside of the transportation context as well. In *Airbnb* v. *San Francisco*, short-term rental platforms Airbnb and HomeAway sued to invalidate a local ordinance imposing liability on platforms that collected booking fees associated with illegal rentals. The platforms argued that they were protected by the Communications Decency Act (CDA) as providers of "interactive computer service[s]" that published third-party content, and argued that the CDA protected them from having to monitor hosts' listings. Rejecting the platforms' motion for a preliminary injunction, the court observed that they were attempting to elide their own active participation in facilitating short-term rentals: "[The platforms] are perfectly free to publish any listing they get from a host and to collect fees for doing so … The Ordinance holds plaintiffs liable only for their own conduct, namely for providing, and collecting a fee for, Booking Services in connection with an unregistered unit."[28]

In the example cases discussed so far, courts have – correctly, in our view – rejected the platforms' efforts to brand themselves as mere providers of technology. But this is not a universal view. For example, the Florida Department of Economic Opportunity concluded that an Uber driver was an independent contractor and accordingly rejected his application for unemployment benefits. The agency characterized Uber as "no more an employer to drivers than an art gallery is to artists,"[29] accepting Uber's description of itself as a "technology platform." Rejecting the *Cotter* and *O'Connor* courts' analysis, the agency concluded that there was little relevance to the fact that Uber needed drivers to make money, writing that "the same is true of all middlemen."[30] And it is likely that other decision-makers have reached similar decisions in private proceedings, including individual arbitrations and other unemployment benefits cases.

Courts generally see platforms like Airbnb and Uber for what, in our view, they often actually are: active intermediaries in transactions between workers or providers and customers, and not mere technology platforms. Still, as the next section discusses, not every platform is the same, and there is a better way for courts to analyze this question.

III RESOLVING THE PLATFORM IDENTITY CRISIS

Two main problems arise from courts' existing approaches to the nature of platform economy enterprises. First, they do not offer a predictable way to distinguish platforms that truly do little more than allow private parties to facilitate their own transactions from those that play an active role in providing services to consumers. And second, they rely mostly on factors that can be manipulated by platforms without changing the core nature of their business operations.

---

[27] *Doe v. Uber Techs.*, 184 F. Supp. 3d 774 (N.D. Cal. 2016) (holding that the plaintiff pled sufficient facts to support claim that Uber was a common carrier).

[28] *Airbnb, Inc. v. City and Cty. of San Francisco*, 217 F. Supp. 3d 1066, 1073 (N.D. Cal. 2016).

[29] *Rasier LLC v. Fla. Dep't of Econ. Opportunity*, Protest of Liability Nos. 0026 2825 90-02, 0026 2834 68-02, & 0026 2850 33-02 (Exec. Dir. Dec. 3, 2015), http://miami herald.typepad.com/files/uber-final-order-12-3-15.pdf, *aff'd on review sub nom.*, *McGillis v. Dep't of Econ. Opportunity*, No. 3D15-2758 (Fla. Dist. Ct. App. Feb. 1, 2017), https://casetext.com/case/mcgillis-v-dept-of-econ-opportunity.

[30] *Rasier LLC v. Fla. Dep't of Econ. Opportunity, supra* note 28, at 2.

Consider the controversy surrounding discrimination by Airbnb hosts. Much of the reason that ire is directed not only at individual hosts, but also at the company, results from Airbnb's involvement in the specific host–guest transaction and the community as a whole. Airbnb encourages users to post photographs and use their real first names to build trust – yet this feature gives would-be discriminators exactly the information they need to discriminate.

Despite Airbnb's protestations that it is merely a platform for connecting people (and that it immediately kicks off hosts who discriminate), its behavior is decidedly different from many "mere" platforms who are its primary competitors. Consider the online reservation systems for hotels like Hilton or Marriott, or aggregation services such as Orbitz, Travelocity, and Kayak. Unlike these companies – which allow customers to book at will provided the hotel has an available room and the booker has a valid credit card – Airbnb's practices evince a much greater level of involvement. The very structure of the business distinguishes it from its competitors. As a result, Airbnb's vocal rejection of discrimination rings hollow: words are one thing, but the company could take action by redesigning its platform to make discrimination impossible.

The same principles apply in the context of ride-hailing platforms. To see why decisions like *Cotter* and *O'Connor* are insufficiently reasoned, consider the following series of events. After the city of Austin, Texas began requiring for-hire ride platforms to perform a fingerprint background check on potential drivers, Uber and Lyft each ceased operating in the city.[31] Into the resulting void stepped a Facebook group called Arcade City Austin/Request A Ride. That group, which grew to 30,000 members, allowed people in need of a ride and people selling rides to find each other and negotiate the terms and conditions under which the ride would be offered. The group also allowed drivers to embed in their profiles "a Facebook or Twitter profile, background check, FBI check, driver's license, proof of physical address, and more," to put riders at ease – though it did not require drivers to provide any of this information.[32] Under the approach of decisions like *Cotter* and *O'Connor*, Facebook is doing no more than providing access to useful technology, and neither Facebook nor the originator of the group is likely to be deemed any more than an employer of any drivers operating in the group – an outcome that is likely to coincide with many readers' (and our) instincts.

But what if, instead of starting a Facebook group, a web developer created a stand-alone webpage that operated in much the same way, except that it charged drivers $1 for every ride successfully booked on the site? Following *Cotter* and *O'Connor*, we might conclude that the fact that the site's only way of making money is through selling rides weighs in favor of finding that the site is more than a platform – it is also a car service. Then, the court's ultimate conclusion about whether the site was a technologically enabled intermediary or a taxi substitute might rest on the site's self-description and marketing efforts – factors that have little to do with the relationship between platform and drivers.

Alternatively, consider the steps that an enterprise like Uber or Lyft might take, following *Cotter* and *O'Connor*, in order to improve their chances of winning the argument that they are technology (and not transportation) companies in the next case. One relatively easy step would be for the enterprise to change its tagline – perhaps from "everyone's private driver" to something more evocative of technology, and less related to driving. Say: "Where lifestyle meets

---

[31] David Kravets, *Uber, Lyft Returning to Austin as Driver-Fingerprinting Dispute Ends*, Ars Technica (May 26, 2017), https://arstechnica.com/tech-policy/2017/05/driver-fingerpinting-fracas-is-over-uber-lyft-returning-to-austin/.

[32] Fitz Tepper, *How a 30K-Member Facebook Group Filled the Void Left by Uber and Lyft in Austin*, TechCrunch (June 7, 2016), https://techcrunch.com/2016/06/07/how-a-30k-member-facebook-group-filled-the-void-left-by-uber-and-lyft-in-austin/.

logistics" – a tagline that Uber actually adopted in 2013.[33] The enterprise might also diversify. Perhaps it could move into meal delivery and other activities that both take advantage of the same technology, and reduce the enterprise's apparent dependence on selling rides. In fact, in a recent misclassification trial involving a GrubHub delivery driver, the company explained that it had done exactly this, arguing that it was not in the food delivery business because it also focuses on helping diners discover new restaurants.[34] And finally, the enterprise might eschew providing direct detailed instructions to workers or providers, and instead substitute a system of informal norm-setting coupled with aggressive performance evaluations by customers. Yet none of these changes gets at the fundamental nature of the enterprise, or its relationship with workers or providers. Rather, these are mainly aesthetic adjustments.

We argue that there is a better way for courts to resolve these platform-or-service-provider quandaries. We begin with the modest proposition that the most important factor in resolving those questions should be about what the enterprises actually do, and not what their carefully designed platforms look like or how they characterize themselves. Accordingly, we urge decision-makers to adopt a functionalist approach to these questions. (Readers who are familiar with Jeremias Prassl's work may be reminded of his functionalist approach to defining employers; our approach here is influenced by and resonant with his, though we focus on a somewhat different question.[35])

To implement such a functionalist approach, courts should compare platform-enabled transactions to analogous transactions that are not facilitated by any platform or other third party. That comparison will in turn allow courts to assess the extent to which the platform is usurping aspects of what would otherwise be a relationship between service provider and customer – in other words, turning what would otherwise be a dyadic relationship between provider and customer into a triadic relationship in which the platform has its own relationships with the other two parties.

To see the advantages of this approach, consider Uber, and its facilitation of relationships between riders and drivers. A purely dyadic relationship between rider and driver would entail three phases: the prospecting phase, in which the rider and driver find each other and negotiate; the service delivery phase, in which the driver actually provides the ride; and the payment and post-ride phase, in which the rider pays for the completed service, and the driver and rider resolve any outstanding disputes or other issues, such as the return of lost items. Each of those phases involves significant decisions to be made by both parties. For example, should the rider insist that the driver provide proof of insurance and bonding? Or should the rider offer a lower fare to a driver who cannot provide those items? Should the driver demand a fare that varies with length of ride, or accept a flat rate, knowing that bad traffic might make the ride unprofitable? During the ride, the driver will have to make decisions about which route to take, knowing that a longer ride might lead to a greater fare, but also risk alienating the passenger. And after the ride, the driver will have to deal with assorted payment systems, or decide whether to demand additional payment if the passenger leaves behind his cell phone.

To list these steps is to realize just how thoroughly Uber usurps the dyadic relationship, reserving most of the decisions described above to itself. Uber passengers cannot decide to accept a lower degree of safety (or even to ride in an older car) in exchange for a cheaper fare; drivers may not refuse short trips or accept physical credit cards in lieu of payment through the

---

[33] Adam Vaccaro, *Uber Isn't a Car Service. It's the Future of Logistics*, Inc. (Dec. 13, 2013), www.inc.com/adam-vaccaro/uber-isnt-a-car-service.html.

[34] Maya Kosoff, *Sued for Underpaying Drivers, GrubHub Claims It Isn't a Food-Delivery Company*, Vanity Fair (Sept. 8, 2017), www.vanityfair.com/news/2017/09/sued-for-underpaying-drivers-grubhub-claims-it-isnt-a-food-delivery-company.

[35] *See generally* Jeremias Prassl, *The Concept of the Employer* (2015); Jeremias Prassl and Martin Risak, *Uber, TaskRabbit, & Co: Platforms as Employers? Rethinking the Legal Analysis of Crowdwork*, 37 Comparative Lab. L. & Pol'y J. 619 (2016).

Uber app; a passenger who leaves behind an item uses the app to contact the driver, who is then directed by Uber to cooperate; and the bidirectional rating system is imposed by Uber, which encourages both parties to rate one another and can be used to suspend or otherwise discipline both drivers and passengers. In other words, the experience of requesting a ride using Uber bears nearly no similarity to venturing out into the open market, because Uber both reserves all of the key decisions to itself, and establishes independent relationships with both riders and drivers. That makes Uber a car service – your private driver – and not just a technology company.

This functionalist approach has several advantages. First, it would not be easily manipulated by platform enterprises. To be sure, enterprises could extract themselves from aspects of their relationships with workers or providers and customers, but that change would require more than an aesthetic adjustment – and would be unlikely, given all the work platforms now do to engineer environments of trust. Second, and related, it allows decision-makers to draw meaningful distinctions between platforms like the Austin Request A Ride group, our hypothetical stand-alone equivalent, and Uber – and makes clear why the stand-alone site is more like Request A Ride than Uber. Third, given the lack of case law instructing courts how to analyze whether a platform is actually a provider, courts could implement this framework today – they need not wait for a legislature to act.

IV CONCLUDING THOUGHTS

Courts would take a big step forward by recognizing and resolving the platform identity crisis. Applying our distinction between merely facilitating a dyadic relationship, and actually participating in a triadic relationship, would solve many of the intellectual dilemmas of the platform economy. It would create a framework for analyzing whether platforms are more like traditional businesses or an entirely new entity, creating a new way of transacting business, would add much-needed clarity to a set of related problems that have developed piecemeal, often in conflicting and confusing ways.

The model we have developed here has implications beyond the specific examples we have discussed. While we have primarily focused on anti-discrimination issues and workers' rights, our framework has implications everywhere platform businesses are involved. The functionalist approach can help to address issues in nearly every substantive area of law. The direction in which we resolve the platform identity crisis has implications for intellectual property, contract law, labor and employment, torts, civil rights, and even criminal law.

More generally, the approach we suggest here has implications even beyond platforms. As new technology emerges, so do new ways of doing business, new relationships between companies and the people with whom they interact, and new legal problems. The way to approach these problems is not one by one, but from the top, from the beginning. If courts and litigators had approached platforms this way from the beginning, we could have avoided a great deal of confusion. Workers would have benefited via greater information about their working conditions. Consumers would have better understood the risks and rewards of using a platform business. And businesses themselves would have benefited by thinking through how they wish to frame their business model. Do they want to benefit from facilitating trust? Or would they rather adopt a more hands-off approach in order to avoid regulation?

Platforms will not be the last stage in the evolution of businesses. And for whatever comes next, the correct approach should be modeled on the one we adopt here – a functionalist one that takes account of the way the new innovation maps onto existing business relations. In this way, future economies can avoid their own identity crisis.

34

Intimacy and Equality in the Sharing Economy

Naomi Schoenbaum[*]

INTRODUCTION

The intimacy on which many sharing-economy transactions are premised holds both promise and peril for those concerned with race and sex equality. Expanding on previous research on intimate work,[1] this chapter explores the significance of intimacy in the sharing economy and the implications for equality. Because of the personal spaces in which sharing-economy transactions are more likely to occur, and because of a reliance on personal traits to enhance trust in these transactions, transacting in the sharing economy disproportionately entails intimacy – the revelation of personal information not typically shared with others. The intimacy of sharing-economy transactions heightens the salience of identity traits to those transactions, in tension with anti-discrimination law's goal of reducing the salience of these traits in the market. In response, sharing-economy platforms have increasingly come to address discrimination by reducing the intimacy of transactions, especially by making transactions more anonymous. This chapter argues that this comes at a cost, not only for the benefits that intimacy brings, but also by foregoing an opportunity to combat discrimination in a way that changes hearts and minds.

This chapter proceeds in three parts. The first part lays the foundation for the relationship between intimacy and equality, explaining how intimacy tends to heighten the salience of identity to transactions, and how these dynamics are particularly important in the sharing economy. The second part explores the historical trajectory of intimacy in the sharing economy. The first phase of the sharing economy was marked by firms' tendency to exploit the intimacy of the transactions that occur there as a means of conferring trust between workers and consumers. As the sharing economy matured and concern about discrimination grew, platforms responded by making transactions more anonymous and less intimate. The third part raises some of the consequences of this shift. In this short space, I refrain from reaching a conclusion, but highlight some of the unique benefits of intimacy that are foregone, as well as some of the costs of this anemic approach to remedying discrimination.

[*] Thanks go to the editors of this volume for inviting me to participate, as well as to participants in the University of Oslo Faculty of Law Welfare, Rights, and Discrimination Research Group Workshop and contributors to this volume who participated in the Workshop for *The Cambridge Handbook of the Law of the Sharing Economy* for offering valuable feedback on this chapter.

[1] Naomi Schoenbaum, *The Law of Intimate Work*, 90 Wash. L. Rev. 1167 (2015).

I INTIMACY AND IDENTITY IN THE SHARING ECONOMY

Intimacy in the market tends to breed discrimination.[2] Intimacy enhances the salience of the service provider (referred to as the worker) and her identity to the consumer of the services (referred to as the consumer).[3] The intimate worker is in many ways inseparable from the intimate services she provides.[4] The worker's identity characteristics "serve as signifiers – that shape expectations about the service they are to receive."[5] For example, the Filipina childcare worker is seen as caring, family-first, and docile.[6] While the signal may not be reliable, it provides a quick shortcut when information is costly and biases run deep.

The identity of the intimate worker signals several types of information to consumers. Identity can signal expertise. A woman may believe that a female gynecologist is better able to understand her problems.[7] Identity can also signal that the intimate worker will be more understanding toward the consumer, leading the consumer to be more comfortable with the worker and even have less concern about mistreatment or discrimination, especially if the worker shares the consumer's identity.[8] A woman might believe that a female gynecologist would have more compassion than a male gynecologist and hold fewer biases against her for choices she has made related to her gynecological health. These signals can also work in reverse, leading intimate workers to have identity preferences for their consumers.[9]

Features of sharing-economy transactions render the transactions there generally more intimate than in the traditional economy, making identity preferences particularly likely to flourish. Perhaps the defining feature of the sharing economy is that it enables the disaggregation of the sale of one's property (e.g., cars, homes) and labor.[10] When it comes to property, this means that sellers are able to sell segments of their own personal property, such as rooms in their homes or rides in their cars, for short segments of time. When it comes to labor, this means that sellers are able to sell smaller segments of their labor. The shift in focus from an impersonal

---

[2] I borrow from economic sociology in my use of the term intimacy. *See* Viviana A. Zelizer, *The Purchase of Intimacy* 14–15 (2005) ("particularized knowledge received, and attention provided by, at least one person – knowledge and attention that are not widely available to third parties").

[3] *See, e.g.,* Harry J. Holzer and Keith R. Ihlanfeldt, *Customer Discrimination and Employment Outcomes for Minority Workers,* 113 Q.J. Econ. 835 (1998) (finding that the racial composition of an establishment's customers has sizable effects on the race of who gets hired in jobs that involve direct contact with customers and hypothesizing that this is due to customer preferences in relationships).

[4] *See* Robin Leidner, *Emotional Labor in Service Work,* 561 Annals Am. Acad. Pol. & Soc. Sci. 81, 83 (1999); Amy S. Wharton, *The Sociology of Emotional Labor,* 35 Ann. Rev. Soc. 147, 152 (2009).

[5] Wharton, *supra* note 4, at 152 (internal quotation marks omitted).

[6] *See* Cameron Lynne Macdonald and David Merrill, Intersectionality in the Emotional Proletariat, *in Service Work: Critical Perspectives* 113, 120–22 (Marek Korczynski and Cameron Lynne Macdonald eds., 2009) (explaining that "racial/ethnic groups are preferred by parents [for caregivers] based on their presumed qualities that are rooted in their ethnicity," and quoting a childcare placement agency owner: "people think that Filipinas are from a different planet where everybody cares about children" (citation omitted)).

[7] *See* Tamar Lewin, *Women's Health Is No Longer a Man's World,* N.Y. Times (Feb. 7, 2001), www.nytimes.com/2001/02/07/us/women-s-health-is-no-longer-a-man-s-world.html.

[8] *See, e.g.,* Jennifer Malat and Mary Ann Hamilton, *Preference for Same-Race Health Care Providers and Perceptions of Interpersonal Discrimination in Health Care,* 47 J. Health & Soc. Behav. 173 (2006); Frederick M. Chen et al., *Patients' Beliefs About Racism, Preferences for Physician Race, and Satisfaction with Care,* 3 Annals Fam. Med. 138 (2005).

[9] *See, e.g., Elane Photography, LLC* v. *Willock,* 309 P.3d 53 (N.M. 2013) (upholding a discrimination challenge to a wedding photographer's refusal to serve gay couple against First Amendment defenses).

[10] *See* Daniel E. Rauch and David Schleicher, *Like Uber, but for Local Governmental Policy: The Future of Local Regulation of the "Sharing Economy,"* at 5–6 (George Mason Univ. Law & Econ. Research Paper Series, Paper No. 15-01), www.law.gmu.edu/assets/files/publications/working_papers/1501.pdf.

transaction with a firm to a personal and often social interaction between individuals – a peer-to-peer transaction[11] – makes the transaction more intimate. This makes the identity of both the buyer and the seller more salient.[12]

The fact that work in the sharing economy occurs outside the typical workplace – often in the worker's home (e.g., Airbnb) or car (e.g., Uber) or the consumer's home (e.g., TaskRabbit) – means that it blurs the boundaries between the "first place," which is the home, the "second place," which is the workplace, and the "third place," communal spaces open to the public.[13] The scripts that govern our behavior take their cues from context. Without a firm and a workplace mediating the transaction, buyers and sellers tend to fall back on scripts of personal interaction that govern less regulated spaces like the home, where our norms still permit discrimination.[14] And transacting online in the sharing economy, without the sense of being monitored, frees participants from the pressure of social norms, including norms of non-discrimination.

Two caveats are in order. First, although the blurring of work and intimacy is not entirely new or unique to the sharing economy, the size of the sharing economy calls these boundaries into question more than ever before.[15] Second, not all transactions in the sharing economy are intimate, and of those that are intimate, some are more intimate than others. Intimacy can vary depending on the structures that platforms put in place, and the preferences of workers and consumers.[16]

II TWO PHASES OF INTIMACY IN THE SHARING ECONOMY

Market transactions present risks for sellers – whether they will be compensated for the goods or services they sell – and for buyers – whether they will get the goods or services they bargained for. In addition to these basic risks of transacting, buyers and sellers may face additional risks, such as the safety risk that arises when the transaction is face to face. Searching for appropriate persons with whom to transact and assessing the reliability of strangers involves significant transaction costs.[17] Firms mitigate these costs by building trust based on reputation.[18]

---

[11] *See generally* Liran Einav et al., *Peer-to-Peer Markets*, 8 Ann. Rev. Econ. 615 (2016) (describing general features of peer-to-peer markets, including increased reliance on reputations of individual workers and consumers rather than firms).

[12] *See* Stacy Perman, *Is Uber Dangerous for Women?* Marie Claire (May 20, 2015), www.marieclaire.com/culture/news/a14480/uber-rides-dangerous-for-women (quoting David Plouffe, then an Uber senior vice president: "[T]he relationship that is most important to an Uber rider is that relationship with their Uber driver, and it's one that they really cherish."); Jenna Wortham, *Ubering While Black*, Medium (Oct. 23, 2014), https://medium.com/matter/ubering-while-black-146db581b9db ("The social nature of the sharing economy makes it more vulnerable to discrimination than the traditional economy").

[13] *See generally* Ray Oldenburg, *The Great Good Place: Cafes, Coffee Shops, Community Centers, Beauty Parlors, General Stores, Bars, Hangouts, and How They Get You Through the Day* (1999); Leo W. Jeffres et al., *The Impact of Third Places on Community Quality of Life*, 4 Applied Res. Quality Life 333, 334 (2009).

[14] Marjorie L. De Vault, *Home and Work: Negotiating Boundaries Through Everyday Life*, 102 Am. J. Soc. 1491, 1491 (1997).

[15] John Hawsworth and Robert Vaughan, *The Sharing Economy–Sizing the Revenue Opportunity*, PWC (2015), www.pwc.co.uk/issues/megatrends/collisions/sharingeconomy/the-sharing-economy-sizing-the-revenue-opportunity.html (estimating the potential value of the five main sharing-economy sectors to be $335 billion by 2015).

[16] *See* Greg Muender, *Uber vs. Lyft: A Former Driver Compares the Two Services*, Pando (Dec. 3, 2014), https://pando.com/2014/12/03/uber-vs-lyft-a-former-driver-compares-the-two-services (contrasting Lyft, which "encourages you to be a good friend," with Uber, which "wants you to be a chauffeur" and encourages "professionalism … from drivers").

[17] *See* Rauch and Schleicher, *supra* note 10, at 9; *see also The Rise of the Sharing Economy: On the Internet, Everything Is for Hire*, The Economist (Mar. 9, 2013), www.economist.com/news/leaders/21573104-internet-everything-hire-rise-sharing-economy.

[18] Benjamin G. Edelman and Michael Luca, *Digital Discrimination: The Case of Airbnb.com*, 9 Am. Econ. J.: App. Econ. 1 (2017), http://pubs.aeaweb.org/doi/pdfplus/10.1257/app.20160213; PWC, *The Sharing Economy, Consumer*

In the sharing economy, technology has facilitated peer-to-peer transactions, reducing the firm's role in matching buyers and sellers.[19] As firms are relied on less, transactions are based more on relationships between the worker and consumer.[20] With these more personal transactions, the need for trust is heightened. This is especially true given the new ways of transacting that the sharing economy presents. People initially thought it strange to trust a stranger to give you a ride or a place to stay. Sharing-economy platforms had to overcome this trust obstacle.

Initially, one of the primary responses to this trust deficit was to make sharing-economy transactions *more* intimate, by replacing trust in the firm with trust in individual workers and consumers.[21] Sharing-economy transactions were made to turn on the individual's characteristics. Workers, consumers, or both create profiles that reveal information about themselves, including their names and photographs, to "help others feel that [they]'re reliable, authentic, and committed to the spirit of [the platform]."[22] Both workers and consumers can rate each other, and ratings feature prominently in online profiles.[23] This shifts the focus of the transaction from one between the consumer and the sharing-economy firm to one between the consumer and the worker.[24]

Still further, some sharing-economy firms emphasized the personal connection between the worker and the consumer. Lyft has used the tagline: "your friend with a car."[25] Tripda, a long-distance ride-sharing platform, highlighted how "[s]haring a ride is fun & social. We connect you with new and interesting people to share a ride with …"[26] Airbnb has sold its service as a way to "creat[e] durable, lasting relationships between host and guests that continue long after

---

Intelligence Series 16, www.pwc.com/us/en/technology/publications/assets/pwc-consumer-intelligence-series-the-sharing-economy.pdf (citing that "69% [of consumers surveyed] say they will not trust sharing-economy companies until they are recommended by someone they trust").

[19] *See* Rauch and Schleicher, *supra* note 10, at 9. However, as detailed below, sharing-economy firms can exert significant control over the matching if they so choose, as, for example, Uber now does by blindly matching drivers and riders based on proximity.

[20] *See* Brishen Rogers, *The Social Costs of Uber*, 82 U. Chi. L. Rev. Dialogue 85, 97 (2015), https://lawreview.uchicago.edu/sites/lawreview.uchicago.edu/files/uploads/Dialogue/Rogers_Dialogue.pdf (discussing how Uber drivers need to establish "micro-relationships" to earn certain ratings).

[21] *See* Rauch and Schleicher, *supra* note 10, at 9.

[22] *See Why Do I Need to Have an Airbnb Profile or Profile Photo?*, Airbnb, www.airbnb.com/help/article/67/why-do-i-need-to-have-an-airbnb-profile-or-profile-photo ("Your profile is a great way for others to learn more about you before they book your space or host you… Whether you're a host or a guest, the more complete your profile is, the more reservations you're likely to book, too… We require all hosts to have a profile photo, and we require all guests to upload a profile photo before making their first reservation."); *Airbnb Announces "Verified Identification,"* Airbnb (Apr. 30, 2013), www.airbnb.nl/press/news/airbnb-announces-verified-identification (explaining that "trust is built on transparency" and that "[w]hen you remove anonymity, it brings out the best in people"); Jamiev2014, *Putting the "Pro" in Profile*, TaskRabbit Blog (Apr. 10, 2013) https://blog.taskrabbit.com/2013/04/10/putting-the-pro-in-profile.

[23] *See* Rauch and Schleicher, *supra* note 10, at 9; *How Are Ratings Calculated*, Uber, https://help.uber.com/h/66ce3340-aa1f-4357-b955-027ef50441d3; Rachel Botsman, *The Changing Rules of Trust in the Digital Age*, Harv. Bus. Rev. (Oct. 20, 2015), https://hbr.org/2015/10/the-changing-rules-of-trust-in-the-digital-age ("I behave differently [at an Airbnb] because of the reputation system in place that means not only do I rate hosts, but they rate me. Trust lies intimately between the perceptions of the two users").

[24] As the founder of RelayRides, a car-sharing marketplace, noted, "You meet great, interesting people. You have great stories." Natasha Singer, *In the Sharing Economy, Workers Find Both Freedom and Uncertainty*, N.Y. Times (Aug. 16, 2014), www.nytimes.com/2014/08/17/technology/in-the-sharing-economy-workers-find-both-freedom-and-uncertainty.html; *see also In the Battle Between Lyft And Uber, The Focus Is On Drivers*, NPR All Tech Considered (Jan. 18, 2016), www.npr.org/sections/alltechconsidered/2016/01/18/463473462/is-uber-good-to-drivers-it-s-relative.

[25] Jason Tanz, *How AirBnB and Lyft Finally Got Americans to Trust Each Other*, Wired (Apr. 23, 2014), www.wired.com/2014/04/trust-in-the-share-economy/.

[26] *How It Works*, Sharing Trip, http://sharingtrip.in/how-it-work.html#. Tripda ceased operations in February 2016. Tripda, https://tripda.com/.

a reservation has ended,"[27] allowing its users to meet "friend[s]" or even a "husband, wife, [or] long lost soul mate."[28]

Some sharing-economy firms took it a step further and relied on identity, especially gender, to build trust in their transactions and make consumers and workers more comfortable with their services. Ride-sharing firms have allowed passengers to select the sex of their driver as a safety measure.[29] One of Uber's primary responses to safety concerns has been to pledge to hire more women drivers.[30] Other sharing-economy firms sent subtler signals about which types of workers should do which types of tasks, with, for example, images of women cleaning and men hauling on their sites.[31]

Then some sharing-economy firms shifted their approach toward intimacy.[32] These firms, including some of the big ones, most prominently Airbnb, started making their transactions less personal and more like those in the traditional economy, and faced calls to do so even more. All told, these changes made sharing-economy transactions more anonymous, especially at the moments when the consumer selects the worker, and the worker accepts the consumer. These changes will be discussed below, but first, I discuss what prompted these changes, to put them in context. While this chapter avoids making definitive causal claims about this shift, it addresses the concern about discrimination, as well as market forces, that have led to – and shaped the nature of – the shift.

Perhaps the most significant factor prompting the depersonalization of sharing-economy transactions has been discrimination.[33] Although sharing-economy firms have strenuously argued that they are not governed by anti-discrimination law, they may still be prompted to address discrimination by other forces. Concerns about discrimination in ride-sharing and home-sharing had long been raised based on the heavy reliance on workers' and consumers' photos and names,[34] and research came to confirm these concerns. A study of Uber and Lyft

---

[27] *See* Laura W. Murphy, *Airbnb's Work to Fight Discrimination and Build Inclusion: A Report Submitted to Airbnb*, at 23, blog.atairbnb (Sept. 8, 2016), http://blog.atairbnb.com/wp-content/uploads/2016/09/REPORT_Airbnbs-Work-to-Fight-Discrimination-and-Build-Inclusion.pdf (explaining this as "Airbnb's overall mission").

[28] Anh-Minh Le, *"When Strangers Meet" Film Contest Winners*, Airbnb Blog (Jan. 27, 2015), http://blog.airbnb.com/when-strangers-meet-film-contest-winners (holding a contest for those who "met someone special through a chance encounter on Airbnb" because "an overwhelming number of couples … met and fell in love through the serendipitous circumstance of an Airbnb").

[29] *See* Hiawatha Bray, *Hitchhiking Goes Digital with Tripda Ride Sharing Service*, Bos. Globe (Nov. 21, 2014), www.bostonglobe.com/business/2014/11/21/hitchhiking-goes-digital-with-tripda-ride-sharing-service/4Jjci QxKybC2FD7HymwxUK/story.html; *Seven Ways to #RideSafe This Season with Sidecar*, Sidecar Blog (Dec. 16, 2014), www.side.cr/seven-ways-to-ride-safe-this-season-with-sidecar ("Seven Ways to Ride Safe this Season (with Sidecar!) Be Choosy: If you prefer to ride in a newer car or with a woman at the wheel, go ahead and choose!").

[30] *See Meet the Uber Team Driving Our Women Partner Program*, Uber (July 27, 2015), http://newsroom.uber.com/2015/07/meet-the-uber-team-driving-our-women-partner-program/ (aiming for one million women drivers globally by 2020).

[31] *See* Naomi Schoenbaum, *Gender and the Sharing Economy*, 43 Fordham Urb. L.J. 1023, 1055–56 (2016).

[32] *See* Megan Rose Dickey, *Here's Airbnb's Plan to Fix Its Racism and Discrimination Problem*, TechCrunch (Sept. 8, 2016), https://techcrunch.com/2016/09/08/airbnb-plan-fix-racism-discrimination.

[33] *See, e.g.*, Katie Benner, *Airbnb Tries to Behave More Like a Hotel*, N.Y. Times (June 17, 2017), www.nytimes.com/2017/06/17/technology/airbnbs-hosts-professional-hotels.html (citing discrimination concerns as one of the factors motivating Airbnb's shifts toward depersonalization); Murphy, *supra* note 27 (cataloguing depersonalizing shifts made by Airbnb in response to discrimination concerns); *Trip Safety: Our Commitment to Riders*, Uber, www.uber.com/ride/safety/ [hereinafter *Trip Safety*] ("All ride requests are blindly matched with the closest available driver. So there is no discrimination based on race, gender, or destination").

[34] *See* Ian Ayres, Mahzarin R. Banaji, and Christine Jolls, *Race Effects on Ebay*, 46 Rand J. Economics 891 (2015) (documenting race discrimination against sellers of baseball cards on Ebay by varying race of person holding the card); Marianne Bertrand and Sendhil Mullainathan, *Are Emily and Greg More Employable than Lakisha and Jamal? A Field Experiment on Labor Market Discrimination*, 94 Am. Econ. Rev. 991, 991–92 (2004).

found that riders with African-American-sounding names waited 35 percent longer for rides and were, in some areas, up to three times as likely to have their ride canceled compared to their white counterparts.[35] That study also found that female passengers in Boston were subjected to longer rides, which produced not only a more expensive ride, but also the opportunity for the driver to "flirt[] to a captive audience."[36] As for Airbnb, another study found that lodging requests by those with black-sounding names were 16 percent less likely than those with white-sounding names to be accepted.[37] Discrimination on Airbnb garnered further attention when, in 2016, a host canceled a booking on a black guest and sent her a slew of racist insults, and the Congressional Black Caucus urged Airbnb to take further action to address discrimination on its platform.[38]

Factors aside from discrimination – especially consumer demand – may also be fueling the shift.[39] Airbnb believes that travelers accustomed to hotels have come to expect that they can have hosts who act like hotel staff members, who blend into the background or who won't be there at all. Note that consumer demand and concerns about discrimination may be linked. Airbnb's expansion depends partly on whether people of different nationalities and ethnicities feel welcome to the platform. And making sure that the firm is open to all can be a boon to business simply as a matter of reputation.

Finally, once the sharing economy matured to a point where sufficient trust had been built in the transactions themselves as well as the firms that offered them, firms might have decided that the business costs of personalization were not worth it. As in the traditional economy, relying too much on relationships between consumers and workers risks the relationship between the consumer and the firm.[40] A firm like Uber ultimately wants riders to keep coming back to Uber rather than to any particular driver on the platform.

As for the shift itself, it has reached across different types of sharing-economy services. In home-sharing, Airbnb has tried to professionalize its more than two million hosts, preparing for guests who just want a place to sleep, not a home to share.[41] Part of the effort is one of standardization, so that hosts have consistent hospitality-grade standards around cleanliness, communications, and cancellations – from removing idiosyncratic toiletries to expanding the instant booking program that allows users to make a reservation without host approval.[42] Among other changes, Airbnb has encouraged "[hosts] to make a bathroom look more like a hotel" and to collect fees and taxes from users, and has added default cancellation policies and check-in and checkout times, "business travel ready" listings with standard amenities like a hairdryer and Wi-Fi and protection against cancellation, and a surge-pricing tool that adjusts rates depending on demand.

Some have suggested additional moves toward depersonalization to target discrimination, including asking Airbnb to remove photographs from its guest profiles and not require them to

[35] Yanbo Ge et al., *Racial and Gender Discrimination in Transportation Network Companies*, NBER Working Paper No. 22776, at 2 (Oct. 2016), www.nber.org/papers/w22776.

[36] *Id.*

[37] *See* Edelman and Luca, *supra* note 18, at 1.

[38] *See* Dickey, *supra* note 32.

[39] *See* Benner, *supra* note 33 (explaining Airbnb's shift to allow instant bookings as based in customer demand, despite hosts' concern about ceding control over who they allowed into their homes). *See generally* Naomi Schoenbaum, *Law and Norms in the Market's Response to Discrimination in the Sharing Economy*, L. & Ethics Hum. Rts. J. (forthcoming 2018) (manuscript on file with author) (discussing the role of anti-discrimination norms and their interaction with market demand in prompting firms' responses to discrimination in the sharing economy).

[40] Schoenbaum, *supra* note 1, at 1212–13.

[41] *See* Benner, *supra* note 33 (one host explains the shift as "Airbnb want[ing] her spare bedroom to be more like a Hilton or a Hyatt, and for her to act like a mini-hotelier").

[42] *Id.*

use their names (or allow the use of a pseudonym).[43] But Airbnb has its limits when it comes to depersonalization. It has continued to define itself as offering a different – and more personal – transaction than a hotel. Airbnb has explained that it would not remove host or guest photos from its site because "photos are an important feature that help build relationships and allow host and guests to get to know one another before a booking begins," which is "far different than merely facilitating an anonymous transaction."[44] Instead, the firm would address discrimination in other ways, including taking more modest steps toward depersonalization, such as "experiment[ing] with reducing the prominence of guest photos in the booking process" and "better featur[ing] objective information" and "reputation-enhancing data such as reviews and verified ID."[45]

New sharing-economy firms have popped up to fill the void that Airbnb has seemed to create in the home-sharing space. These firms specifically aim to combat discrimination through "blind" platforms.[46] Innclusive, a peer-to-peer lodging site, has been developed as a more inclusive alternative to Airbnb. It is specifically designed to "remove the possibility of bias."[47] Until hosts agree to a booking, they cannot see a guest's profile photo or personal information. Instead, they see only their ratings.

Ride-sharing services have also come to rely on anonymity to combat discrimination by limiting access to race- and sex-identifying information about drivers and riders before they are matched.[48] But there are opportunities for both riders and drivers to discriminate *after* a ride is accepted. As for riders, once an Uber rider is matched with a driver, the rider will see the driver's "name, license plate number, photo, and rating – so you know who's picking you up ahead of time."[49] This allows the rider to cancel based on the race or sex of the driver, but at a cost, after having been matched with the driver, and having to wait for another driver. As for drivers, Uber only allows drivers to see a prospective rider's name and photo after accepting a ride request.[50]

---

[43] *See, e.g.,* Jun Li et al., *A Better Way to Fight Discrimination in the Sharing Economy,* Harv. Bus. Rev. (Feb. 27, 2017), https://hbr.org/2017/02/a-better-way-to-fight-discrimination-in-the-sharing-economy.

[44] Murphy, *supra* note 27, at 23.

[45] *Id.* (citing research that "reputation systems like review scores can significantly extend the trust between dissimilar users," and thus that "[m]aking review and other objective data more readily available could help overcome some people's inclination to only trust people who are like them"); Ray Fisman and Michael Luca, *Fixing Discrimination in Online Marketplaces,* Harv. Bus. Rev. (Dec. 2016), https://hbr.org/2016/12/fixing-discrimination-in-online-marketplaces (explaining that HomeAway shows photos only of the property for rent and withholds photos until a later page or does not show them at all).

[46] Katie Benner, *Airbnb Vows to Fight Racism, but Its Users Can't Sue to Prompt Fairness,* N.Y. Times (June 19, 2016) www.nytimes.com/2016/06/20/technology/airbnb-vows-to-fight-racism-but-its-users-cant-sue-to-prompt-fairness .html (discussing Innclusive and Noirbnb as firms marketing themselves as providing safe short-term rentals for people of any race or ethnicity).

[47] Ellen Powell, *How Can the Gig Economy Address Discrimination?* Christian Sci. Mon. (Nov. 2, 2016), www.csmonitor .com/Business/2016/1102/How-can-the-gig-economy-address-discrimination.

[48] *Trip Safety, supra* note 33 (explaining that on Uber "[a]ll ride requests are blindly matched with the closest available driver"); *What Information Do Uber Drivers Know Before They Choose to Pick up a Passenger?,* Quora (updated Apr. 3, 2016), www.quora.com/What-information-do-Uber-drivers-know-before-they-choose-to-pick-up-a-passenger (explaining that drivers used to have access to prospective riders' names before they were matched, which could allow for race or sex discrimination). Some ride-sharing services retain a more personal character. *See* Schoenbaum, *supra* note 31, at 1035 (discussing ways in which Lyft focuses more on the personal nature of the transaction than Uber); *infra* note 50.

[49] *Trip Safety, supra* note 33.

[50] *See* Fisman and Luca, *supra* note 45; Ge et al., *supra* note 35, at 2. Lyft allows access to this rider information before a driver accepts a request. In theory, this should make it easier for Lyft drivers to discriminate against riders. But it appears that Uber drivers are accomplishing the same discrimination – just by canceling *after* the ride has been accepted. *See* Ge et al., *supra* note 35, at 2.

And Uber will ban drivers who cancel too many rides, which may help to reduce the chance that drivers will cancel once they know a rider's identity. It is not clear whether either Uber or Lyft audits rider or driver cancellations for discrimination.[51]

While Uber allows riders and drivers to get in touch with each other, it uses technology that anonymizes phone numbers to keep contact details confidential.[52] This is not only a safety measure, but a depersonalization measure. Riders and drivers cannot get in touch with each other after a ride except through Uber. Importantly, Uber's ultimate goal is to replace drivers with autonomous cars, the end-game of depersonalization.[53]

Notably, Uber and Lyft, like Airbnb, have faced calls for still further anonymity, specifically to stop revealing personal information of riders and drivers even after they have been matched.[54] Both companies have resisted, arguing that the information is needed for trust and safety.[55]

III CONSEQUENCES

The previous section of this chapter described the depersonalization of sharing economy transactions. This section steps back to consider what this shift means for the level of intimacy in transactions in the sharing economy as compared with transactions in the traditional economy, as well as additional consequences of this shift. Initially, it seemed pretty clear that, all told, the sharing economy offered an opportunity for both workers and consumers to find a more intimate version of the same service offered in the traditional economy. After these shifts, that is less clear, and varies more across contexts and platforms.[56]

In the context of lodging, particularly in the case of a shared property, the sharing economy still provides a quite intimate transaction. One Airbnb host said that after the changes the site made depersonalizing the transaction, "she sometimes felt burned out by the complexities of hosting."[57] She explained how in a hotel, various tasks are parceled out across workers – "some employees clean up after guests, while others handle concierge services and make conversation with visitors, while yet another group deals with regulators and bookkeeping" – whereas she was responsible for all of those tasks.[58] "Sometimes I joke that my job is washing sheets and towels, ... [b]ut the right conversation with a guest makes it enriching again."[59] Given the intimacy involved in many of the tasks Airbnb hosts perform, aggregating them in a single worker, particularly when done in her home, makes for a quite intimate endeavor. And

---

[51] *See* Letter from Al Franken, U.S. Senator, to Travis Kalanick, Chief Executive Officer of Uber Technologies, Inc., and Logan Green, Chief Executive Officer of Lyft, Inc. (Nov. 2, 2016), www.franken.senate.gov/files/letter/161102_UberLyft.pdf (asking Uber and Lyft whether they engage in such measures)

[52] *Trip Safety, supra* note 33 ("In many locations around the world, Uber uses technology that anonymizes phone numbers to keep contact details confidential. So when you and your driver need to contact each other, your personal information stays private").

[53] Nayantara Mehta, *Uber Employees Aren't The Only Ones Vulnerable To Discrimination*, Forbes (June 13, 2017), http://fortune.com/2017/06/13/eric-holder-uber/.

[54] *See* Ge et al., *supra* note 35, at 20 (calling for complete rider and driver anonymity by replacing names with numbers).

[55] *See* Megan Rose Dickey, *In Light of Discrimination Concerns, Uber and Lyft Defend Their Policies to Show Rider Names and Photos*, TechCrunch (Dec. 29, 2016), https://techcrunch.com/2016/12/29/uber-lyft-respond-al-franken-about-discrimination.

[56] Variation in the level of intimacy in the sharing economy across platforms providing the same services is not new, but it appears to have increased in degree. *See* Schoenbaum, *supra* note 31, at 1035 (contrasting Uber and Lyft on this dimension).

[57] Benner, *supra* note 33.

[58] *Id.*

[59] *Id.*

Airbnb's decision to double down on intimacy by relying on names and photos and allowing hosts the option to reject guests ensures that it will continue to offer a more intimate experience than a hotel.

But that is not to say that all home-sharing services will inevitably retain substantial intimacy. We can contrast Airbnb with the new home-sharing sites, such as Innclusive, premised precisely in the type of anonymity that Airbnb rejects. When such services provide lodging that is not shared with the host, they do not offer much intimacy beyond a Hilton, for instance.

Ride-sharing has arguably become even less intimate than taking a taxi. Uber's technology disabling drivers and riders from directly contacting each other after the transaction is complete seriously restricts the intimacy involved in the transaction. Given that drivers and riders cannot select each other or stay in touch after the ride is over, intimacy is limited to whatever occurs in the ride itself.[60] Other newer features of ride-sharing meant to enhance safety – such as Share My Trip, which allows drivers[61] and riders[62] to share their location with friends while on a trip – introduce an element of monitoring that reduces the sense of intimacy between driver and rider.

While the apparent ease of addressing discrimination with technologically imposed anonymity seems appealing, achieving equality by reducing intimacy also comes at a cost. The remainder of this chapter will consider these costs, both for the value that intimacy brings to transactions, and for equality itself. In highlighting these costs, I do not mean to suggest that combatting discrimination is not critically important. Instead, I attempt to take a first look at the possible costs of reducing discrimination in the sharing economy by depersonalizing transactions that policymakers should account for when considering strategies to combat discrimination.

First is the cost to intimacy itself. Some who have suggested anonymity as a way to remedy discrimination in the sharing economy have pointed to the famous orchestra study to highlight the important role that anonymity can play in reducing discrimination. In that study, it was found that introducing a blind audition mechanism that disguised the musician's sex substantially increased the rate of women in major orchestras.[63] But the blindness in that circumstance is introduced between the head of the orchestra and the musician, not between the musician and the listener, and, in any event, the relationship between the musician and the listener is already quite anonymous. For many sharing-economy services, by contrast, something is given up when the relationship between worker and consumer is depersonalized.

To be sure, anonymizing a transaction at the moment it is initiated (when the worker is matched with the consumer) does not necessarily foreclose the opportunity for intimacy once the transaction begins (when the worker is renting out a room or providing a ride). For a variety of reasons, though, we can expect that this anonymity, in combination with other intimacy-reducing shifts in the sharing economy, will make such intimacy in transacting less likely.

---

[60] *See* Schoenbaum, *supra* note 1, at 1178 and n. 52 (discussing how repeat interactions enhance intimacy).

[61] *See Share My Trip: A New Feature to Let Loved Ones Know Where You Are*, Uber, www.uber.com/drive/partner-app/share-my-location/ ("Friends can easily see your trip status and where you are on the map, so someone you trust always knows where you are").

[62] *See Rider Safety Tips: Staying Safe While Riding with Uber*, Uber, www.uber.com/info/rider-safety-tips/ ("Share your trip details with a friend. While en route, tap 'Share status' in the app to share your driver's name, photo, license plate, and location with a friend or family member. They can track your trip and see your ETA without downloading the Uber app."); *id.* ("If you're riding alone, sit in the backseat," as "this ... gives you and your driver some personal space.").

[63] *See* Claudia Goldin and Cecilia Rouse, *Orchestrating Impartiality: The Impact of "Blind" Auditions on Female Musicians*, 90 Am. Econ. Rev. 715 (2000).

Anonymity at the outset of the relationship sets the terms of engagement and signals to both parties that what is being provided is the service itself, not the person who does it. The more a consumer is invested in the worker as a person before the transaction begins, the more likely she is to invest in the worker as a person during the transaction as well.[64] The likelihood of intimacy developing during the transaction is further reduced by moves toward depersonalization, like standardizing Airbnb lodging or having Uber passengers sit in the backseat, that affect the transaction while it is under way.[65] Finally, the most valuable forms of intimacy tend to develop over the course of repeat transactions.[66] Shifts by sharing-economy firms, especially ride-sharing firms, barring consumers from selecting workers or workers from selecting consumers, places a practical bar on repeat interactions.[67]

There are costs to both workers and consumers of reducing the intimacy of transactions based on the utility that intimacy provides, in terms of enhancing the efficiency and productivity of the transaction.[68] Intimacy in a transaction primes workers and consumers alike to act altruistically, meaning that each is willing to give more, making the exchange more efficient and the worker more productive.[69] And intimacy greases the wheels for the exchange of additional valuable information that makes for better transactions.[70] For example, if an Airbnb host knows her guest well, she is motivated to create a personalized itinerary for her trip, and has the information necessary to do so.[71]

Some workers and consumers transact in the sharing rather than traditional economy precisely for the intimacy it affords, and the utility this brings them. For example, one Airbnb host explained that she enjoyed the intimacy that went along with renting out her spare bedroom and that made Airbnb "so life-enriching."[72] She ate with guests and even shared a bathroom with them, and developed relationships with guests whom she later visited abroad.[73] As for her guests, she felt that they chose Airbnb for the same reason: " 'People like it here because of how comfortable and at home they feel.' "[74]

These benefits of intimacy between workers and consumers – both personal and productive – are especially important for sharing-economy workers who labor outside a traditional

---

[64] This notion is supported by the psychological principles of commitment and consistency: if a consumer invests in a worker, commitment and consistency suggest that she will continue to invest during the transaction. *See generally* Robert Cialdini, *Influence: The Psychology of Persuasion* 57–113 (2d ed. 1993).

[65] Note there are features pushing in the other direction, such as Uber's "compliments" feature that recognizes valuable intimacy during the ride itself. *See* Mike Truong, *Introducing Compliments*, Uber (Nov. 21, 2016), https://newsroom. uber.com/compliments/ (allowing a rider to give a driver a "compliment" such as "entertaining driver" or "great conversation" on the Uber app).

[66] *See supra* note 61 and accompanying text.

[67] *See id.* UberPool, which provides shared trips with multiple riders, provides the possibility for riders to have more extended intimacy with other riders, but brings its own threats to equality for women. *See* Maggie M. K. Hess, *Dear Fellow Rider, Using Uberpool To Pick Up Dates Is Creepy*, Wash. Post (Sept. 24, 2015), www.washingtonpost.com/ news/soloish/wp/2015/09/24/uberpool-is-not-your-private-dating-service (quoting an Uber spokesperson highlighting that "some riders have landed job interviews, connected with long-lost friends," "found a date" and "even got married after meeting in an uberPOOL," but highlighting the risks of sexual harassment, especially given that a rider might learn where another rider lives).

[68] *See* Schoenbaum, *supra* note 1, at 1180–83.

[69] *Id.*

[70] *Id.*

[71] *See* Benner, *supra* note 33 (describing the experience of one host who thrived on the intimacy that Airbnb afforded and became a "superhost" with Airbnb, who repeatedly went above and beyond to assist guests).

[72] *Id.*

[73] *Id.*

[74] *Id.*

workplace, without any coworkers. These workers will make work connections – which are so important for fulfillment, especially for women workers – either with their consumers or with no one.[75]

There are also costs to the goal of equality. Discrimination is avoided by disabling it: by limiting consumers' access to information about workers that would allow consumers to discriminate, or by limiting workers' access to information about consumers that would allow workers to discriminate. I describe this type of action by firms and by law as a move toward "ignorance as equality."[76] Some forms of ignorance as equality, such as bans on employers asking applicants about protected traits, have long been part of our law.[77] What is new, however, is a turn by market actors like these sharing-economy firms, as well as lawmakers, toward increasing reliance on ignorance to prevent discrimination. In addition to the shift toward anonymity as equality in the sharing economy discussed above,[78] lawmakers have, for example, banned employers from asking about traits like criminal and salary history as a way to avoid a disparate impact on minority and women workers.[79]

While ignorance may provide a short-term prophylactic against customer discrimination, it might not be as effective as it appears at first blush. Discrimination can find other ways into the system. For example, while Innclusive, the anonymous alternative to Airbnb, says it "removes the opportunity for bias" by making guests anonymous, it still relies on ratings.[80] These ratings themselves may be affected by bias.[81] And if customers are able to instantly book Airbnb lodging without host approval, what happens when they arrive on a host's doorstep who refuses to let them in or worse?[82] While anonymity can help to achieve formal equality, it might not achieve more substantive forms of equality.

Perhaps most importantly, ignorance as equality embodies an anemic view of equality that falls far short of the traditional aims of anti-discrimination law. It places a burden on those who believe they are likely to be discriminated against to hide who they are,[83] and to opt in to less intimate versions of a transaction to avoid discrimination, even if this is not their preference.[84] By suggesting that potential victims of discrimination should bear these types of burdens of avoiding discrimination, ignorance as equality sounds the same type of victim-blaming that has been rightly criticized in other areas of life and law.

---

[75] *See* Schoenbaum, *supra* note 1, at 1180–83; Naomi Schoenbaum, *Towards a Law of Coworkers*, 68 Ala. L. Rev. 607, 612–14 (2017).

[76] *See* Naomi Schoenbaum, *Ignorance as Equality* (unpublished work in progress).

[77] *See* Naomi Schoenbaum, *It's Time That You Know: The Shortcomings of Ignorance as Fairness in Employment Law and the Need for an "Information-Shifting" Model*, 30 Harv. J.L. & Gender 99, 100 (2007).

[78] *See supra* Section II.

[79] *See, e.g.*, Michael Alison Chandler, *More State, City Lawmakers Say Salary History Requirements Should Be Banned*, Wash. Post (Nov. 14, 2016), www.washingtonpost.com/local/social-issues/more-state-city-lawmakers-say-salary-history-requirements-should-be-bannedadvocates-for-women-argue-that-the-practice-contributes-to-the-nations-pay-gap/2016/11/14/26cb4366-90be-11e6-9c52-0b10449e33c4_story.html.

[80] *See* Powell, *supra* note 47.

[81] *See* Alex Rosenblat, et al., *Discriminating Tastes: Uber's Customer Ratings as Vehicles for Workplace Discrimination*, 9 Pol'y & Internet 256 (2017).

[82] *See* Brentin Mock, *As Black Travelers Turn Away, Airbnb Creates New Anti-Bias Policies*, CityLab (Sept. 8, 2016), www.citylab.com/equity/2016/09/as-black-travelers-turn-away-airbnb-creates-new-anti-bias-policies/499169/.

[83] Murphy, *supra* note 27, at 23 (explaining that "guests should not be asked or required to hide behind curtains of anonymity when trying to find a place to stay" and that "[t]echnology can bring us together and technology shouldn't ask us to hide who we are").

[84] Katie Benner, *Airbnb Adopts Rules to Fight Discrimination By its Hosts*, N.Y. Times (Sept. 8, 2016), www.nytimes.com/2016/09/09/technology/airbnb-anti-discrimination-rules.html (quoting Professor Jamila Jefferson-Jones as worrying that "[i]f mainly minorities feel comfortable in using instant bookings to reserve rentals on Airbnb, for instance, that could end up creating a two-tiered reservations system").

Finally, ignorance as equality is cynical about the ability to change discriminatory attitudes, and operates by disabling such attitudes rather than challenging them. By taking this approach, it diminishes the educative function of anti-discrimination measures and their historic role in changing norms.[85] So ignorance may have some impact on discrimination, but it might not achieve the ultimate ends of a greater transformation in hearts and minds.[86]

---

[85] *See generally* Kenworthey Bilz and Janice Nadler, Law, Moral Attitudes, and Behavioral Change, *in The Oxford Handbook of Behavioral Economics and Law* 241, 242–43 (Eyal Zamir and Doron Teichman eds., 2014) (discussing how sexual harassment law brought widespread changes in attitudes about appropriate conduct between men and women).

[86] *See, e.g.*, Wendy Scott Brown, *Transformative Desegregation: Liberating Hearts and Minds*, 2 J. Gender, Race & Just. 315 (1999).

35

Discrimination and Short-Term Rentals

Jamila Jefferson-Jones

INTRODUCTION

The allure of the sharing economy prominently includes the promise of freedom from the historical impediments of the traditional economy – racism, sexism, ableism, and ethnocentrism. Airbnb, the market leader among sharing economy short-term rental platforms,[1] touts inclusion through its slogan "Belong Anywhere." Indeed, its iconic logo the "Bélo" is "the universal symbol of belonging."[2] Despite this apparent promise, old economy discrimination has reared its head in the short-term rental segment of the sharing economy.

Prior to deciding whether to accept a booking, short-term rental hosts have the opportunity to examine the prospective guest's profile, which includes the guest's name, and may include a profile picture, if the guest has provided one. Platform users have offered anecdotal evidence that hosts use this profile information to exclude guests based on the guests' racial or ethnic background.[3] Scholars have developed empirical evidence to corroborate these anecdotes. Both the anecdotal and empirical evidence indicates that the sharing economy is susceptible to old-fashioned housing discrimination practices. In the United States, this is particularly true with regard to race-based discrimination against African-Americans who have sought to enter the short-term rental market, whether as hosts or guests.[4]

---

[1] Airbnb boasts that it has connected over 160 million guests with hosted properties in more than 65,000 cities in over 190 countries since its founding in 2008. *About Us*, Airbnb www.airbnb.com/about/about-us. Airbnb offers potential guests options of renting the entire home, a private room (with shared common spaces), or a shared room (also with shared common spaces). Airbnb, www.airbnb.com/s/homes?refinements%5B%5D=homes&allow_override%5B%5D=&s_tag=YkvJcMLj. By comparison, competitor FlipKey (which is owned by TripAdvisor) features 300,000 vacation homes and rooms (but no shared rooms like Airbnb) in over 11,000 cities. *About Us*, FlipKey, www.flipkey.com/pages/about_us.

[2] Airbnb, http://blog.atairbnb.com/belong-anywhere/.

[3] Some African-Americans who have experienced discrimination while trying to secure lodging via Airbnb created the Twitter hashtag #AirbnbWhileBlack to raise awareness about the problem. *See* Shankar Vendantam et al., *#AirbnbWhileBlack: How Hidden Bias Shapes the Sharing Economy*, NPR (Apr. 26, 2016, 12:10 AM ET), www.npr.org/2016/04/26/475623339/-airbnbwhileblack-how-hidden-bias-shapes-the-sharing-economy. The popularity of this hashtag has also spawned a Twitter handle that urges users to "report [their] Case on #airbnbwhileblack" and to "post [their] experiences as we build support against discrimination on @airbnb." Airbnbwhileblack (@airbnbwhileblak), Twitter, https://twitter.com/airbnbwhileblak.

[4] Airbnb uses the term "hosts" to describe its short-term lessors and the term "guests" to describe those who lease via its platform. I will use these terms throughout this chapter to describe short-term lessors and lessees, whether they are Airbnb users or users of another platform.

Two recent Harvard Business School studies validate the anecdotal evidence of short-term rental race-based discrimination against African-Americans. The studies found both that African-American hosts face discrimination from prospective Airbnb guests[5] and that potential African-American guests face discrimination from Airbnb hosts.[6] For example, African-American Airbnb hosts in New York City receive 12 percent less in rental income than non-African-American hosts.[7] This was so even when researchers controlled for neighborhood and rental unit quality.[8] Likewise, prospective African-American Airbnb guests were 16 percent less likely to be successful in securing accommodations than were their white counterparts.[9]

In addition to documenting discrimination against African-Americans on Airbnb, scholars have recently begun to document discrimination against disabled users of short-term rental platforms. For instance, a Rutgers University Study found that those with disabilities also face discrimination in securing lodging on Airbnb.[10] The study focused on four types of disability: (1) blindness; (2) cerebral palsy; (3) dwarfism; and (4) spinal cord injury, finding that individuals in all four categories faced discrimination on the Airbnb platform.[11] Using booking preapproval rates, the study found that only 61 percent of prospective guests with dwarfism, 50 percent of blind prospective guests, 43 percent of those with cerebral palsy, and 25 percent of applicants with spinal cord injury were successful in securing preapproval from Airbnb hosts.[12] These rates compared unfavorably with the 75 percent preapproval rate of non-disabled guests.[13]

Analyzing issues of discrimination in short-term rentals and the applicability of existing US anti-discrimination laws to such rentals rest upon how one categorizes such rentals. Should legal analysis focus upon the roles and actions of individual hosts or instead upon those of the sharing economy firms and their online platforms? If courts are analyzing the actions of individual hosts, should each host be considered an agent of the platform via which she offers lodging or is she more akin to an independent contractor? If, on the other hand, courts focus on the firms and their platforms, should old economy public accommodations laws apply, or should a new paradigm be created to address discrimination in the new economy? Legal scholars have only very recently begun to ask these and similar questions.[14] As of the writing of this chapter, US courts have not yet addressed these issues. Thus, in this chapter, I will discuss the applicability of various US anti-discrimination laws in the short-term rental context in tandem with the question of whether individual hosts or the platform owners should be liable

[5] *See* Benjamin Edelman and Michael Luca, *Digital Discrimination: The Case of Airbnb.com* (Harvard Bus. Sch., Working Paper No. 14–054, 2014), www.hbs.edu/faculty/Publication%20Files/14-054_e3c04a43-c0cf-4ed8-91bf-cb0ea4ba59c6.pdf.

[6] *See* Benjamin Edelman et al., *Racial Discrimination in the Sharing Economy: Evidence from a Field Experiment*, Amer. Econ. J.: Applied Econ. (forthcoming 2017) www.benedelman.org/publications/airbnb-guest-discrimination-2016-09-16.pdf.

[7] Edelman and Luca, *supra* note 5.

[8] *Id.*

[9] Edelman et al., *supra* note 6, at 11–12.

[10] Mason Ameri et al., *No Room in the Inn? Disability Access in the New Sharing Economy*, Rutgers Univ. (2017), http://smlr.rutgers.edu/sites/smlr.rutgers.edu/files/documents/PressReleases/disability_access_in_sharing_economy.pdf.

[11] *Id.*

[12] *Id.* at 11, Figure 1, Table 1.

[13] *Id.*

[14] *See, e.g.*, Jamila Jefferson-Jones, *Shut Out of Airbnb: A Proposal for Remedying Housing Discrimination in the Modern Sharing Economy*, 43 CitySquare, Fordham Urban L.J. (online) 12 (2016); Nancy Leong and Aaron Belzer, *The New Public Accommodations: Race Discrimination in the Platform Economy*, 105 Geo. L.J. 1271 (2017); Michael Todisco, *Share and Share Alike? Considering Racial Discrimination in the Nascent Room-Sharing Economy*, 67 Stan. L. Rev. Online 121 (2015).

for such discrimination. I will specifically focus on discrimination based on race or disability and the various impediments to applying old economy anti-discrimination laws to new economy platforms. This chapter concludes with proposals to address the problem of discrimination in short-term rentals in the future.

I US ANTI-DISCRIMINATION LAWS AND THEIR APPLICABILITY TO SHORT-TERM RENTALS

In the United States, four primary federal statutes protect individuals from housing discrimination in the bricks-and-mortar world: the Civil Rights Act of 1866 (Sections 1981 and 1982 thereof),[15] the Civil Rights Act of 1964 (Title II thereof),[16] the Fair Housing Act (FHA)[17] and the Americans with Disabilities Act (ADA) (Title III thereof).[18] Between them, these statutes provide protection from housing discrimination based upon an individual's race, color, religion, sex, familial status, national origin, and disability. Various state and local laws and ordinances that add protected classes, such as "sexual orientation," "gender identity" or "source of income," supplement and may close the other gaps in federal law.[19]

A Sections 1981 and 1982 of the Civil Rights Act of 1866

The Civil Rights Act of 1866, passed during Reconstruction after the US Civil War, provided rights to newly freed African-Americans. Section 1981 of the Civil Rights Act of 1866 provides that "All persons ... shall have the same right ... to make and enforce contracts and to the full and equal benefit of all laws and protections for the security of persons and property as is enjoyed by white citizens."[20] Section 1982 prohibits racial discrimination in real estate transactions, including rental transactions, providing that "All citizens of the United States shall have the same right, in every State and Territory, as is enjoyed by white citizens thereof, to inherit, purchase, lease, sell, hold, and convey real and personal property."[21] Both sections apply to all racial discrimination perpetrated by both public and private actors regarding contracting and the sale or rental of property.[22]

Although read together, Sections 1981 and 1982 appear as mechanisms to remedy race-based housing discrimination, the standard of proof necessary to successfully make a claim under Sections 1981 and 1982 may prove challenging for the users of short-term rental online platforms. In order to prevail, the plaintiff in a Section 1981 or Section 1982 claim must prove not only that the defendant discriminated, but that he or she *intended* to do so.[23] Proving discriminatory

---

[15] 42 U.S.C. § 1981, §1982 (2014).

[16] § 2000a.

[17] § 3601 et seq.

[18] § 12181 et seq.

[19] *See, e.g.,* Cal. Gov't. Code § 12955 (West 2012); N.Y. Exec. § 296 (McKinney 2016); New Orleans, La., Code art. V, § 86–28 (2017).

[20] 42 U.S.C. § 1981(a) (2014).

[21] *Id.* at § 1982.

[22] *Id.* at § 1981(c) (rights under § 1981 are "protected against impairment by nongovernmental discrimination and impairment under color of State law"); *see also Jones v. Alfred H. Mayer Co.*, 392 U.S. 409 (1968) (clarifying that § 1982 applies to both state and private actors); *Runyon v. McCrary*, 476 U.S. 160 (1976) (clarifying that § 1981 applies to both state and private actors and that it is to be construed in the same manner as § 1982).

[23] *See, e.g., Daniels v. Dillard's, Inc.*, 373 F.3d 885, 887 (8th Cir. 2004).

intent is difficult and may be impossible barring a host's statement affirming such intent (e.g., "I do not rent to non-whites").[24] Rather, a host who intends to discriminate may easily provide a nondiscriminatory pretense for refusing to rent to a prospective guest, such as the timing of the proposed rental or the prospective guest's negative or marginal ratings and/or previous reviews.[25] Moreover, Sections 1981 and 1982, enacted to ensure "participat[ion] in public life regardless of race,"[26] are limited in that they apply only to racial discrimination. Therefore, it is necessary to examine how other anti-discrimination laws – such as Title II of the Civil Rights Act of 1964, the Fair Housing Act, and the Americans with Disabilities Act – may better support claims challenging discrimination on short-term rental platforms.

B Title II of the Civil Rights Act of 1964

Title II of the Civil Rights Act of 1964 (Title II) prohibits racial discrimination in "places of public accommodation" – which the Act defines as "establishments which serve[] the public ... [and whose] operations affect commerce."[27] This includes "any inn, hotel, motel, or other establishment which provides lodging to transient guests."[28] These provisions of Title II offer three ways to conceptualize new economy short-term rentals as "public accommodations" under the statute.

First, short-term rentals are, arguably, the functional equivalents of the establishments listed in Title II.[29] After all, guests who are choosing short-term rentals are those who, had such new economy options not existed, would be staying in an "inn, hotel, motel or other establishment which provides lodging to transient guests." Thus, "[u]nder this analysis, [short-term rentals such as Airbnb] should be considered subject to Title II simply because they are displacing and replacing businesses that are subject to Title II, and because, from the perspective of the consumer, they fulfill exactly the same needs as traditional businesses that are in fact subject to Title II."[30] It would appear, then, that the owners of these "establishments" – the individual hosts who provide lodging via short-term rental platforms – should be subject to Title II, as they are the functional equivalents of innkeepers and hoteliers.

One can also conceptualize the argument of functional equivalency by focusing on the platform firms rather than the individual hosts. Via the Airbnb platform, users have access to nearly as many short-term rental units as are owned by the market leaders in the hotel industry.[31] However, unlike the individual host or old economy lodging companies, Airbnb does not actually own or have any other property interest in the lodging offered on its platform. In this way,

---

[24] In the second part of this chapter, I discuss recent instances where hosts have allegedly explicitly stated that they are refusing to rent to a guest based upon that guest's race. I discuss this issue of the burden of proof under the various anti-discrimination statutes more fully in Section II.A. of this chapter.

[25] Airbnb, for example, uses a system whereby both hosts and guests have the opportunity to both rate and review one another after a stay. Airbnb posts the results of these ratings and reviews on its website. Other prospective hosts and guests use them in choosing future bookings. *But see* Nancy Leong, *New Economy, Old Biases*, 100 Minn. L. Rev. 2153, 2162 (2016) (noting that "sharing economy businesses ... employ ratings systems that risk expression of implicit bias and even magnify its effects."); Leong and Belzer, *supra* note 14 at 1289 ("[C]ertain features of typical ... ratings systems raise concerns about bias and discriminatory behavior").

[26] 42 U.S.C. §§ 1981(a), 1982 (2014).

[27] § 2000a(b)(1).

[28] *Id.*

[29] Leong and Belzer, *supra* note 14 at 1298.

[30] *Id.*

[31] Zainab Mudallal, *Airbnb Will Soon Be Booking More Rooms Than the World's Largest Hotel Chains*, Quartz (Jan. 20, 2015), https://qz.com/329735/airbnb-will-soon-be-booking-more-rooms-than-the-worlds-largest-hotel-chains/.

Airbnb is not like an innkeeper or hotel chain, in that it merely provides a way for individuals to connect and share physical space and experiences.[32]

The second argument for the applicability of Title II in the short-term rental context focuses on the internet itself as a public accommodation. Internet sites as "establishments which serve the public" and which "affect commerce" in their operations, are arguably public accommodations.[33] Some disagreement persists regarding whether Courts should consider all websites places of public accommodation or if they should only consider as such those with a "clear nexus to physical places."[34] This disagreement notwithstanding, short-term rental platforms are clear examples of websites with a physical, real-world nexus and, thus, are good candidates for coverage as public accommodations under Title II. This line of analysis leads to the third argument for Title II applicability. This argument focuses on the way in which the old and new economies intersect on short-term platforms to create situations in which particular websites do not just have links to the physical world, but instead are the *only* means of accessing the real-world functional equivalent of a traditional public accommodation.[35] Such is the case with Airbnb and its ilk.

C The Fair Housing Act

The Fair Housing Act (FHA)[36] was enacted as Title VIII of the Civil Rights Act of 1968 and was subsequently amended in 1988. Section 3604 of the FHA makes it "unlawful [t]o refuse to negotiate for the rental of, or otherwise make unavailable or deny, a dwelling to any person because of race, color, religion, sex, familial status, or national origin."[37] It also declares it "unlawful [t]o represent to any person because of race, color, religion, sex, handicap, familial status, or national origin that any dwelling is not available … when such dwelling is in fact so available."[38] Additionally, the FHA prohibits housing discrimination based upon the "handicap"[39] of a renter, a person intending to reside in the dwelling, or a person associated with the renter or resident.[40] Finally, the FHA mandates that property owners must allow reasonable modifications to the premises and their rental policies in order to accommodate disabled residents.[41]

One can analyze the application of the FHA to instances of discrimination by short-term rental hosts with reference to: (1) individual hosts who offer lodging via online platforms; or (2) the platforms themselves as "brokers" of real estate services under the provisions of the FHA.[42] For instance, Section 3603 of the FHA contains two exemptions that are particularly relevant in the

---

[32] *See* Jefferson-Jones, *supra* note 14 at 12 ("[i]n theory, the housing segment of the sharing economy combines both the community and the trust elements of 'sharing' and the freedom and adventure of the 'experience.'"); Leong and Belzer, *supra* note 14 at 1275 ("Yet, these [sharing economy] businesses do not function like their traditional counterparts. Rather than hosting someone in a hotel, Airbnb connects that person with someone who wants to rent out his or her property and charges a fee for facilitating the connection").

[33] *See generally*, Colin Crawford, *Cyberplace: Defining A Right to Internet Access Through Public Accommodation Law*, 76 Temp. L. Rev. 225 (2003).

[34] Leong and Belzer, *supra* note 14 at 1299 (citations omitted).

[35] *See id.* at 1301–02 ("Although Internet platforms are integral to [the] operation of [sharing economy businesses, they], … are nonetheless intimately linked to physical places that function like public accommodations in the traditional economy… [the company's] online platform is the only way of accessing its physical aspects…").

[36] 42 U.S.C. § 3601 *et seq.* (2014).

[37] *Id.* at § 3604(a).

[38] *Id.* at § 3604(d).

[39] The FHA defines the term "handicap" in the same manner as the term "disability" under the ADA. *See infra* Section I.D.

[40] 42 U.S.C. § 3604(f) (2014).

[41] *Id.*

[42] Jefferson-Jones, *supra* note 14 at 19; *see also* Leong and Belzer, *supra* note 14 at 1310.

short-term rental context: (1) owners of single family homes are exempt, provided that they do not own more than three homes and that the owner does not use a "broker, agent, salesman or … facilities or services of any person in the business of selling or renting dwellings;"[43] and (2) a Mrs. Murphy-like exemption[44] whereby the FHA does not apply to "rooms or units in dwellings containing living quarters occupied or intended to be occupied by no more than four families living independent of each other, *if the owner actually maintains and occupies one of such living quarters as his residence.*"[45]

The FHA makes unlawful, not just discrimination by lessors, but by others engaged in what it terms "residential real estate-related transactions."[46] Such transactions include brokering residential real estate leases.[47] Thus, the first exemption mentioned above should not apply to short-term rental hosts, even those that are the owners of a single-family home. I have previously argued that "[p]latforms such as Airbnb function in the same manner as brokers [in that they] … facilitat[e] host and guest introductions, information exchange, and remuneration."[48] If courts agree with this assessment, "then online platforms like Airbnb would be liable for the discriminatory acts of their users."[49] The law may, however, shield platforms from such liability due to a number of factors that are discussed in Section II of this chapter. The second exemption leaves open the same question as that under Title II: "What constitutes 'occupancy'?"

D The Americans with Disabilities Act

The Americans with Disabilities Act (ADA),[50] passed in 1990, modeled the Civil Rights Act of 1964, including its Title II.[51] Along with the FHA, Title III of the ADA provides to disabled individuals protections against discrimination that may be applicable in the short-term rental context. The ADA defines "disability" as "a physical or mental impairment that substantially limits one or more major life activities…; a record of such impairment; or being regarded as having such an impairment… ."[52] Under Title III, the ADA provides that, "No individual shall be discriminated against on the basis of disability in the full and equal enjoyment of the goods, services, facilities, privileges, advantages, or accommodations of any place of public accommodation by any person who owns, leases (or leases to), or operates a place of public accommodation."[53] Thus, if courts view new economy short-term rentals as the functional equivalent of hotels, accept the internet as a public accommodation, or view sharing economy websites as public accommodations because of their nexus with physical, bricks-and-mortar public accommodations, then the ADA applies equally to discrimination against those with disabilities as would Title II to race-based discrimination.[54] If, on the other hand, courts reject this argument of functional equivalence, then disabled guests facing discrimination will have to seek relief

---

[43] 42 U.S.C § 3603(b)(1) (2014).
[44] *See infra* Section II.B. (discussing the "Mrs. Murphy Exception").
[45] *Id.* at § 3603(2) (emphasis added).
[46] *Id.* at § 3605(a) (providing that it is "unlawful for any person or other entity whose business includes engaging in residential real-estate transaction to discriminate against any person in making available such transactions … because of race, color, religion, sex, handicap, familial status, or national origin").
[47] *Id.* at § 3605(b)(2).
[48] Jefferson-Jones, *supra* note 14, at 21.
[49] *Id.*
[50] 42 U.S.C. § 12101 *et seq.* (2014).
[51] *See supra* Section I.B.
[52] 42 U.S.C. § 12012(1) (2014).
[53] *Id.* at § 12182(a).
[54] *See supra* Section I.B (discussing these arguments more fully).

under the FHA, and their claims would be subject to the exemptions thereunder, as discussed in Section I.C above.

In addition to prohibiting discrimination against the disabled in places of public accommodation, the ADA further requires that public accommodations "make reasonable modifications in policies, practices, and procedures" to accommodate individuals with disabilities unless doing so would "fundamentally alter the nature of the good, service, facility, privilege, advantage or accommodation being offered or would result in an undue burden."[55] For example, this means that policies, such as those that prohibit animals on the premises, that require the payment of fees to have animals, or that limit breeds or sizes of animals, usually violate the ADA because such policies may preclude the use of service or comfort animals by disabled residents.[56] Therefore, just as in the old economy, the failure to modify such policies may also violate the ADA in the short-term rental context.

II IMPEDIMENTS TO SUCCESSFUL CLAIMS OF DISCRIMINATION IN SHORT-TERM RENTALS

There are four major impediments to plaintiffs' bringing successful discrimination claims against short-term hosts and companies: (1) the requisite standards of proof under the various anti-discrimination laws; (2) the "Mrs. Murphy Exemption" to Title II and the FHA; (3) internet exceptionalism, as codified under Section 230 of the Communications Decency Act (CDA); and (4) the terms and conditions of use clauses of most platform-based services. *Selden v. Airbnb, Inc.*[57] and *Hobzek v. HomeAway.com, Inc.*[58] – two recent racial discrimination class action cases – illustrate these four impediments. *Selden* was filed in May 2016 in the United States District Court for the District of Columbia.[59] *Hobzek* was filed in September 2016 in the United States District Court for the Western District of Texas.[60] The same law firm represented both named plaintiffs and submitted similar briefs in both cases.

In *Selden*, the named plaintiff Gregory Selden, who is African-American, claimed that a host named "Paul" in Philadelphia rejected Selden's request for accommodation, stating that the unit was unavailable for the desired dates.[61] Selden's profile on Airbnb included his photograph.[62] Later on the same day the host denied Selden's request, Selden saw the same Philadelphia unit listed as available for the dates in which he had expressed interest.[63] Selden decided to try his own "paired testing"[64] experiment. Selden set up two fictitious

---

[55] 42 U.S.C § 12182(b)(2)(A)(ii) (2014).

[56] HUD Notice FHEO-2013-01, Apr. 25, 2013, https://portal.hud.gov/hudportal/documents/huddoc?id=servanimals_ntcfheo2013-01.pdf. The Rutgers study includes examples of this type of violation. Such instances are discussed in Section II.A.

[57] *Selden v. Airbnb, Inc.*, 2016 WL 6476934 (D.D.C. Nov. 1, 2016) (No. 16-cv-00933-CRC), *appeal dismissed* (D.C. Cir. Feb. 2, 2017) (No. 16-07139), *petition for cert. filed* (U.S. July 14, 2017) (No. 17-00079).

[58] *Hobzek v. HomeAway.com, Inc.*, 2017 WL 476748 (W.D. Tex, Austin Div. 2016), *appeal docketed*, Feb. 22, 2017 (5th Cir. 2016).

[59] Class Action Complaint, *Selden v. Airbnb, Inc.*, 2016 WL 6476934 (D.D.C.) (No. 16-cv-00933-CRC) (*petition for cert. filed* July 14, 2017).

[60] Class Action Complaint, *Hobzek v. HomeAway.com, Inc.*, 2017 WL 476748 (W.D. Tex., Austin Div. Sept. 12, 2016) (No. 16-cv-1058) (*appeal docketed* Feb. 22, 2017) (No. 17-50144).

[61] Second Amended Complaint at 28, 37–38, *Selden v. Airbnb, Inc.* (D.D.C. 2016) (No. 16-cv-00933-CRC).

[62] *Id.* at 33.

[63] *Id.* at 39.

[64] One of the ways of enforcing housing rights in the traditional housing economy is through "paired testing." "Paired testing" is a "methodology in which two testers assume the role of applicants with equivalent social and economic characteristics who differ only in terms of the characteristic being tested for discrimination, such as race, disability

profiles.[65] The first profile was "Jessie," who had demographic information similar to that of Selden.[66] The second profile was "Todd," who was older.[67] Both "Jessie" and "Todd" were white.[68] Both "Jessie" and "Todd" expressed interest in the same accommodation on the same dates as Selden.[69] "Paul" accepted both of the white fictitious Airbnb guests.[70] Selden complained about his experience to both Airbnb and "Paul."[71] Finding neither Paul's nor Airbnb's responses to his complaints of discrimination to be sufficient,[72] he filed suit citing violations of Section 1981, Title II, and the FHA.[73]

The named plaintiff in *Hobzek*, Yvette Hobzek, an African-American woman, claimed she accessed the VRBO website, owned and operated by HomeAway, a subsidiary of Expedia, in order to secure accommodations in New York City.[74] Hobzek attempted to rent a townhouse in Harlem using the website's "instabook" option.[75] The host denied her request, although the property remained listed on the website as available for her requested dates.[76] When Hobzek confronted the host via telephone, he allegedly told her that he does not rent to "her kind."[77]

Although VRBO/HomeAway/Expedia does not require guests to set up profiles containing pictures or any other information beyond their names, a customer service agent told Hobzek the company encouraged hosts to use social media such as Facebook to conduct "background checks."[78] According to Hobzek's complaint, "subsequently and without coincidence, Ms. Hobzek would see [the host] appear on her Facebook page as a potential 'friend' as a result of Facebook's data algorithms."[79] This seemed to indicate to Hobzek that the host had learned of her race by perusing her Facebook page.[80]

Like Selden, Hobzek filed suit, citing violations of Section 1981, Title II, and the FHA.[81] It is, thus, instructive to examine the applicability of these anti-discrimination statutes and the defenses available to both individual hosts and to platform owners.

A *Standards of Proof: Discriminatory Intent Versus Disparate Impact*

As discussed above, plaintiffs seeking relief under Sections 1981 and 1982 must demonstrate that the defendant discriminated intentionally.[82] This burden of proof presents two specific problems: First, a defendant may be able to provide a nondiscriminatory pretext for rejecting

---

status, or marital status." Office of Policy Development and Research, U.S. Department of Housing and Urban Development, *Paired Testing and the Housing Discrimination Studies*, Evidence Matters (2014), www.huduser.gov/portal/periodicals/em/spring14/highlight2.html.

[65] Second Amended Complaint at 40, *Selden v. Airbnb, Inc.* (D.D.C.) (No. 16-cv-00933-CRC).

[66] *Id.* at 41.

[67] *Id.* at 42.

[68] *Id.* at 41–42.

[69] *Id.* at 43.

[70] *Id.* at 44.

[71] *Id.* at 45–46.

[72] "Paul," for instance allegedly told Selden "people like [him] were simply victimizing [themselves]." *Id.* at 46.

[73] *Id.* at 53–81.

[74] Amended Class Action Complaint at 15, 17, *Hobzek v. HomeAway.com, Inc.* (W.D. TX, Austin Div.) (No. 16-cv-1058).

[75] *Id.* at 20–22.

[76] *Id.* at 23–24.

[77] *Id.* at 26–27.

[78] *Id.* at 31.

[79] *Id.*

[80] *See id.* at 54.e., 84.

[81] *Id.* at 61–92.

[82] *See supra* Section I.A.

a potential guest, such as unavailability of the rental premises for the requested dates or negative reviews about or ratings of the guest.[83] It may be difficult for the plaintiff to rebut this nondiscriminatory explanation. Second, even if the plaintiff is able to show that an individual host intentionally discriminated against her, it may not be possible to impute that action to the short-term rental company. Although holding hosts liable for discriminatory conduct is desirable, systemic change is more likely to occur when platform companies are liable for discrimination perpetuated via their platforms.

In both *Selden* and *Hobzek*, the plaintiffs attempted to use Section 1981, not just to hold the hosts liable for their conduct, but also to hold the defendant companies liable for their hosts' discriminatory acts. Selden and Hobzek claimed that the hosts, who they alleged discriminated against them, were the "agents, representatives, or servants" of the defendant platform companies.[84] In doing so, the plaintiffs were signaling their intention to hold Airbnb and HomeAway vicariously liable for their hosts' actions. However, commentators have noted that vicarious liability theory is challenging to apply in the short-term rental context where the indicia of a principal–agent relationship are tenuous.[85] Rather, plaintiffs may be more successful in targeting companies directly by arguing that "the design of the online platforms [and] the use of rating systems" evidences discriminatory intent and that "the reliance on ratings systems' data in the face of demonstrated racial disparities, and other conduct by the company" demonstrates a pattern-or-practice of discrimination.[86] Selden and Hobzek make these and similar claims in addition to their claims of vicarious liability.[87]

Like claims brought under Sections 1981 and 1982, the necessary standard of proof could also be an impediment for plaintiffs bringing claims under Title II. Courts are split on the matter of whether Title II claims require a showing of discriminatory intent, or if instead a showing of disparate impact is sufficient.[88] In jurisdictions requiring proof of discriminatory intent, a prospective guest looking to establish a discrimination claim would face the same challenges as one bringing her claim under Sections 1981 and 1982.[89] However, where the necessary standard of proof is disparate impact, the recent Harvard study showing the disproportionate rejection rate of African-American guests could help to establish such evidence.[90] This same study, along with the Rutgers study[91] could also serve as evidence of disparate impact for a claim brought under the FHA and/or the ADA.

The FHA and the ADA may hold more promise for relief from online host discrimination than Sections 1981 and 1982 and Title II. The United States Supreme Court recently held that the FHA does not require proof of discriminatory intent to establish a prima facie case of

---

[83] *See supra* note 25 and accompanying text.

[84] Second Amended Complaint at 2, 4, 8, 10, 35, 50–51, 65, 79, *Selden v. Airbnb, Inc.* (D.D.C.) (No. 16-cv-00933-CRC); Amended Class Action Complaint at 1, 37–38, 46, 48, 73, 90, *Hobzek v. HomeAway.com, Inc.* (W.D. TX, Austin Div.) (No. 16-cv-1058).

[85] *See* Leong and Belzer, *supra* note 14 at 1312.

[86] *Id.*

[87] Second Amended Complaint at 10, 13, 75, *Selden v. Airbnb, Inc.* (D.D.C.) (No. 16-cv-00933-CRC); Amended Class Action Complaint at 49, 54, 84, *Hobzek v. HomeAway.com, Inc.* (W.D. TX, Austin Div.) (No. 16-cv-1058).

[88] *Compare Olzman v. Lake Hills Swim Club, Inc.*, 495 F.2d 1333, 1340–42 (2d Cir. 1974) (showing of discriminatory intent necessary for Title II claims); *Hardie v. Nat'l Collegiate Athletic Ass'n*, 97 F. Supp. 3d 1163 (S.D. Cal. 2015) (showing of disparate impact insufficient for Title II claims), *with Arguello v. Conoco, Inc.*, 207 F.3d 803, 813 (5th Cir. 2000) (assuming that disparate impact claims are cognizable under Title II); *Robinson v. Power Pizza, Inc.*, 993 F. Supp. 1462, 1465 (M.D. Fla. 1998) (showing of disparate impact sufficient under Title II).

[89] *See supra* Section I.A.

[90] *See supra* notes 5–9 and accompanying text.

[91] *See supra* notes 10–13 and accompanying text; *infra* Section II.D.

discrimination.[92] Instead, a plaintiff bringing suit under the FHA need merely show discriminatory impact or disparate treatment.[93] Likewise, plaintiffs bringing claims under Title III of the ADA do not have to prove that the defendant acted intentionally.[94] Thus, examinations of platform designs and the use of ratings systems, as well as studies like the Harvard and Rutgers studies can be especially useful in establishing claims of discrimination under the FHA and the ADA. In fact, the complaints in both the *Selden* and *Hobzek* cases cite the Harvard study as proof of disparate impact[95] and the Rutgers study exposed many instances that could amount to violations of the ADA.

B The "Mrs. Murphy Exemption" to Title II and the FHA

If courts do find that Title II and/or the FHA cover short-term rentals proffered by individuals, it is nonetheless arguable that some of those bookings are exempt from compliance with these statutes. Section 2000a(b) of Title II exempts rental units in "establishment[s] located within a building which contains not more than five rooms for rent or hire and which is *actually occupied by the provider of such establishment as his residence.*"[96] This exemption, typically referred to as the "Mrs. Murphy Exemption," protects the right of freedom of association of those who supported themselves by "taking in" boarders or lodgers.[97] Section 3603 of the FHA also contains a similar exemption in that its prohibitions against discrimination do not apply to "rooms or units in dwelling containing living quarters occupied or intended to be occupied by no more than four families living independent of each other, *if the owner actually maintains and occupies one of such living quarters as his residence.*"[98] It is easy to identify the number of rooms that a particular host has for rent or hire. Rather, in determining whether the Mrs. Murphy Exemption applies to online short-term rentals, the operative question is, "What does 'actually occupied' mean under these statutes?"[99]

The leading online short-term rental platforms (Airbnb, Flipkey, and VRBO/HomeAway) offer different categories of accommodation, some of which may be eligible for exemption under Title II and/or the FHA. All three platforms offer accommodations that comprise the entire premises, with the host not present in the rental unit. Airbnb and Flipkey, however, also offer private rooms where the owner or other guests may be present in the rental unit and share common areas, such as the kitchen or living room. Finally, Airbnb also offers an option whereby guests may share a bedroom with the host or with other guests, in addition to common areas.

---

[92] *Tex. Dept. of Hous. & Cmty. Aff. v. The Inclusive Cmtys. Project, Inc.*, 135 S.Ct 2507, 2518 (2015).

[93] *Id.*

[94] *Lentini v. Cal. Ctr. for the Arts, Escondido*, 370 F.3d 837, 846–847 (9th Cir. 2004); *Ass'ns for Disabled Ams., Inc. v. Concorde Gaming Corp.*, 158 F. Supp. 2d 1353 (S.D. Fla 2001); *Emery v. Caravan of Dreams*, 879 F. Supp. 640, 643 (N.D. Tex. 1995), *aff'd without opinion sub non Emery v. Dreams Spirits, Inc.*, 85 F.3d 622 (5th Cir. 1996).

[95] Second Amended Complaint, *Selden v. Airbnb, Inc.* (D.D.C.) (No. 16-cv-00933-CRC); Amended Class Action Complaint, *Hobzek v. HomeAway.com, Inc.* (W.D. Tex, Austin Div.) (No. 16-cv-1058).

[96] 42 U.S.C. § 2000a(b)(1) (2014) (emphasis added).

[97] Jefferson-Jones, *supra* note 14 at 19; Todisco, *supra* note 14 at 124–25; *see also* Jamila Jefferson-Jones, *Airbnb and the Housing Segment of the Modern "Sharing Economy": Are Short-Term Rental Restrictions an Unconstitutional Taking?*, 42 Hastings Const. L.Q. 101, 562–64 (2015) (comparing sharing economy short-term rentals to old economy boarding houses). The exemption bears this name because, during congressional hearings, Congress discussed it in terms of a Mrs. Murphy who lived on the premises of her rooming house and who did not wish to rent to African-Americans. *See* House Judiciary Committee Report reprinted in BNA, Inc., *The Civil Rights Act of 1964: What it Means to Employers, Businessmen, Unions, Employees, Minority Groups* 135–287 (1964).

[98] 42 U.S.C. § 3603(2) (2014) (emphasis added); *see supra* Section I.C.

[99] *See* Jefferson-Jones, *supra* note 14 at 18.

Rentals where the host is present in the unit during the rental period appear to be exempt from Title II and the FHA, as this arguably meets the "actually occupied" criterion. However, it is unclear whether a host who rents her entire home on a short-term basis – whether to one guest or to guests with individual bookings who are sharing the common areas – with the intent to return and continue residing in that home after each rental period ends can avail herself of the Mrs. Murphy Exemption.[100] Must the host "actually occupy" the rental unit during the rental term? Alternatively, is an intent to return sufficient to establish actual occupancy? Courts have yet to reach this issue.

C Section 230 of the Communications Decency Act

The Communications Decency Act (CDA)[101] generally protects online platform providers from liability from user-generated content. One of the stated purposes of the CDA is:

> to promote the continued development of the Internet and other interactive computer services and other interactive media; to preserve the vibrant and competitive free market that presently exists for the Internet and other interactive computer services, unfettered by Federal or State regulation; [and] to encourage the development of technologies which maximize user control over what information is received by individuals … who use the Internet and other interactive computer services.[102]

Section 230 of the CDA states that those providing "interactive computer services" shall not be "treated as the publisher or speaker of any information provided by another information content provider."[103] This is the prime example of the codification of "Internet exceptionalism" – the idea that it is "justif[iable] to treat regulation of information dissemination through the Internet differently from regulation of such dissemination through nineteenth- and twentieth-century media, such as print, radio, and television."[104]

Section 230 may bar plaintiffs – whether those plaintiffs are asserting claims under Sections 1981 and/or 1982, Title II, the FHA or the ADA – from doing so successfully against online providers when the providers' users use the platform to violate these anti-discrimination laws. Even if a host uses the platform to state that he will not rent to a guest because of her race or disability, Section 230 may shield the short-term rental company from liability in that the user's speech will not be imputed to the platform company. For this reason, short-term rental platforms lack incentive to police their hosts' compliance with anti-discrimination law.[105]

Courts have yet to address the question of whether the CDA shields sharing economy online platform providers from liability under anti-discrimination statutes. However, the opinions in two cases brought against online platform companies present two judicial lines of thought that are instructive in showing the circumstances under which courts may remove the CDA shield: (1) the US Court of Appeals for the Ninth Circuit's opinion in *Fair Housing Counsel of San Fernando Valley* v. *Roomates.com*[106]; and (2) the US Court of Appeals for the Seventh Circuit's opinion in

---

[100] *See* Todisco, *supra* note 14 at 125; *see also* Jefferson-Jones, *supra* note 14 at 20; Leong and Belzer, *supra* note 14 at 1297.

[101] 47 U.S.C. § 230(c) (2014).

[102] *Id.* at § 230(b)(1)–(3).

[103] *Id.* at § 230(c).

[104] Mark Tushnet, *Internet Exceptionalism: An Overview from General Constitutional Law*, 56 Wm. & Mary L. Rev. 1637, 1638 (2015); *see also* Stephen R. Miller and Jamila Jefferson-Jones, *Airbnb and the Battle Between Internet Exceptionalism and Local Control of Land Use*, 31 Probate & Property 36 (May/June 2017).

[105] Jefferson-Jones, *supra* note 14 at 22; Todisco, *supra* note 14 at 128.

[106] *Fair Hous. Council of San Fernando Valley* v. *Roomates.com, LLC*, 521 F.3d 1157 (9th Cir. 2008).

Chicago Lawyers' Committee for Civil Rights v. *Craigslist*.[107] In *Roomates.com*, the Ninth Circuit held Roomates.com – an online service that helps users find roommates – to be ineligible for CDA protection because its website required users to disclose their gender, sexual orientation, and familial status via pre-filled drop-down boxes.[108] By contrast, the Seventh Circuit found in *Craigslist* the company – an online classifieds service – not liable under the FHA for users' discriminatory posts because the company merely provided a forum for the posting of content that was purely user-generated and did not actually create the content.[109]

Commentators have distinguished between "active developers" and "passive intermediaries" to support the notion that Airbnb is more like the online platform in *Roomates.com* than that in *Craigslist*.[110] Moreover, as noted earlier, Airbnb and companies like it are not just the functional equivalents of hotels, but are also the functional equivalents of real estate brokers and are thus, arguably, covered under Section 3603 of the FHA.[111] Brokers are "by [their] very nature, *active* in [their] facilitation of the transaction, rather than passive."[112]

Despite the importance of the questions of whether anti-discrimination laws apply to short-term rentals or whether the CDA shields providers, there is one major hurdle that has prevented courts' consideration of these issues: the terms and conditions that govern most online platform user agreements. These agreements typically contain clauses that bar class actions and jury trials and compel disputes to be settled via arbitration.

D Terms and Conditions: Arbitration Clauses

Both Airbnb and HomeAway have employed their websites' and apps' terms of use as the first line of defense in the class action discrimination cases brought against them. Airbnb responded to Selden's petition with a "Motion to Compel Arbitration and Dismiss or, In the Alternative, to Stay Pending Arbitration."[113] In it, Airbnb argued that Selden and the other members of the class had agreed to Airbnb's Terms of Service, including its comprehensive arbitration clause, its prohibition against jury trials, and its ban on class actions.[114] The District Court for the District of Columbia agreed with Airbnb, granting its motion.[115] The court's reasoning, based on contract law and its interpretation of Section 2 of the Federal Arbitration Act (FAA),[116] said that "arbitration provisions in electronic contracts – so long as their existence is made reasonably known to consumers – are enforceable in commercial cases and discrimination cases alike."[117] The United States Court of Appeals for the District of Columbia Circuit ruled that the district court's order was not appealable.[118] Selden filed a petition for certiorari in the United States Supreme Court

---

[107] *Chicago Lawyers' Comm. for Civil Rights Under Law, Inc.* v. *Craigslist, Inc.*, 519 F.3d 666 (7th Cir. 2008).

[108] *Roomates.com*, 521 F.3d at 1165.

[109] *Craigslist, Inc.*, 519 F.3d at 670–71.

[110] Leong and Belzer, *supra* note 14 at 1308.

[111] *See supra* Section I.C.

[112] Jefferson-Jones, *supra* note 14 at 23 (emphasis added); *see* Robin Paul Malloy and James Charles Smith, *Real Estate Transactions: Problems, Cases and Materials* 25 (3d ed., 2007) (outlining the activities of real estate brokers as "transactional intermediaries").

[113] Motion to Compel Arbitration and Dismiss or, In the Alternative, to Stay Pending Arbitration, *Selden* v. *Airbnb, Inc.* (D.D.C.) (No. 16-cv-00933-CRC).

[114] *Id.*

[115] *Selden* v. *Airbnb, Inc.*, 2016 WL 6476934 (D.D.C. Nov. 1, 2016).

[116] 9 U.S.C § 2 ("[a] written provision in … a contract evidencing a transaction involving commerce to settle by arbitration a controversy thereafter arising out of such contract … shall be valid, irrevocable, and enforceable, save upon such grounds as exist at law or in equity for the revocation of any contract.").

[117] *Selden* v. *Airbnb, Inc.*, 2016 WL 6476934, *2 (D.D.C. Nov. 1, 2016).

[118] *Selden* v. *Airbnb, Inc.*, 2017 WL 2681950 (D.C. Cir. Feb. 2, 2017).

on July 14, 2017 seeking a review of the circuit court's dismissal, which the Court denied on October 2, 2017.[119]

HomeAway responded to Hobzek's petition with a "Motion to Compel Arbitration and Stay Action."[120] Similarly to Airbnb, HomeAway argued that Hobzek and the other plaintiffs had agreed to the company's Terms and Conditions, which provided, "Any and all Claims will be resolved by binding arbitration, rather than in court," and "Any and all proceedings to resolve Claims will be conducted only on an individual basis and not in a class, consolidated or representative action."[121] Similarly to the court in *Selden*, the *Hobzek* court found that: "The FAA … places arbitration agreements on equal footing with other contracts, and requires courts to enforce them according to their terms."[122] Moreover, the court held that "the parties clearly and unmistakably intended to delegate the power to decide arbitrability to an arbitrator."[123] The district court granted HomeAway's motion, ordering that the defendant submit to arbitration, that the case be stayed pending arbitration and that the parties file status reports regarding the arbitration proceedings every 90 days.[124] Hobzek filed an interlocutory appeal in the Fifth Circuit in February 2017, which the Fifth Circuit dismissed for lack of jurisdiction, finding that the district court's order was "not a final appealable order over which [the Fifth Circuit] has jurisdiction."[125]

III PROPOSALS TO ADDRESS DISCRIMINATION IN SHARING ECONOMY SHORT-TERM RENTALS

The growth of the sharing economy has far outpaced the law's ability to address the various issues this new economy presents, including the issue of discrimination in short-term rentals. Given the recent revelations of discriminatory practices on short-term rental platforms, we must design ways to address this problem. Commentators initially proposed self-regulation by the short-term rental industry as a desirable solution to discriminatory practices on short-term rental platforms.[126] In particular, they suggested redesigning the platforms to mask potential racially identifying information, such as names and photographs, until after booking the lodging.[127] They also suggested that platforms collect data about the race of users, track discriminatory behavior, and sanction users who exhibit such behavior.[128] Finally, they suggest Airbnb modify its ratings system to require that users provide qualitative information, such as comments, to augment quantitative ratings.[129]

In September 2016, in response to pressure from users and commentators, Airbnb voluntarily instituted reforms aimed at addressing discrimination on its platform. However, I, along with other commentators, criticized the reforms as merely cosmetic.[130] Airbnb's reforms included

---

[119] *Selden v. Airbnb, Inc.*, __ S.Ct. __, 2017 WL 3036756 (Mem), 86 USLW 3127 (No. 17–79) (Oct. 2, 2017).

[120] Motion to Compel Arbitration and Stay Action, *Hobzek v. HomeAway.com, Inc.* (W.D. TX, Austin Div.) (No. 16-cv-1058).

[121] *Id.* at ¶ 19.

[122] *Hobzek v. HomeAway.com, Inc.*, 2017 WL 476748, *2 (W.D. TX, Austin Div.) (No. 16-cv-1058).

[123] *Id.* at *5.

[124] *Id.*

[125] *Hobzek v. HomeAway.com, Inc.*, 2017 WL 3630286, *1 (5th Cir. 2017) (No. 17-50144).

[126] Leong and Belzer, *supra* note 14 at 1321–22; Todisco, *supra* note 14 at 128.

[127] Leong and Belzer, *supra* note 14 at 1321; Benjamin Edelman, *Preventing Discrimination at Airbnb* (June 23, 2016), www.benedelman.org/news/062316-1.html.

[128] Leong and Belzer, *supra* note 14 at 1321.

[129] *Id.*

[130] *See* Jamie Condliffe, *Airbnb Isn't Really Confronting Its Racism Problem*, MIT Tech. Rev. (Sept. 12, 2016), www .technologyreview.com/s/602355/airbnb-isnt-really-confronting-its-racism-problem (quoting Benjamin Edelman's and Jamila Jefferson-Jones' critique of Airbnb's new anti-discrimination policy).

mandating that all users affirmatively accept the "Airbnb Community Commitment," eschewing discrimination.[131] Airbnb also committed to diversifying its workforce, composing a team to monitor discrimination on its platform on a full-time basis, and providing anti-bias training for its users.[132] Airbnb, however, did not remove photos and names from the pre-booking process that commentators had identified as likely to facility discrimination. Airbnb justifies its reluctance to eliminate photos and names from the initial booking process on the basis that it built its platform upon trust and user-generated review. It contends that removing names and photos would fundamentally change the Airbnb community and the experience of sharing lodging on its platform.

Due to the reluctance of Airbnb to embrace fully meaningful self-regulation of discrimination, legislative reform may be more effective. In this vein, commentators Nancy Leong and Aaron Belzer suggested two amendments to Title II: First, to make it clear that claims under Title II merely require a showing of disparate impact, rather than of discriminatory intent;[133] and second, to "cover [platform-based businesses] that offer goods and services tantamount to those provided by public accommodations in the traditional economy."[134] This second suggestion reflects the notion that businesses like Airbnb are the functional market equivalents of bricks-and-mortar hotels. As Leong and Belzer note, "In both instances, discrimination affects the end user in the same way by impairing or denying her ability to obtain lodging."[135]

Leong and Belzer also advocate for reporting requirements that platform owners disclose information about their businesses to the Civil Rights Division of the Department of Justice and make that information publically available.[136] For instance, they argue that "Airbnb should be required to disclose the number, cost, size, features, location, and duration of its rentals … [and] should pay a steep penalty for noncompliance."[137] This requirement could work in tandem with Benjamin Edelman's recommendation that Airbnb allow paired testing experiments on its platform.[138] Airbnb currently prohibits such testing and the use of fictitious profiles, such as those created by Gregory Selden and by Edelman's research team at Harvard Business School.[139]

Finally, I, along with other commentators, have proposed an exception to the CDA that would allow members of protected classes to sue platforms when host-users violate anti-discrimination laws.[140] Such an exception would be in line with existing CDA exceptions that balance its guiding policy of internet exceptionalism against other important policies such as the protection of children from exploitation[141] or of intellectual property rights.[142] Since "[p]reventing housing

---

[131] Laura W. Murphy, *Airbnb's Work to Fight Discrimination and Build Inclusion: A Report Submitted to Airbnb* (Sept. 8, 2016), https://blog.atairbnb.com/wp-content/uploads/2016/09/REPORT_Airbnbs-Work-to-Fight-Discrimination-and-Build-Inclusion.pdf.

[132] *Id.*

[133] Leong and Belzer, *supra* note 140 at 1320.

[134] *Id.* at 1318.

[135] *Id.*

[136] *Id.* at 1319.

[137] *Id.*

[138] Edelman, *supra* note 126.

[139] Airbnb, Terms of Service, www.airbnb.com/terms.

[140] Jefferson-Jones, *supra* note 14 at 25; Todisco, *supra* note 14 at 128; *see also* Leong and Belzer, *supra* note 14 at 1321 (arguing that "Congress should either amend section 230 [of the CDA] or specify in Title II that section 230 does not immunize … [platforms] from liability for race discrimination").

[141] 47 U.S.C § 230(e)(1) (2014) ("Nothing in this section shall be construed to impair the enforcement of section 223 or 231 of this title, chapter 71 (relating to obscenity) or 110 (relating to sexual exploitation of children) of Title 18, or any other Federal criminal statute").

[142] *Id.* at § 230(e)(2) ("Nothing in this section shall be construed to limit or expand any law pertaining to intellectual property").

discrimination is also a fundamental policy goal ... online housing discrimination is ripe for inclusion as an exception under the CDA."[143]

With plaintiffs' path to the courts currently blocked by Airbnb and other short-term rental providers' use of arbitration clauses, and given the limited success of self-regulation, legislative solutions present the most direct method of combatting discrimination in the sharing economy. Moreover, amendments to Title II and/or the CDA would "revitalize ... civil rights legislation and send a strong message that discrimination is no more acceptable in the platform economy than in the traditional economy."[144]

CONCLUSION

It remains to be seen whether Congress can gather the political will to enact the legislative changes needed to bring sharing economy anti-discrimination regulation in line with that of the bricks-and-mortar world. Were Congress to do so, the law in the area of housing discrimination could make a giant leap forward toward catching up to the ever-expanding sharing economy.

---

[143] Jefferson-Jones, *supra* note 14 at 25.
[144] Leong and Belzer, *supra* note 14 at 1317.

36

The Sharing Economy and EU Anti-discrimination Law

Nicola Countouris and Luca Ratti

Conçue aujourd'hui sur le modèle cybernétique, la machine à gouverner n'est plus régie par des lois, mais par des programmes assurant son fonctionnement homéostatique.[...] En cela, elle est fidèle à un autre rêve de l'Occident: celui de l'harmonie par le calcul.[1]

INTRODUCTION: WORKING THROUGH ALGORITHMS AND THE MYTH OF "HARMONY BY NUMBERS"

Alain Supiot's description of a dystopian modern world ruled by seemingly neutral, effective, efficient, objective, transparent, yet fundamentally inhumane programs, is sadly, and somewhat ironically, increasingly backed by an emerging amount of data, confirming that the algorithms supporting various service providers in the so-called "sharing economy" are no less biased than the humans that have programmed and operate, or use, them. For instance, it is increasingly clear that the gender pay gap and other forms of unequal treatment are even wider in the sharing economy than in other, comparable, sectors of the "real" economy.[2] While "price discrimination" appears to be predominantly based on gender-related bias,[3] studies increasingly show that race, ethnic origin, and religion/belief also appear to be relevant factors, for instance, when assessing the distribution of work opportunities among so-called "gig-workers." For instance, according to a study conducted in a number of US cities, on-demand drivers are far more likely to be asked for rides if they do not belong to ethnic or religious minorities, two traits that are often inferred from their name and surname, picture, and other personal information provided to the platform to potential "clients."[4] The data altogether suggest how relevant and concrete the risk of discrimination by seemingly facially neutral software is. A benign reading of the problem would be that programmers do not intentionally seek to produce discriminatory outcomes, but that their software, by mirroring and leaving unaddressed the bias and prejudices of their customers, and society at large, perpetuates and reinforces existing discriminations.[5] A less benign reading

---

[1] A. Supiot, *La Gouvernance par les nombres* Ch. 1 (2015).

[2] Arianne Renan Barzilay and Anat Ben-David, *Platform Inequality: Gender in the Gig-Economy*, 47 Seton Hall L. Rev. 393 (2017).

[3] Sara C. Kingsley, Mary L. Gray, and Siddharth Suri, *Monopsony and the Crowd: Labor for Lemons?* 2014 Policy 1 (2016), http://ipp.oii.ox.ac.uk/sites/ipp/files/documents/ Monopsony_and_theCrowd_SCK_MLG_SS.pdf.

[4] Yanbo Ge, Christopher R. Knittel, Don MacKenzie, and Stephen Zoepf, *Racial and Gender Discrimination in Transportation Network Companies*, NBER Working Paper No. 22776, Oct. 2016.

[5] Erika Kovács, *Gender Equality in Virtual Work: The Regulatory Aspects*, paper presented at the LLRN3 Toronto Conference, June 2017, manuscript.

would be that companies operating in the sharing economy design their operations, and the software that supports them, with the full awareness of these pitfalls, but fail to take remedial action and consciously or unconsciously sacrifice fairness on the altar of consumer choice, transparency, and business reason.

A central concern of the present chapter is the extent to which EU law, and more specifically EU equality legislation, is suitably equipped and structured to tackle the old problems generated by discriminatory practices in the seemingly new context provided by the working and service arrangements in the "sharing economy." It is worth noting that the European Parliament itself, while recognizing "that many rules from EU acquis are already applicable to the collaborative economy," also encourage the Commission "to reflect the provisions of the relevant anti-discrimination legislation in the context of further analysis and recommendations in this field."[6] Thus, the following section of this chapter begins by assessing the extent to which working arrangements in the collaborative economy can be analyzed by reference to the traditional categories developed to understand work relations in more conventional sectors of the labor market. Section III moves on to assess the important potential contribution of EU equality law to combatting discriminatory practices in the sharing economy. With a nominally broad scope of application and a dual nature as both an economic right and a fundamental social one, EU anti-discrimination law would be perfectly suited, in principle, to apply to these new forms of work. However, as Section IV will go on to discuss, this potential may go partly unfulfilled, though admittedly mostly because of some inherent structural doctrinal deficiencies affecting EU equality law as interpreted and applied by the Court of Justice of the EU (CJEU), rather than because of some insurmountable complexities and peculiarities affecting work relations in the sharing economy.

I WORKING ARRANGEMENTS IN THE SHARING ECONOMY AND ANTI-DISCRIMINATION LAW – A CONCEPTUAL FRAMEWORK

While the sharing economy is undoubtedly characterized by a large range of different arrangements for the provisions of services and goods, it would appear to us that, among the various forms of digital work coordinated through algorithms, software, and mobile applications, two main models have become, in many ways, prototypical: crowdworking and working on-demand via apps.[7]

The first model is characterized by the fact that an individual or, most likely, a company requests an online platform to search for someone capable of performing a specific, detailed, and digitally based task, at a given rate within a certain period of time. The most well-known and studied[8] global online platform of this kind is arguably Amazon Mechanical Turk, which relies

---

[6] European Parliament, "European Parliament resolution of 15 June 2017 on a European Agenda for the collaborative economy" (P8_TA-PROV(2017)0271), paragraph I.

[7] On the (perhaps flimsy) assumption that platforms operating peer-to-peer property rental and sharing services predominantly involve the exchange of rent for the use of property, with labor, where present, playing a marginal and ancillary role in the contractual transaction, we venture to suggest that the other, main, prototypical form of online platform, best exemplified by service providers such as Airbnb, can be provisionally excluded from the scope of the present chapter, without, however, suggesting that such services are immune from discriminatory practices.

[8] *See* Birgitta Bergvall Kåreborn and Debra Howcroft, *Amazon Mechanical Turk and the Commodification of Labour*, 29 New Tech., Work & Emp. 213 (2014); Miriam A. Cherry, *A Taxonomy of Virtual Work*, 45 Ga. L. Rev. 951 (2011); Miriam A. Cherry, *The Global Dimensions of Virtual Work*, 54 St. Louis Univ. L.J. 471 (2010); Miriam A. Cherry, *Working for (Virtually) Minimum Wage*, 60 Ala. L. Rev. 1077 (2009); Miriam A. Cherry, *Cyber Commodification*, 72 Md. L. Rev. 381 (2013).

on a number of small tasks (named Human Intelligence Tasks, HITs) advertised on the platform by clients (end-users), seeking for someone to perform them. The economic advantage of this kind of arrangement lies in the fact that both the platform and the final user profit from the optimization of resources and the de-synchronization of working and non-working time.[9] While Amazon Mechanical Turk is in many ways the prototype for this kind of crowdsourcing platform,[10] many other providers[11] have developed similar business models and entered comparable arrangements with a plethora of "workers" and final clients, performing the most disparate tasks.

The second model, instead, typically involves the performance of tasks in the "real" world and tends to create "mobile labor markets,"[12] offering their customers a set of different services, from private transport to moving furniture, to cleaning and other small home works: its prototype is the transportation company Uber,[13] but other platforms such as TaskRabbit and Lyft may be classified in the same category.[14]

A substantial difference can be traced between the two models just mentioned: while in the first one, the online platform performs as an intermediary,[15] working on-demand via app involves a more proactive role by the platform, which creates the organizational preconditions for the gigs to be performed, unilaterally fixes the price of the gig or ride, handles the payment transactions, collects and disseminates feedback, and finally retains a commission for the service provided.[16] Empirical analyses show that the algorithm-based management run by online platforms has had the effect of strengthening the power of the platform (and/or the final user) to constantly control the performance of the individual: this can be tested both when the individual's performance happens in the "real" world in real time – such as in the Uber or Lyft model – but also when it comes to controlling, standardizing, and evaluating digital work done via platforms.[17]

Assessing an exponential growth in the use of both forms of work, interpreters and judges have started to question their definition and classification, and to advance concerns on the issues of social protection, commodification,[18] and exploitation.[19] Some have stressed that both forms of work can be seen in the context of a general strategy of employers toward an "organized irresponsibility,"[20] when not also an "exit strategy" for the employer from its labor and social

---

[9]   For a theoretical framework *see* Émilie Genin, *Proposal for a Theoretical Framework for the Analysis of Time Porosity*, 32 Int'l J. Comp. Lab. L. & Indus. Rel. 280 (2016).

[10]   *See also* Eurofound, *New Forms of Employment* 1, 104 (2015), www.eurofound.europa.en/publications/report/2015/working-conditions-labour-market/new-forms-of-employment.

[11]   *See, e.g.,* among the multitude: Crowdflower, Crowdsource, Clikworker, Fiverr, PeoplePerHour, CloudFactory, CrowdComputing Systems, MobileWorks, oDesk, OneSpace.

[12]   *See* Christiano Codagnone, Fabienne Abadie, and Federico Biagi, *The Future of Work in the "Sharing Economy": Market Efficiency and Equitable Opportunities or Unfair Precarisation?* 1, 17–20 (2016), publications.jrc.ec.europa.eu/repository/bitstream/JRC101280/jrc101280.pdf.

[13]   Valerio De Stefano, *The Rise of the "Just-in-Time Workforce": On-Demand Work, Crowdwork, and Labor Protection in the "Gig Economy,"* 37 Comp. Lab. L. & Pol'y J. 471 (2016).

[14]   Jeremias Prassl, *Humans as a Service. The Promise and Perils of Work in the Gig Economy* (2018).

[15]   Luca Ratti, *Online Platforms and Crowdwork in Europe: A Two-step Approach to Expanding Agency Work Provisions?* 38 Comp. Lab. L. & Pol'y J. 477 (2017).

[16]   De Stefano, *supra* note 13.

[17]   The evaluation of individuals' productivity by Upwork, for example, is mainly based on keystrokes. *See* John J. Horton and Prasanna Tambe, *Labor Economists Get Their Microscope: Big Data and Labor Market Analysis*, 3 Big Data 130 (2015).

[18]   Antonio Aloisi, *Commoditized Workers, Case-Study Research on Labor Law Issues Arising from a Set of "On-Demand/Gig Economy" Platforms*, 37 Comp. Lab. L. & Pol'y J. 653 (2016).

[19]   Trebor Scholtz, *Digital Labor: The Internet as Playground and Factory* (2013).

[20]   Hugh Collins, A Review of the Concept of the Employer by Dr. Jeremias Prassl, Lab. L. Blog (Nov. 10, 2016), www.law.ox.ac.uk/content/labour-law-0/blog/2015/11/review-concept-employer-dr-jeremias-prassl.

law obligations.[21] The crucial issue for labor law is to ascertain the legal nature of the relationship – to the extent that there is a "relationship" as opposed to a single, one-off exchange or bargain – established between the online platform, the individual who performs the given tasks, and the final user/client/customer. In virtually all situations, individuals performing via online platforms are formally classified as independent contractors or self-employed people, having no obligation to take up the job/gig/ride, to accomplish it in due time, or to meet the client's satisfaction, let alone direct instructions. All these elements are normally addressed (explicitly) in the legal arrangement that the individual is asked to enter while meeting the job request. The awareness by the platforms of the risks inherent to a reclassification of those relationships is clearly revealed by the accuracy with which platforms draft those legal arrangements: in the Amazon Mechanical Turk "Participation Agreement," for instance, it asks "Requesters" (i.e., the final user) to acknowledge "that, while Providers are agreeing to perform Services for you as independent contractors and not employees, repeated and frequent performance of Services by the same Provider on your behalf could result in reclassification of that employment status."[22]

Even assuming that an employment status can be found in some cases, an apparently insurmountable legal problem appears to be that of identifying the employer, being difficult while not impossible to determine whether it is the platform or the final user to be deemed responsible for providing the employment-related entitlements. The doctrine of joint employment, accepted by appellate courts and administrative bodies in the United States (e.g., the National Labor Relations Board or NLRB), may be suitable to deem the platform to be a joint employer, whose status would fall into the definition of joint employment given by the Fair Labor Standards Act, which finds joint employment "where one employer is acting directly or indirectly in the interest of the other employer."[23] In the European context, however, this doctrine proves to be more problematic, as a consequence of both legislatures and courts conceptualizing the employment relationship from a "single-employer" perspective,[24] with the exceptions of contractual obligations in the context of groups of companies[25] and, in tort law, particularly that of vicarious liability.[26]

Due to the limited acceptance of the co-employment concept in Europe, some other authors propose to rely on the functional concept of the employer, envisaging the application of separate

---

[21]   Wolfgang Däubler and Thomas Klebe, *Die Neue Form der Arbeit – Arbeitgeber auf der Flucht? [The New Form of Work – Employers on the Run?]*, 17 Neue Zeitschrift Für Arbeitsrecht 1032 (2015).

[22]   AMTurk's Participation Agreement, at clause 3.a. Correspondingly, the platform includes in the Agreement an indemnity clause according to which "you will indemnify and hold harmless Amazon Mechanical Turk and its Affiliates (and their respective employees, directors, agents and representatives) from and against any and all claims, costs, losses, damages, judgments, penalties, interest and expenses (including reasonable attorneys' fees) arising out of any claim, action, audit, investigation, inquiry or other proceeding instituted by a person or entity ('Claim') that arises out of or relates to … (iii) your failure to comply with any applicable laws and regulations in connection with your use of the Site." (AMTurk's Participation Agreement, at clause 9.a.).

[23]   C.F.R. § 791.2(b)(2), relying on the initial definition in the FLSA and *Greenberg* v. *Arsenal Building Corp. et al.*, 144 F.2d 292 (2d Cir. 1944). More recently, the NLRB expanded its definition of joint employment, stating: "two or more statutory employers are joint employers of the same statutory employees if they share or codetermine those matters governing the essential terms and conditions of employment." See *Browning-Ferris Indus. of California, Inc.*, 362 N.L.R.B. No. 186, 2 (2015).

[24]   See Jeremias Prassl, *The Concept of the Employer* (2015); Luisa Corazza and Orsola Razzolini, Who is an Employer?, in *Comparative Labour Law* 132 (Matthew W. Finkin and Guy Mundlak eds., 2015).

[25]   This occurs in many Member States, and was also given certain recognition by the CJEU in *Albron Catering*, 2010 E.C.R. C-242/109, 21.

[26]   See Luca Ratti, *Agency Work and the Idea of Dual Employership*, 30 Comp. Lab. L. & Pol'y J. 835 (2009). This result is recognized by most jurisdictions as an application of the policy argument for the protection of the generality of citizens.

rules depending on the different employer function exercised by the putative employing entity.[27] In this interpretation, the analysis of the element of control exercised over the individual in an employment relationship is replaced by an emphasis on whether and to what extent the typical functions of the employer are taken up by the online platform: although many online platforms explicitly reject, in their user agreements, the employer role, one need only look at the functional reality of the arrangement to conclude that the platforms are the employer or, perhaps, a co-employer for different purposes, therefore bearing or sharing the relative obligations, risks, and advantages.[28]

The standard regulatory framework underpinning labor law implies the existence of a subordinate employment relationship, based on long-standing qualification tests.[29] But the practice of crowdworking and working on-demand via apps shows that these tests may not return satisfactory results, partially because the same characteristics of these forms of work tend to change in space and time so constantly as to make them nearly impossible to classify. For this reason some scholars have argued that platform workers should be included in a new, intermediate category, that of quasi-subordinate workers,[30] which would keep with the individual's perception of their work.[31] The advocates of this midway approach often call for legislative intervention to regulate relationships that do not easily fit into that dichotomy.[32] In these terms, the question more resembles that of FedEx drivers,[33] and significantly one court in the United States has already accepted this midway approach with respect to Lyft drivers.[34] But in practice, even in those legal systems where such intermediate categories exist, the difficulties surrounding labeling and the correct classification of working persons are not resolved.[35] The set of rights to be given to those falling in this third category is very much a matter of debate, while equipping it with too generous a set of rights could bring about service providers to indulge in new "avoidance" and misclassification strategies.[36]

In the absence of a single and unified definition of "worker" at the EU level, and with the Court of Justice embracing a binary division between subordinate employees and independent

---

[27] Jeremias Prassl and Martin Risak, *Uber, Task Rabbit, & Co.: Platforms as Employers?* 37 Comp. Lab. L. & Pol'y J. 619 (2016). The authors list at least five of these functions: 1) inception and termination of the employment relationship; 2) receiving labor and its fruits; 3) providing work and pay; 4) managing the enterprise-internal market; and 5) managing the enterprise-external market.

[28] *Id.*

[29] In this sense it should be recalled that normally the online platform provides individuals with job opportunities, exercises general control over their performance (e.g., allowing the final user to retain the work done) and, more generally, unilaterally dictates the terms and conditions of employment. Additionally, the platform allows the final user to monitor the individual's performance at any time, to rate the final result the individual submits, to review the individual's performance, sometimes even allows to take screenshots from the individual's computer and to validate (or not) the individual's intermediate steps or tasks before continuing the collaboration. All these elements call for a classification in terms of employment status instead of independent contractors.

[30] Andrei Hagiu, *Work 3.0: Redefining Jobs and Companies in the Uber Age*, Harv. Bus. Sch. (Sept. 29, 2015), http://hbswk.hbs.edu/item/work-3-0-redefining-jobs-and-companies-in-the-uber-age; Andrei Hagiu and Rob Biederman, *Companies Need an Option Between Contractor and Employee*, Harv. Bus. Sch. (Aug. 21, 2015), https://hbr.org/2015/08/companies-need-an-option-between-contractor-and-employee. See also S. D. Harris and A. B. Krueger, *A Proposal for Modernizing Labor Laws for Twenty-First Century Work: The "Independent Worker"* (2015).

[31] Joan T. A. Gabel and Nancy R. Mansfield, *The Information Revolution and its Impact on the Employment Relationship: An Analysis of the Cyberspace Workplace*, 40 Am. Bus. L J. 304 (2003).

[32] Eva Grosheide and Mark Barenberg, *Minimum Fees for the Self-Employed: A European Response to the "Uber-ized" Economy?* 22 Colum. J. Eur. L. 193 (2016).

[33] Robert Sprague, *Worker (Mis)Classification in the Sharing Economy: Square Pegs Trying to Fit in Round Holes*, 31 A.B.A. J. Lab. & Emp. L. 1, 16 (2015).

[34] *Cotter et al. v. Lyft Inc.*, No. 13-cv-04065-VC (Nd. Cal. 2015).

[35] Prassl and Risak, *supra* note 27, at 288–90; De Stefano, *supra* note 13, at 18–21.

[36] Kovács, supra note 5.

contractors,[37] some reports produced by EU institutions have occasionally referred to intermediate statuses such as "economically dependent work"[38] or "dependent self-employed work,"[39] often in an attempt to engage with various recommendations and policy suggestions produced by a number of international organizations, such as the ILO[40] and the OECD.[41] Paradoxically, however, the heterogeneity of the employment and work relationships falling within these intermediate categories[42] may have further complicated the task of identifying a suitable legal characterization for the increasingly diverse and complex forms of work developing in modern labor markets and human resources management practices.[43]

Unsurprisingly, there is an emerging perception that "no clear consensus has emerged on how the courts will determine employee versus independent contractor status for workers in the on-demand economy," with the legal tests for discerning such status being "largely malleable and based on past precedent [and] largely indeterminate."[44] EU anti-discrimination law, as we shall see, is no exception to this general trend, in spite of a (nominally) broader personal scope of application covering "conditions for access to employment, to self-employment and to occupation."[45]

II EU EQUAL TREATMENT AND ANTI-DISCRIMINATION LAW BETWEEN MARKET REGULATION AND FUNDAMENTAL PRINCIPLES

EU equal treatment legislation is rich and complex, dating back to the establishment of the European Economic Community with the 1957 Treaty of Rome. In trying to break down this multifaceted area of EU social legislation into a limited number of coherent regulatory instruments and principles, it is possible to suggest that EU equality law can potentially interact with the regulation of work in the sharing economy through three distinct dimensions: its fundamental market freedom dimension; its social rights dimension; and its fundamental rights/principle dimension.

To this day, the EU remains a free trade area, or more precisely an internal market operating on the basis of a customs union and a common foreign commercial policy. The most fundamental regulatory principle governing the EU's internal market is the principle of free movement

---

37   *See* Nicola Countouris, *The Concept of "Worker" in European Labour Law: Fragmentation, Autonomy and Scope*, 47 Indus. L. J. 192 (2018), citing in particular the landmark decisions *Allonby* (CJEU, Jan. 13, 2004, case C-256/01, ECLI:EU:C:2004:18), *O'Brien* (CJEU, Mar. 1, 2012, case C-393/10, ECLI:EU:C:2012:110), and *Betriebsrat der Ruhrlandklinik* (CJEU, Nov. 17, 2016, case C-216/15, ECLI:EU:C:2016:883).

38   EU Commission, *Green Paper Modernising Labour Law to Meet the Challenges of the 21st Century* 5–6 (2006), www.europarl.europa.eu/meetdocs/2004_2009/.../com_com(2006)0708_en.pdf.

39   EU Commission, Employment and Social Developments in Europe 2015 86 (2016).

40   ILO, *Non-Standard Forms of Employment* 14–15 (2015), www.ilo.org/wcmsp5/groups/public/@ed_protect/@protrav/@travail/documents/meetingdocument/wcms_336934.pdf.

41   OECD, *OECD Employment Outlook 2014*, 153 (2014), www.oecd.org/els/employmentoutlook-previouseditions.htm.

42   EU Parliament, *Social Protection Rights of Economically Dependent Self-Employed Workers* 8 (2013), adapt.it/professionioggi/docs/Economically_dependent_selfemployment.pdf.

43   A full comparative overview is provided by Nicola Countouris, *The Changing Law of the Employment Relationship* (2007). In particular, on the German concept of *Arbeitnehmeränliche Personen*, *see* Wolfgang Däubler, *Working People in Germany*, 21 Comp. Lab. L & Pol'y J. 77 (1999); Armin Hoeland, *A Comparative Study of the Impact of Electronic Technology on Workplace Disputes: National Report on Germany*, 24 Comp. Lab. L. & Pol'y J. 147 (2005). On the Austrian concept of quasi-subordinate (*freie Dienstnehmer*), *see* Stefanie Watzinger, *Der Freie Dienstvertrag im Arbeits- und Sozialrecht* (2016).

44   Miriam A. Cherry, *Beyond Misclassification: The Digital Transformation of Work*, 37 Comp. Lab. L. & Pol'y J. 577 (2016). at 18.

45   *Cf.* Article 3(1)(a) of Council Directive 2000/43/EC of 29 June 2000 implementing the principle of equal treatment between persons irrespective of racial or ethnic origin.

between goods, services, capital, and economically active persons, sometimes referred to as "the four freedoms."[46] As a general rule, subject to a limited number of exceptions, free movement has historically entailed an obligation not to discriminate between the treatment guaranteed by one EU Member State, for instance, to its own domestic goods or workers and that guaranteed to goods and workers arriving from other Member States. In recent years, the more liberal and pro-market integration principle of "market access" has emerged as a dominant principle in the regulation of the single market,[47] but non-discrimination remains a central tool for the regulation of the EU's market. Identifying activities performed under "collaborative economy" arrangements as "services" will inevitably result in these activities being covered by various areas of EU free movement of services regulation, both general and specific.[48] It is worth noting that a parallel market regulatory function has been historically performed by the EU principle of equal pay, as first enshrined in Article 119 of the Treaty of Rome. Its economic aim, recognized by the ECJ as early as the 1970s, was seeking to "avoid a situation in which undertakings established in states which have actually implemented the principle of equal pay suffer a competitive disadvantage in intra-community competition as compared with undertakings established in states which have not yet eliminated discrimination against women workers as regards pay."[49]

The second dimension of the EU equal treatment principle arguably offers a more conventional analytical standpoint for labor and equality lawyers involved with the regulation of work relations in the sharing economy. EU anti-discrimination law is enshrined in a number of both primary (i.e., Treaty-based) and secondary (i.e., contained in Directives) sources that clearly characterize this area of regulation as a key facet of Social Europe. Within the functioning of the EU's internal market, these provisions may well have retained a dual economic and social aim, but, expanding on a point made by the Court of Justice in respect of "EU equal pay" legislation, it is arguable that "the economic aim […] is secondary to the social aim pursued by the same provision."[50] These provisions range from rules on equal pay for work of equal value and the prohibition of discrimination between men and women,[51] to Directives prohibiting disparate treatment on racial grounds[52] and a range of other protected characteristics.[53] The personal scope of application and internal architecture of these directives varies considerably from instrument to directives. But it is fair to say that the main anti-discrimination Directives have been designed with a view of guaranteeing a very wide coverage of their protective provisions, including in the employment context. So, for instance, the personal scope definitions applicable

---

[46] *See* C. Barnard, *The Substantive Law of the EU: The Four Freedoms* (2016).

[47] *See* G. Davies, Between Market Access and Discrimination: Free Movement as a Right to Fair Conditions of Competition, *in Research Handbook on the Law of the EU's Internal Market* 13 (P. Koutrakos and J. Snell eds., 2017).

[48] *Cf.* European Commission, *A European Agenda for the Collaborative Economy*, COM(2016)356 final, esp. 3–7.

[49] Case 43/75, *Defrenne v. Sabena*, para. 9.

[50] Case C-270/97, *Deutsche Post AG v. Elisabeth Sievers*, Para 57.

[51] Directive 2006/54/EC of the European Parliament and of the Council of 5 July 2006 on the implementation of the principle of equal opportunities and equal treatment of men and women in matters of employment and occupation (recast), [2006] OJ L 204/23; Directive 2004/113/EC of 13 December 2004 implementing the principle of equal treatment between men and women in the access to and supply of goods and services, [2004] OJ L 373/37; and Directive 2010/41/EU of 7 July 2010 on the application of the principle of equal treatment between men and women engaged in an activity in a self-employed capacity and repealing Council Directive 86/613/EEC, [2010] OJ L 180/1. For reasons of convenience, in the remainder of this document, these instruments will be occasionally referred to as "the Recast Directive," "the Goods and Services Directive," and "the Self-Employed Directive," respectively.

[52] Council Directive 2000/43/EC of 29 June 2000 implementing the principle of equal treatment between persons irrespective of racial or ethnic origin [2000] OJ L 180/22.

[53] Council Directive 2000/78/EC of 27 November 2000 establishing a general framework for equal treatment in employment and occupation [2000] OJ L 303/16. *Cf.* E. Ellis and P. Watson, *EU Anti-Discrimination Law* (2012); N. Countouris and M. Freedland, *The Personal Scope of the EU Sex Equality Directives* (2012).

to the equal treatment provisions contained in Article 14 of Directive 2006/54, and Article 3(1) of Directives 2000/43 and 2000/78, are framed as being applicable "in relation to: (a) conditions for access to employment, to self-employment or to occupation, including selection criteria and recruitment conditions, whatever the branch of activity and at all levels of the professional hierarchy, including promotion." This is a very broad personal scope of application that should arguably benefit workers in the sharing economy regardless of their employment status being that of an employee or a self-employed person.

Thirdly, the principles of equal treatment and non-discrimination have also been recognized as general principles of EU law, with a now substantial body of CJEU pronouncements confirming their nature in the context of cases of sex, age, and race discrimination.[54] Equality and non-discrimination between men and women are of course also recognized by Articles 21 and 23 of the Charter of Fundamental Rights of the EU, further consolidating their status as general and fundamental principles of EU law.[55] This status is of paramount importance when assessing the legal effects of non-discrimination that, as other general principles, are applicable in horizontal situations between private parties and requires national judges "when applying provisions of national law, to interpret those provisions in such a way that they may be applied in a manner that is consistent with the [Equality Directives] or, if such an interpretation is not possible, to disapply, where necessary, any provision of national law that is contrary to the general principle prohibiting discrimination."[56]

III THE EQUAL TREATMENT PRINCIPLE, THE REGULATION OF THE EU INTERNAL MARKET, AND THE SHARING ECONOMY

The market-based idea of non-discrimination introduced in the opening paragraphs of the previous section may offer a rather unconventional analytical standpoint for equality lawyers to engage with the regulation of the sharing economy. But it remains crucial to a more rounded, and arguably more precise, understanding of the impact of EU anti-discrimination law, broadly understood, on the "sharing economy" for the simple reason that economic operators in the sharing economy are increasingly being viewed – and arguably correctly so – as service providers and, thus, as falling under the various strands of EU law regulating services in general, and services in specific sectors in particular. The nature of the regulatory regime applicable to particular economic actors in the sharing economy is likely to vary depending on the nature of the activities and services they actually perform. Some could be covered by the Services Directive 2006/123, which allows for a considerable degree of intra-market penetration, though it also excludes some types of services from its application.[57] Some could conceivably be seen as amounting to services of temporary work agencies, and as such falling under the more stringent rules contained and allowed by Directive 2008/104, the Temporary Agency Workers Directive.[58] But some services could be seen as amounting to "information society services," and as such be virtually immune from any national attempt to subject them to stringent regulation, be it by means of authorization regimes or other licensing arrangements.

---

[54] E.g., Case C-144/04, *Mangold v. Rüdiger Helm*; Case C-236/09, *Association belge des Consommateurs Test-Achats ASBL v. Conseil des ministres*; Case C-555/07, *Kücükdeveci v. Swedex GmbH & Co. KG*; Case C-83/14, *CHEZ Razpredelenie Bulgaria AD v. Komisia za zashtita ot diskriminatsia.*

[55] *Cf.* Takis Tridimas, *The General Principles of EU Law* Ch. 2 (2nd ed, 2007).

[56] Case C-441/14, *Dansk Industri v. Estate of Karsten Eigil Rasmussen*, para. 43.

[57] *See* Article 2, excluding, for instance, transport services and services of temporary work agencies.

[58] *Cf.* Ratti, *supra* note 15.

In the recent Opinion by Advocate General Szpunar in Case C-434/15, Uber's core business activity was characterized as offering a "traditional transport service," and "it certainly [could] not be considered to be a ride-sharing platform."[59] As such, the Advocate General went on to exclude it from the application of the Electronic Commerce Directive 2000/31 (which only allows for a very minimal level of restriction to activities performed by "information society services"), but rather as falling within the scope of Article 91 TFEU, and thus lawfully subject to the conditions under which non-resident carriers may operate transport services within the Member States (including, in this case, a national requirement to possess the necessary urban transport licenses and authorizations).

An understanding of particular digital platforms as falling under discrete areas of EU services regulation is also crucially important for the purposes of identifying the nature of the legal relationship between the digital service providers and their work and service providers, and thus ascertain the actual obligations arising upon the platform owners in respect of various areas of social and labor law, including discrimination law, vis-à-vis these workers. Once more, AG Szpunar's Opinion in the *Uber Systems Spain SL* case offers some valuable pointers, noting how Uber pervasively controls various aspects of the transport services it offers, including the price of the services, but also "the conduct of drivers by means of the ratings system and, lastly, over possible exclusion from the platform."[60] The AG cautions us from rushing to suggest that this invariably suggests "that Uber's drivers must necessarily be regarded as its employees. The company may very well provide its services through independent traders who act on its behalf as subcontractors."[61] But the AG is clear in asserting that the "indirect control such as that exercised by Uber [...] makes it possible to manage in a way that is just as – if not more – effective than management based on formal orders given by an employer to his employees and direct control over the carrying out of such orders."[62]

So, economic actors in the sharing economy are more likely than not to be seen as service providers of some particular kind, and thus benefit (to a varying degree depending on the nature of the service they offer) from the right "not to be subject to market access or other requirements ... unless they are not discriminatory, necessary to attain a clearly identified public interest objective, and proportionate to achieving this interest."[63] But they are also likely to see the contractual arrangements they establish with the various personal work and service providers they engage, or whose activities they otherwise orchestrate, as subject to a very close scrutiny for the purposes of ascertaining the extent to which they can be located in the employment or self-employment field, and thus, as we are about to see, as covered by anti-discrimination legislation.

IV EU ANTI-DISCRIMINATION LAW AND THE SHARING ECONOMY

As noted above, at least on paper, EU anti-discrimination law covers in principle a wide range of relationships, including, in some areas, relationship of self-employment, and the existence of a contract of employment may not always be required.[64] However, a number of obstacles do arise from the peculiar judicial understanding by the CJEU of the functioning and operation of anti-discrimination rules, in particular by reference to: the task of identifying a suitable

---

[59] AG Szpunar Opinion in Case C-434/15, *Asociación Profesional Elite Taxi v. Uber Systems Spain SL*, para. 42.
[60] *Id*. at para. 51.
[61] *Id*. at para. 54.
[62] *Id*. at para. 52.
[63] *Cf*. European Commission, *supra* note 48, at 3–4.
[64] CJEU, Jan. 13, 2004, C-256/01, *Allonby*, ECLI:EU:C:2004:18, at 71.

comparator to establish disparate treatment; the complexity of the employing entity, which makes it more difficult to identify a "single source" of the discriminatory treatment; and the substantial unavailability of statistical data for the individual claimant in discrimination cases. These situations will be addressed in this section.

The problem of identifying a suitable comparator is a crucial one as far as EU equality and non-discrimination law are concerned. By and large, a comparator is defined as a person in similar circumstances, who is in a different, more beneficial position than the claimant, as a direct consequence of the existence of one of the protected grounds of discrimination. In EU law, some directives require a real comparator to be found, which is clearly not easy. Others cover a wider range of potential comparators, asking the interpreter to consider also "those [conditions] that would apply if they had been recruited directly by that undertaking to occupy the same job."[65] But the task of identifying a comparator becomes a particularly arduous one when workers are hired under terms of employment that make their work arrangement so peculiar as to become, de facto, uniquely singular. The case of *Wippel* is paradigmatic in that sense, as the female claimant was employed under a "contract which stipulates neither the weekly hours of work nor the manner in which working time is to be organized, but it leaves her the choice of whether to accept or refuse the work offered" (in effect a "zero-hours contract") and was prevented, because of her contract, from comparing herself with a full-time worker because "no full-time worker in the same establishment has the same type of contract or employment relationship."[66] This is likely to emerge as a major hurdle for workers in the sharing economy, precisely because of the increased potential for fragmentation and variation in contractual terms regulating the provision of tasks, gigs, or rides (think of Uber's "dynamic pricing model"). But this also brings to the fore a major contradiction and fallacy of the narrow comparator notion embraced by the CJEU: insisting on a requirement for a broad similarity between the terms and conditions of the claimant and her comparators is illogical, if not perverse, because it typically defeats one of the main purposes of anti-discrimination legislation, which is to prevent discriminatory differences in contractual terms and conditions.

This leads to a second difficulty in targeting an anti-discrimination claim. While assessing the existence of a potential comparator, the CJEU has repeatedly insisted on the existence of a single source of discrimination, noting that "where the differences identified in the pay conditions of workers performing equal work or work of equal value cannot be attributed to a single source, there is no body which is responsible for the inequality and which could restore equal treatment."[67] This restrictive interpretation given by the CJEU in cases such as *Lawrence* and *Allonby* could emerge as a particularly difficult hurdle for crowd-workers and workers on-demand via online apps. We venture to suggest, however, that, in these cases, the online platform (and its owner) ought to be identified as the "source" of discrimination: it is the platform, in practice, that manages the data used by the algorithm and their setting. As opposed to the case of staff agencies acting as intermediaries, in the sharing economy, it is the platform itself that determines unilaterally the conditions of the service provided by the individual. Therefore it should be possible to qualify the platform's position as a single source in the sense used by the CJEU.[68]

---

[65] Article 5, Dir. 2008/104. *See* Gavin Barret, *Shall I Compare Thee To …? On Article 141 EC and Lawrence*, 35 Indus. L.J. 93 (2006).

[66] Case C-313/02, *Wippel*, para. 59–61.

[67] CJEU, Jan. 13, 2004, C-256/01, *Allonby* EU:C:2004:18, at 46, citing CJEU, C-320/00 *Lawrence and Others* EU:C:2002:498, at 18.

[68] Miriam Kullmann, *Platform Work, Gender Equality, and Algorithmic Pay Differences*, paper presented at the LLRN3 Toronto Conference, June 2017, manuscript.

But one last issue comes from the concrete need to render the rights conferred by the treaty and by the relevant directives enforceable. EU anti-discrimination law does not entitle an individual who claims to be discriminated against to have access to all information indicating whether the employer acted correctly and neutrally. Admittedly, as noted in the *Meister* judgment, the refusal to give any information regarding, for instance, the selection process, the conditions of employment, or other data, may be taken into account by the judge in order to establish facts from which discrimination may be inferred.[69] This means that EU legislation does not amend as such the rules provided by the Member States on the burden on proof, which normally put on the claimant the burden to prove the key facts at the base of the claim.[70] While this seems to resolve the asymmetries between the platform and the individual – as the reluctance of the former to make available the huge set of data stored and treated by them is not a procedural obstacle for the claimant's case to progress, in practice it falls short from imposing a duty on the platform to share the relevant data, and thus, de facto, it may hinder the possibility for the claimant to access the information necessary to both make a claim and, once discrimination is inferred, to actually succeed on the merits of the case.[71]

CONCLUSIONS

EU anti-discrimination legislation is often praised as the jewel in the crown of EU social and employment law. Its development is often described as an evolution from formal equality to more substantial forms of equality, aiming at stressing the pivotal role of effectiveness and enforcement of its rules. A further stage in this evolutionary trajectory ought to be what Fredman defines as "transformative equality," a concept that, among other things, refers to the need to include in the personal scope of the application of discrimination law not only employees or disguised employees, but also those casual and non-standard workers that are normally not protected by labor law.[72] The CJEU has a proud record to defend in this context, for instance by reference to its transformative jurisprudence on the rights of pregnant workers.[73]

But, as noted in the previous section, a number of deficiencies continue to affect the architecture of EU anti-discrimination legislation. If left unaddressed, they are likely to affect in a disproportionally adverse manner those workers offering their services through online platforms, both under crowd-working arrangements and by means of an on-demand performance of tasks. An overarching feature of these arrangements is that of presenting the relationship between work providers, users, and intermediary entities – to use three neutral terms – as particularly fragmented and fissured. This effect is produced through the interposition of digital platforms that seemingly increase the fragmentation that is typical of any outsourcing and subcontracting process. To state the obvious, with their emphasis on tasks, rides, and gigs, as opposed to longer term projects or the offer of mutual commitments in terms of future performance, platforms fragment the more relational aspects of work, defeating the establishment of an employment relationship (even an intermittent and discontinuous one). These platforms also fragment the pool of workers, making the identification of a suitable actual comparator an extremely arduous

---

[69] CJEU, 19 April 2012, C-415/10, *Meister* ECLI:EU:C:2012:217.
[70] *Id.*
[71] Kullmann, *supra* note 68. Note that the *Meister* claim was eventually rejected by the referring court. *See* L. Farkas and O. O'Farrell, *Reversion of the Burden of Proof – Practical Dilemmas at the European and National Level* 29 (2015).
[72] Sandra Fredman, Pasts and Futures: EU Equality Law, *in Research Handbook on EU Labour Law* 391 (Alan Bogg, Cathryn Costello, and A. C. L. Davies eds., 2017).
[73] CJEU, Nov. 11, 2011, C-232/09, *Danosa v. LKB Lizings SIA* ECLI:EU:C:2010:674.

task, and, at the same time, they fragment the functions and responsibilities of the employing entity, thus by definition creating multiple potential sources of discriminatory treatment and defeating the "single source" requirement. The argument could be made that the architecture of EU anti-discrimination law was already struggling to cope with some of the more traditional forms of distancing and outsourcing. But the manifest complexities brought about by the emergence of new forms of work in the sharing economy are likely to challenge even further these structural weaknesses of EU equality law.